The Seventeenth Alabama Infantry

THE SEVENTEENTH ALABAMA INFANTRY

A Regimental History and Roster

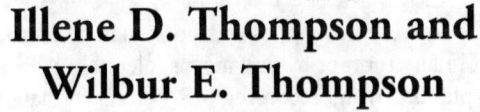

Illene D. Thompson and
Wilbur E. Thompson

HERITAGE BOOKS
2009

HERITAGE BOOKS
AN IMPRINT OF HERITAGE BOOKS, INC.

Books, CDs, and more—Worldwide

For our listing of thousands of titles see our website at
www.HeritageBooks.com

Published 2009 by
HERITAGE BOOKS, INC.
Publishing Division
100 Railroad Ave. #104
Westminster, Maryland 21157

Copyright © 2001 Illene D. Thompson
and Wilbur E. Thompson

All rights reserved. No part of this book may be reproduced or transmitted in any form or by any means, electronic or mechanical, including photocopying, recording or by any information storage and retrieval system without written permission from the author, except for the inclusion of brief quotations in a review.

International Standard Book Numbers
Paperbound: 978-0-7884-1969-0
Clothbound: 978-0-7884-8124-6

To our ancestors
William Winfield Barrington, Co. K 17th Alabama Infantry
John C. Hair, Co. I 53rd Alabama Partisan Rangers
Frederick Kolb Sheffield, Co. C 6th Alabama Infantry
William David Tindal, Co. H 39th Alabama Infantry
James Alford Thompson, Co. C 17th Alabama Infantry

Table of Contents

Acknowledgements	xi
Preface	xiii
Introduction	1
I. Origin and Formation	3
A. Introduction	3
B. Original Staff and Field Officers	3
C. Regimental Commanders	4
D. Staff Officers	8
E. Assignments	10
F. Company A	13
G. Company B	15
H. Company C	17
I. Company D	19
J. Company E	20
K. Company F	24
L. Company G	25
M. Company H	26
N. Company I	28
O. Company K	29
II. Pensacola	33
A. Introduction	33
B. The Continuing Standoff	33
C. Arrival of the 17th Alabama	34
D. Living Conditions	37
E. End of the Stalemate	39
III. Shiloh and the Western Front	41
A. Introduction	41
B. Overview of Important Events, March to August 1862	41
C. Events Leading to the Battle of Shiloh	41
D. Reassignment to the Army of Mississippi	42
E. March to Shiloh	45
F. The Battle of Shiloh	46
G. After Shiloh	51
H. Conclusion	59
IV. Mobile	61
A. Introduction	61
B. Strategic Significance	61
C. Assignment to Mobile	62
D. Duties	63
E. Personal Observations	66
F. Enemy Observations	70
G. Medical Care	71

	H. The Home Front	72
	I. Conclusion	74
V.	Battle for Atlanta	75
	A. Introduction	75
	B. Prologue to Battle	75
	C. The Move to Georgia	77
	D. Battles Involving the 17th	78
	E. Resaca	78
	F. Kennesaw Mountain	82
	G. Peach Tree Creek	86
	H. Ezra Church	90
	I. Siege of Atlanta	92
	J. Retreat from Atlanta	93
	K. After the Atlanta Campaign	95
	L. Where They're Buried	96
VI.	The Battle of Franklin	99
	A. Introduction	99
	B. The March to Tennessee	99
	C. Troop Strength	100
	D. General Walthall's Account of the 17th at Franklin	102
	E. Captain McMillan's Account of the Battle of Franklin	106
	F. Colonel Murphy's Account of the Battle of Franklin	109
	G. A Wounded Soldier	111
	H. Conclusion	112
VII.	The Battle of Nashville	113
	A. Introduction	113
	B. The Preparation for Battle	113
	C. The Battle	115
	D. Retreat	116
	E. Conclusion	118
VIII.	The Final Days	119
	A. Introduction	119
	B. The 17th Alabama in North Carolina	119
	C. General Johnston's View	121
	D. The Last Muster Roll	121
	E. The Men Not There	124
	F. The Long Trek Home	125
	G. Home at Last	126
Appendix I. Description of the Roster		129
	A. Introduction	129
	B. Quality and Limitation of the Service Records	129
	C. Register of the Sick and Wounded of the 17th Alabama	131
	D. Explanation of Terms Used in the Roster	133
	E. Secondary Sources	139

TABLE OF CONTENTS

F. Sources of Additional Information	139
Appendix II. Company A Roster	143
Appendix III. Company B Roster	169
Appendix IV. Company C Roster	199
Appendix V. Company D Roster	229
Appendix VI. Company E Roster	257
Appendix VII. Company F Roster	287
Appendix VIII. Company G Roster	319
Appendix IX. Company H Roster	341
Appendix X. Company I Roster	373
Appendix XI. Company K Roster	397
Appendix XII. Medical Glossary	427
Appendix XIII. Casualty Lists	431
A. Introduction	431
B. Shiloh	431
C. Atlanta	434
D. Franklin	443
F. Nashville	445
Bibliography	451
Index	457

Acknowledgements

Our research on the 17th Alabama began in 1996 and became a compelling quest during the next five years. We have explored many of the facilities in the southeast dedicated to the Civil War and history. During these travels we met many people including historians, archivists, and librarians, all eager to help and share their knowledge.

Our regimental history includes individual data on hundreds of soldiers and covers military assignments and battles in several states. This broad scope necessitates many acknowledgements of assistance and expressions of appreciation.

A very special thanks goes to Annie Crenshaw. She has helped us in so many ways. She willingly shared her knowledge of the Civil War period and of the families of south Alabama. On many occasions she gave us names of people to contact to broaden our knowledge of the men of the 17th Alabama. Her advice and guidance on the presentation of the material has been invaluable.

The lectures and conversations about the Civil War with Robert Davis of Wallace State College greatly enhanced our understanding of that period. Bob Bradley of the Alabama Archives also shared knowledge of the Civil War period, the 17th Alabama and the men of Company H. Dr. Mark A. Weitz of Auburn University (Montgomery) shared knowledge of the Civil War and reviewed historical portions of the book. He also provided encouragement and suggested a broader perspective. Julie Holcomb, archivist, at Navarro College, Corsicana, Texas, graciously provided letters from the Pearce Civil War Collection.

During our numerous visits to the Alabama archives, the staff of the research room was always available to help us locate rosters, letters, diaries, censuses, medical records, and newspaper accounts pertaining to the 17th Alabama. Other public libraries visited within the state included Birmingham, Greenville, Huntsville, Luverne and Troy.

We visited a number of museums and battlefields. We were assisted by Bill Rambo, Confederate Memorial Park, Alabama; David Ogden, Fort Pickens State Park, Florida; Retha Stephens, Kennesaw Mountain National Battlefield, Georgia; Stacy Allen, Shiloh National Battlefield, Tennessee; and David Fraley, Lotz Museum, Franklin, Tennessee. The historians and staff at these facilities provided background on the period when the 17th was assigned to their locale or provided Civil War records not found elsewhere. For example, the Shiloh library has a copy of the 17th Alabama muster roll for June 30, 1862 to August 31, 1862. The information from this muster roll is not available in the regimental service records.

Many unknown volunteers of the Butler County Historical and Genealogical Society have collected and filed information on Butler County soldiers who were members of the 17th Alabama. This information is archived at the Greenville Public Library and includes rosters, censuses, obituaries, and personal information about individual soldiers.

We also visted college libraries throughout the southeast: University of Alabama, Tuscaloosa, AL; Duke University, Durham, NC; Samford University, Birmingham, AL; University of North Carolina, Chapel Hill, NC; and Wallace State College, Hanceville, AL. We visited state archives in Georgia, Mississippi, and Tennessee. We visited the National Archives, Washington, D.C. We express our appreciation to Thomas M. Owen, the first director of the Alabama Archives, Montgomery, AL. In 1904 he loaned to the National Archives his copy of medical records of the 17th Alabama. There are over 3000 medical entries in this document. After a handwritten copy of these medical records was completed, the original was returned to Montgomery. The original register no longer exists.

Our sincere appreciation is also extended to the approximately 100 descendants of 17th Alabama soldiers who made meaningful contributions. These descendants shared family stories and information about their ancestors. In particular, we want to mention Dickey Andress who shared his knowledge of men in Company H, Ron Bridges and Dot Quarles who shared their knowledge of men in Company C, Tim Burgess who shared his knowledge of death and burials of men in the Army of Tennessee, Lewis Ward who shared his knowledge of men in Company F, and Scott Drew who shared his knowledge of men in Company K. A special thanks also goes to the descendants of Frank Robertson of Company E for sharing Robertson's personal letters.

Preface

This book summarizes the involvement of the 17th Alabama Infantry in the four-year civil strife that nearly destroyed the country, but helped shape our nation forever. A synopsis of various battles involving the 17th Alabama is necessarily included to provide part of the framework of how this regiment fit into the overall holocaust.

A primary purpose of this book is to collect into one document the bits and pieces of information available in various state archives, a few special libraries, and official records which document military operations by both Union and Confederate armies. Our efforts do not attempt to rewrite history.

Hundreds of perceptive books have been written in the nearly 150 years since the war's end. Many factual books written by veterans and historians have recorded the complete story of the many glories and sacrifices. These books cover various facets of the wartime era including political, economic, social, military operations, and strategic and tactical decisions, etc. Some books reflect an obvious pride or undeniable bias from either side of the conflict, based on the author's interest or viewpoint.

The 17th Alabama Infantry apparently was not a famous fighting regiment that spawned many glorious writings over the years. The men served as thousands of other men like them served. The 17th Alabama was just a part of the various armies to which they were assigned. During the four years of war, the 17th Alabama served in the Army of Pensacola, the Army of the Mississippi, the Army of the Gulf Coast, and finally in the Army of Tennessee. Their dedication and sacrifices warrant this effort to collect their story for future generations.

Our knowledge of the 17th Alabama began with a great-grandfather we never knew. He was missing in action for about 100 years following a battle at the railroad station in Egypt, Mississippi, in late December 1864. His family belatedly learned of his fate when his military records were found in the National Archives in Washington, D. C., in 1966. He was one of 500 prisoners captured at Egypt Station. He died of pneumonia two weeks later in the military prison hospital in Alton, Illinois.

Our research on the 17th began in 1996 following a visit to the Confederate Memorial Cemetery and monument in Alton. James A. Thompson, Company C, 17th Alabama is listed among 1350 names engraved on the monument. All these men died in the military prison, many of the deaths caused by a smallpox epidemic prevailing in both the prison and in the town of Alton. Research was initiated to learn what brought James Thompson to the battle at Egypt Station. With knowledge of the 17th Alabama's participation in the battles at Franklin and Nashville in December 1864, the burning question intensified: why was James at Egypt Station? Further research revealed that James was part of a special detachment assigned to guard the railroad link in Mississippi to General John Bell Hood's forces in Tennessee. This critical rail link was both Hood's supply line and primary escape route.

The 17th Alabama was formed in south Alabama. Companies B, C, and K were filled primarily by men from Butler County. The remaining seven companies were filled by men from Monroe, Pike, Montgomery, Lowndes, Coosa, Randolph, Russell, and other south Alabama counties. Even though names, dates and locations may vary, the suffering and fates of the men of the 17th Alabama are considered typical of the experiences of Confederate soldiers throughout the war. Ironically this region was untouched by battle and devoid of Union troops for virtually the entire duration of the war. The incursion of Union cavalry during closing months of the war in the spring of 1865 resulted in short term occupation and issuance of paroles as necessary during the final days of the war.

The historical data and personal information presented herein are based on material from various reference books, reports, and personal papers and reflects the authors' interpretation of many source documents.

Additional information on the 17th Alabama surfaced as this book was being finalized for publication even after five years of diligent search of documents. Letters from a member of the 17th were discovered in a family collection; some of them were located within five miles of the authors, and the others were in Alaska. A few days after incorporation of the new information, we learned of eight letters written by an officer on the regimental staff. These letters are part of a Civil War collection at Navarro College in Corsicana, Texas. All the material was significant and portions warranted inclusion in the book. After a few days delay, the book was again finalized for printing. Hopefully circulation of this book will stimulate discovery of more information and documents on the 17th Alabama Infantry.

I. Introduction

This book provides an overview of the 17th Alabama's involvement in the Civil War. Included are geographical assignments, travels, battle engagements, suffering, weariness and sacrifices. The 17th Alabama Infantry was organized September 5, 1861, at Montgomery, Alabama. It was mustered into the Confederate army during September with a full regiment of ten companies and approximately 900 men. The origin and formation of the ten companies is presented in Section II. Personnel listings at the September 1861 mustering were obtained from the original muster rolls where available. For companies F, G, H and I, a partial copy of the initial muster roll was recreated from known enlistment dates for that period, as found in the microfilm data of the service records for the 17th Alabama.

This book is written to honor the memory of the men in the 17th and to provide a focused reference for the 17th Alabama. Summary information from overall military actions already documented in history are included to provide a more complete story and cohesive involvement of the 17th Alabama regiment. The book pays considerable attention to personal aspects of the men as well as their reactions to events surrounding them. Much of their story is told using their own words where available from diaries, letters, and military reports. The letters, in many cases, provide a tortured perspective of the world they were caught up in. Excerpts from the diaries and letters are presented in their original form with grammatical errors and misspelled words.

Although the men of the 17th Alabama were in the same army and embroiled in the same war as other Confederate units, their blessings and ordeals differed from others at various times. Their first regimental assignment in November 1861 was for coastal defense duties at Pensacola, Florida, while the war raged in other places.

The 17th Alabama's initial bloodbath was in the horrific conflict at Shiloh on April 6 and 7, 1862: the shock that jolted both the Union Army and the Confederate Army and gave pause to both sides. Following Shiloh, the 17th was devastated by both the wounds of battle and ravages of disease. In August 1862, they were again assigned to coastal defense duties, this time in Mobile. Although not an enjoyable existence, this was relatively quiet duty while bloody battles raged in other parts of the country.

The comforts of duty in Mobile were suddenly replaced by the hell-on-earth stalemates in northwest Georgia. The 17th Alabama was transferred in April 1864 to provide desperately needed reinforcements to the Army of Tennessee for the Atlanta campaign. This campaign was characterized by months of bloody chase and retreats. After a change of command and a reorganization in July 1864, the 17th Alabama became part of the Army of Tennessee, sharing in its exploits, defeats, and sufferings. Many excellent books have been written which document the battles of the Army of Tennessee.

After Atlanta came the trudging march to northwest Alabama and staging for battles in Tennessee. The book provides a synopsis of the sacrificial slaughter at Franklin, Tennessee, November 30, 1864, and the freezing agony and carnage at Nashville during December 1864. Also included is the aftermath of Franklin and Nashville and significant events up to the end of the war.

A roster of the entire regiment was compiled from many references, including family data from descendants. Individual entries in the roster were made as complete as possible with research material currently available. The data includes date and location for enlistment, disease, injury, capture and imprisonment, and discharge or parole. Date and location of birth, death, and burial are listed if known. The roster contains over 2800 entries and names in each of the ten companies are listed in alphabetical order (Appendices II – XI).

Data on illness, injury, or disease are included on individual entries where applicable. Limited knowledge of medical and health practices 150 years ago also greatly contributed to the suffering and death of men in both armies. A medical register for the 17th Alabama found in the National Archives illustrates the impact of disease on the regiment. The register also helped pinpoint battles the regiment took part in during the Atlanta and Tennessee campaigns of 1864.

Like thousands of other men, members of the 17th served, sacrificed, suffered, and died during the horrific war. Casualty lists from major battles at Shiloh, Atlanta, Franklin, and Nashville were compiled for each company. The known casualties are listed in Appendix XIII and present a picture of the price paid by the 17th Alabama Infantry.

II. Origin and Formation

A. Introduction

The 17th Alabama was mustered into the Confederate Army during September 1861 with a full regiment of ten companies and approximately 900 men. This section provides summary information on the origin of the 17th Alabama, a list of the first appointments of officers and the subsequent replacement of officers. Included are both military and geographical assignments for the 17th throughout the four years of war. The initial muster rolls for the companies on the day in September when they were accepted into the Confederate Army are also listed. Muster rolls for Companies A - D are copies of the initial muster rolls available at the Alabama Archives. Company E and Company H initial muster rolls were reconstructed after the war, each by an officer who was present in September 1861. Initial muster rolls for Companies F, G, I, and K have been reconstructed from various sources currently available.

B. Original Staff and Field Officers

Several years after the war, Captain William W. McMillan wrote an account of his recollections and observation of events during what he called the "War of 1861." A copy is available in the Military Records Division of the Alabama Archives in Montgomery. McMillan was born in 1834 in Old Scotland, Monroe County, Alabama. He graduated in 1856 from the University of Louisiana (now Tulane University). He was a successful physician in Claiborne, Alabama, when the Claiborne Guards, the first company of soldiers in Monroe County, was organized. Dr. McMillan served as the company doctor when the Claiborne Guards were stationed at Fort Morgan. In the summer of 1861, he returned to Monroe County and raised a company of infantry. On September 14, 1861, the company traveled to Montgomery where they were accepted by Colonel Thomas Watts as company H in the 17th Alabama Infantry. McMillan was appointed as captain and commanding officer. McMillan remained with his company throughout the war until his capture at Franklin, Tennessee, on November 30, 1864. McMillan described, in his reminiscences, the organization of the regiment:

"*The Regt. was soon organized the Cos. filling rapidly. The field and staff officers were*
    Col. T. H. Watts
    Lt. Col. R. C. Farris
    Maj. V. S. Murphy
    Adj. W. M. Moon
    W. R. Jones Surgeon
    B. F. Blount Asst. Surgeon
    I. T. Tichenor Chaplain

J. R. Benson Commissay (Commissary)
C. C. Lloyd Qr. Master
Non-commissioned Staff were
S. J. Cummings Sgt Baskins Qr Master Sgt.
Potter Conn(?) Sergt Holt Hospital Steward and Band
The following were the Cos. in order of the rank of their Captains

Co. A   Capt. E. P. Holcombe from Lowndes Co.
Co. B   Capt. T. J. Burnett from Butler Co.
Co. C   Capt. W. D. Perryman from Butler Co.
Co. E   Capt. W. E. White from Randolph Co.
Co. F   Capt. A. L. O'Brien from Montgomery Co.
Co. D   Capt. Bragg from Coosa Co.
Co. D   Capt. Deen from Butler Co.
Co. G   Capt. Thos. Ragland from Russell Co.
Co. H   Capt. W. W. McMillan from Munroe Co.
Co. I   Capt. A. M. Collins from Pike Co.

The Regt. was known thereafter as the 17 Ala. Infantry. I was ninth in rank among the Captains. We remained at Shorter's in Macon Co. organizing and drilling until the 12th of Nov., during which time the fight at Santa Rosa Island occurred."[1]

C. Regimental Commanders

A regiment was commanded by a colonel assisted by a lieutenant colonel and a major. The regimental staff of the 17th Alabama was manned by a series of officers as described below.

Colonel Thomas Hill Watts, the organizer of the 17th Alabama, was their first commander. Watts was born in Greenville, Alabama. He graduated with honors from the University of Virginia in 1840. He passed the bar exam in 1841 and began practicing law in Greenville. In 1842, 1844, and 1845, he was elected to the legislature. In 1848 he moved his practice to Montgomery where he also became a successful planter. He was again elected to the legislature in 1849 and to the state senate in 1853. He was pro-Union in the 1850s, but later played an important role in the secession of Alabama. Defeated in his bid for governor of Alabama in 1861, he turned his attention to organizing and equipping the 17th Alabama Infantry. As commander, he received the title of colonel when the unit was mustered into the Confederate Army in Montgomery during September 1861. His regimental staff included Lieutenant Colonel Robert Clement Fariss and Major Virgil S. Murphy.

Watts remained with the regiment through the initial training period, the move to Pensacola, Florida, November 1861, and the transfer to Corinth,

---

[1] Capt. W. W. McMillan, personal sketch, *Reminiscences of the War of 1861* (SG024896, folder 5, Alabama Archives, Montgomery, AL).

ORIGIN AND FORMATION 5

Mississippi, March 1862. Later in March, he resigned his military position when offered an appointment as attorney general in Jefferson Davis's cabinet. In 1863, Watts was elected governor of Alabama and served in this capacity throughout the turbulent war years.

Consistent with normal succession of rank[2], Lieutenant Colonel Robert C. Fariss was promoted to colonel and appointed commanding officer of the 17th Alabama Infantry when Watts resigned in March 1862. Fariss was born February 1830 at New Canton, Virginia. He attended schools in New Canton and Richmond, and studied medicine in Virginia. Due to declining health, he moved to Montgomery to be near his brother.[3] While living in Montgomery, he enlisted in the 17th Alabama. Shortly after his appointment as colonel, Fariss led the regiment during the battle of Shiloh, April 6 and 7, 1862. He submitted his resignation on April 8 having suffered almost constant pain on the battlefield the previous two days. The brigade surgeon declared Fariss unfit for field duty and his resignation was approved April 13. Fariss returned to Montgomery where he sought a non-combatant position within the Confederacy. In 1863, he applied for an appointment on the Board of Examiners under the Impressment[4] Bill for the state of Alabama. Papers with his service record include a recommendation by Attorney General Watts describing Fariss as a "thorough businessman of unquestionable integrity."[5] It is not known if Fariss received the appointment. Fariss died November 19, 1905.

Major Murphy of Montgomery was another officer in poor health. He had attempted to resign before the battle of Shiloh. However, Colonel Watts refused to accept his resignation. With the resignation of Fariss, Attorney General Watts appointed Murphy regimental commander. Before his appointment as attorney general of the Confederacy, Watts' commanding officer was General Braxton Bragg. Bitter feelings prevailed between Watts and Bragg. General Bragg ignored Watts' assignment of Murphy and replaced Fariss with Colonel J. P. Jones as regimental commander. This turned out to be only a temporary assignment. In July 1862 the War Department declared Bragg's appointment illegal and ordered the regiment to elect their officers. Senior Captain Edward P. Holcombe of Company A was elected commander of the regiment. Holcombe was promoted to lieutenant colonel.

---

[2] *War of the Rebellion: Official Records of Union and Confederate Armies* (OWR) (Washington, DC, 1880-1902), series IV, volume 2, 45: According to acts approved December 11, 1861 and January 22, 1862, promotion was determined by seniority. In military history, seniority usually equated to experience. In the Confederate Army, most officers at the regimental and company level had little training and similar and limited experience.
[3] Thomas Owen, *Dictionary of Alabama Biography* (Spartanburg, SC: The Reprint Co., Publishers, 1978), 560.
[4] Impressment: The forced collection of food, live stock, and other commodities.
[5] *Compiled Service Records of Confederate Soldiers Who Served in Organizations in Alabama*

In the meantime, Murphy had been wounded at Boonsville, Mississippi, in May 1862 and was hospitalized. He had also been put under house arrest by Bragg. August 1, 1862, Murphy wrote from Mississippi, requesting that he be reinstated as regimental commander and be allowed to join his regiment which was on its way to Mobile. Murphy was reassigned to head the 17th Alabama and promoted to colonel. His regimental staff in Mobile, and later in Georgia, included Lieutenant Colonel Holcombe and Major Thomas Jefferson Burnett. With the exception of a long period of illness in 1864, Murphy remained commander of the 17th Alabama until his capture at Franklin November 30, 1864.

Murphy's service record contains numerous letters written in 1863 pertaining to his request for promotion to brigadier general. Many of the letters were written by Murphy himself. There is a long petition signed by members of the Alabama House and Senate. There are also letters from members of his regiment and other officers of the Confederacy.[6] Murphy was never granted the promotion. This may have been a result of his earlier conflict with Bragg in 1862.

Murphy commanded the regiment in Mobile and moved the regiment to Georgia in April 1864 to join the Army of Tennessee. Murphy held the position of brigade commander for several months in the spring of 1864 while Brigadier-General James Cantey was on sick leave. Lieutenant Colonel Holcombe was severely wounded in May 1864 and was on medical furlough. Major Burnett became acting colonel and commander of the 17th Alabama in the absence of Holcombe and while Murphy was acting brigade commander. When Murphy went on sick furlough (dysentery and severe debility) June 27, 1864, Brigadier General Edward O'Neal took over as brigade commander.

Major Thomas Jefferson Burnett was born in Greenville, Alabama, August 30, 1836. He was educated in Greenville and became a successful planter and merchant in Greenville. He was very active in politics before the war.[7] Burnett was severely wounded at the battle of Ezra Church, July 28, 1864. He never really recovered from his wounds and was disabled from further field service. November 29, 1864, he was granted a position in the Confederate government. Governor Thomas Watts wrote, *"Thomas Burnett, a wounded Alabama soldier, is hereby appointed Commissioner of Impressments, for the state of Alabama, under an act of the Confederate Congress to regulate impressments, approved March 26, 1863, in lieu of the Honorable W. W. Mason, resigned."*[8]

On Burnett's regimental staff were the two senior captains of the regiment, Thomas Ragland of Company G as acting lieutenant colonel and

---

[6] Ibid.
[7] Owen, 263.
[8] Letters from Thomas Watts (SG24872, Reel 22, Folder 12, Alabama Archives, Montgomery, AL).

ORIGIN AND FORMATION

McMillan of Company H as acting major. Ragland was killed at Ezra Church. With Murphy and Holcombe still on medical furlough, Captain McMillan was moved up to acting colonel and commander of the regiment. McMillan remained in this position until October when he was relieved by Captain Wiley E. White of Company E. White had been captain of Company E from September 1861 to his capture at Huntsville, Alabama, April 11, 1862. White was exchanged in October 25, 1862, and returned to his unit. McMillan wrote that White relieved him as commander of the regiment October 3, 1864.[9] White's tenure as regimental commander was short. He resigned October 25, 1864.

Brigadier General O'Neal wrote at least one memo in September 1864 requesting that Murphy either return immediately to duty or be dropped from the rolls. At this point Murphy had been absent for three months. O'Neal emphasized that the regiment was being commanded by a captain. Murphy returned to command the 17th Alabama, probably when Captain White resigned. Murphy remained with the regiment until the battle at Franklin, Tennessee, where he was captured November 30, 1864. This ended his fighting days. Murphy remained a prisoner first at Nashville and later at Johnson Island, Ohio, until the end of the war.

McMillan was wounded at Franklin, November 30, 1864, and finally captured December 17 when the Confederates retreated from Nashville with the Union Army in pursuit. These events resulted in Captain John Bolling Jr. of Company C, now senior company captain, becoming the officer in charge of the regiment. Bolling led the 17th Alabama during the battle of Nashville where he was captured, December 15, 1864. He remained a prisoner at Johnson's Island, Ohio, until the end of the war.

Bolling was born and educated in Greenville, Alabama. He entered the Confederate Army immediately after graduation and initially held the rank of first lieutenant. He was appointed captain of Company C after the battle of Shiloh and served in that position until the battle of Franklin. After his return home to Greenville in 1865, he read law and went into practice with his father. He was a well respected member of the community. He died May 11, 1898, in Tuscaloosa and was buried at Magnolia Cemetery in Greenville.[10]

After the battles of Franklin and Nashville, the 17th Alabama was reduced in size to a skeleton force. This small force moved into North Carolina in early 1865. At that time they were commanded by Lieutenant Colonel Holcombe. Holcombe had recovered from his wounds suffered in the Atlanta Campaign in 1864 and was able to rejoin his unit in 1865. He was now the senior officer remaining on active duty. He was listed present with the rank of colonel and commanding officer of the regiment at the surrender at Greensboro, North Carolina, April 1865.

---

[9] McMillan sketch.
[10] "Civil War Veterans' Obituaries", *Butler County Historical and Genealogical Society* (April 2000), 12.

The following men were made staff officers in the final days of the war. John F. Tate of Company G was promoted to lieutenant colonel and A. J. Milner of Company F to major, both on April 20, 1865. Tate had joined the 17th Alabama in September 1861 as an officer. He was a doctor by profession, but during war time, chose to lead men into battle. In 1911 Tate was mayor of Hurtsboro, Alabama. Milner first enlisted in the 5th Georgia Regiment in August 1861 as a private. In January 1863, he transferred to the 33rd Alabama Regiment where he reached the rank of captain. He was aide de camp to Brigadier General Lowery. He served as acting assistant inspector general of his brigade. It was after the consolidation of the 17th and 33rd that he became a major on the regimental staff.[11]

D. Staff Officers

A regimental commander was also assisted by several other officers including an adjutant, quartermaster, surgeon, assistant surgeon, and chaplain.

1. Adjutant
- Captain William L. Moon was appointed adjutant for the regiment March 7, 1862. It is not known when Moon resigned.
- Captain J. L McIntyre of Company G was appointed acting adjutant July 24, 1862.
- Lieutenant W. H. McMillan of Company H was acting adjutant when he was killed at the battle of Ezra Church, July 28, 1864. McMillan was probably a temporary replacement for Samuel Cummings. Cummings was on sick furlough during the summer of 1864 recovering from wounds.
- Lieutenant Samuel J. Cummings was appointed adjutant, September 1, 1862. Cummings was born in Baltimore, Maryland, September 1821. He was a lawyer, educated in Baltimore and Plymouth, England. He relocated to Monroeville, Alabama, in 1842. He was active in politics. After the war, he practiced law in Birmingham where he died in 1893.[12]

2. Quartermaster
- Captain C. C. Lloyd was listed as quartermaster for the regiment when it reported to Montgomery in September 1861. Lloyd resigned January 7, 1862.
- Captain B. F. Reed was appointed as Lloyd's replacement January 7, 1862. Reed was a member of the regiment as late as the summer of 1864.
- Captain James Moreland served as acting quartermaster for an unknown period.

---

[11] "Maj. W. J. Milner". *Butler County Historical and Genealogical Society* (July 1998), 51.
[12] Owen, 440

ORIGIN AND FORMATION

3. **Commissary**
Captain James R. Benson was appointed regimental commissary September 11, 1861. He was relieved of duty by order of the Secretary of War July 31, 1863. An invoice of subsistence stores turned over to Captain Benson at Pensacola on December 31, 1861 included the following: 16 barrels of pork, 122 barrels of flour, 15,210 lbs. of fresh beef, 2973 lbs. of bacon, 6136 lbs. of corn meal, 1745 lbs. of rice, 660 lbs. of coffee, 320 lbs. of candles, 662 gals. of molasses, 166 gals. of vinegar, and 1030 lbs. of dried apples.[13]

4. **Chaplain**
- Reverend Isaac T. Tichenor was the first know chaplain for the 17th Alabama regiment. Tichenor was a Baptist minister who served as pastor to churches in Mississippi, Tennessee, Kentucky, and Alabama before the Civil War. In the early years of the war, he served as chaplain of the 17th Alabama Regiment. He resigned after the battle of Shiloh and became president of the Montevallo Coal Mining Company in Shelby County, Alabama.[14] He later became president of the Agricultural and Mechanical College in Auburn, Alabama, now known as Auburn University.
- Joshua J. Groce replaced Reverend Tichenor as chaplain October 20, 1862. Groce was born in Green County in 1836 and was a minister before the Civil War. He enlisted in the 17th Alabama May 10, 1862, at Corinth, Mississippi. He was hospitalized during June 1862 and served as a fifth sergeant from July to October. On October 10, 1862, Groce was reassigned as chaplain of the 17th Alabama. He remained with the regiment until his capture at Franklin, Tennessee, December 17, 1864. From there he was imprisoned at Camp Chase, Ohio, where he was paroled June 11, 1865.

5. **Surgeon**
- B. F. Blount was listed as acting surgeon when the regiment was formed in 1861.[15]
- Michael J. Bolan was listed as acting surgeon of the regiment. He was probably captured at Shiloh, Tennessee, in April 1862. He was taken ill and admitted to the hospital on board USA Hospital Steamer Empress April 15, 1862. He was later sent to a general hospital. By June 25, 1862, he was imprisoned at Camp Douglas, Illinois.[16]
- J. S. Jenkins was born in 1818 in Colleton, South Carolina. He was a physician before the war and was enlisted by Captain W. W. McMillan of Company H October 16, 1861. He was listed as acting assistant

---

[13] *Compiled Service Records of Confederate Soldiers Who Served in Organizations in Alabama*
[14] *The Alabama 17th, Isaac Taylor Tichenor and a Sabbath Event* (SG024895, folder 11, Alabama Archives, Montgomery, AL).
[15] McMillan sketch.
[16] *Compiled Service Records of Confederate Soldiers Who Served in Organizations in Alabama*

surgeon to Surgeon Jones during the month of January 1862. He was granted a disability discharge March 22, 1862, at Corinth, Mississippi.
- W. R. Jones was listed as surgeon when the regiment was formed in September 1861[17] and on the January regimental returns for 1862[18]
- John Washington Keyes was a physician and practicing dentist in Montgomery when the war began. In November 1862, he resigned as first lieutenant in the 60th Alabama and was assigned as surgeon of the 17th Alabama. After the war, he and his family moved to Rio de Janeiro, Brazil, where he became dentist to the emperor Dom Pedro and his royal family. In the late 1870s he returned to Alabama. He later moved to Wewahitchka, Florida, where he died.[19]
- M. J. Rice was appointed as assistant surgeon by General Bragg May 6, 1862.[20] He was listed as assistant surgeon, April 30, 1864.[21]
- William A. Walton of Company C studied at Tulane Medical School in New Orleans to become a medical doctor. After receiving his degree he returned to Butler County where he began his practice. He entered the 17th Alabama as a private September 7, 1862. In November 1863 he became a regimental surgeon and first lieutenant by order of Colonel Murphy. He remained with the regiment for the remainder of the war. After the surrender he returned to Butler County where he continued his medical practice at Mashville.
- A. F. Watson of Company F was appointed surgeon by General Bragg May 6, 1862, and division surgeon July 22, 1864.[22]

Captain McMillan of Company H, Captains Thomas McCane and Leonidas Pentecost of Company K, and Major Fariss were all trained as doctors before the war began. All four of these men chose to support the Confederacy in a military role rather than a medical role.

E. Assignments

During the War, the regiment assignment changed as the Confederate Army was reorganized. Below is a list of assignments found in Confederate records.[23]

September – October 1861
    Walker's Brigade
October 1861
    Army of Pensacola

---

[17] McMillan sketch.
[18] Thomas Watts, *January Returns 17th Alabama Regiment (Shiloh National Park, Unpublished).*
[19] Owen, 973.
[20] Edward Crenshaw, "The Diary of Edward Crenshaw", *The Alabama Historical Quarterly* (Fall 1930)
[21] Joseph Jones, "Roster of Medical Officers of the Army of Tennessee," *Southern Historical Papers*, Book 22 (1894): 165.
[22] *Compiled Service Records of Confederate Soldiers Who Served in Organizations in Alabama*
[23] Stewart Sifakis, *Compendium of the Confederate Armies* (New York, NY: Facts on File, 1992).

ORIGIN AND FORMATION

    Dept. of Alabama and West Florida - Major-General Braxton Bragg
        Gladden Brigade – Brigadier-General A. H. Gladden
            17th Alabama – Colonel Thomas H. Watts

February 1, 1862
    Dept. of Alabama and West Florida - Major-General Braxton Bragg
        Army of Pensacola - Brigadier-General Sam Jones
            17th Alabama - Colonel Thomas H. Watts

April 7, 1862
    Army of the Mississippi - Major-General Braxton Bragg
        2nd Army Corps
            2nd Division
                3rd Brigade - Brigadier-General John K. Jackson
                      17th Alabama - Lt.-Colonel Robert C. Fariss

June 30, 1862
    Army of the Mississippi - Major-General Braxton Bragg
        Reserve Corps - Brigadier-General J. M. Withers
            3rd Brigade - Brigadier-General John K. Jackson
                17th Alabama – Colonel J. P. Jones

October 31, 1862
    District of the Gulf - Major-General John H. Forney
        Army of Mobile - Brigadier-General J. E. Slaughter
            17th Alabama – Colonel V. S. Murphey

April 1863
    Department of the Gulf – Major-General S. B. Buckner
        Western Division – Brigadier-General William W. Mackall
            1st Brigade – Brigadier-General James E. Slaughter
                17th Alabama – Colonel V. S. Murphey

August 10, 1863
    Department of the Gulf - Major-General Dabney H. Maury
        1st Brigade – Brigadier-General James Cantey
            17th Alabama – Colonel V. S. Murphey

September 30, 1863
    Department of the Gulf - Major-General Dabney H. Maury
        1st Brigade – Brigadier-General James Cantey
            17th Alabama – Colonel V. S. Murphey

January 20, 1864
    Department of the Gulf - Major-General Dabney H. Maury
        Cantey's Brigade - Brigadier-General James Cantey
            17th Alabama - Colonel V. S. Murphey

June 10, 1864
    Army of Mississippi[24] – Lieutenant-General Leonidas Polk

---

[24] OWR, serial 74, 646: Previously called Army of the Mississippi, by June 1864 called Army of Mississippi. In April 1864 some divisions of the Army of Mississippi moved to Georgia to reinforce the Army of Tennessee in its defense of Atlanta from Sherman.

12 THE SEVENTEENTH ALABAMA INFANTRY

  Cantey's Division - Brigadier-General James Cantey
   2nd Brigade – Colonel V. S. Murphey
    17th Alabama – Major Thomas J. Burnett
June 30, 1864
  Army of Mississippi - Major-General William W. Loring
   Walthall's Division – Major-General Edward C. Walthall
    2nd Brigade - Brigadier-General James Cantey
     17th Alabama – Major Thomas J. Burnett
July 10, 1864
  Army of Mississippi - Major-General William W. Loring
   Walthall's Division - Major-General Edward C. Walthall
    Cantey's Brigade – Colonel Edward A. O'Neal
     17th Alabama - Colonel V. S. Murphey
July 31, 1864
  Army of Tennessee[25] – General John Bell Hood
   Stewart's Corps – Major-General Benjamin F. Cheatham
    Walthall's Division - Major-General Edward C. Walthall
     Cantey's Brigade - Colonel Edward A. O'Neal
      17th Alabama – Captain Thomas A. McCane
August 31, 1864
  Army of Tennessee – General John Bell Hood
   Stewart's Corps – Lieutenant-General Alexander P. Stewart
    Walthall's Division – Major-General Edward C. Walthall
     Cantey's Brigade - Colonel Edward A. O'Neal
      17th Alabama – Capt. W. W. McMillan[26]
November 1, 1864
  Army of Tennessee – General John Bell Hood
   Stewart's Corps – Lieutenant-General Alexander P. Stewart
    Walthall's Division – Major-General Edward C. Walthall
     Cantey's Brigade - Brigadier Charles M. Shelley
      17th Alabama – Colonel V. S. Murphey
December 10, 1864
  Army of Tennessee – General John Bell Hood
   Stewart's Corps – Lieutenant-General Alexander P. Stewart
    Walthall's Division - Major-General Edward C. Walthall
     Cantey's Brigade – Brigadier-General Charles M. Shelley
      17th Alabama – Captain John Bolling, Jr.
March 31, 1865

---

[25] Ibid, 665: When General Hood replaced General Joseph Johnston as commander of the Army of Tennessee, the army was reorganized and Cantey's brigade became part of the Army of Tennessee.

[26] McCane and McMillan were temporary replacements for Colonel Murphy. McMillan was replaced on October 3, 1864, by Captain Wiley E. White. White resigned October 25, 1864, when Colonel Murphy returned to duty.

ORIGIN AND FORMATION 13

> Army of Tennessee - Lieutenant-General Alexander P. Stewart
> Stewart's Corps - Major-General Edward C. Walthall
> Loring's Division – Brigadier-General George D. Johnston
> Quarles' Brigade – Captain Sol. Jones
> 17th Alabama Consolidated - Captain Benjamin Screws

April 9, 1865
> Army of Tennessee – General Joseph Johnston
> Hardee's Corps – Lieutenant-General William J. Hardee
> Loring's Division – Major-General William W. Loring
> Shelley's Brigade – Brigadier-General Charles M. Shelley
> 17th Alabama – Colonel Edward P. Holcombe

F. Company A

Muster Roll of Captain E. P. Holcombe's Company A, September 5, 1861[27], from Lowndes County and known as Bartow Avengers.

Officers

E. P. Holcombe	Captain
W. L. Moon	1st Lieutenant
C. E. Sadler	2nd Lieutenant
R. M. Williamson	Jr. 2nd Lieutenant
J. C. Bright	1st Sergeant
H. G. Hartley	2nd Sergeant
T. F. Davidson	3rd Sergeant
Alford Robinson	4th Sergeant
Whitman Coltin	1st Corporal
Jordan Shanks	2nd Corporal
James M. Davis	3rd Corporal
F. A. Hambrick	4th Corporal

Privates

Aaron, William	Acree, Joseph S.
Adams, Martin	Adams, Solomon
Adams, Stephen	Autrey, Elmo
Balt, Erasmus	Baltzer, Daniel
Bodeford, John	Boutwell, Wm. Arnold
Brown, John R	Canady, William
Cleeman, William	Cotrell, Young A.
Cowles, Thomas	Davis, Joseph Greene
Davis, Joseph T.	Dean, J. M.
Dean, R.	Dyer, J. B.
Edings, C. T.	Edwards, William

---

[27] *17th Alabama Muster Rolls* (SG024896, folder 21, Alabama Archives, Montgomery, AL).

Gill, John	Gill, Marion
Goodwin, M. W.	Hall, Marshall
Hatcher, W. J.	Hawkins, H. S.
Hawkins, James	Hawkins, R. F.
Holiday, Newtin	Jones, David P.
King, Jas. L.	Lawrence, David S.
Lawrence, Jasper	Leach, Richard
Lee, Oliver	Lee, W. H. C.
McPherin, Jas.	McShoe, William
Moorer, Mansin	Murphy, Jas. G.
Nealy, Benja. C.	Numan, William
Owen, Wade	Peacock, Jno. J.
Perdue, Whitman	Philpot, S. W.
Pitts, Henry W.	Scallion, Augustus
Smith, Henry	Smith, Moses
Smith, W. P.	Spanks, Geo. P.
Spanks, John	Spanks, Monne
Spivey, Joshua	Stewart, Benj. F.
Sullivan, Elbert	Taylor, D.B.
Taylor, J. M.	Taylor, John
Till, William	Vernell, Calvin.
Walker, Frank L.	Weatherford, Stephen
White, James	Williams, Geo. W.

Edward P. Holcombe was elected captain of Company A September 5, 1861. He was senior captain of the regiment. This placed him first in line for advancement to the regimental staff. He was promoted to lieutenant colonel July 25, 1862. He was absent from the 17th Alabama in 1864 after the battle of Resaca, Georgia, in May recovering from his wounds. In April 1865 he was promoted to colonel and appointed commander of the 17th Alabama.

F. A. Hambrick was appointed captain of the company to replace the vacancy left by Holcombe. Appointment of company commanders was usually the responsibility of the regimental staff. In this instance, the promotion of Hambrick was on orders from General Braxton Bragg.[28] This was not considered a legal appointment by the regimental staff. He was replaced in July 1862 when General John K. Jackson appointed C. E. Sadler as commanding officer of Company A after Holcombe was promoted. Hambrick continued with Company A until he was wounded at Kennesaw Mountain in July of 1864. He died soon after.

---

[28] Correspondence dated November 14, 1864, in service record of C. E. Sadler.

Sadler, as first lieutenant of Company A, was the logical person to replace Holcombe as company commander. He held this position during the battle of Shiloh. Sadler was severely wounded at Shiloh April 6, 1862. Although he never quite recovered from his wounds, he remained commander of his unit for the next couple of years. He was hospitalized in March 1864 because of the wounds suffered at Shiloh and was placed on furlough in May 1864. He requested that he be allowed to retire and was placed on extended furlough. His papers appointing him captain of Company A in 1862 had been lost or destroyed which probably delayed his retirement and the appointment of a successor. Sadler survived the war and was paroled in Montgomery May 24, 1865, which indicates he was not at the surrender with his unit.

G. Company B

Muster Roll of Captain Jeptha J. Deen's Company B, September 14, 1861[29], from Butler County:

Officers

Deen, Jeptha, 42	Captain
Norris, Esum L., 25	1st Lieutenant
Parker, Benjamin J., 29	2nd Lieutenant
Williams, Thomas, 20	2nd Lieutenant
Edgar, Adams. H., 41	1st Sergeant
Deal, James. F., 24	2nd Sergeant
Norris, John F., 19	3rd Sergeant
Arant, Elvin P., 23	4th Sergeant
Ansley, John A., 21	1st Corporal
Parker, John T., 25	2nd Corporal
Jackson, Geo. L., 18	3rd Corporal
Lee, Geo. W., 20	4th Corporal

Privates

Barrett, Melvin T., 19
Black, James H., 23
Blackman, Chapman, 37
Brent, Joseph, 43
Carnethan, Joseph, 28
Coleman, Charles
Coleman, Jesse, 28
Deen, Wm. K., 25
Foster, Hosey W., 18
Galloway, Eli, 22

Bishop, Columbus F., 32
Black, Wm. H., 26
Braswell, Wm., 29
Brooks, Wm. F, 23
Caton, Alfred D.
Coleman, Geo. T., 17
Davis, John W., 27
Eubanks, Jesse H., 20
Fowler, Wm. A., 20
Gardner, John, 23

---

[29] Ibid.

Garrett, Henry C., 22
Grantham, Thos J., 19
Green, James, 19
Griswold, Clemmons R., 28
Halso, Stephen, 20
Hawthorn, John R., 24
Hudson, Wm. W., 16
Johnson, James H.
Jones, Thomas B., 21
Kirven, John F., 22
Lee, John D., 20
Lewis, John H., 21
Manley, Charles J., 34
Maxey, Wm., 33
Moore, Augustus W., 18
Morris, John M., 25
Mosley, Chapman L., 20
Norris, Alex F.
Owens, Robert G., 17
Pittman, Robt. C., 20
Rambo, John R., 20
Redd, Joshua, 43
Stanley, Wm. Henry, 16
Stewart, William D., 34
Thomas, James M., 19
Townsend, Samuel, 22
Tyner, Joseph A., 21
Walker, Felix G., 27
Warren, George W., 18
Watson, Jesse M., 24
Williamson, John, 36
Williamson, S. E., 20
Worthington, Wm. A., 20

Garrett, Nathan G., 17
Grantham, Wm., 19
Griffin, John H., 20
Griswold, Oba, 31
Hambrick, John F. N., 21
Hodges, David L., 21
Johnson, Geo. S., 23
Jolley, Henry M., 21
Kirksey, William D., 21
Lee, George, 19
Lee, Wm., 18
Major, Daniel, 24
Mathew, John L., 36
Miniard, John, 20
Morison, S., 18
Morris, Wm. J., 22
Nicholas, Jasper P., 24
Norris, William A., 25
Pearson, James H., 22
Porter, Tho. M. J., 27
Ramsey, James M., 20
Stallings, Archie M., 19
Stewart, Lewis C., 23
Taylor, William, 19
Tisdale, Marshal S., 18
Tyner, Elijah S., 22
Vardell, Milton G., 20
Ware, David, 21
Watson, Anderson J., 23
Wiggins, Wm. H.
Williamson, Madison, 17
Worthington, Alex, 22

Jeptha J. Deen was captain of Company B when the unit was mustered into the Confederate Army in September 1861. He resigned May 2, 1862, after the battle of Shiloh.

The next captain of the company was T. J. Barrett. General Braxton Bragg transferred Barrett from the 6th Georgia Regiment and appointed him captain of Company C May 12, 1862. On June 26, 1862, Bragg transferred him to Company B. Bragg relieved Barrett of his position July 24, 1862. In 1863, Barrett was appointed first lieutenant and ordinance officer of Jackson's Brigade.

ORIGIN AND FORMATION

James S. Moreland was appointed captain July 23, 1862, replacing Barrett. He was transferred from Company K to become captain of Company B July 26, 1862. Moreland was captured at Resaca, Georgia, May 1864, and imprisoned at Johnson Island, Ohio, where he was paroled June 16, 1865.

It is not known who commanded the company after Resaca. However, Major Thomas J. Burnett, acting commander of the 17th Alabama, on May 21, expected that William Turner Dunklin would be appointed captain of Company B.[30] This occurred after Captain James Moreland was captured and Lieutenant Benjamin Parker was killed at Resaca.

H. Company C

Muster Roll of Captain Walter D. Perryman's Company C, September 14, 1861[31], from Butler County and known as the Butler Rifles:

Officers

Perryman, Walter D., 37	Captain (resigned)
Bolling, John Jr., 21	1st Lieutenant
Trawick, LaFayette W., 32	2nd Lieutenant
Payne, John K., 19	3rd Lieutenant
Lloyd, Cary C., 27	1st Sergeant
Perry, Robt., 20	2nd Sergeant
Goodson, Peter, 26	3rd Sergeant
Wallace, John	4th Sergeant
Peterson, William T., 27	1st Corporal
Stevens, Edward, 25	2nd Corporal
Skipper, John W., 44	3rd Corporal
Seale, Henry R., 20	4th Corporal

Privates

Andrews, Marion J., 24
Bailey, Geo. W., 20
Burton, Benjamin F., 22
Conner, William H., 18
Davis, Alfred, 20
Driver, John W., 25
Dukes, James F., 18
Frost, Henry, 20
Gafford, Thomas G., 26
Harrison, John A., 21
Henderson, Josiah H., 18
Atchinson, Theophilus, 28
Boggus, Henry J., 25
Cater, Josiah, 38
Creach, Sidney S., 19
Dendy, Buford W., 20
Dugan, James, 25
Earnest, James, 20
Frost, Josiah, 20
Harper, Henry S., 30
Harrison, Moses, 18
Hendricks, Yapley, 38

---

[30] Burnett (Thomas Jefferson) Papers, 1862-1864, *Pearce Civil War Collection* (Navarro College, Corsicana, Texas).
[31] 17th Alabama Muster Rolls.

Hernden, William, 30
Hester, Louis A., 18
Jay, James W., 32
Johnson, Julius F., 22
Kelly, John H., 18
Lord, Lewis M., 25
McCrary, John A., 29
Milton, Jacob C., 31
Pace, Thomas E., 21
Parker, Gardner G., 30
Perry, James, 38
Philyaw, Thomas J., 18
Powell, William H., 25
Rayburn, Richard, 19
Sims, Robert M., 18
Smith, Thomas J., 18
Smyth, Andrew C., 34
Stringer, Robt. J. K., 18
Thompson, John J., 19
Troutman, Soloman H., 24
Wallace, Samuel G., 21
Willis, James S., 21

Hester, Daniel E., 19
Howard, John D., 18
Johnson, James H., 21
Kelly, Andrew J., 25
Lary, LaFayette, 35
McCormack, John D., 28
Miller, Isaiah G., 18
Nicholas, Shadrack, 35
Pace, William B., 24
Payne, Ira E., 18
Petty, James A. M., 35
Pierce, Frank M., 25
Ramsay, Neal O., 21
Sanders, Thomas J., 25
Singleton, John W., 23
Smith, William, 22
Spurlock, John T., 20
Talley, Littleton, 18
Troutman, Newton
Wallace, Abram F., 20
Williamson, William, 23

Walter D. Perryman was elected captain of Company C September 9, 1861, and resigned May 2, 1862.

General Braxton Bragg appointed T. J. Barrett captain of Company C May 12, 1862. Then Bragg transferred Barrett to Company B June 26, 1862.

John Bolling Jr. was promoted to captain of the company June 22, 1862. He remained in this position until after the battle of Franklin, November 30, 1864, when he was promoted to commander of the regiment. He led the regiment in the battle of Nashville December 15, 1864, when he was captured. He was imprisoned at Johnson Island, Ohio, where he was paroled June 16, 1865.

John L. Powell was promoted to captain of Company C April 10, 1865, during the final reorganization.

I. Company D

Muster Roll of Captain Thomas Coke Bragg's Company D, September 17, 1861,[32] from Coosa County:

---

[32] Ibid.

ORIGIN AND FORMATION

Officers

Bragg, Thomas C., 35	Captain (resigned)
Thaxton, Dixon S., 25	1st Lieutenant
Hester, John A., 24	2nd Lieutenant
Hull, Wm. D., 24	Jr. 2nd Lieutenant
Rush, Warren R., 24	1st Sergeant
Callaway, Joseph W., 20	2nd Sergeant
Adkins, John T., 18	3rd Sergeant
Holland, Robert M., 27	4th Sergeant
Stewart, Seaborn M., 30	1st Corporal
Storey, Newton A., 19	2nd Corporal
Lauderdale, John T., 18	3rd Corporal
Lee, William W., 23	4th Corporal

Privates

Balentine, Isaac, 18
Blankenship, Abner J., 28
Carony, Green B.
Crew, William C., 20
Downs, Joshua, 35
Duke, George W., 18
Fleming, Wm. J., 18
Gillelund, Wm., 20
Gresham, Whitten R., 18
Hendrix, James, 20
Hines, Thomas G., 23
Hull, Nathaniel, 21
Jackson, Wm. M., 24
Jones, Julius, 18
Kincade, Wm. B., 23
Letlow, Bulger F., 22
Lewis, Jas. H., 21
Linsey, William, 19
Mayo, Elisha M., 18
McQueen, Norman, 21
Norwood, Jas. M., 25
Pate, William A., 18
Peek, Benjamin F., 19
Pickett, Jas. W., 26
Rawls, Wm. B.
Roberts, William J., 18
Rush, John B., 20
Shaw, William, 19
Stewart, Geo. W. S., 19
Barnett, John B., 33
Bryant, William, 20
Collier, C., 24
Crumpter, Paschal A., 18
Downs, Shelley, 30
Durden, William W., 18
Gary, Augustus S., 28
Glenn, John, 18
Hadmond, James N.
Hester, Alfred L., 20
Hull, Joseph B., 18
Ingram, Samuel A., 18
Johnson, Samuel A., 20
Kimbrough, Thos. M., 28
Ledbetter, James M., 23
Letlow, Thos. B., 19
Lewis, Wm. P., 21
Macon, Wm. H., 18
McNair, John B., 23
Monroe, Benjamin P., 20
Pate, Thos. M., 19
Paylant, Andrew H., 21
Peoples, John, 19
Powell, Edmond J., 20
Reves, Wm., 22
Robertson, Josiah, 18
Sharp, Jas. G., 18
Smith, William H., 20
Stewart, Nathaniel W., 26

Stewart, Samuel D.
Stewart, Wm., 32
Taylor, Wm. R. H., 20
Thompson, Zebeder, 19
Warrick, Henry J., 22
Wilson, Elias, 19

Stewart, Sanders S., 19
Taylor, Evens, 18
Thomas, Wm. H., 32
Thorenton, Horatio M., 22
Whetsone, Joseph, 26

T. C. Bragg was elected captain of Company D September 17, 1861. He resigned in 1862 due to poor health. He had been a teacher before the Civil War. Know as Professor Thomas C. Bragg, he purchased Central Institute, Baptist male school in Coosa County, in 1860 for $4,025. He returned to the school in 1862. He suspended the school for a while in 1865. He then reopened the school for two years before selling it and moving to Montgomery.[33]

First Lieutenant Dixon S. Thaxton resigned December 1861. Consequently Second Lieutenant John A. Hester was promoted to captain of the company January 28, 1862. He was captured May 27, 1864, at Dallas, Georgia. Hester was imprisoned at Johnson Island, Ohio, where he was paroled at the end of the war.

A. J. Simpson held the rank of captain. He was listed as a captain and in Company D at the surrender at Greensboro, North Carolina, April 1865. It can only be assumed that he, at some point, replaced Captain Hester after Hester's capture.

J. Company E

Company E was the Dowdell Rangers from Randolph County. Wiley E. White, better known as Dose White of Roanoke, made up a company of 86 men in July and August 1861. The original company was composed of the following men:

Officers

White, Wiley E., 29,	Captain
Reed (Reid), B. F., 30	1st Lieutenant
Weathers, B. F., 22	2nd Lieutenant
Robertson, J. D., 23	2nd Lieutenant
Stitt, Robert S., 20	1st Sergeant
Cullens, George W., 26	2nd Sergeant
Collier, Squire T., 31	3rd Sergeant
Barrett, Thos. D, 31	4th Sergeant
Hester, John, 22	1st Corporal
Gauntt, Elisha L., 28	2nd Corporal

---

[33] Rev. George E. Brewer, "Professor Thomas Coke Bragg", *The Alabama Historical Quarterly*, Spring and Summer 1942.

ORIGIN AND FORMATION 21

Wheeler, John, 28 — 3rd Corporal
Green, Tandy H., 24 — 4th Corporal
Hollingsworth, T., 18 — Musician
Daniel, Newton, 18 — Musician

Privates

Arnold, Thos., 27
Barton, Enoch, 43
Boyd, Elias, 25
Burson, David J., 18
Copeland, Thomas J., 23
Dabney, Garlin, 28
Edwards, John W., 29
Fincher, Alex B., 33
Harrell, Sam, 29
Head, Richard, 23
Hester, Jeremiah, 24
Hodges, James M., 25
Hood, Onan A., 20
Hornsby, Noah D., 29
Hutchens, Henry, 35
Jenkins, William, 18
Kitchens, John, 18
Mayfield, B. W., 31
Miller, Wm. J., 20
Moon, John G., 21
Moon, Levi T., 18
Norred, Joshua,, 25
Owen, Alphus, 34
Pike, Thomas, 21
Robertson, Andrew, 18
Skinner, James, 19
Slaughter, John, 18
Spears, Wm. C., 24
Swann, Nathaniel J., 27
Taylor, George, 21
Upchurch, Hobson, 18
Vaughan, Samuel, 18
Wadkins, James, 50
Weathers, Thomas, 18
Weaver, John, 22
White, Henry C.
Young, Joel, 20

Baker, W. H., 19
Blair, J. W., 21
Braziel, James P., 18
Camp, Izah C., 22
Copeland, Wm. C., 45
Davis, David L., 23
Etheridge, Harrison P., 45
Fincher, William A., 18
Hawthorn, Hugh
Head, Samuel, 20
Hodges, Bennett, 22
Holder, Theophilus, 18
Hornesby, J. M.
Hunt, Gilbert, 18
Hutchens, J. D., 18
Johnson, Robert, 18
Mattox, Benj. P., 18
Mayo, Louie, 21
Milton, John F., 28
Moon, Josiah F., 25
Newman, Samuel, 25
Osburn, John L., 22
Pate, R. S.
Rice, Wm. P., 23
Shelmet, Andrew, 24
Skipper, Hiram, 26
Smith, Lewis, 21
Stitt, Thomas, 18
Talley, John, 21
Townsend, Harris, 19
Upchurch, John W. H., 19
Vinson, Micajah, 34
Walden, W. W., 43
Weaver, James, 53
Weaver, Richard, 21
Young, Jiles, 22

Captain Wiley E. White was elected captain of Company E September 14, 1861. Four days after the battle of Shiloh, he was captured at Huntsville, Alabama. Lieutenant Benjamin F. Weathers was temporarily appointed captain and commanding officer of Company E when Captain White was captured. In the meantime, White was moved to Sandusky, Ohio, May 24, and sent to Vicksburg, Mississippi, for exchange September 1, 1862. He was returned to duty with his unit and relieved Weathers as captain and commander of Company E October 25, 1862.[34] White remained with his company for two years and resigned October 25, 1864.

Weathers was born in Fayetteville, Georgia, and moved with his family to Alabama in 1842. He was living in Randolph County in 1861 when Company E was organized. He was appointed second lieutenant September 1861 and first lieutenant January 1862. Weathers remained in Company E until his capture at Franklin, Tennessee, November 30, 1864. In 1931, still living in Randolph County, Weathers wrote a series of articles for the *Roanoke Leader* describing his involvement in the Civil War. As part of the series of articles, Weathers describes the first weeks of duty in Company E:

"We drilled to teach the men how to keep in step as a soldier in marching.

In July a fine dinner was given the Company at Corn House Creek by people of that community. We marched the four miles in August. A dinner was given the company at Rocks Mills. We were having a fine time as soldiers. In August Captain White called the company together and ordered an election of officers, as follows: Wiley E. White, captain; B. F. Reed, first lieutenant; B. F. Weathers, second lieutenant; J. D. Roberts, third lieutenant.

Captain White reported to Gov. Moore that his company was organized and ready for action. Gov. Moore then issued commissions naming the company as the Dowdell Rangers. Thomas J. Judge was at that time engaged in forming a regiment. He sent bolts of gray cloth to be cut and made into uniforms for the company. They had to be made by the women. It took them some time to get them ready. In the meantime Col. Judge had completed his regiment. So it was September the 9th when the company left Roanoke. The day was full of excitement. Many were present to bid farewell to friends and their sons. In the evening as the company lined up to leave Miss Fannie White, a niece of Captain Abose White, (now Mrs. Fannie Pool), presented a very large pound cake to the company as a token of her heart's feelings for the company. Her brother was one of the company.

Mrs. John A. Moore, a very intelligent woman, made the presentation speech, the writer responding, after which the command, "Forward

---

[34] *Compiled Service Records*, See B. F. Weathers.

March," was given, and we marched five miles to Bethel and camped in the church. We had a wagon loaded with supper and breakfast. The cake was cut and each one got a piece. A detail guard was made and posted, with instructions not to let any one pass without giving the countersign "Chickahominy."

Next morning the company was ordered to fall into line for roll call. After the roll call the command, "Right face, forward march!" was given. Some of the boys were singing, "The girl I left behind." Just before we got to Fredonia we met a wagon and learned that two of Captain Smith's men had died in camp in Virginia and were being sent back to Roanoke for burial – Slay and Adcock. The whole company was made sad.

We got to Fredonia at 11 a.m. The citizens had prepared a rich bountiful dinner on a long table in J. M. Robertson's yard for the company. We left about 1 p.m. on a 11-mile march to West Point. We got there about sundown and spent the night at the hotel. We were treated royally. The West point people are noted for their generosity.

Sept. 11th we boarded a train for Montgomery. At Opelika Captain Tom Ragland, of Russell County, joined us. When we got to Montgomery Thomas H. Watts met us at the depot and marched us to an artesian well on Commerce Street, gave us dinner and blankets and marched us to the fair grounds for the night. Next day he sent us to the Johnson Warehouse at the Pensacola depot.

On the 18th of September the regiment was completed.

The regiment on the 18th of September was mustered into the Confederate service for three years, or during the war. The regiment moved to Shorter Station, 23 miles east of Montgomery, went in camp in an old field and drilled for six weeks. Camp was in Macon County, a few miles from Tuskegee. The citizens were very kind, many of them bringing us wagon loads of all kinds of vegetables."[35]

K. Company F

Company commander was Captain Andrew L. O'Brien. The company was from Montgomery County and was known as the Winter Greys. A partial list of the initial muster roll has been recreated from known enlistment dates prior to mustering in to the regiment in September 1861. This information was extracted from the data found on the microfilm of the service records for the 17th Alabama.

Officers

O'Brien, Andrew	Captain
Roberts, A. F. E.	1st Lieutenant
Skipper, William	2nd Lieutenant

---

[35] B. F. Weathers, "War History of General Weathers," *Roanoke Leader*, Roanoke, AL (1931).

Addison, Abijah	Sergeant
Bray, Henry B.	Sergeant
Matthews, Albert T.	Sergeant
Moore, W. H.	Sergeant
Sharp, James M.	Sergeant
Bailey, Wesley F.	Corporal
Croxton, Robert A.	Corporal
Hayle, George W.	Corporal
Jones, Owen	Corporal
Owen, Jones	Corporal
Wilson, M. W.	Corporal
Shunackel, William	Musician

Privates

Albright, Charles	Anderson, W., Sr.
Baker, J. H.	Blount, C. W.
Bock, F. R. W.	Butler, Thomas
Champion, H. M.	Coll, Hugh
Collins, Jeremiah	Evans, E. A.
Fields, Gabriel	Grayor, H. T.
Hall, H. P.	Harrison, Martin
Lovett, Joseph	McHugh, John
McMillon, Charles B.	Miller, Edward
Mings, James W.	Monfee, Francis
Odom, L. S.	Owen, James Madison
Owen, Thomas F.	Sharp, John O.
Shoemaker, W. H.	Skipper, William
Taylor, W. B.	Terry, Thomas
Webb, C. C.	Webb, W. H.

Andrew O'Brien was elected captain of Company F September 17, 1861. He was severely wounded July 28, 1864, at the battle of Ezra Church near Atlanta. The injury was to his left foot and his right ankle. It is doubtful that he was ever able to lead his men again. However, no record can be found as to his successor as commander of Company F.

L. Company G

The commander for Company G was Captain Thomas Ragland. The company was from Russell County. A partial list of the initial muster roll has been recreated from known enlistment dates prior to mustering in to the regiment in September 1861. This information was extracted from the data found on the microfilm of the service records for the 17th Alabama.

Officers

Ragland, Thomas	Captain
Leonard, B. F.	1st Lieutenant
Leonard, G. F.	2nd Lieutenant
Johnson, L. S.	Master Sergeant
Johnson, R. W.	Sergeant
Smith, Charles J.	Sergeant
Wynn, R. A.	Sergeant
Bussey, J. C.	Corporal
Elbern, Joseph W.	Corporal
Wynne, John T.	Corporal

Privates

Barker, Jesse M.	Broadwaters, Thomas J.
Bussey, James	Carden, William Tarrentine
Chadwick, Augustus H.	Chadwick, John L.
Chadwick, Rickerson	Chappell, Abram
Crenshaw, James E.	Davis, James D.
Elder, James	Goff, Matthew
Gray, T. J.	Johnson, Henry M.
Lollis, John	Lollis, W. A.
Lunsford, Blanton	O'Ferrell, J. W.
Porter, Joe Day	Porter, John T.
Sasser, John W.	Sasser, Joseph J.
Sharpton, Alexander	Sharpton, William E.
Simmons, A. D.	Spinks, William
Teat, J. H.	Treadway, James M.
White, J. F.	Williams, D. M.
Wilson, W. C.	Wynne, Lemuel
Wynne, William H.	Geeslin, Benjamin F.
Mote, James	

Thomas Ragland was elected captain September 25, 1861. He was killed July 28, 1864, at the battle of Ezra Church near Atlanta.

John F. Tate was appointed second lieutenant October 25, 1861, and first lieutenant May 17, 1862. He was promoted to captain and commander of Company G after the death of Ragland. He was promoted to lieutenant colonel April 20, 1865, and was on the regimental staff at the surrender.

J. L. McIntyre was appointed captain July 24, 1862. He was listed as captain at the time of the surrender at Greensboro, North Carolina.

M. Company H

The commander of Company H was Captain W. W. McMillan. The company was from Monroe County. McMillan provided a list of the initial muster roll for Company H when it was mustered into the 17th Alabama regiment in September 1861:

Officers

McMillan, W. W.	Captain
Andress, R. M.	1st Lieutenant
McCorvey, A. B.	2nd Lieutenant
Wiggins, T. S.	Brev. 2nd Lieutenant
Davison, Jas. M.	1st Sergeant
McMillan, B. F.	2nd Lieutenant
Richardson, W. H.	3rd Lieutenant
Bloxam, H. C.	4th Lieutenant
Andress, Hugh M.	1st Corporal
Perry, R.	2nd Corporal
Black, Jno. M.	3rd Corporal
Andress, W. R.	4th Corporal
Cummings, Samuel McL	Musician
Johnson, S. A.	Musician

Privates

Andress, G. D.	Biggs, W. J.
Black, James	Black, John
Boyles, W. J.	Bradbury, J. W.
Brent, W. T.	Brown, N. B.
Burnett, O. S.	Carter, C. M.
Carter, J. W.	Cummings, S. J.
Davison, J. N.	Davison, W. M.
Deason, W. M.	Deese, C. H.
Eddins, F. M.	Eddins, J. B.
Eddins, R. H.	Fountain, H. S.
Fountain, P. C.	Gordon, J. J.
Jenkins, J. S.	Jenkins, Ralph (Amateur)
Johnson, L.	Lewis, T. F.
McMillan, Malcolm	McMillan, W. H.
Newberry, W. T.	Powell, Henry
Preston, J. E.	Raines, T. H.
Rives, B. S.	Rives, J. H.
Roberts, E. M.	Rumbly, T. A.
Salter, G. W.	Salter, J. C.
Salter, Simon	Sinquefield, James
Stevens, W. C.	Talbert, G. W.
Terraptin, Henry	Thames, N. C.
Wiggins, J. T.	Wiggins, N. J.

W. W. McMillan was appointed captain of Company H October 25, 1861. He remained in charge of the company until wounded at the battle of Franklin, November 30, 1864. He was captured after the battle of Nashville. He was imprisoned at Camp Chase, Ohio, where he remained until the end of the war.

In a journal written by Captain McMillan, he provided information about the origins of Company H of the 17th Alabama:

"*The citizens of the neighborhood met and organized a military Co. of which I was chosen Captain. I knew nothing of Military Tactics, neither indeed did any of the Co. We met weekly for drill. I had a considerable practice, but found time to study "Hardie".^{36} Frequently drawing on the hours which should have been devoted to sleep, for that purpose. The Co. "The Scotland Home Guard"^{37} numbered about 60. We drilled weekly until the latter part of July, when intelligence from "The Battle of Manasas" reached us. The terrible excitement which thrilled the whole country at that time is indescribable. No longer was there any doubt that we were to have a bloody battle - no one could tell how fierce and terrible a struggle. At the request of about 30 of our Home Guard, I commenced raising a Co. of Inf. and in about 6 weeks completed it, and were accepted by Col. Thos. H. Watts who was authorized by the War Department of the C. S. to raise a regiment of Inf. for Service during the War.*

On the morning of the 24 Sept. 1860,^{38} we bade a tearful adieu to the loved ones at home and left for Evergreen on the Illinois Fla. R.R. A great many of our friends accompanied us there, and a few even to Montgomery. At Evergreen we took the cars, and arrived at Montgomery on the morning of 25 at 8 o'clock. Col. Watts met us at the Depot, and invited the whole Co. to breakfast at the Exchange Hotel. After breakfast we marched to the fairgrounds and proceeded to organize the Co. I was elected Capt. by acclamation, the other officers and non-commissioned officers were voted viva voce, all having opposition.... We remained at the Fairgrounds that night and in the morning went to Shorter's Depot on the Mont. and West Point R.R. where the Regt. was rendezvousing."^{39}

N. Company I

The first commander of Company I was Captain A. M. Collins. The company was from Pike County and was known as the Pike Rangers. A partial list of the initial muster roll has been recreated from known enlistment dates prior to mustering in to the regiment in September 1861.

---

[36] Hardie is a reference to a book on military procedure.
[37] Company H was also known as the Scotland Invincibles.
[38] The year was 1861.
[39] McMillan sketch.

This information was extracted from the data found on the microfilm of the service records for the 17th Alabama.

Officers

Collins, A. M.	Captain
Bones, John Samuel	Lieutenant
Brumby, T. P. G.	1st Lieutenant
Guthrie, Albert M.	Sergeant
McLaurine, Christopher	Sergeant
Wright, William J.	Sergeant
Hale, George	Corporal

Privates

Adams, John B.	Adams, Robert B.
Cheatham James	Cogburn, Jesse M.
Dorman, John A.	Downing, Joseph T.
Faulkner, William J.	Gray, Daniel
Harden, Allen	Hale, George W.
Hall, James	Hammonds, Wylie
Harris, John T.	Head, Adolphus M.
Head, William L.	Hogan, George W.
Hogan, William	Hogan, Wyatt
Jackson, Joseph B.	Joiner, Thomas B.
McLane, Henry A.	McWhorter, Ezekiel A.
Ozier, James N.	Padgett, John
Rainer, Joel	Rawls, Oliver L.
Roberds, William R.	Saunders, John Henry
Smith, Saul	Spoon, James H.
Thomas, G. W.	Thomas, Ira
Thompson, Augustus L.	Townsand, Jefferson C.
Ward, John W.	Ward, Sampson M.
White, John L.	Williams, Stanford J.
Williford, John T.	Wright, Thomas

A. Marion Collins was the first captain of Company I. He resigned May 16, 1862.

John Samuel Bones was appointed captain May 10, 1862. He was severely wounded in the left thigh at the battle of Peachtree Creek near Atlanta July 20, 1864, and furloughed from the hospital with his wounds. He was examined at Augusta, Georgia, on April 11, 1865. At that time, he was recommended for retirement to the Invalid Corps - physical disability from gunshot wound.

John H. Rainier was listed as captain in Company I at the surrender at Greensboro, North Carolina.

O. Company K

The commander of Company K was Captain Thomas J. Burnett. The company was from Butler County and was known as the Butler True Blues. A partial list of the initial muster roll has been recreated from known enlistment dates prior to mustering in to the regiment in September 1861. This information was extracted from the data found on the microfilm of the service records for the 17th Alabama.

Officers

Burnett, Thomas J.	Captain
Cody, Columbus J.	2nd Lieutenant
Crenshaw, Edward	2nd Lieutenant
Dunklin, William T.	2nd Lieutenant
Martin, James L.	Lieutenant
McCane, Thomas A.	Lieutenant
Pentecost, Leonidas	2nd Lieutenant
Boan, Frederick	Sergeant
Coleman, Walter	Sergeant
Durden, W. W.	Sergeant
King, Thomas C.	1st Sergeant

Privates

Albritton, John E.	Albritton, P. L.
Ballard, John A.	Bennett, Jeremiah
Blackman, George W.	Blackman, Hardy
Bonnell, Andrew J.	Burke, P. J.
Cheatham, John H.	Clark, James T.
Cleghorn, Henry S.	Clements, W. H.
Coatney, William R.	Cody, Jackson, V. P.
Cubstead, Azbury	Cubstead, John
Daniel, Frederick	Defee, William T.
Dewberry, William	Donaldson, John W.
Donaldson, William H.	Fort, George W.
Gafford, Milton	Golson, John C.
Golson, George F.	Gore, Samuel J.
Hammonds, Wylie H.	Harrison, Daniel
Harrison, J. J. N.	Harrison, James W.
Harrison, Levi	Harvill, Samuel
Harvill, William	Heaton, Frank M.
Hinson, William C.	Huggins, James L.
Hughes, Singleton	Hughes, William W.

Jones, Charles C.
Jordan, George W.
Kirpatrick, William M.
Leysath, Erskine
Majors, Henry
Martin, John M.
McCoy, William J. R.
Meredith, E. W.
Moseley, Robert
Newton, Thomas Edmund
Odom, L. S.
Peagler, George W.
Perdue, Lorenzo B.
Pitts, John
Potter, William
Rogers, William James
Sanders, W. J.
Seale, James K.
Seawright, John R.
Sheppard, Thomas
Sims, W. H. S.
Skipper, Joseph
Smith, William J.
Staggers, John N.
Thigpen, George W.
Tippett, J. M.
Wallace, George
Watson, William V. R.
Wight, J. M.
Williams, Daniel
Wynsdick, T. R.

Jones, Joseph S.
Kerbee, James D.
Knight, L. Samson
Long, Henry J.
Majors, Samuel D.
McCory, James R.
McKellar, Felix G.
Moseley, John L.
Newton, Benjamin Jaspar
Norris, John A.
Payne, William J.
Peagler, Martin G.
Perry, John T.
Potter, Thomas F.
Reid, Hillory
Rozier, John L. B.
Scott, William
Seawright, George A.
Sheppard, J. M.
Sheppard, William F.
Skipper, Alexander
Sloane, J. B.
Solomon, Francis M.
Taylor, John H.
Tierney, Frank
Vernon, Obadiah
Watson, William J.
Whisker, Daniel W.
Wilbur, James
Williams, Reason

Thomas J. Burnett was appointed captain of Company K September 1861. As a member of the legislature, he was granted a leave of absence from the 17th during the legislature session November 26, 1861. He was promoted to major May 1862, but failed to pass examination. The July 1862 muster roll for the unit states he was commissioned and assigned to duty, but found incompetent and suspended while waiting action of the war department. Burnett served on the regimental staff while at Mobile and during the Atlanta campaign. See C. Regimental Commanders.

Thomas McCane was promoted to captain of the unit July 1862. He was captured at the battle of Franklin, Tennessee, November 30, 1864.

McCane was imprisoned at Johnson Island, Ohio, where he was paroled at the end of the war.

Leonidas Pentecost was appointed second lieutenant September 9, 1861, and first lieutenant July 30, 1862. He was wounded during May 1864 in the Atlanta Campaign. Pentecost was promoted to captain and commander of Company K after McCane was captured. Pentecost was present at the surrender at Greensboro, North Carolina.

Edward Crenshaw, an officer in Company K, was a native of Butler County. Crenshaw had attended the University of Alabama for two years. He then transferred to the University of Virginia law school in 1861 when he left school to enlist. He was elected lieutenant with Company K in 1861. He almost died of typhoid fever at Corinth in May 1862, but recovered and returned to his company by July. March 1863, he was transferred and promoted to captain of Company B in the 58th Alabama Infantry. After being severely wounded in the face at the battle of Chicamauga, he was appointed second lieutenant in the Confederate Marines Corps. He later was promoted to first lieutenant and assigned to the Confederate privateer, "Tallahassee". This vessel captured about 40 Union vessels during the war. Crenshaw kept a diary of his war experiences. In his diary he describes the origins of Company K:

"Found Mr. T. J. Burnett raising a company for the war. He persuaded me to join his company. The company was organized with one hundred and forty names on the rolls on the 31st day of August 1861. I was elected junior Second Lieutenant by acclamation. Were ordered to Montgomery and arrived there on the 7th day of September 1861. We were mustered into the Confederate States service for the War as Company "K" 17th Alabama regiment, Col T. H. Watts on the 9th day of September 1861....

Regiment went into camp of instruction near Cross Keys and Shorter's Depot on the Montgomery and West Point railroad in Macon County, Ala. Our camp was in a beautiful location near the residence of Mr. Conrad Webb. Charles Metzler Van Echlin, formerly an officer in the French army and now an officer in our regular army, was the instructor of our regiment. He was a very fine officer and a clever gentleman. He messed with us (joined us for meals).

Dr. T. A. McCane was first lieutenant of my company, and Dr. L. M. Pentecost was second senior lieutenant. Thomas King was first sergeant; F. S. Cone, second sergeant; Wm. Dunklin, third sergeant; Wm. V. R. Watson, 4th sergeant; and John Clow, fifth sergeant. Wm. C. Hinson was first corporal; T. E. Newton, second corporal; Thomas Shepherd, third; and I. H. Taylor fourth. John Payne was 3rd sergeant when the company was first mustered in and Turner Dunklin was 4th. We had no 5th sergeant then. W. V. R. Watson was soon afterwards appointed. John Payne was soon discharged, and John Clow was appointed 5th sergeant. We remained in *camp in instruction in Macon County from Sept. 14, 1861, to November 15, 1861."* [40]

---

[40] Crenshaw diary, 261.

III. Pensacola

A. Introduction

In the early days leading up to the Civil War, Pensacola, as a port city with the associated forts and Navy Yard, was considered property of Florida. Pensacola was situated on the best harbor on the Gulf Coast. Unfortunately, the United States felt it had a claim on the area as well. This section presents a brief history of events that took place at Pensacola before the Confederates decided the removal of the Union presence would be too costly and the troops at Pensacola were best used elsewhere. In addition, some insight is presented on the activities of the 17th Alabama while assigned to Pensacola.

B. The Continuing Standoff

In January 1861 when Florida seceded from the Union, the governor of Florida ordered the Florida militia to seize and occupy any forts or arsenals then manned by Union troops. The Navy Yard at Pensacola, in addition to the neighboring Forts Pickens[41], Barrancas[42], and McRee[43] with their associated batteries, was on the list of facilities to be seized. Before action could be taken by Florida militia, all Federal troops in the Pensacola area were moved to Fort Pickens on Santa Rosa Island which was on the southern side of Pensacola Bay. Fort Pickens was considered the most defensible of the military facilities. An attempt was made by the Federal troops to remove or destroy all equipment at the evacuated forts and Navy Yard, but there was not enough time. The Navy Yard and nearby Forts Barrancas and McRee on the northern side of Pensacola Bay were surrendered to the state of Florida on January 12, 1861.

There followed a long stalemate that included an unofficial truce between the Confederate troops controlling the captured facilities and the Union troops at Fort Pickens. Initially each side was manned by a limited number of poorly equipped troops. By the end of February, the Florida militia was joined by units from other Confederate states.

On March 7, 1861, President Jefferson Davis appointed Brigadier General Braxton Bragg as the commander of all troops in the Pensacola area. Bragg was a North Carolinian, a graduate of West Point, and a veteran of the Mexican War. By October 1861, Bragg's command was extended to include the Confederate troops in Mobile. Bragg possessed a strict approach to discipline and was generally not well-liked by his men. The new units arriving in Pensacola were composed of men who were untrained and

---

[41] Fort Pickens has been partially restored and is maintained by the National Park Service.
[42] Fort Barrancas was restored in the 1970s and is maintained by the National Park Service. It is located on the Pensacola Naval Air Station.
[43] Fort McRee no longer exists

undisciplined. Under Bragg's command, they were organized, drilled, and disciplined until they became battle-ready units.

Neither side controlled Pensacola Bay, but neither side could use Pensacola Bay. From Fort Pickens, Union guns prevented Confederate ships from entering the Bay. From Forts McRee and Barrancas, Confederate guns prevented Union ships from entering the Bay. Union supplies reaching Fort Pickens were delivered by ship from the south side, the Gulf side, of Santa Rosa Island. Confederate supplies were delivered over land to Pensacola and then moved to Forts McRee and Barrancas and Navy Yard.

General Bragg was frequently urged to capture Fort Pickens. He steadfastly refused. He lacked confidence in the troops under his command, and he probably overestimated the strength of the Union troops at Fort Pickens. As time passed, more Union troops and more equipment arrived at Fort Pickens. Emergencies throughout the Confederacy kept Pensacola at a low priority. Bragg was not provided with food, guns, ammunition and other supplies required. Manpower was another problem. Periodically units trained at Pensacola were transferred to Virginia or Tennessee, and more untrained units were sent to Pensacola.

By early October, Bragg heard rumors that Fort Pickens was planning a bombardment on the Confederates. He decided it was time for the Confederates to launch a surprise attack. After dark on October 8, 1861, more than 1,000 Confederates crossed Pensacola Bay and landed east of Fort Pickens on the side most vulnerable with the least defenses. By daybreak on October 9, the Confederates exchanged fire with some few Union soldiers and destroyed most of the easterly Union camp. This camp was located about one mile east of Fort Pickens and was manned by the 6th New York Volunteers. After a signal from Bragg, the troops moved back in the direction of their boats with Union troops in pursuit. The most casualties occurred during the escape back across the Bay. There were possibly as many as 90 Confederate casualties and 70 Union casualties. The Confederates were back in Pensacola by 11 AM. Colonel Harvey Brown, the Union commander of Fort Pickens at that time, began making plans to avenge the attack by the Confederates.[44]

C. Arrival of the 17th Alabama.

On November 14, 1861, the 17th Alabama Infantry under command of Colonel Watts was ordered to leave their training camp near Shorter's Depot, Macon County, Alabama, and report to Pensacola, Florida. When the regiment arrived in Pensacola, it numbered about 900 men. The 17th

---

[44] George Pearce, *Pensacola During the Civil War* (Gainesville, FL: University Press of Florida, 2000), 116-118.

Alabama was assigned to Brigadier General Adley Hogan Gladden's brigade under General Bragg.

The 17th Alabama was exposed to Bragg's lack of concern for the welfare of enlisted soldiers on their arrival at Pensacola. Colonel Watts requested that the 17th Alabama be given permission "*to remain near the city of Pensacola where there was a healthy location and good water, urging as a reason that there was a great deal of sickness in the regiment.* Gen. Bragg replied in his usual laconic style '*Move your regiment immediately to the Navy Yard.*'"[45] This would not be the last unpleasant encounter between Colonel Watts and General Bragg.

Within a few days of the arrival of the 17th Alabama at Pensacola, Colonel Brown was ready to attack the Confederates. On November 22, 1861, Fort Pickens and Union ships in the area began a bombardment of Fort McRee. Shells hit the sand batteries and the fort. Within a few hours, the guns at Fort McRee were quiet. The Union bombardment was directed at Confederate facilities from Fort McRee eastward to the Navy Yard, a distance of several miles. All Confederate batteries fired in return. The battle went on until dark. Colonel Brown estimated that his guns fired a shot every 15 to 20 minutes, while the Confederate batteries were considerably slower.[46] The next day the Union bombardment began again and continued for most of the day. Damage on the Confederate side of the Bay was extensive, but minor on the Union side.

In his journal Captain McMillan placed Company H initially on Big Bayou about three quarters of a mile in the rear of Fort Barrancas[47]. In his narrative on the 17th Alabama, McMillan discusses the bombardment: "*On 21 Nov I heard my first gun. Dr. S. C. Jenkins, a member of my Co., and myself had been visiting some men who were sick with measles at the Naval Hospital. We had just left to return when the Steamer Time from Pensacola which was just landing at the Navy Yard was fired into from Ft. Pickens: and I for the first time heard the shrill shriek of a shell, a noise which I was destined to become so familiar with. I was a mere spectator of the Bombardment as our Regt. had charge of no batteries. It was a grand scene particularly at night. On the night of the 21st, I was detailed with a hundred men to make repairs on Ft. McRea which had suffered pretty severely during the day. The firing was kept up on 22 nearly all day.*

The Navy Yard with nearly all its splendid buildings was destroyed. Our loss was only 6 or 7 killed, and the damage to our Forts soon repaired."[48]

---

[45] Crenshaw Diary
[46] Pearce, 136.
[47] This location probably was at the Advanced Redoubt, a fortication built to provide protection from an attack by land. This redoubt still exists, but has not been restored. It is located on Taylor Road northeast of Fort Barrancas.
[48] McMillan sketch.

In his own words, Lieutenant Weathers of Company E further described the effect of the bombardment on the 17th Alabama: *"The 17th Alabama regiment was located back of fort Barrancas. It is an old Spanish fort*[49] *constructed, it seems, with a view of defense against an attack of a Navy fleet. Fort McCrary*[50] *was built on the sandbar below the light house by the United States.*

The regiment was present at the bombardment in November and in January. But few of the men had ever heard the roar of cannon and when the Federals at Fort Pickens began to bombard, it so excited the men that they were almost crazy. They expected to see the enemy coming like wild buffaloes. The drums beat, men fell into line with their muskets, the regiment formed with fixed bayonets. Men were saying, 'If I am killed, send my watch to my wife or my mother', and at the time not an enemy within two miles.

Fort McCrary had been damaged and a detail of 100 men was sent to repair the fort, the writer in command of the detail. We worked all night, filling sand bags, piling them against the walls of the fort. A magazine had been crushed by a cannon ball. Six men were trapped and smothered. We dug them out. They were warm and limber.

A large rifle cannon had to be mounted on top of Fort Barrancas and trained on Fort Pickens. With a strong rope we pulled it to Fort Barrancas. Company E was given command of the fort. The beach out for some distance was flat, ordinarily the water was about ten or fifteen inches deep."[51]

The Union bombardment ended late on November 23. This bombardment caused extensive damage to the villages of Warrington[52] and Woolsey, both located just beyond Confederate batteries. Confederate casualties included seven dead and eight wounded.

On January 1, 1862, when a naval vessel was seen tied up at the Confederate Navy Yard, for the first time since the November bombardment, Colonel Brown at Fort Pickens showed his displeasure. He ordered the firing of three rounds at the vessel. Forty-five minutes later, Confederate batteries responded. Thus began another day-long bombardment. This time Fort Pickens had bigger guns that fired with greater accuracy. The damage was extensive.

This would be the last battle the 17th Alabama would witness at Pensacola. For the next couple of months, life at Pensacola would remain tense but quiet.

---

[49] Fort Barrancas was originally built by the Spanish about 1797. The American fort was built using the old Spanish fort as a base. Building was done from 1839 to 1844. In January 1861 only one Federal artillery company of 50 men was stationed at Fort Barrancas. These men were evacuated to Fort Pickens.
[50] Fort McCrary refers to Fort McRee.
[51] Weathers war history.
[52] The village of Warrington in 1861 was positioned directly west of the Navy Yard. Many years later, Warrington was moved north to make room for the expansion of the naval facilities.

January 29, 1862, Colonel Watts described to his daughter the facilities along the coast of Florida, *"About once in every ten days it becomes my duty as officer of the day to make, in military parlance, the Grand Rounds, i.e., to visit all the sentinels, guard tents and batteries on the beach. This has to be done between 12 o'clock M. and daylight. When the moon shines this is very pleasant. I take two or three gentlemen to act as my escort, and we travel around the meanderings of the Bay, in sight of Fort Pickens...There is a Light-house here built of brick, tapering up for 200 feet or more, and from the top of it the whole surrounding country can be seen; the Perdido Bay – the bayou or sort of inland lake on which my encampment is situated, can be seen distinctly, stretching for miles through green pine forests. Fort Barrancas, Redoubt, the Navy Yard, Warrington and Woolsey (villages near the Navy Yard) and Pensacola (eight or nine miles off) can be seen by one coup d'ei. Then there is a good glass through which you can see Fort Pickens and all the soldiers there, and the large vessels blockading the Port. The top of this Light-house is reached by a spiral flight of one hundred and eighty five steps..."*[53]

D. Living Conditions

From Captain McMillan, it is known that the 17th Alabama drilled in infantry and in heavy artillery at the forts and batteries under the charge of the 1st Alabama Regiment. After the bombardment in November, men of the 17th spent time rebuilding batteries and repairing damage to the facilities. Captain McMillan and Lieutenant Weathers each wrote that they were in command of a detail of 100 men to make repairs at Fort McRee.

Lieutenant Crenshaw of Company K, in his diary, described living conditions for the regiment at the Navy Yard, *"We were ordered into camp in a low swampy place on a disagreeable bayou back from the Navy Yard and half a mile distant. Nearly one hundred of our regiment died in less than three months from diseases acquired at this camp – or at least their death was brought about by this unhealthy situation. We at last got permission to move out of camp a short distance to a higher place. Companies K and I were so sickly that they were sent to the little village of Warrenton near the Navy Yard which had been deserted by its inhabitants during the first bombardment of the Navy Yard and our land batteries by Fort Pickens."*[54] Although the swampy location certainly contributed to the disease suffered by members of the 17th Alabama, the first three months of an enlistment were normally a time of adjustment and frequent illness.

Crenshaw continued, *"We occupied good comfortable houses and very soon there was a great improvement in the health of our two companies. The regiment was slowly improving. We had a most delightful time during our stay in Warrenton. The officers of our company occupied an elegant*

---
[53] Thomas Watts folder, Alabama Archives, Montgomery, Al.
[54] Crenshaw diary.

little house with four rooms – with necessary kitchen and out houses. We had two servants in our mess. Capt. Burnett's boy Pete, and my boy Lewis, who had been presented to me by my grandfather on my first entering the service. While we were at Warrenton Mrs. Burnett visited us and stayed several days. We enjoyed her visit very much. The day she left we were ordered to relieve Capt. Baker's Eufaula company, of Col. Clayton's 1st Ala. Regiment, in charge of a mortar battery on a line with and between the Marine Hospital and the Marine Barracks. We had nice comfortable houses here, also and good water. We remained in charge of this battery until our regiment was ordered to Corinth, Miss., on the 15th day of March 1862. While in Pensacola we were drilled in infantry and heavy artillery tactics. We were first Brigadier-General Gladden's brigade, he was sent away to Mobile, and Col. Jno. K. Jackson of the 5th Ga. Regiment was promoted and put in command of the brigade. Liked Gladden better than Jackson though he was rough. Col. Watts and Gen. Bragg did not get along well at all. They were always having trouble with each other. An intense dislike seemed to have sprung up between them. I think both were to blame."[55]

Sergeant Henry Bray of Company F wrote on January 29, 1862 from Camp Gladden in O'Bannonville, Florida, about the sickness, *"We had about 95 men when we came here and we haven't more than 75 now. We have had bad luck since we came here. It seems like our men never will get well again or quit dying."*[56] O'Bannonville was the site of the Army of Pensacola headquarters before the evacuation of Pensacola.

On February 19, 1862, Bray wrote again, *"I have a good house to stay in and a soft plank to sleep on which is more than many a poor soldier can say for there is some companies in our regiment that have no houses to stay in yet. The colonel gave our company the praise as being the best drilled and most gentlemanly and keep ourselves the cleanest of any company in the regiment."*[57]

The 17th Alabama numbered about 900 men when it first arrived at Pensacola in November. During the four months the regiment was located at Pensacola, the muster roll was in a constant state of change. No draft law had been passed. Many men eagerly joined the Confederate Army early on because of their zeal to fight for the cause without full realization of the commitment they were making to a life in the military. Consequently some thought they could leave as easily as they joined. Many who enlisted quickly found they were not fit for military life; this resulted in numerous discharges or resignations. In addition, the problem of epidemics and disease claimed an untold number of men.

---

[55] Ibid.
[56] Henry Bray, letters, transcribed and edited by Mark Anderson (Box 26, folder 7N, Alabama Archives, Montgomery, AL).
[57] Ibid.

The 17th Alabama remained in Pensacola until March 29, 1862, when it was ordered to Bethel Station, Tennessee. The regiment was assigned to the Army of the Mississippi under the command of General A. S. Johnston, Bragg's Corps, Withers' Division, and the Third Brigade, commanded by Brigadier-General J. K. Jackson. As they moved from Pensacola to Tennessee, it is unknown how many men were in the regiment, but all were volunteers. They were on their way to Corinth and Shiloh.

E. End of the Stalemate

By May 1862, the decision was made for all Confederate forces to abandon Pensacola, the Navy Yard, and the forts. After the defeat at Shiloh, they realized the well-trained men occupying Pensacola could be put to better use elsewhere. Confederate troops completely burned or destroyed everything at the Navy Yard, Fort Barrancas, and Fort McRee when they abandoned Pensacola. The evacuation of Confederate troops undermined the morale of the Confederate population of south Alabama and the panhandle of Florida and placed them in a vulnerable position. Union forces were now able to bring in more troops and strengthen their position. Federal troops from Pensacola also assisted the troops from Fort Morgan in their attack and defeat of Mobile in the summer of 1864. Raids by Union cavalry, such as Major-General Frederick Steele's command, also penetrated northward into Alabama from Pensacola in the closing months of the war.

IV. Shiloh and the Western Front

A. Introduction

The battle of Shiloh was the real indoctrination for the men of the 17th Alabama into the horrors of war. This section covers the period from March 1862 to August 1862 and describes the events leading up to the battle of Shiloh. General background information from published references is included to provide an overview of this important engagement that had a devastating impact on both sides. Confederate preparations for battle and some portions of the battle are depicted using words of members of the 17th Alabama who were present. The combatants' words also describe the situation after the battle and the retreat from Shiloh. Their letters reveal first-hand the horrific conditions and deprivation endured by these brave men who were inexperienced soldiers.

B. Overview of Important Events, March 1862 to August 1862

March 7	Departure from Pensacola, Florida, and reassignment to Corinth, Mississippi
March 14	Arrival at Corinth, Mississippi
April 3	March to Shiloh and Pittsburg Landing, Tennessee
April 6 & 7	Battle of Shiloh
April 8	Retreat to Monterey, Tennessee, and return to Corinth, Mississippi
May 10	Skirmish at Farmington, Mississippi
May 29	Evacuation of Corinth and retreat to Tupelo, Mississippi
July 5	Move to Saltillo, Mississippi
August 1	Departure and reassignment to Mobile, Alabama

C. Events Leading to the Battle of Shiloh.

In 1862 the Confederate commander of the Army of the Mississippi was General Albert S. Johnston. At the beginning of the Civil War, Johnston was considered one of the finest soldiers, North or South. As the second ranking general in the Confederate Army he was given command of the western theater of operations. It was Johnston's responsibility to defend a 400 mile line from the Mississippi River running through the middle of Kentucky to the Cumberland Gap at the Tennessee line in the western theater. This was an impossible task considering the length of the line and the number of troops and guns available to Johnston. Brigadier-General U. S. Grant, with his Union Army of the Tennessee, had been slowly advancing south through Kentucky and Tennessee. Grant had captured Fort Henry on the Tennessee River and Fort Donelson on the Cumberland River on February 6 and February 16, 1862, respectively. Both forts were in the northern part of Tennessee, almost on the Tennessee-Kentucky line. Loss of the two forts closed the important Confederate access to the Ohio and

Mississippi Rivers from central and eastern Tennessee. Johnston was then forced to remove his army from Kentucky, to retreat through Tennessee, and to evacuate Nashville. In March 1862, Johnston gathered his scattered Army of the Mississippi at Corinth, Mississippi. It was here that he planned to defend the Memphis and Charleston Railroad, the Confederacy's only east-west cross-country rail link.

General P. G. T. Beauregard was Johnston's second in command. He graduated from West Point in 1838 and was a veteran of the Mexican War. He had commanded the forces that bombarded Fort Sumter in April 1861 and fought at First Manassas in July. In March 1862, Beauregard was amassing troops in the area of Corinth. These were troops reassigned from other areas of the west. By March 1862, the Army of the Mississippi had grown to almost 45,000 men.

At the same time, Grant's Army of the Tennessee was arriving at Pittsburg Landing, Tennessee, on the Tennessee River. Grant's men, about 40,000 in number, were sick and weary from their long drive south through Kentucky and Tennessee. Pittsburg Landing was considered an ideal location for Grant's troops to rest and recover while they waited for reinforcements. Major General Don Carlos Buell, with the Union Army of the Ohio, was on his way to join Grant. The Army of the Ohio was traveling from Nashville and consisted of about 25,000 men. Combining the forces of 65,000 men from the Army of the Tennessee and the Army of Ohio, Grant planned to move south and attack Johnston at Corinth. To capture Corinth would be a major victory for the Federals, a victory that would isolate Memphis from the eastern front.

Pittsburg Landing was less than 25 miles from Corinth, where Johnston was finalizing his plan for stopping Grant - a surprise attack on Grant before Buell and his army could reach Pittsburg Landing.

D. Reassignment to the Army of the Mississippi

On March 7, 1862, the 17th Alabama Infantry was ordered to transfer immediately to Corinth. Fortunately the Mobile and Ohio Railroad was a direct line from Mobile to Corinth. The 17th Alabama joined the 9th, 18th and 19th Alabama and the 2nd Texas Infantries to form a brigade commanded by Brigadier-General John K. Jackson, a brigade assigned to the Army of the Mississippi.

Captain McMillan, commander of Company H, provided an account of the reassignment of the 17th Alabama and some of the problems the regiment and their officers encountered once they arrived at Corinth.

"On 7 March 1862, our Regt. which had been at work almost incessantly, day and night, dismounting guns preparatory to the evacuation of Pensacola -- was ordered to Corinth, Miss., where Beauregard was concentrating all the forces in the West. We reached Corinth via M. & O. R.

R.⁵⁸ *on 14th and were sent to Bethel Station, Tenn. From Bethel we marched to Purdy McNairy Co., and from this time our experiences as soldiers really began. At Pensacola we had comfortable cabins, and the furniture saved from the Navy Yard at its burning enabled us to fix up in a style of elegance. The weather was splendid and vegetation was putting out freely.*

When we arrived at Bethel it had been raining two or three days; the creeks were swollen and the mud, as mud only can be where troops are marching, and to add to our discomfit the wind was blowing and soon commenced sleeting. We bivouaced in some old fields. No tents, no cooking utensils, nor indeed anything to cook. We remained in this condition two days when we returned to Bethel where we met our baggage. We remained here a day or two, and received orders to proceed to Corinth. As the weather was still very inclemental, and we were ordered to go without baggage and the result of the trip to Purdy had been about 100 added to the sick list: Col. Watts refused to go, his subordinates sustained him and the Regt. did not move. All the officers were placed in arrest by Gidden,⁵⁹ our Brig. Gen., but the next day were released and the Regt. with its baggage proceeded to Corinth where we were attached to Brigade of Brig. Gen. Jno. K. Jackson, Withers division, Bragg's Corps. All the field officers and Senior Capts. were again put under arrest. Now we had all been guilty of downright mutiny, but in our undisciplined conditions and utter ignorance of military affairs, we were ignorant of the fact." ⁶⁰

John Witherspoon DuBose in his notes on the 17ᵗʰ Alabama commented on this same incident:

"On March 7th, 1862, the regiment was sent from its comfortable quarters at Pensacola, to fields about Bethel, Purdy, Corinth and Shiloh. Here they were in chilling rains and deep mud without shelters of any kind, separated for a time from their baggage, cooking utensils, and other comforts. It was in this state of distress that Colonel Watts and the officers of the regiment refused obedience to orders to move to another point, and were put under arrest. Just after being placed under arrest Colonel Watts received his appointment as Attorney General of the Confederate States, in President Davis Cabinet. This was from the head of the army and overrode the other orders and he accepted. Lieut. Col. R. C. Farris succeeded to the command of the regiment. In the report of the organization of the Army of the Mississippi for April 6-7, the brigade of General J. K. Jackson, which was the Third Brigade of Wither's Division, General Braggs's Second Corps, consisted of

   17th Alabama, Lieut. Col. Robert C. Farris
   18th Alabama, Col. Eli S. Shorter

---

⁵⁸ Mobile and Ohio Railroad
⁵⁹ Brigadier-General A. H. Gladden
⁶⁰ McMillan sketch.

> 19th Alabama, Col. Joseph Wheeler
> 9th Alabama Battalion
> Arkansas Battalion
> 2nd Texas, Col. J. C. Moore
> Girardy's Battery"[61]

Lieutenant Edward Crenshaw in his diary described the movements of the 17th Alabama around Corinth for the same time period, *"Sometime in March, 1862, about the 15th our regiment was ordered to Corinth, Mississippi, at which place Gen. Beauregard was then collecting an army. Not long after we reached there Gen. A. S. Johnston arrived with the remains of his army and assumed the command. Our brigade made a reconnaissance to Purday, Tennessee, but did not discover the enemy. We suffered a great deal from exposure to the weather."* Crenshaw described the conflict between Colonel Watts and General Gladden. It was a difficult situation. The 17th Alabama had recently moved from the comfortable climate around Pensacola to the cold, wet, miserable weather in northeast Mississippi. For these men, everything that could go wrong went wrong. Colonel Watts' defiance of orders issued by General Gladden, something not done in the military, caused further impact on the men. This resulted in the arrest of all the officers of the 17th Alabama. Morale dipped very low.

In Crenshaw's words, *"But Brig. Gen. Patton Anderson having interfered persuaded Col. Watts to consent to obey the order but as soon as the regiment reached Corinth, Col. Watts, Lieut. Col. Farriss, Major Murphy and Senior Captain E. P. Holcombe were placed under close arrest and Maj. Farrow of the 1st Louisiana Regulars was put in Command of the regiments...Col. Watts and the other officers of our regiment were kept under arrest some days when they wrote an ample apology acknowledging their fault, &c., and they were relieved from arrest and restored to duty again...Gens. Bragg and Gladden and Jackson were always severe on our regiment on account of the trouble with Col. Watts and the bad state of discipline engendered thereby, and the notorious incompetency of the majority of the officers."*[62]

Captain Thomas Jefferson Burnett of Company K wrote his wife, Ann, from Corinth, March 23. He told of preparations for battle. *"We have concentrated at this place a very large army now at least 40,000 and arriving daily. Gens. Beauregard, Johnston, Polk, Bragg & a host of others are here assembled and have the poor soldiers out in large numbers daily making fortifications &c preparatory it would seem for a great battle, but still the enemy are at the river eighteen miles away, and I cannot form an idea as to what may be our next movements. Tomorrow we may be sent*

---

[61] John W. DuBose, *History of Seventeenth Alabama Infantry* (SG024896, folder 4, Alabama Archives, Montgomery, AL), 1930.
[62] Crenshaw diary.

some where else. Our regiment is out to day two miles off digging trenches and but for the fact that I am an officer of the day I could not have an opportunity to scribble you a line, and I am now writing in my tent shut up close & so dark that I can scarely see the lines & snowing outside rapidly – but I do not think will fall in sufficient quantity to obstruct the roads &c."[63]

In his letter Burnett described the incident between Bragg and the officers of the 17th Alabama, the close arrest and the appointment of Watts as Attorney General. *"We have heard that Col Watts has been appointed Atty Gen in the Presidents Cabinet & we gave a shout for him & what makes it better was appointed over Gen Braggs brother and I am satisfied Gen Bragg has been pressing this arrest. If there is no mistake in the Col appointed then will be a vacancy & if so I will be selected Major of the Reg."*[64] Burnett also commented on the effect of the rain, wind, sleet, and snow described earlier. *"The exposure of the past two weeks has put fully half our Reg on the sick list to day I had about 20 reported & some Cos as many as 40."*[65]

E. March to Shiloh

In his journal, Captain McMillan continued, *"Col. Watts remained over a week in close arrest during which he rec'd the appointment of Atty. Gen. of the Confederate States. Our field officers were released on making public acknowledgment of their mistake. Major Murphy being in feeble health resigned. We were encamped about 2 miles east of Corinth on the Purdy road, for about two weeks. It was a disagreeable fortnight. On the 3rd of Apr. the order to cook 3 days rations and prepare to march was given. We filed off in the direction of the Tennessee River reaching Monterey that night. The next day we only went about 6 miles camping near the 'Mickey House*[66]*'. On Sat. 5, we moved forward about 5 miles."* [67]

Johnston was ready to stop Grant and provide the South with a needed victory on the western front. Johnston gave the order to move forward from Corinth on April 3. The march was postponed by one day because of delayed orders and stormy weather. Once on the march, progress was slow due to the inexperience of the marchers and the bad roads, described by one soldier as meandering cow paths. By the evening of April 5, the Confederates were encamped within two miles of the Union position. This was one day later than Johnston had planned. The late arrival was of great concern to Beauregard. He feared that Buell had already joined Grant, and the Confederate battle plan would fail. Buell was in near proximity and could have joined Grant, but neither Grant nor Buell felt any urgency. The Union soldiers had been in training while resting at Pittsburg Landing. No

---

[63] Burnett papers.
[64] Ibid.
[65] Ibid.
[66] Mickey House is listed on current Tennessee maps as Michie.
[67] McMillan sketch.

orders were issued to build entrenchments because, in Grant's plan, Pittsburg Landing was not to be a battlefield. The stop there was for rest, recovery, drill, and training in preparations for a planned attack on the Confederates at Corinth. Grant and his officers were so confident of their position that they did not send out scouting parties, and the few assigned pickets were positioned close to camp. The Yankees had no idea that Johnston's Army of the Mississippi was camped within two miles of the Union camp; ready to strike early on the morning of the 6th.

F. The Battle of Shiloh

On the morning of April 6th, Buell was still some distance from Pittsburg Landing. As the Confederates approached the Union camp, they were surprised by a small enemy patrol. Their sudden exchange initiated the fighting to start earlier than planned. The Army of the Mississippi, screaming the rebel yell as they poured out of the woods near the Shiloh Church, took the Union camp by complete surprise. Many of the troops on both sides were inexperienced which caused much confusion during various engagements at Shiloh. The 17th Alabama had never seen anything like the battle of Shiloh. The Union army fought hard to hold their position, but the Confederates were dogged in their efforts to push the Yankees back to the Tennessee River at Pittsburg Landing.

Captain McMillan reported on the battle of Shiloh. During the afternoon of April 5, *"Hardies Corps had passed us and we were awakened early on the morning of the 6th by sharp picket firing in advance. The sun rose clear, and the beautiful Spring Sabbath day suggested thoughts of church bells ringing - but such thoughts were soon dissipated by the deafening roar of artillery, for Hardie's Corps had surprised them in their camps. A sharp fight took place, but the enemy soon fled in confusion, leaving their breakfast smoking and half eaten. Here Gen. A. S. Johnston rode down our line and informed us that we had won a great victory. We felt mortified that Hardie's troops had all the glory, and were really sorry that the fighting (so we thought) was over. We were standing in line when a shell from a field piece came tearing through the trees a few feet above us. We were ordered to "lie Down" and for nearly a half hour patiently bore the infliction, but Col. Girandy's battery which was attached to our brigade finally came up through the woods, took position and silenced things in a few minutes. We were then marched out by the right flank, taking position on the right of Hardie's Column which was nearly all the time engaged. About two o'clock, our brigade came on the Yanks thoroughly posted among some small hills. A stubborn fight in the open fields, lasting about 2 hours ensued."* [68]

---

[68] McMillan sketch.

By mid-afternoon the Union army had retreated to a peach orchard with the Confederates in pursuit. Here a long hard battle was fought and many lives were lost on both sides. The 17th Alabama Infantry took part in the battle at the Hornet's Nest, where the bullets flew with the intensity of swarms of hornets. Brigadier-General Jackson included the 17th Alabama in his report of April 6, complimenting them on their actions and crediting them with capturing two stands of colors.[69]

Captain McMillan described the involvement of Company H in the battle on April 6th, *"We then charged them and continued to drive them through the day. They stood through at every available point, and contested the group and late in the evening, we had a desperate fight in the open field, lasting about half an hour, in which our brigade was repulsed for a few minutes. It was at this place that Prentis' Brigade was captured,[70] and the 17 and 18 Alabama guarded them about 15 minutes until some cavalry came up.[71]*

We then went forward again, and soon came under the fire of the Gunboats in the Tenn. their shells however did little damage. We had now driven the Yankees under the river bank and around Pittsburg landing, and it is said might have captured the whole of Grant's Army, if we had pushed forward. This might have had great influence on the destiny of the afterwards celebrated Ullyses: but Pshaw! I think it probable they might have been captured, as they must have been badly demoralized after retreating all day. We wasted this precious time until night in a useless cannonade."[72]

Lieutenant Crenshaw described the involvement of Company K on the afternoon of the 6th, *"We were soon heavily engaged and 12 or 15 men struck down by shells, among them Lt. Sadler of Lowndes. But the enemy were soon driving from this place and we were moved further to the right, where we became heavily engaged, our regiment being placed in a very perilous position part of the time, exposed to fire from three directions at same time. At this point Sgt. Bob Mosely (who was killed afterwards) captured and wounded first Lt. Col. of 50 Ill. Regt. Between our two regts. during a short lull in the fire. He fired on us 3 times when we both pulled him down on him simultaneously breaking his leg. We had a hot fight at this point for over an hour when we broke the Yankees, and then double-quicked by our left flank to the assistance of Breckenridge's Div. In the center which had been in reserve and was just engaged and was being sorely pressed. Gladden's wasted troops and Gage's Mobile battery were nobly sustaining*

---

[69] OWR, Serial 10, 553-6. This agrees with Tichenor's letter to Attorney General Thomas Watts. See below.
[70] OWR, Serial 10, 553-6, in Jackson's report he shows his brigade, including the 17th Alabama, was main factor in the capture of Prentis' brigade of 1500 prisoners. Note: Prentis actually was a division commander of the 6th U. S. Division, not a brigade commander.
[71] Ibid, Withers says they were sent to Corinth under Shorter's 18th Ala.
[72] McMillan sketch.

them, when we rushed in front of them and swept forward driving the Yankees before us. Three times we retired without ammunition in face of their hot fire, for they made a gallant stand in the center, and went in again, until to our combined efforts Prentiss Div. surrendered and were sent to the rear under guard. We pressed on driving the Yankees to the River-in sight of their gunboats and our artillery playing havoc at short range. Until dark when the troops being in some confusion resulting from so many different lines being crowded together in so narrow a space we were ordered to our old positions for the night... Our company went into battle 40 strong and lost 17...Chaplain Tichenor fought gallantly in my company and was wounded by a spent bullet... "*[73]* Lieutenant Crenshaw was taken ill with typhoid fever in early May and did not return to duty until June 28 in Tupelo.

Reverend I. T. Tichenor was a Baptist minister who served as pastor to churches in Mississippi, Tennessee, Kentucky, and Alabama before the Civil War. In the early years of the war, he served as chaplain of the 17th Alabama Regiment. He resigned after the battle of Shiloh and became president of the Montevallo Coal Mining Company in Shelby County, Alabama.[74] He later became president of the Agricultural and Mechanical College in Auburn, Alabama, now known as Auburn University. Having been present and active at the battle of Shiloh, Chaplain Tichenor wrote to Attorney General Thomas Watts on April 18, 1862, from Corinth about the events of April 6. *"The loss of our regiment in killed on the field was thirteen; wounded and missing, one hundred and seventeen more than one-third of the number we carried into the field. Accurate information obtained on the ground, and from prisoners, satisfies me that we fought all day five times our number and with 300 men, killed and wounded not less than 1000 Yankees.*

The dead Yankees in front of our Regiment, where we first met the Enemy, counted after the fight 352. Capt. Cummings, of Jackson's staff, says they were piled three deep others say it looked as if a regiment had dressed up and laid down. Most of them were shot in the head; this was caused by the fact that the enemy were formed in three lines of battle, one behind the other, and the front were lying down. During the engagement we were under a cross fire on the left wing from three directions. Under it the boys wavered. I had been wounded, and was sitting down, but seeing them waver, I sprang to my feet, took off my hat, waved it over my head, walked up and down the line, and, they say, 'preached them a sermon.'

I reminded them that it was Sunday; that, at that hour (11-1/2 o'clock) all their home folks were praying for them; 'Tom Watts,' (excuse the familiar way in which I employed so distinguished a name) had told me that

---

[73] Crenshaw diary.
[74] *The Alabama 17th, Isaac Taylor Tichenor and a Sabbath Event* (SG024895, folder 11, Alabama Archives, Montgomery, AL).

he would listen with an eager ear to hear from the 17th; and shouting your name far over the roar of battle, I called upon them to stand there, and die, if need be, for their country. The effect was evident.—Every man stood to his post—every eye flashed and every heart beat high with desperate resolve to conquer or die. They piled that ground with Yankees slain.[75]

Colonel I am satisfied—more than satisfied—with the results of my labours as Chaplain of the 17th. I feel in my heart a consciousness, that in no other position could I have served the cause of my God or my country as well; and I am more that recompensed for all my toils and privations." [76] Tichenor also stated in his letter, "Enclosed I send you a copy of a petition to the Secretary of War asking that the two flags[77], taken in the great battle of Shiloh by our Regiment, may be transferred to Gov. Shorter to be placed in the Capitol at Montgomery. I feel that I need not ask you to do all you can to have this petition granted. They are both marked on the stripe just below the blue field, <u>Captured by the 17th Alabama, at Shiloh, April 6, 1862.</u> One is a beautiful silk flag, the other a large cotton one."

The Confederates fought valiantly all day on April 6, but they could not quite push the Federals back to the river for a complete victory. General Johnston had been fatally wounded in the afternoon, which placed Beauregard, Johnston's second in command, in charge. The hour was late and the troops exhausted. The decision was made that the Confederates would reorganize the next morning to finish the job. Beauregard believed the next day would only require a 'mopping up' and sent a telegram off to Richmond declaring a complete victory. The Confederate cavalry in North Alabama reported that Buell was headed for north Alabama and not Pittsburg Landing. From this report Beauregard assumed that all he had to do was finish off what was left of Grant's army. The Federals actually had sent one brigade to North Alabama as a decoy. The rest of Buell's army was, indeed, headed for Pittsburg Landing.

The night was miserable for both armies. The torrential rains made it impossible for either side to give any attention to their dead and their wounded lying in agony in the fields and woods. The total casualties numbered over 10,000. The Federal gunboats fired cannon at regular intervals throughout the night. All this coupled with the thunder and

---

[75] Years later, Private William Jasper Fleming of Company D wrote in his *Civil War Reminiscences* that Tichenor *"walked up and down the line of the foremost rank exhorting the men and firing their enthusiasm by his bravery and oratory, 'Remember my friends, what you are fighting for, your wives and children, your homes, your sacred altar.'"*

[76] Isaac Taylor Tichenor, letter (SG024896, folder 1,Alabama Archives, Montgomery, AL). Tichenor resigned later that month. He stated in his resignation, *"In the recent battle of Shiloh I took part with the gallant men of this command achieving the glorious victory...I have the satisfaction of knowing that my conduct on that bloody day met the ... approval of every officer and private in the Regiment...I can no longer consent to hold my present position. My resignation will be forwarded..."*

[77] Captain Andrew O'Brien of Company F mentions these two flags in a memo, dated April 16th 1862, *"On investigation I find that the flags were found in the Enemys Second Camp.* Capt. Holcombe *acting Lt. Col. Found one & Sergeant Watson of Co. K the other."* A copy of the memo is located in O'Brien's service record.

lightning made sleep impossible. Under cover of cannon and unknown to the Confederates, Buell's men were ferried across the Tennessee River at Pittsburg Landing.

The Confederates were supported by Nathan Bedford Forrest and his cavalry. Forrest was a Tennessee native. In spite of his very limited education, he was a very successful planter and slave dealer. During the outset of war, he raised and equipped his own battalion of mounted troops. He fought at Shiloh, Chattanooga, and in the Tennessee campaign in 1864. He ended the war as a lieutenant general and became president of the Selma, Marion and Memphis railroad.

At Shiloh Forrest's scouts discovered what the Federals were doing. With night-time conditions, the torrential rains with the thunder and lightening, and the steady cannon fire, Forrest could not find Beauregard to warn him. None of the Confederate generals he talked to would react until they received orders directly from Beauregard.

When morning came, the Confederates remained totally exhausted, scattered, and disorganized. Many of the men had left the battlefield during the night. Most of the men had not been issued additional ammunition and were not equipped for another battle. The Confederates were definitely not battle-ready troops, while the Federals had 25,000 fresh troops ready to take back whatever ground had been lost on the previous day. The Federals struck at daylight. The Confederates put up a gallant effort. By mid-morning the Confederates were again an organized army making a defensive stand. However by early afternoon Beauregard realized the hopelessness of the situation and reluctantly ordered the men to retreat.

Captain McMillan described conditions on April 7, *"Buell arrived during the night. Our men were straggling over the Yankee Camps which were rich with booty.[78] Buell and Grant combined, attacking our forces at daylight on the 7th. Our shattered and scattered columns retired slowly, fighting like heroes and during the day lost about the same ground they had gained the day before. We fell back that night to Monterey: It had rained considerably, and the mud was awful, but on the 8th we were behind our entrenchment at Corinth."*[79]

Lt. Crenshaw reported on the 17th Alabama's contribution at Shiloh, *"The battle of Shiloh was fought on the 6th and 7th of April with great slaughter and bravery on both sides. Our Regiment went into the battle a little over 300 strong and had 130 officers and men killed*[80] *on Sunday the 6th of April, not being engaged the next day, but detailed by Gen. Beauregard as a rear guard to pick up stragglers and send them to the front. Our ardor and anxiety had been considerably cooled by the first day's work,*

---

[78] Food, clothing, weapons, etc.
[79] McMillan sketch.
[80] This should be 140 casualties, i.e., killed, wounded, captured, or missing.

and we did not grumble at all being assigned to this duty in the rear of the line of battle."[81]

The number of casualties for the 17th Alabama would have been much greater, but for the fact that they had been delegated to serve as a rear guard on April 7. This assignment is confirmed in a report by Brigadier-General Jackson on April 26, 1862, when he stated that *"in the darkness the brigade was scattered, the 17th going back to the position of the morning, and was no more in the battle, but on the 7th temporarily with Breckenridge used by him in stopping stragglers."*[82] See Appendix XIII for the list of casualties at Shiloh for the 17th Alabama.

G. After Shiloh

From Shiloh the army slowly retreated to Monterey and then back to Corinth. In Captain McMillan's words, *"Our brigade Jackson's were ordered back on the 9th to Monterey on Picket. Our Regt. lost 125 killed and wounded.*[83] *My Co. lost killed Corp. H. M. Andress and Private E. M. Roberts. Wounded Lt. R. M. Andress, Private J. H. Rives, B. S. Rives, T. F. Lewis, Jas. Black, H. M. Rumbly, and James Andress. Private Lewis was captured.*[84] *...Remaining at Monterey for a few days on picket, we returned to Corinth where we were engaged in fortifying."*[85]

The Army of the Mississippi remained in Corinth for about six weeks. In that time they fought only one skirmish at Farmington on May 10th, losing few men.[86] Corinth was a strategic location that had to be held. The east-west railroad to Memphis ran through Corinth. Along with the weary troops from the battle of Shiloh, Beauregard was given brigades from various points around the south. By early May he had 70,000 troops. However, the number of duty-ready men was much less than 70,000. The many wounded (estimated at about 8,000) at Shiloh were recovering and not fit for duty. Living conditions in Corinth were terrible. An inadequate, befouled water supply caused thousands of men to fall ill with dysentery and typhoid. Almost as many men died of disease at Corinth as had been killed

---

[81] Crenshaw diary.
[82] OWR Serial 10, 553.
[83] OWR, ibid, 395. The brigade is shown to have lost 86 killed, 364 wounded and 194 missing. Quite a different statement appears on page 535 ibid, but the number reported killed is evidently a misprint for it makes the killed 835, wounded 365, and missing 213."
[84] He did not list Lt. A. B. McCorveys, Privates Neil McCorvey and Thomas Rains who were also wounded.
[85] DuBose history: *"On page 789, ib., the organization of the brigade on June 30th shows the 19th Ala. eliminated; the 21st and the 24th Ala. added; as also the 5th Ga. and Burtwell's Battery. Captain B. F. Weathers of Roanoke, Ala. says that in a short time after the battle of Shiloh, the field officers all being away, the 17th Alabama was commanded most of the time until its return to Mobile in the early days of August 1862, by Col. Jones whose given name is not remembered and who held apparently a commission in the army without a definite command."*
[86] Although it was not reported in official records, Captain McMillan of Company H and Private Bray of Company F both mention fighting at Framington by some part of the 17th.

at the battle of Shiloh.[87] As one soldier described the situation, "All water courses went dry and we used water out of filthy pools."

Shortly after the battle of Shiloh, Colonel Farris resigned as commander of the 17th Alabama. The personal struggle begun in Pensacola continued between Colonel Watts and General Bragg. Watts was now Attorney General Watts. Watts had refused to accept the resignation requested by Major V. S. Murphy before the battle of Shiloh. Instead he promoted him to colonel and assigned him as a replacement for Colonel Farris. General Bragg ignored this appointment by arresting Murphy and placing Colonel J. P. Jones in command of the 17th.

Samuel M. Cummings enlisted as a musician with the 17th Alabama at the age of 13. He was a member of Company G, and his father an officer in Company H. He joined the regiment September 25, 1861, and celebrated his 14th birthday in February while the 17th was located at Pensacola. On April 15, 1862, after the battle of Shiloh, his mother wrote a letter to Samuel's commanding officer and a letter to Jefferson Davis. Her letters were a plea for a discharge for her son. She gave various reasons. Her husband had been in the service of the Confederacy for seven months. Her brother who had been attending "our farm" had enlisted. She needed her son to help her on the home front. She mentioned Samuel's age and described his state of mind and body after the horrors of Shiloh: *"His health has been bad and since the regiment moved to Corinth the fatigue and labor of the marches and the great exposure have much affected his health. Since the battle of the 6th and 7th of this month he has been almost entirely unable to do any duty. My husband has also been in the service and has been for the last seven months."*[88] There is no doubt that many members of the 17th Alabama, much older than young Samuel Cummings, were deeply affected, mentally and physically, by the reality of the war.

Corporal Henry Bray of Company F wrote from Corinth on May 17th, 1862. *"My dear Brother I seat myself this evening to Answer your welcome...Bud I have no news to write you of much importance—only that the same day you started to write me, wich was the 9th of may, that very same day I was out at farmington (a village five miles east of Corinth). a fight wich lasted a very short time before we drove the yankeys from their holes and made them take the bush. bud there is no use of talking, the yankeys can't fight in the bushes like the rebels. bud I am one of the greatest bush fighters now of the age I can charge bayonetts over a brush*

---

[87] OWR, Serial 10, 791-2, Serial 25, 484: On May 28, 1862, prior to the evacuation of Corinth, the Army of the Mississippi reported a total of 74,547 troops. Of these 26% (19,449) were listed as sick, 15% (11,517) absent with leave and 4% (2880) absent without leave. On June 9, after the move to Tupelo, the army of Mississippi reported a total of 62,747 men. The total listed as sick was 23% (14,320), absent with leave was 13% (7,913) and absent without leave was 4% (2,286). On July 1, 1862, conditions had not improved. The total was 66,484 men. The list of sick totaled 27% (17,966), absent with leave 10% (6,552) and absent without leave (1,985).
[88] Compiled Service Records of Confederate Soldiers Who Served in Organizations in Alabama.

heep in double quick time after a yankey and make him show me the bottom of his foot mighty quick. bud, in the fight at farmington we only lost one man killed and one wounded in our Regement bud, I thought we would have had a fight here before this time. the great Corinth fight, but the chance looks very slim now and I don't believe the yankeys ever intend to fight us in our intrenchment's but if they do they will get whirped woser than what they did at the battle of Shiloh bud I have not got that box you sent me yet but I sent down town this evening to see about it bud don't none of you take on about me not having no clothes and no tobacca to chaw, for I can go naked and chaw leaves. And fight yanks with a good stomache for I get plenty to eat such as Bacon and Bull beef or mule...."[89]

Captain Burnett of Company K wrote his wife, Ann, from near Corinth, May 20, 1862. He had just returned with the regiment after three days on picket duty. *"...such a time no regiment ever had picketing. Ann I honestly believe that the portion of the picket put under my charge as Senior Capt. 120 men, and I verily believe there were 3,000 rounds fired at us by the Yankees and I believe my command fired fully as many. We killed quite a number say perhaps twenty, and strange to say we only lost one from Co. I.*

We had decidedly the advantage of position & the best sharp shooters by far. Darling I had rather had fought the Shiloh battle than to have undergone what we have in the past three days.

Now that it is over it is funny to think about how we dodged & jumped from tree to tree & but for the advantage of ours, having an abundance of big timber, they would have gotten us badly – I wish I had time to write you more. I suppose you will be astonished to know that only one man in my command killed & shot at three thousand times – It is this we shot at least 400 yds & every man of ours behind trees & only when it became necessary to change position or fall back for water &c And we afraid to venture on the Yankees for fear they had a large reserve & vice versa...We leave again in a few minutes for the enemy – and in all probability will be in a battle. But I trust the same kind providence will protect me."[90]

Major General Henry W. Halleck, commander of the Union western action, joined Grant and Buell at Corinth. The combined Union armies numbered more that 100,000 men. Their officers included Grant, Sherman, Sheridan, Buell, Pope, Rosecrans, George H. Thomas, and James B. McPherson. Halleck slowly extended the Union lines around the city and brought in big guns. After Shiloh, Beauregard had stated, "If defeated here, we lose the whole Mississippi Valley and probably our cause." However, the Confederate postion reached a point where he had no choice. Halleck tightened the noose around the Confederate troops such that Beauregard was forced to evacuate Corinth. On May 29, Beauregard began an orderly retreat from Corinth. Anything of value the Confederates could not take

---

[89] Bray letters.
[90] Burnett papers.

with them was destroyed. Ammunition, guns, food, medical supplies, personal belongings, and tents were all sacrificed. Nothing was left for the Federals when they took over Corinth. Leaving the diseased city to the Federals, the Confederates retreated down the Mobile and Ohio Railroad to Tupelo, the next major station.

McMillan wrote of the move, "*We evacuated Corinth on 29th May, falling back to Tupelo. Our brigade again did picket duty at Clear Creek, and fought a skirmish at Blackland. Our Regt., however not being engaged, as we were making an effort to get to the rear while the fight was going on. We then went on duty at Tupelo, and remained until the 5th of July....*"[91] During the evacuation of Corinth, Colonel V. S. Murphy, temporary commander of the 17^{th,} Alabama, was wounded at Boonsville, Mississippi.

When the 17th Alabama finally arrived at Tupelo, conditions were a great improvement over Corinth for the many sick and wounded soldiers. However, recovery of the sick and wounded was slow. Confederate Service Records identify many of the soldiers of the 17th Alabama who were hospitalized from either wounds or disease, or who died or were discharged during the month of June 1862. Currently archived at Shiloh National Battle Park is a muster roll for the period July and August of 1862. This record lists additional soldiers of the 17th who were hospitalized, died and discharged during the summer months. The muster roll gives an exact account of the men who were present or absent for a given period.

After the battle of Shiloh, Columbus, Mississippi, was selected as the hospital center for treatment of the wounded and sick of the Army of Mississippi and the Army of Tennessee. As the train loads of sick and wounded arrived from points north of Columbus, existing buildings were converted into hospitals. These conversins included the Gilmer Hotel, Odd Fellows building, the concert hall, Columbus Female Institute, and the amphitheatre at the fair grounds. The buildings were all soon filled to capacity. Next came the creation of cemeteries for interment of the many soldiers who died there. The death rate ran as high as 25 to 30 per day.[92]

John A. Bolling, Greenville, Alabama, was a first lieutenant in Company C when he wrote two letters from Tupelo, Mississippi, during June of 1862. On June 22nd when Captain Walter D. Perryman resigned as commanding officer of Company C, Bolling was promoted to captain and assigned as a replacement for Perryman. Bolling would later become commander of the 17th Alabama in December 1864 for the battle of Nashville where he was captured. On June 9, 1862, Bolling wrote his wife, "*I recd your letter of the 25th May which gave me much pleasure but I am very sorry to know that you had only recd one from me when I have written*

---

[91] McMillan sketch
[92] W. L. Lipscomb, *A History of Columbus, Mississippi, During the 19th Century* (Birmingham, AL: Press of Dispatch, 1909).

every week since I have been in the service with one exception and would have wrote then but we were on the march all the time ...well the day after I wrote my last we went off to the entrenchments as usual and then on picket where we had the pleasure of running the detestable Yankees once they came up within a quarter of a mile of the entrenchment and dove in our pickets of the 10th South Carolina Regt and four companys of our Regt were sent out to reestablish the posts and our Co. was one of them and I was selected a front guard to advance about 600 yards in front of the Co and...the bullets rained about me worse than hail but thank the Lord no body was hurt and I am still in hopes of one day seeing you and the children yet tho I have many risks to run.

.....and staid until the next night at 10 0'c when we commenced our retreat from Corinth and marched all night and only travel four miles, that however was owing to the long train of wagons that was in front of us; we marched three days and only came 20 miles where we landed late Sunday evening and remained there until Tuesday 12 o'c when we were ordered back three miles to skirmish as the Yankees were following us and stood there until Friday noon when we left for this field where we landed Saturday evening and in fact we will stay here several days to rest as we are very much fatigued with our march.

I have never seen such destruction as when we left bed quilts, blankets, pants, shirts...I got a pair pants and drawers...we had all of our tents sent off before we left Corinth and they were all burned up on account of there being so much to move that they could not do it all in time to keep the Yankees from getting things. I had borrowed a roundabout of Joe Barnett to wear and put both my coats in the tent with my valise and got them all burned. I was not allowed to carry any thing on a march more than a knap sack and only one suit of clothes in that...."[93]

On June 13th Bolling wrote his wife again, *"I have nothing new to write only since we left Corinth our health has much improved tho it is not from high living you may believe we get only an ounce of bacon per day and a lb pickled beef which is so salt that we have to boil it through three...before we can eat it. So upon the whole we are living pretty hard and I guess it will not be any better at least for this year as we cant get any bacon from Tennessee...we have had plenty of pork and fresh beef since we began our retreat from Corinth but we had it all to broil and that without salt so you know it is not good. Crops in this section of country are very backward tho they look green and ...we burned up all the cotton as we came from Corinth to this place. I lost my bed quilt and both my coats in the retreat so I am coatless myself only as I borrow. I neglected to tell you that my blanket was stolen from me the first night I got to Corinth, but when I was sent to the hospital some person in their hurry getting off the cars left me a much better*

---

[93] John Bolling, letters, (Rare Book, Manuscript and Special Collections Library, Duke University, Durham, NC).

one and before we left Corinth I got one of the best coverlets you ever saw and if I get a chance I shall send it to you...we are living under bush arbours and will for some time as our tents are all burned we drill from 7 to 9? o'c then rest until 10 and drill till eleven and then rest till four and drill till 5 and at 6 we go on dress parade...."[94] The clothes and tents and other personal items burned at Corinth were not items that the Confederate military could replace. These items would have to be replaced from home sources, if possible.

In June 1862, Henry Bray sent two letters written from Camp Jackson at Tupelo Station, Mississippi. On the 13th, he wrote, " *....Ma, I have not got that box you sent me and never shall for I am pretty sertain that it got destroyed in Corinth. ma, the soldiers has a bad chance now for when anything is sent to them they never have the chance to go look after them. without forty different names to a furlough and then when you get to the fortieth one, he refuses to sign it.*

ma, I have a bad chance now for I am first corporal and every one of our Sargeants is sick and I have to Act Orderly Sergeant and I have my hands full from 5 ock in the morning til 8 ock at night ...

...Ma, when I sent that money by Brodenan I thought I was sending by a responsible man but I am sorry to say he proved the reverse a graded rascol. But ma, when I draw again I will try and send it so that it will reach you...."[95]

On the 23rd, Bray wrote, "*....ma, times is dull here; no yankeys to fight and, of corse, no news. I am getting along pretty fine on slap jacks and ash cakes. we had some coffee this morning which is the first we have had since April and it went mighty well for you know what a great coffee drinker I am.*

...Ma, if you see any of the Boys coming to camps I wish you would send me an old hat of some sort for I have nothing but a cap and the sun has Burn me nearly black and there is no chance of Buying a hat here Ma I wish I could be with you to set water melons this year, But I am fraid I wont get to see one this year much more to eat one, but set them ma and save the seed and maby I will be home in time to plant next year ...P. S. Ma, excuse this pencil writing for my ink got spilled and mine was all that was in the company."[96]

On July 3rd, Bray wrote his last letter from Tupelo, "*....I get plenty to eat such as it is but we don't get any coffee now nor much bacon we get half rations of cornmeal now but we get no sifter and the bran about chokes me and scratches my throat like forty but it all helps to fill up and I suppose that's all the confedracy cares for so the keep our belly full with something.*

---

[94] Ibid.
[95] Bray letters.
[96] Ibid.

Ma, the box you sent down for Sergeant Call to fetch to me, he forgot it and left it at Capt. O'Brien's store and the hat you sent by Lieutenant Bryant got stolen. His carpet sack was broken open and a pair of boots and shirt and my hat was taken out of it; but I got the pants and tobacco you sent by Andrewson Evans and I tell you I was glad to get them. The pants fit me to the notch.

ma Andrewson is going off to the hospital sick again this evening. they are sending off all the sick in the country to hospitals that are not able to stand a march. ma we will not stay here much longer for they are making preperrations to move somewhere and I think it is back to corinth or tennessee. I hope it is to whirp the confouded yankey thieving scoundles clean out of dixie and end this evil and barbarous warfare. but never will I lay down my musket until the inhuman scoundrels are driven from our sweet Isle or I am laid low with the rest of our brave Shiloh men....

ma, I am sorry to tell you that my fourth of July furlough comes up missing and the captain is off now, too, and even if he were here he couldn't give me a furlough. If he could have done it, I would have been home long ere this.

ma, it is near dress parade so I must come to a close...[97]"

On July 5th, the division, commanded by Brigadier-General J. M. Withers, moved to Saltillo, just north of Tupelo on the Mobile and Ohio Railroad. Withers Division included Jackson's Brigade and the 17th Alabama. While the men had been suffering for water on the prairies of Mississippi, at Saltillo they had plenty of water of an excellent quality.

Private James Alford Thompson was an overseer at Monterey in Butler County before his enlistment in Company C May 10, 1862. He enlisted as a substitute for his employer, F. W. Crenshaw of 'The Ridge' in Butler County. On July 20, 1862, he wrote Crenshaw from Camp Jackson near Saltillo, Mississippi, "...I have nothing of much importance to write to you. Times is dull and hard here and some right smart sickness and some deaths here. I tell you a sick man here has but little attention paid to him here for we have a very sorry doctor in our regiment. We had better have none than to have him for if you go to him when you are sick he will curse you and tell you to go away...They drill us very hard and they don't feed well at all. It is half rations and double duty all the time though I have stood it very well with the exception of three days and that was when we marched up here from Tupelo. That nearly killed me...."[98] On the 17th Alabama muster rolls for the months of July and August 1862, Private Thompson was one of many members of the 17th Alabama who was listed as sick in the hospital.

Lieutenant Crenshaw explained the appointment of officers before the 17th moved to their next assignment in Mobile, "*Under Braggs appointment: J. P. Jones was Col.: John Ryan was Lt. Col.: S. A. Moreno Maj.: S. S.

---

[97] Ibid.
[98] James A. Thompson, letters (Private collection, Crenshaw family of Greenville, Alabama).

Harris Adj.: *A. F. Watson Surgeon: M. Rice Asst. Surgeon. These officers continued to act for 2 mos....*

Capts. Holcombe and Burnett, who had both been absent at Home contended that they were entitled to the place of Lt. Col. and Major, by promotion, and right of seniority, and whilst stationed at Tupelo, Miss., an order from the War Dept. was received, declaring Gen. Braggs appointment in the field illegal and elections were ordered to fill vacancies in the Companies. Capt. Holcombe was promoted to Lt. Col., and took command of the Regt. versus Jones. The examining committee refused to promote Capt. Burnett. The Co. officers as well as I recollect at that time July '62 were as follows –

Company A	C. E. Sadler Capt., F. A. Hambrick 1st Lt., S. A. Verdery 2nd Lt., J. L. Bright Brev. 2nd Lt.
Company B	James L. Moreland Capt., W. T. Dunklin 1st Lt.,· B. Williams 2nd Lt., Porter Brev. 2nd Lt.
Company C	Jno. Bolling Capt., Jno. L. Powell 1st Lt., Jno. Harrison 2nd Lt., B. W. Dowdy Brev. 2nd Lt.
Company D	Jno. A. Hester Capt., W. D. Hull 1st Lt., ____ Rush 2nd Lt.
Company E	B. F. Weathers Capt.
Company F	A. L. O'Brien Capt., J. B. Johnson 1st Lt., Thos. Holfain 2nd Lt., T. S. O'Brien Brev. 2nd Lt.
Company G	Thos. Ragland Capt., Jno. F. Tate 1st Lt., W. D. Tate 2nd Lt., J. L. McIntire Brev. 2nd Lt.
Company H	W. W. McMillan Capt., R. M. Andress 1st Lt., C. L. Harrell 2nd Lt., W. J. Robison Brev 2nd Lt.
Company I	Jno. S. Bones Capt., J. H. Raines 1st Lt., ____ Lancaster 2nd Lt., C. McLaurin Brev 2nd Lt.
Company K	T. A. McCane Capt., L. M. Pentacost 1st Lt., Ed Crenshaw 2nd Lt., C. J. Cody Brev 2nd Lt."[99]

On August 1, 1862, Colonel Murphy whose appointment as commanding officer of the 17th Alabama by Attorney General Watts was opposed by General Bragg, wrote from Okolona, Mississippi. "*I have the honor to respectfully represent to the Col. Comdg, this post that I was arrested here on the 17th day of June 1862 while under surgical treatment for a wound received at Boonsville on the 30th day of May. No charges have been performed against me as far as I know. My regiment leaves today for Mobile, Al., under orders to report their for duty. I am discharged from the hospital and desire to accompany my command...I therefore respectfully request the Col. Comdg. To parole me...to my command and to report*

---

[99] Crenshaw diary.

myself to the Comdg. General at Mobile under arrest."[100] Murphy was granted permission to go to Mobile with his command.

H. Conclusion

After spending several months of their enlistment in the comparatively quiet confines of Pensacola, Florida, the 17th Alabama experienced the horrors of battle at Shiloh and Corinth. Poorly equipped and lacking experience, they met the enemy bravely, fought well, and suffered greatly.

Where are those brave men who died on the battlefield at Shiloh? Beauregard officially reported 1,728 killed, left behind when the Confederate army retreated on April 7. The next day Beauregard sent a request to Grant to remove the Confederate dead. Grant refused. Because of the condition of the dead and the warm weather, he had assigned Union soldiers to bury the dead of both armies immediately. The dead of both armies were buried in trenches and large pits. Five of the common graves of the Confederate soldiers have been identified and marked with appropriate monuments in the Shiloh National Military Park. Many of the Confederates who died of wounds or disease after the battle of Shiloh were buried in cemeteries in Columbus, Lauderdale and other towns in Mississippi.

The ranks of the 17th Alabama were diminished by the battle of Shiloh, by the spread of disease at Corinth and Tupelo, and by desertion. Desertion had become a severe problem in the Confederacy that would continue throughout the war. The number of desertions tended to peak after a battle as disastrous as Shiloh. Another cause of desertion was animosity towards the general in command, and there was certainly much animosity towards General Bragg. Bragg complained about deserters in 1862, *"Our armies are gradually but certainly melting away whilst we are getting no reinforcements, no recruits and cannot see a source from which they are to come. Some of my regiments are down to 100 privates for duty."*[101] There is no official record of how many men deserted the 17th Alabama after Shiloh.[102] Although men continued to volunteer, the numbers were not sufficient to fill the needs of the various armies. A draft law was passed on April 16, 1862, requiring that all men, ages 18 to 35, residing in the Confederate states enlist in military service.

---

[100] *The Compiled Service Records of Confederate Soldiers who Served Organizations from the State of Alabama.*
[101] OWR, series I, volume xix, part ii, 407.
[102] Bessie Martin, *Desertion of Alabama Troops from the Confederate Army* (New York: AMS Press, Inc., 1966). A record book labeled "Deserters of Alabama" was maintained during the war, but the book disappeared after the war and has never been found.

In August of 1862, the morale of the men of the 17th Alabama was low and disease was still a problem. After five months in northeast Mississippi, the regiment was reassigned to Mobile.

V. Mobile

A. Introduction

The strategic importance of the city of Mobile throughout the war demanded particular attention and revised tactics by both Confederate and Union leaders. Examples of specific actions are summarized in this section along with troop assignments. Evolving duties at Mobile are described including personal observations by Confederate troops assigned there. Military hospitals and personnel sicknesses are briefly summarized. Union observations by a Union scout and undercover activities by a Confederate deserter are included.

B. Strategic Significance

Mobile, as both a strategic rail center and a major port for blockade runners, was critical to the defense of the Confederacy. Mobile was the link between the eastern and western sections of the Confederacy. Early in the war the Confederate government realized that it was impossible to protect its entire coastline. Mobile was one of the exceptions. Much effort was put into strengthening the defenses of Mobile. The construction of entrenchments surrounding Mobile for light artillery and infantry and the various batteries in Mobile Bay deterred the Federals for years from mounting major attacks against Mobile. In addition, the need for Federal troops in other areas took precedent over Mobile until late in the war.

To illustrate the importance of Mobile as a rail center, consider the part it played in transferring 25,000 troops from Tupelo, Mississippi, to Chattanooga, in the summer of 1862 after the loss of Shiloh and Corinth. The Army of Mississippi located in Tupelo was needed to reinforce troops in Chattanooga. The route to Chattanooga was via the Mobile and Ohio Railroad from Tupelo to Mobile. From Mobile, the troops loaded onto a steamer to Tensas Landing east across Mobile Bay. At Tensas Landing, the troops boarded another train on the Mobile and Great Northern railroad to Pollard, Alabama. At Pollard, the train switched to the Alabama and Florida Railroad which took the troops to Montgomery and finally Chattanooga.

In 1865 near the war's end, the defeated Army of Tennessee followed the same route. Many of the men moved from northeast Mississippi south through Mobile and then north through Montgomery to join the Confederate forces in North Carolina for a last attempt to stop Sherman's advance. The Confederacy maintained their control of Mobile through most of the war. It was not until March 1865 that Union forces made a serious attack against Mobile. With no reinforcements available, the Confederate forces were unable to hold Mobile. On April 10 the Confederate army began evacuating the city that finally fell to the Union forces.

C. Assignment to Mobile

Confederate forces in Chattanooga were in critical need of reinforcements in the summer of 1862. To meet this need, 25,000 members of the Army of Mississippi left northeast Mississippi for Chattanooga, passing through Mobile. Three regiments were left at Mobile to replace the troops moved earlier to Chattanooga. These three regiments, the 17th, 18th, and 21st Alabama, became part of Brigadier-General John H. Forney's brigade.

Due to bad health in early 1863, Forney was forced to resign as brigade commander. The 17th was next placed under the command of Brigadier-General James Cantey. Cantey was a South Carolinian and a lawyer. He had served in the military during the Mexican War where he was wounded. Prior to the Civil War, he was a planter living in Alabama. Although he commanded a Confederate brigade and then a division, he was plagued by ill health and was frequently on leave from his command. Cantey's Brigade first consisted of the 17th, 21st, and 29th Alabama regiments and the 37th Mississippi. In late 1863, the brigade was reorganized to include the 1st, 17th, 26th, and 29th Alabama regiments and the 37th Mississippi.

By 1863 all troops at Mobile were part of the Department of the Gulf, under the command of Major General Dabney Maury. Maury was a Virginian and a graduate of the University of Virginia and West Point. When the war began, he was assistant adjutant general of the Department of New Mexico on the frontier. After turning in his resignation to the US Army, he held several positions in the Confederacy. In April 1863, Jefferson Davis sent him to Mobile to replace Major General Buckner as commander of the Department of the Gulf. He held this position to the end of the war.

John Witherspoon Dubose writing about the 17th Alabama stated that the regiment *"was without incidents of interest while on garrison duty about Mobile after its return to that place in the summer."* It certainly was without incident compared to the battle of Shiloh.

While in Mobile many of the men were retrained as artillerist. The regiment spent their time drilling and building fortifications around the city of Mobile and manning the defensive positions in the area. Company A was assigned to Pinto Island Battery from August 1862 to April 1863 and to Battery Gladden in Florida during September and October 1863.[103] Company B was assigned to Fort Apalachee during November and December of 1862.[104] Company K was assigned to city redoubt #10 in Mobile during May and June of 1863.[105] From letters and diaries included

---

[103] *The Compiled Service Records of Confederate Soldiers who Served Organizations from the State of Alabama.* Pinto Island was renamed Battery Gladden in June 1863 by General Maury.
[104] Ibid. Fort Apalachee refers to Apalachee Battery, renamed to Battery Tracy in June 1863 by General Maury.
[105] Ibid.

in this section, it is known that other companies were temporarily assigned to the Pinto Island, Spanish River[106] and Bay Shore Batteries. Different companies spent time in Mississippi protecting bridges and the Mobile and Ohio Railroad when needed. Captain McMillan mentioned Company H going to Mississippi temporarily as did Private Bray of Company F. Some companies of the 17th spent time at Pollard, Alabama, monitoring activities at Pensacola.

D. Duties

In August 1862 Lieutenant Crenshaw of Company K discussed duties of the 17th while in Mobile, *"In camp at Mobile, Alabama, on the Bay Shell Road, we have charge of a line of Batteries extending from the old Light House for some distance down the Shell Road. We were drilled a great deal in Heavy Artillery and the officers had recitation under the Regular Army Officers...Our company (Company K) had a battery (No. 3 on the Shell Road) of two rifled 32 pounders. We were in Brig. Gen. J. E. Slaughter's command.... Soon after our arrival in Mobile two companies of our regiment, Capt. Sadler's (Company A) and Capt. O'Brien's (Company F) were detached and ordered to two beautiful batteries in the Bay just below Mobile, know as Spanish River Battery and Pinto Island Battery. Soon Capt. O'Brien's company was relieved and ordered back to the regiment; but Capt. Sadler remained at "Pinto."*

The 17th reorganized on 25th July at Saltillo, Miss., and all of Bragg's appointments were thrown out with a few exceptions who were elected to fill vacancies. In this way the reg't got some very good officers after all...."[107]

After arriving in Mobile in August 1862, McMillan of Company H wrote, *"Here our Regt. was placed in charge of Pinto Island, Spanish River, and Bay Shore Batteries, drilled in Heavy Artillery, as well as Infantry. My Co. (Company H) had charge of Bay Shore Battery No. 1, near the second toll gate on Bay Shell road. The battery consisted of one ten inch, and one 8 inch collunbriad and a smooth bore 32 pounder. After city fortifications were finished, Redoubts took the place of these batteries, and I was placed in command of Redoubts. Nos. 1 and 2 on bay shell road and near the foot of St. Lawrence St. Our camp was immediately at the foot of St. L, and was called Camp Forney in honor of our Brig. Gen. We remained there just one year, and were camped during the winter of '63 near Spring Hill. Whilst stationed at these places we were twice sent up into Miss: once to meet Grierson's raid, and again when Sherman invaded the state. We also made a campaign through Conecuh Co., which walk I shall always charge to the acts of Alfred Holley Esq. a renegade from Covington Co.*

---

[106] Spanish River Battery was renamed Battery McIntosh in June 1863 by General Maury.
[107] Crenshaw diary.

During our stay in Mobile we were commanded by the following Gens. in the order in which they are placed. Brig. Gen. J. H. Forney, afterwards Maj. Gen.; Brig. Gen. G. Cummings; Brig. Gen. L. E. Slaughter; Maj. Gen. S. B. Buckner; Maj. Gen. D. H. Maury; Brig. Gen. Cantey. During our 18 mos. sojourn in Mobile we were very pleasantly situated. The duty was light and we had comfortable quarters, and generally were tolerably well fed; besides many of us were near enough home to have a great many necessaries as well as luxuries sent from there. Our friends could visit us, and we could also go home occasionally." [108]

On July 23, 1863, Major General Maury wrote from Mobile that four companies of the 17th were on duty guarding bridges near Quitman, Red Bluff, Shubuta and Bucatunna Stations[109] of the Mobile and Ohio Railroad. Maury wanted the men of the 17th returned because they were artillerists. He requested other troops to take over their duty guarding the bridges. In the memo, he also requested that no more prisoners be sent to Mobile. They interfered with transportation and consumed scarce supplies. He also reported that a large naval force was assembling at Pensacola and requested 12,000-15,000 reinforcements at Mobile.[110] There were no reinforcements to send him.

On September 4, 1863, a "bread riot" occurred. A group of several hundred poor women of the city of Mobile demonstrated against a shortage of food and other supplies. The goods were available in limited quantities. However prices were so high, there was an element of the population that could not afford the barest of necessities.[111] These women marched into the city and broke into stores taking food and supplies they needed. General Maury ordered the 17th Alabama Infantry to put down the riot. The regiment refused to obey the order. Fortunately the civil authorities took control of the situation before the day was out.

Frank Robertson of Company E wrote from Pascagoula, Mississippi, on January 18, 1864. In his letter he indicated that he (and his company) left Camp Cantey (in Mobile) on January 4. He described the difficulties he encountered on the trip. He described wading through water for four days *"...and the deepest water I waded was up to my arms I waded for a mile that cold day from half thi deep to waste deep Tha was a big sleat on the ground at that time you cant tell how we suffered..."*[112] He did not explain why his unit was at Pascagoula. There had been some activity by Union forces in the Pascagoula area in December, but they were gone by December 26.

---

[108] McMillan sketch.
[109] These were all towns in extreme eastern Mississippi below Meridian.
[110] OWR, Serial 42.
[111] Arthur W. Bergeron Jr., *Confederate Mobile* (Oxford, MS: University Press of Mississippi, 1991), 101.
[112] Frank Robertson, letters (Private collection).

According to their muster roll for January – February 1864, Company H marched from Mobile to Pollard, Alabama, on February 4, 1864. This was a distance of 80 miles. They returned on February 12, 1864. Also in February 1864, Cantey's Brigade provided defense for the southern section of Mobile and Ohio Railroad. The brigade was assigned to prevent General William T. Sherman and his army from continuing their advance toward Mobile. The bridge at DeSoto, Mississippi, was destroyed, but as soon as the enemy was aware of Cantey's approach, they retreated. Cantey reported from Bucatunna on February 20th that the enemy left Enterprise heading back to Meridian.[113] Company H was included in this mission. Noted on their muster roll was their march from Mobile to Bucatunna, February 12, 1864. The distance was 71 miles. They returned to Mobile February 25, 1864.

In March 1864, General Maury reported on the February mission. He stated that he had sent General Cantey and his brigade *"up the Mobile and Ohio Railroad with orders to attack and drive back any raiding party and to delay and obstruct Sherman's advance, if it should be found that he was really advancing on Mobile that route. I held re-enforcements ready for General Cantey..."*[114]

A bulletin posted by Governor Watts indicates the uncertainty and the frame of mind in Mobile in February 14, 1864:

"TO THE PEOPLE OF MOBILE

Your city is about to be attacked by the Enemy. Mobile must be defended at every hazard and to the last extremity. To do this effectively, all who cannot fight must leave the city. The brave defenders of the city can fight with more energy and enthusiasm when they feel assured that the MOBILE WOMEN AND CHILDREN are out of danger. I appeal to the patriotic NON-COMBATANTS to leave for the interior. The people of the interior towns and the planters in the country will receive and provide support for all who go. The patriotic of this city will see the importance and necessity of heeding this call.

Those who love this CITY and the glorious CAUSE in which we fight will not hesitate to obey the calls which patriotism makes.

Thomas H. Watts
Governor of Alabama"[115]

Capt. McMillan reported, *"In March '64 we broke up camp at Mobile and went to Pollard where we were thrown into a brigade composed of 17 Ala., 21 Ala. Col. C. D. Anderson, 29 Ala. J. F. Conalley and 37 Miss. Col. O. S. Holland, so with Reynolds brigade of Tennesseans formed a new*

---

[113] OWR, Serial 48
[114] OWR, Serial 57
[115] Letters from Governor Thomas Watts Watts (SG24872, Reel 20, Folder 11, Alabama Archives, Montgomery, AL).

division commanded by Brig. Gen. J. Cantey. Our brigade (Canteys) being commanded by Col. V. S. Murphy. During this time many changes had taken place in our Regt."[116] Pollard, Alabama, was a strategic point for the Confederacy, located about 75 miles northeast of Mobile along the Mobile and Great Northern Railroad. The brigade's assignment at Pollard was to observe the Union forces at Pensacola and to protect the Confederate line in Mobile from attacks launched from Pensacola.

In April 1864, Cantey's Brigade was ordered to reinforce the Army of Tennessee. On April 20 the brigade left Pollard and the Mobile area, headed for northern Georgia.

E. Personal Observations

Lieutenant Crenshaw of Company K described life in camp in August 1862, "...*We had a beautiful and healthy camp. Most of the officers and men had tents walled up and floored with plank with cloth doors, and in the winter most of the officers bought small stoves and put in their tents. A great many of the men and officers had houses. We were very comfortable. I spent decidedly the most pleasant winter of the War, at Mobile.*"[117]

Captain Thomas J. Burnett wrote to his wife, Ann, October 4, 1862. He had just received word that very dear family friends had been killed in battle. Obviously the death of one of his friends had deeply affected him. He wrote, "*Well we will have to console ourselves with the reflection that he died as every brave soldier prefers to die: on the battlefield, and that he fell with his face to the foe endeavoring to drive back from southern soil those ruthless invaders of our dearest rights.*

My Dear Ann, I at this time have more determination to fight out this war than ever, and avenge his death....but it is the sad affliction which has visited nearly every family in this bleeding country of ours. I feel this morning almost persuaded to say that I wish we had submitted, no I will never say it for it would be the utterance of a lie for we could never more have lived in peace and unity with them, and I never will live with them on any terms. Give me separate independence or give me death is and shall ever be my sentiments.

God knows it tries my weak heart though and that sorely too receive such tidings. That boy would have laid down his life in combat for me at any time, and I pray God that I may yet have the opportunity to avenge his death, and besides darling there is no turning back, you have doubtless read that <u>Old Demon's</u> *proclamation, in which he says our property is to be liberated on the 1st day of January 1863. Let his minions come we will fight him as long as a man remains.*

---

[116] McMillan sketch.
[117] Crenshaw diary.

Bear up under this affliction and console yourself with the glorious truth that he gave up his life for his bleeding country, that he has fallen nobly defending the dearest rights of us all."[118]

Henry Bray of Company F wrote to his mother on November 4, 1862, from Camp Forney, "....*Ma I would have Answered your letter sooner but I was on guard the day I received it and the next day I had to drill all day. They have made a artillery Company of owrs and given us a battery of flying artillery and they drill us six hours ever day now.*

I tell you what they are putting us through, making us pay for owr corn dodger (a form of fried cornbread similar to a large hush puppy) *owr instructor give us the praise of being the most intelligent and learn the quickest of any set of men he ever had learn, Ma tell Cousin Judge* (Williamson) *he must come down and see me, for I would like to see him very much and there is no chance for me to come to see him unless We have a fight here soon and then if I should get half killed or wounded they might let me come home and I don't think the fight is long off. From all appearance before we will have to face the music again...*"[119]

James Alford Thompson of Company C wrote home from Camp Forney near Mobile. On December 6, 1862, he wrote, "......*I seat myself this morning to let you know I received your kind letter that was dated the 29th of Nov...I have not got much to write to you more than we have got some cold weather now. It is good to save meat now that* (unreadable) *is ready to kill. Time is lively here in camp. The boys drink a heap of whiskey. They have to pay 50 cents a drink for it...You wrote you wish I had of been there to eat possum with you. I would been very glad to have been there for I would give a dollar to get a good bait of possum and yam potato for I love them dearly. They eat the same down here some times, but they sell so high they ask for 2 dollars for a common old possum....*"[120]

On March 15, 1863, Thompson wrote to his employer, F. W. Crenshaw of Butler County, "....*I think the measles have not got out of me yet. I have just received your letter that was dated July 27th 1862. I don't know where it has been all this time. I have nothing of importance to write. Everything is quiet here. There is some talk of this regiment being ordered to Tennessee. I don't know whether it will go or not. I hope I won't have to go from here. I don't want to leave here if I can help it...I tell you times is very hard about something to eat. It is two and three days at a time when we don't get any meat. If it gets much harder I don't know what we will do. I wish this war would come to a close....*"[121]

---

[118] Burnett papers.
[119] Bray letters
[120] James A. Thompson, letters (Private collection, Thompson family of Greenville, Alabama).
[121] James A. Thompson, letters (Private collection, Crenshaw family of Greenville, Alabama).

On May 8, 1863, Bray wrote of Company F being temporarily on duty in Mississippi: "....*Ma I am very sorry to inform you that I am very unwell at this time I was taken sick a day after I wrote you the last letter. I had contracted a very bad cold while I was up in Miss. From getting very wet Several times, and since then I have suffered very much from the fever and head ach and at this time I have the bloody flux pretty bad...Ma I have nothing of very much importance to write you. There was a day or two after we came back from Miss. Strong talk of our going back again. The Yankees were advancing in heavy colum down the railroad (*Mobile and Ohio), *and that it would require owr Regimunt to repulse them but it has all died out I don't think there is any thing of it now Ma you Said that you had heard that al the women and children were ordered away from Mobile and that thet were expecting a fight here Ma there is nothing of it, and I don't See any prospects of a fight here now that there was eight months ago....*"[122]

On May 26, 1863, Thompson wrote again, "*Everything is quiet. It seems that our army is in great spirits at Vicksburg. They seem to think we can hold that place very easy. They are bringing out the Militia down here to defend Mobile. They are a fine bunch of them here, but they want to depend on like we old volunteers. They ain't drilled. I think the prospects for us staying here is very good. Gel Slaughter says we will stay here as long as there is any troops needed here...I heard the hog colrey* (cholera) *has killed a great many hogs up in your settlement.*[123] *I was very sorry to hear it for meat is scarce there. It had not got among my hogs the last time I heard from there, but I expect it in every letter I get...*"

On record are three letters from Private Peter McGowin of Company I. The first letter was written to his wife from Fort Gindrat[124] on June 14th, 1863. "*Dear wife as the boat is about to start to the post office I hasten to write to you a few lines to inform you that we will leave this place tomorrow morning for Mobile, where it is said we will be stationed at a fortification called a redout, about two miles above the city on the Mobile and Ohio Railroad.*

I am glad we are going to leave here because it is the most uncomfortable place I ever was at I believe, the quarters are as hot as a fire room and the musquitos so bad one can't rest

I have been a little unwell since I wrote to you but not seriously ill. I am taking medicine now and feel like I will soon be as well as ever."

On September 16, 1863, Peter McGowin wrote his wife from Camp Pelham near Mobile. "*I seat myself this evening to inform you that I am well except cold, sore throat, etc. which is getting better...It seems that they*

---

[122] Bray letters.
[123] The words your settlement refers to "The Ridge" in Butler County. By this time Alabama farmers had switched from cotton to corn and Alabama led the Confederacy in hog production.
[124] Fort Gindrat was Gindrat Battery located on Blakely Island. Gindrat Battery was later renamed to Huger Battery.

are having a kind of breaking up of troops here, our Regt. Except those companies in charge of the water batteries, has been relieved from duties here, and it is said that the balance of us will be in a few days. I don't know the cause of the change some say it is to have the health of the regiment improved. When relieved from here we will go out about 8 miles for the City of camp, I don't know what will be our duty.

You remember I wrote to pa. To have for myself and Jas. Each a pair of shoes made, and I believe I forgot to mention the size, we want No. 7. Tell him if he has not yet had it done to have a good pair of shoes though I don't think we'll be sent far from here..."

On December 10, 1863, he wrote his brothers from Camp Cantey near Mobile, *"....I am in tolerable good health though for sometime past I have been a little on the puny order, my stomach has been considerably deranged some, nothing I eat seems to agree with me and I have the heartburn a great deal and very bad....we have been building us a "shanty" to live in which is now about complete. If we stay here all winter we will be very comfortable situated. Our ratins are very poor and skanty, but as long as we stay here I expect to get things from home to keep from suffering....*

You requested me to give you all the war news I have, but I have none more than you know. My opinion about the war is that if it continues twelve to eighteen months longer we will achieve our independence, that is if we hold out prospectively that long. They I think will give it up, but if they succeed I think it will be brought to a focus in six months, though I know nothing and my opinion is worth nothing....

P. S. When I came from home I brought three shoats to camp and they are doing as well as you could expect on the slop and stuff gathered about camp."

Peter McGowin, age 30, died of typhoid fever December 10, 1863, nine days after this letter was written. His widow traveled to Mobile and took her husband's body home. He is buried in Foshee Cemetery near Grab Mill, Alabama.

Frank Robertson, a private of Company E, wrote a number of letters to his wife, Martha, during 1863. Copies of many of these letters still exist.[125] His letters are probably typical of letters written by many soldiers in the 17th Alabama. In each letter he wrote how much he wanted to see Martha and the children, how much he wanted to go home. He described his health which, at best, was improving. He complained of daily headaches, chills, aching all over, and lethargy. Although conditions at home were difficult, Martha obviously never complained. Robertson commented how glad he was to hear from her and how glad to hear *"you was all well and getting along well."*

---

[125] Robertson letters.

He frequently complained about conditions in Mobile. On August 13, 1863, he wrote, *"We don't get but very little at this time we draw one pound a quarter of bacon for seven days and a little syrup and a little soap and candle we don't draw no flower nor sugar we draw a little bull beef and it will stick to a tree if you will throw it agan it and so you may know what kind of beef we get to eat hear in camp and sometimes we don't get non-at-all."* Probably Frank's meager food rations were supplemented by food from home. In one of his letters, Frank mentioned a visit to camp by Martha. He also wrote of a future visit to camp by his parents.

Frank wrote, *"I can study back and think how much we use to live and thought that we seed bad times but gest think of them and now it all most brake my heart to think about it."* By October 6, he wrote about his chances of a visit home. Although furloughs had been granted, he doubted that he would be granted one anytime soon because *"many of the men given a furlough stay gone so long that they may soon quit giving furloughs."*

F. Enemy Observations

On September 1, 1863, Union correspondence included a letter from a deserter from Company C, Tennessee Light Artillery. He had been in Mobile and described the Confederate strength there. He mentioned the 17th Alabama and the 29th Alabama, *"and three batteries, one battery four guns and the other four guns each, and probably 200 cavalry... There are nineteen forts around the city, mounting three siege guns each, 32-pounders and larger, besides three light guns, 4 or 6 pounders. In the bay there are only three batteries heavy guns—about 2 miles from the city down the bay. Two rams in the bay finished, mounting six heavy guns each. On the Pensacola side about three batteries, heavy guns. Forts are all manned and batteries also, exclusive of force mentioned before...There are three or more floating batteries in the harbor of Mobile, well manned. The intention is, in case they are overpowered, to sink them in the harbor to impede navigation. There is a new English breech-loading gun on the point near Fort Morgan, a light gun for long range."*[126]

On October 1, 1863, a letter was sent to Major General Halleck, General-in-chief of the Union army, Washington, D.C. It included a report from a Union scout who had recently returned from the south. The scout mentioned the 17th and 29th Alabama as located in part of the city of Mobile. He described the defenses in the area of Mobile, *"The fortifications around Mobile, Ala., about 5 miles from the city, are three broad and deep ditches, which run all around the city. No. 1 has the entrance on the southeast side. No. 2 is situated on the east side of the river opposite St. Michael Street, the entrance being on the south side.*

---

[126] OWR, Serial 52, 280-1.

Going down the river with the Mobile and Great Northern Railroad boat, and as the boat turns to the left to get into the bay (which takes it to the river running to Tensas, the landing of the Mobile and Great Northern Railroad, on the right end of that turn is situated a battery of three 32-pounder rifled guns and on 10-inch. This is called the Spanish battery. A little down the bay, on the left, is one battery of six 32-pounders, called Pinto's battery. Between this and Fort Morgan are four more batteries, at Choctaw, Cedar Plain, Grand Spell, and Light-House battery. All these have six guns, 32-pounders, rifled...I spoke with many men in Mobile who are in official employment; they told me the place could be taken by land...."[127]

G. Medical Care

Military hospitals included the United States Marine Hospital opened on November 3, 1861 and called the Ross Hospital. The Mobile City Hospital was turned over to the military and named Cantey Hospital. In 1862 a convalescent hospital was built near Mobile at Spring Hill. The capacity was about 100 soldiers.[128]

A medical register[129] exists for the 17th Alabama Infantry for the period, December 1, 1863 to November 30, 1864. This register presents a record of the health of the troops while in Mobile during December 1863 through April 20, 1864, when they left Mobile and moved to northwest Georgia. Company A did not appear on the medical register until March. This might indicate that they were not stationed in the Mobile area during those months. Other assignments during this period could have been at Pollard or guarding the railroad in Mississippi.

Measles were not reported on the medical register until January – six cases in Company E and one case each in Companies G and K. By April the epidemic was over with one case in Company H and two cases in Company A. During the first four months of 1864, 83 cases of rubeola were reported within the 17th Alabama. During the month of March, 30 cases were transferred to the general hospital in Greenville, Alabama. All others were moved to the hospital in either Mobile or Spring Hill.

Fever was a major health problem throughout the war. A diagnosis of "feb int" indicated intermittent fever that meant an attack of malaria or other fever characterized by intervals of elevated temperature separated by intervals of normal temperature. "Feb int tert" was an intermittent fever that occurred every three days. "Feb int quotid" was an intermittent fever that occurred every day. From December 1, 1863 to April 30, 1864, the hospital

---

[127] OWR, Serial 50, 4-7
[128] Bergeron, ibid.
[129] *Register of Sick and Wounded of the 17th Alabama Volunteers*, handwritten, National Archives, Washington, DC, 1907.

register has record of about 350 cases of feb int tert and about 300 cases of feb int quotid. Company B was the hardest hit with over 100 cases.

H. The Home Front

By the end of 1862, it was obvious that the war was not going well. There was no end in sight. The draft was still in effect. However, the draft law was modified October 11, 1862, to exempt from service anyone owning 20 or more slaves. This was not a popular amendment. To many, this was indication that this war was a rich man's war and poor man's fight and another factor that lowered morale.

The blockade of Confederate ports was taking its toll, not only on supplies for the military, but on every aspect of life on the home front. The South was an agricultural region, supported by its production of cotton. It was totally dependent on imports, largely from the Northern states earlier or from Europe. What the South might have produced with materials on hand, it lacked man power to do, most of the men had volunteered or were conscripted into the Confederate Army.

In March, Captain Thomas Jefferson Burnett had written his wife, Ann, *"When I get to thinking about the condition of things at home I think it is too hard on you, and the only thing that does reconcile me is to look around and see thousands & tens of thousands similarly situates and then say to myself it must be so for a time. There is scarely a day that I do not hear some acquaintance say that he will be ruined if he does not get to go home and see after his affairs, & others mentioning some sad occurrence with his family left behind him."*[130]

There was a shortage of food. More acres were planted in edible crops, but the men were not there to help cultivate and harvest. There was a shortage of seeds, an item commonly imported from the North. With a shortage of feed for animals, there was a shortage of meat. Even though available supplies of beef and pork were very limited, much of it was impressed to feed the armies. At home a substitute for beef or pork was mule, wild game, pets, etc. There was frequent difficulty in moving excess stores from areas with abundant crops to other areas where food was desperately needed. Wagons were scare, and train service sadly lacking.

Cooking supplies, such as spices, salt, pepper, sugar, flavoring, vinegar, baking soda, coffee, flour, were all in short supply. Southern women, out of necessity, became very creative in finding substitutes. Many household effects, such as cooking utensils, dishes, furniture, silverware, lamps, were no longer available. Families made do with what they had. Any new clothing, bedding, bandages, or uniforms were created from old clothes or old cloth or new cloth spun and woven in the home. There was a shortage of building materials, such as nails, screws, lumber, locks, tools, etc. There

---

[130] Burnett papers, March 23, 1862.

was a shortage of paper and glue for books, newspapers, stationary, postage stamps, wrapping paper, and school supplies. Candles, combs, brushes, ink, leather, medicine, pen, pencil, razors, shoes, soap, toiletries, and the list goes on and on of items that could no longer be purchased. Life on the home front declined at a rapid pace.[131]

The military was affected by these same shortages. On December 7, 1862, Governor Jno. Gill Shorter issued an appeal to the women of Alabama, *"The Troops of this State who are bravely defending your liberties in the mountains of Virginia and Tennessee are suffering for Blankets. The Confederate Government is unable to supply them in sufficient quantity. I must appeal to the women of Alabama who have so well sustained their part in this revolution, to give up their carpets, their remaining blankets, and such other suitable bed clothing as thay can spare to the cause of Independence. A ready response to this appeal is certain to increase the efficiency of our troops and alleviate their sufferings. It may save the lives of thousands..."*[132] Governor Watts sent 100 pairs of shoes to Pollard in the spring of 1864. He wrote, *"I regret that I cannot let the regiment have more. But Alabama has not the ability to furnish all her soldiers with shoes."*[133]

Impressment was another major problem on the home front. Impressment was the act of forcibly taking goods and persons for public service, in this case for the Confederate Army. Governor Watts was against impressment, but was powerless to stop it. Men were assigned to roam the countryside impressing goods for the military. However some of these men carried impressments too far. Watts reported cases where corn and fodder was impressed where it could not be spared. He wrote about corn and fodder impressed that had been contracted to the county to feed indigent families. In one case Watts wrote about a group of soldiers who impressed considerably more than they could use. They then impressed the wagons and stock to pull the wagons so that they could take their newly acquired goods to Georgia with them. They went so far as to impress drivers for the wagons. Frequently plow stock were impressed during the season they were needed for crop production. Horses and mules were sometimes impressed in the middle of the night. Frequently goods and stock were impressed by men who had no legal right.[134]

The number of desertions from the army increased throughout the Confederacy. Men knew they were needed back home to help their families, many of whom were starving. Many of the deserters were not

---

[131] Mary Elizabeth Massey, *Ersatz in the Confederacy* (Columbia, SC: University of South Carolina Press, 1952).
[132] Mobile *Register and Advertiser*, December 17, 1862 (Alabama Archives, Montgomery, AL).
[133] Letters from Governor Watts. (Reel 21, Folder 12-13).
[134] Letters from Governor Watts, ibid. (Folder 14).

cowards. They were torn between their duty to the Confederate cause and their duty to their families. On September 5, 1863, The Independent of Gainesville, Alabama, published an article titled "List of Deserters." The list was released by Cantey's Brigade on August 27, 1863. It offered a $30 reward for "apprehension and delivery or confinement in any safe Jail within this State of any of the following deserters." The list contained the names of 60 men from the 17th Alabama, giving a brief description, occupation and age. In the spring of 1863, the Confederate Army was at its peak strength with the largest enrollment and the lowest percentage of absentees.[135] Absentees included absent with leave, absent without leave, and prisoners of war. By the fall of 1863, the Secretary of War indicated that the effective force, the men present and able to fight, was between half and two-thirds of the total enrollment.[136] The problem of desertion is discussed further in Appendix I.

Colonel Murphy of the 17th Alabama wrote Governor Watts February 14, 1864, asking help for a friend, *"...of Selma with her two children desire to obtain a passport or permission from you to leave the state and go North. Her husband deserted his country and went North more than one year ago and she has determined to follow him. I can arrange for her to pass through General Polk's lines with your approval. Please do me the kindness and favor to sent me your approval."*[137]

I. Conclusion

While the 17th Alabama was in Mobile, they played an important role in the defense of the Confederacy. The work was hard. Along with military drills, the construction of entrenchments continued for many months as General Maury expanded the defenses around Mobile and increased the size of the batteries. The men of the 17th Alabama were homesick and worried about their families. Food supplies were barely tolerable, and the inadequate diet undermined their health. The men attempted to supplement the army food with food from home when possible. The living conditions were crowded and unsanitary which bred disease, a continuing problem. However, things would become much worse when they were transferred from Mobile to northwest Georgia and joined forces with the Army of Tennessee.

---

[135] OWR, Series iv, volume ii, 530.
[136] Ibid, Series iv, volume ii, 995.
[137] Letters from Governor Watts. (Reel 20, Folder 8).

VI. The Atlanta Campaign

A. Introduction

The strategic significance of Atlanta was critical to the Confederacy and winning the battle was vital. The 17th Alabama Infantry was heavily involved in the Atlanta campaign. The struggle between the Confederate Army of Tennessee and three Union armies raged for five months, April to October 1864. This campaign involved many separate battles in various locations, but Atlanta was always the goal. Battles involving the 17th Alabama Infantry are featured in this section. Again, words of participants are used wherever possible to best describe the impact on soldiers caught up in the horror of that time.

B. Prologue to Battle

In September 1863, the Army of Tennessee, under the direction of General Bragg, defeated the Army of the Cumberland commanded by General William S. Rosecrans at the Battle of Chickamauga. This battle resulted in the retreat of Union forces to Chattanooga, with the Confederates in hot pursuit. From strong defensive positions on Missionary Ridge and Lookout Mountain, Bragg and his army placed the Union army under siege. He also had control of the Union supply line and planned to starve the enemy into submission. Because of the retreat at Chickamauga and the critical situation at Chattanooga, Rosecrans was replaced by Major General George Thomas. In the meantime, General Grant had been promoted to commander of the Military Department of the Mississippi. He took active charge of the activities at Chattanooga. It was at this point that General William T. Sherman and the Union Army of the Tennessee was brought over from Mississippi. With skillful planning and determination, the Union troops redeemed themselves for the failure at Chickamauga and defeated the Confederates at Chattanooga. On November 25, 1863, the determined Union forces stormed a seemingly unconquerable position, crumbling the Confederate line into a swift retreat.

After the defeat at Chattanooga, a change was made in the Confederate Army. On December 18, 1863, President Davis assigned General Joseph E. Johnson to replace General Bragg as commander of the Army of Tennessee. Johnston was a Virginian and had graduated from West Point in 1829. Early in the war, he headed the Army of the Shenandoah and later the Army of Northern Virginia. Johnston was wounded at the battle of Seven Pines in 1862 and was replaced by Robert E. Lee. After his recovery in 1863, Johnston commanded the Army of Tennessee during the Vicksburg campaign. Bragg replaced Johnston after Johnston's failure at Vicksburg. Now Davis reluctantaly replaced Bragg with Johnston. Although highly intelligent and capable, Johnston had a reputation of not taking an offensive position. He preferred the defensive postion or retreating. Also Johnson's career was handicapped throughout the war by a continuing feud with Jeff Davis.

The Army of Tennessee wintered in Dalton, Georgia. Johnston had been handed a demoralized and poorly equipped army after the defeat at Missionary Ridge. During the first couple of months of his command, Johnston did much to improve the situation and won the confidence and admiration of his men. The men were granted leaves of absence allowing them to visit their families. Many men who had temporarily deserted after the defeat slowly returned to their units which helped their numbers. However, the Confederate Army still was numerically inferior to the Union Army. In an attempt to remedy this situation, the Confederate draft law was modified in early 1864. On January 18, the draft age was changed to include men from 18 to 45. On February 18, the draft age was changed to include men from 17 to 50.

The Confederates anticipated an offensive campaign into northwest Georgia by the Union army sometime in the spring of 1864. By the time spring arrived, General Grant had been called away from Tennessee to Washington, D. C., where he was promoted to supreme commander of all Union armies. Grant placed Sherman in command of the Union forces in Chattanooga and instructed Sherman to wage an offensive campaign against Johnston into the enemy territory. Sherman's destination was Atlanta. Atlanta was a vital center for the Confederate arsenal, foundries, warehouses, and manufacturing. It was the distribution point for war goods and food supplies and the railroad crossroads of the southeast. One historian described Atlanta as a town of critical military, logistical, and political importance.[138]

One estimate of the opposing forces in the Atlanta campaign was that the Union army outnumbered the Confederate army two to one. General Sherman led an army of about 120,000 troops who were well supplied. General Johnston led an army of about 60,000 men who lacked many of the essentials of war. It will never be known exactly what the true ratio was. Numbers vary from one history book to another. They all agree on one point – the Confederate Army of Tennessee was drastically outnumbered. During the Atlanta campaign the Confederates faced three Union armies: the Army of the Tennessee commanded by General James B. McPherson, the Army of the Cumberland commanded by General George Thomas, and the Army of the Ohio commanded by General John M. Schofield. McPherson was killed at Atlanta and was replaced by General Oliver O. Howard.

---

[138] Thomas L. Connelly, *Autumn of Glory, The Army of Tennessee* (Baton Rouge, LA: Louisiana State University Press, 1971).

C. The Move to Georgia

Captain McMillan in his writings on the War of 1861 stated that Cantey's Brigade, including the 17th Alabama, left Pollard, Alabama, on April 20, 1864, headed for Atlanta to join the Army of Tennessee. When the brigade left Pollard, it was commanded by Colonel Virgil S. Murphy, a temporary replacement for General Cantey who was on medical furlough. The brigade remained in Atlanta for one day and then moved on to Rome, Georgia, where they remained for ten days.[139]

In a letter written April 27 from Rome by Colonel Murphy, he described the trip from Pollard to Rome, *"We had a disagreeable time Moving being packed like sardines in Boxcars. Yet the move was not as bad as Some we have had, for the weather was good and we stopped one night in Montgomery and slept. With the exception of that and a few hours at Atlanta, we were subjected to the "Sardine" prison the whole time. We left Pollard Thursday Morning last and arrived here Sunday."*[140]

Colonel Murphy continues, *"I am very much pleased with this place. We now belong to the Army of Tennessee, but there are no other troops Stationed at this point except our brigade and the Cavalry in front.... There are batteries built on hills around one hundred and ninety to two hundred and fifty feet above the plain...I was saddened by the sight of the humbler but very numerous hillocks which cover the ashes of Martyrs to the cause in which we are engaged. At the battle of Murfreesboro and afterwards there were large hospitals here, and many of the wounded heroes of that fight and others now lie peacefully sleeping in this beautiful Mountain Cemetery."*[141]

Thomas J. Burnett entered the war as a captain and commanding officer of Company K when the company was organized in September 1861. He was placed on the regimental staff in 1862 and eventually promoted to major. He was placed in command of the 17th Alabama in May 1864 while Colonel Murphy replaced Cantey as brigade commander and Lieutenant-Colonel Holcombe, the second in command, was severely wounded at Resaca. Burnett held the position of regimental commander until he was severely wounded at the battle of Ezra Church on July 28, 1864. He never fully recovered from his wounds and probably never returned to duty.

Major Burnett wrote his wife, Ann, from near Rome, Georgia, April 30, 1864. As in all his letters, he expressed concern for conditions on the home front. He talked of his longing to return home and his hopes for the future. He also asked Ann to send him money for items he had bought to send her, but had no money to pay for them. *"...we can not draw a cent for our pay*

---

[139] McMillan sketch.
[140] Colonel Virgil S. Murphy, letters, (Kennesaw Mountain National Park, Kennesaw Mountain, GA).
[141] Ibid.

yet & do not know when we can."¹⁴² At this point, with Cantey's Brigade positioned near Rome, General Johnston with the remainder of the army was positioned 30 miles north at Dalton. Burnett wrote of conditions near Rome, *"The people here have been kind and sociable and have visited us and invited us in to see them and to dine &c &c. I have done so with Col. Murphy on two occasions & enjoyed my dinner much...If we can stay here we will be truly blessed for it is a healthy and pleasant location. All is quiet along the line yet, but great anxiety felt by Gen Johnston. I have seen several dispatches from him. We dispatched him that we could hold this place against any force. Nature has done a great deal for us here. It's natural fortification or defenses are fine and we are also making strong artificial works – We are anxious to be held here and to fight here if it becomes necessary. I have heard from our army in Dalton and we never were in so fine a condition and all are eager for the movement. They do not fear an attack at Dalton, but fear that the enemy are amassing their troops to flank us and force Genl Johnston to fall back and and that is why Genl J expresses so much anxiety about this place & the right. He wants to force the enemy to fight us where we are..I will keep you posted of all our movements. I shall if the hour of trial comes try to discharge my whole duty and pray that I will have your fervent and unceasing prayers for my safety..."*¹⁴³

D. Battles Involving the 17th

May 9	Skirmish at Resaca
May 12-15	Battle of Resaca
May 17 - 22	Fight at Cassville
May 25	Fight at New Hope
June 15 – 30	Kennesaw Mountain
July 20	Battle of Peachtree Creek
July 28	Battle at Ezra Church
Aug 31 – Sept 1	Battle of Jonesboro
Sept 2	Union occupation of Atlanta

E. Resaca

The first assignment in the campaign on May 5, 1864 included orders for Cantey's Brigade to move out to the Resaca area, a distance of over 30 miles northeast of Rome. Cantey's Brigade was reported to total over 2500 men.¹⁴⁴ Cantey's Brigade plus Quarles Brigade and Reynold's Brigade made up Walthall's Division which was commanded by Major-General

---

[142] Burnett papers.
[143] Ibid.
[144] *OWR*, Serial 74, 676. On April 30, 1864, the reported size of Cantey's Brigade (17th Alabama, 26th Alabama, and 37th Mississippi) was 1543 effective present, 1830 aggregate present, and 2540 aggregate present and absent.

Edward C. Walthall. Walthall was born in Virginia and raised in Mississippi. Before the war, he was a lawyer and a district attorney. He entered the war as a first lieutenant in Company H, 15th Mississippi Regiment. He was a brigade commander by the summer of 1863 and eventually was a division commander with the appropriate title of major general.

Walthall's Division arrived at the Ostenaula River where they camped before their first skirmish with the enemy on May 9. Hooker's Corps critically outnumbered the Confederate forces, but the approach of troops from General John Bell Hood's Corps saved the day. This encounter was described by Captain McMillan, *"We bivouacked about one mile below the town (Resaca) on the Ostenaula River, until the ninth of May, when Hookers Corps having passed through Snake Creek Gap attacked us. We had a brisk skirmish with them, but Reynolds brigade from below and Vaughn's from Dalton joined us during the fight."* [145]

Another eyewitness account written from Resaca described the events of May 9th; *"We were in line of battle at this place, or rather in our fortification. Loring's division is here and Canty's Brigade from Mobile, and Vaughn from Cheatham's division. This place is fifteen miles from Dalton, where the railroad crosses the Coosa River, a very important post. The enemy came in sight, five thousand strong, on Monday, skirmished with Canty, but Vaughn coming down on the train the enemy seemed to have taken a scare and left that night, about five miles towards a gap in the hills, where they are entrenched...Canty lost eight killed and seventy-six wounded."* [146]

Major Burnett gave his account of the events of May 9th, *"We were all rejoicing over the news from the Trans-Miss Department, and our bright prospects in Virginia and I wanted you to know that we were all jubilant at our prospects, although dangers were threatening us. We were ordered yesterday morning to pack and were ready for Dalton but the enemy were then trying to turn our left flank & we were ordered to remain here. They came in five miles of our Camp this morning and quite a cavalry fight ensued. We drove their pickets and captured sixteen of the enemy. We lay on our arms all night and have been in line of battle all day to this hour, noon, but I do not think that we will have anything to do to day...We lived well at Rome but the past four days corn bread and bacon is all except for a few almonds.*[147]

Resaca was the first heavy fighting involving the 17th Alabama Infantry since the battle at Shiloh in April 1862. It was the first heavy fighting ever

---

[145] McMillan sketch.
[146] "A Captured Letter." *Southern Bivouac*, June 1886, 67.
[147] Burnett papers.

for the many newer recruits. With the departure of the enemy on the 9th, the 17th Alabama moved into Resaca where the brigade dug in and prepared fortifications in case the enemy returned. Resaca was a major battlefield during May 12, 13, 14 and 15. The brigade suffered severe losses. On the 16th the Confederates retreated from Resaca to Cassville. The army remained in Cassville during May 19-22 fighting daily. Again the enemy outflanked the Confederates forcing them to retreat again. The army first retreated to Altoona Mountain and then to New Hope Church[148] fighting skirmishes along the way.

McMillan described the above events, *"We ...remained at Resaca fortifying until the 12th when the enemy having flanked Johnston at Dalton attacked us again. We however now constituted the left of Johnston's line, and participated in the fights of the 12, 13, 14 and 15th of May. Lt. Parker of Co. B was killed. Lt. Col. Holcombe was severely wounded by a fragment of a shell. Sargt. Newberry, Privates Hornbeck, Hudson, Monahan, Raines and Rives of my Co. were wounded. Lt. Andress was struck and Lt. Robison painfully wounded in the shoulder while on picket.*

On the 16th we retreated to a point a short distance below Calhoun, on the 17th went to Cassville via Adairsville. At Cassville I was engaged in a heavy picket fight, and barely escaped being killed and captured. From here we retreated across the Etowah River to Altoona Mountain, where we (Company H) remained three days, and went to New Hope Church arriving just too late to participate in the fight of the 25th of May 1864."[149]

Major Burnett served as acting commander of the 17th Alabama while Colonel Murphy was acting commander of Cantey's Brigade. One of Burnett's letters was written on May 21 from Altoona, 40 miles from Atlanta. He shared his frustation as a commanding officer during this trying time. He wrote his wife, *"The past sixteen days have been filled with many events of consequence to the soldier and the people at home.*

Our Army in that time has fallen back and left behind them sixty miles of beautiful country. I might say truthfully the prettiest and most productive portion of Georgia to be pillaged by our enemys, beautiful and flourishing town of Rome, where we met with so much hospitality have been completely sacked. I am told that the furniture beds and every thing belonging to private residences were broken, torn up and piled in the streets. We have left behind many little flourishing towns & fine residences that I suppose are utterly destroyed now. But Darling all the military men Genl Johnston at the head say that we are going to demolish them and that soon. This I have no doubt is the opinion of my own and my judgement is we ought to have forced them to fight us. We have evidently offered them battle three times and they have continued to march around our left Flank. I pray God that

---

[148] A Methodist chapel near Dallas, Georgia.
[149] McMillan sketch.

Genl Johnston may be right for I want this campaign ended. I wanted to go to Va for the reason that this army is too much disposed it seems to me to fall back, and I cannot yet understand when they Flank us, why we cannot flank them. The news we received from Va & the Trans Mississippi Department is very cheering indeed. I heard a Yankee prisoner that we captured two nights ago say that it was published in General Orders in their Army that we abandoned Richmond and that the people of North Carolina would not allow President Davis & Gen Lee transportation on their Rail Roads & that Banks in La & Ark had glowingly triumphed over us. My God what a people we have to deal with when they will resort to such lies to cheer their soldiers.

...It was at Cassville where we were all in line of battle and when I read Genl Johnston's Battle Order to my command that was decidedly the heaviest shelling we have had yet and we had no protection. We lost several men, among the killed was Mr. Ellis[150] of my old company, a good soldier & Christian. He was from the eastern side of the county. Sargt Shanks of Co. A Holcomb's old Co was severely wounded, to of Co F & one of Co E that I now remember. Capt Moreland of Co B is missing and probably killed. Lieut Parker killed poor fellow was charging bravely when he fell and Turner[151] will now be Capt of that Co I expect. He should come back as soon as possible and take charge of the Co. Well I have great cause to be thankful & and I am truly so for my safety thus far. And though we have labored day & night marching every night for a week & superintending fortications. I have not been sick a minute when about one third of the officers & men have failed and many gone to the rear.

I learn that it is rumored that the Regt did not stand fire. All I have to say is that it is a base slander. The Regt was ordered to make one charge or rather the reserve of the Regt that were just in trenches. I lead them took the hill we were ordered to and held it for more than two hours & that too often other troops had left us and never left until out Genl sent a second order to me to fall back that the enemy were flanking me. I took out about 200 men and officers and had about 40 killed and wounded. The Gen; complimented me for the gallantry of the charge and darling of all Some contemptible person I think started that report just to annoy us and not intending it seriously.

We have been under fire more or less for eight days in the past twelve and never have we left any position until directly ordered & also for the 29th Ala they have acted as gallantly as any Regt could and held their posts as picket or skirmishers under as heavy a fire as was ever directed against any Regt not only balls but shell, grape shot and every conceivable missile of

---

[150] Private Radford Ellis of Company K
[151] Probably William Turner Dunklin

death and lost nearly 100 killed & wounded. Their conduct was matter of remark by Genl Johnston himself – Show this to Dan and if he thinks that such stuff prevails in this county to have a note published in the Greenville paper, or the substance of my remarks to you. As to myself I would not notice the report of stay at home people but I do not want the Regt or Brigade to suffer by cowardly tongues."[152]

The regimental medical register for the 17th Alabama Infantry listed 63 soldiers wounded or killed during the month of May, which reflects the magnitude of the casualties at Resaca and other battles. The register also reveals the level of sickness during that same period – 25 cases of debilitas, 110 cases of diarrhea, 150 cases of dysentery and 75 cases of other illnesses. Inadequate diet and unsanitary conditions took their toll.

Brigadier-General Jeff C. Davis was a Union officer in the 2nd Division of the Army of the Cumberland. On May 28, 1864, he wrote from Washington's House, Georgia, *"The operations of yesterday of this division I have the honor to report as follows: I moved on the Marietta road in Support of McPherson, skirmishing with the enemy and gradually driving him back until my main line could not longer be advanced without separatin from McPherson's right. This brought my left in front of a gap passing through the mountain on the right of the road...The enemy could be seen all day felling timber and digging rifle-pits along the crest of the hill, and this morning have a battery commanding the road from the top of the hill between me and Hooker...The enemy attacked McCook's brigade last night, and after a sharp fight were repulsed, leaving in our possession a few wounded and 27 prisoners, 1 captain*[153] *among them. They belong to Seventeenth Alabama, of Polk's corps, and say that Johnston's whole force is here...."*[154]

Governor Watts was very optimistic for the Confederate cause. On May 18, 1864, he wrote, *"I trust that their (Alabamians) sufferings will soon be over. The wonderful successes of our armies this spring, have changed – greatly – the aspect of our affairs, The total destruction of the Yankee armies – west of the Mississippi and their defeats in North Carolina, and in Virginia, and the near approach of another defeat in north Georgia will soon give the best assurance of a speedy Independence and peace. Tell our people to be of good cheer."*[155]

F. Kennesaw Mountain

The Union Army applied constant pressure on the Confederates. The Confederates, strengthened by reinforcements such as Cantey's Brigade,

---

[152] Burnett papers.
[153] This refers to Captain James S. Moreland of Company B.
[154] OWR, Serial 75, 334.
[155] Governor Watts letters (SG24872, Reel 20, Folder 14).

were usually able to repel each Union assault. However Sherman continuously tried to prevent the Confederates access to their supply line, the Western and Atlantic Railroad. With this goal in mind, Sherman attempted to outflank them at every opportunity and made steady advancements ever pushing south towards Atlanta, the ultimate prize. In spite of the enemy's superior numbers, Johnston was able to escape each of Sherman's flanking maneuvers. However, the steady retreat by the Confederates was a severe blow to morale. Much of the movement was done at night, through difficult and dangerous terrain that was unknown, mountainous, and heavily wooded. The Confederates were on a continuous cycle of retreat, dig, build new entrenchments, defend the new position, and be outflanked. When not on the march at night, they were constantly on alert for activity by the enemy. In addition, rations were in short supply. Foraging was a necessary activity to supplement their meager rations. The citizens of Alabama were asked to do their part to alleviate the shortage of rations. On May 20, 1864, Governor Watts reminded the citizens of Alabama that the armies required any surplus of meat the citizens had over *"one-quarter pound per day per adult and one-eighth pound per day per child uner 12 years of age."*[156]

Thomas A. Rumbley was a private in company H. In 1893 he wrote in the *Claiborne Southerner*, Claiborne, Alabama, of an incident that occurred during the Atlanta Campaign. *"In the Spring of 1864, there was a detail of men in each company in our brigade sent to charge a picket line of the Federals at the foot of Lone Mountain*[157] *at night. Our orders were to roll at least one large rock each ahead. We formed a line at the top of the mountain, Lt. Colonel Morris of the 26th Alabama Regiment was our commander, and Col. V. S. Murphey of the 17th Alabama, acted as General. The command was given, the rocks rolled, and we followed. The Yankees poured a heavy fire into us and everyone of our men were killed as they went down the mountain, except five: Lt. Wm. Jesse Robison, B. F. McMillan, a preacher named Belcher*[158]*, myself and one other...Belcher grabbed one of the Yankees, his gun fired and the Yankee fell. I ordered him to give up his arms; and he handed over his sword and Navy six-shooter, and said, 'Come on boys, let's surrender'.*

Thirteen men came from behind large rocks and surrendered. One of the officers said his name was Arbor of the 154th Illinois Regiment. Lt. Robison ordered McMillan and me to escort the prisoners back to camp, and as we went up the mountain one of them said, 'I had no idea I could

---

[156] Ibid. (Reel 21, Folder 14).
[157] This was either Pine Mountain or Lost Mountain.
[158] This was probably E. M. Belcher of Company H. Robison and McMillan were also in Company H.

ever be scared as bad as I was tonight. There were only five of you, and I could have killed you all'"!

McMillan wrote that the regiment retreated on June 3, first to "Lost" Mountain and then to "Pine" Mountain. By June 15, the Confederates had retreated to Kennesaw Mountain. They held this position until the first week of July, fighting skirmishes every day. Kennesaw was a natural for a defensive position. Where the terrain lacked adequate defensive protection, the Confederates created excellent fortifications. The weather was in their favor. A long rainy period slowed Sherman's advancement giving the Confederates more time to build a strong defense line. When Sherman arrived at Kennesaw, he decided on a full-scale offensive assault. He underestimated Confederate strength, and the Confederates repelled each attack. The battle of Kennesaw Mountain was fought in four segments: Big Kennesaw, Little Kennesaw, Pigeon Hill and Cheatham Hill. Cantey's Brigade took part in the Big Kennesaw segment.

In June 1864, Major Burnett wrote three letters from the vicinity of Kennesaw Mountain. The first, written to his wife on June 15, told of the death of General Leonidas Polk, his corps commander. Burnett wrote, "*It was our sad lot to receive the intelligence of the death of our Lt. Genl Leonidas Polk our Corps Commander. He was killed by an accidental shot yesterday morning about ¼ miles from me and on the left of Gen Quall's line who is in our Division by a stray shot from one of the enemys field pieces. The wound was a fearful one, shot through the body by a solid shot and both arms shot off – He was at the time in consultation with Gens Johnston & Hardee. He was the highest ranking officer next to Johnston in this army – The ways of Providence are tryly mysterious. There was scarely a skirmish going on at the time & the enemy only occasionally firing a random shot trying to find our lines & firing without any sort of accuracy & I do not think had thrown a shell or solid shot within two hundred yards of our lines save that particular shot.*

I had been impressed with the opinion that Lt. Genr Polk was a slow & rather plodding man, but he was a learned great & good man and deplore his loss very much. It seemed to have thrown a gloom over our entire Corps and I suppose the entire Army."[159]

Major Burnett wrote again on June 18. He confided that he had "*to some extent lost my appetite & coarse cold corn bread & bacon absolutely sickens me to look at, for we have had it so long with out variation*". He told his wife not to send him anymore meat because he knew she did not have it to spare. Instead he requested vegetables, flour, bread, and butter. He complained about his pretended friends who paid off their debts to him with "*Confederate trash that he could not use any other way.*" He told of being at the foot of Kennesaw Mountain and "*about two miles from the*

---

[159] Burnett papers.

summit. I am told it is a beautiful view of both armies but I cannot get off to see it. Many Ladies & Old Gentlemen ...come up daily & look down upon the dirty soldiers of both parties."[160]

Two days later Burnett sent a letter to his children in Greenville. Obviously his position had changed because the letter was written from *"On the top of Kennesaw Mt., 2 miles from the pretty little town of Marietta."* Burnett wrote, *"I thought I would write you a short letter this morning and tell you about the large mountain I am on today. It is about 1,000 feet high above the valley and you can see rocks on it as big as our house.*

If you were here and on top you could see fifty miles around you, that is, as far as from Greenville to Montgomery. You could see the town of Marietta and the city of Atlanta 25 miles away... You could also see the Yankees and our army, you could see our cannons fire at the Yankees and theirs fire at us. We have had up to this time today one poor man killed and six wounded in this brigade, but we have killed more of their men because we are above them and have the best chance, and our men can beat them shooting. We are not falling back because the Yankees can whip us but because they won't fight, but go round us...."[161]

Colonel Murphy wrote from Kennesaw Mountain on June 21, *"...since I wrote to you we have moved our line somewhat, and litteraly "gone up" – to the top of Kennesaw Mountain. We have dug nine ditches in the Campaign and only fought in one of them (at New Hope Church). We are well entrenched now and have plenty loose rocks. And I think it would take more Yankees than you could pack into a fifty acre field to move us from our position... It is not our fault however that we have not fought them in all our ditches, as the enemy very prudently avoids them. The weather has been very unfavorable for Military Operations recently. We have had rain every day, but one or two since the 31st of May. The roads are almost impassable and it still Continues to rain. It is bad on soldiers. We have no tents and no covering but "the canopy of Heaven." And it leaks mighty bad when it rains. The scenery from the top of the Mountain is really grand and will repay in some measure for being shot at so much. On the Northern side villages of Yankee tents can be seen, and their Maneuverings, Marchings and Counter Marching is plainly visible...*

We continue to fight after the same fashion. Shelling and skirmishing daily. Occasionally the Yankees make a feeble effort to charge our works, but invariably get so badly used that they are loosing all taste for such sport. And prisoners say that an order has been read to them saying they would not be required to charge breastworks anymore. If that is so I cant imagine how Gen. Sherman proposes to get to Atlanta. Some men are killed

---

[160] Ibid.
[161] Major Thomas Burnett, letter, *Marietta, Georgia, Journal,* November 13, 1924.

and wounded everyday. And as Gen. Johnston said in his report some time ago, the aggregate fighting and casualties are as great as if a general battle had been fought."[162]

Frank Robertson of Company E wrote a letter from Georgia, probably during the month of June. His words described conditions there. "...we don't get to sleep a bit hardly tall we are up night and day and rite under the shells and bullets all the time but I am getting use to them all tho I am very tired of hearing them ther is a grate many killed and wounded Ever day that passes by this company is all rite yet all though tha is here a grate many wounded but none killed.....Martha I will tell something concerning our fate here we don't get nothing to eat but a little meat and bread and not more than half a nough of it a tall Martha I have got on the same clothes that I wore off from home yet and never had them washed at all and now we is low as howgs...."[163]

The 17th Alabama Regimental medical register listed only 15 casualties for the month of June. The regimental medical register also contained entries of 95 cases of dysentery, 108 cases of fever, 120 cases of diarrhea, 22 cases of debilitas, and 55 cases of other illnesses. Added to their problems of limited rations and unsanitary conditions was the constant rain. Men in all armies fighting in Georgia in June 1864 ate, slept, marched, and fought in the rain and mud.

On June 27, Colonel Murphy took ill and was temporarily relieved of command of the brigade. Colonel Edward Asbury O'Neal of the 26th Alabama took command of Cantey's Brigade. O'Neal was born in Madison County, Alabama. He graduated from LaGrange College, Georgia, and was admitted to the bar. He was a leading advocate of secession. Early in the war he enlisted in the 9th Alabama Infantry. O'Neal was promoted to colonel and led the 26th Alabama Infantry in Virginia. He and the 26th Alabama were transferred to the Army of Tennessee in 1864.

G. Peachtree Creek

In spite of the success at Kennesaw Mountain, General Johnston found that the Confederates were once again in danger of being outflanked and cut off from their supply line. On July 2, with the rains gone and the roads closer to passable, the Confederates began another retreat south. By the night of July 3, Cantey's Brigade had passed through Marietta and was entrenched on the railroad at Vinings Station. Skirmishes continued daily, and during the first several days of July the 17th Alabama lost at least 23 killed or wounded. On July 9th the Confederates crossed the Chattahoochee River and dug in along Peachtree Creek where Johnston planned to make a stand. Once the citizens realized that the Confederates were just northwest

---
[162] Murphy letters.
[163] Robertson letters.

of Atlanta and the Union Army occupied Marietta, evacuation of Atlanta began.

A letter was written by Private J. B. Sanders of the 37th Mississippi Infantry, part of Cantey's Brigade, to his wife on July 15. "*Sherman is too strong for Johnston's force to attack him, he will march around our army again which he does he will compel Johnston to fall back into the city and then if Sherman gets the railroad from West Point to Macon he (Johnston) will have to fall back where to I have no idea. Johnston is having everything moved out of Atlanta to Macon so as to loose nothing but the place if he has to abandon it. I believe Johnston is doing all in his power to save our country and unless the people do turn out and stand by those who are risking their health and lives to drive this enemy hard back we are a Lost and Ruined People....*"[164]

True to his reputation, Johnston fought a defensive war and retreated 100 miles in 60 days that brought the battle line to Atlanta. President Jefferson Davis wanted a commander who would go on the offensive and stop Sherman's advance on Atlanta. Johnston's motivation was to prevent a major confrontation and heavy casualties until the battle lines were more to his advantage. He never found that advantage line. Davis communicated with General Robert E. Lee on the subject of replacing Johnston. Lee agreed that Johnston probably should be replaced, but considered a change of command in the middle of the Atlanta Campaign very poor timing. Davis wrote Johnston one last time requesting a plan of attack to save Atlanta. Johnston responded on July 16, "*...As the enemy has double our number, we must be on the defensive. My plan of operations must, therefore, depend upon that of the enemy. It is mainly to watch for an opportunity to fight to advantage. We are trying to put Atlanta in condition to be held for a day or two by the Georgia militia, that army movements may be freer and wider.*"[165] Davis knew that the Georgia militia could not hold Atlanta for any length of time. They were too small and inexperienced to stop Sherman. In spite of Lee's recommendation, on July 18, Davis appointed General John Bell Hood to replace Johnston, a controversial decision.

Hood was an ambitious general and a close friend of Jeff Davis. During the Atlanta campaign, Hood was privately critical of Johnston and shared his opinions with Davis. He zealously sought the position of commanding general of the Army of Tennessee. Hood was a highly respected soldier on the battlefield, but had no experience commanding an entire army. He had no interest in the details of organization or administration.

General John Bell Hood was a graduate of West Point. He was born in Kentucky, but commanded a Texas unit at the outset of the Civil War. He

---

[164] "Sanders (J. B.) Papers," letters (Mississippi State Archives, Jackson, MS).
[165] OWR, Volume 8, Part 5, 883

had a distinguished career in the Virginia Campaign. He was severely wounded twice. He lost use of his arm at Gettysburg and lost a leg at Chickamauga. He rose from a first lieutenant in 1861 to become a full general in July 1864. Hood previously fought with the Army of Northern Virginia. He replaced Johnston, a man much loved by his troops. The change in command was not met with enthusiasm by the officers or troops and had a severe impact on morale. Dislike or distrust of a commanding officer was one of the major causes of desertion.

Quoting Colonel O'Neal's report, *"During this time, on the 17th of July General Johnston was ordered to turn the command of the army over to General J. B. Hood, to the great regret of the whole army, and which resulted in the destruction of a fine army which had unbounded confidence in itself to what its leader would call upon them for, and that the defeat of the foe was only a question of time under their matchless leader."* [166]

On July 20, Hood went on the offensive with about half the Army of Tennessee at the battle of Peachtree Creek. It was Hood's intent to surprise General George Thomas and the Army of the Cumberland as they crossed Peachtree Creek. Hood's men were late and most of the Union troops had crossed the creek when the Confederates finally attacked. Hood lost about 5000 men and gained nothing. Thomas lost about 2000 men. Cantey's Brigade, commanded by Colonel O'Neal, was present at Peachtree Creek. O'Neal wrote about the 37th Mississippi and three companies of the 17th Alabama. These men fought a good fight but were not supported by troops to their right. They were forced to retreat when they were about to be outflanked. They re-formed and began another charge, but still did not have the support they needed.

In his report of the Peachtree Creek Battle on July 20th, 1864, Colonel O'Neal stated that Major Thomas J. Burnett was in command of the 17th Alabama on that day, and was the right center of the line of the brigade. He further stated: *"The line being formed, the command forward was given, and we advanced a short distance quietly, when our pickets becoming hotly engaged, I gave the command to charge the enemy and continued forward and drive every obstacle before them, which order was obeyed with a cheer, driving a heavy line of skirmishes and one of battle. The ground over which we advanced was very rough and the bushes and undergrowth dense and tangled, yet the line was well formed and advanced in good order, except on the left, where from some misapprehension, some one gave the command "guide left", which threw the Twenty-ninth Alabama Regiment too far to the left, and left too much ground for the sharpshooters and the Twenty-Sixth Alabama Regiment to cover, attenuating their line almost to a skirmish line. We continued to push forward driving the enemy before us, and advanced to within a short distance of some works the enemy had thrown up, having*

---

[166] OWR, Serial 74, 742.

passed a line to our right some hundred yards. This line was crescent-formed, which fact was not discovered till we emerged from the dense wood into an open field. The Thirty-Seventh Mississippi and the three right companies[167] of the Seventeenth Alabama Regiment had swung around by a right wheel to face this line in the field, and had commenced a heavy and telling fire on it, when it was discovered we were not supported by the troops on our right, who had failed for some cause to come up, and that we were being flanked and enfiladed by a battery.

In danger of being flanked and captured the brigade fell back, not in very good order but was soon rallied and formed, when a second charge was made, aided by the Twenty-fourth South Carolina Regiment (Lieutenant Colonel Jones commanding) and the second corps of sharpshooters, Captain W. H. Lindsay, Twenty-sixth Alabama Regiment; but being unsupported were compelled again to fall back and take another position, where we remained till ordered back to the position in the trenches which we had left in the morning. We drove the enemy nearly a mile, captured some of his works, and had punished him severely....

In justice to the brigade which I for the first time had the honor to command in battle, and to the other troops in this division, I must say, that if the whole of our line had pressed forward with the same energy and determination which the troops of this division did, we would have carried the day and driven the enemy in confusion across the creek...

we captured a number of prisoners (293), including several officers, a list of whom has already been sent in. Inclosed I send you a list of casualties, which shows our loss to be 279 killed, wounded, and missing."

[168] O'Neal was referring to the number of casualties for the brigade. Known killed or wounded at Peachtree Creek in the 17th Alabama numbered about 75 men lost from all companies.

W. I. Mothershead, a private in Company F, wrote on the 23rd about the battle on the 20th, "*The battle is still raging, our company has lost most all killed and wounded, our regiment behaved well, swept all before it.*" [169] Mothershead died September 2, 1864, at a hospital in Macon, Georgia.

The battle at Peachtree Creek was the first of four attacks that General Hood would command in the next few days, attacks that would decide the fate of Atlanta. At least three of the four attacks failed due to a delay before orders were carried out. These delays diminished the effectiveness of the original battle plan. On July 21 the Confederates retreated and moved closer to Atlanta. On July 22 Hood went on the offensive again. No gain was

---

[167] The right three companies are normally companies D, F, and A.
[168] OWR, Serial 74, 741-2. The battle of Peach Tree Creek is discussed in more detail by General Walthall, Serial 74, 925.
[169] W. I. Mothershead, letter, (SG024896, folder 5, Alabama Archives, Montgomery, AL).

made, and Hood lost 8,000 men. On July 27, a third attempt was made. Again, no gain, and Hood lost 2500 men.

H. Ezra Church

On July 28, Cantey's Brigade took part in the engagement at Poor-House on Lick Skillet Road. This was also known as the battle of Ezra Church. Ezra Methodist Chapel was located in west Atlanta in the area of the current Mozley Park. It was here that Hood decided to make his fourth offensive attack since his appointment as commander of the Army of Tennessee. Walthall's Division including the 17th Alabama arrived as ordered after a forced march in the mid-day heat of a July day in Georgia. They faced an enemy well entrenched and fortified, an enemy who had already repulsed one Confederate division. Initially General John C. Brown's Division suffered many casualties. Then Walthall's Division was ordered forward, advancing over Brown's dead and wounded. The enemy was still well entrenched and fortified. Walthall's Division suffered the same fate as Brown's Division, repulsed with many casualties.

On this day Sherman lost about 600 men, while Hood lost about 5000 men and again gained nothing. The morale of the Army of Tennessee reached a new low. The battle of Ezra Church has been described as a one-sided slaughter. Another major cause of desertion was loss of confidence in the military leadership after a succession of defeats with many casualties and no successes. A report on the Army of Tennessee revealed that the number of deserters in July 1864 was approximately 20% of the rolls.[170]

Captain McMillan who had been absent (dysentery) from the regiment for almost a month returned on the 28th. He gave his account of the battle of Ezra Church: *"I reached my company about 10 or 11 oclock on the 28th of July, and was quietly lying down listening to the men relate their hairbreadth escapes on the 20th when we were ordered to "fall in". We were then occupying Atlanta to which place they had fallen back during my absence. We marched by the left flank until we reached Lickskillet road, where the entrenchments crossed it, and passed out through the entrenchments. We now thought we were going to make a reconnaissance, but soon the order to double quick was given, and in a few minutes afterwards I heard brisk firing from small arms. We were marched and countermarched very rapidly, and finally it seemed that the General was satisfied with our position. The heat was almost intolerable; the firing in our front was now very heavy. We were ordered to lie down as the bullets were coming very thick, but as the line was in an open field with nothing to shield us from the burning rays of the sun, we suffered intensely from the heat, especially as we were fatigued by our previous rapid marching. I felt the heat more severely, as I had just returned from the Hospital and was still*

---

[170] Martin, 37.

suffering from weariness from my recent illness. Major Burnett commanded, Capt. Ragland acted as Lt. Col. and I as Major.

The brigade (Deas I think) which was in our front was repulsed, and our brigade commanded by Col. E. A. O'Neal was now ordered forward. Our line charged them, but found them thoroughly posted behind piles of rails and in good position. We were also repulsed but falling back about one hundred yards continued to fight until the brigade was almost decimated. Capt. Ragland, Lt. W. H. McMillan Co. H (acting Adjutant) and Lt. Harrison of Co. C were killed. Major Burnett was severely wounded in the shoulder. Capt. O'Brien lost a leg. I was painfully wounded in the right hand. Capt. J. N. Dovroon and privates N. J. Robison and D. Faulkenberry of my Co. killed, and many others wounded. The loss in our Regt. amounted to 180 out of 300. The Division (Walthalls) lost 1150 killed and wounded. This was the battle of the "Poor House". It was a shocking affair and I think our Generals were ashamed of it, as I noticed very little was said in relation to the affair."[171] Gen. Walthall stated, "My command was promptly put in motion, left in front, and soon was halted nearly opposite Ezra church and a line formed for attack by Lieutenant-General Stewart's order, the left retreating on the road by which I moved out, and the right slightly thrown not far from the Poor-House." [172]

Of the battle of July 28th, Colonel O'Neal wrote: "For more than two hours the sanguinary conflict raged with great fury and slaughter, and finding it impossible to dislodge him from his position, I saw to the major-general commanding for assistance. General Quarles was ordered up. He obeyed the order with alacrity. His troops came up in splendid style and at once opened on the enemy a heavy fire; but even with this additional force it was found impossible to break his (the enemy's) line although at one time some parts of our line gained a footing in forty or fifty yards of the enemy...during the whole of this sanguinary conflict the officers (field and line) and the men, with some exceptions, behaved with the coolness and intrepidity of veterans and held their ground with a steady and stubborn courage worthy of the highest admiration and I trust it will not be deemed envious? to say what truth demands should be stated, that if the troops on the right of our division had moved forward and kept pace with our line of battle, the enemy would have been driven from his position if not routed....Among the slain we have to mourn the loss of some valuable officers, Captain Ragland, 17th Alabama, and Captain Hanna, 29th Alabama Regiment, two gallant and meritorious officers are among the killed. I cannot close this report without acknowledging my obligations to Captain S. B. Smith of the 16th Alabama Regiment, and Capt. Tate, 17th Alabama

---

[171] McMillan sketch.
[172] OWR, Serial 74, 927.

Regiment and Sergeant Major Banks, who were acting on my staff in the absence of the regular staff. Each behaved with gallantry, and faithfully performed his duties."[173]

Robert Croxton, a sergeant in Company F, wrote from Atlanta on July 31, "We came out today, the fight lasted for 1 or 2 hours. I mean we was into it that length of time myself. As for the rest it was going on all the evening on our wing, we tried to storm their work, and did. They were too many for us and they having breastworks on us too, we lost a great many men. T. J. McKey was slightly wounded, but he was not broke, a ball struck him in the back of the shoulder and knocked him down, all our Officers was wounded Johns and Halpin slight but Capt. O'Brien I am afraid, will loose his foot. He was shot through the ankle and foot. So we have but 19 men in the company for duty, besides James Sharp and myself...."[174]

After the battle at Ezra Church, 115 men from the 17th Alabama were listed as killed or wounded according to the regimental medical register. This does not include the men captured and missing. The 17th Alabama hospital register for July listed 18 cases of dysentery, 86 cases of fever, 44 cases of diarrhea, 19 cases of debilitas, and 11 cases of other illnesses.

I. Siege of Atlanta

For the next four weeks, there were no major battles. The Confederates destroyed railroad lines north of Atlanta in an attempt to cut off Sherman's supply line from Tennessee. Sherman's men repaired a railroad as rapidly as it was destroyed. The Confederates built a 12 mile defensive ring around Atlanta that Sherman had no intention of attacking. Instead Sherman concentrated on destroying the Confederate supply lines to the east, south and west. As part of the Union strategy, starting on August 9, Atlanta was bombarded continuously by Sherman's siege guns.

In a letter to his wife, Elizabeth, on August 14, J. B. Sanders wrote from Atlanta, "It is through the mercy of God that I am permitted to write once more to let you know that I am still in the land of the living....of provisions we draw a pound and a quarter of bread and a half pound of good bacon per day and every third day we draw a half pound of cooked beef but we are tired out on such a Diet..."[175]

On August 24, 1864, James Alford Thompson, Company C, wrote his wife, Mary, from Atlanta: ...This leaves one tolerable well in body – but not in mind. I hope this may reach you and find you all well. I have no news much to write more than times is very hard here yet, but I don't know how long it will last... ...Mary, I want to see you all so bad I don't know what to do. Tell your pap to save all the fodder he can and all the peas he can for

---

[173] Ibid, 943.
[174] Robert Croxton, letters (SG024896, folder 1, Alabama Archives, Montgomery, AL).
[175] Sanders letters.

everything will sell at a high price and that is all the chance to get any money. I don't know when we will draw any and save all the ground peas he can and push your hogs..."[176]

Thompson indicated he was well in body. However there was much sickness through out the summer of 1864 from heat exhaustion in both armies. The unsanitary conditions persisted with these two huge armies encamped in such a small area. Lack of rations was another problem. Foraging was a constant necessity and a dangerous excursion for many soldiers. Both armies were plagued with scurvy, a condition that improved when Georgia's 1864 corn crop was available.

Thompson also indicated that he was not well in mind. Like so many other soldiers at the time, he was probably in a state of depression. He certainly had reason to be. Homesickness was one probable factor. The extreme fatigue, hunger, and poor diet would break down any soldier's resistance to depression. Other contributing factors were losing comrades in battle and the continuing lack of success stopping Sherman. Thompson's comment on saving all the fodder and peas to sell reflects his concern about money. The money a soldier drew for his service in the army was $11 a month. The value of Confederate money had dropped so low that $11 didn't buy much, and the government payroll was months late.

According to the hospital register, the 17th lost 31 men killed or wounded in the month of August. The register entries for August 19 listed cases of dysentery, 38 cases of fever, 78 cases of diarrhea, 8 cases of debilitas, and 72 cases of other illnesses.

Following the four week stand-off, the fate of Atlanta would be quickly resolved. By August 26, General Hood had completed preparations for his next battle. He was ready to attack Sherman's army when he discovered that the Union army had left the Atlanta area. The citizens of Atlanta were jubilant. The Yankees were gone. Actually Sherman had sent General Howard south with the Army of the Tennessee to cut off the Macon and Western Railroad. Sherman's strategy was to force Hood to send some of his troops after Howard. That action would weaken Atlanta's defenses. His plan worked. Hood sent Hardee's Corps and Lee's Corps south to Jonesboro on the night of August 30. Fighting began on the afternoon of August 31, and by September 1, the Confederates had met defeat at Jonesboro.[177] Hood finally realized that Atlanta was lost.

J. Retreat from Atlanta

Hood evacuated Atlanta on September 1. During the Confederate evacuation of Atlanta Hood's army torched off 101 rail cars loaded with

---
[176] Thompson letters.
[177] The 17th Alabama was not at Jonesboro.

high explosives to keep them from falling into enemy hands. The blasts were so forceful that they helped destroy the main industrial center of Atlanta. The widespread devastation of Atlanta resulted from actions taken by both the Union and Confederate armies. The extensive barrage by Sherman's guns, the destruction of war materials and supplies by Hood's troops, and the destruction by Sherman's troops after the fall of Atlanta left the town in ruins. During the Atlanta campaign, the loss of men (wounded, captured and killed) totaled over 31,000 Union troops and about 35,000 Confederate troops.

Hood moved his Army of Tennessee south to Lovejoy Station. J. B. Sanders wrote from 30 miles south of Atlanta, *"Stewart's Corps was cut off and left in Atlanta, but made its escape by a force march day and night around by the right flank. We march between 40 and 50 miles with out Rest or Sleep the enemy following close on our heels they captured a great many of our men that was sick and worn down..."*[178]

On September 20, Hood moved his army in the direction of West Point, Georgia, in anticipation of Sherman moving to the Alabama manufacturing area. On September 21, Hood was located at Palmetto, Georgia, where he met with Jefferson Davis. They made plans to destroy Sherman's supply line to Chattanooga. They hoped that this would lure Sherman north or his men would starve. If Sherman pursued Hood, Hood hoped to battle smaller segments of Sherman's army throughout northwest Georgia. On September 24, Hood made plans to seize the Western and Atlantic Railroad south of Atlanta. If Sherman responded by moving north with forces too strong for Hood, Hood would head for the area around Gadsden, Alabama. If Sherman moved south, Hood would follow.

A letter written from the ditches of Palmetto September 24 tells much about the condition of the Army of Tennessee, *"...I wrote to you on the 14th of this month we were then at lovejoy road we left love(joy) on the 18th and arrived here on the 20th and went to ditching. The yankees are not near us I think we just came here to fortify to be ready for them we have completed our ditches and there is talk of us going in camps again. We have had to fortify so much on this campaign that we have almost become perfect it don't take us long to throw up good breastworks...this is the ninth works that were made this year....Sister I had a good dinner today or it was what we called a good dinner in camp cornbread and beef fried ham pumpkin and sweet potatoes. We had to eat cold bread all this campaign from the 19th of May until the 7th of Sept I never tasted a mouthful of bread but what had been baked a day or more....I have had good clothes and have had all the time But I have been so dirty at times that I would have been ashamed to go in any ladies house...I wrote you on the 14th the 15th was fast day we fasted and gave our rations to the destitute citizens of Atlanta. We have had a*

---
[178] Sanders letters.

great many fast days but I am sorry to confess to you that this was the first one I ever observed...the army destroys a great lot where ever they go. We had destroyed almost everything before us on this campaign where ever we threw up breastworks all of the houses that were in front of the works were torn or burnt down and all of the rails that were near were used in fortifying and for fire wood.... "[179]

On October 1, Hood headed his army north backtracking much of the path Johnston had traveled only a few months earlier. On October 3, the Confederates attacked the Union garrison at Big Shanty – victory for the Confederates. On October 5, the Confederates attacked at Altoona – victory for the Federals. Sherman had now reached Kennesaw Mountain. On October 8, Hood was at Cedartown. He now intended to destroy Sherman's communications at Chattanooga, Stevenson, and Bridgeport, Alabama, and then meet the enemy in north Georgia. On October 9, Hood met with his new commander, General Pierre G. Beauregard. They agreed it was important to keep up the morale of the Army of Tennessee by not entering a battle, unless the Confederates had the advantage of size or position. On October 11, Hood was at Resaca threatening Union troops there. On October 13, the Confederates captured a garrison at Dalton and destroyed 25 miles of railroad. It was immediately rebuilt by Sherman's men.

McMillan described their route, "*After dark we fell back behind our works and kept up picket fighting until Sherman flanked us on the left and we retreated (on the 1st day of Sept. I think) to Lovejoy Station about 30 miles south of Atlanta, remaining at Lovejoy until the 18th of September, when we were moved around via Fayetteville to Palmetto on the Atlanta and West Point RR. We entrenched there but on the 27th of Sept. we crossed the Chatahoochie and commenced flanking Sherman by the same route by which we had been flanked out of Atlanta. We moved around cautiously and struck the R. Road at "Big Shanty" a station above Kennesaw Mountain, and took up about 9 miles of the road and captured the garrison of 80 men. We then marched back by way of Lost Mountain where we encamped. Here rather a remarkable coincident occurred. Our Brigade reached the base of the Mountain about dark, as we had done after the fight at New Hope Church 5 months before, and marched up to the top of the Mountain and encamped, and next morning, like,*

"*The King of France with Ten Thousand men
Marched up the hill then down again.*"

After Maj. Burnett was wounded, I was thrown in command of the Regt. and continued to command it until the 3rd day of Oct. when I was relieved by Capt. W. E. White. From Lost Mountain we continued our march via New Hope Church and Pumpkin Vine Creek around Rome,

---

[179] Jessie McQuigg, letter (Tutwiler Collection, Birmingham Public Library, Birmingham, AL).

crossing the Coosa River at Coosa, and again struck the Rail Road. Co. E. A. O'Neal was relieved of the command of the Brigade about this time by Brig. Gen. C. M. Shelley.[180] *We next captured Tilton above Resaca, Dalton and Tunnel Hill, and about 1000 prisoners, over 800 of whom were Negroes, and tore up 10 or 12 miles more of Rail Road."*[181]

K. After the Atlanta Campaign

Hood and the Army of Tennessee had reached the northwest corner of Georgia, back where the Atlanta campaign began in April. At the beginning of the Atlanta campaign, the Union Army had about 100,000 men and the Confederates about 45,000. At the height of the campaign, with reinforcements, the Union army probably had a maximum of 120,00 men and the Confederates about 65,000. By October, the Confederate Army of Tennessee numbered about 35,000. It had been diminished in size by the casualties of battle, by disease, and by desertion.

In September, Hood sent letters to the governors of the Confederacy requesting more men. Governor Watts replied on September 19, *"Your letter of the 14th inst was received by me yesterday. I regret to have to inform you that I have no more troops to send you. I have no authority, under the law, to send any of the Militia beyond the limits of the state."*[182] Two days later Watts replied to Governor Brown of Georgia who also requested more troops to help remove Sherman and his army from Georgia. Watts sent Brown a copy of the letter he had sent to Hood.[183]

With the Union army in Georgia numbering about 80,000, Hood made the decision that the Army of Tennessee was not ready to face an army as big and as well-equipped as Sherman's army. Hood turned his army west and moved into Alabama. Hood had a new plan - to retake Nashville and then head north into Yankee country. The fight for Atlanta was ended. With the Confederate army headed north away from Atlanta, General Sherman began his infamous "march to the sea."

L. Where They're Buried

Where were those brave men buried, the brave soldiers who died in the various engagements during the Atlanta campaign? They were buried on the battlefields where they fell in mass graves or in graves with markers no longer visible.

Union military reports throughout the Atlanta Campaign of 1864 mentioned burials of Confederate casualties. After a battle in May, a Union officer reported, *"We buried of the enemy's dead in my front over 300*

---

[180] DuBose history: "He was appointed Oct 2d, See Serial 79, 782."
[181] McMillan sketch.
[182] Letters from Governor Watts, ibid. (Reel 22, Folder 9). Much of the militia was boys between 17 and 18 and men over 45.
[183] Ibid.

bodies."[184] In late June from Kennesaw Mountain, Lieutenant Colonel Cyrus E. Briant, 88th Indiana Infantry, reported that "...*rebel dead lying outside of our works for some days and smell very bad; tried to compromise long enough to have them buried, but they would not allow us.*"[185]

After the battle of Peachtree on July 22, the number of causalities was staggering. Major General John A. Logan, 15th Army Corps, wrote, "...*the number of their dead buried in front of the Fifteenth Corps up to this hour is 360, and the commanding officer reports as many more as yet unburied, burying parties being still at work.*"[186] "Major General Grenville M. Dodge, Sixteenth Army Corps, reported, "*During the engagement on my front, prisoners were taken from 49 different regiments, 8 brigades, and 3 divisions; 351 prisoners were captured, not including those taken by Colonel Mersey's brigade on the line of the Fifteenth Corps, 8 battle-flags, and some 1,300 muskets were captured and turned over; 422 of the enemy's dead were buried in my front.*"[187] Major General Frank P. Blair of the Seventeenth Army Corps wrote, "*On the morning after the fight the enemy sent a flag of truce to bury their dead, and we buried and delivered over to the enemy to be buried of their dead between 900 and 1,000.*"[188] Colonel Benjamin Harrison, 70th Indiana Infantry, wrote, "*The enemy's dead to the number of 150 were left within our lines and buried by us, while several hundred others were seen upon the open field between the lines, but could not be reached for burial. Among the dead buried were 1 lieutenant-colonel, 2 majors, 2 captains, and 3 lieutenants.*"[189]

After the battle of Ezra Church on July 28, the number of Confederate casualties was again staggering. Colonel Harrison reported, "*These assaults occurred from noon until about 4 p.m., when the enemy disappeared, leaving his dead and wounded in our hands. As many as 642 dead were counted and buried, and still others are known to have been buried which were not counted by the regularly detailed burial parties.*"[190] Major General Logan, 15th Army Corps, reported, "*One hundred and six prisoners were captured not including 73 wounded, who have been removed to hospitals and are being taken care of by our surgeons. Five hundred and sixty-five rebels have been already buried, and about 200 yet supposed to be unburied. A large number were already buried and about 200 yet supposed to be unburied. A large number were undoubtedly carried away during the night, as the enemy did not withdraw until nearly daylight.*"[191]

---

[184] OWR, Serial 74, 35.
[185] Ibid, Serial 72, 542.
[186] Ibid, Serial 74, 21.
[187] Ibid, 372.
[188] Ibid.
[189] Ibid, Serial 73, 347.
[190] Ibid, Serial 72, 78.
[191] Ibid, Serial 74, 86.

After the battle of Atlanta on September 1, Colonel Theodore Jones of the 30th Ohio Infantry reported, *"During the night of the 1st of September 120 of their dead were buried, and several were left unburied when we marched in pursuit of the enemy on the morning of September."*[192]

---

[192] Ibid, 294.

VII. The Battle of Franklin

A. Introduction

General Hood turned his back on Sherman in Georgia after the multiple defeats during the Atlanta campaign. Hood then selected Nashville as his next objective. By recapturing Nashville after many months of occupation by the Union Army, Hood hoped that he could gain the position he wanted, as one of the great generals of the Confederacy. After Nashville, he might head north to the Ohio River into enemy territory. Or he could head east where he would join Lee and assist in the defeat of the Union Army in the east. Hood had great plans. This section briefly describes Hood's march into Tennessee and the battle of Franklin, and conveys the conditions, which the 17th Alabama Infantry endured during that period.

Although there has been little written about the 17th Alabama's involvement after Atlanta, they can be tracked as a unit in the Army of Tennessee. The 17th was in Cantey/Shelley's brigade that was part of Walthall's Division and Stewart's corps. Tracking the brigade, division, and corps through the record books provides an accurate view of the path of the 17th Alabama during October and November of 1864.

Cantey's Brigade remained intact with new leadership. On September 13, 1864, while Hood was at Lovejoy Station, Georgia, Hood officially requested that Colonel Charles Miller Shelley be placed in command of Cantey's brigade. Cantey was in poor health and was unable to continue as brigade commander. Shelley was born in Tennessee and was an Alabama architect before the war. He served as captain at the battle of Bull Run. He then raised a regiment and fought in the western theater. He was captured during the Vicksburg Campaign. After prisoner exchange, Shelley fought at Chickamauga and the Atlanta Campaign and advanced to brigadier general in September 1864.

In this section, Walthall's report on Shelley's brigade at Franklin gives some detail of the brigade's involvement. Captain McMillan of Company H and Colonel Murphy, commander of the 17th Alabama, draw a vivid picture of the horrors of Franklin.

B. The March to Tennessee

By October 19, 1864, Hood had moved his army to Gadsden where his waiting supply train was located. Here Hood met with General Beauregard to establish actions for the Army of Tennessee. The Confederates were planning to cross the Tennessee River with Nashville as their destination. More than half the men in the Army of Tennessee were Tennessee natives. The news they were headed for Tennessee was cause for much celebrating. Sherman was moving east through Georgia and was no longer a threat to the Army of Tennessee. Sherman suspected that Hood would move his army to Nashville. After the capture of Atlanta, Sherman had assigned General

George Thomas, commanding officer of the Army of the Cumberland, responsibility for the safety of Nashville.

Hood's plan on October 19 was to cross the Tennessee River at Guntersville, Alabama. On October 22, the Confederates left Gadsden with 20 days rations. When they arrived at Guntersville, Hood changed his mind about the location for crossing the Tennessee River. He believed he needed the presence of cavalry when his army crossed the river. Not only was General Nathan Bedford Forrest not there with his cavalry division, the river was higher than expected for that time of year. Hood and his army continued their march in a westerly direction, south of the Tennessee River. There were no railroads in that part of the state, and the entire route was covered on foot and in all kinds of weather. Eighteen miles a day was considered an average march. All available wagons were used for moving supplies and wounded. This was a long difficult march through poor country with poor rations and poor foraging. One private wrote that he existed on three sinkers[193] a day.

On October 27, Hood passed near Decatur, which was a possible crossing point. However, he decided the Union garrison at Decatur was too strong to attack and continued west. At Courtland on October 28, Hood made the decision that his men were too poorly equipped to cross the river there.

Tuscumbia was finally selected as the crossing point. On October 30, the Army of Tennessee began arriving in the Tuscumbia/Florence area of north Alabama. The army was now 100 miles further west than Hood's original plan. This placed the army within ten miles of the Memphis and Charleston Railroad, which connected with the Mobile and Ohio Railroad. This rail link from the south through Mississippi was now Hood's supply line. Another element of Hood's plan was to acquire a two-week supply of ammunition, rations, and other essentials. He optimistically planned that future supplies would be obtained from the enemy in Nashville and surrounding areas..

C. Troop Strength

In September when Hood made plans to move on Nashville, President Davis promised fifteen to twenty thousand reinforcements from the Army of Mississippi. In Tuscumbia Hood learned the promised reinforcements were not available. Those men were needed to cover the state of Mississippi and to protect Hood's supply line through Mississippi. Instead of additional troops, Hood was forced to supply men from the Army of Tennessee to augment the troops in Mississippi who were protecting the Mobile and Ohio Railroad.

---

[193] Definition of a sinker: a biscuit made from unbolted flour without any milk, grease, salt, or soda.

At Tuscumbia, Hood no longer had the army he had in July when he replaced Johnston as commander of the Army of Tennessee. On July 10, official records listed the effective number of soldiers present in the Army of Tennessee as 50,932 (aggregate present and absent at 134,254).[194] On September 10, after the loss of Atlanta, official records listed 39,238 effective men present (aggregate present and absent at 124,847).[195] During the next two months when Hood fought small skirmishes in northwest Georgia and moved his troops in the direction of Nashville, the numbers dropped again. On November 6, official records listed 30,599 effective men present (aggregate present and absent at 96,481).[196]

If Hood was to be successful at Nashville, he desperately needed more men. There were few new recruits available. What the Confederacy needed was the return of the thousands of men who were absent without leave. This included men who had gone home to see about their families; men who had lost confidence in General Hood; men who could no longer face the carnage; men who no longer had the strength or will to fight. These were some of the men Alabama Governor Watts encouraged to return to duty. Watts distributed a message to all newspapers within the state which he hoped would be published at the same time:

"*To Alabama Soldiers Absent from their Commands*
Many of you have, doubtless, remained at home after the expiration of your furloughs, without intervention to desert the cause of your country, and you have failed to return to your commands for fear of the penalty to which you may be subjected. Many of you have left your commands without leave, under the mistaken notion that the highest duty required you to provide sustenance and protection to your families. Some have been prompted to leave by one motive and some by others. Very few, I am persuaded, have left with the intent to abandon the cause of the South.

I have received letters from several expressing sorrow for their past neglect of duty, and a wish to return to their commands if any assurance could be given that they would not receive the extreme penalty of the law.

At this time our cause needs all men able and willing to bear arms in its defense. The best recommendation to those who have hereunto fore neglected their duty is a prompt acknowledgement of their fault, manifested by their prompt return to duty. That there may be no obstacle in the way of those who really desire to serve their country, I am authorized to say that all who will, without delay, voluntarily return to their commands, will receive a lenient and merciful consideration; and that none, who so return within 40 days from this date, will have penalty of death inflicted on them.

---

[194] OWR, Serial 74, 678. Absent indicates men who were prisoners of war, absent with leave, and absent without leave.
[195] OWR, Serial 79,829.
[196] OWR, Serial 93, 678.

I promise all, who will heed this appeal, to use by best exertions for their good."[197]

During the long delay, the Union Army in Nashville brought in supplies and reinforcements from Georgia, Kentucky, Missouri, etc. The weather turned very cold and very wet, the beginning of a harsh winter. The Army of Tennessee was not equipped for winter weather. The troops were poorly clothed and many were barefoot. In spite of the weather and the condition of the troops, Hood made the decision on November 18 to move on to Nashville. After completing railroad repairs that made possible the delivery of supplies and ammunition for the coming campaign, the Army of Tennessee began the long march north over pontoon bridges across the Tennessee River.

D. General Walthall's Account of the 17th Alabama at Franklin

Stewart's Corps was the first to cross the river. Although scheduled to cross on November 19, they were delayed one day due to weather. Walthall described crossing the river at south Florence *"on a pontoon bridge and went on with the corps (*Stewart's) *by a route intermediate between Lawrenceburg and Waynesborough, over roads so bad that it was almost impossible for the artillery to move at all, the teams being very poor and greatly exhausted from constant and excessive service. Until we struck the old Nashville road heavy details (sometimes one, and often two regiments) were required to move with the artillery to assist in getting up the hills. After this we got along with less difficulty..."*[198] Some days they marched as many as 18 miles. The men not only suffered from the weather conditions, they also suffered much from pangs of hunger. Lieutenant Benjamin Weathers of Company F reported that the food issue on the march to Franklin was three ears of corn per man per day.[199] And some days there was only corn meal.

General John M. Schofield and the Army of the Ohio were located at Pulaski, Tennessee, a precarious position with the Army of Tennessee so near. Thomas ordered Schofield to Nashville to furnish reinforcements there for the pending battle with Hood. Thomas further ordered Schofield not to engage the enemy in route to Nashville. A key element of Hood's plan was to position his army between Schofield and Thomas to keep them from combining their armies. Some units of Hood's Army of Tennessee and Schofield's Army of the Ohio engaged in skirmishes at Columbia and in the area of Spring Hill.

On November 29, Walthall's division was ordered to bivouac near the Franklin Pike about a mile above Spring Hill. Unfortunately for the

---

[197] "The Independent American." *Pike County, Alabama, Civil War News,* November 18, 1864.
[198] OWR, Serial 93, 720-21.
[199] Weathers articles.

Confederates, they missed their chance at Spring Hill. It was the big blunder of the Tennessee campaign when Schofield and his army, headed for Nashville, were able to quietly march past the Army of Tennessee in the middle of the night at Spring Hill. The next morning, November 30, 1864, when Hood was made aware of what had happened, he was furious. He berated his officers and men alike, declaring that they all were cowards. He hastily moved the Army of Tennessee towards Franklin. Waiting for them at Franklin was General Schofield and the Army of the Ohio. Although Schofield was still under orders to move to Nashville without engaging in battle with the enemy, he realized he had to stop and fight Hood at Franklin. Schofield selected the battlefield – strong earthworks on the southern edge of town. The fighting at Franklin did not begin until late afternoon. Just before sunset, more than 25,000 Confederate soldiers charged almost half a mile across an open field into the fire of the well-fortified earthworks of Schofield's army. The battle was a slaughter that ended after dark. In the morning Schofield and his army were gone again; on the way to finally join Thomas at Nashville.

A lack of bravery was not the cause of the Confederate defeat. The battlefield was Scofield's selection and a disadvantage for the Confederates. It was a long charge across open terrain to reach the enemy. Historians have questioned Hood's decision to attack under these conditions.

Much has been written about Hood's physical and mental condition the last months of 1864. Physically he had deteriorated. The loss of the use of one arm and the loss of a leg made mobility difficult and very painful. His mental capability was probably impaired by the alcohol and drugs consumed to dull his continuing pain. Hood was forced to rely on reports by his officers rather than being able to observe the activities of his army. He was frequently out-of-touch with what was happening. Closer observation or better information might have resulted in Hood aborting the charge at Franklin. Instead, wave after wave of men charged across the open field with the same devastating results.

In his report of the battle, Walthall wrote of his division, *"now numbering but 1400 guns, was the center of the corps, and presented two brigades front (Quarles' on the right and Reynolds' on the left), with Cantey's, under command of Gen. C. M. Shelley, in reserve. The advance was ordered at 4 o'clock."*[200] During the advance, Reynolds' brigade was hindered by briar thicket so extensive that it prevented him from holding his line. Consequently, Shelley with his brigade moved up in Reynolds' position on the left.

General Walthall described the conduct of Brigadier-General Shelley and his brigade (which included the 17th) during the battle of Franklin:

---

[3] OWR, ibid.

"Brigadier-General Shelley came promptly upon the line, and in a few moments afterward, when the entire line was rectified, the advance was resumed. Both officers and men seemed fully alive to the importance of beating the enemy here at any cost, and the line moved steadily forward until it neared his outer works, and then fell upon it so impetuously that the opposing force gave way without even retarding the advance and retired in disorder to the strong intrenchments in rear. There was an extensive, open, and almost unbroken plain between the outer and inner lines, across which we must pass to reach the latter. This was done under far the most deadly fire of both small-arms and artillery that I have ever seen troops subjected to. Terribly torn at every step by an oblique fire from the battery advantageously posted at the enemy's left, no less than by the destructive fire in front, moved on and did not falter till, just to the right of the pike, it reached the abatis fronting the works. Over this no organized force could go, and here the main body of my command, both front line and reserve, was repulsed in confusion; but over this obstacle, impossible for a solid line, many officers and men (among them former Brigadier-General Shelley) made their way, and some, crossing the ditch in its rear, were captured and others killed or wounded in the effort to mount the embankment. Numbers of every brigade gained the ditch and there continued the struggle with but the earth-works separating them from the enemy until late in the night." [201]

There were many casualties (wounded, captured, and killed) in the 17th Alabama at Franklin. See Appendix xiii for a list of known casualties at Franklin. Records at that point in the war were not well maintained or were lost. The losses by Shelley's brigade were estimated at 432 killed and 1100 wounded. This does not include the captured or missing. Shelley escaped injury, but his horse was shot from under him, and his clothing was pierced by seven bullets. Quarles Brigade, also of Walthall's Division and fighting alongside Shelley's, suffered heavy losses. Many officers, down to the rank of captain, were casualties at Franklin. When the last shot was finally fired, what remained was a ghastly scene. Many of the wounded and dead, those brave, courageous men were lying in the open field where the charge began. Many of the wounded and dead soldiers and their horses had fallen where shot, piled one on top of another, in front of the enemy earthworks. At the end of the battle, six of Hood's generals were dead and the Confederates had suffered over 7,000 casualties. The words of Captain McMillan of Company H and Colonel Murphy of the 17th Alabama describe the bravery and the horror of that long night. Excerpts from their diaries are presented in sections E and F.

---

[201] OWR, ibid.

E. Captain McMillan's Account of the Battle of Franklin

Captain McMillan described the Army of Tennessee's journey to Tennessee and what he saw and experienced during the battle of Franklin:

"*Passing through Dug Gap we marched via Subligna, Lafayette and Gaylesville to Gadsden, from there via Summerville to Decatur. Here we remained for two or three days, skirmished with the garrison and gunboats, and passed on down the line of Rail Road via Leighton, Courtland and etc. to Tuscumbia which place we reached on the 31st day of October. Here we remained in camp two weeks, and moved over to South Florence and encamped five or six days, and on the 20th of Nov. crossed the Tennessee River. Nothing remarkable happened, but cold and fatiguing marches, as we were crossing the mountains of North Alabama and Tennessee. We passed Mt. Peasant the Polk neighborhood and the residence of General Pillow and arrived at Columbia on the 26th of Nov. - skirmished with the enemy, on the 29th flanked them, crossing the Duck River above the town, and striking the Nashville R. Road at Spring Hill.*

Here occurred the famous "Faus pas"[202] *of allowing the enemy to march by after having him, as it were, completely in our power. Who was to blame? The commanding officers of the army surely, though I would willingly attribute it to some one else, if I could, as he has sins enough to bear. I think he should have been on the ground when a point of so much importance was to be gained, and not leave its performance to any subordinate entirely. Doubtless the subordinate (Cheatham) was also much to blame. He commanded the Corps that should have cut off the enemy's retreat, he failed and ought to have lost his reputation. Hood commanded Cheatham and failed to see his order executed, and lost a battle - an army - perhaps a nation.*

Nothing was left for Hood to do on the next morning (the 30th) but to follow up the flying Federals. We came up with them about 12 o'clock at Franklin, where they had become entrenched. Lee's Corps had been left at Columbia, but Hood began immediately to make dispositions for an attack. This was to be my last battle in the mighty war in which we were engaged, and I approach a description of it with a heavy heart.

It was about 4 oclock I suppose before the troops were in position, and ordered to charge. Never did men fight better, indeed they seemed to be desperately (unreadable) brave. They rushed upon the first line and swept the enemy before them, and with loud hazzas approached the stronger and inner works. They were met by a murderous fire of shell, grape and musketry but still they went on, hundreds going down before the tremendous

---

[202] The "faus pas" was allowing Schofield's Army of the Ohio to pass by the Army of Tennessee during the night of November 29. Hood had ordered Cheatham and his corps to stop Schofield. For whatever reason this did not happen.

hailstorm of lead and iron. The works were reached and captured in some places, but the Southern troops were finally repulsed.

I had gotten within about 10 paces of the works and so thoroughly excited that I had forgotten the surrounding danger and was thinking of what I should do on reaching the ditch. I had concluded to pick up one of the muskets lying around and use the bayonet on the blue coats, when I was struck on the left thigh with a musket ball, making a severe wound about 10 inches in length but not breaking the bone, although completely paralyzing the whole limb. I was running at the time and as the ball struck me I fell, my face striking the ground. My first impression was that I had been struck by a cannon ball, as I was nearly in front of a piece, constantly firing. I knew that I was past locomotion and my professional instinct led me to place my thumb on the femur artery as I though my thigh was torn all to pieces and I knew if so I must soon bleed to death. With the other hand I proceeded to examine the wound and satisfying myself that I was in no immediate danger, and being unable to walk I stretched myself on the ground with my head on my arm to rest, as I was exhausted from the race in the charge. While lying in this position, a ball passed thru my right hand or wrist inflicting a very painful wound cutting the ulna artery, from which I lost a great deal of blood. Another ball passed through my blanket just grazing my ribs; another glanced my left shoulder, but neither of the last did much damage. I lay in this position through the whole fight, with my teeth firmly clenched. I looked at the stream of fire under the head logs expecting every minute to be my last on earth. Besides the balls which struck me, others were constantly striking the earth near enough to throw dirt in my face. A kind Providence had decreed that I was to be spared yet awhile.

After the repulse of our men they fell back to the outer line, which had been captured and still kept up firing, I had a mortal dread of being captured, and determined to keep my position until dark - it was then sundown - and crawl back to our line, but as the firing grew slack the men behind the Yankee ditches began to peep over the breastworks, and seeing me alive, ordered me to go over, threatening to shoot me if I did not. Nothing was left for me but to comply, and as I was crawling over the breastwork, a cowardly little scoundrel who was afraid to risk his head high enough to see what he was shooting at, fired his piece in my face, burning me considerably with the powder, I abused him for shooting a man after he had surrendered, but he disclaimed any intention of shooting me and about that time our men opening a brisk fire, I was hurried to the rear, an Irishman under each arm supporting me. I was carried through the town and across Harpseth River, and placed under guard together with 20 or 30 others.

I found several of my Regt. and among them my Sergt. Jas. M. Davison. I felt very much exhausted from fatigue and the excitement, together with the *shock from my wounds, as well as the loss of blood. The Yankees had no stimulants or opium, or at least would give me none, and would not allow us to build a fire for fear of attracting the fire of the Southern troops. The ground was wet and the weather cold. Davison spread his blanket on the ground, and we both lay on it and covered with mine, but it seemed I would freeze. I do not think I ever spent a more miserable night than the 30 of Nov on the Battle Field. About midnight all who were able to walk were sent back to Nashville: the guard was not drawn from the rest, and it was evident that they were preparing to retreat.* (Schofield's army was leaving Franklin for Nashville. Any prisoner, including McMillan, who could not walk was left behind in Franklin.) *The last of them retired, and set fire to the R. R. bridge. The squad of disabled men, among whom I was, were in rear of the bridge, and in line of the fire. The shells burst uncomfortable near to us, but with Davison's assistance I crawled a few feet and got behind a ledge of rocks which protected me from further harm.*

After daylight, Davison[203]*, who was always an indefatigable forager, found coffee, sugar, coffee pot and cups: indeed he soon had a pretty respectable start for a commissary collected around us from the debris of the Yankee camp. Some of those who were best able, built us a fire, and under its influence of its genial warmth and the (unreadable) stimulus of the genuine coffee, to which we had been a stranger for some time. We almost forgot the terrors of the night before, and were comparatively comfortable and happy. Our men were engaged burying the dead, and collecting the wounded on the other side of the river.*

It was near night on the 1st Dec., before I was taken to town, and cared for, but even then I only rec'd a drink of whiskey, and dose of morphine, passing the night on a hard floor, surrounded by 20 or 30 of wounded groaning men. We had no hospital stores, but the generous citizens of Franklin threw open their doors and fed and nursed us. On the morning of the 2nd Dec., the Surgeon of our Regt. found me and moved me to the hotel of Mr. Crutcher, where I remained until the 25th of Dec. I am deeply indebted to Mr. C and family for their kindness, which could not have been exceeded by my own family. I would have been other than human not to appreciate it. I had heard of my brother's death (killed at Franklin), *and was suffering severely with my wounds, but the idea of being in the hands of our people, and kindly cared for, went far to sustain me in my severe trails."*[204]

Captain McMillan was wounded and hospitalized at Franklin where he remained until the defeat at Nashville. He was captured on December 25th

---

[203] Sergeant James Miller Davison, like Captain McMillan, was left behind when Schofield's army moved on to Nashville. Davison, like McMillan, would be captured again when the Union Army came back through Franklin after the Battle of Nashville on December 17.
[204] McMillan sketch.

as the Confederates retreated from Nashville with the Union Army in pursuit.

Thomas A. Rumbley, a private in McMillan's company, described some of the horror at Franklin, his words passed down by his son, Hector. He spoke of the hunger, "*The most horrible story I ever heard him tell was about the desperate Battle of Franklin, where the soldiers became so hungry they cut up a horse that had been dead for days and ate it...*" He spoke of the carnage, "*...and when they dug ditches for breastworks, the blood oozed down the ditches where the trenches were made. He said the dead lay stacked in piles.*"[205]

F. Colonel Virgil S. Murphy's Account of the Battle of Franklin

Colonel Virgil S. Murphy, commanding officer of the 17th Alabama, was captured at the battle of Franklin. While he was a prisoner he kept a diary. The diary began the day of the battle of Franklin and continued through February 17, 1865. In his diary he vividly described his experience at Franklin:

"*I was captured in the conclusion of the battle of Franklin Tenn Nov 30th 1864 about 7 P.M. It was commenced by the Confederates at 4 1/2 P.M. and raged with unexamplid fury, intensified by national hatred and rendered sanguinary by bitter wrongs endured. The Confederates debauched from their adjacent heights upon a level plain and attacking vigorously the Yankees in works, swept their lines like a tempest. The enemy huddled crowded, bewildered and confused by this bold and resistless charge, some sought safety in flight while others dropped their arms from their nerveless hands and stood stupified and amazed while many found homes in the soil they had desecrated. Utter* (unreadable) *and confusion added to the enthusiasm which victory always inspires. With flashing eyes and vengeance darting from every glance the Confederates moved on in unbroken column through an open field against the second and almost impregnable lines of works. The enemy amassed four deep in places behind these formidable works awaited* (unreadable) *with* (unreadable) *trepidation our approach. Expansive flashes of fire followed by deafening reports and the hurtling storm of gunfire and cannister ploughing pitilessly through the advancing column indicated the position of their cannon. Shells darting athwart the horizon cavorting angrily in the air and forming strange lines before exploding among us, did not break the cadence of the step. Firm steady and with bated breath was the Co. advanced under a severe and murderous fire of musketry and artillery. Men fell like leaves before an autumn blast but their surviving comrades closed ranks with Spartan heroism and with a shout that rung far above the din of continuous hosts*

---

[205] *The Monroe Journal Centennial Edition, 1866 – 1966* (Monroe County, AL: privately published, 1966).

THE BATTLE OF FRANKLIN

(unreadable), *they flung themselves defiantly before their ramparts and were repulsed bleeding torn and decimated. Like old ocean waves stirred by the angry winds of heaven the billows lash the rockbound shores but to* (unreadable) *not to retreat. It being sure and swift destruction* (unreadable) *active and* (unreadable), *men and officers sought protection under cover of the works and continued to fight with unabated vigor and undiminished confidence. The assailants and the beseiged now grappled in fierce array across the works, vibrating and oscillating, as it was swayed alternately by the tide of success or repulse. The annals of chivalry never exhibited more disparate valor, heroic courage, distinguished gallantry or more charming nonchallance to death. Men officers* (unreadable) *with powder. Their clothes torn in rents and dyed in blood with their hair straming in the storm of battle, not a muscle blanched by a view of death, walked those works, with a step as firm and elastic as a lovir amid flowers, waving their swords or brandishing their muskets, cheering the lukewarm and disappointed, rallying the wavering and unsteady and performing prodigies of valor. Another line of battle came up and was hurled like a thunderbolt upon the frowning battlements only to share the horrible fate of its predecessor. Hastily banners floated upon the same parapet and the fitful glare of musketry disclosed faces in close proximity, replete with passive enthusiasm and determination. Guns loaded with the missiles of death were thrown over the works and fired aimlessly assailant and assailed charges and counterchanges made with varying success until the whole line was illuminated by the jets and flashes of fire from the guns. The incessant and unceasing roar of the musketry mingled with the hoarse sullen peals of the artillery and the shouts of the soldiery enveloped in a dense smoke made the* (unreadable) *grand in its* (unreadable) *and sublime in its terror. The field was strewn with the dead and the Columbia turnpike ran with the* (unreadable) *purest blood of our heroic land. The* (unreadable)*ment of the works was wet with human gore, and men disfigured mutilated and dying lay upon them while the carnage raged around them. It was the carnival of death. The charge was more desperate than at Balaklana, the contest as bloody as Eylau or Austirlily and the field as* (unreadable) *for courage as Iena Laudi or Waterloo. Adams fell with his steed striding the works like a centaur. Cliburne the Stonewall of the West, the chevalier Bay sans* (unreadable) *sans reproach fell in the wave of his devisive Granberry Strahl* (unreadable) *have gone on to that celestial sphere* (unreadable) *the sacred* (unreadable) *of our bleeding country. The author was in the front line and surrounded in the thickest of the grand terrific combat for two hours. When our line was shattered and decimated by the heavy musketry which poured into us, I sought shelter under the cover of the works and sat down at the mouth of an embrasure. With a few comrades we soon rendered their artillery useless and superfluous. They were shotted and once more bold and audacious than cautious or discret, advanced with lighted pri*(unreadable) *to fire them but fell to rise no more. Finally when our cartidges were exhasuted and our men were robbing a dead Yankee of an additional supply the Yankee suceeded by violent exertions in winning back one piece, and not being able to elevate or aim it fired it directly through the works. Huge fragments of timber were vomited forth particles of earth literally covered us limbs were wrenched from their stems, and nine of our men swept unheralded into eternity. To remain in this occumbent and dangerous position was worse than death. The fire measureably slackened and organizing the surviving men, a bold and determined effort was made to enter, capture and drive the defenders from their position. Forward was the watch word and the men bounded over like infuriated demons and were either shot down on the summit of the works or were secured transfixed on bayonets. The conflict was brief bloody and decisive. I was a prisoner. After the storm, came the calm, after superhuman exertions, reprise, after passion, coolness, after excitement, composure. The muscles relax from their unnatural tensions, blood flows back into its accustomed channel mental and physical frustration follows and the mind comtemplating the perilous scene shudders with horror at the abyss human hands has just created. The battle ceased and both sides withdraw silently from the fatal field, as if shunning and avoiding the unholy ground where "death came careening upon every breeze. But the glowing mournful and touching part of "grim visaged war" was yet to be performed. The earth had to receive its dead, our country had received its sacrifice and God had received their noble spirits. The sharp agonizing cry of the wounded pierced the still night air, the low gutteral death rattle was borne upon the coming zephrs=deaths cold dues settled upon lofty brows when external hands should relieve the chaplet of immortality and the gentle blushed with shame while down upon "man inhumanity to man"*

*The Battle of Franklin will live in history. It is a monument as induring as time to southern valor. It was the most magnificent display of gallantry in the record of military annals since the empire and the consulate. Each man was a (*unreadable*) in himself shedding lustre upon his arms and his country. Immortal spirits were born there in an hour, ran their brief glorious career and perished with the sword and musket clutched in their hands. It will be a Mecca for patriotic pilgrimage and posterity* (unreadable) *to the sacred remains of the fallen heroes like the Spartan mothers to the mausoleum at Thermopylan go and learn how men can die for freedom justice and inherited rights.*

While we lost more men in Killed and wounded, the enemy suffered severely in morale and prisoners and while we failed in repeated attempts to successfully capture their inner works, it was nevertheless a complete triumph to our arms; for the enemy retreated in disorder under the friendly cover of night, sadly crippled and disgusted with Southern steel. Our gain was not commensurate with our loss but who knew that God was awaiting the spirit of the peerless Cleburn. A spider web across the threshold of a cave saved Mahomet from his (unreadable) *and the destinies of the world were changed. Had the penalties of the* (unreadable) *laws been faithfully executed literature would have lost Shakespeare and drama* (unreadable) *and* (unreadable)*. Had Hood succeeded, Nashville would have opened her gates to the head of his victorious legions and the throat of Tennessee released from the humiliating grasp of a remorseless despotism. It was worth the hazard. Its failure does not diminish the value of the prize. The same blow delivered with equal power at Spring Hill or Thompson station would have yielded us dominion over Tennessee at Franklin it gave a few miles of territory because the hour and event did not meet. A failure to obey our order lost to us a noble commonwealth.*

I was conducted by my captor Capt. Coogin to the presence of Col. Rousseau 16th Kentucky Infantry and placed under guard in rear of the position we had assailed. I immediately experienced a sense of loneliness and despondency and my mind searching back, sought in vain for an avenus of escape in the secret conflict through which I had passed almost unscathed."[206]

G. A Wounded Soldier

Private James B. Stanley was a resident of Greenville and a member of Company C. He was severely wounded at the Battle of Franklin. His medical experience after the battle was explained in detail in an article written 100 years after the battle by Anne Seckler of Auburn University. She wrote that Stanley *"was hit three times...One bullet went entirely through his lower arm, without doing permanent damage; another nicked the same arm, and a third struck high in the upper arm, and lodged inside."* He found his way to the McGavock house that had become a hospital as the battle raged all around it.

The article continued, *"A doctor ignored the young soldier's two lesser wounds, but undertook to remove the bullet from the upper arm. He ran a probe into the wound, located the bullet far upon the shoulder and took out the bullet. The doctor had no medication of any kind. He took out his own pocket handkerchief, and pushed it through the wound, all the way, pulling it through and out of the hole in the shoulder which he had opened to remove the bullet."* Stanley then had the choice of sleeping on the floor of the McGavock house or going home. Fortunately he chose to leave.

---

[206] Virgil S. Murphy, *Diary, November 30, 1864 - February 17, 1865* (Wilson Library, University of North Carolina, Chapel Hill, NC).

Somewhere on his way home, he found refuge where he was nursed back to health. Stanley survived the war and lived until 1934, working as editor of *The Greenville Advocate* most of those years.[207]

H. Conclusion

Six generals killed, six generals severely injured and 7,000 troops lost, yet Hood claimed victory. It is impossible to imagine the condition, both mental and physical, of the survivors of Franklin. They saw their comrades die. They lost many of their leaders. They gave their all, but were drastically overwhelmed. Now Hood asked for more. He led them on to Nashville to face superior numbers, and a well-entrenched and well-supplied enemy. Hood still desperately wanted a win at Nashville. As one historian has said, Hood was too weak to fight and too stubborn to quit.

Where are those brave men who died on the battlefield at Franklin? They were buried in graves where they fell. Some time later, citizens of Franklin moved the Confederate soldiers that could be found, each to their own grave in McGavock Cemetery in Franklin. Unfortunately, most of these men lie in unmarked graves. The winter of 1864 was a terrible winter, and many of the original markers were used for firewood.

---

[207] Anne Seckler, "The Battle of Franklin", Publication unknown, November 1964.

VIII. The Battle of Nashville

A. Introduction

At Nashville, the Army of Tennessee faced the beginning of the end of the war. This section summarizes the conditions of the battle arena in which the 17th Alabama Infantry found itself in December 1864. There are few sources of information for the 17th at Nashville. There is no mention of the 17th Alabama during the battle of Nashville in the *War of the Rebellion*. No muster rolls for the 17th have been found for that period, no hospital records nor any regimental records. No letters have been found from this regiment nor diaries addressing the Nashville campaign. Captain McMillan, whose memories tracked the 17th Alabama through Shiloh, Mobile, Atlanta, and Franklin, was not present at Nashville. He was lying severely wounded in a hospital back in Franklin. Union prison records provide a list of about 160 men from the 17th Alabama captured at Nashville. Walthall's report of his division and of Shelley's brigade indicates the approximate battle positions of the 17th Alabama. Official records provide information on the strength of Cantey/Shelley's Brigade. On December 9, 1864, the brigade had 732[208] effective soldiers present, after losing 190[209] men at Franklin. How many of these men were in the 17th Alabama is unknown.

B. Preparation for Battle

On December 1, 1864, what was left of the Army of Tennessee moved out of Franklin and headed for Nashville. They would face the combined forces of General George Thomas with the Army of the Cumberland, plus General Schofield with his Army of the Ohio, recently arrived from Franklin. The next day the Army of Tennessee arrived at Nashville and took position in front of the Nashville defense line. Nashville had been occupied by the Union army since February of 1862 and was well fortified. It was probably the best fortified town in the South. General Thomas had about 70,000 men, well equipped, well fed and ready for battle. The Confederates numbered less than 25,000. They were poorly equipped, poorly fed, and demoralized after their many defeats. The Union army was prepared for an immediate attack by the Confederates. They could be confident the Confederates would not be successful because of the overwhelming Union forces and fortification.

The Confederates' first order of business was to build entrenchments and redoubts. Hood was preparing for a defensive position in the upcoming battle instead of his usual offensive tactic. During the first week of December, only minor skirmishes broke out periodically along the lines. Hood was in dire need of additional men, and, on December 6, requested an

---

[208] OWR, Serial 93, 680.
[209] Ibid, 726. This included men killed, wounded, and missing.

exchange of prisoners. The request was denied. Thomas' reply indicated that all his prisoners had been taken north. On December 7, Hood sent another request to General Beauregard for additional troops. Beauregard had moved from Tuscumbia to Montgomery when Hood began his march into Tennessee in November. Beauregard could not help Hood because there were no troops available from other parts of the Confederacy.

On December 10, official records for the Army of Tennessee list the effective total of soldiers present at 23,053[210] (aggregate present and absent at 96,863). This was a loss of about 7,000 men following the battle of Franklin. The Confederate ranks were further reduced by other logistical or mission requirements. While at Nashville, Hood sent General Forrest and his cavalry east to Murfreesboro to entice Thomas to send some of his troops after Forrest and away from Nashville.

Supplying the troops was a big problem. Hood's plan to have the railroad running from Alabama to Nashville didn't happen. It only ran as far north as Franklin. It was necessary to send troops south from Nashville to bring back supplies from Franklin. Hood sent men looking for recruits. Hood sent men looking for supplies for the army. Hood sent one brigade off to build a fort on the Tennessee River. He had barely 20,000 men when the fighting began on December 15th. While Hood's army was being depleted, Thomas was given time to bring in more men and more supplies. Thomas had staffed up to 70,000 men when the fighting started, but only used about 55,000 at the Battle of Nashville. Along with overwhelming manpower, newer firepower was also available. Some of the Union troops were equipped with repeating rifles that had not been provided to soldiers in the earlier phases of the war.

The weather in Nashville was warm, dry, and beautiful during the entire first week of December. On the 7th, the weather suddenly changed. First the wind, then the rain and cold moved in. On the 8th, the wind continued and the temperature dropped drastically. The ground froze solid. Hood in his daily log mentioned that Lieutenant General Lee had driven pickets back from their line. No mention of the weather. On the 9th, both armies were busy fighting the elements and trying to exist in the extreme cold. Hood's daily entry stated that it was all quiet in front.[211]

On the 10th, Hood entered in his log a report that Stewart and Lee's corps moved their line back *"for the purpose of convenience to wood. No change otherwise."* He does not mention the suffering of his men in the bitter cold. Many of these men had no tents, few blankets, and were poorly clothed. Many of the men were in rags and barefoot. Stewart and Lee moved their men back from the front lines to gain access to a wooded area. Both armies were stripping Nashville of its trees and anything that would

---

[210] Ibid, 679.
[211] Ibid, 669.

burn. On December 11th through the 14th, Hood wrote that there was no change to report. Again, he did not mention that the ground was covered by a layer of ice. General Thomas describes the situation on the 12th: *"I have the troops ready to make the attack on the enemy as soon as the sleet which now covers the ground has melted sufficiently to enable the men to march. As the whole country is now covered with a sheet of ice so hard and slippery it is utterly impossible for troops to ascent the slopes, or even to move over level ground in anything like order. It has taken the entire day to place my cavalry in position and it has only been finally effected with eminent risk and many serious accidents, resulting from the number of horses falling with their riders on the roads. Under these circumstances I believe an attack at this time would only result in a useless sacrifice of life."*[212]

D. The Battle

The Army of Tennessee was severely outnumbered. Hood could not obtain the necessary reinforcements from Beauregard. Earlier he truly believed that once he entered the state, the citizens of Tennessee would come forward with many new recruits. This did not happen. The Confederates were stretched very thin with gaping holes facing the long Union line. Walthall told of manning redoubts *"with detachments of 100 men, with artillery, to resist any effort that might be made to turn the left flank of the army. Between some of these points there were considerable intervals; in one case as much as 1200 yards or more."* Walthall furnished 100 men from Quarles brigade to man one redoubt and 100 men from Shelley's brigade to man another. By the 15th, the temperature had risen to a more comfortable level; which melted the ice, and Thomas attacked. The Confederates fought valiantly, but their numbers were too few facing an enemy of too many. The redoubt manned by soldiers from Shelley's brigade was captured. By the end of the day all the redoubts were taken by the enemy. Union troops then turned the captured guns on the Confederate infantry. The left wing of the Confederate army collapsed and the Army of Tennessee retreated.

Thomas believed the battle was over, but Hood was still not finished. In the dark of night, the Confederates moved south two miles. The men then spent the rest of the night cutting down trees and building entrenchments along the new defensive line. Hood realized his line of defense on the 15th was too long. He shortened the defensive line for the battle on the 16th and took advantage of the hilly countryside in placing his troops. To the surprise of the Union army, the Confederates were waiting for them on the morning of the 16th.

---

[212] Ibid, 155

Initially the battle progressed in the Confederates' favor. Shelley's Brigade (including the 17th Alabama Infantry) was located on top of Shy's Hill with 12 other brigades. Hood considered Shy's Hill as his strongest sector because of its height and steep slopes. Hood gradually moved brigades from Shy's Hill to reinforce some weaker areas of his line. By mid-afternoon five brigades had been removed and the remaining brigades had to overextend their men to cover the vacated areas. For example, Shelley's Brigade (which probably continued to include the 17th Alabama) had to extend their line to cover the area vacated by Reynolds' Brigade. To further complicate the problem, it was found that some of the defenses on Shy's Hill had been completed in haste and were no deterrent to an attacking force.

At about three in the afternoon, an attack against Shy's Hill began. The Union army threw many men and fire power against Shy's Hill. Scaling the steep slopes was not an easy task, and many Federals lost their lives there. When they reached the top they were met with fierce fighting. Shelley's Brigade put up a valiant fight and thought the attack repulsed. However the attackers broke the line to Shelley's left, and two brigades fled the battle that allowed more Federals to reach the top. Shy's Hill turned into chaos. The chaos spread to the main line. The Army of Tennessee was in a disorganized retreat. The retreat was led by the soldiers and could not be stopped by their commanders. The battle for Nashville was over. Hood had lost the prize.[213]

It is not known how many men were lost in Shelley's Brigade or in the 17th Alabama. Because of their position on Shy's Hill, it is likely that the casualty list was extensive. From available records, it is known that at least 170 members of the 17th were captured at Nashville (See Appendix xiii). Few records have been found of the dead or wounded in the 17th at Nashville or in the retreat from Nashville. An estimate of the number of the Army of Tennessee captured by the Federals was about 4500 and the killed and wounded at about 1500.

E. Retreat

The retreat continued for several days with Union troops in pursuit. The night of the 17th was spent in Spring Hill. The next day the army began the retreat across the Duck River on the pontoon bridge at Columbia. The weather was severely cold, and the retreat was through mud. The men were exhausted, hungry and demoralized. So many of the men were barefoot, their feet gashed by the frozen ruts, that they left a bloody trail through Tennessee. On December 20th, General Hood assigned Walthall *"with a special command to be organized for that purpose, to report to Major-General Forrest to aid in covering the retreat of the army, then in motion*

---

[213] Stanley Horn, *The Army of Tennessee* (New York, NY: The Bobbs-Merrill Company, 1941), 415-416

toward Pulaski, his purpose being to cross the Tennessee River near Bainbridge, if practicable."[214] The Confederates were retracing their route back to the Tennessee River at Bainbridge, Alabama, four miles northeast of Florence. Walthall's special command consisted of about 1900 men from carefully selected brigades. Walthall's men plus Forrest's cavalry of 3,000 men were responsible for covering the retreat to the crossing at Bainbridge. Walthall and Forrest engaged in numerous skirmishes and engagements with the Union army who were following them as the Confederate army moved south. The Army of Tennessee crossed the river on the 25th and 26th of December. Forrest Crossed on the 28th and Walthall on the 29th. From Bainbridge, Hood's Army of Tennessee moved through Tuscumbia, Iuka, Burnsville and south to Tupelo arriving there on January 8.

Walthall reported, *"The remnant of my command (a division), after this campaign of unprecedented peril and hardship, reduced by its battles and exposure, worn and weary with its travel and its toil, numbered less when it reached its rest near Tupelo than one of its brigades had done eight months before*[215] *...The limits of such a report as is expected at this time do not enable me to make full mention of the hard marches and severe duties...accomplished by my command during the time which it refers, nor to do more than refer to the privations and trials bravely borne by my troops, ill clad and often shoeless, campaigning in the depths of a rigorous winter in Tennessee; but it is due to the officers who commanded the several brigades under me, and the artillery battalion which served with me, and the men they commanded, having witnessed their courage and endurance, their self-sacrifice and their fidelity, during the trial and dangers of this severe campaign, that I should here record my high appreciation of their conduct and services, and accord to them with my thanks my unqualified approval.....*"[216]

Capt. McMillan of Company H provided his personal view of the end of the war for him: *"The Battle of Nashville had occurred on 15 and 16 Dec. Hoods army had been routed: he had retreated across the Tenn. And I was again a prisoner (*as were many of the other wounded Confederates left in Franklin after the earlier battle there). *On the morning of Dec 25th I was sent by R. R. to Nashville, where I began an existence truly miserable, as it is possible for a man to experience....*

I remained in Nashville until Mar 1st 1865, by which time I was able to walk on crutches. I was then sent to Louisville Ky., and kept in Military Barracks for 10 days; from there I was sent to Camp Chase, near Columbus, Ohio, by way of Indianapolis, Ind. I remained there only 7 days, when I was

---

[214] OWR, ibid, 724
[215] Eight months before was the Battle of Resaca and the beginning of the Atlanta Campaign.
[216] OWR, ibid.

*paroled, and sent to Richmond by way of Baltimore. After being paroled we were given nearly as much as we would eat (*unreadable*) for 5 or 6 days. I ate a lb. of raw bacon and 1-1/2 lb. of hard tack daily....*"[217]

E. Conclusion

In the last six weeks of 1864 the Army of Tennessee had marched over 700 miles and fought in two major battles plus several skirmishes. These soldiers had done their best, and for now they could do no more. It was time to heal their wounds and raise their spirits. Not only had they endured the wounds of battle, but many also suffered frostbite, malnutrition, and disease. Those injured and capable of travel were sent home to recover. Others spent time healing in hospitals in Mississippi. Survivors would later reorganize and move on to North Carolina to make a last attempt to stop Sherman.

On January 3, Hood sent a telegram from Corinth to Beauregard, *"The army has re-crossed the Tennessee River without material loss since the battle of Franklin. It will be assembled in a few days in the vicinity of Tupelo to be supplied with shoes and clothing and to obtain forage for the animals."*[218] Beauregard arrived in Tupelo on January 15 and saw what little was left of the Army of Tennessee. It no longer looked like an army. This telegram and Hood's earlier reports on conditions at Nashville before the battle reflect Hood's incompetence at this point in his career. Was he deliberately deceptive? Was he so out-of-touch with the reality of the situation? Or was he mentally impaired by his ailing body? Or by the alcohol and drugs required by his physical condition? Why could Hood not comprehend the terrible state of the Army of Tennessee?

What of the brave men who died at Nashville? Where are they buried? Many were buried where they fell. Others who died of wounds at Nashville were first buried in the Old City Cemetery. In 1969, remains of over 1500 Confederate soldiers were moved to a mass grave called Confederate Circle at Mt. Olivet Cemetery in downtown Nashville. The site is marked by beautiful monument.

---

[217] McMillan sketch.
[218] OWR, ibid, 757.

IX. The Final Days

A. Introduction

The war was nearing an end. This section briefly describes the 17th Alabama's involvement in the final days of the Civil War and covers the period from January 1865 to surrender in late April. As in previous chapters, there are few Confederate records to describe the activities of the 17th Alabama as the war was ending. Union records list the names of about 275 soldiers in the 17th Alabama who were paroled at Greensboro, North Carolina. The names are listed in this chapter to recognize those known to have fought to the end. After the long ordeal of war, they were also confronted with the long trek home and the devastation awaiting them.

B. The 17th Alabama in North Carolina

On January 20, 1865, Hood's Army of Tennessee was greatly diminished in size. Official records state that the aggregate present and absent was 77,366. While the aggregate present was 25,053, the number present for duty was only 18,708. There are no records to indicate how many of the 52,313 aggregate absent were killed, captured, wounded, or absent without leave.[219]

By January 25, 1865, a part of the Army of Tennessee, Cheatham's Corps, left Tupelo, Mississippi, headed for South Carolina with whatever men were available at that time. They were to join General Joseph Johnston who had been reappointed to replace General Hood as commander of the Army of Tennessee. Stewart's Corps followed January 30. It was not an easy task to move a corps from Tupelo to South Carolina. Rail transportation had deteriorated to a desperate situation. The trip started with the men marching from Tupelo to Meridian, Mississippi. From there they traveled by train to Selma, Alabama. The next leg of the trip was by boat to Montgomery where the men boarded the train for Columbus, Georgia. From Columbus, they marched to Macon, then to Milledgeville and then to Mayfield. At Mayfield they boarded another train to Augusta. They completed the journey by marching from Augusta to Newberry, South Carolina.

A communication to General Beauregard on February 25, 1865, stated that Shelley's Brigade might be retained at Augusta, Georgia, in case the state troops were removed.[220] It is uncertain if Shelley's Brigade included the 17th Alabama at that time. By March 31, 1865, the 17th Alabama was assigned to Quarles' Brigade, Walthall's Division, at Smithfield, North Carolina.[221]

---

[219] OWR, Series IV, volume III, 989.
[220] OWR, Serial 93, 1273.
[221] OWR, Serial 100, 765.

General Sherman entered North Carolina in early March. Johnston's army was positioned at Bentonville, south of Raleigh, and on March 20, Johnston and the Army of Tennessee attacked Sherman's left wing. It was to be Johnston's last major battle. His army waged a good fight, but could not stop Sherman's advance. Sherman then pulled together his entire army which outnumbered Johnston's army four to one. With this force, Sherman proceeded to surround the Army of Tennessee. The fighting days of the last Confederate army were over. Johnston began a retreat, first to Raleigh, then to Chapel Hill, to Salem and finally to Greensboro, North Carolina.

On April 7, 1865, official records indicate that Johnson's Army of Tennessee consisted of effective men present at 8,953 men. On April 9, 1865, at General Johnston's insistence, Shelley's Brigade was reorganized to include the following regiments:

- 1st Alabama Regiment that consisted of the consolidated 16th, 33rd, and 45th Alabama Regiments led by Colonel Robert H. Abercrombie
- 17th Alabama led by Colonel Edward P. Holcombe
- 27th Alabama Regiment that consisted of the 27th, 35th, 49th, 55th, and 57th Alabama Regiments led by Colonel Edward McAlexander.[222]

After the reorganization, the Army of Tennessee moved again, arriving in Raleigh on April 11th and then to Greensboro. In Greensboro, President Davis and his cabinet were informed of the surrender of Robert E. Lee and the Army of Northern Virginia that had taken place on April 9th. Soon these surrendered troops of the Army of Northern Virginia were passing through Greensboro. After some heated discussions, the President and his cabinet ordered Johnston to begin surrender negotiations.

The negotiations on the surrender of Johnston's army were conducted between Generals Joseph E. Johnston and William T. Sherman. There was some delay because of interference from Washington; but the terms were finally agreed upon by April 26. Negotiations for the surrender and signing took place at Danville Station. Thus ended the long, bitter, disastrous war. These battle scarred soldiers began their journey home in the early days of May 1865. Soldiers of the Army of Tennessee remaining on duty presented their arms and were paroled at Greensboro. They were provided with some rations and furnished railroad transportation where it existed and for as far as it would go. They were ordered to return to their respective states, and once there to be disbanded. The soldiers were told to turn in to their state authorities the one-seventh of their guns that General Sherman had allowed them to retain for use on their way home.[223]

---

[222] Ibid, 773.
[223] Jacob D. Cox, *The March to the Sea, Franklin and Nashville* (Wilmington, NC: Broadfoot Publishing Company, 1989), 216-217.

C. General Johnston's View

In 1874, Johnston wrote *Narrative of Military Operations, Directed, During the Late War Between the States*, giving his view of what happened. In the book, he talks about what he thought his mission was when he replaced Hood as commander of the Army of Tennessee in January 1865. He said that he accepted the appointment *"with a full consciousness on my part, however, that we could have no other object, in continuing the war, than to obtain fair terms of peace; for the Southern cause must have appeared hopeless then, to all intelligent and dispassionate Southern men. I therefore resumed the duties of my military grade with no hope beyond that of contributing to obtain peace on such conditions as, under the circumstances, ought to satisfy the Southern people and their Government."*[224]

According to Johnston, the remains of the Army of Tennessee, healing their wounds in Mississippi, were called back to battle when Sherman invaded South Carolina from the south. Some of the men arrived with their division. Others made their way across Georgia from their homes to follow Johnston. The men were poorly armed as much of their arms were left in Tennessee, and the South was unable to produce guns in sufficient quantities. Food supplies were sparse, and much of the available food for the military in North Carolina was designated for Lee's army in Virginia. Moving troops and supplies was difficult due to the shortage of wagons and rail. Johnston and the Army of Tennessee was hardly a threat to Sherman and his army.

Johnston had no doubt about the loyalty of the Southern individual. They gave so much for so long, but in the end, in his opinion, *"after the Confederate currency had become almost worthless—when a soldier's month's pay would scarely buy one meal for his family"*, that was when the soldier had to make a hard choice. He often chose duty to his family over military service.[225]

D. The Last Muster Roll

In *The Compiled Service Records of Confederate Soldiers Who Served Organizations from the State of Alabama*, the Union parole records provide a list of over 270 soldiers from the 17th Alabama. These men were present at the surrender of the Army of Tennessee at Greensboro in April 1865. It should not be assumed that these were the only members of the 17th who were present at the time of surrender. It is estimated that as many as 4,000 Confederate soldiers left the army and headed home when the armistice was

---

[224] Joseph E. Johnston, *Narrative of Military Operations* (New York, NY: D. Appleton and Company, 1874).
[225] Ibid.

signed. They left out of fear that they would become prisoners of war. There is no way to know how many men from the 17th headed home without surrendering. The list below is probably a list of the majority of what was left of the 17th Alabama Regiment. The list contains the names of the brave men of the 17th who remained with the Army of Tennessee to the bitter end.

The number of men in the 17th Alabama paroled at Greensboro according to Union parole records numbered 278: Company A – 15, Company B – 43, Company C – 24, Company D – 29, Company E – 36, Company F – 46, Company G – 25, Company H – 16, Company I – 22, Company K – 22. An asterisk indicates a soldier who was on the original muster roll.

Company A

Bozeman, Walter	Holcomb, Edward*	Sills, John H.
Buffington, A. E.	Montgomery, John A.	Taliaferro, Edward T.
Buffington, T. P.	Murphy, James G.*	Taylor, Joseph M.*
Davis, Joseph G.*	Shanks, A. M.	Walker, Napolean B.
Edwards, William*	Shanks, John	Williams, A. M.

Company B

Ansley, J. C.	Kuykendall, J. H.	Smalwood, W. F.
Ansley, John S.	Lee, John H.*	Smith, J. H.
Arant, Calvin L.	Maxey, William*	Stallings, Archa M.*
Blair, Jasper	McCaskell, F. R.	Stallings, J. L.
Bowden, J. S.	McIntire, John N.	Stephens, S. W.
Dees, J. H.	McKinsey, J. T.	Taylor, W. Henderson
Easterling, William B.	McKinsey, William	Taylor, William H.*
Garrett, Thomas J.	Moore, J. G.	Tyner, Josiah*
Goldsmith, J. C.	Morris, William L.	Vardell, Milton G.*
Heard, J. W.	Moseley, William	Watson, J.
Hearn, W. A.	Palmer, A. L.	Wiggins, James C.
Hughes, N.	Powell, J. W.	Williamson, Thomas
Jernigan, J. P.	Rigsby, Philo D.	Willoughby, William
Jernigan, William	Roberson, J. L.	
Kelly, J. M.	Roberson, N. F.	

Company C

Cheatham, D. H.	Pace, Russell F.	Stanly, J. T.
Cornathan, George	Parker, W. W.	Thagard, Andrew J.
Davidson, J. S.	Parmer, R. F.	Thompson, Calvin C.
Dendy, Lawson	Powell, John L.	Tyner, T. C.
Jay, James W.*	Smith, William R.*	Wallace, Abram*
Jones, J. B.	Spradley, James E.	Walton, William A.
Kendrick, R.	Spurlock, Thomas	Williamson, J. W.
Maney, William	Stallings, J. T.	Wright, Stephen M.

THE FINAL DAYS

Anderson, F. F.
Bennett. G. H.
Boswell, T. J.
Brown, A.
Bruner, J. D.
Cox, James A.
Darden, William W.*
Duffie, W. G.
Edward, C. L.
Galaway, H. J.

Company D
Gillilond, William*
Grimmer, E. M.
Jolly, J. C.
Lecroy, William D.
Lee, John H.
Lewis, B. G.
McCook, D. A.
McNair, John B.
Musslewhite, J. E.
Peacock, Simon

Pelew, J. R.
Riley, William
Rutherford, Samuel
Simpson, A. J.
Stephen, J. W. H.
Walker, W. E.
Whitehead, W. H.
Wilson, Henry
Wilson, Robert

Alexander, W. A. J.
Bales, Newton
Benefield, Calab Cox
Bohanan, James
Bohanan, W. R.
Cassells, G. H.
Cooper, John G.
Ellington, George W.
Fincher, N. E.
Gauntt, E. T.
Harrell, Samuel H.*
Harris, James A.
Heldebrand, Vanburen

Company E
Hodge, Bennett
Hodges, William
Holder, Jose D.
Hornesby, Noah D.
Hudson T. J.
Johnston, J. H.
Kinion, J. A.
McDanel, K.
McDaniel, Josiah
McDaniel, Samuel
Milton, John F.*
Pate, R. S.*
Robinson, Joseph R.

Skipper, Hiram*
Swan, James A.
Swan, S. L. G.
Taylor, W. J.
Vowell, J. C.
Watson, Samuel H.
Weathers, James A.
Weathers, Thomas*
White, David C.
Williams, Basil B.
Williamson, Thomas J.

Adams, D.
Addison, Moses B.
Amason, C. O.
Amason, W. F.
Armer, W. M.
Blair, G. M.
Boothe, W. D.
Boyd, J. M.
Bray, Henry B. *
Caffey, E. C.
Caffey, W. V.
Champion, H. M.*
Conger, R. E.
Cook, W. M.
Courtney, B. F.
Courtney, S. J.

Company F
Cumbie, J. T.
Cumbie, W. A.
Cumbie, W. B.
Dickey, C. K.
Goynes, H.
Goynes, J. T.
Green, J.
Gregory, J. A.
Halso, John William
Hicks, A. J.
Howell, W. T.
Huffman, A. J.
Huffman, B. H.
Jolly, J. H.
Kettner, G.
Larkins, J. S.

McCampbell, J.
McLellan, Charles W.*
Mickler, W. C.
Milner, W. J.
Moore, W. H.*
Mustin, William
Norman, W. R.
Pettis, Samuel
Rushton, J. H.
Scogin, E. B.
Smith, A. J.
Stoudenmeir, D.
Tankersley, J. R.
Webb, C. C.*

Company G

Anderson, G. W.
Barker, Jesse M.*
Broadwater, T. J.*
Bryant, W. S.
Cassidy, J. L.
Chadwick, John L*.
Chadwick, Rufus N.
Haggins, H. C.
Harris, William J.

Martin, John
McIntyre, J. L.
McTyre, W. C.
Paul, William
Porter, Joe Day*
Porter, John T.*
Porter, W. M.
Pruitt, Miles S.
Sasser, John W.*

Sasser, Joseph J.*
Sasser, W. P.
Tate, John F.
Treadway, Henry C.
Wilkerson, Freeman W.
Woodward, W. J.
Wynne, Clem

Company H

Anthony J. C.
Biggs, W. J.*
Carter, James W.
Daily, S. F.
Dunn, Anthony W.
Eddins, R. H.*

Grace, J. A.
Harvel, W. D.
Jenkins, A. E.
Kearley, A.
Murray, James H.
Raiford, L. H.

Rumbley, Thomas A.*
Slaughter, Samuel H.
Templin, Charles
Thames, Newby C.*

Company I

Alford, H. J.
Adison, M.
Bickerstall, R. A.
Bristow, James W.
Brown, Enoch F.
Cheatham, James*
Edwards, W. J.
Gray, Daniel J.*

Green, William S.
Harris, J. P.
Hickman, J. M.
Jackson, Joseph B.*
Jenkins, Jenkins E.
King, John
Murphy, B. F.
Ozier, J. N.*

Rainier, Joel H.*
Rawls, Olivier L.*
Roberds, William R.*
Ready, S. W.
Schofield, John J.
Thomas, W. T.

Company K

Bunkley, B. J.
Coker, William P.
Durden, W. W.*
Golson, James A.
Harrison, Daniel*
Huse, D.
Lauderdale, J.
Martin, James L.

McKinney, E. H.
Mullala, J.
Pentecost, Leonidas*
Prewitt, H. H.
Prewitt, J. W.
Ray, Andrew
Reid, Hillory*
Seawright, John R.*

Sheppard, Thomas H.*
Smith, John B.
Smith, J. W.
Steward, J. J.
Stubbs, Alexander G.
Tierney, Frank*

E. The Men Not There

Many of the 17th Alabama could not be at Greensboro. Many brave soldiers were left lying on a battlefield in Georgia or Tennessee. Others had died of sickness or wounds during the war. Others had left the army to return home to help their suffering families. Many had survived the battles of Franklin and Nashville to reach Tupelo in January 1865, but had been sent home on furlough to recuperate. Some of these men were unable to rejoin their regiment. How many instances were there like James Raines of Company H. In 1921 he stated that he was on furlough January 1865, at home in Monroe County. He could not get back to his regiment because it was in North Carolina. *"I and 14 other soldiers including W. J. Robison the 1st lt. of my co. They asked Montgomery if they could send a train to get us and they* (Montgomery) *told him they couldn't. So he* (Robison) *told us that we would hafta go back home."*[226] Men not paroled at Greensboro were required to present themselves for parole elsewhere. The service records of the 17th Alabama lists many men granted parole at Montgomery, as well as other towns in south Alabama. Henry Pleasant Yarborough of Company F remained in Franklin after the battle as a member of the burial detail. When the Army of Tennessee returned to Tupelo after Nashville Yarborough was hospitalized. He finally was furloughed, sent home, and arrived in Montgomery weak from hunger and illness. He was too ill to rejoin his regiment before the surrender and finally was granted a parole in Montgomery at the end of the war.[227]

F. The Long Trek Home

The Confederate soldiers captured and imprisoned during the war were paroled after the armistice and sent home. Two examples of the circuitous and lengthy route home from a Federal prison are described below.

1st Lieutenant Benjamin Weathers of Company E was paroled on June 19, 1865, Johnson Island, Ohio. After being given three days rations, he was put on a boat for Sandusky. From Sandusky he traveled by rail car to Cincinnati. Next, he traveled by boat to Louisville, and another train to Nashville and on to Chattanooga arriving on June 24. *"I went through the tunnel* (at Chattanooga) *on top of a box car. The sparks fell all over me. From Dalton to the Chattahoochee River I had to walk much of the way. Got to Atlanta June the 25th, spent the day waiting for the train to West Point.*

On the 26th day of June I had not heard from my people at home in over eight months. I learned that all of my brothers had gotten home unhurt. My friend Askew lived seven miles from West Point, so I went home with him and spent the night. June the twenty-seventh I walked to Roanoke – 18 miles. Bob Pate was in town. A friend lent me a horse and Pate and I got home."[228]

---

[226] *1921 Confederate Soldiers Census*
[227] "Col. H. P. Yarborough." *Montgomery Advertiser*, 1931
[228] "War History of Gen. Weathers." *Roanoke Leader*, Roanoke, Alabama, September 23, 1931. Note: This article was written 66 years after 1st Lieutenant Weathers returned home. A letter found in Weathers service record was written May 15, 1865, in prison at Johnson Island, Ohio. May 15 was after the surrender, but a month before Weathers' release. *"I have the honor to make the following request of you. It you will comply with it you can oblige me very much by doing so. On or about the 26th of last month I*

Captain W. W. McMillan was wounded and captured at Franklin, November 30, 1864. He wrote that he was imprisoned in Nashville until "*Mar 1st 1865, by which time I was able to walk on crutches. I was then sent to Louisville, Ky., and kept in the Military Barracks 10 days; from there I was sent to Camp Chase, near Columbus, Ohio, by way of Indianapolis, Ind. I remained there only 7 days, when I was paroled, and sent to Richmond by way of Baltimore. After being paroled we were given nearly as much as we would eat for 5 or 6 days. I ate a lb. of raw bacon and 1-1/2 lb. of hard tack daily.*

Arriving at Richmond a few days before its surrender, we rec'd leave of absence for 30 days and started home. At Chester, S.C., R.R. communication had been broken by Sherman, and I proceeded by Newberry C. H. thence by R. R. to Abbeville, there private conveyance again to Wash., Ga. I then had uninterrupted R.R. conveyance with the exception of a short gap near Atlanta, to Opelika, where I met Wilson's raid, which had captured Selma and Montgomery. I then went to Columbus Ga., expecting to go by way of Union Springs to Montgomery, and get in Wilson's rear, but he reached Columbus soon after our train did capturing the place on 16 April. I now went back to Macon Ga., and from there to Eufaula, Ala. Here I got a wagon and proceeded to Troy in Pike Co. where we heard of the fall of Mobile and that the whole of South Ala. Was covered with the enemy. Some gentlemen of Wilcox, among them Dr. Frank Hamilton, and Augustus Powell, were running their horses and negroes out of the way of Stules army, as they passed up to Montgomery. They gave me a horse, and I helped them flank the enemy at Greenville, and we reached Pine Apple, without further adventure. Powell sent me down to Priceville, and S. D. Andress a member of my Co. sent me from there home which place I reached 3 May 1865, having been over 30 days on route from Richmond."[229]

G. Home at Last

After all the suffering in battle: the disease, the crippled bodies, the death, the long marches, surviving the elements, poor clothing, and lack of rations, the men were finally home. However home was not the place they had left three or four years earlier. There was devastation; not just the destruction of battle that befell many cities and towns, but extreme deprivation. Where the Confederacy had been, the economy was shattered.

---

received a Suit of Clothin from a friend of Brooklyn, N. Y. also a letter stating that they had forwards ten Dollars to Me and Directed it to the care of the officer who approved the permit. Maj. Linell was then Supt. Prison. The Permit was also approved by your Self. I will enclose my friends Letter to you so you can see and make the necessary enquiries and inform me. I received all the articles mentioned except two combs which I had the permit for and the ten dollars in money. Will you please have the two combs sent in to me and oblige your friend. N. B. also one toothbrush I did not receive." Weathers signed the letter as 1st Lieutenant.

[229] McMillan sketch.

There was hunger and critical shortages of most things essential for life. This cruel fate would continue for many years as families struggled to rebuild their lives; with many loved ones gone forever.

Appendix I. Description of the Regimental Roster

A. Introduction

Appendices II through XI contain the roster of each of the ten companies in the 17th Alabama Infantry. This section defines the contents of the roster and the quality and limitation of the data. The basis for the roster was extracted from the microfilm of *The Compiled Service Records of Confederate Soldiers Who Served Organizations from the State of Alabama*. Further research uncovered forty additional sources of information pertaining to members of the 17th Alabama. This data was added to the entry for the appropriate member in *italics* to distinguish this information from the Service Record data. Sources for the additional information are listed at the end of this section. Information from descendants of various individual soldiers is also included. The quality and accuracy of the sources of information for the regimental roster are varied.

B. Quality and Limitation of the Compiled Service Records

The service records of each regiment in the Confederate Army were compiled at the beginning of the 20th Century by the Federal government. The service records of individual soldiers were composed of information gleaned from any documents available to the government pertaining to each individual. Available, in this case, refers to assorted Confederate documents accumulated by the government and stored in the Office of the War Department in Washington, D. C., after the Civil War. The documents included enlistment records, muster rolls, hospital records, discharge papers, prisoner of war records, parole records, letters, pay roll records, etc. Many records pertaining to the Confederate soldiers were lost or destroyed during the war, or never released to the U. S. Government. Consequently, the service records for individual soldiers are far from complete.

Records often contained duplicate entries for the same person because of the variations in name spelling. Some variations in spelling are bolded and combined into a single entry in the rosters in this book. Variations in spelling and the use of initials instead of full names presented a challenge many years ago to the compilers of the service records. This had to be a mammoth effort and involved the work of many people. Conversely there are instances where more than one person is represented under a single entry. During the process of extracting data for this roster, it was found that legibility of handwritings varied widely. The quality of each roll of microfilm varied as well. For example, much of the third roll of film covering soldiers whose last names began with F through Hi is overexposed and very difficult to read.

The service record information in this roster should be treated as a people-finder or secondary source. It is recommended that the original microfilm be read for verification and to obtain additional data. Errors were made during the original compiling of the service records. Errors were made by the authors when reading the microfilm and compiling this roster for the 17th Alabama.

Not all the information in the service record for each soldier has been included here. Types of information omitted include payment records, officers' correspondence and requisition requests. Personal descriptions found on discharge papers and parole papers granted in Montgomery have also been omitted. Personal descriptions include height, color of eyes, hair and complexion. Most, but not all, of the hospital information was extracted and included in this book.

Diaries, letters and records of the 17th are sadly lacking, having been lost during battles or intentionally destroyed. Many men destroyed letters to prevent the enemy from reading the letters if they were caught or killed. Many surviving records have been victims of the intervening years. Thomas M. Owen of the Alabama Archives in 1905 actively solicited documents from survivors of the Civil War. Below is the response of one member of the 17th Alabama, a lawyer in Brewton, Alabama. This response describes one example of missing records:

"Nov 4, 1905

Dear Sir:

I have your circular card – addressed to me as "of Co. H 17th Ala CSA

I was First Sergt of that Co. and in the line of my duty kept the muster rolls and other records of the Co. in a knapsack carried by my darkey boy on the march (It was too heavy for me to carry in addition to my other equipment). At the evacuation of Atlanta I lost my darkey and my knapsack and with it all the company records. The active campaign thence forward to Franklin where I was wounded and put out of the ring permanently left me no facilities for supplying lost papers. Indeed from Atlanta on to the end every exercise except marching and shooting Yankees was greatly simplified and I remember that I called the roll of Co. "H" from memory. However, one of the companys muster rolls made in March 1864 just before we were ordered from Mobile to Dalton came to my hands some while back and I send you that to keep until called for by myself or Lt. L. A. Rumbley. This you know only covers the names of members the Co. at the date of making that report. I have a copy of a diary kept by Capt. McMillan showing a complete roster of the Co. from its mustering in service until its disbandment at Greensboro, N.C. But this is not "original"

The only other original paper I have is my parole delivered to me at Pt. Lookout, Md. June 7, 1865 when I was released, and this I presume would not be of interest or worth its room in the Ala. Dept. of Archives.

I thank you personally for the interest you are taking in preserving the record of the deeds of the men with whom I consorted and walked and suffered and sorrowed and bled and rejoiced. The investment in 65 looked as if it was all a miserable loss, but some of us have lived to receive grateful installments of interest in the precious appreciation our sons are manifesting for the struggle we made for the honor of their name and the land that was to be their inheritance.

If I find any other records of use to you I will try and get them into your hands.

Yours truly   James M. Davison
1st Sergt. Co. "H" 17 Ala Inf." [230]

C. Register of the Sick and Wounded - 17th Alabama Volunteers

The *Register of the Sick and Wounded of the 17th Alabama Volunteers* is the second most important input to the roster. The *Register* covers the period from December 1, 1863, through November 30, 1864, and contains over 3000 entries. During this period the 17th Alabama was located at Mobile, moved to Georgia, suffered through the Atlanta Campaign, traveled across Alabama to Tuscumbia and then into Tennessee to Franklin. The last day of the journal was November 30, 1864, when the 17th Alabama took part in the battle of Franklin.

The medical register is available at the National Archives in Washington, D.C. The copy of the *Register* located at the National Archives is not a microfilm copy, but a book of large journal size. The existing copy of the register was hand-copied from the original record that was loaned to Washington, D.C., by Thomas M. Owen of Montgomery, Alabama, and returned to Owen on completion. The copy was prepared under the direction of the Military Secretary's Office of the War Department in July 1904. The original copy of the *Register* probably no longer exists.[231] There are obvious errors in the spelling of names. Again, those doing the copying in 1904 probably had difficulty interpreting the handwriting on the original. At times it was difficult to extract the data, i.e., interpreting the information. The book is in excellent condition, but the recording was done by different people with different handwriting skills.

The medical register lists each time a soldier in the 17th Alabama reported to the regimental medical unit with any ailment. The information for each entry includes name, rank, company, diagnosis, date admitted, and columns for comments. The comments column was rarely used. The information is in chronological order by month, but within a month each company is grouped separately. The diagnosis for each soldier is often a term understood mainly by the medical staff. Appendix XII contains a glossary of medical terms with definitions.

---

[230] James M. Davison, letter, SG024896, Alabama Archives, Montgomery, AL.
[231] There is also a microfilm copy (F326.M2M3) of the *Register* located in the library at Wallace State College, Hanceville, Alabama.

Each regiment of at least 1000 men was assigned a medical unit that included one surgeon and one assistant surgeon. All doctors were labeled surgeons, but at that time very few doctors in either army had any experience as a surgeon. In many cases, they received on-the-job training. See Section II for a list of surgeons known to have been assigned to the 17th Alabama.

The medical unit followed the regiment to each assignment and each battle. In the Army of Tennessee, sick call was held fifteen minutes after reveille. At that time the sick were attended to by the regimental medical staff and sent to the field hospital if necessary. This action was then recorded in a journal, information available in the *Register* for the one year of December 1, 1863 to November 30, 1864. The concept of a field hospital as a 'mobile' unit became common practice sometime in late 1862. Originally a field hospital's responsibility was to tend to the needs of a single regiment.[232] However, the shortage of medicine, wagons, tents, surgeons, etc., soon made it necessary to extend a field unit to tend the needs of an entire division. Any soldier with a contagious disease, a serious illness, or a long recovery period was sent from the field hospital to a general hospital, or even home to recuperate. While the field hospital tended to the medical needs of a soldier of a single division, the general hospital accepted soldiers from any regiment. During the battle of Atlanta, the wounded or seriously ill were generally moved by rail to a hospital in Macon, Georgia, or Montgomery, Alabama. After the battle of Nashville and the retreat to Mississippi, the soldiers that were not sent home to recuperate from illness or wounds were hospitalized in Mississippi. When possible, a soldier was sent to a general hospital in or near his hometown.

Confederate general hospitals tended to be located along railroad lines. General hospitals in Alabama were located in Auburn, Demopolis, Eufaula, Greenville, Mobile, Montgomery, Selma, Shelby Springs, Spring Hill, Talladega, Tuscaloosa, and Uniontown. During the Atlanta campaign, many of the sick and wounded of the 17th Alabama were moved from the field hospital to a hospital in Macon. There also is record of some men being moved to hospitals in LaGrange and in Montgomery. The policy, where possible, assigned soldiers to a general hospital or ward containing men from their state.

Medical entries recorded from December 1863 through April 1864 occurred while the regiment was located in the area of Mobile. The medical records traced the 17th Regiment to Georgia through the various battles, and later on to Franklin. The medical records place the 17th at the battle of Resaca when so many wounded reported to the regimental medical staff. The medical records place the 17th at the battle of Peachtree Creek and Ezra

---

[232] J. Julian Chisolm, M. D., *A Manual of Military Surgery for the Use of Surgeons in the Confederate States Army*, (Columbia: Evans and Cogswell, 1864), 58-63.

Church, again with its report of the wounded and dead. On November 30th, 1864, the last day of the register, the medical records reveal the horror of Franklin with large numbers of mortally wounded and dead.

There are almost 400 entries of wounded in the register during this twelve-month period. However the numbers for diarrhea and dysentery are much higher. These two illnesses were the major causes of death during the war. It was not known how to prevent diarrhea and dysentery at that time, nor was it known how to cure these two illnesses. The numbers for fevers (feb int tert, feb int quotid, etc.) were also extremely high. The physicians did not know how to differentiate between typhoid fever, malaria, or other fevers, and there was no known cure.

For many soldiers, their service record revealed only that they were members of the 17th Alabama. An entry in the regimental medical register augments a soldier's record of service. Where he reported to the regimental medical unit as late as January 1864 with fever, it confirms that he survived the Battle of Shiloh and the extreme sickness in Mississippi in 1862. If he reported to the regimental medical unit in the summer of 1864, he obviously took part in the Battle of Atlanta. That he reported to the hospital in the fall of 1864 is an indication he had survived the traumas of the Atlanta campaign. With the absence of a detailed record of an individual soldier's involvement in the war, any little piece of information is valuable.

D. Explanation of Terms Used in the Roster

Summary explanations are provided for terms used in various Civil War documents, i.e., deserted, discharged, enlisted, furloughed, and paroled. Many instances in the reference documents, terms are loosely applied or used in a more general sense. The following descriptions are provided to clarify, in part, the terms as used during the Civil War and hopefully assist the reader in interpreting some of the data.

1. Absent Without Leave

The word "deserter" appears periodically in the roster. There were soldiers in both armies who permanently deserted.

There were also soldiers who temporarily left their command, i.e. were absent without leave. Many of the men in the Confederate Army had little knowledge or respect for strict military policy. They joined the army to fight for the Confederate cause, a cause they believed in. However, if there was a need to go home for some indefinite period, they went. It was common practice for the ranks to diminish, for example, during crop planting time, or if there was an emergency. Times were hard at home, and became progressively worse as the war continued. There was a shortage of everything. What the families back home could not produce, it was difficult to buy even if they had the money. Money was another scarce item. Towards the end of the war when a soldier received his monthly pay, which was infrequent, the money was barely sufficient to feed a family for a couple of days.

Impressment of crops and livestock caused further hardship. June 1864, Governor Watts reported on a complaint received. It involved a poor, but industrious family in central Alabama. The father was 72 years old. He had five sons, two died in the army, two were still in the army, and one was in Arkansas, probably in the army. The crop had been made entirely by the old man's daughters. Members of several companies were camped nearby and found the crop. The soldiers took the entire crop with no regards to the needs of the family. The soldiers declared that they did not care who made it. That they wanted it and would have it.[233]

The families back home wrote their husbands of the terrible conditions, often begging their husbands for help. As the war progressed, and the need for men in the Confederate Army became so critical, furloughs were only granted for those not fit for field duty, i.e., too weak from disease or wounds. Many of the men had to make the difficult choice between the Confederate cause or the welfare of their loved ones.

The situation on the home front became desperate. With all the able-bodied husbands, fathers, sons, brothers, cousins off at war, there were no men at home to help with the labor-intensive chores. Slave owners were the exception and in the minority. In the later days of the war, the stealthy return of a soldier from the battlefield was welcomed. Huddleston family traditions tells how Thomas Huddleston and his wife hid deserters in a cave in their well, allowing the men to rest there until they were ready to continue on their way.

Another cause of desertion was dissatisfaction with commanding officers, from the captain of a company to the generals. Dissatisfaction with General Bragg at Shiloh, and later in Mississippi and Tennessee caused a number of men to leave in disgust. When General Hood replaced General Johnston in the Atlanta campaign, morale in the Army of Tennessee dropped to a new low. The defeat at Atlanta, the carnage at Franklin and the destruction of the Army of Tennessee at Nashville, all probably precipitated additional desertions.

No matter why the decision was made to leave their unit, frequently these men returned voluntarily. Others were rounded up by the cavalry. Still others were rounded up by the enemy. Many instances of men in the roster who were listed as absent without leave later were documented as active members of their company.

There were Confederate prisoners who took the oath of allegiance long before the actual surrender and/or joined the Union Army or Navy.

---

[233] Letters from Governor Watts (SG24782, Reel 21, folder 13).

This was often a matter of self-preservation, depending on how bad prison conditions were. The following is an example of a Confederate soldier imprisoned at Camp Douglas, Illinois: He was captured near Atlanta in July 1864 and arrived at Camp Douglas in August. In December his record states that he *"claims to have been loyal. Enlisted through false representation. Was captured and desires to take the Oath of Allegiance to the U. S. and become a loyal citizen."* April 1, 1865, he joined the 6th US Volunteers.[234] After November 1863, the option to take the oath of allegiance was severely curtailed by the Union authorities. After that time, a soldier had to be able to prove that he was a deserter, or he had to enlist in a Federal unit. He was then assigned to a unit located in the West protecting the frontier or fighting Indians. This was assurance the soldier would not return to the Confederate Army.

The term "deserter" was often applied inappropriately in the service records and is very misleading. There were soldiers who were detained because they were separated from their unit while foraging for food, cut-off by the enemy, or late in returning from the hospital or furlough. Others were not present with their unit because they had been killed, wounded or captured. John A. Watson of Company A is an example of a soldier inappropriately as a deserter. His name appeared on a list of deserters September 5, 1864. He reported to his unit on October 24, 1863, where it was determined that his right leg was paralyzed. He was granted a medical discharge November 14, 1863.

Because of the growing number of desertions and the desperate need for men in the army, on August 1, 1863, Jefferson Davis offered amnesty to anyone absent without leave. The manpower problems continued to worsen. The draft law was amended January 18, 1864, to include all men between the ages of 18 and 45. One month later the age was extended to men between 17 and 50.

2. Discharged

A discharge during the war was primarily issued for one of the following reasons:
  a. Disability – Caused by either the wounds of battle or one of the diseases prevalent in both armies during the war. Many discharges were temporary, issued to allow the soldier to go home to recuperate.
  b. Promotion – In a number of cases when an officer was promoted, he resigned and then was commissioned with the new rank.
  c. Substitute – A soldier could hire another man to substitute for him in the army.

---

[234] *Compiled Service Records of Confederate Soldiers Who Served in Organizations in Alabama*

d. Death – On rare occasions a soldier was given a discharge if it was proven that he had died. The discharge process was a method of settling an account, i.e., back pay, commutation money, pension to the widow, etc.
   e. Age – A number of discharges recorded in the service records of the 17th Alabama were for soldiers who were either under age or over age.

The discharge records found in the personal papers for the 17th Regiment cover only the period of late 1861 into 1863. One can only assume that discharges were granted after that period and that the records were lost.

Frequently the roster in Appendices II - XI will list a soldier as discharged, but the next sentence will give more information on the service of the soldier at a later time. Often a soldier was discharged because he was unable to fight whether due to illness or severity of his wounds. Later the soldier would return to his regiment after he had recovered.

In the early days of the war neither army, north or south, had enlistment requirements and physical exams were cursory. Anyone who wanted to enlist was accepted. Consequently there were numerous cases where a soldier was discharged within weeks of his enlistment. In some cases, individuals who had enlisted were found to be too young or too old and were discharged. The younger volunteers would return later when they reached an acceptable age.

It did not take long to realize that some of the eager enlistees were physically unfit to withstand army life. New troops experiencing some form of sickness was a common occurrence during their first weeks of service. The new troops from rural areas suffered more sickness than men from urban areas. Men from rural areas were more likely to have been free of exposure to infantile diseases such as measles, mumps, etc. and they were less likely to have been vaccinated. Outbreaks of measles disrupted many rural units in both the Union and Confederate armies. Terrible hygienic conditions were also the cause of much of the sickness. Men were granted disability discharges or died within weeks of enlistment.

3. Enlisted

Frequently there is conflicting information on when and where a soldier enlisted. One explanation is that the soldier signed up with a recruitment officer in his home town, but his enlistment was not official until some days later, perhaps when he arrived at the camp of the company he was assigned to.

Early in the war, an enlistee signed up for a specified period, such as six months or a year. Later in the war, the enlistment period was for the duration of the war. For the men of the 17th Alabama that enlisted in the early months of the war (fall of 1861), the Confederacy looked to them to reenlist in the fall of 1862. Service records for the 17th Alabama rarely reflect more than one enlistment. For example, James M. Davison is listed on the initial muster roll for Company H in September 1861. His service record states that he enlisted October 24, 1862, i.e., this was when he reenlisted.

Early in the war, companies were often recruited within a single county. Friends, neighbors, relatives enlisted in the same company. In the spring of 1862, the conscription law was passed and all men were to be drafted. If a soldier enlisted he could select his regiment and company. If he was drafted, he was placed in a unit selected by the government.

4. Furlough

Most furloughs listed in the following rosters were medical furloughs. Rarely was a soldier granted a leave of absence for any reason other than medical. Confederate leadership was concerned that once a soldier was allowed to go home, he might be reluctant to return. Another reason for limiting furloughs was the logistics. Transportation throughout the south was difficult. While the 17th Alabama was located in Mobile and Pensacola, the route home was direct. From northeast Mississippi, Atlanta, and middle Tennessee, it was a long, difficult and circuitous route to south Alabama. The shortage of manpower in the Confederacy was an additional reason to limit furloughs.

Edward C. Miller of Company F was granted a 20 day sick furlough on January 9, 1862, and sent home to Montgomery. He was given a permit to carry with him addressed *"To All Whom It May Concern. The bearer hereof E. C. Miller a private of Capt. A. G. O'Briens Company 17th Reg. Ala Vol aged 20 years, five feet ten inches high fair complexion, blue eyes, light hair, and by profession a farmer, born in county of Montgomery and enlisted at Montgomery in the State of Alabama in the 14th of September 1861 to serve during the war, is hereby permitted to go to his house in the county of Montgomery he having received a sick furlough from the 9th day of January 1862 to the 29th day of January 1862 at which period he will rejoin his Company or Regiment at Camp Gladden or wherever it then may be, or be considered a deserter. Subsistence has been furnished Said E. C. Miller to the 9th day of January 1862 and no pay."* The letter was signed by Captain O'Brien and by O'Brien's commanding officer General Gladden. There was an additional note on the bottom of the letter in another handwriting, *"Departed this life 12 January 1862."*[235]

---
[235] Ibid.

Furloughs for members of the 17th Alabama are listed in the roster predominantly for specific time periods. January 1862 while the 17th was assigned to Pensacola and surrounding forts, there was obviously much sickness and many soldiers in the 17th were sent home on sick furlough. June 1862 after the move from Corinth to Tupelo, Mississippi, many men were suffering from disease contracted in Corinth or from wounds received at Shiloh. When possible men were sent home on sick furlough to recover. In the summer of 1864, the sick and wounded were sent home from hospitals in Macon, Georgia, and surrounding areas. In January and February of 1865 after the retreat from Nashville, the sick and wounded were sent home from hospitals at West Point, Lauderdale and Tupelo, Mississippi. Many of these men were unable to return to their regiment.

5. Paroled

At the end of the war, every Southern male was required to swear an "oath of allegiance" to the Federal government. Towns listed in the roster where soldiers in the 17th Alabama typically were paroled included Montgomery, Greenville, Citronella, and Talladega, Alabama. Members of the 17th Alabama present at the surrender of the Army of Tennessee were paroled at Greensboro, North Carolina, and sent home. For two months after the surrender, Confederate soldiers imprisoned in northern prisons took the oath and were released to find their way home. During the last two months of the war, Union cavalry occupied south Alabama, the home of the men of the 17th. Those captured by Union troops were also required to take the oath and were paroled. The remaining members of the 17th, whether home on furlough or men no longer members of the Confederate Army, were required to report to the occupation forces and take the oath of allegiance.

6. Extra Duty

The roster includes numerous references to extra duty, detached duty or detailed for specific assignments. Soldiers who were detailed to work in the hospital either as a nurse or cook were probably hospitalized soldiers. These men were recuperating from disease or wounds and were probably not ready for field duty, but were able to work in the hospital. Other men were given extra duty as carpenters, laborers, and mechanics. This occurred in Mobile where the 17th Alabama was involved in the building of fortifications. Some of the men were on detached duty to Montgomery as clerks. Others were detailed as teamsters and wagoners. Extra duty often meant extra pay. There is information on extra pay on a soldier's service record, but has not been included in the roster.

E. Secondary Sources

This information must be considered as secondary and informative, but not error free. Some of the information was recorded long after the fact when memories had faded and details forgotten. It is all valuable information none-the-less. The *1907 Alabama Confederate Soldier Census, 1921 Confederates Census*, and the list of Confederate Veterans who attended the reunion in Greenville in 1897 are proof that specific soldiers survived the war.

The work of many individuals and researchers supplied information on when and where many members of the 17th Alabama died and were buried. Deaths and/or burial locations associated with a battle have been recorded in *The Battle of Shiloh, Civil War and Reconstruction Casualties, Listing of Confederate Soldiers' Cemetery, Franklin, Tennessee*, and *Confederate Graves Roster*. Soldiers that died in the hospital during the war are recorded in *Deaths of Confederate Soldiers in Confederate Hospitals* and *Hospitals, Columbus, Mississippi: Alabama Deaths*. Deaths and/or burials of Confederate prisoners of war are listed in *Alabama Confederate Soldiers and Sailors Who Died as POWs* and *Confederate POWs Buried in Northern Cemeteries*. In addition to individuals who shared information from cemeteries they have visited, burial sites of numerous soldiers who survived the war are listed in *Confederate Veterans Buried in Clay, Cleburne, and Randolph Counties, Service Records of Veterans Buried at the Confederate Soldiers Home of Alabama*, and "Confederate Soldiers Buried in the Old Cemetery".

Books covering the Civil War period in the counties of Butler, Pike, Randolph, and Monroe provided information not found elsewhere. Newspaper clippings on file in the Butler County Historical Society Research Room of the Butler County Library were another valuable resource. Last, but not least, the roster contains personal information supplied by descendants of over 100 soldiers of the 17th Alabama.

F. Sources for Additional Information

1. *1907 Alabama Confederate Soldier Census.* Cullman, AL: Gregarth Publishing Co.
2. Listing of Confederate Soldiers' (McGavock) Cemetery, Franklin, Tennessee. SG11134, SG11135, Alabama Archives, Montgomery, AL.
3. Hahn, Marilyn Davis. *Butler County in the Nineteenth Century.* Birmingham: Privately published, 1978.
4. "The Heirs of Anderson Seale, Ransom Seale, and William Henry Seale." *Butler County Historical and Genealogical Society Quarterly,* April 1997: 27.

5. Crenshaw, Edward. "Report of Killed and Wounded, and Missing in the 17th Alabama Regiment, commanded by Colonel R. C. Farris in the Engagement of the 6th and 7th of April." SG024896, Folder 1, Alabama Archives, Montgomery, Alabama, photocopied.
6. Watkins, Raymond W. *Deaths of Confederate Soldiers in Confederate Hospitals.* Meridian, MS: Lauderdale County Department of Archives and History, 1989.
7. "Registered Soldiers (Confederate Veterans)." *Greenville Advocate,* Greenville, AL, July 11, 1906.
8. Farmer, Margaret P. *Record of Confederate Soldiers, 1861-1865, Pike County, Alabama.* Abbeville, AL: Privately published, 1962.
9. *Medical and Surgical History of the Civil War.* Wilmington, NC: Broadfoot Publishing Co., 1999.
10. *Alabama Confederate Soldiers and Sailors Who Died as POWs,* SG11134, SG11135, Alabama Archives, Montgomery, Alabama.
11. *Civil War and Reconstruction Casualties,* SG11134 – SG11137, Alabama Archives, Montgomery, Alabama.
12. *Muster Roll, 17th Alabama Regiment, June 30, 1862 – August 31, 1862.* Shiloh National Park, Shiloh, Tennessee, 17th Alabama folder, photocopied.
13. Notes on Company H, 17th Alabama Regiment. 17th Alabama Infantry folder, Alabama Archives, Montgomery, AL.
14. Harrison Cemetery, Butler County, Alabama.
15. Crenshaw County, Alabama, Cemeteries.
16. Ronald Bridges: South Alabama Cemetery research
17. *Register of Sick and Wounded of the 17th Alabama Volunteers.* 1907. National Archives, Washington, D.C., Filed as Chapter VIII, Volume 5, handwritten journal.
18. "List of Deserters." *The Independent,* Gainesville, AL. September 5, 1863. Alabama Archives, Montgomery, AL.
19. 17th Alabama Regimental folder. Butler County Historical Society Research Room, Butler County Library, Greenville, AL.
20. *1907 Confederate Veterans (Survivors) Questionnaire.* Alabama Archives, Montgomery, AL.
21. *Hospitals, Columbus, Mississippi: Alabama Deaths.* Alabama Archives, Montgomery, AL, Folder 14A.
22. *Hospitals, Augusta, Georgia.* SG11143, Folder 13, Alabama Archives, Montgomery, AL.
23. Igmire, Frances and Carolyn Ericson. *Confederate POWs Buried in Northern Cemeteries.* Nacogdoches, TX: Privately printed, 1984.
24. UDC, Georgia Division. *Confederate Graves Roster.* Atlanta: Privately printed, 1999.

DESCRIPTION OF THE ROSTER

25. Watkins, Raymond. *Deaths of Confederate Soldiers in Confederate Hospitals.* Meridian, MS: Lauderdale County Department of Archives and History, 1989.
26. Laney, Mildred Smith. *Confederate Veterans, Buried in Clay, Cleburne, and Randolph Counties.* Anniston, AL: Privately published, 1987.
27. Rambo, William. *Service records of Veterans Buried at the Confederate Soldiers Home of Alabama.* Privately published, 1992.
28. "Roster of Confederate Veterans Reunion at Greenville, Alabama, August 21, 1897." *The Living Truth*, Greenville, AL, August 21, 1897.
29. *Greenville Advocate* clippings. Butler County Historical Society Research Room, Butler County Library, Greenville, AL, 17th Alabama folder.
30. Personal records shared by descendants of the 17th Alabama.
31. "Confederate Veterans Reunion." *Greenville Advocate*, Greenville, AL, March 10, 1897.
32. *List of Officers and Men of Company H, 17th Alabama.* SG024896, Folder 8, Alabama Archives, Montgomery, AL.
33. Herren, Diane S. *Randolph County, Alabama, and the Confederacy.* Woodland, AL: Southern Roots, 1992.
34. Forsyth Confederate Cemetery, Forsyth, Georgia.
35. "Confederate Soldiers Buried in the Old Cemetery." *Butler County Historical and Genealogical Society Quarterly*, March 1989: 3.
36. *Company H Muster Roll, December 1, 1863 – February 29, 1864.* 17th Alabama Regiment, Box 9x, Alabama Archives, Montgomery, AL.
37. *1921 Confederate Soldiers' Census.* Alabama Archives, Montgomery, AL, Microfilm.
38. Files, Lotz Museum, Franklin, Tennessee.
39. Tim Burgess, Confederate research.
40. William James Andress: *Monroe Journal Centennial Edition*, Monroe County Cemetery research.
41. *The Heritage of Butler County, Alabama.* Clanton, AL: Heritage Publishing Consultants, 2001.
42. Watts, Thomas. "January 1862 Return, 17th Alabama." Shiloh National Park, Shiloh, TN, Unpublished.
43. Family Files, Butler County Historical Society Research Room, Butler County Library, Greenville, AL.

Appendix II. Company A Roster

Aaron, William, Private, enlisted at Montgomery September 5, 1861. He was 5'6 and born in Lowndes County in 1840. He was placed on sick furlough January 30, 1862. [12]*He was listed as absent and sick during the summer of 1862.*

[17]**Aceman, J. M.,** *Private, reported to the regimental medical unit June 1, 1864, with acute dysentery.*

Acreman, G. M., Private, enlisted November 27, 1863, at Mobile. He was 5'11, a farmer, and born in Lowndes County in 1845. [17]*He reported to the regimental medical unit on March 30, 1864, diagnosis was catarrhus.* Also spelled **Ackerman**.

Adams, John, Private, enlisted June 16, 1863, at Mobile. He was 5'8, a farmer, and born in 1828 in Lowndes County. He was hospitalized in Mobile during September and November of 1863. [17]*He reported to the regimental medical unit three times in 1864. On August 26 and September 5, the diagnosis was nephritis. He was sent to the general hospital on September 6. He reported sick November 15 with acute diarrhea.*

Adams, John Z., Private, enlisted March 5, 1863, at Mobile, 5'10. He was hospitalized in Mobile October 25, 1863. He was paroled June 1, 1865.

Adams, Solomon, Private, enlisted September 5, 1861. He was six foot tall and from Lowndes County. He was listed as a deserter, but was reinstated in July 1862. He was granted a disability discharge on August 18, 1862, but rejoined his company sometime later. [17]*He reported to the regimental medical unit July 5, 1864, with acute diarrhea and again July 17, diagnosis feb remitt.* He temporarily transferred to the general hospital at Macon, Georgia, July 19, 1864, and then transferred home to Lowndes County July 23, 1864. He was paroled on May 11, 1865, at Montgomery.

Adams, Stephen J., Private, died before July 1862.

Adams, Vincent T., Private, enlisted July 15, 1862. He was hospitalized in Mobile during September and November of 1863. [17]*He reported to the regimental medical unit June 15, 1864, diagnosis was feb int tert.* He received a slight wound to the head during the battle of Franklin, Tennessee, November 30, 1864. [30]*Adams whose nickname was Dock was born March 9, 1831, Alabama, to Vincent and Rebecca Norred Adams. He and his wife, Mary Catherine Shanks, were members of Hopewell Methodist Church, Lowndes County. He died August 15, 1895 and is buried in Palmyra Cemetery.*

Alexander, William E., Private, was hospitalized in Mobile February 25, 1864, for 7 days with chronic rheumatism. [17]***W. A. Alexander** reported to the regimental medical unit with chronic diarrhea and was then sent to the general hospital on July 18, 1864.*

Anderson, W., Private, was captured at Pittsburg, Tennessee, April 8, 1862, after the battle of Shiloh. He was imprisoned at Camp Douglas, Illinois, where he later died.

Andrews, Daniel W., Private, enlisted March 5, 1863, at Mobile. [17]*He reported to the regimental medical unit March 1, 1864, diagnosis was feb int quotid. He reported again March 18 with rubeola and was immediately sent to the general hospital [6] in Greenville where he died March 27, 1864.*

Andsly, Benjamin T., Private, enlisted March 5, 1863, at Mobile, and was 6 foot tall. Also spelled **Ansly, Ansley, Andly**

[17]***Avant, Wm.,*** *Private, reported to the regimental medical unit March 14, 1864, diagnosis feb int quotid. He reported again on March 18 with pneumonia and was sent to the general hospital the following day.*

Autrey, Arias, Private, enlisted September 5, 1861, at Montgomery. He was granted a disability discharge July 5, 1862.

Banks, James P., Private, enlisted March 5, 1863, at Mobile. [17]*In May 1864, probably during the battle at Resaca, he reported to the regimental medical unit with a slight wound to the abdomen. In mid-June he returned to the regimental medical unit, diagnosis feb int tert, and was sent to the general hospital the next day.*

Battle, E. C., Private, was discharged May 25, 1862.

Blankenship, Eli, Private, enlisted November 1, 1862 at Mobile. [17]*He was wounded on July 28, 1864, at the battle of Ezra Church. After reporting to the regimental medical unit, he was moved to the general hospital on July 31.* Captured December 15, 1864, at Nashville, he was imprisoned at Camp Douglas, Illinois. [20]*He was born 1834 in Warren County, Georgia, and was living in Henry County in 1907.*

Bodiford, Aley, Private, enlisted April 17, 1862, at Greenville. He was 5'8 and did extra duty as a carpenter. He was working as a nurse in the hospital during June 1862. On August 19, 1862, he was located at Pinto Island Battery. [12]*He was hospitalized during July-August 1862.* [17]*He was listed as seeking medical treatment four times in 1864. On March 29, diagnosis was feb int quotid; April 1, feb int quotid; and June 28, debilitas. On August 12, he suffered a severe wound (left foot) during the Atlanta campaign. He was transferred to a general hospital August 14.* [30]*He was born October 14, 1812, South Carolina to Alexander and Christina Watson Bodiford. He survived his wife, Eleanor Hollingshead, who died in 1878. He is probably buried in the Highland Home area of Lowndes County, Alabama.* Also listed as **Alex Bodiford.**

Bodiford, Isham, Private, 6'1, enlisted March 1, 1862 at Mobile. He entered the hospital in Mobile September 22, 1863; diagnosis was debility. He was released from the hospital on October 2, but returned

COMPANY A

on October 11, 1863. He was placed on medical furlough on October 16, and was sent to the general hospital in Greenville, Alabama. [17] *He reported to the regimental medical unit twice in 1864. In September, the diagnosis was acute dysentery, and on November3 feb int tert.* He was paroled May 23, 1865. He was a member of the Crenshaw County Veteran's Association in 1890.

Bodiford, John Jasper, Private, enlisted at Montgomery September 5, 1861. He was hospitalized at Ross Hospital in Mobile September 20, 1863, diagnosis was feb int tert. [17] *He reported to the regimental medical unit March 18, 1864, the diagnosis morti cutis.* He died May 23, 1864; [30] *and was buried at Macon, Georgia. He was born December 20, 1839, Alabama, to Aley G. and Eleanor Hollingshead Bodiford. His father was also a member of Company A.*

Bodiford, William Preston, Private, enlisted September 1, 1862 at Mobile. He was 5'7 and from Lowndes County. He was admitted to the hospital several times in 1863. [17] *He was listed as seeking medical treatment several times in 1864. On March 18, the diagnosis was debilitas. On March 27, the diagnosis was chronic hepatitis and he moved to the hospital in Greenville. On April 25, the diagnosis was debilitas, and he was immediately sent to the general hospital.* He was sent to the hospital in Macon, Georgia, with chronic diarrhea. While at Ocmulgee Hospital in Macon, Georgia, he was placed on medical furlough. Diagnosis was chronic diarrhea and general debility. He was sent home to Lowndes County for 60 days. [17] *On October 9, the diagnosis was acute rheumatism. After eight days he was sent to the general hospital.* He was paroled May 23, 1865, at Montgomery. [28] *He attended the Confederate Veteran Reunion held in Greenville on August 21, 1897.* [1] *Born October 9, 1841, at Rocky Mount, Lowndes County, he was living in Butler County in 1907.*

Boutwell, William Arnold, Private, enlisted September 15, 1861, at Montgomery. [17] *He reported to the regimental medical unit three times in 1864. On March 2 and May 2, the diagnosis was feb int tert and on November 3, catarrhus. He was sent to the general hospital on November 14.* He was paroled June 1, 1865, at Montgomery. [1] *Born October 22, 1841 in Troy, Pike County, he was living in Palmira, Lowndes County, in 1907.* [37] *In 1921 he stated he took part in the battles of Shiloh, Atlanta, Kennesaw Mountain, and Nashville.* His pension record states that he was wounded at Shiloh.

Bozeman, Walter, Private, enlisted September 24, 1862, at Mobile. He was listed as sick in the Ross Hospital at Mobile, on the muster roll for September-October 1862. [17] *He reported to the regimental medical unit twice in 1864. On April 2, diagnosis was feb int tert and on April 17, acute diarrhea when he was immediately sent to the general hospital.*

He was at the surrender at Greensboro, North Carolina, April 26, 1865. [1]*He was born August 22, 1844, at Hickory Grove in Lowndes County. He was granted parole at Greensboro, North Carolina, in April 1865. He was living in at Montgomery in 1907.* [37]*In the 1921 Confederate Soldiers Census he stated he was born August 22, 1844, at Mt. Caramel in Montgomery County. He listed battles he fought in: Resaca, New Hope Church, Kennesaw Mountain, "all over Atlanta," all in Georgia and Columbus, Spring Hill, Franklin, and Nashville, all in Tennessee. He also stated that he was wounded at Franklin.*

Branch, Noah, Private, enlisted September 15, 1862, at Montgomery.

Bright, J. C., 2nd Lieutenant, enlisted September 61, at Montgomery. [17]*He reported to the regimental medical unit on September 9, 1864, diagnosis was debilitas, and transferred to the general hospital the same day.* He retired September 17, 1864, "Totally disqualified."

Brooks, John T., Private, enlisted September 14, 1861, at Montgomery. [12]*He was hospitalized at Spring Hill Hospital in Mobile August 1862.* Also listed as **Thomas J. Brooks**

Brown, John, Private, was captured May 20, 1864, Cassville, Georgia, and imprisoned at Rock Island, Illinois.

Brown, John R., Private, enlisted September 5, 1861, at Montgomery. He was captured April 7, 1862, at Pittsburg Landing, Tennessee, and imprisoned at Camp Douglas, Illinois.

Brown, Joseph, Private, was a musician. He was placed on sick furlough January 31, 1862, and sent to Lowndes County. He was captured at Cassville, Georgia, May 20, 1864, and imprisoned at Rock Island, Illinois. He was released from Rock Island and sent to Louisville, Kentucky, May 30, 1864.

Broxton, George W., Private, enlisted September 15, 1862, at Mobile. He was admitted to Ross Hospital in Mobile on September 21, 1863. He remained in the hospital until December. Also listed as **Braxton.**

Buck, George W., Private, 5 foot 5, enlisted September 5, 1861, at Montgomery. [17]*He is listed on the regimental medical register three times in 1864. On March 16 the diagnosis was feb int tert. On July 4 diagnosis was acute diarrhea. On August 8, during the siege of Atlanta, he was wounded in the right hip.* He was discharged June 5, 1865, at Montgomery. Also listed as **T. W. Buck**

Buck, James, Private, [17]*was severely wounded in the hip at the battle of Resaca. He reported to the regimental medical unit in early May* and died September 29, 1864, Greensboro, Georgia. *Also listed as **J. K. Buck.***

Buffington, Alfred E., Private, enlisted November 10, 1863, at Mobile. [17]*He reported to the regimental medical unit April 3, 1864, diagnosis was feb int quotid.* ***S. E. Buffington*** *reported to the regimental medical* unit and moved to the general hospital September 4, 1864, diagnosis acute diarrhea. He was at the surrender at Greensboro, North Carolina, April 26, 1865.

Buffington, Thomas P., Private, enlisted February 9, 1863. [17]*He reported to the regimental medical unit with acute dysentery on June 3, 1864. He was at the surrender at Greensboro, North Carolina, April 26, 1865.* [20]*He was born March 3, 1835, at Farmersville in Lowndes County. In 1907 he was living at Excel, Monroe County.*

Callaway, Henry H., Private, enlisted February 1, 1863, at Greenville, Alabama. He was born in 1846, Russell County. He was granted a disability discharge May 16, 1862.

Cannon, W. S., Private.

Cany, John O., Private, 5'5, was granted parole June 15, 1865, at Montgomery. [20]*He was born January 24, 1840, at Bragg's Store, Lowndes County. He was living in Conecuh County in 1907.* Also listed as **Coney**

Carnes, J. F., Private, enlisted November 3, 1861, at Camp Davis. He was a farmer, born in Lauderdale County. He died August 17, 1862 in a hospital at Mobile, leaving a widow, Martha J. Carnes.

Causey, J. W., Private, was paroled May 20, 1865, at Montgomery.

[17] **Clarke, John**, *Private, reported to the regimental medical unit on May 4, 1864, diagnosis was feb int quotid.*

Cluman, William, Private, was discharged December 5, 1861.

Cocheran, F. G., Private, was paroled May 22, 1865, at Montgomery. [17]*He reported to the regimental medical unit on March 14, 1864, suffering with chronic diarrhea. He was transferred to the general hospital at Greenville.*

[17]**Cocherel, J. W.**, *Private, reported to the regimental medical unit November 13, 1864, diagnosis was sub luxatio.*

Cochran, George Washington, Private, enlisted at Mobile August 17, 1863. A farmer, he was born in Abbeville District, South Carolina, in 1822. [17]*He reported to the regimental medical unit on March 22, 1864, suffering from rubeola and was sent to the general hospital in Greenville on March 26. He returned to the regimental medical unit on July 4, 1864, diagnosis was acute diarrhea. He transferred to the general hospital July 6.* [17]**G. W. Cawthron**, *Private, reported to the regimental medical unit June 23, 1864, diagnosis was acute dysentery.*

Coley, J., Private, was captured in 1862 at Fort Donelson.

Colvin, D. K., Private, 5 foot 7, [17]*reported to the regimental medical unit with acute dysentery in September 1864.* He was granted parole May 26, 1865, at Montgomery. Also listed as **DeVan Calvin, D. K. Calvin.**

Cotrell, Y. J., Private, [12]*enlisted September 5, 1861, at Montgomery. He was hospitalized June 1862.* [12]*He died at Columbus, Mississippi, during the summer of 1862.* Also spelled **Cottrill**.

Cottingham, Alex H., Private, 6', [17]*was listed on the regimental medical register three times in 1864. On March 19, diagnosis was feb int quotid; on June 23, diagnosis was acute dysentery; and on August 28, diagnosis was acute diarrhea.* He was a prisoner of war and was granted parole May 26, 1865. Also listed as **A. H., A. J. Cottingham**

Cottingham, James W., Private, enlisted August 14, 1863, at Mobile. He was 5'7, a farmer, and born in 1822 in Bibb County.

Cotton, Eldred M., Private, enlisted July 29, 1863, at Mobile. He was 5'7, a farmer, and born in 1845 in Lowndes County. [17] *He reported to the regimental medical unit November 3, 1864, with a case of scorbutis.*

Cotton, Whitman, Private, enlisted September 5, 1861, at Montgomery. He was hospitalized June 1862 while in Mississippi. [12]*The muster roll for July-August 1862 listed Cotton as a 1st corporal and absent without leave.* He reported to Ross Hospital in Mobile with fever several times in September and October of 1863. He was sent to the general hospital in Greenville, Alabama, October 16, 1863. [17]*He is listed on the regimental medical register five times in 1864. On June 20, the diagnosis was contusis. On July 5, the diagnosis was feb int tert. By July 11, the diagnosis was ischria et dysuria which required an immediate transfer to the general hospital. On September 30, the diagnosis was acute dysentery and on November 13, acute diarrhea.* [20]*He was born June 9, 1833, at Edgefield County, South Carolina. In 1907 he listed his residence as Skinerton, Monroe County.* Also listed as **Whitman Colton**

Cowles, F. A., Private, died January 12, 1862, in a hospital in Pensacola, leaving father, A. D. Cowles, of Lowndes County.

Cretrett, J. C., Private.

Davidson, T. F., 3rd Sergeant, enlisted September 5, 1861, at Montgomery. He was hospitalized during June 1862 while in Mississippi.

[20]**Davis, James Madison**, *Private, enlisted at Montgomery September 1, 1861. He was born July 5, 1843, Salem, Chambers County. In 1907 he was living in Florala, Covington County.*

Davis, James T., Private, enlisted September 5, 1861, at Montgomery. [17]*J. T. Davis was listed on the regimental medical register four times in 1864. On June 23, the diagnosis was acute dysentery and on July 31 and August 2, feb int quotid. After the battle of Franklin, Tennessee, on November 30, 1864, he was admitted to the hospital with a shell wound to his right side.*

Davis, Joseph G., Private, enlisted September 5, 1861, at Montgomery. [17]*He was listed on the regimental medical register three times in 1864. On March 3, the diagnosis was feb int quotid, on March 18, catarrhus, and on April 18, feb int quotid.* After capture on July 4, 1864, at Chattahoochie, Georgia, he was transferred for exchange February 26, 1865, and sent to Camp Morton, Indiana. He was paroled at Greensboro, North Carolina, at the end of the war. Also listed as **Joseph I. Davis**

[1]***Davis, Joseph L.,*** *Private, was born February 12, 1847 in Lowndes County. He was granted parole April 28, 1865, at Montgomery. He was living in Luverne, Crenshaw County, in 1907.*

Davis, R. C., Private, was paid January 31, 1864 for service for the period September 1 to December 31, 1863

Davis, Ransom L., Private, enlisted February 14, 1862, at O'Bannonville. He was captured at Pittsburg Landing, Tennessee, April 8, 1862, and imprisoned at Camp Douglas, Illinois. [1]*He was exchanged at Vicksburg, Mississippi, during September 1862.* [30]*He reenlisted the same month in company D while the 17th Alabama was at Mobile. Captured at Nashville,* [1]*December 16, 1864, he was imprisoned at Camp Douglas, Illinois, where he was paroled June 20, 1865.* [1]*He was born January 11, 1831, in South Carolina.*

[14]***Davis, Robert F.,*** *Private, was born July 19, 1843, Lowndes County. When wounded at Franklin, Tennessee, on November 30, 1864, he lost part of his left hand. He was granted parole May 1865 at Montgomery and was living in Luverne, Crenshaw County, in 1907.*

Day, B. F., Private.

Day, James A. W., Private, enlisted February 9, 1862, at Fort Deposit. He was 5'8 and born in 1836, Abbeville District, South Carolina.

Day, John F., Private, enlisted January 22, 1862, at Fort Deposit. He was 5'7 and born in 1839 in Lowndes County.

Day, William B., Private, enlisted February 26, 1862, Ft. Deposit. He was 5'11, a farmer, and born in 1844 in Lowndes County.

Dean, James R., Private, enlisted September 5, 1861, at Montgomery.

Dean, Sumter, Private, was 5'10 and from Lowndes County. [17]*During March 1864 he reported to the regimental medical unit twice. On the 10th, the diagnosis was feb int tert. On the 17th he was suffering from acute dysentery and was sent to the general hospital in Greenville on the 21st.* He was captured December 15, 1864, at Nashville and imprisoned at Camp Douglas, Illinois. [15]*He was buried at Black Rock Cemetery in Crenshaw County.*

Defraites, John, Private, was 5'1 and from New Orleans. [17]*He was listed on the regimental medical register three times in 1864. On May 2, the diagnosis was phlegmon, on September 12, acute diarrhea, and in*

September, acute dysentery. Captured on October 15, 1864, at Blue Mountain Road, Georgia, he was imprisoned at Camp Douglas, Illinois.

Denniston, John, Private, enlisted December 24, 1862, at Mobile.

Donalson, E. R., Private, enlisted August 14, 1863, at Mobile. A farmer, he was 5'11 and born in 1819 in Edgefield County, South Carolina. [17]*He was listed on the regimental medical register June 30, 1864; diagnosis was debilitas, and November 3, diagnosis irritatis spinatis*

Dorman, Ephraim, Private, was enlisted January 16, 1862. [12]*He was discharged January 28, 1862: underage.*

Dyer, J. B., Private, [12]*was on extra duty at the Gladdenville Commissary January 1862.*

Eddings, C. F., Private, enlisted September 5, 1861, at Montgomery.

Edwards, F. M., drummer, enlisted June 21, 1863, at Mobile. He was 5'9 and born 1849 in Mississippi.

Edwards, Lyman D., Corporal, enlisted at Montgomery, September 9, 1861. His home was in Lowndes County. He was captured December 15, 1864, at Nashville and imprisoned at Camp Douglas, Illinois, where he was discharged June 19, 1865.

Edwards, William James, Private, enlisted at Montgomery, September 22, 1861. He was granted parole at Greensboro, North Carolina, April 1865. [30]*He was born October 19, 1829. He married Harriet A. Thompson. He died February 15, 1876, Chidester, Arkansas.*

Evans, Lemuel, Private, enlisted at Mobile. [17]*He reported to the regimental medical unit with rubeola March 28, 1864. He transferred to the general hospital at Greenville on March 30.*

[17]***Evans, T. J.,*** *Private, reported to the regimental medical unit with rubeola March 18, 1864. He transferred to the general hospital in Greenville, Alabama, March 21.*

Ferris, James M., Sergeant, was wounded in the leg at the battle of Shiloh, Tennessee, April 6-7, 1862.

[17]***Fields, M. J.,*** *Private, arrived at the regimental medical unit October 3, 1864, with acute diarrhea, and was transferred to the general hospital October 15.*

Finnell, Jesse M., Private, enlisted February 2, 1863, at Mobile. He worked extra duty as a laborer. He was hospitalized in Mobile October 31, 1863, diagnosis was feb int quotid.

Floyd, E. H., Private, received pay for the period February 11, 1862 to June 6, 1862.

Fonville, James B., Private, [17]*arrived at the regimental medical unit March 26, 1864, with pneumonia and was transferred to the general hospital at Greenville on March 29.* He was captured July 4, 1864, Chattahoochie,

Georgia, and imprisoned at Camp Morton, Indiana. He was transferred for exchange March 4, 1865. He was granted a furlough from a Richmond Hospital March 13, 1865, for 30 days. Also spelled **J. B. Foreville**

Gandy, G. L., Private.
Gant, G. T., Private, was admitted to Way Hospital, Meridian, Mississippi, with wounds, and granted a furlough from the hospital January 11, 1865.
Gauntt, A. T., Private, [17]*reported to the regimental medical unit June 1, 1864, diagnosis feb int tert, and transferred to a general hospital the next day.*
Gibson, M. B., Private.
Gill, J., Private, [12]*enlisted September 5, 1861..*
Gingles, Harry S., Private, 5'9, enlisted March 5, 1863 in Mobile. He worked extra duty as a laborer. [17]*He was listed on the regimental medical register five times in 1864. On April 19, he was suffering with ulcers. On May 2 the diagnosis was feb int quotid, and on June 4 and July 3, acute diarrhea. On July 28, during the battle at Ezra Church near Atlanta, he suffered a severe wound to his left wrist. He was sent to the general hospital on the 31st.* He was paroled in May 1865 at Montgomery.
Goodwin, Henry C., Private, enlisted March 5, 1863, at Mobile. He was 5'9, a farmer, and born in 1825, Butler County. He was granted a disability discharge on May 29, 1863. He was hospitalized with acute dysentery at Ross Hospital in Mobile, September 28, 1863. He was paroled June 1, 1865, at Montgomery.
Goodwin, Wiley, Private, died in the hospital January 21, 1862 (while stationed at Pensacola).
[17]*W. R. Goodwin was listed on the regimental medical register June 9, 1864, with acute dysentery and was transferred to the general hospital June 10. W. R. Goodman was listed on the regimental medical register August 6, 1864, diagnosis feb int quotid.* Note: Either of these men could be William Goodwin.
Goodwin, William, Private, enlisted September 15, 1862, at Mobile. He was sick in the hospital at Mobile, October 30, 1863, diagnosis debility. Also spelled **Godwin, Goodin**
Grachak, R. I., Private, took the oath of allegiance November 1, 1864, at Tullahoma, Tennessee.
Green, Doctor J., Private, enlisted February 12, 1863 at Mobile.
Gregg, James M., Private, enlisted February 5, 1863, at Montgomery.
[17]*He was listed on the regimental medical register March 28, 1864, diagnosis chronic hepatitis, and on April 1, debilitas. He was given a*

15-day furlough on April 15. He was granted parole June 1, 1865, at Montgomery.

Hall, M. H., Corporal, died June 1862.

Hambrick, F. A., 1st Lieutenant, was hospitalized during June 1862 while in Mississippi. He was promoted to captain July 23, 1862. [17]*He was listed on the regimental medical register July 2, 1864, after being severely wounded (thigh) during the battle at Kennesaw Mountain. He was immediately sent to the general hospital where his leg was amputated. He did not recover and died at the age of 29 years.*

Hamson, S. C., Private, was hospitalized June 1862 while in northeast Mississippi.

Harris, George, Private, was captured July 1864 at Marietta, Georgia. He was imprisoned at Camp Douglas, Illinois, where he was paroled at end of war.

Harris, Joseph A., Private, enlisted April 1863 at Mobile. [17]*reported to the regimental medical unit April 14, 1864, with rubeola and transferred to the general hospital April 17.* He was paroled at Montgomery on June 1, 1865.

Harrison, J., Private, was captured February 16, 1862, at Fort Donelson. He was imprisoned and died at Camp Douglas, Illinois. Note: This soldier is probably listed in the wrong regiment as the 17th never fought at Fort Donelson.

Hartley, Hiram G., Sergeant, enlisted September 5, 1861, at Montgomery. He lost an arm fighting near Tupelo, Mississippi, during June 1862. [17]*Listed as a lieutenant, he was listed on the regimental medical register July 28, 1864. He was slightly wounded (shoulder) during the fighting at Ezra Church in Atlanta. He was transferred to the general hospital on July 31.* [39]*Mortally wounded at Franklin, Tennessee, November 30, 1864, he was buried at McGavock Cemetery, Section 75 number112.*

[17]**Hartly, Green B.,** *Lieutenant, was listed on the regimental medical register after being severely wounded (left hip) at the battle of Franklin, Tennessee, on November 30, 1864.*

Hatcher, William J., Private, enlisted September 5, 1861, at Montgomery. He was hospitalized June 1862 while in northeast Mississippi. [17]*He was listed on the regimental medical register March 19, 1864, diagnosis feb int quotid.* He entered Way Hospital, Meridian, Mississippi, January 13, 1865. He had been wounded, probably during the Tennessee campaign, and was placed on medical furlough. He was captured at Greenville, Alabama, April 27, 1865.

Hawkins, Hanel S., Private, enlisted September 5, 1861, at Montgomery. He was assigned as a nurse in the hospital June 1862. [17]*He was listed on the regimental medical register on September 5, 1864, diagnosis was* *feb int tert*, and was transferred to the general hospital on September 6. He entered St. Mary's Hospital, West Point, Mississippi, January 13, 1865, diagnosis was feb int. He was paroled at Montgomery May 26, 1865.

Hawkins, James A., Private, enlisted September 5, 1861, at Montgomery. He was hospitalized during June 1862 in Mobile where he later died leaving father, S. M. Hawkins

Hawkins, J. S., Private, [17]*was listed on the regimental medical register June 23, 1864, diagnosis was feb int quotid. He was sent to the general hospital June 24.* He was admitted to St. Mary's Hospital, West Point, Mississippi, January 13, 1865, diagnosis diarrhea. He was paroled at Montgomery during May 1865.

Hawkins, Joseph L., Private, [1]*enlisted November 1863 at Mobile. He was paroled April 28, 1865, Montgomery. He was born February 12, 1847, Lowndes County. He* [8]*was from Pike County.* [28]*He was present at the Confederate Veteran Reunion in Greenville on August 27, 1897.* [1]*He was living in Luverne in 1907.*

Hawkins, Robert F., Private, enlisted September 5, 1861, at Montgomery. He was granted a medical furlough December 1861 and sent to Pike County. [17]*He was listed on the regimental medical register after suffering a severe wound (left hand) during the battle of Franklin, Tennessee, November 30, 1864.* He was paroled at Montgomery May 26, 1865. [20]*Born July 19, 1843, he was living in Luverne, Crenshaw County, in 1907.*

Hawkins, Vincent Thomas, Private, enlisted [12]*May 10, 1862, at Greenville.* He was hospitalized June 1862 and was given a disability discharge August 8, 1862. He [1]*enlisted in the 6th Alabama in August 1862. He was living in Fort Deposit in 1907 and 1921. He was born August 21, 1831, at Mt. Willing, Lowndes County.* Also listed as **Vansant Hawkins**.

[17]***Heath, George**, Private, was listed on the regimental medical register March 7, 1864, diagnosis was gonorrhea.*

Heinbaak, W. T., Private, 6', was born in 1816 and was from New Orleans. He surrendered at Citronelle, Alabama, May 4, 1865.

Hendrick, Elijah W., Private, [17]*was listed on the regimental medical register on April 3, 1864, suffering with constipation. He returned on April 16, diagnosis was scorbutus.* He was paroled at Montgomery May 26, 1865.

Holcombe, Edward P., Colonel, was elected captain September 5, 1861. He took the rank of lieutenant colonel April 25, 1862. [17]*He was severely wounded in the chest in May 1864, probably during the battle for Resaca, Georgia.* He was granted a medical furlough May 14, 1864.

He was present at the surrender at Greensboro, North Carolina, April 26, 1865, with the rank of colonel.

Holcomb, Milton S., Private, [12]*enlisted October 5, 1861.* A student, he was born in 1845 in LaFounch, Louisiana. He originally joined Company H. He was hospitalized June 1862. [12]*He was discharged July 27, 1862.* He was promoted to ensign on April 10, 1864. He was paroled July 27, 1865, New Orleans. [17]*He was listed on the regimental medical register four times during 1864. On June 8, he complained of acute diarrhea. On July 11, the diagnosis was feb int quotid. He was granted a 30-day furlough on July 14. However on July 28, 1864, he reported to the hospital again with a slight wound to his left breast, incurred at the Battle of Ezra Church near Atlanta. He was sent to the general hospital to recover on July 31. He reported to the medical unit on August 26, diagnosis psoriosis.* Note: Probably two men.

Holladay, W. J., Private, 5'8, [17]*was listed on the regimental medical register four times in 1864. On April 29, diagnosis was paronychia; on May 3, abscessus; June 30, acute dysentery; and November 30, acute diarrhea.* He was paroled June 2, 1865, at Montgomery.

Holliday, George W., Private, enlisted October 22, 1863, at Mobile. [17]*He was listed on the regimental medical register three times in 1864. On April 6 and May 5, diagnosis was feb int tert; and November 3, catarrhus. He was sent to the general hospital on November 12.* He was granted parole May 20, 1865, at Montgomery. [7]*He registered as a Confederate veteran in Butler County, July 4, 1906.*

Holliday, Nathan F., Private, enlisted May 5, 1863, at Mobile. [17]*He was listed on the regimental medical register on March 28 with rubeola and was transferred to the general hospital in Greenville, March 31.* He was captured December 28, 1864, at Egypt Station, Mississippi, and imprisoned at Alton, Illinois. He was sent to Point Lookout on February 26, 1865 for exchange. He was hospitalized in Richmond, Virginia, March 13, 1865, where he died of pneumonia on March 14, 1865. Also listed as, **A. F. Holliday, H. F. Holloday.**

Holliday, Newton J., Private, enlisted September 5, 1861, at Montgomery (5'9). [17]*He was listed on the regimental medical register on September 13, 1864, with rubeola.* He was granted parole June 2, 1865, at Montgomery. [1]*He was born August 31, 1841, at Greenville, Alabama. He resided in Drane, Lowndes County, in 1907.* [15]*He is buried in Mt. Willing Cemetery, Lowndes County.* [37]*In 1921 he stated he took part in the battle of Shiloh, Tennessee, April 6-7, 1862.*

Howard, Henry Malone, [1]*Private, was born November 20, 1844, in Lowndesboro, Lowndes County, where he was living in 1907.* [17]*He was listed on the regimental medical register June 2, 1864, diagnosis was*

COMPANY A   155

acute diarrhea, and in October, acute dysentery. He was transferred to the general hospital on October 31.

Hudson, James, Private, was born in 1839 in Clarke County. He was hospitalized at Ross Hospital, Mobile, September 24, 1863, diagnosis feb int quotid. He was granted a medical discharge December 5, 1863. He later returned to this unit. He was granted sick furlough July 26, 1864, at Macon, Georgia, and sent home to Lowndes County.

Hudson, Joseph, Private, enlisted March 5, 1863, at Mobile. He was put on extra duty as a laborer during August 1863. [17]*He was listed on the regimental medical register with acute diarrhea June 3, 1864.* He was transferred to the general hospital on June 18, 1864, in Macon, Georgia, after being wounded (thigh).

Hughes, William, Private, enlisted September 5, 1861, at Montgomery. He was hospitalized June 1862 [12]*and discharged August 25, 1862.*

Hurd, T. J., Private, was admitted to Way Hospital, Meridian, Mississippi, January 29, 1865.

Hurley, Michael, Private, enlisted November 4, 1862, at Mobile. He was hospitalized in Mobile in the fall of 1863. [17]*He was listed on the regimental medical register suffering with acute diarrhea April 4, 1864* (while in Mobile). *He was transferred to the general hospital (*Stonewall Hospital, Montgomery) *on April 20.*

Hutson, Daniel, Private, was wounded and captured at the battle of Shiloh, Tennessee. He died April 16, 1862, Presbyterian Church Hospital Paducah, Kentucky.

[17]**Jackson, A. J.,** *Private, was listed on the regimental medical register in September of 1864, diagnosis was feb int tert.*

Jackson, William S., Private, enlisted October 1, 1861, at Camp Davis. His home was in Butler County. He was granted a medical furlough January 31, 1862, and sent home to Lowndes County. He was granted parole June 9, 1865. Also listed **M. S. Jackson**

[17] *Jackson, W. L., Private, was listed on the regimental medical register three times in 1864. On June 13, diagnosis was debilitas and he was transferred to the general hospital on the 14th. On November 3, his problem was acute diarrhea, and on November 13, feb int tert.*

Johnston, Enoch G., Private, enlisted November 1862, at Mobile. [17]*He was listed on the regimental medical register four times in 1864. On April 18, diagnosis was feb int quotid, on August 13, acute diarrhea, on August 16, feb int tert and on September 21, feb int quotid. On the last admittance, he was transferred to the general hospital the same day.* He was granted parole at Montgomery June 10, 1865.

Johnston, James D., Private, enlisted November 1, 1862, at Mobile. Born 1829 in Harris County, Georgia, he was granted a disability discharge November 19, 1863.
Jones, D. P., Private, died January 28, 1862, [12]*at the hospital in Pensacola.*
Jones, W., Private, was captured February 16, 1862, at Fort Donelson [10]*and was sent to Camp Douglas, Illinois, where he died May 3, 1862.* Note: this soldier is probably listed in the wrong regiment as the 17th never fought at Fort Donelson.

Kaough, James, Private, enlisted September 13, 1862, at Mobile.
Kelley, Franklin., Private, died 1862-63.
[10]***Kennedy, Benjamin, F.**, enlisted February 1865 at Mobile. He was born July 1, 1851* (this is probably the wrong year if he enlisted in 1865.), *at Hayneville, Lowndes County, and was living in Montgomery in 1907.*
Kennedy, William L., Private, enlisted September 5, 1861, at Montgomery. He was granted parole May 30, 1865.
King, James S., Private, 5'6, enlisted September 5, 1861, at Montgomery. He was hospitalized May 21, 1864, in Macon, Georgia, [17]*with acute diarrhea. On July 28, 1864, he was wounded in the abdomen at the battle of Ezra church near Atlanta. He was sent to the general hospital on July 31 to recuperate.* His home was in Lowndes County. He was paroled May 1865.
King, William E., Private, 5'6, enlisted March 29, 1862, Greenville, Alabama. He was hospitalized June 1862. [12]*He was listed as absent without leave on the muster roll for July-August 1862.* He was hospitalized in Greenville from March to September in 1864. He was paroled May 1865. [20]*He was born April 24, 1844, Bullock County and living in Coffee County in 1907.* Also listed as **Ellis King.**

Lawrence, D. S., Private, enlisted September 3, 1861, at Montgomery. He was hospitalized in June 1862 and captured in Lowndes County, May 1865.
Lawrence, James M., Private, enlisted November 1862, at Mobile. He was a musician. [17]*He was listed on the regimental medical register April 3, 1864, with rubeola and June 18, 1864, with an acute case of dysentery. He transferred to the general hospital June 19, 1864.* He was granted parole June 22, 1865. [7]*He registered as a Confederate veteran in Butler County July 4, 1906.*
[12]***Lawrence, Jasper**, Private, enlisted September 5, 1861, Montgomery.*
[17]*As a corporal, he was listed on the regimental medical register April 1, 1864, diagnosis was feb int tert. He was transferred to the general hospital April 22. As a private he was listed on the regimental medical*

register July 7, diagnosis debilitas. He moved to the general hospital the next day.

Lawrence, Joseph, Private, enlisted September 5, 1861, at Montgomery.

Leach, Richard F., Private, enlisted September 5, 1861, at Montgomery. [12]*He was listed as sick and absent from his company during the summer of 1862.* [17]*He was killed July 20, 1864, at the battle of Peachtree Creek in Atlanta.*

Lee, Ollin Talbot B., Private, enlisted September 5, 1861, at Montgomery. [17]*He was listed on the regimental medical register March 8, 1864, with a case of scabies.* He was captured July 3, 1864, at Marietta, Georgia, and imprisoned at Camp Douglas, Illinois.

Lee, W. H. C., Private, a signal operator, enlisted September 5, 1861, at Montgomery. He was hospitalized June 1862 in northeast Mississippi.

Lewis, D. J., Private. Also listed as **James A. Lewis**

Mastin, Z. T., Private, enlisted October 15, 1861, at Camp Davis. He was furloughed April 9, 1863, for 20 days. He was a musician. [17]*He was listed on the regimental medical register with a fever (feb int tert) on March 22, 1864, and again (feb int quotid) on April 11. He was granted a furlough April 13, 1864, for 20 days.* Also listed as **Gas T. Mastin.**

McCord, George E., Private, enlisted February 7, 1863, at Mobile. He was appointed Ordnance Sergeant September 16, 1863.

McCrae, W. W. L., Private, enlisted September 3, 1861, at Mobile. [17]*He was listed on the regimental medical register March 3, 1864, with a case of dysentery.* He was admitted to Stonewall Hospital, Montgomery, November 14, 1864.

McCree, W. W., Private, enlisted August 15, 1862, Camp Watts. [17]*He was listed on the regimental medical register with a case of roseola April 16, 1864.*

McEntyre, J. L., Private, was hospitalized with rubeola in Mobile from February 15, 1864 to March 18, 1864.

McFerrin, James, Sergeant, enlisted September 5, 1861, at Montgomery. He served as a nurse during January and February of 1862. He was granted a 20-day furlough from Ross Hospital in Mobile September 19, 1863, diagnosis remit fever. [17]*He was listed on the regimental medical register with acute dysentery June 20, 1864, when he was sent to the general hospital.* He was granted a parole June 1, 1865, at Montgomery. [30]*He was born May 2, 1822, South Carolina. He married (1) Anne Bruner and (2) Suvilla Bruner. He died February 4, 1896, Georgiana, Butler County, and was buried at Oakwood Cemetery, Lowndes County.*

McQueen, George W., Private, enlisted June 2, 1862, at Montgomery. He was a farmer, 5'7, and born 1832 in Lowndes County. He was discharged October 25, 1862: provided John Dennison as substitute.

McShores, William, Private, enlisted September 5, 1861, at Montgomery. [17]*He was listed on the regimental medical register four times in 1864. On March 22 and March 24, the diagnosis was febris typhoid. On the 24th he was sent to the general hospital in Greenville, Alabama. On April 27, the diagnosis was phlegmon. On July 20 he was severely wounded (left thigh) at the battle of Peachtree Creek in Atlanta. He transferred to the general hospital where his leg was amputated.*

Montgomery, John A., Private, enlisted April 10, 1862, Corinth, Mississippi, [12]*a re-enlistment from the 3rd Alabama.* He was hospitalized October 12-17, 1863, in Mobile. He was granted parole at Greensboro, North Carolina, May 1, 1865. He was listed in Company I at the surrender.

Moon, David N., Private, was captured April 7, 1862, Pittsburg Landing, Tennessee. He died from a gunshot wound, May 7, 1862, at General Hospital #4, Louisville, Kentucky, a Union hospital. [23]*He was buried in Cave Hill Cemetery, Louisville, May 7.*

Moon, William L., enlisted and elected 1st lieutenant September 5, 1861. He was appointed adjutant March 7, 1862.

Moore, Daniel, Private, [8]*was from Pike County.* He was seriously wounded at the battle of Shiloh, Tennessee, and reported missing in April 1862.

Moorer, Mancil R. P., Private, enlisted September 5, 1861, at Montgomery. He was placed on sick furlough January 19, 1862, and sent to Lowndes County. He was granted a disability discharge July 5, 1862. [1]*He re-enlisted in the 6th Alabama Regiment in 1862. He was born February 19, 1831, at Braggs, Lowndes County, where he was living in 1907.*

Morrison, John A., Private, enlisted March 5, 1863, at Mobile. He was a merchant, 5'8, and born in 1837 Lincoln County, North Carolina. He was granted a disability discharge June 8, 1863.

Murphy, James G., Private, enlisted September 5, 1861, at Montgomery. [17]*He was listed on the regimental medical register January 6, 1864, diagnosis acute diarrhea.* Listed as a second lieutenant, he was paroled at Greensboro, North Carolina, May 1865.

[17]***Murphey, S. G.,*** *Private, was listed on the regimental medical register on June 23, 1864, diagnosis feb int quotid, and moved to the general hospital the next day.*

[17]***Newman, C. B.,*** *Private, was listed on the regimental medical register April 25, 1864, with a case of parotitis.*

Newman, Joseph C., Private, enlisted December 26, 1863, at Mobile. He was hospitalized with fever on February 4, 1862, at Mobile. [17]*He was listed on the regimental medical register on March 31, 1864, with acute dysentery and on April 2 with chronic diarrhea. In April he was sent to*

COMPANY A

Demopolis to recover. On September 5, the diagnosis was feb int quotid, and he transferred to the general hospital the next day. He was granted parole May 24, 1865, at Montgomery.

Newman, S. M., Private, [17]*was listed on the regimental medical register September 4, 1864, with acute dysentery and debilitas. He was listed on the 6th, diagnosis feb int quotid, and was sent to the general hospital on the 9th.* He was paroled May 24, 1865, at Montgomery. Also listed as **S. N. Newman.**

Newman, William, Private, enlisted September 5, 1861, at Montgomery. While at Pensacola, he was granted a medical furlough that expired January 2, 1862. He had been sent to Pike County. [17]*He was listed on the regimental medical register and transferred to the general hospital June 20, 1864, diagnosis feb int quotid. He entered the hospital with the same diagnosis on November 7.* He was paroled May 24, 1865, at Montgomery. Also listed as **W. D. Newman.**

Ordianne, G. H., Private, 5'9, was granted parole May 17, 1865, at Montgomery. Also spelled **Ordione**

Overton, H. G., Private, was admitted to Chattanooga Hospital with a fracture of the right femur that was amputated by a Confederate surgeon. [9]*He was admitted to the hospital on November 25, 1863.* Note: This would have been in Mobile.

Owen, L. C., Private, enlisted January 27, 1862, Greenville. He transferred to the 9th Alabama Battalion, March 13, 1863.

Owens, Hugh, Private, enlisted November 1, 1862, at Mobile. [17]*He was listed on the regimental medical register June 4, 1864, with acute dysentery and again two days later with feb int quotid. He was sent to the general hospital on the 9th.* He died October 7, 1864, at Augusta, Georgia.

[24]***Owens, Henry,*** *was buried in the Madison City Old Cemetery, Madison, Georgia, on June 14, 1864.*

Owens, Wade, Private, enlisted September 5, 1861, at Montgomery. He was hospitalized in Mobile for 5 days, September 24, 1863. [17]*After reporting to the regimental medical unit on March 18, 1864, with rubeola, he was sent from Mobile to a hospital in Greenville. He again was listed on the regimental medical register August 13, 1864, with acute diarrhea.* He was paroled May 25, 1865, at Montgomery.

Packer, Robert F., Private, enlisted November 1, 1862, at Mobile.

Palmer, John, Private, enlisted August October 1863, at Mobile. He was 5'7, a farmer, and born 1822 in Edgefield County, South Carolina. He was hospitalized October 12, 1863 at Mobile. [17]***John Palmore*** *was listed on the regimental medical register with debilitas June 5, 1864.*

Jno. Palmore was listed on the regimental medical register June 10, 1864, and was transferred the next day to the general hospital. He was paroled May 1865, Selma, Alabama.

Palmer, M. B, Private, Captured April 10, 1865, near Benton, Alabama. [17]*M. R. Palmer* reported to the regimental medical unit in September 1864, diagnosis feb int tert. *M. R. Palmore* was diagnosed with rubeola by the regimental medical staff April 3, 1864, and was sent to the general hospital the same day. [7]He registered as a Confederate soldier in Butler County on July 4, 1906.

Peacock, John A., Private, enlisted September 5, 1861, at Montgomery, 5"11. [17]*J. A. Peacock* entered the general hospital July 30, 1864, diagnosis feb int quotid, and September 30, 1864, diagnosis feb int tert. He was granted parole June 1, 1865, at Montgomery.

Peacock, M., Private, enlisted February 14, 1862, Pensacola, Florida. He transferred to the 1st Alabama Regiment, November 18, 1862.

Pearson, David J., Private, enlisted March 1, 1863, at Mobile. He was admitted to Ross Hospital, Mobile, September 22, 1863, for 10 days. He was sent to a general hospital October 28, 1863. [17]*He was listed on the regimental medical register March 26, 1864, diagnosis feb int quotid, and again April 29, diagnosis feb int tert. J. D. Pearson* was diagnosed with pleuritis May 5, 1864. He died November 29, 1864, Corinth, Mississippi.

Perdue, Morris W., Private, enlisted September 5, 1861, at Montgomery. [17]*He was listed on the regimental medical register May 3, 1864, diagnosis catarrhus, and June 11, 1864, feb int quotid.* He was granted parole June 7, 1865, at Montgomery.

Pettry, D., Private.

Pickenpack, E. J., Private, enlisted June 1, 1863, at Mobile.

Pimell, C.C., Private, was detailed as a nurse in the hospital.

Pittman, J. W., Private, enlisted March 1, 1863, at Mobile. He was hospitalized in Mobile on July 28, 1863, for seven days and on July 11, 1863 for one day.

Pitts, Harvey E., Private, enlisted September 5, 1861, at Montgomery. [17]*H. W. Pitts* was listed on the regimental medical register June 10, 1864, diagnosis feb int quotid, and was sent to the general hospital the next day.

Powell, William F., Private.

Pridgeon, S. J., Private, enlisted November 1, 1862, at Mobile. He was 5'8 and born in 1837 in Dooley County, Georgia. He was granted a disability discharge December 8, 1862.

Pruitt, William T., Private, enlisted November 5, 1863, at Mobile. He was 5'11, a farmer, and born in 1823, Lowndes County.

COMPANY A

Randbrar, J. L., Private, was hospitalized at Meridian, Mississippi, January 15, 1862.

[17]***Reynolds, McCode or MacCode,*** *Private, was listed on the regimental medical register twice in 1864. On April 13, the diagnosis was catarrhus and on September 28, acute diarrhea.*

Rison, F. A., Private.

Roberson, Alfred B., Sergeant, enlisted September 5, 1861, at Montgomery. His home was Lowndes County. [17]*He was listed on the regimental medical register March 15, diagnosis was feb int tert; March 27, neuralgia; and September 10, acute diarrhea.* On July 28, 1864, he was slightly wounded (right thigh) at the battle of Ezra Church near Atlanta. He was sent to the general hospital July 31 to recuperate. He was captured December 15, 1864, in Nashville. He was imprisoned at Camp Douglas, Illinois, where he was paroled at the end of the war. Also spelled **Robertson, Robinson, Robison**

Roberson, Frank, Private, enlisted December 14, 1861, O'Bannonville, Florida (near Pensacola). He was granted a sick furlough in January 1862 and sent home to Lowndes County. Also spelled **Robinson, Robison.**

Sadler, C. E., Captain, was promoted from 2nd lieutenant to 1st lieutenant September 5, 1861, and then promoted from 1st lieutenant to captain March 7, 1862. He was placed on sick leave January 1862 and sent to Lowndes County. He was seriously wounded (side) at the battle of Shiloh, Tennessee, April 7, 1862. [17]*He was listed on the regimental medical register on March 18, 1864, because of wounds received at Shiloh two years earlier.* He was transferred from Mobile to the general hospital in Greenville, Alabama, March 21. He was granted a certification of retirement dated May 13, 1864, suffering from wounds at Shiloh (lots of information in his service record). He was furloughed by the medical board August 20, 1864. He appeared before the retiring board at Lovejoy Station, Georgia, on September 18, 1864. He reported to Florence (where the 17th Alabama was located) November 14, 1864, having lost papers that appointed him as captain of Company A. He was granted parole May 24, 1865, at Montgomery. Sadler died October 29, 1906.

Scallions, A. D., Private, (5'8) enlisted September 5, 1861, at Montgomery. He was granted sick furlough November 14, 1861 to January 12, 1862. He was wounded near Corinth, Mississippi, during April 1862. [17]*He was listed on the regimental medical register three times in 1864. On March 30, the diagnosis was debilitas, on August 4, feb int quotid, and on October 3, feb int tert.* He was granted a parole June 1, 1865, at Montgomery. Also spelled **Scallon, Scanlins.**

Schley, Jacob L., Private, enlisted June 1862, at Mobile. His home was in Lowndes County. He was hospitalized in Montgomery during November 1864. He was hospitalized in Macon, Georgia, during March 1865; diagnosis was ascites.

Sellers, Hugh M., Private, enlisted February 17, 1863, at Mobile. He was hospitalized in Mobile on September 3, 1863, for 5 days and on September 28, 1863, for 7 days. Also listed as **Hewitt M. Sellers**

Sellers, William J., Private, enlisted August October 1863, at Mobile. He was 5'6, a farmer, and was born in 1845 in Montgomery. His home was in Lowndes County. He was hospitalized in Mobile September 13, 1863, for two days. He was hospitalized in Macon, Georgia, May 21, 1864, for two days, diagnosis was acute dysentery. [17] *He was listed on the regimental medical register twice in 1864. On April 25, the diagnosis was acute dysentery. On June 7, the diagnosis was feb int quotid. He was sent on to the general hospital the same day.*

Selman, Thomas B., Private, enlisted December 23, 1862, at Mobile. Also listed as **Thomas D. Selman.**

Sexton, A. C., Private, 5'8, granted parole June 2, 1865 in Montgomery.
[17]*A. E. Sexton was listed on the regimental medical register on April 7, 1864, diagnosis feb int quotid*

Shanks, A. M., Private, enlisted September 5, 1861, at Montgomery. He was wounded at the battle of Shiloh, Tennessee, in April 1862. He was hospitalized in Mobile October 20, 1863. He was paroled at Greensboro, North Carolina, April 1865.

Shanks, G. P., Private, enlisted September 5, 1861, at Montgomery. He was discharged July 4, 1862.

Shanks, James Jordan, Sergeant, enlisted September 5, 1861, at Montgomery. He was promoted to sergeant July 23, 1862. He was hospitalized October 25, 1863. [17]*He was listed on the regimental medical register April 2, 1864, diagnosis feb int tert. After the battle of Resaca on May 5, he reported to the regimental hospital with a slight wound (foot).* [30]*Family tradition states that he was killed at the battle of Franklin, Tennessee.* [10]*A planter, he was born October 23, 1838.* [30]*He was born October 23, 1838 to Robert M. and Martha McFerrin Shanks. His wife was Margaret E. Bruner.*

Shanks, John, Private, enlisted August 10, 1863, at Mobile. He was 6'1, a farmer, and born in 1821 in Abbeville, South Carolina. He was hospitalized in Mobile September 8, 1863, for 9 days and September 22, 1863, for 15 days. He was also hospitalized in Mobile October 17, 1863, and in Macon, Georgia, November 9, 1864. He was paroled at Greensboro, North Carolina, April 1865. [17]***John Shanks** was listed on the regimental medical register August 13, 1864, diagnosis was irritatis spinatis, and in September, acute rheumatism. **Jno. Shanks** was listed*

April 25, 1864, diagnosis was pleuritis. (Note: See John Wesley Shanks below.) *On October 9, the diagnosis was feb int tert. He was transferred to the general hospital on October 15.*

Shanks, John W., Private, enlisted September 5, 1861, at Montgomery. [17]*G. W. Shanks was diagnosed with pneumonia on April 10, 1864. He was transferred to the general hospital two days later.* [17]*On July 28, 1864, at the battle of Ezra Church in Atlanta,* **Jno. Shanks** *was slightly wounded in both legs and was sent to the general hospital on July 31.* [20]*In 1907,* **John W. Shanks** *stated that he was wounded July 1864 in both legs and was never able to do service again.* He was hospitalized with wounds at Meridian, Mississippi, March 24, 1865. He was 5'11 and paroled at Montgomery on May 30, 1865. [37]***John Wesley Shanks** was born April 17, 1841, in Lowndes County. He was living in St. Clair County in 1921 when he stated he took part in the battles of Atlanta, New Hope Church and Marietta, Georgia. He also stated he was wounded July 28, 1864, at Atlanta.* (See John Shanks above.)

[17] **Shanks, Marshall Henry,** *Private, is listed on the regimental medical register six times in 1864. On March 22, diagnosis was debilitas; on April 17, acute dysentery; on May 3, debilitas; and on August 19, feb int tert. In October, the diagnosis was again feb int tert when he was transferred tot the general hospital October 31. On November 13, diagnosis was feb int tert.* [37]*He was born March 1, 1847, in Lowndes County. He was living in Mt. Willing, Lowndes County in 1921 when he stated he took part in the battles of Resaca, New Hope Church, Kennesaw Mountain, Atlanta, Franklin, and Nashville*

Shields, Milton J., Private, enlisted February 14, 1862, O'Bannonville, Florida, near Pensacola. He was slightly wounded in the arm at the battle of Shiloh, Tennessee, April 1862. He was hospitalized October 30, 1863, at Mobile. [17]*He was slightly wounded (face) at the battle of Peachtree Creek on July 20, 1864, and sent to the general hospital on the 21st. As a corporal, he was listed on the regimental medical register in September, diagnosis feb int tert.*

Shores, William H., Private, was hospitalized in Mobile January 27, 1864, diagnosis was an ulcer. This is probably the **W. M. Shores** [24]*buried at Stonewall Confederate Cemetery in Griffin, Georgia.*

Sills, John H., Private, enlisted November 1, 1862, at Mobile. [17]*He was listed on the regimental medical register on July 4, 1864, with an acute case of diarrhea. He was back in the hospital on the 18th, diagnosis feb int quotid and sent on to the general hospital two days later. On November 3, 1864, he reported to the regimental hospital, diagnosis feb int tert, and was sent to the general hospital on the 12th.* He was paroled at Greensboro, North Carolina, April 1865.

Sloan, D. B., Private, enlisted December 1, 1863, at Mobile. He was 5'8, a farmer, and born 1845 in Lowndes County. [17]*He was listed on the regimental medical register six times in 1864. With a case of rubeola on March 30, he was placed in the general hospital on the 31st. On April 20, the diagnosis was debilitas; on May 3, parotitis; on July 6, acute diarrhea; on August 2, feb int tert and on November 3, catarrhus.* See Service Records for G. M. Acreman.

Sloan, Hugh, Private, enlisted August 14, 1863, at Mobile. He was 5'11, a farmer, and born in 1820 in Duplin County, North Carolina. His home was in Lowndes County. [17] *He was listed on the regimental medical register three times in 1864. On March 10, the diagnosis was feb int quotid; on September 4, debilitas; and on November 3, acute diarrhea.*

Smith, W. B., Private, captured April 6, 1862, at Pittsburg Landing, Tennessee, he was imprisoned at Camp Douglas, Illinois, where he died June 10, 1862.

Spivey, J. J., Private, was granted sick furlough January 21, 1862, for 20 days and sent home to Lowndes County. He was discharged May 25, 1862.

Stewart, B. F., Private, died January 26, 1862, at the hospital in Pensacola.

Stewart, John M., Private, enlisted January 10, 1862, at Fayetteville. [12]*He transferred from the 5th Alabama April 26, 1862.*

Stewart, William M., Private, enlisted September 5, 1862, at Mobile. He died March 4, 1863, in Mobile.

Stringfellow, George, Private, enlisted December 1, 1863, at Mobile. He was 5'8, a farmer, and born in 1838, Lowndes County. [17]*He was listed on the regimental medical register April 27 and May 3, 1864, diagnosis parotitis.*

Stringfellow, Thomas W., Private, enlisted March 1, 1863, at Mobile.

Sullivan, E., Private, died January 11, 1862, at the hospital in Pensacola.

Sullivan, James M., Private, enlisted March 5, 1863, at Mobile. He was hospitalized in Mobile October 29, 1863. [17]*He was hospitalized on March 18, 1864, with a case of rubeola and sent to the general hospital in Greenville on the 19th.* This may be the **J. W. Sullivan** [24]*buried at Rose Hill Cemetery in Macon, Georgia, on June 6 or September 6, 1864, grave 104.*

[1]***Taliaferro, Edward Taylor,*** *Private, was born March 10, 1845, at Rose Hill, Orange County, Virginia. He was paroled at Greensboro, North Carolina, April 1865. He was living in Birmingham in 1907.*

Taylor, Charles P., Private, enlisted December 20, 1861, at Newbern, northwest of Selma, Alabama. He was 5', a farmer, and born in 1846 in Cherokee County. [12]*He transferred from the 5th Alabama Battalion on*

April 26, 1862. He was discharged December 23, 1862. [20]*He was born July 13, 1840, and was living in Fayette in 1907.*

Taylor, Dixon L., Private, enlisted March 29, 1862, at Greenville. He was admitted to Ross Hospital in Mobile September 13, 1863, diagnosis was feb int tert. [17]*He was severely wounded in the left thigh on July 28, 1864, at the battle of Ezra Church near Atlanta and was sent to the general hospital on the 31st.* He was 5'11, a farmer, and was born in 1837 in Lowndes County.

Taylor, George T., Private, enlisted July 20, 1863, at Mobile. He was 5'5, a farmer, and born in 1845 in Montgomery County. [17]*He was listed on the regimental medical register with an acute case of diarrhea on the 3rd and 16th of August in 1864.*

Taylor, James P., Private, transferred from the 5th Alabama Battalion on April 26, 1862. He was discharged December 23, 1862: expiration of service.

Taylor, Joseph M., Private, enlisted September 5, 1861, at Montgomery. He was placed on sick furlough January 1862. He was promoted to 4th corporal on September 23, 1862, to 3rd corporal on March 22, 1863, and to sergeant on November 1864. [17]*He reported at the regimental medical unit March 15, 1864, diagnosis was feb int tert and again in October with acute rheumatism. He was sent to the general hospital October 31.* He was listed as first lieutenant when paroled at Greensboro, North Carolina, April 1865.

Taylor, John, Private, enlisted September 5, 1861, at Montgomery. He was placed on sick furlough January 29, 1862, for 20 days and sent home to Lowndes County. [17]***John Taylor** was listed the regimental medical register June 23, 1864, diagnosis feb int tert. He was wounded in the left hip at the battle of Peachtree Creek, Georgia, July 20, 1864. He was sent to the general hospital the next day.* Note: This could be **John P. Taylor** below. Captured December 16, 1864, at Nashville, he was imprisoned at Camp Douglas, Illinois, where he died December 30, 1864. He was buried in lot number 366-2 at Chicago City Cemetery.

Taylor, John P., Private, enlisted December 20, 1861, Newbern, northwest of Selma, Alabama. He was 5'6, a farmer, and born in 1845 in Cherokee County. He was discharged December 23, 1862. [17]*He was listed on the regimental medical register three times in 1864. On July 1, diagnosis was hemeralopia; on July 30, acute colitis; and on August 7, feb int tert.* [22]*He died in a hospital in Augusta, Georgia, probably in 1864.*

Taylor, Samuel B., Corporal, enlisted September 5, 1861, at Montgomery. He was promoted from 3rd corporal to 2nd corporal March 22, 1863. He was a sergeant by April 1862 when he was wounded in his left thigh at the battle of Shiloh, Tennessee. [12]*He was listed as absent without* *leave on the muster roll for July-August 1862.* He was hospitalized with tonsillitis March 13, 1864. [17]*He was listed on the regimental medical register May 2, 1864, again with tonsillitis. He was severely wounded in the thigh on July 20, 1864, at the battle of Peachtree Creek, Georgia, and was left on the field.* He probably was captured at Peachtree Creek as he died in a Union hospital October 20, 1864. He was single and may have died in Chattanooga.

Taylor, William Alexander, Private, [12]*enlisted September 1861, Montgomery. He was discharged July 5, 1862.* He re-enlisted September 26, 1862, at Mobile. He was 5'8 and from Lowndes County. [17]*The regimental medical records indicate that he reported to the hospital six times in 1864. On March 4 and April 1, diagnosis was feb int tert; on both April 13 and June 15, phlegmon; and on July 3, feb int quotid. During the battle at Ezra Church in Atlanta July 28, he was wounded (right side and back).* He was hospitalized at the general hospital in Macon, Georgia, during August 1864 with a gunshot wound to spine that he received at Altoona, Georgia. He was paroled on June 22, 1865. [10]*He was born October 17, 1842, in Lowndes County, and living in Montgomery in 1907.*

Thigpen, David M., Private, enlisted January 31, 1863, at Mobile, 5'8. He was hospitalized with debility October 5, 1863, for 7 days. He was placed on sick furlough from Mobile December 1, 1863, for 30 days. He was hospitalized in Mobile February 14, 1864, for ulcers for 3 days. He was granted parole June 1865.

Thompson, James S., Private, was hospitalized October 6, 1863, in Mobile. [6]*He died in a Mobile hospital October 24, 1863.*

Thornton, John E., Private, enlisted May 10, 1862, Greenville. He was 5'11, a farmer, and born January 18, 1836, in Conecuh County. [17]*He was listed on the regimental medical register on July 3, diagnosis feb int tert. He was listed on July 28, 1864 with a severe wound to the left side, which occurred at the battle of Ezra Church in Atlanta. He was sent to the general hospital on the 31st to recover.* Granted parole June 5, 1865 in Montgomery. [10]*He was living in Butler County in 1907.*

Till, William T., Private, enlisted September 5, 1861, at Montgomery. He was 5'5 and paroled June 15, 1865, Montgomery. [20]*He was born August 17, 1839, at Bragg's Store, Lowndes County, and living in Caledonia, Wilcox County in 1907.* [30]*His parents were Jacob and Eliza Ward Till. His wife was Jane Autry. He died April 8, 1914, Wilcox County.*

Tomlinson, J. S., Private, enlisted February 8, 1863, at Mobile. He was 5'11, a farmer, and born in 1826 in Lowndes County. He died in Mobile October 24, 1863, leaving mother, Malinda Tomlinson. Also listed as **J. C. Tomlinson**

Tomlinson, William B., Private, enlisted October 1, 1861, at Camp Davis. He was captured December 17, 1864, at Franklin, Tennessee. He was imprisoned at Camp Chase, Ohio, where he died of pneumonia March 18, 1865, [10]*and is buried in lot number 1701.*

Turner, William, Private, enlisted October 1, 1861, at Camp Davis. His father was A. R. Turner. [12]*He died in the hospital at Lauderdale, Mississippi, February 12, 1862.*

Verdery, Samuel A., 2nd Lieutenant, elected July 23, 1862. [17]*He suffered a severe face wound at the battle of Franklin, Tennessee, November 30, 1864.* He was granted a medical furlough February 5, 1865, while hospitalized at Way Hospital, Meridian, Mississippi.

Vernell, Calvin C., Private, enlisted September 5, 1861, at Montgomery. He was hospitalized at Mobile July 22, 1863, for a month. [17]*He was listed on the regimental medical register March 22, 1864, diagnosis abscessus. He was listed again August 18, 1864, with an acute case of diarrhea.* [30]*He applied for a pension in Lincoln County, Tennessee (See Application #S2153). Also spelled* **Varnell, Vernelle.**

Walker, Franklin L., Private, was granted sick furlough January 2, 1862, and sent home to Lowndes County.

Walker, Napoleon B., Private, enlisted December 23, 1862, at Mobile. He was hospitalized in Mobile September 28, 1863, for 10 days. [17]*He was listed on the regimental medical register four times in 1864. On April 3, diagnosis was catarrhus. On April 15, diagnosis was rubeola, and he was sent to the general hospital April 17. On August 30, diagnosis was feb int quotid. On September 4, diagnosis was feb remitt, and he was sent to general hospital on same day.* He was paroled at Greensboro, North Carolina, April 1865.

Watson, F. M., Private, 5'10, enlisted June 6, 1863, at Mobile. He was born about 1846 in Tallapoosa. He was discharged March 23, 1864: under 18. He was paroled June 6, 1865, in Montgomery. Also listed as **J. M. Watson**

Watson, John A., Private, enlisted November 1, 1862, at Mobile. He was 5'9, a farmer, and born in 1834 in Greene County, Georgia. He was listed as a deserter September 5, 1863. He reported to his company October 24, 1863, bringing evidence of sickness. He was discharged November 14, 1863, reason: his right leg was paralyzed.

Weatherford, Stephen, Private, was seriously wounded (hip) at the battle of Shiloh, Tennessee, April 1862. He was reported missing February 17, 1863. Mother, Louisa M. Shackleford, applied for death benefits.

Weaver, D. F., Private, was granted parole May 21, 1865 at Talladega.

Wetherford, James, Private, died of a gunshot wound April 18, 1862, on the Steamer Imperial on the way to St. Louis after being captured at the battle of Shiloh, Tennessee. [10]*He was buried at St. Louis, lot number #4982.*

White, James, Private, enlisted September 5, 1861, at Montgomery,

Wiggins, W. D., Private, 5'7, [17]*was listed on the regimental medical register, diagnosis was feb int quotid, May 5 and July 3, 1864. On November 11, 1864, he was listed again, acute dysentery.* He was paroled May 30, 1865.

Williams, A. M., Private, enlisted March 1, 1862, at Greenville, Alabama. He was at the surrender at Greensboro, North Carolina, April 1865.

Williams, G. W., Private, enlisted September 5, 1861, at Montgomery. He was hospitalized June 1862. [12]*He died during the summer of 1862.*

Williams, John, Private, was hospitalized in Mobile February 24, 1864 with hypertrophy of the heart. He was placed on sick furlough March 1, 1864 for 30 days. He was hospitalized March 28 to April 14, 1864. He was hospitalized July 14 to July 20, 1864. Medical certification, dated April 20, 1864 stated he was unable to perform duties of soldier in field due to organic disease of heart, a permanent disability and was recommended for detail as an engineer.

Williamson, R. M., 2nd Lieutenant, was appointed September 5, 1861, and resigned April 30, 1862, at Corinth, Mississippi.

Wilson, David R., Private, was 5'9 and enlisted January 28, 1863. He was hospitalized at Ross Hospital, Mobile, April 22, 1863, for five months. [17]*He was listed on the regimental medical register on March 6, 1864, diagnosis feb int tert, and on September 25, 1864, fibris typhoides and was admitted to the general hospital the next day.* He was paroled June 5, 1865, Montgomery. [28]*He was present at the Confederate Veterans Reunion in Greenville August 21, 1897. He was living in Butler County July 4, 1906.* [30]*David Wilson was born May 9, 1825. He transferred from Company G, 9th Alabama Infantry. His home was in Buckaloo, Alabama. He died May 22, 1910, and was buried at Shiloh Primitive Baptist Church.*

Wingate, W. A., Private, was captured at South Mountain, Georgia, July 4, 1864, and imprisoned at Point Lookout, Virginia.

Wright, James N., Private, 6', enlisted September 15, 1862, at Mobile. [17]*He was listed on the regimental medical register with acute diarrhea on August 7, 1864, and on April 9, 1864, with acute dysentery. He was sent to the general hospital on April 12.* He was paroled June 19, 1865, Montgomery. [17]***Jas. M. Wright** received a head wound at the battle of Franklin, Tennessee, November 30, 1864.*

Wright, Joseph T., Private, enlisted September 15, 1862, at Mobile

Appendix III. Company B Roster

[17]**Ansley, J. C.**, Private, was listed on the regimental hospital register five times. The first was December 6, 1863, diagnosis feb int quotid. In 1864, he reported on January 12 and February 28, diagnosis feb int tert. On August 3, he reported to the hospital with acute dysentery. J. Ansley reported on January 30, diagnosis feb int quotid. J. H. Ansley reported on January 18, diagnosis catarrhus. [31]He was listed as a member of Company C at the surrender April 26, 1865, at Greensboro, North Carolina.

Ansley, John S., Corporal, enlisted at Montgomery September 14, 1861. [17]He was listed on the regimental medical register January 29, 1864, diagnosis was feb int tert; February 14, feb int tert; and March 9, acute dysentery. On November 9, he was diagnosed November 9 with pneumonia and transferred to the general hospital. [31]He was at the surrender April 26, 1865, Greensboro, North Carolina, listed as a member of Company C.

Ansley, Josiah, Private, was admitted to Ross Hospital in Mobile September 1, 1863, for 30 days and on January 20, 1864, for six days, diagnosis was feb int quotid. [17]He was listed on the regimental medical register December 24, 1863, diagnosis was feb int tert.

Arant, Calvin L., Private, enlisted September 6, 1862, at South Butler. [17]He was listed on the regimental medical register February 18, diagnosis was colica and November 3, 1864, icterus. He moved to the general hospital on November 19. He was hospitalized with wounds in Meridian, Mississippi, January 18, 1865. [31]He was at the surrender April 26, 1865, at Greensboro, North Carolina, listed as a member of Company C. [30]He was born May 7, 1834, to Jacob and Barbara Till Arant. He married (1)Eveline McCormack and (2)Mary Caroline Williams. He was living in South Butler in 1870, in Georgiana in 1880, and in Butler County in 1900. He died February 19, 1907. Also listed as **Aaron**.

Arant, Elvin P., Sergeant, enlisted September 14, 1861, at Montgomery. [17]He was listed on the regimental medical register in 1864 with acute diarrhea on June 15 and August 19 and September 11, with feb int tert.

Autrey, Benjamin F., Private, [17]was listed on the regimental medical register five times in 1864. In May he was diagnosed with acute diarrhea and was declared missing. On June 9, he had acute diarrhea and was sent to the general hospital two days later. On July 5, the diagnosis was feb remitt. He was transferred to the general hospital the next day. On September 12, the diagnosis was feb int quotid. On November 3, the diagnosis was contusio. He was captured at Nashville, December 15, 1864. He died of pneumonia February 1, 1865, at Camp Douglas, Illinois, and was buried in lot number 656, Block 2, Chicago

City Cemetery. [30]*Autrey was born in 1846, Butler County, to Robert and Elizabeth Till Autrey.*

Baird, Isaac R., Private, died September 16, 1864.
Baldwin, Jesse, Private, enlisted November 26, 1861, at Pensacola. [17]*He was listed on the regimental medical register four times with the same diagnosis, feb int tert: December 25, 1863, January 23, February 23, and March 29, 1864. On April 22,1864, the diagnosis was feb int quotid.*
Barnes, Julius E., Private, enlisted September 9, 1861, at Montgomery. He was 5'7 and born in 1841 in Dallas County. He was appointed second lieutenant in May 1862. [3]*In 1921, he was living in Wilcox County and stated that he fought at the battle of Shiloh.*
Barrett, T. J., Captain, enlisted in the 6th Georgia Regiment May 11, 1861, as first lieutenant. He resigned January 20, 1862. By special order he was appointed captain of Company C, 17th Alabama by General Braxton Bragg May 4, 1862. Bragg transferred him to Company B from C June 26, 1862. Barrett resigned June 25, 1862. He was appointed first lieutenant and ordnance officer of Jackson's Brigade March 7, 1863. He was at the surrender at Greensboro, North Carolina, April 26, 1865.
Barrett, J. R., Private, was a prisoner in 1862. [17]*He was listed on the regimental medical register three times in 1864. The diagnosis was pertussis on July 1, acute diarrhea on August 9, and catarrhus on August 20..*
Barrett, Melvin T., Private, enlisted September 14, 1861, at Montgomery. [17]*He was listed on the regimental medical register: December 17, 1863, diagnosis was feb int quotid, and June 15, 1864, phlegomon. Also listed as* **T. M. Baviett.**
[17]***Barrett, T. M.**, Private, was listed on the regimental medical register four times in 1864: January 5, the diagnosis was catarrhus; February 2 and March 25, feb int quotid; and November 5, acute diarrhea.*
Barrett, William R., Private, enlisted September 7, 1862, Mobile. [17]*He was listed on the regimental medical register January 18, 1864; diagnosis was neuralgia. He was transferred to the general hospital on the 20th. He was listed again February 24, 1864, diagnosis was feb typhoides. He was transferred to the general hospital at Mobile on the 25th.* **Ruffin Barrett** *reported to the hospital on June 18, diagnosis catarrhus.*
Barton, M. C., Private, was discharged December 17, 1861.
Beesley, Abram, Private, enlisted September 6, 1862, at South Butler. [17]*He was listed on the regimental medical register December 10 and 27, 1863, diagnosis feb int tert. On March 20, 1864, diagnosis was acute dysentery, and on April 26, feb int quotid. In May, probably at the*

battle of Resaca, Georgia, he suffered a slight wound in the shoulder. On June 1, he reported to the hospital with pneumonia and was sent to the general hospital the next day. He was captured April 25, 1865, at Greenville, Alabama. Also listed as **Beasley, Bensley.**

Bishop, Columbus T., Sergeant, enlisted September 14, 1861, at Montgomery. He died in Mobile September 27, 1862.

Black, James A., Private, enlisted September 14, 1861, at Montgomery. He was 5'10 and born in 1837, Troupe County, Georgia. He was hospitalized in June 1862 and discharged July 30, 1862. [17]*He was listed on the regimental medical register March 17, 1864, with acute dysentery.* [24]*He died May 29, 1864, and is buried at Rose Hill Cemetery, Macon, Georgia.*

Black, William H., Private, enlisted September 14, 1861, at Montgomery. He was hospitalized during June 1862. [17]*He was listed on the regimental medical register with chronic rheum December 16, 1863, and February 14, 1864.* He was returned to duty April 18, 1864, and was turned over to the commandant for punishment – practiced deception and feigned disease. [17]*He was slightly wounded in the left arm August 18, 1864, during the Atlanta campaign.* He was 6' and paroled June 6, 1865, at Montgomery.

Blackman, Chapman, Private, enlisted at Montgomery September 14, 1861. His home was in Butler County. [17]*He was listed on the regimental medical register on March 27 and April 25, 1864, diagnosis was feb int quotid.* He received a lead bullet in his left hip during the Atlanta campaign. He was admitted to the general hospital August 2, 1864, at Macon, Georgia, where he died. [24]*He was buried in the Rose Hill Cemetery in Macon.*

Blair, Jasper, Private, enlisted May 1, 1862, at Greenville. He was at the surrender at Greensboro, North Carolina, April 26, 1865.

Bowden, J. S., Sergeant, enlisted in 1862, at Georgiana. He was at the surrender at Greensboro, North Carolina, April 26, 1865.

Braswell, James, Private, enlisted September 7, 1862, at Montgomery.

Braswill, William, Private, enlisted September 14, 1861, at Montgomery. [17]*He was listed on the regimental medical register February 16, 1864, diagnosis was feb int quotid, and March 18 with acute dysentery.* He was wounded twice: a slight hand wound in May 1864, probably at the battle of Resaca, Georgia; and a severe wound to the left chest on June 23, at Kennesaw Mountain, Georgia. [28]*He attended the Confederate Veteran Reunion in Greenville on August 21, 1897.*

Brent, Joseph, Private, enlisted September 14, 1861, at Montgomery. He was hospitalized June 1862 and died June 11, 1862, at Pottsville, Mississippi.

Brewer, Judson, Private, enlisted March 9, 1862, at Greenville.

Brooks, Samuel E., Private, enlisted September 6, 1862, at South Butler. He was hospitalized at Ross Hospital, Mobile, September 4, 1863; diagnosis was int fever. *[17]He was listed on the regimental medical register in 1864: June 21, diagnosis was feb int quotid, and November 6, contusio.* He was 5'3 and paroled June 10, 1865, at Montgomery.

Brooks, W. F., Private, enlisted September 14, 1861, at Montgomery. He died July 30, 1862, at a hospital in Gainesville, [25]*where he was buried.*

Buffington, George J., Private, enlisted October 1, 1862, in Clark County. He died of pneumonia November 24, 1862, [6]*in a Mobile hospital and* [25]*is buried at Magnolia Cemetery in Mobile.*

Cannon, Abraham, Private, enlisted September 14, 1861, at Montgomery. He was 6'2 and born in 1827 in Montgomery.

Carathan, George, B., Private, [17]*was listed on the regimental medical register with rubeola February 23, 1864, and transferred to the Mobile general hospital two days later.* [11]*He was born in Marion County, Georgia, and was living in Butler County in 1907.*

Carathan, Joseph, Private, enlisted September 14, 1861, at Montgomery. His home was in Butler County. He was wounded at the battle of Shiloh, Tennessee, in April 1862. [17]*He was listed on the regimental medical register July 30, 1864, with rubeola; August 6, diagnosis was feb int tert; and August 29, acute dysentery.* Captured at Nashville December 15, 1864, he was imprisoned at Camp Douglas, Illinois.

Castleburey, J. W. P., Private.

Caton, Alfred D., Private, enlisted September 14, 1861, at Montgomery. He was granted sick furlough on January 25, 1862, for 20 days and sent to Covington County. Also spelled **Catin**.

Clark, James R., Private, resided in Butler County. [17]*He was listed on the regimental medical register on December 28, 1863; diagnosis was nephritis. He was listed five times in 1864: on January 28 with chronic rheumatism; on February 6, feb int quotid; on February 17, acute dysentery; and on April 15, orchitis.* His hand was severely wounded in May, probably at the battle of Resaca, Georgia. He was hospitalized February 21, 1864, Mobile, diagnosis was debility and dropsy, and August 9, 1864 in Macon, Georgia. He was hospitalized February 20, 1865, in Meridian, Mississippi, and was granted a 60-day furlough February 28. He was sent home to Georgiana, Butler County, diagnosis was disease of the heart.

Coleman, Charles, Private, enlisted September 14, 1861, at Montgomery. [17]*He was listed on the regimental hospital register five times: December 20, 1863, the diagnosis was icterus; March 28, 1864, morbi cutis, August 3 and September 30, acute dysentery, and on November 8, pneumonia.* He was 5'11 and was paroled June 3, 1865, at

Montgomery. [28]*He attended the Confederate Veteran Reunion in Greenville on August 21, 1897.*

Coleman, George T., Private, enlisted at Montgomery, September 14, 1861. [17]*He was listed on the regimental medical register on June 10, 1864, with pneumonia and moved to the general hospital the next day.* He was captured December 16, 1864, at Nashville and imprisoned at Camp Chase, Ohio, where he died of pneumonia March 26,1865. [10]*He was buried in lot number 1759.*

Coleman, J. R., Private, enlisted October 2, 1861, at Greenville. [17]*He was listed on the regimental medical register February 14, 1864, with acute dysentery; March 9, contusio; and June 4, acute dysentery. He was transferred to the general hospital June 6.* He was 5'4, a farmer, and born in 1845 in Butler County.

Coleman, Jesse, Private, enlisted September 14, 1861, at Montgomery. On January 7, 1862, he was granted a medical furlough for 20 days and sent home to Rockford, Alabama. [17]*He was listed on the regimental medical register four times in 1864: February 5, diagnosis was pleuritis; on April 13, vulnus contusio; on August 3 with acute dysentery. In May he was slightly wounded on the forehead during the battle of Resaca, Georgia.* He was captured at Nashville December 16, 1864, and imprisoned at Camp Douglas, Illinois.

[17]**Connor, George**, *Private, was listed on the regimental medical register June 6 with acute diarrhea, and moved to the general hospital June 9, 1864.*

[7]**Conway, John**, *Private, registered as a veteran in Butler County July 4, 1906.*

Cook, J. D., Private, was 5'5 and paroled May 26, 1865, at Montgomery.

Cook, James Russell, Private, [17]*was listed on the regimental medical register on September 6, 1864, with acute dysentery.* [10]*He enlisted on April 15, 1863, at Blakeley, near Mobile. He was born March 28, 1831, Henry County, Georgia. He was living in Butler County in 1907.* [37]*Living in Opp in 1921, he stated that he took part in battles at New Hope and Atlanta.*

Crenshaw, Howell, Private, enlisted September 7, 1862, at Mobile. [10]*He registered as a veteran in Butler County on September 4, 1906.* [10]*He was born July 10, 1831, Warren County, Georgia.* [37]*He was living in Evergreen in 1921.*

[1]**Cubstead, John W.**, *Private, enlisted August 10, 1861, at Greenville and transferred to the 25th Alabama. He was born April 22, 1840, South Carolina.*

Davis, Bradley D., Private, enlisted September 6, 1862, at South Butler. [17]*He was listed on the regimental medical register on December 14,*

1863; diagnosis was catarrhus, on January 4, 1864, feb int tert. He was admitted to the general hospital with pneumonia on January 7 and died January 12, 1864.

Davis, Jasper Horrie, Private, enlisted February 4, 1863, Butler County, [17]*He was listed on the regimental medical register in 1864 with acute diarrhea on April 14, June 21, July 9, August 19, and August 29. He was paroled June 7, 1865, at Montgomery.* [30]*He was from South Butler, Alabama. He was probably related to Bradley D. Davis. He applied for a pension June 7, 1900, which was granted July 13 of the same year. At that time his post office address was Lumber Mills, Alabama, and his wife's name was Amanda.*

[17]**Davis, Lewis**, Private, *was listed on the regimental medical register March 18, 1864, diagnosis was rubeola. He was sent to the general hospital in Greenville March 20.* **L. C. Davis** *was listed July 4, 1864, with acute dysentery and was moved to the general hospital two days later. He was listed September 6, 1864, with chronic diarrhea and was moved to the general hospital the same day.*

[19]**Davis, Sam**, *was killed at Franklin, Tennessee, on November 30, 1864.*

Deal, J. F., Sergeant, enlisted September 14, 1861, at Montgomery.

Deal, William J., Private, died April 17, 1862, at Andalusia, Alabama, of wounds in his arms and sides received at the battle Shiloh, Tennessee, April 7, 1862.

Deans, John J., Private, enlisted December 1863, at Mobile. [17]*He was listed on the regimental medical register on December 25, 1863, with pneumonia. He reported again to the hospital July 28, 1864, with wounds to his right arm received at the battle of Ezra Church during the siege of Atlanta. He transferred to the general hospital on July 31.* He was 5'11, a farmer, and born in 1845 in Covington County.

Deans, Jeptha J., Captain, resigned May 2, 1862, after the battle of Shiloh, Tennessee. Also spelled **Deane, Deens**.

Decken, William, Private, enlisted September 10, 1862. He was discharged May 12, 1863: provided a substitute. He obviously rejoined his unit, as he was admitted to Ross Hospital in Mobile, September 27, 1863. He was sent to the general hospital in Greenville, Alabama. Later he returned to duty. He was captured December 15, 1864, at Nashville. He was imprisoned at Camp Douglas, Illinois, where he took the oath of allegiance and became a legal US citizen in February 1865. He was discharged by the US Army May 8, 1865. He was a farmer, born in 1825, Washington County, Georgia, and a resident of Butler County at the time of his enlistment.

Deens, William H., Private, enlisted September 14, 1861, at Montgomery. He was 5'2, born in 1818, and lived in Monroe County. [17]*He was listed on the regimental medical register seven times in 1864. On January 6* and 24, diagnosis was feb int tert. On March 16, August 5 and 13, diagnosis was acute dysentery. On July 29, it was phlegmon. Finally November 8, he suffered with acute diarrhea. Captured December 15, 1864, at Nashville, he was imprisoned at Camp Douglas, Illinois, where he died March 16, 1865. He was buried in lot number 963 at the Chicago City Cemetery. Also spelled **Deans, Dean**

Dees, J. H., Private, enlisted 1862, at Greenville. He was paroled May 1, 1865, Greensboro, North Carolina.

Dees, W. R., Private, enlisted March 1, 1862, at Greenville.

Denis, J. J., Private, was paroled June 6, 1865, at Montgomery.

Dewberry, Thomas, Private, enlisted May 8, 1862, at Greenville.

[17]**Dickens, W. J.**, Private, was listed on the regimental medical register February 19, 1864, with acute diarrhea. **Wm. Dickens** was listed February 17, diagnosis feb int tert, and June 4 with acute dysentery, and moved to the general hospital June 5. **Jas. Dickens** was listed December 10, 1863, with pneumonia and transferred to the general hospital December 12. Note: This may be more than one soldier.

[17]**Doswell, W. J.**, Sergeant, was listed on the regimental medical register in May 1864 after being wounded on the forehead, probably at the battle of Resaca, Georgia. He was listed with acute dysentery on August 23, and September 30, 1864. He was listed again November 11, diagnosis catarrhus. Also spelled **Daswell, Dozwell.**

[17]**Dunklin, W. T.**, Lieutenant, was listed on the regimental medical register five times. On December 15, 1863, diagnosis was feb int tert. On February 28, March 3, and July 4, 1864, the diagnosis was feb int quotid. On April 12, the diagnosis was debilitas. He was moved to the general hospital July 6. [28]He attended the Confederate Veteran Reunion in Greenville, August 21, 1897. [7]He registered as a veteran in Butler County on July 4, 1906. Note: He transferred from Company K in 1862. See Company K for more information.

Easterling, William B., Private, enlisted March 1, 1862, at Greenville. He was paroled at the end of the war at Greensboro, North Carolina.

Edgar, Adam A., Sergeant, enlisted September 14, 1861, at Montgomery.

Ewing, Samuel T., Private, [17]was listed on the regimental medical register on August 10, 1864. He was severely wounded in the right forearm during the battle of Franklin, Tennessee, on November 30, 1864. His arm was later amputated. He was paroled June 17, 1865, at Montgomery. [1]He was born March 3, 1826, Hancock County, Georgia, and was living in Pigeon Creek, Crenshaw County, in 1907. [7]He registered as a veteran in Butler County on July 4, 1906. [19]His parents were Jonathan and Nancy Turner Ewing. Also spelled **Erving.**

Fagan, Nicholas, Private, enlisted October 1863, at Mobile. He was 5'9 and born in 1815 in Ireland. He was hospitalized in Jackson, Mississippi, during August and September 1864; diagnosis was debilitas. See Service Records for J. R. Coleman

Fail, Boling, Private, [17]*was listed on the regimental medical register three times, December 5, 1863, January 6 and 26, 1864, diagnosis was feb int tert.* He died in a Mobile Hospital of congestive fever February 19, 1864. He was buried in Magnolia Cemetery, Mobile, row 12, lot G42.

Fail, H. W., Private, was discharged June 17, 1862.

[17]***Flowers, Henry,*** *Private, was listed on the regimental medical register in 1864. On January 15, the diagnosis was ulcus, and he immediately transferred to the general hospital. On March 20, the diagnosis was chronic ulcus, and he transferred to a general hospital in Greenville March 30.*

Fowler, William A. O., Private, enlisted at Montgomery, September 14, 1861. His home was in Butler County. Captured December 15, 1864, at Nashville, he was imprisoned at Camp Douglas, Illinois, where he was granted a parole June 19, 1865.

Franklin, B. J., 2nd Lieutenant. He was transferred, appointed 2nd lieutenant, and assigned to the 17th Alabama by General Bragg, June 6, 1862.

Free, William B., Private, enlisted March 9, 1862, at Greenville. He was granted a furlough December 27, 1862 to January 3, 1863. By May 11, 1863, he was listed as a member of Company E, 9th Alabama Battalion. By September 19, 1863, he was a member of Company E, 58th Alabama Infantry. [30]*He was born June 14, 1845, Patogaville, Georgia, and died June 14, 1832, Brenham, Texas.*

Galloway, Eli, Private, lost an arm at the battle of Shiloh, Tennessee, April 1862.

Gallaway, Walter C., Private, was hospitalized at Hill Hospital, Cuthbert, Georgia, fourth quarter 1864. He was a resident of Butler County. [17]*C. Galloway was listed on the regimental medical register on January 28, 1864, diagnosis feb int quotid. W. Galloway was listed on the register June 9, diagnosis acute dysentery and transferred to the general hospital June 10, 1864.* **Walter Galloway** *was listed on the register April 20,1864, diagnosis was feb int quotid.*

Gandy, William, Private, was discharged December 5, 1861.

Gantham, Jno., Private.

Gardner, John, Private, enlisted September 14, 1861, at Montgomery. He was listed as sick in the hospital in Mobile during December 1862. He died in a Mobile hospital September 20, 1863. [25]*He is buried at Magnolia Cemetery, Mobile.*

Garrett, James B., Private, [17]*was listed on the regimental medical register twice in 1864: on June 20 with acute dysentery and August 26 with acute diarrhea.* He was captured December 15, 1864, at Nashville and was imprisoned at Camp Douglas, Illinois. His home was in Butler County. Also listed as **Garnet.**

Garrett, Henry C., Private, enlisted September 14, 1861, at Montgomery. He was 5'10, a farmer, and born in 1839, Stewart County, Georgia. He was severely wounded (thigh) at the battle of Shiloh, Tennessee, April 6, 1862. He was hospitalized June 1862. He was absent without leave in October 1862; reason: home sick. He was discharged November 30, 1862. Also listed as **W. C. Garrett**

Garrett, J. D., Private, was paroled June 11, 1865, at Montgomery.

Garrett, William G., Private, enlisted at Montgomery September 14, 1861.

Garrett, Nathaniel G., Private, enlisted at Montgomery September 14, 1861. [17]*He was listed on the regimental medical register December 13, 1863, diagnosis was feb int quotid. He was listed three times in early 1864: January 7, diagnosis was catarrhus; February 28 and March 1, feb int tert.* [39]*He was captured at Nashville.* He was paroled at Montgomery May 30, 1865. Also listed as **N. J. Garrett, W.G. Garrett**

Garrett, Thomas J., Private, enlisted October 1, 1861, at Camp Davis. [17]*He was listed on the regimental medical register on December 2, 1863, diagnosis feb int quotid. He was listed on the register three times in 1864: January 25, feb int tert; February 23, feb int quotid; and August 16, acute diarrhea.* [31]*He was at the surrender April 26, 1865, at Greensboro, North Carolina, and listed as a member of Company C.*

Goldsmith, J. C., Private, enlisted March 1, 1862. He was paroled at Greensboro, North Carolina.

Grantham, George W., Private, enlisted January 6, 1862, at Camp Gladden. He was born in 1844 in Stewart County, Georgia. He was hospitalized in June 1862 and granted a disability discharge on July 10, 1862. [17]*He was listed on the regimental medical register on September 29, 1864, and sent to the general hospital the same day.* He died January 26, 1865, [6]*at a Montgomery hospital.*

Grantham, John, Private, enlisted September 3, 1862, at Mobile, as a substitute for D. W. Brooks. He was 5'10 and was paroled June 6, 1865, at Montgomery. [17]*He was listed on the regimental medical register on January 15, 1864; diagnosis was chronic rheum.* He was granted a furlough from Way Hospital, Meridian, Mississippi, February 1865; diagnosis was wounds probably received in the Tennessee campaign.

Grantham, Thomas J., Private, 5'7, enlisted at Montgomery September 14, 1861. He was hospitalized June 1862. [17]*He was listed on the regimental* medical register August 17, 1864, acute diarrhea, and November 3, 1864, acute rheum. He was paroled June 17, 1865, at Montgomery.

Green, James, Private, was discharged December 5, 1861.

Griffin, John H., Private, enlisted September 14, 1861, at Montgomery. [17]*He was severely wounded in the left elbow July 28, 1864, at the battle of Ezra Church near Atlanta. He was transferred to the general hospital July 31.* Also listed as **J. Graffin**.

Griffin, Samuel L., Private, [17]*was listed on the regimental medical register with acute dysentery on August 8, 1864.* Captured December 15, 1864, at Nashville, he was imprisoned at Camp Douglas, Illinois, where he died February 5, 1865. He was buried in Block 3 of the Chicago City Cemetery.

Griswold, Clemmons R., Private, was hospitalized June 1862 and discharged on July 30, 1862. [30]*He was born in 1832. His spouse was Sarah Caroline Nixon. He died February 22, 1912, Covington, County.*

Griswold, Obediah, Private, [30]*was born 1830 in Georgia. He was married to Nancy Fortner or Falkner and died between January 1875 and November 1877.*

Hagins, Benjamin, Private, was hospitalized in Mobile September 1, 1863, for 10 days; diagnosis feb int tert.

Hall, John A., Private, was hospitalized May 27, 1862, at Jackson, Mississippi.

Hallford, Julius, Private, enlisted September 6, 1862, at South Butler. The muster roll for November and December 1862 lists Hallford as sick in quarters.

Hamric, John F. M., Corporal, enlisted September 14, 1861, at Mobile. His home was in Butler County. Captured November 30, 1864, at Franklin, Tennessee, he was imprisoned at Camp Douglas, Illinois. [28]*He attended the Confederate Veterans Reunion in Greenville on August 21, 1897.* Also listed as **Hamrick, J. M. F. Hambrick, John Hamick, Hunbrick, B. F. M.**

Hamrick, George W., Private, enlisted September 7, 1862, at Mobile. He was absent on leave at Blakely, near Mobile, December 1862. [17]*He was listed on the regimental medical register February 24 and June 17, 1864. Each time the diagnosis was feb int quotid, and he was sent to the general hospital the next day.*

Hardy, W. R., Private, was discharged December 5, 1861.

Hartnell, William, Private, was captured in Tennessee, May 12, 1862.

Hawthorne, John R., Private, was discharged in March 1862. He was born in 1834 in Butler County. He died April 2, 1862, at Corinth, Mississippi, leaving widow, Narcussus M. Hawthorne.

[17]**Hays, Geo.**, *Private, was listed on the regimental medical register three times in 1864: January 18, diagnosis was catarrhus; February 24, acute diarrhea; and April 20, chronic rheum. He was sent to the general hospital April 22.* Sergeant **George Hays** is listed in Company K.

Heard, J. W., Private, enlisted March 1862, at Greenville. He was paroled at Greensboro, North Carolina, April 1865.

Hearn, W. A., Private, enlisted March 1862, Greenville. He was at the surrender at Greensboro, North Carolina.

[17]**Henderson, W. E.**, *Private, was listed on the regimental medical register on July 29, 1864, diagnosis was feb int quotid.*

Hendrick, J. M., Private, was paroled in 1865 at Talladega.

Hendrix, William, Private, enlisted September 14, 1861, at Montgomery. He was 5'8, a farmer and born in 1826 in Hale County. He was discharged September 15, 1862.

Hodge, David L., Private, enlisted September 14, 1861, at Montgomery. [17]*He was listed on the regimental medical register on July 4, 1864, diagnosis was feb int quotid.*

Hodges, James M., Private, enlisted September 6, 1862, South Butler. [17]*He was listed on the regimental medical register September 30, 1864, with acute diarrhea. G. M. Hodges was listed on the register July 9, diagnosis feb int tert, and moved to the general hospital the next day.*

[20]**Holliman, James H.**, *was born January 28, 1839, in Tuscaloosa. He enlisted April 1862 after the battle of Shiloh, Tennessee. He was promoted to lieutenant September 1862. He was captured November 1863 (*Should be 1864, at the battle of Franklin, Tennessee, which occurred on November 30) *and was imprisoned at Johnson Island, Ohio, until June 13,1865. He was living in Fayette County in 1907.*

Hover, Henry J., Private, was paroled June 20, 1865, at Montgomery.

Hudson, C. H., Private, [36]*was listed as hospitalized on the muster roll for December 1863 through February 1864.* [17]*He suffered a severe* (gun shot) *wound to his thigh* [32]*at Resaca on the 14th and died May 27, 1864.*

[17]**Hudson, F. C.**, *Private, was listed on the regimental medical register February 9, 1864, diagnosis febris congestion, and moved to the general hospital on the 11th.*

Hudson, Francis M., Private, enlisted October 29, 1862, at Mobile, as a substitute. He had died by June 16, 1864, leaving his father, Eli Hudson.

Hudson, William W., Private, enlisted September 14, 1861, at Montgomery. [17]*He was listed on the regimental medical register December 1 and 16, 1863, and January 6, 1864. The diagnosis was feb int tert.*

Hughes, N., Captain, enlisted March 14, 1862. He was paroled May 1865 at Greensboro, North Carolina.

Jackson, George L., Corporal, enlisted at Montgomery September 14, 1861. [17]*He was listed on the regimental medical register December 10, 1863, diagnosis was feb int tert.* He was captured July 28, 1864, at the battle of Ezra Church near Atlanta. [9]*The same day at the age of 21 he was admitted to a Union hospital where his leg was amputated the next day.* He was released to the provost marshal on December 1, 1864 and imprisoned at Camp Douglas, Illinois. He was a sergeant at the time of his capture. He had been released by March 22, 1865, and was hospitalized in Richmond.

James, William H., Private, lived in Butler County. He was hospitalized with ulcers in Macon, Georgia, November 8, 1864.

Jernigan, D. P., Sergeant, March 1, 1862, at Greenville. He was paroled May 1865 at Greensboro, North Carolina.

Jernigan, William, Private, enlisted March 1, 1864, at Greenville. He was paroled May 1865 at Greensboro, North Carolina.

Johnson, Daniel R., Private, enlisted June 8, 1863. [17]*He was listed on the regimental medical register with acute diarrhea January 5, 1864.* He died March 16, 1864, at the Greenville general hospital leaving mother, E. D. Thomas. He was born in 1846 in Decatur, Georgia.

Johnson, George W., Private, enlisted October 10, 1861, at Camp Davis. He was hospitalized January 1862 and June 1862. He died by November 1862.

Johnson, James H., Sergeant, September 14, 1861, at Montgomery. [17]*He was listed on the regimental medical register January 25, 1864, diagnosis contusio.* As a second lieutenant, he was dropped from the regimental roster February 17, 1865, absent without leave.

Johns, John B., 1st Lieutenant, was wounded at the battle of Shiloh, Tennessee, April 6, 1862. He was appointed second lieutenant on May 4, 1862. On August 4, 1862, he was granted a 20-day furlough and sent to Montgomery. [17]*He suffered a slight injury to his left foot, July 28, 1864, at the battle of Ezra Church near Atlanta. He was transferred to the general hospital on the 31st.*

Jolly, Hardy, Private, was discharged June 17, 1862.

Jones, Isham B., Private, enlisted September 14, 1861. He was detailed as a nurse in the regimental hospital at Camp Forney, Mobile, during July through December 1862.

Jones, John E., Private, enlisted September 6, 1861, at South Butler. [17]*He was listed on the regimental medical register on February 14, 1864, diagnosis debilitas.*

Jones, W. H., Private, enlisted December 4, 1862, at South Butler. [17]*In 1864 he was listed on the regimental medical register three times: January 21, the diagnosis was feb int tert; April 23, ulcus; and July 8,* debilitas. *He was sent to the general hospital April 25. He was paroled at Montgomery May 1865.* [30]*This is probably William Henry Jones, twin brother of Wiley W. Jones of Company H. William was born November 12, 1823, near Brooklyn, Conecuh County, to Elbert and Elizabeth Bensley Jones. His wife was Martha Perkins Rhodes. He died November 15, 1899, and is buried at Jones' Mill, Monroe County.*

Jones, William, Private, enlisted October 1, 1862, Clarke County. He was hospitalized in Mobile September 1, 1863, diagnosis remitt fever. [17]*He was listed on the regimental medical register February 3, 1864; diagnosis was pleuritis. He was transferred to Spring Hill general hospital, Mobile, February 8. He was listed on the register March 30 and in September, diagnosis acute diarrhea. In November, he was listed on the register, acute colitis.* He was captured April 26, 1865, at Greenville.

Jordan, Nathan, Private, 5'9, was born in 1821 in Georgia. [17]*He was listed on the regimental medical register in 1864; diagnosis was catarrhus February 3 and June 13. On June 14 he was sent to the general hospital. He was wounded in the toe in May 1864, probably at the battle of Resaca, Georgia. He died July 19, 1864, at Eufaula.* See Service Records for Wiley H. Tynes.

Jordon, John F., Private, enlisted November 1863, at Greenville. He was 5'10, a farmer, and born 1845 in Montgomery. See Service Records for J. R. Coleman. [17]*He was listed on the regimental medical register December 17, 1863, diagnosis acute rheum, and July 17, 1864, with acute diarrhea.* He was paroled June 7, 1865, at Montgomery.

[17]**Jordan, Thomas**, *Private, was listed on the regimental medical register December 20, 1863, diagnosis acute rheum, and transferred to the general hospital on the 23rd. He was listed on the register August 7, 1864, with acute diarrhea.*

Jourdan, James M., Private, enlisted September 7, 1861, at Mobile. He was paroled June 7, 1865, at Montgomery. Also listed as **J. M. Jordon**

Kelly, J. M., Private, was discharged on December 5, 1861. He enlisted March 1, 1864, at Greenville. He was paroled May 1865 Greensboro, North Carolina.

Kelsoe, Daniel, Private, was discharged on December 5, 1861.

Kimbro, J. B., Private, 5'4, was paroled June 20, 1865. Also listed as **J. P. Kimbro.**

Kimbrough, William D., Private.

Kirksy, Willis D., Private, enlisted September 14, 1861, at Montgomery. [17]*He was severely injured in his left hip by a minnie ball at the battle of Peachtree Creek near Atlanta July 20, 1864, and was transferred to the* *general hospital the next day.* He died August 5, 1864, at Gilmer Hospital in Georgia. Also listed as **Willis P. Kirksy.**

Kirksey, Isaac M., Private, enlisted October 17, 1863, at Mobile. He was 5'11 and born in 1819 in South Carolina. [17]*He was listed on the regimental medical register on June 13, 1864, and transferred to the general hospital on the 14th, diagnosis catarrhus.* See personal papers for Willis.

Kirvin, John F., Private, enlisted September 14, 1861, at Montgomery. [42]*He was on special duty as wagoner January 1862.* He was listed as deserted from Tupelo, Mississippi, on June 28, 1862. Also listed as **John F. Kirkin.**

Kuykendall, J. H., Private, enlisted March 1, 1864, at Greenville. He was paroled May 1865 at Greensboro, North Carolina.

Lee, George W., Private, died December 15, 1861. He served as a corporal. He was discharged due to bad health. He later enlisted in Company C, 37th Alabama. He was born October 30, 1841.

Lee, John D., Private, enlisted September 14, 1861, at Montgomery. He was born in Butler County. He was wounded and captured at the battle of Shiloh, Tennessee, on April 7, 1862. Imprisoned at Camp Chase, Ohio, he was exchanged on August 25, 1862. He was captured December 28, 1864, at a battle at the railroad station at Egypt, Mississippi. He was imprisoned at Alton, Illinois, where he died of pneumonia February 1, 1865.

Lee, John H., Private, enlisted May 1, 1862, at Corinth, Mississippi. [17]*On December 11, 1863, he was listed on the regimental medical register, diagnosis was feb int tert. He was listed again on the register in 1864: on June 12 with acute diarrhea and on September 13 with acute dysentery.* He was paroled May 1865 at Greensboro, North Carolina.

[17]**Leflore, J. W.**, *Private, was listed on the regimental medical register in 1864 with acute diarrhea: on July 1, August 10, and August 23.* Also spelled **Laflore.**

Leslie, Charles W., Private, enlisted January 25, 1862. He was born in 1844, was a clerk, 5'5, and lived in Mobile. [17]*He was listed on the regimental medical register March 19, diagnosis was feb int quotid, and September 10,1864, feb in tert.* He was captured December 15, 1864, at Nashville, and imprisoned at Camp Douglas, Illinois. See Service Records for Daniel R. Johnson. Also spelled **Lessure.**

[17]**Loftin, J. W.**, *Private, was listed on the regimental medical register on June 15, 1864, diagnosis was phlegmon.*

Lim, J. B., Private.

[17]**Lynn, N. B.**, *Private, is listed on the regimental hospital register seven times. Four times with a diagnosis of feb int tert, he reported to the*

regimental unit December 21, 1863, January 18, 1864, January 28 (**L. B. Lynn**), and March 19. He also reported February 23 (**N. D. Lynn**), diagnosis chronic ulcus; August 3, debilitas; and September 18, chronic rheum.

Majors, Benjamin Shadrick, Private, enlisted September 6, 1862, at South Butler. [17]He was listed on the regimental medical register December 14, 1863, diagnosis was catarrhus. He was listed on the register twice in 1864. On January 31, diagnosis was feb int tert, and on August 13, constipatio. He was captured December 15, 1864, at Nashville and imprisoned at Camp Douglas, Illinois. [28]He attended the Confederate Veterans Reunion in Greenville on August 21, 1897. [30]He was born April 27, 1830 to Jonathan and Mary Matilda Mathews Majors. His wife was Elizabeth Wall. He was blind at his death March 10, 1899. He is buried at New Prospect Cemetery, Butler County.

Majors, Daniel M., Private, enlisted September 14, 1861, at Montgomery. His home was in Butler County. [17]He was listed on the regimental medical register December 21, 1863, diagnosis feb int tert, and again March 21, 1864. He suffered a flesh wound on his left arm August 3, 1864, during the siege of Atlanta. At that time he was listed as a deserter (probably only missing after the battle). [30]Family tradition states that he was wounded when a rifle bullet broke his left wrist July 20, 1864, and that he was wounded a second time when a shell fragment hit his right leg. He spent time at a hospital in Columbus, Georgia. He eventually was granted a convalescent furlough and sent to Montgomery which is where he was when his regiment surrendered. He was admitted to Ocmulgee Hospital in Macon, Georgia. He was paroled May 8, 1865. [30]After the war his left arm was basically useless from his war wound, as it was deformed and crippled. He applied for a pension in 1905 and 1906. He was born December 23, 1836, Dale County, Alabama, to to John and Serena Cook Majors. His wife was Susan Ann Frances Majors, a cousin. He died April 27, 1918, Escambia County, Florida, and is buried at Clopton Cemetery, Pensacola. His wife applied for a pension after his death.\

Majors, James, Private, (5'9) enlisted October 9, 1863, at Camp Cantey in Mobile. He was born 1821 in Henry County. [17]He was listed on the regimental medical register December 12, 1863, diagnosis feb int quotid. He was paroled at Montgomery June 8, 1865. [30]He was born in 1828, Georgia, to Jonathan and Mary Matilda Mathews Majors. His wife was Sophronia Beasley. He died in 1865 of war related injuries in either Dale or Crenshaw County.

Majors, James Cornelius, Private, (5'5) enlisted May 13, 1862, Corinth, Mississippi. He was hospitalized June 1862. He reenlisted October 9,

1863, at Camp Cantey in Mobile. He was discharged October 22, 1863, debility. He was born in 1845, Dale County, Alabama, [30]*to John and Serena Matilda Cook Majors. His spouse was Frances Elizabeth Daniel.*

Majors, Jonathan, Private, 5'11, enlisted July 20, 1863, at Greenville. He was born in 1841 in Butler County and was granted a disability discharge November 5, 1863. [30]*He was born April 5, 1841, to John and Serena Cook Majors.*

Majors, Joseph, Private, (5'6) enlisted October 9, 1863, at Greenville, Alabama. [17]*He was killed July 28, 1864, at the battle of Ezra Church in Atlanta.* [30]*He was born in 1846, Dale County, Alabama, to James and Sophronia Beasley Majors.*

Manley, Charles J., Private, enlisted September 4, 1861, at Montgomery. He was assigned as a nurse in the hospital during June 1862. [17]*He was listed on the regimental medical register June 16, 1864, with acute diarrhea. He moved to the general hospital the next day. He was wounded (back of neck) August 2, 1864, during the siege of Atlanta. He was moved to the general hospital on August 8.* **Joseph Manley** *was listed on the regimental medical register on July 31 with colitis.* After fighting at Nashville, Charles was hospitalized at West Point and Meridian, Mississippi, and in Macon, Georgia. He was captured in the Spring of 1865 in Macon, Georgia.

Mathews, John L., Private, 5'7, enlisted at Montgomery September 4, 1861. He was hospitalized June 1862. He was born in 1828 in South Carolina and died June 15, 1862, Lauderdale County, Mississippi.

Maxey, William, Private, enlisted September 14, 1861, at Montgomery. He was employed on extra duty at Batteries Tracey and Huger in June 1863. [17]*He was severely wounded in the thigh, probably at the battle of Resaca, Georgia, in May 1864.* [31]*He was listed as a member of Company C at the surrender April 26, 1865, at Greensboro, North Carolina.* [30]*He was born in 1830 and died in September or October 1878 in Butler County. His wife, Eliza Maxey, applied for a pension May 17, 1899.*

McCaskell, F. R., Private, enlisted March 8, 1862, at Greenville. Parole was granted at Greensboro, North Carolina, in May 1865.

McClure, George H., Sergeant, was discharged May 14, 1863. [17]*He was listed on the regimental medical register February 28, 1864, with opthalmia. He was killed July 20, 1864, at the battle of Peachtree Creek near Atlanta.* [30]*He was born February 8, 1829, Monroe County. A memorial marker is located at McClure Cemetery, Butler County.*

McIntire, John N., Private, lived in Conecuh. [17]*He is listed on the regimental medical register February 28, 1864, and* **(J. M. McIntire)** *April 10, diagnosis was neuralgia. On July 1, he was listed on the* *register with acute dysentery and sent to the general hospital the next day. He (J. C. McIntire) suffered a flesh wound to his left arm August 10, 1864, during the siege of Atlanta. He diagnosed with scabies on September 12 and on October 9, 1864. He was moved to the general hospital on October 15.* [31]*He was listed as a member of Company C at the surrender April 26, 1865, at Greensboro, North Carolina.* Also listed as **John N. McIntyre**.

McKinsey, J. T., Sergeant, March 17, 1862, at Greenville. He was paroled at Greensboro, North Carolina, May 1865.

McKinsey, William, Private, enlisted February 1, 1862, at Greenville. He was paroled May 1865 at Greensboro, North Carolina.

[17]***McPhearson, J. W.**, Private, was killed July 20, 1864, at the battle of Peach Tree Creek near Atlanta.*

McPherson, Arnold, Private, enlisted May 1, 1862, at Corinth, Mississippi.

Mills, R. B., Private, enlisted March 8, 1862, at Greenville.

Mims, Basil M., Private, was captured December 15, 1864, at Nashville and imprisoned at Camp Douglas, Illinois.

Minoyard, John, Private, was discharged December 5, 1861.

Moore, Augustus W., Private, enlisted at Montgomery September 14, 1861. He was born in 1844, Conecuh County. He died of brain fever November 19, 1862, at Camp Forney Hospital, Mobile. He left father, Allen W. Moore.

Moore, J. G., Private, enlisted March 1, 1864, at Greenville. He was paroled at Greensboro, North Carolina, May 1865.

Moreland, James S., Captain, was 5'8 and born in 1828. His home was in Mobile. He transferred from Company K to B July 26, 1862. He was elected captain July 24, 1862. [17]*He was listed on the regimental medical register on December 30, 1863; diagnosis was neuralgia.* Captured May 16, 1864, at Resaca, Georgia, he was imprisoned at Johnson Island, Ohio, where he took the oath of allegiance on June 15, 1865.

Morris, John M., Private, enlisted September 14, 1861, at Montgomery. He was hospitalized June 1862. [17]*He was listed on the regimental medical register twice in 1864: August 4, diagnosis was lithitis, and on September 30, dysuria.* He was paroled May 1, 1865, at Greenville.

Morris, William L., Private, enlisted September 14, 1861, at Montgomery. His home was Cherokee County. He was placed on detailed service driving wagons at Chattanooga, during July and August of 1862. He was working as a teamster at Mobile during November and December 1862. He was hospitalized with bronchitis July 22, 1864, at Macon, Georgia. He was present at the surrender in Greensboro, North Carolina, April 26, 1865, listed as a member of Company C. [28]*He attended a Confederate Reunion in Greenville on August 21, 1897.* [10]*He* was born September 15, 1838, in Chester County, South Carolina. He was living in Butler County in 1907.

Morrow, Abram S., Private, enlisted September 14, 1861, at Montgomery. [17] He was listed on the regimental medical register twice with diagnosis feb int tert: on December 12, 1863, and January 22, 1864. He also reported to the regimental medical unit with acute diarrhea: July 30 and August 16, 1864. He was listed on the regimental medical register on December 4, 1863; diagnosis was morbi cutis.

Moseley, William, Private, enlisted March 1, 1862, at Greenville. He was paroled May 1, 1865, Greensboro, North Carolina.

Mosely, C. L., Private, died January 20, 1862, in the hospital.

Nichols, James, Private, enlisted September 7, 1862, at Mobile. [17] He was listed on the regimental medical register in 1864. On January 30, the diagnosis was feb int tert, on February 8, debilitas, and on April 14, feb int quotid. [37] He was born April 8, 1844, in Covington County and was living in Covington County in 1921. He took part in battles at Resaca, Cassville, New Hope Church, near Marietta, and near Columbus. He was slightly wounded in 1865 near Columbus, Georgia.

Nichols, Jasper N., Private, enlisted September 14, 1861, at Montgomery. He was employed as a teamster for Companies B and I. [17] He was listed on the regimental medical register on January 28, diagnosis constipatio. [10] He was living in Butler County in 1907.

Norris, Alexander, Private, enlisted September 14, 1861, at Montgomery. He was granted a medical furlough January 25, 1862, for 20 days and was sent to Butler County. [17] He was listed on the regimental medical register three times with feb int tert: December 4, December 27, 1863 and January 25, 1864. He reported to the hospital on February 5, diagnosis was feb remitt, and transferred to the general hospital at Spring Hill, Mobile February 8. He was hospitalized February 17, 1864, in Mobile. Captured December 15, 1864, Nashville, he was imprisoned Camp Douglas, Illinois. [7] He registered as a veteran at Butler County July 4, 1906.

Norris, John F., Private, died March 7, 1862.

Norris, William A., Private, enlisted September 14, 1861, at Montgomery. His home was in Tallapoosa County. He was placed on sick furlough January 3, 1862 for 20 days and sent to Butler County. [17] He was listed on the regimental medical register December 13, 1863, diagnosis was feb int tert. He was hospitalized with acute dysentery June 5, 1864, at Macon, Georgia. He was captured December 15, 1864, at the battle of Nashville and imprisoned at Camp Douglas, Illinois. Also listed as **W. H. Norris**

COMPANY B

Owens Robert E., Private, musician, was the father of Robert P. Owens. He was severely wounded in the mouth at the battle of Ezra Church July 28, 1864, during the siege of Atlanta. He was sent to the general hospital on the 31st. [30]*He was a patient at Ladies Hospital, Montgomery, December 22, 1865. He was born in 1817. He died December 30, 1894, and is buried in the Ebenezer Cemetery in Butler County.*

Owens, Robert Phillip, Private, enlisted September 14, 1861, at Montgomery. He was severely wounded at the battle of Shiloh, Tennessee, in April 1862. He was appointed musician October 1, 1862. He was listed on the muster rolls of the 17th Alabama July through December of 1862. [17]*He was listed on the regimental medical register February 9, 1864, diagnosis was odontalgia and again June 21, 1864, with acute diarrhea.* [30]*He was mortally wounded at Franklin, Tennessee, and was sent to a hospital, possibly at Columbia, Tennessee, where he died November 1864. He is buried in Rosehill cemetery in Columbia. He was born 1844, son of Robert E. Owens.* [41]*A memorial marker was placed in Ebenezer Cemetery, Pigeon Creek, Alabama.*

Palmer, A. L., Sergeant, enlisted March 16, 1862, Georgiana. He was paroled May 1, 1865, at Greensboro, North Carolina.

Palmer, H. G., Private, was paroled June 17,1863. [17]*He was listed on the regimental medical register on February 6, 1864; diagnosis was spinal irritation. He returned to the regimental medical unit with the same problem on March 10 and was transferred to the general hospital two days later. He returned on June 2 with acute dysentery.* He was paroled June 20, 1865. **H. J. Palmer** was wounded and hospitalized January 13, 1863, at Meridian, Mississippi. Also spelled **Parmer.**

Palmer, R., Private, was hospitalized at Meridian, Mississippi, January 7, 1865. [7]*R. F. Parmer registered as a veteran in Butler County, July 4, 1906.*

Parker, Benjamin J., 1st Lieutenant, enlisted at Montgomery September 14, 1861. He was elected 2nd lieutenant September 8, 1861, and promoted to 1st lieutenant June 1, 1862. [17]*He was listed on the regimental medical register December 15, 1863, and January 4, 1864, diagnosis feb int tert. He reported to the regimental medical unit February 14 and April 5, diagnosis feb int quotid. He was killed by a minnie ball to the left breast in May14, 1864, at the battle of Resaca, Georgia.* [24]*He is buried in the Resaca Confederate Cemetery.*

Parker, John T., Corporal, enlisted September 14, 1861, at Montgomery, from Butler County. [17]*He was listed on the regimental medical register on August 23, 1864; diagnosis was constipatio.* Captured December 15,

1864, Nashville, he was imprisoned at Camp Douglas, Illinois. Letter of inquiry was written on February 10, 1953.

[17]**Parker, Wm.**, *Private, was listed on the regimental medical register on July 8, 1864, diagnosis colica.* He was wounded (left hand) August 17, 1864, during the siege of Atlanta.

Payne, John S., Sergeant, was discharged December 16, 1861.

Pearson, James H., Private, was killed at the battle of Shiloh, Tennessee, April 7, 1862, breast wound. Also spelled **Pierson**.

Phillips, John W., Private, enlisted August 24, 1863, Butler County. He was 5'9, a farmer, and born in North Carolina. [17]*He was listed on the regimental medical register on February 13 and March 10, 1864: diagnosis was feb int tert, April 29, diagnosis phlegmon.* Captured May 27, 1864, Dallas, Georgia, he was imprisoned at Rock Island, Illinois. After his release he was hospitalized on March 12, 1865, at Richmond, Virginia. See Service Records for Daniel R. Johnson.

Pittman, Robert C., Private, enlisted September 14, 1861, at Mobile. His home was in Butler County. [17]*He was listed on the regimental hospital register five times. On December 25, 1863, the diagnosis was ulcus. On January 15, 1864, diagnosis was feb int tert, on February 6, feb int quotid, On August 26, the diagnosis was acute diarrhea, and in September, contusio.* He was paroled May 9, 1865, at Meridian, Mississippi.

Pittman, William, Private, enlisted September 6, 1862, South Butler. He was 5'11, a farmer, and born in 1828 in Butler County. He was granted a disability discharge November 11, 1863.

Pitts, Davis W., Private, enlisted August 5, 1863, at Mobile. A farmer, 5'8, he was born in 1822 in Newberry County, South Carolina. [17]*He was listed on the regimental medical register four times in 1864. On January 5, the diagnosis was acute dysentery; February 3, feb int quotid; February 28 and March 4, catarrhus.* Also listed as **David Pitts**.

Porter, Thomas M. J., 2nd Lieutenant, enlisted September 14, 1861, at Montgomery. He was 6'1, born in 1833, and lived in Georgiana, Butler County, Alabama. He was wounded in the stomach at the battle of Shiloh, Tennessee, April 7, 1862. He was elected second lieutenant, September 5, 1862. [17]*He was listed on the regimental medical register three times in 1864 with the diagnosis feb int tert. On January 17 when he was transferred to the general hospital the next day, February 2 when he was moved six days later, and March 21. He also was on the list for March 10, diagnosis was debilitas, and April 5, feb int quotid.* Captured November 30, 1864, at the battle of Franklin, Tennessee, he was imprisoned at Johnson Island where he took the oath of allegiance June 1, 1865.

COMPANY B

Powell, J. W., Private, was paroled May 1865 Greensboro, North Carolina.

Rambo, John R., Private, enlisted September 14, 1861, at Montgomery. He was placed on sick furlough January 2, 1862, for 20 days and sent to Butler County. He was commissioned a sergeant in 1863. He was hospitalized at Mobile September 2, 1863, for 5 days. [17]*He was listed on the regimental medical register in December 1863: on the 4th, diagnosis was feb int quotid; on the 27th, parrychia. On January 1, 1864, he was listed again, diagnosis feb int tert; on March 30, morbi cutis; and on April 24, catarrhus. The regimental register listed him as killed by minnie ball to arm and chest in May 1864* [19]*at the battle of Resaca, Georgia.*

Ramsay, James M., Private, was discharged December 5, 1861.

Redd, Joshua, Private, [42]*was on special duty as wagoner January 1862.*

Rhodes, James W., Private, enlisted September 7, 1862, at Mobile. He was detached to the signal corps on December 10, 1862. [17]*He was listed on the regimental medical register on July 9, 1864; diagnosis was anasarca. He was wounded in the hand in May 1864, probably at the battle of Resaca, Georgia.* Captured December 15, 1864, at Nashville, he was imprisoned at Camp Douglas, Illinois. Also spelled **Rhoades**.

Rhodes, Newton N., Private, was discharged November 3, 1863.

Rigsby, Benjamin, Private, enlisted September 6, 1862, at South Butler. [17]*He was listed on the regimental medical register three times in 1864, diagnosis was feb int quotid: February 3, March 7, and June 21. He was also listed July 11; diagnosis was phlegmon. He was listed July 28, 1864, after being severely wounded in the right shoulder, during the battle at Ezra Church at Atlanta.* [30]*Probably B. Rigsby who was born in 1843 to Noah and Frances Grizzle Rigsby and brother of Philo D. Rigsby.*

Rigsby, Phil D., Corporal, enlisted October 26, 1861, at Camp Davis. Hospitalized in Mobile during January 1862, he was granted a sick furlough for 20 days and sent home to Butler County. [17]*He was listed on the regimental medical register five times in 1864. On March 19, April 12, and July 29, the diagnosis was feb int tert. On August 9, diagnosis feb int quotid. Wounded in his left side during the siege of Atlanta, he reported to the hospital on August 17, 1864.* [31]*He was listed as a member of Company C at the surrender April 26, 1865, at Greensboro, North Carolina.* He was listed as a corporal when he was paroled May 1, 1865, Greensboro, North Carolina. [28]*He attended the Confederate Veterans Reunion in Greenville August 21, 1897.* [30]*He was born in 1841 to Noah and Frances Grizzle (Griswold) Rigsby. He married Frances Arant and died in 1909.* Also listed as **Phillip B., P. B., P. D. Rigsby**.

Robbins, Solomon E., Private, lived in Coosa County. [17]*He was listed on the regimental medical register on June 11, 1864, and was immediately transferred to the general hospital. The diagnosis was anemia. He sustained a wound to the abdomen July 28 at the battle of Ezra Church in the Atlanta area. The wound was described as slight. He was transferred to the general hospital on July 31.* He died August 26, 1864, Macon, Georgia. [24]*He is buried in Rose Hill Cemetery in Macon.*

Roberson, J. L., 2nd Lieutenant, was paroled May 1865 at Greensboro, North Carolina.

Roberson, N. F., Private, was paroled May 1865 at Greensboro, North Carolina.

Scott, S. H., Private, enlisted October 10, 1861, at Camp Davis. He was dropped from rolls in December 1862 when it was learned that he had died in the hospital.

[17]**Scruggs, E. F.,** *was listed on the regimental medical register on April 18, 1864, diagnosis was feb int tert.*

Scruggs, J. W. F., Private, worked as carpenter on a major's winter quarters during January 1863. He may have transferred to 18th Alabama Infantry, Company F.

Sellers, Daniel B., Private, 5'3, enlisted May 1, 1862, at Corinth, Mississippi. [17]*He was listed on the regimental medical register in 1864; diagnosis was feb int tert on July 8 and September 30.* He was hospitalized at West Point, Mississippi, January 1865 and paroled June 1, 1865, at Montgomery. [30]*Family tradition states that he was wounded July 28, 1864, at Peachtree Creek near Atlanta, and November 30, 1864, at Franklin, Tennessee.* [10]*He was born August 10, 1834, at Haynesville, Lowndes County. He listed his home as Butler County in 1907. His spouse was Margaret Parker.* [30]*He died April 16, 1918, and is buried at Pleasant Hill Cemetery in Butler County.*

Shea, Patrick, Private, lived in Baldwin County. [17]*Sick with pneumonia, he was listed on the regimental medical register on February 14, 1864, and was moved the same day to Ross Hospital, Mobile. He was diagnosed with acute dysentery April 27, 1864, with acute dysentery, and with debilitas, August 10, 1864.* Captured December 15, 1864, at Nashville, he was imprisoned at Camp Douglas, Illinois.

Shell, G. E., Private, was paroled June 23, 1865, at Montgomery. Also listed as **Sherl.**

Sheppard, James, Private, was slightly wounded at the battle of Shiloh, Tennessee, in April 1862.

[17]**Shine, Wm. P.,** *Private, was listed on the regimental medical register on January 5, 1864. He moved to the general hospital the next day, diagnosis was catarrhus. He was listed again, February 14,1864, and*

was placed on medical furlough February 18 for 15 days, diagnosis debilitas.

Shreves, J. S., Private, died in 1862.

Singer, John, Private, [17]*was listed on the regimental medical register December 7, 1863, diagnosis was abscessus and on April 5, 1864, syph consec. He reported to the hospital again in May, diagnosis was feb int quotid, and was listed as missing. On June 11 he reported to the hospital with acute diarrhea.* He was paroled May 30, 1865, at Montgomery.

Sisk, J. N., Private, enlisted September 15, 1862, Larkenville, Alabama.

Smalwood, W. F., Private, enlisted March 1, 1862, at Greenville. He was paroled May 1865 at Greensboro, North Carolina.

Smith, F. C., Private, enlisted February 1, 1864, at Greenville.

Smith, J. H., Corporal, enlisted March 17, 1862, at Greenville. [17]*Jas. Smith was listed on the regimental medical register on January 24, 1864, diagnosis was feb int tert.* He was paroled May 1865 at Greensboro, North Carolina.

Stallings, Archa M., Private, enlisted September 14, 1861, at Montgomery. [17]*He was listed on the regimental medical register four times in 1864. On March 31 and April 8, the diagnosis was feb int tert. He reported June 24 and transferred to the general hospital the same day. He reported on November 3 and transferred on November 14, diagnosis acute rheum.* [31]*He was listed as a member of Company C at the surrender April 26, 1865, at Greensboro, North Carolina*, where he was paroled.

Stallings, Henry Chambers, Private, [19]*enlisted at Montgomery May 1, 1863.* His service record says to see **H. C. Nalling**, but the record does not exist. [17]*He was listed on the regimental medical register March 11, 1864; diagnosis was acute rheumatism, sent to the general hospital the next day. He was wounded in the right wrist July 28, at the battle of Ezra Church near Atlanta. He was transferred to the general hospital July 31.* [19]*He was born February 6, 1845, to Daniel and Nancy H. Lane Stallings. He was paroled in Montgomery May 1865.* [28]*He attended the Confederate Veterans Reunion in Greenville August 21, 1897.* [37]*He was born in Oakey Streak, Butler County. In 1921 he was living in Honoraville, Crenshaw County. At that time he stated he took part in battles at Peachtree Creek and Atlanta in 1864.*

Stallings, J. L., Private, enlisted March 21, 1862, at Greenville. [17]*On December 30, 1863,* **Jo Stallings** *was listed on the regimental medical register; diagnosis was herpes circ. On February 7,* **Jas. Stallings** *was listed with acute dysentery. In September* **J. T. Stallings** *was listed on the register, diagnosis was debilitas.* He was paroled May 1865 at

Greensboro, North Carolina. [19]*His parents were Daniel and Nancy Lane Stallings.*

Stanley, Jno. T., Private, [17]*was listed on the regimental medical register on November 5, 1864, with acute diarrhea.* Wounded, probably at the Tennessee Campaign, he was admitted to Way Hospital at Meridian, Mississippi, in early 1865 and granted a furlough.

Stanley, William H., Sr., Private, enlisted June 25, 1863, at Mobile. He was born in 1816 in North Carolina, a farmer, and 5'4. [17]*The regimental hospital register lists the following:* **Henry Stanley**, *February 5, 1864, diagnosis feb int quotid, transferred to the general hospital in Mobile on February 11.* **W. H. Stanley**, *July 4, diagnosis scalp wound, transferred to the general hospital the next day.* **W. H. Stanley**, *July 28, was killed on field, at the battle of Ezra Church, in the Atlanta area.* **W. H. Stanly**, *November 5, was listed on the medical register, diagnosis contusio.* Note: One of the last two entries was misidentified.

Stephens, James, Private, enlisted December 20, 1861, at Camp Gladden. He was appointed 5th Sergeant October 1, 1862. [17]*He was listed on the regimental medical register June 18, 1864, diagnosis was feb int quotid, and moved to the general hospital the next day.* Also spelled **Stevens**.

Stephens, Roswell, Private, enlisted August 16, 1862, at Camp Forney. [17]*He was listed on the regimental medical register twice in 1864. On March 11, the diagnosis was acute rheumatism, and on June 18, feb remitt.* Also spelled **Stevens**.

Stephens, S. W., Private, enlisted February 1, 1864, at Rough & Ready, Georgia. He was paroled May 1865 at Greensboro, North Carolina.

Stewart, Charles H., Private, enlisted January 6, 1862, at Camp Gladden, Pensacola, Florida. He died March 27, 1862, in Corinth, Mississippi. He was a mechanic before the war and was born in 1832 in Butler County

Stewart, Lewis C., Private, enlisted September 14, 1861, at Montgomery. [17]*He was listed on the regimental medical register five times in 1864. On January 18, February 1, and February 20, the diagnosis was feb int tert. On March 9, the diagnosis was feb int quotid. On March 11, he reported to the medical unit with acute dysentery and transferred to the general hospital at Spring Hill the next day.* He was paroled May 30, 1865 in Montgomery. Also spelled **Stuart, Stuard**.

Stewart, S. C., Private.

Stewart, William D., Private, 5,6, enlisted at Montgomery September 14, 1861. [17]*He was listed on the regimental medical register on February 11, 1864, diagnosis was debilitas, and transferred to the general hospital in Greenville, Alabama, the next day. He was listed again with pneumonia June 9 and moved to the general hospital June 11.* He was paroled May 30, 1865, at Montgomery. Also spelled **Stuart**.

[17]*Swaner, F. M.*, Private, was listed on the regimental medical register on January 27, 1864, diagnosis was feb int tert.

Taylor, William Hillary, Private, enlisted March 8, 1862, at Greenville. He was discharged on May 16, 1863. He was paroled May 1865 at Greensboro, North Carolina.

Taylor, W. Henderson, Private, enlisted March 21, 1862. He was paroled May 1865 at Greensboro, North Carolina.

Taylor, William, Private, reported to the hospital January 1862 and died the same year. He may be buried in Barrancas National Cemetery, listed as T..., W. B 17TH ALA INF or T..., W.T. PVT B 17TH

Thomas, Daniel, Private, [17]*was listed on the regimental medical register June 11, 1864, with acute diarrhea.* He was captured at Nashville, December 15, 1864, and imprisoned at Camp Douglas, Illinois. He died January 11, 1865, of pneumonia and was buried in lot number 447 block 2, Chicago City Cemetery.

Thomas, James M., Private, was discharged December 5, 1861.

Thornton, John, Private, enlisted December 20, 1861, at Newbern. He was hospitalized June 1862.

Till, Daniel Green, Private, enlisted September 6, 1862, South Butler. [17]*D. G. Till was listed on the regimental medical register on January 23, 1864; diagnosis was neuralgia. G. D. Till was diagnosed with feb int remitt on July 26, 1864.* [10]*He was born April 22, 1838, in Butler County and was living in Butler County in 1907.* [30]*His parents were Daniel and Rosana Hungerpillar Till. He was a long time resident of Butler County. He died May 10, 1928. He and his wife, Nancy, are buried at Mount Pleasant Baptist Church Cemetery.*

Tisdale, Marshall, Private, 5'6, was a farmer, and born in 1843 in Conecuh County. He died November 27, 1861, leaving father, John A. Tisdale and brother, T. A. Tisdale. He may have been buried at Barrancas National Cemetery, listed as T..., N. PVT B 17th ALA INF.

Tisdale, Samuel, Private, [17]*was listed on the regimental medical register five times in 1864. On January 28, 1864, the diagnosis was catarrhus. On June 15 and July 4, he had acute dysentery. On August 13, he had chronic diarrhea. In October, the diagnosis was debilitas and he was moved to the general hospital on October 21.* He was paroled May 24, 1865, at Montgomery.

Townsand, Samuel W., Private, enlisted at Montgomery September 14, 1861. He was listed as a deserter December 1, 1862.

Tyner, Elijah S., Sergeant, enlisted September 14, 1861, Montgomery. He was granted a furlough June 1862. He was Accounting Commissary Sergeant November and December 1862. In October 1863, he applied to be relieved of service because he was a minister of the gospel.

Letters relating to the application are part of his service record on microfilm.

Tyner, Josiah, Private, enlisted September 14, 1861, at Montgomery. [17]*He was wounded in the arm in May 1864, probably at the battle of Resaca, Georgia. He was wounded in the arm July 28 at the battle of Ezra Church near Atlanta and was transferred to the general hospital.* [31]*He was listed as a member of Company C April 26, 1865, at Greensboro, North Carolina, and* was paroled May 1865. Also listed as **Joseph Tyner.**

Tyner, Wiley H., Private, enlisted October 20, 1863, Butler County. He was born in 1826 in Alabama, a farmer, and 5'11. [17]*In February 29, 1864,* **Wm. H. Tynes** *was listed on the regimental medical register; diagnosis was chronic ulcus. On March 4,* **W. H. Tynes** *reported to the hospital; diagnosis was ulcus. On July 6,* **W. H. Tynes,** *was listed on the regimental medical register and transferred to the general hospital the next day; diagnosis feb int quotid.* He was paroled June 1, 1865, at Montgomery. Also listed as **Jyner.**

Vardell, Milton G., Sergeant, September 14, 1861, at Montgomery. He was placed on medical furlough January 25, 1862, for 20 days and sent to Butler County. His was slightly wounded (arm) at the battle of Shiloh, Tennessee, in April 1862. [17]*He was listed on the regimental medical register on April 4, 1864, and placed on furlough April 8 for 30 days; diagnosis was debilitas. .* [31]*He was listed as a member of company C at the surrender April 26, 1865, at Greensboro, North Carolina, and* was paroled May 1865 at Greensboro. He was listed as a 2nd lieutenant when paroled. Also spelled **Verdell.**

[17]**Vardelle, R. J.,** *Private, was listed on the regimental medical register on August 8, 1864, with acute dysentery.*

Walker, Felix G., Private, enlisted September 14, 1862, at Montgomery. [17]*He was listed on the regimental medical register on July 7, 1864, diagnosis was feb int quotid.* Captured July 20, 1864, near Atlanta, he was imprisoned at Camp Douglas, Illinois, where he applied to take the oath of allegiance. He joined the 6th US Volunteer Infantry on April 3, 1865.

Wall, Andrew J., Private, cards filed with the 17th Georgia.

Wallace, Samuel H., Private, was hospitalized at Mobile September 22, 1863, and sent home to Greenville September 27, 1863. He was hospitalized at Mobile February 18, 1864, for 9 days. [17] *He was listed on the regimental medical register twice more in 1864: on April 23, diagnosis was icterus, and on June 20, acute dysentery.* Also spelled **Waller.**

[17]**Waller, W. S.**, *Private, was listed on the regimental medical register on December 23, 1863, diagnosis was feb int tert.* May be **Wallace**.

Walling, H. C., Private, was paroled June 8, 1865, at Montgomery.

Ward, John W., Private, enlisted December 20, 1861, at Newbern. He was hospitalized June 1862.

Ward, Soloman A., Private, enlisted December 20, 1861, at Newbern, northwest of Selma, Alabama.

Ware, David, Private, enlisted September 14, 1861, at Montgomery. He was 5'5, a farmer, and born 1836. He died in Corinth, Mississippi, March 30, 1862, leaving mother, June Ware.

Warren, George W., Private, enlisted at Montgomery September 14, 1861. He suffered a slight breast wound at the battle of Shiloh, Tennessee, April 1862. He died September 28, 1863, in Mobile leaving mother, Mary Warren.

Watson, Andrew Jackson, Private, enlisted September 14, 1861, at Montgomery. He was placed on sick furlough for 20 days January 25, 1861, and sent home to Butler County. [17]*He was listed on the regimental medical register twice in 1864: on February 5, diagnosis was catarrhus, and on July 13, debilitas. A. M. Watson also reported to the medical unit January 24, diagnosis was feb int tert.* Captured December 17, 1865, at Brentwood, Tennessee, he was imprisoned Camp Chase, Ohio, where he was paroled June 1865. [30]*He was called Jack.* He was born February 2, 1837, son of Gilbert and Nancy Proctor Watson. His friend, Benjamin Robert Tobias, died at Camp Chase. After the war, Watson delivered a letter to Tobias' widow, Mary. He fell in love and married Mary. Watson filed for a pension June 28, 1905. The pension was granted August 5, 1905. He died October 29, 1915. His wife filed for a pension January 14, 1916 and again December 20, 1920. Watson's brothers, William Russell and Jesse, were also in Company B.

[17]**Watson, J.**, *Private. J. G. Watson was listed on the regimental medical register on June 18, 1864; diagnosis was morbi cutis. J. R. Watson was listed on the regimental medical register on September 18 and transferred to the general hospital the same day. J. S. Watson was listed on the regimental medical register three times in 1864: February 29, diagnosis was lumbago; June 22, scabies; and July 25, morbi cutis. Jas. S. Watson was listed March 5, diagnosis lumbago.* [31]*He was listed as a member of company C at the surrender April 26, 1865, at Greensboro, North Carolina.*

Watson, Jesse M., Private, died in the hospital at Pensacola, Florida, on January 9, 1862. His parents were Gilbert and Nancy Proctor Watson. His brothers, William Russell and Andrew Jackson Watson, were also in Company B.

Watson, William Russell, Private, enlisted September 6, 1862, at South Butler. He was hospitalized at Mobile February 18, 1864. [17]*He was listed on the regimental medical register five times in 1864: January 18, diagnosis was acute diarrhea; February 14, feb int tert; March 24, acute dysentery; April 16, catarrhus; and July 5, feb int tert. He transferred to the general hospital on July 6.* He was captured April 27, 1865, at Greenville. [30]*He was born ca 1831 in Georgia, son of Gilbert and Nancy Proctor Watson. His wife was Ann Elizabeth Fulton. He died October 7, 1916, Escambia, Alabama, and buried in Union Cemetery near Georgiana. His brothers, Andrew Jackson and Hesse Watson, were also in Company B.*
Weeks, W. A., Private, enlisted December 20, 1861, at Newbern, northwest of Selma, Alabama. He was discharged July 5, 1862.
Wigg, W. K., Private, was working at the brick ovens in June 1862.
Wiggins, James C., Private, enlisted August 18, 1863, at Mobile. He was 5'8, a farmer, and born in 1844 in Butler County. [17]*He was listed on the regimental medical register on December 1, 1863, diagnosis was feb int tert.* He was paroled May 1865 at Greensboro, North Carolina.
Wiggins, J. E., Private, enlisted March 8, 1862, at Georgiana.
Wiggins, William K., Private, enlisted at Montgomery September 14, 1861. [42]*He was on special duty at the brick oven January 1862.* He was 5'7, a farmer, and born in 1843 in Butler County.
Williams, Benjamin, Private, enlisted at Pensacola, Florida, November 5, 1861. [17]*He was listed on the regimental medical register on December 26, 1863, diagnosis was feb int tert.* Captured December 15, 1864, at Nashville, he was imprisoned Camp Douglas, Illinois. He died February 15, 1865, and was buried in lot number 801 block 3 at Chicago City Cemetery. He was listed as a corporal when captured.
Williams, M. W., Private, was discharged December 5, 1861.
Williams, Thomas, 2nd Lieutenant, enlisted September 14, 1861. He was elected September 7, 1861, and appointed 2nd lieutenant September 14, 1861. His file includes an interesting letter dated July 17, 1862.
Williams, William, Private, lived in Butler County. [17]*He was listed on the regimental medical register three times in 1864. On February 19 and June 21, the diagnosis was feb int quotid. On September 10, he had chronic diarrhea.* Captured December 15, 1864, in Nashville, he was imprisoned at Camp Douglas, Illinois, where he was paroled June 1865.
Williamson, James B., Private, enlisted October 10, 1861, at Camp Davis. He was hospitalized June 1862, and reported dead by Colonel V. S. Murphy.
Williamson, John, Private, enlisted September 14, 1861, at Montgomery. He was listed in the hospital in Mobile in December 1862. He was hospitalized in Mobile September 5, 1863, and February 27, 1864, for 4

weeks. [17]*He was listed on the regimental medical register three times with the complaint feb int tert: on December 9, 1863, on February 1, 1864, when he was transferred to the general hospital in Spring Hill, near Mobile, and on April 1. He was diagnosed with acute dysentery January 27, 1864, and with debilitas March 26, 1864. On November 30, during the battle of Franklin, he was slightly wounded on the right ankle.* He was also hospitalized in Meridian, Mississippi, January 12, 1865. [24]*He was born January 31, 1847, died on August 6, 1927, and is buried in the Oakey Streak Methodist Church Cemetery in Butler County.*

Williamson, John W., Private, enlisted September 7, 1862, at Mobile. [17]*He was listed on the regimental medical register on November 5, 1864; diagnosis was morbi cutis.* He was hospitalized in Mobile January 12, 1865, and transferred to Marion, Ala. [10]*He was born June 24, 1840, in Covington County. He was living in Butler County in 1907.*

Williamson, S. J., Private, (5'7), [1]*enlisted March 1861 in Butler County.* He was discharged July 5, 1862. [17]*He was severely wounded in the right thigh and hand during the battle at Ezra Church on July 28, 1864. He was moved to the general hospital on the 31st.* [1]*He was furloughed until paroled* May 6, 1865, at Montgomery. [1]*He was born February 6, 1841, in Butler County. He was living in Mobile in 1907.* Also listed as **Stephens James Williamson.**

Williamson, Thomas, Private, enlisted February 1, 1864, at Greenville. He was paroled May 1865 at Greensboro, North Carolina.

Williamson, T. J., Private, enlisted September 14, 1861, at Montgomery.

Willioughby, William, Private, enlisted March 8, 1862, at Greenville. He was paroled May 1865 at Greensboro, North Carolina.

Wood, J., Private, was hospitalized June 1862.

Wood, Samuel McN., Private, enlisted March 1, 1862, at Tuscumbia and died later that year.

Worthington, William A., Private, enlisted at Montgomery September 14, 1861. He was hospitalized June 1862. He was listed on the muster roll for September-October 1862 as hospitalized at Columbus, Mississippi. On the November-December 1862 muster roll, he was reported deceased by Colonel V. S. Murphy. [6]*He died of dropsy in Columbus, Mississippi, on August 8, 1862.* Also spelled **Worrington.**

Young, J. Berry, Private, was hospitalized June 1862. In December 1862, he was reported deceased by Colonel V. S. Murphy and removed from rolls.

Appendix IV. Company C

Alford, J. R., Private, enlisted September 7, 1862, at Camp Forney. He was born in 1845 and was from Butler County. [17]*On January 27, 1864, he was listed on the regimental medical register; diagnosis was ulcus.* He was wounded in the hip and captured December 15, 1864, near Nashville, Tennessee. He was imprisoned at Camp Chase, Ohio, where he was paroled on June 12, 1865.

Anderson, H., Private, [12]*enlisted December 20, 1861, Newbern.* He reenlisted September 25, 1862, at Camp Forney. [12]*He was listed as sick in the camp hospital in northeast Mississippi during the summer of 1862.*

Armstrong, Henry C., Private, was captured at Gaylesville, Cherokee County, Alabama, and imprisoned at Camp Douglas, Illinois. It is also recorded that he was captured at Dirt Town, Georgia. He died December 19, 1864, leaving a wife, Mrs. G. Armstrong of Autauga County. [17]*H. S. Armstrong was listed on the regimental medical register on December 26, 1863, diagnosis was feb int quotid.* Also listed as **Henry D. Armstrong.**

Armstrong, Max, Private, enlisted September 7, 1862, at Camp Forney. [17]*He was listed on the regimental medical register on July 4, 1864, after being hit in the arm by a shell. He was listed as 27 years old and a farmer. He returned to his company, but died on the field on July 28, 1864, at the battle at Ezra Church during the siege of Atlanta.*

[17]***Arnold, M. H.**, Private, was listed on the regimental medical register on January 23, 1864, diagnosis was parotitis. On February 1,* **M. C.** *Arnold was listed on the regimental medical register with feb remitt and was immediately sent to the hospital at Spring Hill in Mobile.*

Atkinson, Theophilus, Private, enlisted at Montgomery September 14, 1861, age 28. [42]*He was placed on furlough January 5, 1862, and sent to Butler County for 21 days.* [17]*He was listed on the regimental medical register in 1864. In January the diagnosis was constipatio, and in April, feb int tert.* He was 6'2 and paroled at Montgomery.

Bailey, Geo. M., Private, enlisted September 14, 1861, age 20. He died March 28, 1862, at Corinth, Mississippi. He was survived by his father, Isaac.

Bailey, J. T., Private, enlisted September 1862, at Camp Forney. [17]*He was listed on the regimental medical register four times in 1864. On January 22, diagnosis was acute diarrhea; on June 15 and 27, feb int quotid; and in November, acute diarrhea.* He was captured December 15, 1864, near Nashville and imprisoned at Camp Douglas, Illinois. He was promoted to corporal on April 17, 1866, in the United States Army at Ft. Leavenworth, Kansas. He applied for a pension in 1911 and 1915.

Barnes, Jethrow, Private, enlisted December 20, 1861, at Montgomery. He was born in 1830 in Fayette County, Alabama. He was 5'11 and received a medical discharge September 20, 1862.

Bell, Jere, Private, enlisted September 7, 1862, at Camp Forney. [17]*He was listed on the regimental medical register with pneumonia April 16, 1864. Wounded on July 28, 1864, at the battle of Ezra Church at Atlanta (a slight wound to his left foot), he was sent to the general hospital July 31.*

Belton, Sol. D., Private, enlisted December 4, 1862, at Camp Forney. [17]*He was listed on the regimental medical register with acute dysentery April 20, 1864.* He was 5'6 and was paroled at Montgomery, June 6, 1865. Also spelled **Betton**.

Berry, F. M., Private, [12]*enlisted February 17, 1862, Fayetteville, Talladega County. He was listed as sick and absent from his company during the summer of 1862 while located in northeast Mississippi.* [6]*He died in the hospital at Okolona, Mississippi, October 1, 1862.*

Berry, William, Private, enlisted February 27, 1862, at Fayetteville, Talladega County. He was discharged December 27, 1862.

Black, J., Private, enlisted December 28, 1861, at Newbern, northwest of Selma, Alabama. [12]*He was listed as sick and absent from his company during the summer of 1862 while located in northeast Mississippi.*

Bobo, F., Private, enlisted September 25, 1862, at Camp Forney. [12]*He was listed as sick and absent from his company during the summer of 1862 while located in northeast Mississippi.*

Bodright, P., Private, 5'2, was paroled May 26, 1865, at Montgomery.

Boggs, Isah, Private, was discharged February 5, 1861.

Boggus, Henry J., Private, [12]*enlisted September 14, 1861.* [19]*He was a member of Company B when it was organized in 1861 and was listed as Henry Boggs, age 25.* [42]*He was placed on furlough January 17, 1862, for 14 days and sent to Butler County.* He was hospitalized during the month of June 1862. He was granted a disability discharge on July 21, 1862, but reenlisted on February 4, 1863. [17]*He was listed on the regimental medical register March 14, 1864; diagnosis was catarrhus. He transferred to the general hospital in Greenville on March 22.* He survived the war and was paroled in April 1865. [43]*He was born May 24, 1838, and died March 15, 1890. He was buried in Mercer Cemetery, 5 miles northwest of Luling, Texas. He married Sarah Jane Thomas.*

Boggus, James Carter, Private, enlisted September 7, 1862, at Camp Forney. [17]*He reported four times to the regimental medical unit in 1864. On January 14, the diagnosis was catarrhus and on March 1, feb int quotid. On March 20 and April 15, he had pneumonia and was sent to the general hospital a few days later.* He was captured April 25, 1865, at Greenville. [30]*He was born May 8, 1836, Georgia. He was* married to Mary Elizabeth Turner. He died June 1, 1894, Caldwell County, Texas, and was buried in the Mercer/Boggus Cemetery. His widow applied for a pension in 1909.

Bolling, John Jr., Captain, enlisted September 14, 1861, at Montgomery. He was born in 1840. Bolling was promoted to captain of Company C June 22, 1862. [17]*He was listed on the regimental medical register on June 3, 1864, with an acute case of dysentery. He was transferred to the general hospital the next day.* He was captured December 15, 1864, near Nashville and imprisoned at Johnson's Island, Ohio, where he was paroled June 16, 1865. Reference card: see manuscript #2457. [29]*He died May 11, 1898.*

Bradford, T. H., Private, was born in 1835 in Clarke County. He was 5'10 and discharged June 1, 1863.

Braydon, William E., Private, enlisted September 7, 1862, at Camp Forney. He was assigned to a Mobile hospital as assistant cook March 1, 1863. [17]*He was listed on the regimental medical register five times from December 1863 to September 1864. On December 5, the diagnosis was feb int quotid, and on December 10, neuralgia. On April 24, he had an acute case of dysentery, on June 20, acute diarrhea, and on September 18, an abscess.* He was captured December 15, 1864, near Nashville and was imprisoned at Camp Douglas, Illinois. [20]*He was born in Wilcox County July 25, 1839. He was living in Luverne, Crenshaw County, in 1907.*

[1]***Bradley, William E.***, Private, enlisted September 5, 1862, at Montgomery. He was born in Wilcox County. He was captured on December 15, 1864, near Nashville. He was imprisoned at Camp Douglas, Illinois, where he was paroled on June 15, 1865. He was living in Luverne, Crenshaw County, in 1907

Brooks, Leonard M., Private, [17]*was listed on the regimental medical register November 3, 1864, with a case of parotitis.* He was captured December 15, 1864, near Nashville and imprisoned at Camp Douglas, Illinois.

[18]***Brown, H. G.***, Private, was described as *46 years old, blue eyes, auburn hair, fair complexion, 5 foot 9 inches, a seaman, and a deserter September 5, 1863.*

Brown, J. A., Private, enlisted September 25, 1861, at Camp Forney. He was hospitalized June 1862. He was listed as present on the muster rolls for the period September – December 1862.

Buist, James, Private.

Burks, Columbus A., Private, enlisted December 20, 1861. [6]*He died in the hospital at Okolona, Mississippi, October 1, 1862.*

Caple, William L., Private, enlisted February 17, 1861, at Fayetteville, Talladega County, Alabama. He reenlisted March 1862 in the 58th Alabama.

Carter, A. W., Private

Cater, Josiah, Private, 5'10, was paroled June 7, 1865, at Montgomery.

Chambers, John E., Private, enlisted September 19, 1863, at Camden. He was 5'9, a farmer, and born in 1845 in Wilcox County. [17]*He was listed on the regimental medical register three times in 1864. On January 2, the diagnosis was feb int tert, on April 4, catarrhus, and on September 12, bronchitis. He transferred to the general hospital September 23.* He was captured December 15, 1864, near Nashville and was imprisoned at Camp Douglas, Illinois.

Chambers, William F., Private, was captured December 15, 1864, near Nashville. He was imprisoned at Camp Douglas, Illinois, where he died February 3, 1865. He was buried in lot no. 667, block 2, Chicago City Cemetery.

Cheatham, D. H., Private, enlisted April 15, 1864, at Pollard. [17]*He was listed on the regimental medical register on April 27, 1864; diagnosis was neuralgia.* [31]*He was at the surrender at Greensboro, North Carolina, on April 26, 1865.*

Cheatham, William Alexander, Private, enlisted February 2, 1863, at Greenville. [17]*He was listed on the regimental medical register four times in 1864. On January 1 his complaint was debilitas. He was placed on furlough for 15 days. He was diagnosed with dyspepsia January 28 and with debilitas March 30. He had pneumonia and was sent to the general hospital October 30.* He was captured December 15, 1864, near Nashville. He was imprisoned at Camp Douglas, Illinois, where he died of pneumonia April 22, 1865. He was buried in lot no. 1099, block 2, Chicago City Cemetery.

Coleman, James, was hospitalized at LaGrange, Georgia, June 7, 1864.

Connelly, John, [18]*Private, was described as 47 years old, blue eyes, red hair, fair complexion, 5 feet 7 inches, laborer, and a deserter in "The Independent", Gainesville, Alabama, September 5, 1863.*

Conner, William H., Private, enlisted September 14, 1861, at Montgomery. He was wounded at the battle of Shiloh, Tennessee, April 1862. [28]*He was present at the Confederate Veterans Reunion in Greenville August 21, 1897.* [7]*He registered as a veteran in Butler County on July 4, 1906.*

Corley, Andrew. B., Private, enlisted September 14, 1861, at Montgomery. Early in the war, he was employed at the Montgomery Arsenal. He was captured December 24, 1864, near Columbia, Tennessee. He was imprisoned at Camp Chase, Ohio, where he was paroled May 5, 1865. He was born in 1826 and lived in Butler County. Also listed as **Conley** and **Cooley**.

Cornathan, George, Private, enlisted September 5, 1862, at Mobile. [17]*He was listed on the regimental medical register June 2, 1864, with acute dysentery, and April 13, 1864, diagnosis catarrhus. The regimental hospital records indicate that he suffered a severe wound to his arm and was left on the field on July 20, 1864, at the battle of Peachtree Creek, Georgia.* [31]*He was at the surrender April 26, 1865, at Greensboro, North Carolina, and was listed as a member of Company C. Also spelled* **Cawthron, Carnahan, Carnothan.**
Cox, Odom, Private, enlisted February 2, 1863, at Greenville. [17]*He was listed on the regimental medical register in 1864. Diagnosis was neuralgia on February 11, catarrhus on April 17, and acute dysentery on August 3. He was sent to the general hospital on August 18, diagnosis was feb remitt and debilitas.* He was captured, took the oath of allegiance, and released April 22, 1865, at Greenville. [4]*He died March 1868, leaving wife, Martha Seale Cox.*
Creach, Sidney S., Private, enlisted September 4, 1861, at Montgomery. [12]*He was listed as absent on furlough during the summer of 1862.* [17]*He was listed on the regimental medical register July 17, 1864, with a case of acute diarrhea.* He was captured December 15, 1864, near Nashville, Tennessee. Imprisonment was at Camp Douglas, Illinois, where he died February 1, 1865 of pneumonia, and was buried in lot number 546, Chicago City Cemetery. Also listed as **Sidney L. Creech** and **S. L. Cruch.**
Creech, Francis Lafayette, Private, [1]*reenlisted during the Fall of 1862 in Greenville.* [12]*He was listed as sick and absent from his company during the summer of 1862 while located in northeast Mississippi.* [17]*He was listed on the regimental medical register January 29, 1864; diagnosis was catarrhus.* He was captured December 15, 1864, near Nashville and was imprisoned at Camp Douglas, Illinois. [1]*After Camp Douglas, he was sent to Richmond, Virginia, and later paroled.* [1]*He was born November 29, 1845, near Clayton.* [28]*He was present at the Confederate Veteran Reunion in Greenville, August 21, 1897.* [7]*F. L. Creech registered as a veteran in Butler County on July 4, 1906.* [37]*In 1921 he stated he was engaged in battles at Resaca, Cassville, Spring Hill, Franklin, Nashville, and Decatur, Alabama, and wounded at Resaca.* [24]*He died May 24, 1926, and is buried at Hartley Cemetery in Butler County.*
Cunningham, W. R., Private, [12]*enlisted December 20, 1861, Newbern, Perry County. On the muster roll for July-August 1862, he was listed as absent sick.*

Damper, Elijah, Private, 5'10, [17]*was diagnosed with feb int quotid September 29, 1864, and was immediately sent to the general hospital.*

He was paroled May 4, 1865, at Montgomery. Also spelled as **Dampier, Dampeir.**

Davidson, J. S., Private, enlisted September 5, 1862, Mobile. [17]*He was listed on the regimental medical register December 8, 1863, diagnosis feb int tert. On January 18, 1864, diagnosis feb int quotid, and February 23, diagnosis debilitas.* He was present at the surrender at Greensboro, North Carolina, April 26, 1865, where he was paroled.

Davis, Isaiah, Private, enlisted September 14, 1861, Montgomery. He was born 1830 in Lowndes County. He was granted a medical furlough January 1862 for 19 days and sent to Butler County. He was hospitalized June 1862. [17]*He reported to the regimental medical unit June 2, 1864, with acute dysentery. He suffered a shell wound (right chest) during the battle at Kennesaw Mountain, Georgia, June 20, 1864.*

Davis, R. G., Private, enlisted September 20, 1862, at Camp Forney.

Davis, R. J., Private.

Dendy, Buford W., 2nd Lieutenant, 5'8, enlisted September 14, 1861, at Montgomery. He was born in 1832 and lived in Greenville. [12]*He was listed as sick and absent from his company during the summer of 1862 while located in northeast Mississippi.* [17]*After being wounded on July 20, 1864, in the right thigh at Peachtree Creek near Atlanta, he was sent to the general hospital the next day.* He was captured December 15, 1864, near Nashville and imprisoned on Johnson Island, Ohio. Also listed as **Buford W. Dandy.**

Dendy, Lawson, Private, enlisted July 4, 1863, at Greenville. He was 5'8, a farmer, and born in 1845 in Pike County. See Service Records for David Blackman of the 54th Alabama Infantry. [17]*On January 29, 1864, he reported to the regimental medical unit with an acute case of dysentery. On April 14, 1864, he returned to the medical unit and was transferred to the general hospital April 22.* [31]*He was at the surrender April 26, 1865, at Greensboro, North Carolina.* Also listed as **Dandy.**

Dodson, George W., Private, enlisted December 20, 1861, at Newbern, northwest of Selma, Alabama.

Dodson, N. J., Private, enlisted December 20, 1861, at Newbern, northwest of Selma, Alabama.

Dorson, George W., Private, was hospitalized June 1862.

Driver, James M., Sergeant, enlisted November 11, 1863. He was 6', a grocer, and born in 1825 in Chambers County. [17]*He was listed on the regimental medical register during November 1864 with acute diarrhea.* Captured December 15, 1864, near Nashville, he was imprisoned at Camp Douglas, Illinois. His home was in Chambers County.

Driver, John W., Private, enlisted September 14, 1861, at Montgomery. Placed on medical furlough January 13, 1862, he was sent home to Butler County for 18 days. [17]*Jno. M. Driver was listed on the*

COMPANY C

regimental medical unit June 25, 1864, diagnosis was abscessus. **J. W. Driver** was listed on the regimental medical unit five times in 1864. On January 31, the diagnosis was diarrhea; on February 11, catarrhus; on August 7, feb int quotid; on August 19, feb int tert; and on September 4, neuralgia.

Dugan, James F., Private, was discharged September 17, 1861. [12]*He was listed as absent on furlough during the summer of 1862 while located in northeast Mississippi.* [17]*James Dugan was listed on the regimental medical register three times in 1864 with the same complaint, feb int tert, on April 23, August 8, and 26. He was severely wounded in the left arm and middle finger during the battle of Franklin on November 30. His arm was amputated below the elbow.*

Dukes, James F., Private, enlisted September 14, 1861, at Montgomery. He was paroled May 22, 1865, at Montgomery.

Earnest, James J., Private, enlisted September 14, 1861, at Montgomery. [12]*He was listed as absent sick on the muster rolls for July-August 1862.* [17]*He was listed on the regimental medical register on February 24, 1864, diagnosis was feb int quotid.* He died of pneumonia May 27, 1864. Also spelled **Ernst**.

Elliot, A. M., Private, enlisted February 12, 1863, at Camp Davis. He was 6'1, a farmer and born 1829 in Butler County. [17]*He was listed on the regimental medical register in August and September of 1864, diagnosis feb int tert.* He was paroled May 24, 1865, at Montgomery

Fales, L., Private, also listed as **L. Tales** with no additional information.

Flowers, J. D., Private, [17]*was listed on the regimental medical register March 16, 1864; diagnosis was feb int tert.* Captured December 15, 1864, near Nashville, he was imprisoned at Camp Douglas, Illinois, until the end of the war. His home was Butler County. [7]*J. D. Flowers registered as a veteran in Butler County on July 4, 1906.* [28]*He died July 23, 1924.*

Frost, Henry, Private, enlisted September 14, 1861, Montgomery. He was hospitalized June 2, 1862. [17]*He was listed on the regimental medical register June 26, 1864, diagnosis was feb int quotid, and July 10, pneumonia. He transferred to the general hospital July 11.* [19]*He was listed as a member of Company C when it was organized in 1861.*

Frost, James, Private, [12]*enlisted September 14, 1861, Montgomery. He was granted a sick furlough for 15 days January 1862 and sent home to Butler County.* He was [5]*reported as slightly wounded at the battle of Shiloh, Tennessee, on April 6-7, 1862.* [12]*He was listed as sick and absent from his company during July-August 1862 while located in northeast Mississippi.* [17]*He was listed on the regimental medical* register September 30, 1864; diagnosis was acute dysentery. He was captured December 15, 1864, near Nashville. Imprisonment was at Camp Douglas, Illinois, where he died April 8, 1865. Burial was in lot number 1044, block 3 at Chicago City Cemetery.

[17] **Frost, Joseph**, Private, reported to the regimental medical unit June 24, 1864 with a case of scabies and immediately transferred to the general hospital. May be **Josiah Frost.**

Frost, Josiah, Private, [12]enlisted September 14, 1861. He was listed on the muster roll for July-August 1862 as sick in the camp hospital. He reenlisted September 19, 1862, at Montgomery. He was 6' and born in 1841 in Butler County and received a disability discharge November 2, 1862. [17]He was listed on the regimental medical unit August 13, 1864, diagnosis irr spinatis & diarrhea and again on September 13, catarrhus.

[17] **Frost, W. H.**, Private, was wounded in May 1864, possibly at the battle of Resaca, Georgia. He died June 29, 1864, probably of the wounds received the previous month.

Ganus, Thomas J., Private, [20]enlisted in November 1863 in Greenville, Alabama. [17]He was listed on the regimental medical register twice in 1864: March 26, diagnosis was feb int tert, and June 24, diagnosis was feb int quotid. He was transferred to the general hospital on the 24th. [20]He was born at Midway, Barbour County, Alabama, November 4, 1845 and living in Monroe County, Alabama, in 1907. He was paroled at Greenville April 25, 1865. A copy of his Parole of Honor is stored in the Alabama archives in Montgomery and signed by Ganus.

Goodson, Peter, Sergeant, enlisted September 14, 1861. On the muster roll for September-October 1862, he was listed as sick in the hospital. [17]Sgt. **C. Goodson** was listed on the regimental medical register on March 28, 1864, feb int tert. Sgt. **P. C. Goodson** entered the hospital on June 15, acute diarrhea. Sgt. **Peter Goodson** was killed instantly by a minnie ball to the skull on July 8, 1864, during the siege of Atlanta..

Graibeck, Ripley J., Private.

Grayden, Henry Sterling, Private, enlisted September 15, 1862, at Camp Forney. He was hospitalized during June 1862 and given a disability discharge December 1862. [17]From December 1863 to November 1864, he was listed on the regimental medical register seven times. On December 22, the diagnosis was feb int quotid. On January 27, February 11, and June 15, the diagnosis was feb int tert. On August 17, the diagnosis was acute diarrhea, in September, parotitis, and November, acute dysentery. He was detailed as a mechanic. He was paroled at Montgomery June 16, 1865. [1]He was born March 15, 1837, in Butler County. He served until the surrender and resided in Butler

County in 1907. ⁷*He registered as a Confederate veteran in Butler County on July 4, 1906.* ¹⁹*He died May 7, 1908, and was buried in the cemetery adjacent to Antioch Church.*

Grayden, William A., Private, enlisted September 15, 1862, at Camp Forney. ¹⁷ *He was listed on the regimental medical register four times between December 1863 and July 1864. On December 12, the diagnosis was debilitas. He was granted a furlough December 18 for 20 days. On March 31, the diagnosis was catarrhus, and on April 19, feb int tert. At the battle of Peachtree Creek on July 20, he was slightly wounded in the thigh. He was moved to the general hospital the next day. He was paroled in Montgomery June 14, 1865.* ¹⁶*He was born March 12, 1828, died January 2, 1902, and is buried at Spring Creek Cemetery, Butler County.*

Green, Edward, Private, ¹²*enlisted November 1, 1861, at Camp Davis. He was listed as sick and absent from his company during the summer of 1862 while located in northeast Mississippi.*

Hall, Benton, Private, was hospitalized in Mobile February 18, 1864. ¹⁷*He was listed on the regimental medical records on the following dates: February 6, diagnosis phthisis pulm and sent to a hospital at Spring Hill; February 17, diagnosis rubeola and sent to the general hospital on the 18th; March 4, diagnosis acute dysentery and sent to a hospital at Spring Hill on the 12th. He was paroled at Selma, Alabama, in June 1865.*

Harrison, J. E., Private, enlisted November 24, 1863. A farmer, 5'9, he was born 1817 in Montgomery County. See Service Records for Driver. ¹⁷*He was listed on the regimental medical register on January 6, diagnosis was catarrhus; on June 21, feb int quotid; on August 11, acute diarrhea. **J. K. Harrison** was listed on February 26, diagnosis feb int quotid. He was captured and paroled at Greenville in April 1865.* Could be **John K. Harrison**.

Harrison, John A., 2nd Lieutenant, was born in 1837 in Butler County. ¹⁹*His name was on Company C roster when it was organized in September of 1861. He was promoted July 1862.* ¹⁷*Wounded in the chest, he was killed at the battle of Ezra Church in Atlanta July 28, 1864, age 21 years 2 months 29 days. His brother, Moses J., was also in Company C.* ⁴³*He was born April 29, 1840, Butler County, to Williamson and Amanda Elizabeth Smith Harrison. Unmarried.*

Harrison, John R., Private, enlisted September 7, 1862, at Camp Forney. ¹⁷*He was listed on the regimental medical register on February 1, 1864, diagnosis was feb int quotid. He was paroled at Montgomery June 3, 1865.*

Harrison, Moses J., Private, enlisted September 14, 1861, at Montgomery. On the muster rolls for July-August 1863, Moses was listed as sick in quarters. [17]*He was slightly wounded (side) in May 1864 during the Atlanta campaign. He was listed on the regimental medical register September 13, diagnosis feb int quotid. He was killed at Franklin, Tennessee, on November 30, 1864, age 20 years 7 months 8 days.* [30]*His place of burial is unknown. A memorial marker is located at the Harrison Cemetery in Butler County. His brother, John A. Harrison, was also in Company C.* [43]*He was born August 4, 1844, Butler County, son of Williamson and Amanda Elizabeth Smith Harrison. Unmarried.*

Head, Oliver J., Corporal, enlisted November 11, 1863, at Montgomery. A farmer, 5'8, he was born in 1819, Jasper County, Georgia.

Henderson, Isaiah H., Private, 5'10, enlisted September 14, 1861, at Montgomery. He was born in 1847 in Butler County. [17]*He was hospitalized December 27, 1863 and February 3, 1864, diagnosis was feb int tert.* He was captured December 16, 1864, at Nashville and imprisoned at Camp Chase, Ohio, where he was paroled at the end of the war. Also listed as **John H. Henderson.**

Hendricks, Tapley, Private, died in the hospital June 11, 1862. [19]*His name is on the roster of Company C when it was organized in September of 1861.*

Herbert, R. L., Private.

Hernden, William, Private, was granted a sick furlough January 7, 1862 for 14 days and sent to Butler County. He was wounded and died at the battle of Shiloh, Tennessee, April 1862.

Hester, D. E., Private, enlisted September 1, 1863, at Greenville. He was 5'3 and born 1839 in Butler County. [17]***Daniel** was listed on the regimental medical register on April 14, 1864 and transferred to the general hospital on the 23rd, diagnosis debilitas.* He was granted parole in 1865 at Montgomery. [28]***D. L.** was present at the Confederate Veteran Reunion in Greenville, August 21, 1897.* [7]***D. L.** Hester registered as a Confederate Veteran in Butler County on July 4, 1906.*

Hester, L. A., Private, reenlisted September 7, 1862, at Camp Forney. [19]***Louis A.** was listed on roster of Company C when it was organized in September of 1861.* **Lewis** was discharged on December 5, 1861. He was listed as present on the muster rolls in 1862 and 1863. [17]***L. A.** was listed on the regimental medical register on April 13, 1864, diagnosis debilitas. He was killed by a rifle ball to the neck in May of 1864, probably at the battle of Resaca, Georgia.*

Holland, David J., Private, enlisted December 13, 1863, in Greenville. A farmer at 5'5, he was born [1]*November 11, 1844, in Greenville,* Butler County. [17]*He was listed on the regimental medical register March 8, 1864, with rubeola and sent to the general hospital at Spring Hill near*

Mobile March 10. He was listed on the regimental medical register four more times in 1864. On June 2, the diagnosis was feb int tert; on June 11, acute diarrhea; on September 11, feb int tert; and on November 3, acute rheum. **D. G.** was hospitalized March 31, 1864; diagnosis was debilitas. He was captured May 30, 1865, at Montgomery. [1]*He resided in Palsburg, Crenshaw County, in 1907.* [15]*He died July 1, 1916, and is buried in Old Providence Cemetery, Crenshaw County.*

Holland, J. H., Private, 6', was born 1841 in Butler County. He was granted a sick furlough January 27, 1862, for 15 days and sent to Butler County. He was killed by a shot to the head at the battle of Shiloh, Tennessee, on April 1862. Papers under J. H. are listed under the names **J. H., H. J., and Harrison Holland.**

Howard, John D., drummer, was discharged April 3, 1863, reason: underage. [19]*His name is on roster of Company C when it was organized in September of 1861.*

Jackson, William B. Jr., Private, was born in 1833 in Marengo County. He earned a discharge May 12, 1863, by providing a substitute.

Jay, James W., Private, [12]*enlisted September 14, 1861, Montgomery.* He reenlisted November 14, 1863, in Montgomery. He was at the surrender at Greensboro, North Carolina, April 26, 1865, listed in Company K.

Johnson, James, Private, 5'11, enlisted December 17, 1863, in Greenville. A wheelwright, he was born in 1827 in Barnwell District, South Carolina. [17]*J. L. Johnson was listed on the regimental medical unit on June 4 with an acute case of diarrhea, and J. A. Johnson on June 11 also with acute diarrhea.*

Johnson, J. E., Private, enlisted September 7, 1862, at Camp Forney. [17]*He was listed on the regimental medical unit June 21, 1864, diagnosis feb int quotid. Jos. E. Johnsons was killed July 20, 1864, at the battle of Peachtree Creek during the siege of Atlanta.*

Jones, J. B., Private, enlisted during September of 1861 at Montgomery. His parole was granted at Greensboro, North Carolina, May 1865.

Kelly, Andrew J., Private, enlisted September 14, 1861, at Montgomery. He was born in 1838 in Butler County. He was granted a discharge on January 14, 1863, reason: deafness and disability.

[17]**Kendrick, J. H.**, *Private, was listed on the regimental medical register September 4, 1864, with chronic diarrhea.*

Kendrick, R., Private, enlisted November 1, 1862, at Camp Davis. He was paroled in April 1865, at Greensboro, North Carolina.

Kent, T. A., Private, was hospitalized in June 1862.

Kent, T. J., Private, enlisted September 10, 1861. [17]*Listed as a sergeant, he was listed on the regimental medical register on August 2, 1864; diagnosis was anthrax.*

Kite, Bankston, Private, enlisted September 1861, at Montgomery. [42]*He was placed on furlough November 13, 1861, for two days and sent to Butler County.* [12]*He was listed as sick and absent from his company during the summer of 1862 while located in northeast Mississippi.* He was granted a medical furlough November 13, 1862, for 20 days and sent to Butler County and for another 20 days January 5, 1863. On June 13, 1864, he was granted a medical furlough from LaGrange, Georgia.

Laney, George, Private, 5'7, took the oath of allegiance, September 27, 1863.

Lary, LaFayette, Private, died July 11, 1862, [6]*at Lauderdale Springs, Mississippi,* leaving mother or widow, Louisa Lary. [19]*His name is on roster of Company C when it was organized in September of 1861.* [12]*He was listed as **Lafayette Largo** on the regiment muster rolls for July-August 1862.*

Lines, J. B., Private. See Julius F. Sims.

Lintern, H., Private, reported to the hospital in Richmond, Virginia, May 12, 1864.

Living, W. J., Private, enlisted August 15, 1863, at Mobile. A shoemaker and 6', he was born in 1823 in Pike County. See Service Records for Samuel Scipper. [3]*Could be **Leva**.*

Lowery, George W., Private, enlisted September 1862, at Camp Forney. [1]*He was born September 28, 1844, in Butler County.* [17]*He was listed on the regimental medical register on June 11, 1864, diagnosis was feb int quotid.* He was captured July 14, 1864, at Stone Mountain (Oxford), Georgia, and imprisoned at Camp Chase, Ohio. [1]*He was paroled in April 1865.* He listed Luverne in Crenshaw County as his home in 1907 [37]*and again in 1921 when he stated he took part in the battles of Resaca and Kennesaw Mountain.*

Lowery, H. B., Private, enlisted February 27, 1862, at Greenville.

Lowery, James, Private, enlisted September 21, 1861, at Camp Davis. He was granted sick furlough January 7, 1862, for 24 days and sent to Butler County. [17]*On the regimental hospital records he was listed as a 2nd Corporal. He reported on January 12, 1864, diagnosis was feb int tert, and on February 11, 1864, feb int quotid.* He was paroled on May 31, 1865. [20]*He was born July 7, 1840, in an area that became Crenshaw County in the late 1860s. He was living in Marengo County in 1907 and in 1921.* [37]*On the 1921 Confederate Soldiers Census he stated that he took part in the battle of Shiloh and two battles and the*

retreat from Dalton, Georgia, to Atlanta in 1864. In 1865 he "was on way to Lee's Army and was cut off as Surrender came."
[39]**Lowery, J. H.**, Pvt., was wounded at Nashville December 1864.
Lowery, R. B., Private, enlisted February 27, 1862, at Greenville.
Lowery, Thomas H., Private, enlisted September 24, 1861, at Camp Davis. He was hospitalized in June 1862.
Lowery, Wiley, Private, enlisted February 27, 1862, Greenville. [12]*He was listed as sick in quarters during the summer of 1862 while located in northeast Mississippi.* [1]*Wiley W. Lowery Jr. was born July 1839 at Catoma Creek, Montgomery County. He served until the surrender and resided in Butler County in 1907.* [7]*He registered as a Confederate veteran in Butler County on July 4, 1906.*

Maney, William, Private, enlisted September 14, 1861, at Montgomery and was paroled at Greensboro, North Carolina, in May 1865.
Mapes, John W., Private, enlisted September 24, 1861, at Camp Davis. He was wounded at the battle of Shiloh, Tennessee, April 1862 and hospitalized in June of the same year. [17]*He was listed on the regimental medical register on December 6, 1863, diagnosis was feb int quotid, and on January 31, 1864, constipatio.* He was paroled June 19, 1865. [16]*He was buried in Mitchell Cemetery, Crenshaw County, no headstone.* Also listed as **J. M. Mapes**.
[16]**Mapes, William James**, Private, *was born April 17, 1836. He died October 2, 1879, and was buried at Rocky Mount Cemetery, Crenshaw County.*
Mash, David J., Private, enlisted February 3, 1863, at Greenville. A farmer and 5'11, he was born in 1844 in Fayette County, Georgia. [17]*He was listed on the regimental medical register on December 5, 1863, diagnosis was feb int quotid, and on December 20, feb int tert. He was reported to the regimental medical unit January 7, 1864, and was transferred to the general hospital the next day, diagnosis feb int tert. He was listed on the regimental medical register and then the hospital at Spring Hill on March 11, diagnosis debilitas.* He was disabled due to tuberculosis and was granted a medical discharge September 23, 1864. [28]*He attended the Confederate Veteran Reunion at Greenville August 21, 1897.* [30]*He was born February 23, 1844, Fayette County, Georgia. He ran a gristmill in Mashville, Butler County. His wife was Sophronia Gholson. He died April 1, 1905, and was buried in St. Paul's Cemetery, Butler County.*
McCormack, John D., Private, was discharged December 5, 1861. [19]*His name is on roster of Company C when it was organized in September of 1861.*

McCrary, John A., Private, enlisted September 14, 1861, at Montgomery. [17]*He was listed on the regimental medical register January 6, 1864, diagnosis chronic rheum, and transferred to the general hospital the next day. **Jno. McCrary** reported to the regimental medical unit December 30, 1863, diagnosis ebrietas. **J. R. McCrary** reported with the same illness on January 3, 1864.* He was paroled June 1865.

McIntyre, J. N., Private, enlisted February 20, 1863, at Mobile.

McLellan, George F., Private, enlisted December 20, 1861, at Newbern, Perry County. Also listed as **George F. McClelland**.

[17] **Melton, J. P.**, *Sergeant, was listed on the regimental medical register July 2, 1864 and in September 1864, diagnosis was feb int quotid. He was sent to the general hospital on July 4. Could be **Milton**.*

Mercer, Seth, Private, [1]*enlisted February 16, 1864, at Greenville.* [17]*He was listed on the regimental medical register on June 21, 1864, with acute diarrhea.* He was hospitalized January 12, 1865, at West Point, Mississippi. He was captured and paroled April 29, 1865, at Greenville. [1]*He was born October 26, 1826, in Darlington District, South Carolina. He resided in Butler County in 1907. From The Shells of Pigeon Creek: His parents were Noah and Catherine Mercer. His wife was Irene Fails.* Also listed as **Murser**.

Miller, Isaiah G., Private, enlisted September 14, 1861, at Montgomery. He was hospitalized in June 1862. [12]*He was again listed as sick in camp during the July-August muster rolls while located in northeast Mississippi.* [17] *I. J. Miller was listed on the regimental medical register January 25, 1864, diagnosis feb int tert. I. G. Miller reported March 16, 1864, diagnosis acute diarrhea.* He was captured June 5, 1864, at New Hope Church, Georgia, and transferred for exchange, March 15, 1865. Also listed as **Ira G., Isaac G. Miller**

Miller, J. T., Private, enlisted September 7, 1862, at Camp Forney. He was hospitalized in July 1863. From Greenville he was granted a disability furlough on June 8, 1864, for 60 days, diagnosis chronic diarrhea.

[17]**Miller, T. J.**, *Private, was listed on the regimental medical register April 14, 1864, diagnosis feb int tert.*

Milton, Berryman, Private, enlisted September 7, 1862, at Camp Forney. [17]*He was listed on the regimental medical register January 31, 1864, diagnosis was feb int tert.*

Milton, Jacob C., Private, enlisted September 14, 1861, at Greenville. He was captured at Pittsburg Landing, Tennessee, on April 7, 1862, during the battle of Shiloh, where he was wounded in the thigh. Imprisonment was at Camp Chase, Ohio, where he was transferred to Vicksburg, Mississippi, for prisoner exchange August 25, 1862. [17] *He was listed on the regimental medical register twice in December 1863, on the 3rd when the diagnosis was feb int quotid and on the 19th when the* diagnosis was constipacio. In 1864, he was listed three times. On March 15, the diagnosis was catarrhus, on April 14, feb int tert, and on November 3, acute rheum.

Milton, R. B., Private, was discharged December 5, 1861.

Milton, William L., Private, 5'10, enlisted January 1863, Camp Forney. He was born in 1826 and lived in Lowndes County. [17]*He was slightly wounded in the arm during May 1864, probably at the battle of Resaca, Georgia.* He was captured December 17, 1864, at Franklin, Tennessee, and imprisoned at Camp Chase, Ohio, where he took the oath of allegiance June 12, 1865. Also spelled **Melton**.

Moon, J. J. C., Private, died at a hospital in Jackson, Mississippi. Note: He may have been in Company E.

[17]***Morgan, J. W.***, *Private, could be either **James W. Morgan** or **John W. Morgan** below. J. W. was listed on the regimental medical register six times in 1864.* On January 20, the diagnosis was feb int tert; on February 11, feb int quotid; on March 19, contusia; on August 4, anasarca; in September, chronic diarrhea; and on October 6, acute diarrhea. On October 15, he was sent to the general hospital. [28]*He attended the Confederate Veteran Reunion August 21, 1897.*

Morgan, James W., Private, 5'9, enlisted November 3, 1862, Camp Forney. [17]*He was slightly wounded in his side during May 1864, probably during the battle of Resaca, Georgia. He was listed on the regimental medical register on July 5; diagnosis was cephalolgia.* He was paroled June 16, 1865, at Montgomery. [7]*He registered as a Confederate Veteran in Butler County on July 4, 1906.* [30]*He applied for a pension in 1916.* In his pension application, he stated that after he was wounded (this could be at Resaca or later) he was detailed to the engineering corps, located at Selma, Alabama. In December of 1864, he was not with his unit at Nashville, but was with the wagon train headed for Mississippi. When he finally reached Selma again, he was sent home, probably March 1865. He was born November 11, 1830, and married Celia Ann Easterling. He died November 13, 1919, in Butler County. See J. W. Morgan above. [43]*He was the son of Thomas and Nancy M. Morgan.*

Morgan, J. E., Private, enlisted November 9, 1862, at Camp Forney.

Morgan, John A., Private, enlisted November 3, 1862, at Camp Forney. [17]*He was listed on the regimental medical register on December 22, diagnosis was feb int tert.* He was captured and paroled at Greenville, May 1865.

Morgan, John W., Private, enlisted February 12, 1862, at Camp Forney and lived in Butler County. [17]*He was listed on the regimental medical register at least three times in 1864. On April 2, he was suffering with pneumonia and was sent to the general hospital on the 18th. On April*

28, the diagnosis was debilitas, and on July 10, feb int tert. He was hospitalized June 3, 1864, at Macon County, Georgia. [28]*He attended the Confederate Veteran Reunion in Greenville on August 21, 1897. See* **J. W. Morgan** *above.*

Nichols, Christopher, Private. See 30th Alabama for information. [17]*Also listed as* **C. C. Nichols, Nicholls**. *He is listed on the regimental register ten times for the period December 1863 to August 1864. On December 28 and February 3, the diagnosis was catarrhus. On January 30 and July 11, the diagnosis was feb int tert. On February 17, the diagnosis was rubeola. He was sent to the general hospital February 18. On April 29 and June 4, the diagnosis was acute dysentery. On June 23, the diagnosis was debilitas. On August 4, the diagnosis was acute diarrhea. On August 16 during the siege of Atlanta, he suffered a slight chest wound.*

Nichols, Shadrick, Private, enlisted September 14, 1861, at Montgomery. Also listed as **S. Nicholas**. [17]*He is listed on the regimental medical register five times between December 1863 and March 1864. On December 27, the diagnosis was fit int quotid; December 31 and January, oedema; January 26, feb int tert; and March 22, feb int quotid.*

Northcut, H. L., Private, enlisted December 20, 1861, at Newbern, Perry County. [12]*He was hospitalized the summer of 1862 while located in northeast Mississippi.* He reenlisted September 25, 1862, at Camp Forney.

Odom, William, Private, enlisted September 7, 1862, at Camp Forney. He died October 29, 1863, at Miller General Hospital, Spring Hill in Mobile.

Owens, Miami J., Private, was captured December 15, 1864, at Nashville and imprisoned at Camp Douglas, Illinois.

Pace, G. W., Private, was discharged January 15, 1862, reason: disability.

Pace, Joseph W., Private, enlisted September 4, 1862, Choctaw County. He entered Ross Hospital in Mobile February 14, 1864, diagnosis: ulcer. He was sent to the general hospital in Greenville, February 18.

Pace, Russell F., Private, enlisted September 7, 1862, at Camp Forney. [17]*He was listed on the regimental medical register December 4, 1863, diagnosis was catarrhus, and April 28, 1864.* [31]*He was at the surrender April 26, 1865, at Greensboro, North Carolina.*

Pace, Thomas E., Private, enlisted September 14, 1861, at Montgomery.

Pace, William B., Private, enlisted September 14, 1861, at Montgomery. He was born in 1837 and lived in Butler County. He was promoted to sergeant March 18, 1863. [17]*He was listed on the regimental medical* *register December 9, 1863, diagnosis was feb int tert, February 4, 1864, catarrhus, and April 10, tonsilitis.* He was captured December 16, 1864, at Nashville. He was imprisoned at Johnson Island, Ohio, where he was paroled June 17, 1865 and listed as 6'. Also spelled **Pack**.

Palland, T. B., Private, 5'9, was paroled June 17, 1865, at Montgomery.

Parker, Gardner G., Private, enlisted September 14, 1861, at Montgomery. He worked as a teamster and was commissioned as sergeant June 1862. [17]*He was listed on the regimental medical register December 11, 1863; diagnosis was anthrax. He was slightly wounded (right little finger) July 28, 1864, at the battle at Ezra Church near Atlanta. He was sent to the general hospital on the 31st.* He was captured December 15, 1864, at Nashville and imprisoned at Camp Douglas, Illinois, where he died May 5, 1865. He was buried in lot number 1122, in block 3, at Chicago City Cemetery.

Parker, W. W., Private, enlisted January 16, 1864, at Mobile. [31]*He was at the surrender April 26, 1865, at Greensboro, North Carolina.*

Parmer, R. F., Private, enlisted January 25, 1865, in Greenville. [31]*R. T. Parmer was at the surrender April 26, 1865, at Greensboro, North Carolina.*

Payne, J. E., Private, lived in Butler County. Granted a sick furlough January 8, 1862, he was sent to Butler County for 23 days.

Payne, Ira Ellis, Private, 5'11, enlisted September 14, 1861, at Montgomery. He died June 24, 1862, in a hospital in [35]*Enterprise, Mississippi, of typhoid fever. He is buried in the Old Cemetery in Greenville. He was born May 18, 1844, in Butler County, son of John and Frances Gafford Payne.*

Payne, John, 2nd Lieutenant, 5'11, enlisted September 9, 1861, at Greenville. He was elected 2nd lieutenant September 14, 1861, and promoted February 23, 1862. [35]*He was born April 4, 1842, in Butler County, to parents John and Frances Gafford Payne. He died June 19, 1862, of typhoid fever at Dr. Witherspoon's near Crawford, Mississippi. He is buried in the Old Cemetery in Greenville.*

Perdue, J. H., Private, enlisted December 29, 1863, at Greenville. [17]*He was wounded in the ankle in May 1864, probably at the battle of Resaca, Georgia.* He was captured and paroled April 22, 1865 in Greenville.

Perry, Benjamin, Private, enlisted August 3, 1863, in Greenville. He was 5'9, a farmer, and born in 1819 at Edgefield County, South Carolina. He was hospitalized with disease June 22, 1864, at Macon, Georgia, and transferred June 24 to Butler County. [17]*According to the regimental medical register, diagnosis was chronic diarrhea. He was listed on the regimental register seven more times. On December 17, 1863, and April 6, 1864, diagnosis was catarrhus. All other entries occurred in 1864. On February 26, the diagnosis was rubeola; March 10, debilitas;*

August 13, acute diarrhea; September 18, paratitis; and November 3, contusio. On September 18, he was transferred to the general hospital. He was captured December 15, 1864, at Nashville and imprisoned at Camp Douglas, Illinois, where he died of smallpox February 22, 1865.

Perry, James, Private, enlisted August 3, 1863, Greenville. He was 5'6, a farmer and born 1823 in Abbeville District, South Carolina. He was discharged on December 5, 1861. He was hospitalized November 10, 1864, at Jackson, Mississippi. Capture and parole occurred on April 26, 1865.

Perry, Robert L., Sergeant, enlisted September 14, 1861, at Montgomery. [17]*He was listed on the regimental medical register four times with fever, December 3, 1863, and January 11, February 26, and August 7, 1864.* He was captured and paroled April 26, 1865, at Greenville. [28]*He attended the Confederate Veteran Reunion on August 21, 1897.* [41]*Robert was born in 1840 to John and Harriet Allis Davis Perry. His wife was Edna Permelia Smyth. He died January 1, 1901.*

Perry, William, Private, [17]*was listed on the regimental medical register with acute diarrhea August 30, 1864.* He was captured December 15, 1864, at Nashville and imprisoned at Camp Douglas, Illinois. He applied to take the oath of allegiance. He died of measles February 2, 1865, and was buried in lot no. 674, block 2, at Chicago City Cemetery.

Perryman, Walter D., Captain, was elected captain September 9, 1861, and resigned May 2, 1862.

Peterson, Thomas A., Private, enlisted September 12, 1862, at Camp Forney. His home was Butler County. [17]*He was listed on the regimental medical register June 2 and 4, 1864, with acute dysentery. He was wounded (left thigh) July 28, 1864, at the battle of Ezra Church near Atlanta. He was transferred July 31 to the general hospital.* He was captured December 15, 1864, near Nashville. Imprisonment was at Camp Douglas, Illinois, where he was discharged June 17, 1865.

Peterson, William R., Private, enlisted at Montgomery, September 14, 1861. [17]*He was listed on the regimental medical register March 27 and June 18, 1864, with fever.* He was captured December 17, 1864, Nashville. Imprisonment was at Camp Chase, Ohio, where he died of pneumonia February 2, 1865, and was buried in lot number 916. Also spelled **Patterson**.

Petty, J. A. H., Private, enlisted September 1861, at Montgomery. He was arrested for desertion December 24, 1862. [3]*Probably **James A. M. Petty**.*

Philyaw, Thomas J., Private, enlisted September 14, 1861, at Montgomery. Also spelled **Philyan, Philgan**.

Pierce, Frank M., Private, enlisted September 14, 1861, at Montgomery. [17]*He was listed on the regimental medical register on June 18, 1864, diagnosis was feb int tert, and on August 4 with acute dysentery.*
Pierce, R. W., Private, 5'8, enlisted September 7, 1861, at Camp Forney. [17]*He was listed on the regimental medical register twice in 1864, July 30 with acute dysentery and August 3 with acute diarrhea.* He was paroled June 19, 1865, at Montgomery. Also listed as **W. R. Pierce, Pearce.**
Pitman, Absolum, died June 1, 1862, at the general hospital in Macon, Mississippi.
Pollard, Everett, Private, enlisted September 9, 1862, at Camp Forney. [17]*He was listed on the regimental medical register December 13, 1863, diagnosis feb int quotid, January 1, 1864, debilitas, and January 17, feb int tert. He was wounded in the left shoulder August 10, 1864 during the siege of Atlanta and was sent to the general hospital the same day.* He was hospitalized August 22, 1864, having been wounded with a U.S. ball in arm. His home was in Greenville. [7]*He was born September 3, 1830, in Butler County, where he resided in 1907.* [28]*He was present at the Confederate Veteran Reunion in Greenville on August 21, 1897.*
[7]*He registered as a Confederate Veteran in Butler County July 4, 1906.*
Pollard, T. B., Private, [17]*was listed on the regimental medical register on February 1, 1864, with erysipelas and transferred to the hospital at Spring Hill the same day. He was listed on the regimental medical register April 25, diagnosis catarrhus, and June 20, acute diarrhea.* He was paroled June 17, 1865, at Montgomery, listed as 5'9. [28]*He was present at the Confederate Veterans Reunion in Greenville August 21, 1897.* Also spelled **Palland.**
Posey, George H., Corporal, enlisted September 14, 1861, at Montgomery. [17]*In September 1864, he held the rank of sergeant when he was listed on the regimental medical register with acute diarrhea.* [2] *He was killed at Franklin, Tennessee, November 30, 1864, and buried in Confederate Soldiers Cemetery (McGavock Cemetery) Section 69, lot 23, Franklin.*
Powell, D. M., Private, was discharged April 3, 1863.
Powell, James F., Private, enlisted April 1, 1862, at Greenville. [12]*He was listed as sick and absent during the summer of 1862 while located in northeast Mississippi.*
Powell, John L., 1st Lieutenant, enlisted April 1, 1862, at Greenville. He was elected 1st Lieutenant on July 25, 1862. [17]*He was wounded (toe of left foot) July 20, 1864, at the battle of Peachtree Creek near Atlanta. He was sent to the general hospital on the 21st where the doctors amputated. He was listed on the regimental medical register in September, diagnosis debilitas.* He was promoted to captain April 10, 1865. [31]*He was at the surrender April 26, 1865, at Greensboro, North*

Carolina and paroled May 1, 1865. [28]*He was present at the Confederate Veterans Reunion in Greenville August 21, 1897.*

Powell, William H., Private, enlisted September 14, 1861, at Montgomery. He was wounded at a battle near Corinth, Mississippi, May 1862. He was absent on sick furlough for 30 days, August 9, 1863, and finally discharged September 24, 1863.

Rhodes, George W., Private and musician, enlisted September 24, 1861, Camp Davis (5'6). [42]*He was placed on furlough January 18, 1862, and sent to Butler County.* He was captured December 17, 1864, Franklin, Tennessee. Imprisonment was at Camp Chase, Ohio, where he took oath of allegiance, May 1865. Bradleyton, Crenshaw County, was his home in 1907. [1]*He was born July 14, 1840, in Butler County.* [30]*His parents were George Washington and Theresa Welch Rhodes. He died June 1, 1907.*

Rhodes, John D., Private, enlisted September 19, 1862, at Camp Forney. [17]*He was listed on the regimental medical register June 29, 1864, with acute diarrhea.* He was paroled June 11, 1865, Montgomery, listed as 6'1. [16]*He was born August 21, 1844. He died April 23, 1915, and was buried at Live Oak United Methodist Church, Patsburg, Crenshaw County.* [30]*His parents were George Washington and Mary Lowery Rhodes.*

Rodgers, Harvy, Private, enlisted March 1865, at Camp Forney. He was hospitalized September 23 to October 3, 1863, with fever. [17]*He was listed on the regimental medical register twice: on December 26, 1863, diagnosis orchitis, and on January 26, 1864, diagnosis catarrhus.* He was hospitalized February 25 to March 18, 1864, with rubeola. He was furloughed June 29, 1864, for 60 days, to Millville, Butler County, after being sick four months with extreme emancipation and debility. He was captured May 28, 1865, at Union Springs, Alabama, and paroled June 2, 1865, at Montgomery. Also listed as **H. W., Herdy W., H. M. Rogers**

Rodgers, Wesley D., Private, enlisted September 24, 1861, at Camp Davis. [42]*He was placed on furlough January 7, 1862, for 12 days and sent to Butler County.* [17]*He was listed on the regimental medical register twice in September of 1864: on the 14th, diagnosis phlegmon, and on the 18th, diagnosis feb int quotid.* He was paroled June 19, 1865, Montgomery. [37]*He was born September 9, 1840, Salsada, Butler County. In 1921 he was living in Montgomery. He listed battles he fought in as Shiloh, Resaca, Atlanta, and Franklin.* Also listed as **N. C. Rogers, W. D. Rogers, Roggers.**

[17]***Rogers, W.**, Private, was listed on the regimental medical register February 23, 1864, diagnosis feb int tert.* Could be either **Wm. Rogers, Wesley Rodgers.**

COMPANY C

[17]**Rogers, Wm.,** Private, was listed on the regimental medical register January 25, 1864, diagnosis catarrhus.

Rose, J. A., Private, was paroled June 18, 1865, at Montgomery. Also spelled **J. A. Rhodes.**

Russell, Henry C., Private, was hospitalized February 17, 1864, in a Mobile hospital for nine days.

Russell, Samuel Tines, Private, enlisted September 7, 1862, at Camp Forney. He was hospitalized February 8, 1864, in Mobile. [17]*He was wounded in the right shoulder by a minnie ball July 20, 1864, at the battle at Peachtree Creek near Atlanta. He was sent to the general hospital on the 21st.* [16]*He was born December 23, 1832. He died December 25, 1907, and is buried at Pigeon Creek, Crenshaw County.*

Sapp, Allen H., Private, enlisted February 27, 1862, Greenville. He was hospitalized during June 1862. He was paroled June 20, 1865, Montgomery, listed as 5'5.

Sapp, John A., Private, enlisted February 27, 1862, at Greenville.

Scipper, Samuel, Private, enlisted August 1, 1863, at Greenville (6'2). A farmer, he was born 1822 in Montgomery County. [17]*He was listed on the regimental medical register on January 24 and February 1, 1864, with pneumonia. He died February 11, 1864.* [30]*He married Mary Jane Thagard. He was born June 12, 1822, Fuller's Crossroad, Crenshaw County. He was buried at Yorktown, Virginia.* Also spelled **Skipper**

Seale, Cornelius H., Private, enlisted September 7, 1862, a at Camp Forney. [17]*He was severely wounded in the arm in May 1864, probably at the battle of Resaca. He was captured December 15, 1864, at Nashville and imprisoned at Camp Douglas, Illinois. His occupation was overseer. He was listed as sergeant when captured in 1864.* Also spelled **Seal, Seals.**

Seale, Elias A., Private, enlisted May 22, 1862, at Greenville. [17]*He was listed on the regimental medical register June 5, 1864, acute dysentery, and August 21, chronic diarrhea. He reported June 13, diagnosis feb int tert, and sent to the general hospital June 14. He was captured and paroled April 27, 1865, Greenville.* [4]*He was home sick when the war ended. He was born in 1834, died in 1903, and is buried in Brewton, Alabama.*

Seale, Henry O., Corporal, enlisted September 14, 1861, at Montgomery, an overseer. [17]*He was listed on the regimental medical register July 13, 1864, diagnosis feb int tert. At that time he was still listed as a private. He was captured July 20, 1864 at Peachtree Creek near Atlanta. He was imprisoned at Camp Douglas, Illinois, where he was discharged June 17, 1865.* [28]*He was present at the Confederate Veterans Reunion in Greenville August 21, 1897.*

[17]**Seale, O. E.,** *Private, reported to the regimental register December 14, 1864, diagnosis feb int quotid.*
Shepherd, J. T., Private, enlisted August 24, 1863, at Randolph.
Shirlock, J. T., Private, suffered a slight wound to his arm at the battle of Shiloh, Tennessee, April 1862. Could this be **Thomas J. Spurlock**?
Sims, Julius F., Private, enlisted August 4, 1864, at Greenville. [17] *He was listed on the regimental medical register September 21, 1864, diagnosis feb int quotid, and October 30, 1864, acute diarrhea. He transferred to the general hospital October 31.* He was hospitalized at Mobile, November 5, 1864. He was granted parole June 6, 1865, Montgomery.
Sims, Robert M., Private, enlisted September 14, 1861, Greenville. He was placed on sick furlough January 20, 1862 for 15 days and sent to Butler County. He was wounded (abdomen) at Shiloh, Tennessee, April 6, 1862. [17]*He was listed on the regimental medical register three times in 1864. On March 22, the diagnosis was feb int quotid; on September 6, acute diarrhea; and on October 30, feb int quotid. He was sent to the general hospital October 31.* He was listed as sergeant by November 1864 when he was hospitalized in Montgomery with acute dysentery. He was paroled June 7, 1865, Montgomery.
Singleton, John W., Private, enlisted September 7, 1862, at Camp Forney. He was discharged December 5, 1861. [17]*He was listed on the regimental medical register January 19, 1864, with acute diarrhea. He was wounded June 16 and sent to the general hospital the next day.* He was paroled June 1865 at Selma.
Skipper, George, Private, enlisted September 15, 1862, at Camp Forney. [17]*He was listed on the regimental medical register December 5, 1864, diagnosis feb int quotid. He was wounded in the right leg and knee joint July 4, 1864, during the siege of Atlanta. His leg was amputated just above the knee, and he was sent to the general hospital on the 5th. He was listed as a farmer and 19 years old.* He was captured April 28, 1865, Union Springs. He was paroled on the march to Montgomery.
Skipper, John W., Private, enlisted September 14, 1861, at Montgomery. He was promoted to 4th corporal by September 1862 and sergeant by July 1863. He died March 1864, Mobile. [17]*J. W. Skipper was listed on the regimental medical register three times in 1864. On January 23, the diagnosis was gonorrhea, and on September 12, neuralgia. On October 30, he suffered a severe wound to the hip that was labeled as accidental. He was transferred to the general hospital on the 31st.* Note: Must be two people.
[17]**Smith, Jeff,** *Private, was listed on the regimental medical register June 3, 1864, with acute dysentery.* [24]*This may be the J. F. Smith of Company C, 17th Alabama, buried at Rose Hill Cemetery, grave 49, Macon, Georgia, September 4, 1864.*

Smith, John A, Private, enlisted September 7, 1862, at Camp Forney. [17]*Suffering with an acute case of diarrhea, he was listed on the regimental medical register February 29, 1864.* He was put on sick furlough from Macon, Georgia, for 30 days. He was captured April 25, 1865, at Greenville.

Smith, William N., Private, enlisted December 20, 1861, at Newbern, Perry County. He was assigned from the 5th Battery but never joined the 17th Alabama. [6]*He died in the hospital at Okolona, Mississippi, October 1, 1862.*

Smith, William R., Private, enlisted July 14, 1861, at Montgomery. [12]*He was listed as sick in quarters during the summer of 1862 while located in northeast Mississippi.* [17] *He was listed on the regimental medical register twice in December of 1863: on the 3rd, diagnosis was feb int quotid, and on the 15th with colica. On March 3, 1864, he had acute dysentery. On July 28, 1864, he suffered a severe wound (left thigh), probably received during the battle at Peachtree Creek during the Atlanta campaign. He was sent to the general hospital three days later. His last recorded visit to the regimental medical unit was on November 5, diagnosis morbi cutis.* [31]*He was at the surrender April 26, 1865, at Greensboro, North Carolina, where he was paroled May 1865.*

Smyth, A. C., Private, was discharged February 3, 1862. [19]*His name was on the roster of Company C when it was organized in September of 1861.*

Smyth, Robert J., Sr., Private, [12]*enlisted November 16, 1861, Camp Gladden, Florida.* He reenlisted December 11, 1863, at Greenville (5'6). A farmer, he was born December 18, 1845, Butler County. [17]*He was listed on the regimental medical register December 29, 1863, and March 1, 1864, diagnosis pneumonia and feb int quotid, respectively.* [1]*He was living in Butler Co. in 1907.* [28]*He attended the Confederate Veterans Reunion in Greenville August 21, 1897.*

Sowell, Robert L., Private, enlisted November 16, 1861, at Glidden. He was placed on sick furlough January 14, 1862, and sent to Butler County for 17 days. [6]*He died in the hospital in Mobile.*

[17]***Spradley, G. H.,*** Private, was listed on the regimental medical register December 10, 1863, suffering with pneumonia.

Spradley, James Erwin, Private, enlisted October 30, 1863, Greenville. [17]*He was listed on the regimental medical register while in Mobile on March 21, 1864, with rubeola. Two days later he was transferred to the general hospital at Greenville. He was diagnosed with pneumonia on April 20, 1864, and moved to the general hospital the next day. On July 4, he was wounded in the right leg during the siege of Atlanta. He was listed as a farmer and 18 years old. On July 28, he was suffering from acute diarrhea. On August 3, the diagnosis was feb int tert. He was diagnosed with acute diarrhea on September 21 and transferred to the* *general hospital two days later.* ³¹*He was at the surrender April 26, 1865, at Greensboro, North Carolina.* ¹⁶*He was born October 1, 1846, Lowndes County. He died June 17, 1893, and is buried at Live Oak Cemetery, Patsburg Crenshaw County.*

Spradley, Manning C., Private, enlisted November 18, 1863, Greenville (5'9). A farmer, he was born 1819, Kershaw District, South Carolina. ¹⁷*He reported to the regimental medical unit January 26 and February 23, 1864, with fever. He was severely wounded (arm) July 20 at the battle of Peachtree Creek near Atlanta. His arm was amputated, and he was sent to the general hospital to recuperate.* He was captured May 14, 1865 at Centerville and paroled June 15, 1865, Montgomery. ¹⁶*He appeared before Judge James T. Leeper, Shelby County July 26, 1887, to apply for a pension for relief by soldiers maimed or disabled: lost arm.*

¹⁷**Spradley, Samuel,** Private, *reported to the general hospital January 23, 1863, diagnosis phisis pulm.*

Spradly, Thomas Harrison, Private, enlisted September 24, 1861, Camp Davis (5'6). ¹*He was born February 22, 1842, at Raner, Montgomery County.* He was paroled May 31, 1865, Montgomery. *His home was Luverne, Crenshaw County, 1907.* ¹⁶*He died June 30, 1919, and was buried at Live Oak United Methodist Cemetery, Patsburg,Crenshaw County.*

Spurlock, Thomas J., Private, enlisted September 14, 1861, at Montgomery. He was paroled May 1865, Greensboro, North Carolina. ⁵*J. T. was slightly wounded at the battle of Shiloh, Tennessee, in April 1862. Is this same as J. T. Shirlock?* ¹⁷ *T. J. reported on December 7, 1863, diagnosis debility, and sent to the general hospital on the 10th. J. T. was listed on the regimental medical register on November 5, 1864, diagnosis feb int tert.* ³¹*J. T was at the surrender April 26, 1865, at Greensboro, North Carolina. His rank was second sergeant at the time of the surrender.* ⁴³*Thomas Spurlock was living in Lincoln County, Louisiana, in 1911.*

Stallings, J. T., Private, enlisted January 28, 1863, Mobile. ³¹*He was at the surrender April 26, 1865, at Greensboro, North Carolina.* He was paroled May 1865, Greensboro.

Stallings, R. R., Private, enlisted February 11, 1863, at Mobile. He was transferred to the engineer troops on August 30, 1863. His records list him as a prisoner of war on May 18, 1865, Columbus, Mississippi. See Service Records for Ripley J. Traweek

Standaland, Lawson K., Private, enlisted March 11, 1862, at Mobile. He died May 13, 1862, Tupelo, Mississippi, leaving father, Hugh Standaland of Pike County. Also spelled **Standland, Staniland.**

Stanley, C. D., Private, [17]*was severely wounded in his right hand on July 28, 1864, at the battle of Ezra Church near Atlanta. He was sent to the general hospital to recover on the 31st.* He surrendered and was paroled May 26, 1865, at Augusta, Georgia.

Stanley, James B., Private, enlisted February 13, 1863, at Greenville. [17]*He is listed on the register of the regimental hospital September 30, 1864, diagnosis feb int quotid. His right arm was severely injured on November 30, 1864, at the battle of Franklin, Tennessee.* He surrendered and was paroled May 26, 1865, Augusta, Georgia. [28]*He was present at the Confederate Veterans Reunion in Greenville August 21, 1897,* [7]*and registered as a Confederate veteran in Butler County on July 4, 1906.*

Stanley, James Henry, [1]*enlisted December 1862 at Mobile. He was born August 8, 1844, in Lowndes County. He served until his surrender at Augusta, Georgia, in 1865, and was living in Butler County in 1907.*

Stanly, J. T., Private, enlisted April 7, 1864, at Pollard. [31]*He was at the surrender April 26, 1865, at Greensboro, North Carolina, and* was paroled at Greensboro May 1865.

Stevens, Edward, Private, was discharged on July 4, 1862, by the medical board.

Stewart, D. M., Private, enlisted February 2, 1863, at Greenville. [17]*On June 20, 1864, he was sent to the general hospital to recover from anemia. On August 17, he was listed on the regimental medical register with acute diarrhea. On November 30, 1864, at Franklin, Tennessee, he received a severe wound to the left foot and leg. The leg was removed below the knee.* [8]*Daniel M. Stewart was killed at the battle of Franklin.* Also spelled **Steward.**

[17]**Stewart, E. M.**, Private, *was listed on the regimental medical register on January 24, 1864, diagnosis abscessus.*

Stewart, Hillery, Private, enlisted September 7, 1862. [17]*He was listed on the regimental medical register three times in 1864 in the regimental hospital. On March 6, the diagnosis was neuralgia; on the 20th, feb int tert; and on June 23, debilitas.* He was captured July 3, 1864, at Kennesaw Mountain, Georgia, and exchanged. He was captured November 3, 1864, Decatur, Alabama, and imprisoned at Camp Douglas, Illinois. He claimed he had deserted and requested to take the oath of allegiance while at Camp Douglas. He enlisted in the 6th US Volunteers.

Stringer, Anderson T., Private, [1]*enlisted April 1864. He was born March 17, 1847, in Butler County.* [17]*He was listed on the regimental medical register August 21, 1864, with chronic diarrhea, and in September with acute diarrhea. He was captured December 15, 1864, near Nashville. Imprisonment was at Camp Douglas, Illinois, where he was paroled*

June 15, 1865. His residence was Honoraville, Crenshaw County, in 1907. In the 1907 Confederate Veterans Census, he was listed as **Anson T. Stringer.**

Stringer, Robert J. A., Private, enlisted September 14, 1861, at Montgomery. [1]*He was born January 27, 1843, in Butler County.* He was given a disability discharge September 9, 1863, reason: pneumonia caused collapse of right lung. [1]*His residence was Honoraville, Crenshaw County, in 1907.* [7]*He registered as a Confederate veteran in Butler County July 4, 1906.*

Stuckey, John Q., enlisted February 3, 1863, at Greenville. [17]*He was listed on the regimental medical register on January 25, 1864, with acute diarrhea, and on March 31, diagnosis debilitas.*

Tales, L., Private, also listed as **Fales** with no additional information.

Tally, Josiah, Private, [17]*was listed on the regimental medical register three times in 1864. On March 20, the diagnosis was feb int tert. On July 28, 1864, he suffered a head wound at the battle of Ezra Church near Atlanta. He transferred to the general hospital on the 31st. On September 21, he was hospitalized with acute diarrhea.* He was captured and paroled at Greenville, Alabama, April 28, 1865. [28]*He was present at the Confederate Veterans Reunion in Greenville August 21, 1897.* [19]*He died October 9, 1921, and was buried at Antioch Cemetery in Greenville.*

Thagard, Andrew Jackson, Private, enlisted August 10, 1863, at Greenville. He was 5'9, a farmer, and born 1845 in Butler County. [17] *He was listed on the regimental medical register December 22, 1863, diagnosis was feb int tert. He was listed six times in 1864. On January 28, diagnosis was acute diarrhea; April 29, catarrhus; June 3, acute dysentery; June 13, feb int tert; August 26, neuralgia; and November 6, feb int tert.* [31]*He was at the surrender April 26, 1865, at Greensboro, North Carolina.* [30]*He was called Jack. He was born October 4, 1845, and married Mrs. Elizabeth Smith. He died July 13, 1897 and is buried at Damascus Cemetery, Butler County.*

Thagard, Warren Robert, Private, [30]*enlisted September 7, 1862, and was called Dock. He was born April 25, 1833, Alabama. He married (1) Elizabeth Jane Reese and (2) Sarah Permelia Doughty. He died October 29, 1911, and was buried in Magnolia Cemetery, Greenville, Alabama.*

Thompson, Calvin Clay, Private, [1]*first enlisted August 1861 at Monterey in J. S. Powers Company of Home Guards where he served until the company was disbanded in December 1861. He again enlisted December 1862 at Greenville in J. B. Goldsmith's Company of State Troopers until it was disbanded in December 1863. He enlisted January*

COMPANY C

26, 1864, at Greenville in the 17th Alabama. He was born in 1844 and lived in Butler County. [17]He was listed on the regimental medical register on March 20, 1864, diagnosis morbi cutis. He was hospitalized on August 23, 1864, at Macon, Georgia. [31]He was at the surrender April 26, 1865, at Greensboro, North Carolina, and paroled May 1865. [28]He was present at the Confederate Veterans Reunion in Greenville August 21, 1897. He resided in Butler County in 1907. [30]He was born April 25, 1844, Butler County, to Warren and Mary Hays Thompson. His wife was Mary L. Little. He died April 23, 1917. His brothers, James Alford and John Jefferson Thompson, were also in the Company C.

Thompson, James Alford, Private, enlisted May 13, 1862, Greenville. He was born August 18, 1835 in Butler County. [12]He was listed as sick in the camp hospital during the summer of 1862 while located in northeast Mississippi. [17]He was listed on the regimental medical register on February 7, 1864, diagnosis catarrhus. He was again admitted on October 9 with acute diarrhea. He was then transferred to the general hospital to recover. He was captured December 28, 1864, Egypt, Mississippi, and imprisoned at Alton, Illinois, where he died of pneumonia, January 22, 1865. [30]He was born August 13, 1835, Butler County, to Warren and Mary Hays Thompson. His wife was Mary Anne Chancellor. His brothers, Calvin Clay and John Jefferson Thompson, were also in Company C.

Thompson, John Jefferson, Private, enlisted September 14, 1861, at Montgomery. He was born December 13, 1841 in Butler County. He was detailed for duty in the signal corp. He was granted sick furlough January 14, 1862 for 17 days to Butler County. [17] He was listed on the regimental medical register with acute dysentery on February 12, 1864. He was hospitalized January 17, 1865, Meridian, Mississippi. [1]He was captured at Macon, Georgia, April 10, 1865, and paroled April 17, 1865. [28]He was present at the Confederate Veterans Reunion in Greenville August 21, 1897. He resided in 1907 in Butler County. [37]In 1921 he listed battles he took part in as Corinth, Shiloh, Resaca, New Hope Church, and Nashville. [30]He was born December 13, 1840, Butler County, to Warren and Mary Hays Thompson. His wife was Amanda Campbell. He died June 1, 1923. His brothers, James Alford and Calvin Clay Thompson, were also in Company C.

Thornton, K. H., Private, enlisted February 5, 1862. [17]He was listed on the regimental medical register in 1864: on February 8, diagnosis abscessus, and on November 4, diagnosis contusio. He was listed July 20, 1864, wounded in the left arm by a shell at the battle of Peachtree Creek near Atlanta. He was sent to the general hospital the next day. He was a corporal when granted parole June 6, 1865, at Montgomery.

^{30}He married (1) Margaret Lee and (2) Louisa Alabama Hall. Also listed as **H. K.**

^{17}**Thornton, R. N.**, Private, was listed on the regimental medical register January 26, 1864, diagnosis abscessus

Trainem, Joseph, Private, enlisted November 29, 1863, at Greenville. A farmer, 5'10, he was born 1845 in Butler County. ^{17}*He was listed on the regimental medical register on June 4, 1864, with acute diarrhea.* Also spelled **Tranham.**

Trainum, James F., Private, was captured June 5, 1864 at New Hope Church, Georgia, and imprisoned at Camp Chase, Ohio. He died January 3, 1865, ^{5}and was buried in lot number 697 at Camp Chase. Also spelled **Trainwin, Trainman**

Traweek, Ripley J., Private, ^{12}*enlisted March 15, 1862, Greenville.* He reenlisted February 3, 1863, at Greenville. He was 5'11, a blacksmith, and born 1836 in either Butler County or Wilcox County. He was hospitalized during the month of June 1862. ^{12}*He was granted a disability discharge July 4, 1862.* ^{17}*He was listed on the regimental medical register December 4, 1863. He reported to the regimental medical unit in 1864, diagnosis chronic rheum: March 20, April 1 when he was sent to Demopolis, and again on September 18 when he was sent to the general hospital.* He was hospitalized with wounds January 10, 1865. He was paroled June 14, 1865, at Montgomery.

Trawick, L. W., 2nd Lieutenant, was elected September 14, 1861.

Troutman, Newton C., Private, enlisted September 14, 1861, at Montgomery. He was 5'6 and born 1841. He was granted sick furlough on January 18, 1862, for 15 days to Butler County. ^{17}*He was listed on the regimental medical register February 6, 1864; diagnosis was acute rheum. He was immediately transferred to the Spring Hill hospital in Mobile. He was diagnosed February 28, 1864, with acute diarrhea and transferred to the general hospital in Mobile.* He was captured December 16, 1864, at Nashville and imprisoned at Camp Chase, Ohio. Parole was granted June 5, 1865. Also spelled **Trotman.**

Troutman, Sol. H., Private, enlisted September 14, 1861, at Montgomery. ^{17}*He was listed on the regimental medical register July 9, 1864, diagnosis feb remitt, and transferred to the general hospital two days later.* He was captured April 26, 1865, at Greenville. See Service Records for B. A. Vaugh.

^{17}**Tucker, W. H.**, Private, was listed on the regimental medical register December 1, 1863, with a case of lumbago.

Turner, Joseph, Private, was captured June 5, 1864 at New Hope Church, Georgia.

Tyner, T. C., Private, enlisted October 23, 1863, at Mobile. He was 5'6, a farmer, and born 1845 in Macon County, Georgia. [31]*He was at the surrender April 26, 1865, at Greensboro, North Carolina.*

Vice, John R., Private, enlisted June 1, 1862, at Mobile. He was hospitalized at Mobile February 17, 1862, and sent to Greenville on February 29, 1862. [17]*He was listed on the regimental medical register on April 15, 1864, diagnosis catarrhus.* He was captured and paroled June 23, 1865, Demopolis, Alabama. Also spelled **Vise**.

Vines, William, Private, enlisted September 24, 1862, at Camp Forney. He was hospitalized June 1862.

Wallace, Abram F., Private, enlisted September 14, 1861, at Montgomery. He was hospitalized during June 1862. [12]*He was listed as sick in the camp hospital during the summer of 1862 while located in northeast Mississippi.* [17]*As private, he was listed on the regimental medical register on February 21, 1864; diagnosis acute dysentery. As a sergeant he was diagnosed with feb int tert on April 23, and as a private on June 25, diagnosis was debilitas.* He was hospitalized on February 18, 1864, at Montgomery and later transferred to the hospital at Auburn, Alabama. [31]*He was at the surrender April 26, 1865, at Greensboro, North Carolina.*

[17]**Wallace, A. G.**, Private, *was listed on the regimental medical register on February 14, 1864, diagnosis gonorrhea.*

[17]**Wallace, H. F.**, Private, *was listed on the regimental medical register March 9, 1864, diagnosis feb int quotid.*

Wallace, Samuel G., Sergeant, enlisted at Montgomery, September 14, 1861. He was hospitalized during June 1862. [17]*He was listed on the regimental medical register on March 21, diagnosis feb int tert, rank private. On April 8, diagnosis was feb int quotid.* He was captured July 20, 1864, probably at the battle of Peachtree Creek near Atlanta. He was imprisoned at Camp Douglas, Illinois, where he enlisted in the 5th US Volunteer Infantry on April 14, 1865. [28]*He was present at the Confederate Veterans Reunion in Greenville August 21, 1897.*

Walton, William Allen, Private, enlisted September 7, 1862, at Camp Forney. In November 1863, he was appointed a regimental surgeon and promoted to first lieutenant. He was paroled at Greensboro, North Carolina, May 1865. [30]*He was born May 3, 1838, Lowndes County. He married Frances Thagard Ellington. He died March 9, 1878, and is buried in Damsacus Cemetery, Butler County.*

Ward, James N., Private, enlisted September 24, 1862, at Camp Forney. [20]*He was born June 2, 1839, in Fayette County where he was living in 1907.*

Ward, J. M., Private, enlisted December 20, 1861, at Newbern, Perry County. He was hospitalized during June 1862.

Watson, J. A., Private, enlisted February 3, 1863, at Mobile.

Weaver, J. M., Private, enlisted September 5, 1862, at Camp Forney. [17]*He was listed on the regimental medical register on December 8, 1863, diagnosis was debility; on August 13, feb int tert; and on February 12, 1864, acute dysentery.*

Weeks, C. M., Private, enlisted September 24, 1862, at Camp Forney. He was hospitalized during June 1862.

Westley, Rogers, Private, enlisted in 1863, at Greenville. He was 5'8, a farmer, and born in 1826 in Butler County.

White, B. R., Private, was paroled May 2, 1865.

Williamson, J. W., Private, enlisted August 20, 1862, at Greenville. [31]*He was at the surrender April 26, 1865, at Greensboro, North Carolina.*

Willis, James Thomas, Private, enlisted on September 14, 1861, at Montgomery. [1]*He was born on September 26, 1845, in Marlboro District, South Carolina.* He was captured December 15, 1864, at Nashville and imprisoned at Camp Douglas, Illinois, *where he was paroled. He resided in Fort Deposit, Lowndes County, in 1907* [37]*and in 1921. In the 1921 Confederate soldiers Census he stated that he moved to Alabama in 1849. He listed Shiloh, Atlanta, Franklin, and Nashville as battles he fought in. He was a farmer.*

Wright, Stephen M., Private, enlisted January 9, 1863, at Greenville. [31]*He was at the surrender April 26, 1865, at Greensboro, North Carolina.* [24]*He is buried in the Magnolia Cemetery in Greenville.*

Wyche, George D., Private, enlisted September 7, 1862, at Camp Forney. He was born in 1840 in Georgia. Wounded at Franklin November 30, 1864, he was captured there December 18, 1864, and hospitalized in Nashville. He died in Nashville on April 13, 1865, leaving his widow, Mary Wyche of Honoraville. He was buried in Nashville City Cemetery and later moved to Mt. Olivet Cemetery in the Confederate Circle in Nashville.

[17]**Wyche, J. D.,** *Private, was listed on the regimental medical register August 26, 1864, with acute diarrhea.*

Appendix V. Company D

Adams, John, Private, enlisted September 17, 1861, at Montgomery. He was 5'6 and born in 1843 in Coweta County, Georgia. He entered Ross Hospital in Mobile October 13, 1863; diagnosis was debility.

Adkins, John F., Sergeant, 5'8, enlisted at Montgomery September 17, 1861. He was placed on medical furlough January 16, 1862, for 15 days and sent to Goodwater, Alabama. [17]*As second sergeant, his name appeared on the regimental medical register January 17, 1864, diagnosis was feb int tert. As first sergeant his name appeared on the register February 11, 1864. During the battle of Ezra Church on July 28, he sustained a severe wound to his right thigh and a slight wound to the left thigh.* He was paroled May 19, 1865. Also listed as **John T. Adkins, Atkins**

Adkins, Rufus G., Private, lived in Coosa County. [17]*He was listed on the regimental medical register February 23, 1864, with rubeola and was sent to the general hospital at Mobile three days later. He was listed again April 5, 1864. He was granted a medical furlough April 20 for 20 days. He was listed June 23, 1864, diagnosis was feb int tert. He reported to the hospital with a slight wound (jaw) July 20, 1864, received at the battle of Peachtree Creek near Atlanta. He was sent to the general hospital the next day.* Captured December 15, 1864, near Nashville, he was imprisoned at Camp Douglas, Illinois. He was paroled in 1865. He applied for a pension in Texas and died in San Antonio.

[17]**Alexander, W. H.,** *Private, was listed on the regimental medical register December 30, 1863, and January 3, 1864, diagnosis was catarrhus.*

Anderson, F. F., Private, enlisted March 11, 1862, at Clopton, Alabama. He was at the surrender at Greensboro, North Carolina, April 26, 1865.

Ashworth, William M., Private, enlisted March 1, 1863, at Mobile. He was captured April 20, 1865, at Macon, Georgia.

Balentine, Isack, Private, enlisted September 17, 1861, at Montgomery. [41]*He died July 24, 1862, while the 17th was still in northeast Mississippi, and is buried at Gainesville, Alabama.*

Banister, David Monroe, Private, 5'6, enlisted November 15, 1861, Macon County. [17]*His name appeared on the regimental medical register on December 12, 1863, diagnosis feb int quotid. He reported sick again January 21, 1864, diagnosis feb int tert.* [30]*He lost an eye while on retreat at night at Kennesaw Mountain, Georgia,* where he was captured July 3, 1864. He was imprisoned at Camp Morton, Indiana, where he took the Oath of Allegiance May 18, 1865. [30]*While there he related that he was so hungry he "even helped eat part of a dog." He learned to read and write while at Camp Morton. After the war he went to Dayton,*

Ohio, because he "had no home to go to". He married (1) Permelia Alexander and (2) Sarah Odella Messenger. He eventually moved to Davidson County, Tennessee where he died July 28, 1926. He was buried in the Banister family cemetery. He was later relocated to Mt. Juliet Cemetery, Wilson County, Tennessee. His brother, J. J., and father, William M., are listed below. Also listed as **D. M. Bannister.**

Banister, John J., Private, 5'8, [30]*enlisted September 1861 at Montgomery.* [17]*He was listed on the regimental medical register twice in December of 1863: on the 14th with feb int quotid and on the 22nd with dysentery. During the first four months of 1864, he appears on the regimental register seven times. On January 5 and 19, February 9, March 29 and April 30, diagnosis was feb int tert. On February 25, diagnosis was feb int quotid, and on March 1, debilitas.* [30]*He was captured near Atlanta September 1864, and imprisoned at Fort Pickens, Florida.* He was paroled at Montgomery at the end of the war. [30]*In 1860, he lived in Wetumpka, Coosa County. After the war he moved to Early, Floyd County, Georgia. His brother, David M., and his father, William M., were also members of the 17th Alabama.* [24]***J. J. Bannister,** 17th Alabama, was buried in the Pisgah Cemetery, Floyd County. He was born about 1840 and died September 20, 1924.*

Banister, William M., Private, enlisted September 10, 1862, at Mobile. [17]*His name is listed on the regimental medical register March 20, 1864, diagnosis acute diarrhea.* He was admitted to Ocmulgee Hospital, Macon, Georgia, May 21, 1864, (acute dysentery) and returned to duty two days later. Wounded (lower 3rd femur) July 29, 1864, during the siege of Atlanta, he underwent an amputation and died August 4, 1864. [30]*He was born in Georgia. He was living in Wetumpka, Coosa County, in 1860. His sons, David M. and John J. Banister, were also in Company D.*

Barnett, John B., Private, enlisted September 17, 1861, at Montgomery. [20]*He was born November 29, 1842, in Spartanburg, South Carolina. He transferred to the engineering corp. In 1907 he was living in Glen Mary, Marion County.*

Bennett, G. M., Private, enlisted July 20, 1863, at Harrison, Tennessee, and was paroled at Greensboro, North Carolina, at the end of the war.

Blankenship, Abner J., Private, [12]*died January 7, 1862, in the hospital in Pensacola.*

Boswell, T. J., Private, enlisted March 13, 1862, at Greenville. He was at the surrender at Greensboro, North Carolina, April 26, 1865.

Bragg, T. C., Captain, enlisted September 17, 1861. He was granted leave for 25 days January 8, 1862 while in Mobile.

Briant, C. G., Private. His service record references J. T. Bryant.

Briant, J. G., Private. His record references J. T. Bryant.

Brown, A., Private, enlisted February 1, 1862, at Florence. He was paroled at Greensboro, North Carolina, May 1, 1865.

[18]***Brown, Thomas****, Private, was listed in September 1863 as 45 years old, grey eyes, dark hair, fair complexion, 5'8, a laborer, and deserter.*

Bruner, J. W., Private, enlisted at Rock Head, Alabama, December 14, 1861. He was at the surrender at Greensboro, North Carolina, April 26, 1865.

Bryant, John D., Private, was granted parole May 27, 1865, at Talladega. Also listed as **John L. Bryant.**

Bryant, William, Private, suffered a head wound [5]*at Shiloh, Tennessee April 1862.*

Bryant, Zac T., Private, [17]*received a severe wound to the right thigh July 20, 1864, at the battle at Peachtree Creek near Atlanta. He moved to a general hospital the next day.* He was paroled May 27, 1865.

Buckelew, James, Private, enlisted October 7, 1862, Clark County. He was captured December 19, 1864, at Nashville and imprisoned at Camp Douglas, Illinois.

Burk, James S., Private, enlisted August 19, 1863, at Mobile. He was 5'5, a farmer, and born in 1822 in Georgia. See Service Records for S. H. Clyett.

[17]***Burke, James D.****, Private, was listed on the regimental medical register on December 11, 1863, diagnosis was debilitas. He was listed on the register six times in 1864. On January 23, March 10, and July 4, the diagnosis was feb int quotid. He was moved to general hospital July 12. On February 2, the diagnosis was dysentery. On February 11 and March 31, the diagnosis was feb int tert.*

[17]***Burk, William L.****, Private, was listed on the regimental medical register five times in 1864. On April 9 and June 22, the diagnosis was feb int quotid. On January 6, diagnosis was acute dysentery, on March 15, feb int tert, and on August 26, acute diarrhea.* [1]*He was born March 20, 1836, near Carrolton, Carroll County, Georgia. He was living in Rock Mills, Randolph County, in 1907.* [26]*He was paroled April 26, 1865. He died March 19, 1917 and was buried in an unmarked grave in Param Baptist Church Cemetery, Randolph County.*

Bush, John B., Private, was discharged December 17, 1861.

Caffey, Alberto H., 2nd Lieutenant, 5'10, [12]*was listed as absent from duty during the summer of 1862 having suffered wounds at the battle of Shiloh, Tennessee, on April 6-7.* [17]*He was listed on the regimental medical register April 20, 1864, diagnosis was feb int tert and July 14, 1864, feb int quotid. He sustained a severe wound to his right thigh August 15, 1864, during the siege of Atlanta, and was furloughed from* the hospital to Montgomery. He was paroled at Montgomery May 20, 1865. Also spelled **Coffee, Coffey**.

[10]**Caigle, N. H.,** Private, died March 16, 1865, at Camp Chase, Ohio, and was buried in lot number 1682.

Callaway, J. W., 1st Sergeant, enlisted September 17, 1861, at Camp Watts, and was later granted a disability discharge. He was 5'10, a farmer, and born in 1842 in Meriweather County, Georgia.

Carlisle, J. B., Private, 5'7, [17]was listed on the regimental medical register November 3, 1864, diagnosis was feb int tert. He was moved to the general hospital November 14. He was paroled May 8, 1865, at Montgomery.

Carlisle, Robert, Private, resided in Coosa County. [17]He was listed on the regimental medical register February 4, 1864; diagnosis was acute rheum. He was listed with acute diarrhea July 2, 1864. He was hospitalized in Macon, Georgia, July 22, 1864, with jaundice.

[10]**Carman, D. A.,** Private, died July 5, 1862, at Camp Douglas, Illinois, where he was a prisoner. Note: He probably was captured at the battle of Shiloh, Tennessee, in April 1862.

Causey, G. B, Private, was captured April 7, 1862, at Pittsburg Landing, Tennessee, and died October 1862 ([10]June, 10, 1862) at Camp Douglas, Illinois.

Causey, J. W., Private, was granted parole May 20, 1865, at Montgomery. Also spelled **Cansey**.

Channel, G. W., Private, was granted parole May 26, 1865, at Talladega.

Christian, William H., Private, enlisted August 20, 1862, at Autauga, and died in 1863.

[17]**Clesby, S.,** Private, was listed on the regimental medical register February 22, 1864, with rubeola, and was immediately transferred to a general hospital. His name appeared on the register March 8, diagnosis was catarrhus. **Stephen Clisby** was listed on the register April 4 with acute diarrhea. **Saml. H. Clisby** was killed on July 20, 1864, at the battle of Peachtree Creek near Atlanta.

Clyett, S. H., Private, enlisted September 6, 1861, Coosa County. He was described as 5'9 with gray eyes, fair complexion, light hair, farmer, and was born in Coosa County in 1845.

[17]**Clyatt, Thomas H.,** Private, was listed on the regimental medical register March 8, 1864, with rubeola, and transferred to the general hospital at Spring Hill, Alabama, March 10. He appeared again on the hospital records April 14, diagnosis was debilitas; June 18, diagnosis feb int tert; June 23, diagnosis was pneumonia.

Collier, Jugertha E., Corporal, enlisted at Montgomery September 17, 1861. [42]He was granted a furlough January 17, 1862, for 15 days and sent to Rockford, Alabama. Also spelled **Collin**.

Conner, David A., Private, enlisted March 20, 1862, at Corinth, Mississippi. He was captured April 7, 1862, Pittsburg Landing, Tennessee, and imprisoned at Camp Douglas, Illinois. [17]*He was listed on the regimental medical register three times in 1864.* (He obviously was released from the Northern prison). *On January 10, the diagnosis was neuralgia. On July 18, the diagnosis was feb int quotid, and he was transferred to the general hospital the next day. He was sick in September, diagnosis rheumat acute.* Parole was granted May 25, 1865, at Talladega. Also spelled **Coner, Connor.**

[17]***Conner, James,*** *Private, was listed on the regimental medical register twice with diagnosis feb int tert: December 15, 1863, and January 22, 1864. He reported sick again April 1, 1864, with pneumonia and July 1, 1864, with acute diarrhea.*

Conner, William J., Private, [17]*was listed on the regimental medical register twice in 1864. On February 2 the diagnosis was parotitis and on March 29 catarrhus.* He was captured September 2, 1864, at Jonesboro, Georgia. Imprisonment was at Camp Douglas, Illinois, where he enlisted in the 6th US Volunteers, May 6, 1865.

Conner, William S., Private.

[17]***Cook, W. F.,*** *Private, was listed on the regimental medical register on December 19, 1864, diagnosis was sub luxatio. He reported to the hospital again in June. On the 15th the diagnosis was feb int quotid. On the 18th the diagnosis was feb remitt. He was transferred to the general hospital the next day.*

Cook, Wiley H., Private, [37]*enlisted September 16, 1863, at Roanoke, Alabama.* [17]*He sustained a slight wound to his left arm on July 28, 1864, at the battle of Ezra Church near Atlanta. He was transferred July 31 to the general hospital. He was listed on the regimental medical register on August 8 with acute diarrhea.* He was captured December 15, 1864, at Nashville, and imprisoned at Camp Douglas, Illinois. [37]*He was born June 30, 1844, Pike County, Georgia. In the 1921 Confederate Soldiers Census, he stated that he fought in battles from Resaca to Atlanta, and at Franklin and Nashville. In 1921 he was living in Roanoke.*

Cooley, Jno. S., Private, [17]*was listed on the regimental medical register on March 16, 1864, diagnosis was feb int tert. On April 1 he reported sick; diagnosis was debilitas. He was placed on medical furlough on the 5th for 30 days. In September he reported again, diagnosis was icterus.* He was granted parole June 28, 1865, at Talladega.

[17]***Corley, Benjamin,*** *Private, was listed on the regimental medical register December 18, 1863, diagnosis was feb int quotid. He reported again March 16, 1864, diagnosis orchitis, and was sent to the hospital in*

Greenville on the 19th. [10]*He was listed as a prisoner of war from Pike County.*

Corprell, Charles S., Private, enlisted September 1, 1862, at Mobile.

Cox, James A., Private, enlisted March 11, 1862, at Clopton. He was paroled at Greensboro, North Carolina, May 1865.

Crew, William C., Private, died April 1862, at the battle of Shiloh. The original muster roll for Company D in September 1861 includes William Crew, born 1841.

Crumpter, Paschal A., Private, was placed on sick furlough on January 7, 1862, for 20 days and sent to Rockfort, Alabama. The original muster roll for Company D in September 1861 includes Crumpter, born 1843. Also spelled **Crumpton**.

[17]***Cummins, J. L.***, *Private, was listed on the regimental medical register with acute dysentery, November 3, 1864.*

[18]***Daff, Robert***, *Private, was listed in September 1863 as 46 years old, blue eyes, black hair, fair complexion, 5'10, a laborer, and deserter.*

Danagan, James, Private, surrendered May 4, 1865, at Citronella, Alabama. He was 5'9, lived in Clarke County, and was born in 1834.

Darden, William W., private, enlisted September 17, 1861, Montgomery.

Deans, J. J., Private. Probably **John Jefferson Deans**. Also listed as **J. J. Deens**.

Dixon, J. R., Private, enlisted December 6, 1861, at Montgomery.

Dodson, James E., Private, enlisted December 28, 1861, Greene County. [12]*He was listed as sick and absent from his company during the summer of 1862 while located in northeast Mississippi.*

Downs, Joshua, Private, enlisted September 17, 1861, at Montgomery. He was 5'10 and born in 1826, Newton County, Georgia.

Downs, Shelley E., Private, enlisted September 17, 1861, at Montgomery. [17]*On December 20, 1863, he was listed on the regimental medical register; diagnosis was lumbago. On January 28, 1864, his complaint was catarrhus, on March 18, acute dysentery and on August 26, acute diarrhea.* Captured December 15, 1864, at Nashville, he was imprisoned at Camp Douglas, Illinois. **Also spelled Downdes.**

Duffie, W. G., Private, enlisted December 6, 1862, at Montgomery. He was paroled at Greensboro, North Carolina, May 1865.

Duke, George H., Private, was discharged September 17, 1861.

Durden, Anderson J., Private, [17]*was listed on the regimental medical register four times in 1864. On February 27, the diagnosis was rubeola, and he was immediately sent to the general hospital. On July 24 diagnosis was feb int quotid, and again he was sent to a general hospital. On June 21 and November 2, his complaint was acute dysentery.* He was captured December 15, 1864, at Nashville and imprisoned at Camp Douglas, Illinois. He died on January 20, 1865, and was buried in lot number 516, Block 26, Chicago City Cemetery. Also listed as **Darden, Andrew Derden.**

Durden, William Watson, Private, enlisted September 17, 1861, at Montgomery. [17]*On December 1, 1863, he was listed on the regimental medical register, diagnosis syph prim. On February 27, 1864, the diagnosis was feb int quotid. On July 28, as a corporal, he sustained a severe wound to the right side of his face at the battle of Ezra Church near Atlanta, and moved to the general hospital on July 31.* [20]*He was born December 6, 1843, at Prattville, Autauga County. He was paroled at Greensboro, North Carolina. In 1907 he was living in Manning, Coosa, County. Also spelled* **Darden.**

Eason, John Clark, Private, enlisted December 29 1862, at Talladega. He was 6' and born in 1836, Forsythe County, Georgia. He was granted a disability discharge February 2, 1863, reason: [37]*leg wound received on the drill field. He was born November 29, 1844, in Fayette County, Georgia. In 1921 he was living in Alpine, Alabama.*

Easterling, E., Private, enlisted August 20, 1862, Autauga County. [17]*He sustained a severe wound to his right hand and was listed on the regimental medical register July 28, 1864, at the battle of Ezra Church near Atlanta. On July 31, he was transferred to the general hospital in Macon, Georgia. His ring finger on his right hand was amputated. He was paroled in Montgomery, May 26, 1865.*

Edward, C. L., Private, enlisted December 1, 1862, at Montgomery. He was paroled at Greensboro, North Carolina, at the end of the war.

[17]**Edwards, T.,** *Private, sustained a slight flesh wound to his leg during May 1864, possibly at the battle of Resaca, Georgia.*

[20]**Esom, James Marion,** *was born March 13, 1840, at Jonesboro, Fayette County, Georgia. He was paroled at Dallas, Alabama, and was living in St. Clair County in 1907.*

Fleming, William Jasper, Corporal, enlisted September 17, 1861, at Montgomery. He was sick in the hospital in Mobile August 1862. He was absent with leave January 1863 to Coosa County. He was captured December 15, 1864, at Nashville and imprisoned at Camp Douglas, Illinois. He was listed as 18 when he mustered in September 17, 1861. [30]*He was born September 19, 1838, to John and Anne Safalo Stuart Fleming. He married Mary Elizabeth Albea. He died November 30, 1914.*

Foster, J. M., Private, was hospitalized in Mississippi during June 1862.

Foster, Joel E., Private, enlisted February 17, 1862, Fayette County. [12]*He was listed as sick and absent from his company during the summer of*

1862 while located in northeast Mississippi. The September-October 1862 muster roll stated that Foster had transferred from the 5th Alabama April 23, 1862, but never reported to the 17th Alabama.

Galaway, H. J., Private, enlisted March 11, 1862, at Clopton, Alabama. He was listed as absent without leave June 28, 1862. He was paroled at Greensboro, North Carolina, April 1865.

Gay, Augustus S., Private, enlisted September 17, 1861, at Montgomery, age 28. Also listed as **Gary.**

Gillilond, William, Private, enlisted September 17, 1861, at Montgomery. He was hospitalized in Mississippi during June 1862. [12]*He was listed as absent on leave from his company during the summer of 1862 still in Mississippi.* [17]*He was listed on the regimental medical register four times in 1864. On January 4, the diagnosis was feb int tert. On March 28 and April 1, his complaint was debilitas. On April 5, he was placed on a medical furlough for 30 days. He sustained a severe wound to his hand August 14 during the siege of Atlanta. He was transferred to the general hospital August 19.* He was paroled at Greensboro, North Carolina, May 1, 1865. Also spelled **Gillaland, Gilliland, Gilleland.**

Glover, Alfred L., Private, enlisted February 17, 1862, Fayette County. He was hospitalized in Mississippi during June 1862. [12]*He was listed as absent on leave during the summer of 1862 while still in Mississippi.*

Graham, Thomas M., Private, [17]*was listed on the regimental medical register twice in December 1863. On the 18th, the diagnosis was feb int quotid, and on the 22nd, debilitas. On January 6, 1864, his diagnosis was debilitas and on April 29, feb int tert. On July 1 during the siege of Atlanta, he sustained a severe wound to his thigh, and was sent to the general hospital.* He was a farmer, born in 1844, and 5'8. He was granted parole May 19, 1865, at Montgomery.

Gresham, Whitten R., Private, died in the hospital January 2, 1862, [12]*in a hospital in Pensacola.* The original muster roll for Company D included Gresham, age 18. He is buried at Barrancas National Cemetery.

Grimmer, E. M., Sergeant, enlisted in Montgomery. He was paroled at Greensboro, North Carolina, May 1865.

Groce, Joshua J., Private, enlisted May 10, 1862, at Corinth, Mississippi. A chaplain, he was born in 1836, in Green County. He was hospitalized in Mississippi during June 1862. He served as 5th sergeant from July to October 1862. He was discharged and appointed chaplain October 20, 1862. He was captured December 17, 1864, Franklin, Tennessee, and imprisoned at Camp Chase, Ohio. He was paroled June 11, 1865. More papers in service record on microfilm. Also spelled **Grace.**

Guin, H. M., Private, was from Greene County. [12]*He enlisted September 7, 1861, Montgomery. He transferred to the Sharpshooters July 1, 1862.*

[17]***Gulledge, A. J.***, Private, was listed on the regimental medical register March 22, 1864, diagnosis was acute diarrhea. ***J. A. Gulledge*** was listed on the regimental medical register February 24, 1864, with pneumonia. He was transferred to the general hospital in Mobile on the 26th. ***W. A. J. Gulledge***, was listed on the regimental medical register August 23, 1864, with acute diarrhea. He may have been a member of 13th Alabama, Company H.

[12]***Ham, Bright A.***, Private, enlisted February 17, 1862, Fayette County. He transferred to Company B, 58th Alabama.

[12]***Ham, L. W. B.***, Private, enlisted February 17, 1862, Fayette County. He was listed on the muster roll for July-August 1862 as sick in the hospital.

Hamer, D. P., Private, entered Way Hospital, Meridian, Mississippi, with wounds, January 1865. He was then placed on furlough. Note: He was wounded during the Tennessee campaign.

[17]***Hammock, T. J.***, Private, was listed on the regimental medical register February 9, 1864, with acute diarrhea. He may have been in Company K, 59th Alabama.

[17]***Hammock, W. T.***, Private, was listed on the regimental medical register three times in 1864. On January 24, the diagnosis was constipacio; on February 28, acute dysentery; and on April 9, feb int quotid.

Hanny, D. J., Private, was hospitalized June 12, 1864. He died June 23, 1864, at Ocmulgee Hospital, Macon, Georgia.

Harmon, James B., Private, [17]*was listed on the regimental medical register three times in 1864. On April 28 his complaint was acute dysentery; August 5, acute diarrhea; and August 19, catarrhus. He transferred to the general hospital August 22.* He was captured December 15, 1864, at Nashville and imprisoned at Camp Douglas, Illinois. Also listed as **James B. Hammond.**

Harrington, H. M., Private, was hospitalized in Mississippi during June 1862.

Harris, James F., Private, enlisted February 17, 1862, Fayette County. Also listed as **John F. Harris**

Harris, James M., Private, enlisted December 27, 1861, Greene County.

Haynes, Henry C., Private, lived in Coosa County and was hospitalized May 21, 1864, Macon, Georgia. He was paroled in Montgomery May 24, 1865.

Heller, M., Private, enlisted December 6, 1862, at Mobile. He was a merchant, born 1827 in Germany.

Henderson, James A., Private, enlisted August 1, 1861, Randolph County. [17]*He was listed on the regimental medical register December 18, 1863. He was granted a medical furlough three days later for 30 days;*

diagnosis was debilitas. [33]He died August 19, 1889. His wife later applied for a pension.

[17]**Henderson, W. E.**, Private, was listed on the regimental medical rolls eight times. On December 25, 1863, the diagnosis was feb int tert, as it was, when he reported again January 2, 1864. Two weeks later the diagnosis was feb int quotid. On April 24 the diagnosis was sub luxatio. On June 2 and 22 his complaint was acute dysentery. When he reported on June 27, he was sent to the general hospital the next day, diagnosis feb int tert. He was last listed July 13 with acute diarrhea.

Hendrix, Jones, Private, enlisted September 14, 1861, at Montgomery, age 20. [17]He was listed on the regimental medical register April 19, 1864, diagnosis was feb int quotid.

Hester, Alfred Lafayette, Private, enlisted at Montgomery September 17, 1861. He was placed on furlough during June 1862. He was appointed 4th sergeant by summer of 1862. [17]He first was listed on the regimental medical register in Mobile March 8 and April 3, 1864, diagnosis was feb in tert. He sustained a wound to his right arm July 28, at the battle of Ezra Church near Atlanta. He was transferred to the general hospital July 31. He was paroled May 1865, at Montgomery. [20]He was born October 8, 1841, Coosa County. He was living in Elmore County in 1907. [30]His parents were Abram and Margaret Everton Hester, and he was married to Alice Washburn. He died in 1920 and was buried at Wetumpka City Cemetery, Wetumpka, Alabama.

[11]**Hester, George F.**, Sergeant, enlisted May 10, 1862, at Monroe. He died July 24, 1862, [12]at Gainesville, Alabama. [41]His grave or memorial marker is located Socapatoy Cemetery, Coosa Co.

Hester, John A., 2nd Lieutenant, was born in 1836 and appointed second lieutenant September 7, 1861. He was promoted to captain January 29, 1862. He was captured May 27, 1864, at Dallas, Georgia, and imprisoned at Johnson Island, Ohio, where he took the oath of allegiance June 14, 1865. He was born in 1836.

Hines, Thomas G., Private, was listed on the original muster for Company D on September 17, 1861, age 23. He was discharged December 1861.

Hinton, T. A., Private, enlisted January 8, 1863, at Talladega and was discharged June 8, 1863. He was born in 1849, Leon---ala, Ala.

Hochmeister, Fritz, Private, enlisted December 16, 1862, at Mobile.

Holiman, James W., Sergeant, was 5'9 and born in 1839, Forsythe County, Georgia.

Holland, Robert M., Sergeant, enlisted at Montgomery September 17, 1861, and died July 17, 1862, at Saltillo, Mississippi.

[17]**Hollingshead, J.**, Private, was listed on the regimental medical register June 2, 1864, and transferred to the general hospital the next day, diagnosis feb remitt. He was listed again September 18 with chronic

diarrhea and immediately transferred to the general hospital. [24]*He was buried at the Linnwood Community Cemetery, Columbus, Georgia.*

Hollingshead, Moses, Private, [17]*was listed on the regimental medical register three times in 1864: January 26, the diagnosis was feb int tert; February 26, feb int tert; and June 22, acute dysentery.* He was captured December 15, 1864, at Nashville, and imprisoned at Camp Douglas, Illinois. He was paroled from the hospital at Louisville, Kentucky, on June 29, 1865.

Hollimond, James F., Private, enlisted December 26, 1861, Greene County. He was hospitalized in Mississippi during June 1862. Also spelled **Holleman.**

Homes, W. T., Private, enlisted August 20, 1862, Chambers County.

Horis, J. M., Private, was hospitalized in Mississippi during June 1862.

Horn, Bright, Private, enlisted February 17, 1862, Fayette County. He was hospitalized in Mississippi during June 1862.

Horn, D. W. B., Private, enlisted February 17, 1862, Fayette County. He was hospitalized in Mississippi during June 1862.

Huddleston, David F., Private, enlisted September 13, 1862, at Mobile. [17]*He was severely wounded in his left side, probably at Kennesaw Mountain, and was listed on the regimental medical register on June 24, 1864.* [30]*He was born in 1837 to William Berry and Mary Jane Howard Huddleston. He applied for a pension with the state of Texas (#31021) where he stated that he was a prisoner at Rock Island, Illinois, at the end of the war.*

[17]**Huddleston, T. M.,** Private, [30]*enlisted September 1862, Lamar, Randolph County.* [17]*He was severely wounded in his left thigh in May 1864, possibly during the battle of Resaca, Georgia.* [30]*He was severely wounded in the shoulder at Calhoun, Georgia, probably May or June 1864, and was probably discharged at that time. He was at home with wounds at the surrender. He was paroled May 1865, Atlanta, Georgia. He was born in 1827 to William Berry and Mary Jane Howard Huddleston. He married (1) Lucinda J. Cates, (2) Mary Jane Parmer, (3) Senie Vergilin Parmer. Thomas was a farmer and helped his father run a supply store. In 1897 he was living in Sewell (*now known as Bethel*), Randolph County.* [33]*He survived the war and applied for a pension.*

Hudmon, James Neal, Private, enlisted at Montgomery September 17, 1861. He was hospitalized in Mississippi during June 1862. [20]*He was born June 24, 1843, Coosa County. He was paroled April 15, 1864, at Augusta, Georgia. He was living in Elmore County in 1907.* Also spelled **Hadmond.**

[17]**Hughes, B.**, *Private, was listed on the regimental medical register June 13, 1864, and sent to the general hospital June 14, diagnosis feb int quotid.*

Hull, Joseph B., Private, enlisted September 17, 1861, at Montgomery, age 18. He was hospitalized in Mississippi during June 1862. Also spelled **Hall**.

Hull, M. G., Private

Hull, Nathaniel G., Private, was listed on the original muster roll for Company D September 17, 1861, age 21. He was discharged December 17, 1861.

[17]**Hull, Thad**, *Private, was listed on the regimental medical register November 20, 1864, and transferred to the general hospital November 29, diagnosis feb int quotid.*

Hull, William D., Lieutenant, was 5'7, born in 1838, and lived in Buychville, Alabama. He was elected second lieutenant September 17, 1861. He was elected first lieutenant on January 28, 1862. He was hospitalized in Mississippi during June 1862. [17]*He was listed on the regimental medical register with acute diarrhea twice in 1864; June 16 when he was transferred to the general hospital the next day, and again August 14.* He was captured December 15, 1864, at Nashville and imprisoned at Johnson Island, Ohio, where he was paroled June 6, 1865.

Ingram, Samuel J., Private, enlisted September 17, 1861, at Montgomery. He was captured July 28, 1864, at the battle of Ezra Church near Atlanta. He was hospitalized July 29, 1864, at Nashville where he lost a leg and was later imprisoned at Camp Douglas, Illinois. He was paroled May 1865, at Montgomery.

Jackson, B. F., Private, died December 19, 1862, at Mobile [25]*and is buried in Magnolia Cemetery in Mobile.*

[12]*Jackson, D. W., Private, enlisted September 16, 1861, Montgomery.*

Jackson, Hilrey, Private, paroled May 1865, at Montgomery.

[17]*Jackson, J. S., Private, was listed on the regimental medical register March 14, 1864, diagnosis was feb int quotid.*

Jackson, James T., Private, enlisted October 4, 1862, Clarke County. He was 6', a farmer and born in 1843, Clarke County. He was granted a disability discharge June 8, 1863. He was captured December 15, 1864, at Nashville, and imprisoned at Camp Douglas, Illinois. After his release, he was hospitalized in April 1865 at Richmond.

Jackson, William M., Private, enlisted at Montgomery September 17, 1861, age 24. He was detailed as a nurse during January and June 1862. [17]*He was listed on the regimental medical register three times with the same diagnosis of feb int tert: December 14, 1863, April 13 and June 18,*

1864. On July 4, 1864, during the siege of Atlanta he was severely wounded in both shoulders and his spine. He was not doing well when he was sent to the general hospital. He was a farmer.

Jenkins, D. S., Private, enlisted February 17, 1862, Fayette County.

[12]**Jenkins, D. S.,** Private, enlisted February 17, 1862, Fayette County.

Jenkins, Samuel W., Private, enlisted December 21, 1861, Fayette County. He was hospitalized in Mississippi during June 1862.

[17]**Johnson, J. A.,** Private, was listed on the regimental medical register April 14, 1864, diagnosis was feb int tert.

[12]**Johnson, Joseph D.,** Private, enlisted September 20, 1861, Montgomery.

Johnson, J. F., Private, enlisted December 11, 1862, at Mobile. He was a carpenter, born in 1811 in Manchester, England.

[17]**Johnson, J. L.,** Private, was listed on the regimental medical register March 5, 1864, diagnosis was feb int quotid. He died after being hit in the head and neck May 1864, possibly at the battle of Resaca, Georgia.

Johnson, Joseph S., Private, enlisted September 20, 1861, at Montgomery.

Johnson, Samuel A., Corporal, enlisted at Montgomery September 17, 1861, age 20. Also listed as **Johnston.**

Johnson, Thomas, Private, [17]was listed on the regimental medical register with acute diarrhea on February 7 and March 21, 1864. He was paroled at Talladega in 1865.

[17]**Johnson, Wm.,** Private, was listed on the regimental medical register June 17, 1864, with pneumonia and sent to the general hospital June 18.

Johnsten, Joseph, Private, enlisted December 11, 1861, at Mobile.

Jolly, J. C., 2nd Lieutenant, enlisted March 14, 1862, Greenville, and was paroled at Greensboro, North Carolina, April 1865.

Jones, Julius, Private, enlisted September 17, 1861, at Montgomery, age 18.

[12]He was discharged July 3, 1862, at Tupelo, Mississippi.

[17]**Jones, William R.,** Private, was listed on the regimental medical register twice in 1864. On March 30, his problem was pneumonia. He was sent to the general hospital at Greenville the next day. On November 30, he was severely wounded (bowels), at the battle of Franklin, Tennessee.

Jonyes, J. S., Private, was admitted to the hospital at Meridian, Mississippi, January 30, 1865, with wounds received during the Tennessee campaign.

[18]**Kelly, Michael,** Private, was listed in September 1863 as 46 years old, grey eyes, dark hair, fair complexion, 5'8, a laborer, and deserter.

Kershratter, James, Private, was born in 1825, Shelby County. He was granted a disability discharge February 12, 1863.

Kimbrough, T. H., Private, was discharged December 17, 1861.

Kinkade, William B., Private, enlisted at Montgomery September 17, 1861, age 23 and a resident of Coosa County. He was hospitalized at Macon,

Georgia, May 21, 1864. [17]*He was severely wounded in his right side July 28, 1864, at the battle of Ezra Church in Atlanta. He was moved to the general hospital July 31.* Also spelled **Kinkode, Cincade, Kincade.**

Kirkland, Calvin, Private, enlisted December 21, 1862, Randolph County. [17]*He was listed on the regimental medical register March 28, 1864, diagnosis was feb int tert, and April 11, diagnosis oedema. He was sent to the general hospital April 25, 1864.*

[17]**Kirkland, J.**, *Private, was listed on the regimental medical register with acute diarrhea April 17, 1864.*

Konkle, John, Private, enlisted October 8, 1862, Coosa County. [17]*He suffered a slight wound to his hand during May 1864, possibly at the battle of Resaca, Georgia. He was listed on the regimental medical register June 6, 1864, with acute dysentery and was transferred to the general hospital three days later.*

Kuykendall, William E., Private, enlisted at Fayette County, December 20, 1861. Also spelled **Kurlendoll.**

Lacoste, L, Private, was hospitalized in Mississippi during June 1862.

Lake, James M., Private, 5'8, enlisted August 13, 1863, Coosa County. [17]*He was listed on the regimental medical register three times in 1864: January 4, diagnosis was acute diarrhea and February 9, catarrhus. He suffered a slight wound in his right hand July 28, at the battle of Ezra Church. He was transferred to the general hospital three days later. He was paroled May 1865. He was born in 1845 in Coosa County.*

Lane, Henry S., Private, [17] *was listed on the regimental medical register January 17 and February 14, 1864, diagnosis was feb int tert. He was listed March 20, diagnosis catarrhus, and in November with acute diarrhea. He was also listed June 22 when he was transferred to the general hospital, diagnosis unknown.* He was captured December 15, 1864, at Nashville and imprisoned at Camp Douglas, Illinois. He was hospitalized in Richmond March 20, 1865, after his release. [26]*He was born in 1823. He died April 7, 1880, and was buried in an unmarked grave at Rane's Chapel Cemetery in Randolph County.*

Lane, James M., Private, enlisted December 20, 1861, Green County. He was hospitalized in Mississippi during June 1862. **Also** listed as **James McLane.**

Lane, John H., Private, [17]*was listed on the regimental medical register April 26, 1864, diagnosis was catarrhus.* He was captured December 15, 1864, at Nashville and imprisoned at Camp Douglas, Illinois.

[12]**Lane, Louis,** *Private enlisted December 20, 1861, from Green County.*

Lauderdale, John F., Sergeant, enlisted at Montgomery September 17, 1861. [5]*He was slightly wounded at Shiloh, Tennessee, in 1862.* [17]*He was listed on the regimental medical register seven times in 1864. On*

January 16 (sergeant), February 13 (sergeant), and March 3 (private), diagnosis was feb int tert. On July 9 (private) the diagnosis was anasarca; August 26 (private), acute diarrhea; September 13 (sergeant), acute dysentery; and in November, acute diarrhea. [2]***J. S. Lauderdale*** *died November 30, 1864, (at the battle of Franklin, Tennessee) and is buried lot number 128, section 76, McGavock Cemetery, Franklin.*

Lecroy, William D., Private, enlisted September 15, 1862, Coosa County. [17]*He was listed on the regimental medical register January 29, 1864; diagnosis was contusio.* He was paroled at Greensboro, North Carolina, April 1865. Also listed as **W. D. Leacroy.**

Ledbetter, James M., Private, was listed on the original muster roll of Company D September 17, 1861, age 23. He died April 14, 1862, at a hospital in Grenada, Mississippi.

[17]**Lee, John H.** *Private, was listed on the regimental medical register on December 6, 1863, diagnosis was feb int tert.* [31]*He was listed in Company C at the surrender, April 26, 1865, at Greensboro, North Carolina.*

Letlow, Andrew J., Private, enlisted August 4, 1862, Coosa County.

Letlow, Bulger F., Private, enlisted September 17, 1861, at Montgomery, age 22. He was hospitalized in Mississippi during June 1862. [17]*He was listed on the regimental medical register five times in 1864. On January 7, the diagnosis was catarrhus; on April 19, acute dysentery; and on June 21, acute diarrhea. He sustained a slight wound to his left arm on June 20. He was moved to the general hospital the next day. During November he returned to the hospital suffering with an old wound.* He was captured December 16, 1864, at Nashville and imprisoned at Camp Chase, Ohio. Also spelled **Belcher.**

Letlow, Thomas B., Private, enlisted September 17, 1861, at Montgomery, age 19, from Coosa County. [17]*He was listed on the regimental medical register five times during 1864. On March 7, the diagnosis was phlegmon; on June 21, July 9, and August 5, the diagnosis was acute diarrhea; and on September 6, acute dysentery.* He was captured December 15, 1864, at Nashville and imprisoned at Camp Douglas, Illinois. Also spelled **Leglow, Ledlow, Ludlin, Ludlow.**

Lewis, B. G., Corporal, enlisted March 12, 1862, at Covington. He was at the surrender at Greensboro, North Carolina, April 26, 1865.

Lewis, D. C., Private, was paroled May 22, 1865, at Talladega.

Lewis, G. F., Private, [17]*was listed on the regimental medical register on December 12, 1863, diagnosis was debilitas. He returned to the regimental hospital four times in 1864. On April 29, the diagnosis was abscessus, and on July 31, debilitas. On August 5 and during*

November, the diagnosis was acute diarrhea. He was paroled May 24, 1865.

Lewis, H. H., Private

Lewis, James H., Private, enlisted September 17, 1861, at Montgomery, age 21 and a musician. [17]*He was listed on the regimental medical register five times in 1864. On January 25 and March 14, diagnosis was feb int tert. On February 6, March 3, and April 15, diagnosis was feb int quotid.*

Lewis, M. P., Private, enlisted April 20, 1864, at Dalton, Georgia.

[20]***Lewis, Richard Henry,** was born in 1846 in Coosa County. In 1907 he was living at Goodwater, Clay County.* [1]*He enlisted in 1863 at Socapatoy, Alabama. He was paroled at the end of the war at Talladega.*

Lewis, William Pinckney, Private, was listed on the original muster roll for Company D on September 17, 1861, age 21. He was killed at Shiloh, Tennessee, on April 7, 1862.

Lindsay, Noah J., Private, was listed on the original muster roll for Company D on September 17, 1861, age 21. [17]*He was listed on the regimental medical register twice in 1864. On July 31, the diagnosis was phlegmon. On August 13, the diagnosis was hepatitis.* He was captured September 7, 1864, Atlanta and imprisoned at Camp Douglas, Illinois, where he enlisted in the 6th US Volunteers in April 1865.

Lindsey, William M., Private, enlisted at Montgomery September 17, 1861, age 19. [17]*He was listed on the regimental medical register twice in 1864. On June 13, the diagnosis was chronic rheum, and he was moved to the general hospital the next day. On October 3, the diagnosis was acute rheum, and he was moved to the general hospital on October 15.*

Littlejohn, W. B., Private, enlisted August 20, 1862, Autauga County.

Livingston, Abraham Richard, Private, [20]*He enlisted September 3, 1862, at Mobile.* [17]*He was listed on the regimental medical register December 1, 1863; diagnosis was catarrhus. On December 12 his complaint was acute dysentery. On April 14, 1864, the diagnosis was otalgia. On June 11, his complaint with acute dysentery and he was immediately transferred to the general hospital. On July 20, at the battle of Peachtree Creek near Atlanta, he was severely injured in his left arm by a minnie ball. He was sent to the general hospital the next day. On March 8,1864,* **Richard Livingston** *was listed on the regimental medical register with rubeola.* [20]*He was born February 10, 1845, in Coosa County. He was living in Coosa County in 1907.*

Lorroon, G. Private, was a prisoner of war. He was granted a parole at Macon, Georgia, April 27, 1865. A copy of his parole papers is stored at Alabama Archives.

Lucas, Lorenzo, Private, enlisted December 20, 1861, Green County.

Lucas, William M., Private, enlisted December 20, 1861, Green County. He was hospitalized in Mississippi during June 1862.

[17]***Lynn, N. B.***, *Private, was listed on the regimental medical register on February 21, 1864, diagnosis was abscessus, and June 13, feb int tert. He was moved to the general hospital June 14.*

Macon, William H., Private, enlisted September 17, 1861, at Montgomery, age 18. He was granted a medical furlough January 12, 1862, for 20 days and sent to Wetumpka. He was discharged August 18, 1862. [17]*He was listed on the regimental medical register June 2, 1864; diagnosis was acute dysentery. On July 20, 1864, at the battle of Peachtree Creek near Atlanta, he suffered a wound to his right hand. He was moved to the general hospital July 21.*

Maoro, R. P., Private, enlisted April 17, 1862, at Montgomery. He was listed at Macon, Georgia, on the muster roll for November-December 1864.

Mason, Henry P., Private, enlisted February 17, 1862, Fayette County. He was hospitalized in Mississippi during June 1862. [12]*He was listed on the muster roll for July-August 1862 as sick in the hospital.* Also listed as **Hiram P. Mason.**

Mason, James B., Private, enlisted February 17, 1862, Fayette County. He was hospitalized in Mississippi during June 1862. Also listed as **L. B. Mason**

[18]***Mayhor, William***, *Private, was listed in September 1863 as 47 years old, blue eyes, sandy hair, fair complexion, 5'6, a laborer, and deserter.*

Mayo, Elisha M., Private, enlisted September 17, 1861, at Montgomery, age 18. He was hospitalized in Mississippi during June 1862 and died July 24, 1862, General Hospital, Macon, Mississippi.

McCall, Clarence Osbourn, Private, [30]*enlisted Augus 1861, Coosa County.* [17]*He was listed on the regimental medical register three times in 1864. On February 26, diagnosis was feb int quotid, and in September, feb int tert. On October 9, he was accidentally shot in the left shoulder. He was sent to the general hospital October 15.* [30]*He was born December 13, 1836, in Georgia. He died of complications from his wounds July 20, 1867, possibly in Nixburg, Alabama. He was married to Luisiana Napier. Family tradition states that James B. McCall of Company I was his brother.*

McCook, D. A., Private, enlisted March 11, 1862, at Clopton, Alabama, and was paroled in Greensboro, North Carolina, at the end of the war.

McCullough, George W., Private, [17]*was listed on the regimental medical register February 14, 1864, diagnosis was dysentery.* He was placed on medical furlough March 8, 1864, for 30 days. He was paroled May 17, 1865, at Montgomery. Also spelled **McCollough**

McElrath, James, Private, [17]*was listed on the regimental medical register February 23, 1864, with rubeola. He was transferred to the general hospital the next day. He listed again April 12, diagnosis feb int tert, and in October, diagnosis acute rheum.* Also spelled **McIlrath.**

McKelay, S. M., Private, was granted parole May 20, 1865, at Talladega.

[17]***McNair, A. H.,*** *Private, was listed on the regimental medical register December 1, 1863, with congestion of the brain. He died two days later.*

McNair, Daniel, Private, was captured April 7, 1862, at Shiloh, Tennessee. He died from a gun shot wound April 23, 1862, at Camp Dennison. His father filed a claim. [10]*He was buried at Camp Chase, Ohio, lot number 2125.*

McNair, John B., Private, enlisted September 16, 1861, at Montgomery, age 23. He was placed on sick furlough January 8, 1862, for 20 days and sent to Goodwater. His home was Coosa County. [17]*He was listed on the regimental medical register July 3,1864; diagnosis was acute dysentery. He was moved to the general hospital on July 11. He was listed August 9, diagnosis phlegmon.* He was hospitalized October 24, 1864, in Macon, Georgia. He was paroled at Greensboro, North Carolina, April 1865.

McQueen, Norman L., Private, enlisted September 17, 1861, at Montgomery, age 21. [12]*He was listed on the muster roll for July-August 1862 as sick in the hospital in Gainesville, Alabama.*

Mills, Charles, Private, was from Coosa County. He was captured December 15, 1864, at Nashville and imprisoned at Camp Douglas, Illinois.

Mitchell, Luther C., Private, died 1862 [6]*at Okolona, Mississippi.*

[17]***Mitchel, P. H.,*** *Private, was listed on the regimental medical register January 19, 1864, diagnosis was feb int tert.*

Mitchell, Thomas H., Private, enlisted August 9, 1862, Coosa County. [17]*He was listed on the regimental medical register three times in 1864. On February 9 (4th sergeant), diagnosis was feb int tert. On August 9 (sergeant), the diagnosis was phlegmon. On September 11 (private), the diagnosis was feb int tert.* He was captured November 30, 1864, at Franklin, Tennessee, and imprisoned at Camp Douglas, Illinois.

Mizzels, Joseph, Private, (5'9) enlisted on September 4, 1863, in Coosa County, his home county. [17]*He was listed on the regimental medical register three times in 1864. On July 31, the diagnosis was acute colitis; August 6, acute diarrhea; and October 3, debilitas. He was moved to a general hospital October 11.* He was captured April 12, 1865, Salisbury, North Carolina. He was imprisoned at Camp Chase, Ohio, where he took the oath of allegiance on June 13, 1865. [30]*He was* born December 25, 1819, Wilkinson County, Georgia. He died March 14,1899, Goodwater, Coosa County. Also spelled **Measles**.

Monk, John Samuel, Private, was from Coosa County. [17]*He was listed on the regimental medical register five times in 1864. On March 9 and July 4, the diagnosis was acute dysentery. He was transferred to the general hospital the next day. On June 21, the diagnosis was feb int quotid. On September 13 and in November, the diagnosis was acute diarrhea.* He was hospitalized in Macon, Georgia, with dysentery July 5, 1864. [2]*He died November 30, 1864, at the battle of Franklin, Tennessee. He is buried in section 69, McGavock Cemetery, Franklin.*

Monk, Joseph Rufus, Private, [37]*enlisted during April of 1864 in Coosa County.* [17]*He was listed on the regimental medical register June 21, 1864; diagnosis was acute diarrhea.* He was captured December 15, 1864, at Nashville and imprisoned at Camp Douglas, Illinois. [20]*He was born April 17, 1846, Davidson, Tallapoosa County. He was paroled June 22, 1865, and was living in Coosa County in 1907.* [30]*He was the son of John Samuel Monk.* [37]*In 1921 he was still living in Coosa County and stated that he had fought in the battles of New Hope Church, Lost Mountain, Kennesaw Mountain, Resaca, Atlanta, Franklin and Nashville.*

Mullaney, William J., Private, was from Randolph County. [17]*He was listed on the regimental medical register on June 22, 1864, with acute dysentery. In July 1864 during the Atlanta campaign, he was slightly wounded in the right arm. The minnie ball was extracted on the field. He was sent to the general hospital on July 5* at Macon, Georgia. He was placed on medical furlough July 8 for 30 days. [17]*He was slightly wounded in the face at the battle of Franklin, Tennessee, on November 30, 1864.* Also spelled **Mullaly**.

Munroe, Benjamin P., Private, [12]*enlisted September 17, 1861, Montgomery, age 20.* [17]*He was listed on the regimental medical register July 12, 1864; diagnosis was acute diarrhea.* [17]*He was wounded in the left thigh July 28, 1864, at the battle of Ezra Church near Atlanta. He transferred to the general hospital July 31.* He may have been captured at Atlanta. Also spelled **Monroe**.

[18]***Murray, William,** Private, was listed in September 1863 as 47 years old, blue eyes, dark hair, fair complexion, 5'4, a laborer, and deserter.*

Musgrove, John W. Jr., Private, enlisted February 17, 1862, Fayette County. He transferred from the 5th Battalion on April 23, 1862. He never reported to the 17th and was listed as a deserter. He was hospitalized in Mississippi during June 1862.

Musgrove, John W. Sr., Private, enlisted December 20, 1861, Fayette County. He transferred from the 5th Battalion on April 23, 1862. He never reported to the 17th and was listed as a deserter. He was hospitalized in Mississippi during June 1862.

Musslewhite, J. E., Private, enlisted March 11, 1863, at Clopton. He was paroled on May 1, 1865, at Greensboro, North Carolina.

[17]***Norris, A. F.,*** *Private, was listed on the regimental medical register December 4, 1863, diagnosis was feb int tert.*

[28]***Norris, B. L.,*** *was present at the Confederate Veterans Reunion in Greenville August 21, 1897.*

Norwood, James M., Private, was on the original muster roll for Company D September 17, 1861, age 25. He died at home January 11, 1862.

Odioran, William W., Private, enlisted at Montgomery November 29, 1861, and was discharged September 28, 1862. **Also spelled Odiomi.** See Company H.

Ogburn, W. H., Private, enlisted October 18, 1863, Chattanooga.

Oliver, H. M., Private, was missing after the battle at Shiloh, Tennessee, April 1862.

[17]***Owen, W. F.,*** *Private, was listed on the regimental medical register on June 11, 1864, diagnosis was acute diarrhea.*

Pate, Thomas M., Private, enlisted September 17, 1861, at Montgomery, age 19, and was from Mt. Olive, Coosa County. [17]*On July 28, 1864, at the battle of Ezra Church near Atlanta, he sustained a severe wound (left wrist). He transferred to the general hospital on July 31.* He was hospitalized August 1864, at Macon, Georgia, with a fracture (ulna). [17]*He was listed on the regimental medical register on November 3, 1864, diagnosis feb int tert, and moved to the general hospital November 14.* Captured December 15, 1864, at Nashville, he was imprisoned at Camp Douglas, Illinois. He was paroled and transferred to City Point, Virginia, on March 1865. He was hospitalized March 21, 1865, at Richmond and moved to Fort Lee, Virginia, March 25, 1865. He was again paroled on June 3, 1865, at Talladega.

Pate, William A., Private, was on the original muster roll for Company D September 17, 1861, age 18. He was discharged December 17, 1861.

Peacock, Simon, Private, enlisted March 11, 1862, at Clopton, Alabama. He was paroled May 1, 1865, Greensboro, North Carolina.

Pelew, J. R., Private, enlisted March 11, 1862, at Clopton, Alabama. He was paroled May 1, 1865, Greensboro, North Carolina.

Pennington, L. or S., Private, was hospitalized March 3, 1865, at Richmond, Virginia.

Peoples, Benjamin P., Private, 5'9, enlisted December 1, 1862, at Mobile. [17]*He was listed on the regimental medical register June 23, 1864, with* *acute diarrhea.* On July 28, 1864, at the battle of Ezra Church near Atlanta, he sustained a slight wound to his left side. He was listed on the regimental medical register and then transferred to the general hospital July 31. He was granted parole June 1, 1865, at Montgomery.

[12] **Peoples, John A.**, Private, enlisted September 17, 1861, Montgomery, age 19. [17] *He was killed July 31, 1864, probably at the battle of Ezra Church near Atlanta.*

Pinkett, J. W., Private, was on the original muster roll for Company D September 17, 1861, age 26.

Pool, A, Private, was captured April 1865.

Poor, Newton M., Private, was 6'2, a farmer, and born in 1834 Anderson County, South Carolina. He was discharged February 12, 1863: disability.

Powell, Andrew J., Private, enlisted September 19, 1862, at Montgomery. He was 5'6 and born in 1834 in Macon, Georgia. [17] *He was listed on the regimental medical register December 9, 1863, diagnosis was acute diarrhea and January 16, 1864, feb int quotid.* He was granted a parole May 15, 1865, at Montgomery.

Powell, Edmund, Private, enlisted September 17, 1861, at Montgomery, age 19. He died July 15, 1862, at Grenada, Mississippi.

Powell, J., Private

Price, Frederick F., Private, enlisted September 12, 1862, at Montgomery. He was on detached duty at the Ordnance Department at Mobile during November and December of 1862.

Price, George J., Private, enlisted September 4, 1862, Autauga County. [17] *He was listed on the regimental medical register twice in 1864 with acute diarrhea, on August 8 and September 12.* [10] *He died January 14, 1865, at Louisville, Kentucky.*

Prickett, James W., Private, 5'7, enlisted at Montgomery September 17, 1861. He was granted a medical furlough on January 6, 1862, for 15 days and sent to Berrryville. [17] *He was listed on the regimental medical register on January 25, 1864, diagnosis was opthalmia, and on June 15, feb int quotid. He sustained a slight wound (left hand) July 20, 1864, at the battle of Peachtree Creek near Atlanta. He was transferred to the general hospital June 21.* He was paroled at Montgomery May 1865.

Prickett, W. F., Private, enlisted at Mobile. He was 5'5 and born in 1847 in Georgia. [17] *He was listed on the regimental medical register seven times in 1864. On January 5, the diagnosis was acute diarrhea. On March 11 and 26, the diagnosis was feb int quotid. On July 10, the diagnosis was parotitis. During September, he suffered from bronchitis. On November 30 during the battle at Franklin, Tennessee, he sustained a slight wound to the little finger on his left hand.* He was granted May 18, 1865, at Montgomery. Also spelled **Puckett.**

Pruett, George J., Private, enlisted August 1, 1862, Coosa County. [17]*He was listed on the regimental medical register four times in 1864. On January 15 and February 2, diagnosis was catarrhus. On June 3 and September 13, diagnosis was acute diarrhea.* He was wounded and captured December 15, 1864, at Nashville. He was sent to a Louisville prison hospital where he died January 14, 1865, of diphtheria. He was buried at Cave Hill Cemetery, Louisville, Lot 6, and Range 62. [30]*He was born in 1830.*

Pruett, H. H., Private, enlisted April 8, 1862, Coosa County. [17]*He was listed on the regimental medical register twice in 1864. On June 18, diagnosis was feb int tert, and on July 9, feb int quotid.*

Purdey, J. H., Private, was placed on medical leave from LaGrange Hospital, July 5, 1864 for 30 days. [17]*James Purdy was listed on the regimental medical register January 5, 1864, diagnosis catarrhus. J. H. Purdey was listed on the regimental medical register January 31, 1864, with dyspepsia. On September 29,* **H. J. Purdy** *was listed, diagnosis neuralgia.* He was hospitalized May 5, 1865, Jackson, Mississippi. He was paroled May 24, 1865, at Talladega.

Pylant, A. H., was promoted January 27, 1862, to second lieutenant.

Rawles, J. C., Private, 5'5, was paroled May 17, 1865, at Montgomery.

Rawles, J. P., Private, enlisted March 7, Corinth. He was 5'8, a physician, and born 1838 at Buryville, Alabama.

Rawls, William B., Private, enlisted September 17, 1861, at Montgomery. [42]*He was granted a furlough and sent to Burksville, Alabama, January 12, 1862, for 20 days.* He was captured June 2, 1864, New Hope Church, Georgia, and imprisoned at Rock Island, Illinois. He took the oath of allegiance on October 25, 1864, but his request to join the US Army was denied. He was 5'10 and from Coosa County.

Reeves, William, Private, enlisted September 17, 1861, at Montgomery, age 22. He was 5'10 and born in 1830 in Jasper County, Georgia. He was discharged October 3, 1862: provided a substitute.

[17]***Richardson, W. C.,*** *Private, was killed July 20, 1864, at the battle of Peach Tree Creek near Atlanta.*

Riese, Henry, Private, enlisted August 13, 1862, at Mobile. [17]*He was listed on the regimental medical register on September 21, 1864; diagnosis was fistula.* Also spelled **Reese.**

Riley, William, Private, enlisted March 11, 1862, at Clopton, Alabama. Parole was granted May 1865, Greensboro, North Carolina.

Robbins, Howell R., Private, [20]*enlisted on August 1, 1863, at Mobile.* [37]*His assignment while in Mobile included guard duty building breastworks.* [17]*He was listed on the regimental medical register on April 1, 1864; diagnosis was organic disease of the heart.* [20]*He was discharged April*

19, 1864, at Pollard, and was living in Coosa County in 1907. He was born September 1, 1846, at Nixburg, Coosa County. [37]He was born August 1, 1845, in Coosa County. In 1921 he was living in Goodwater.

Roberts, William P., Private, enlisted September 17, 1861, at Montgomery.

Robertson, William M., Private, was 5'10 and born in 1846 in Scotland. He was discharged September 22, 1862, disability.

[18]**Robinson, James,** Private, was listed in September 1863 as 46 years old, blue eyes, dark hair, fair complexion, 5'9, a laborer, and deserter.

Robinson, Josiah, Private, was on the original muster roll for Company D September 17, 1861, age 18. He was discharged December 17, 1861.

Ruse, Henry, Private, **Also spelled Riese.**

Rush, George W., Private, enlisted November 20, 1862, Coosa County. He was 6'1, born 1826 in South Carolina, and a teamster. [17]*He was listed on the regimental medical register December 26, 1863, January 10 and 21, 1864, and February 6, diagnosis was feb int tert. He was listed again April 3, diagnosis phthitis pulmon. He was discharged April 19.*

Rush, Warren R., Lieutenant, enlisted at Montgomery September 17, 1861. He was 6'1 and born in 1833, in Montgomery County. He was severely wounded (jaw) at the battle at Shiloh, Tennessee, in April 1862. He was promoted from first sergeant to second lieutenant January 29, 1862.

Russell, Moses Richardson, Private, was discharged April 10, 1863. [30]*He enlisted in 1862 in Mobile. According to "Memoirs of Georgia", volume 1, 439-440, he was born in 1835, Coweta County, Georgia, to Harris and Leah Steed Russell. He was a school teacher. During the war he was disabled by sickness and sent a substitute. He was buried at Old Camp Methodist Church near Carrollton, Carroll County, Georgia.*

Rutherford, Samuel, Private, enlisted March 13, 1862, at Montgomery, and was paroled at Greensboro, North Carolina, April 1865.

Sharp, James E., Private, enlisted September 17, 1861, at Montgomery. [42]*He was granted a furlough and sent to Traveler's Rest January 16, 1862, for 15 days.* He died December 4, 1862.

Sharpton, J. G., Private, was paroled June 1865 at Selma.

Shaw, Joseph P., Private, was discharged April 10, 1863.

Shaw, William J., Private, enlisted September 17, 1861, at Montgomery, age 19, and did not survive the war.

[12]**Shirey, Aran,** *Private, enlisted May 10, 1862, Corinth, Mississippi. On the muster roll for July-August 1862, he was listed as sick in the hospital at Enterprise, Mississippi.*

Simpson, A. J., Captain, enlisted March 11, 1862, at Clopton, Alabama. He was granted parole May 1865, Greensboro, North Carolina.

Sinclair, Daniel, Private, enlisted October 4, 1862, Clark County. [17]*He was listed on the regimental medical register three times in 1864. On March*

20, diagnosis was feb int tert. On June 3 and June 25, diagnosis was acute dysentery. He was discharged November 1864. He was captured and took oath of allegiance on November 15, 1864, at Talladega.

Skipper, James H., Private, enlisted September 17, 1861, at Mobile. He was hospitalized December 1, 1864, at Macon, Georgia. His home was in Butler County.

Smallwood, James A. I., Private, enlisted October 18, 1862, Coosa County. [17]*He sustained a wound to the intestines on July 20, at the battle of Peach Tree Creek, and died at the brigade hospital July 21.*

[17]***Smith, C. A.,*** *Private, was listed on the regimental medical register twice in 1864. On March 7, diagnosis was feb int quotid and August 16, constipatio.*

[17]***Smith, J. W.,*** *Private, was listed on the regimental medical register July 4, 1864, with acute diarrhea, and sent to the general hospital July 6.*

Smith, W., Private

Smith, William H. W., Private, enlisted August 21, 1862, Coosa County. He was captured December 15, 1864, at Nashville and imprisoned at Camp Douglas, Illinois.

Spear, James A., Private, [17]*was listed on the regimental medical register twice in 1864. On July 3, the diagnosis was feb int quotid. He was moved to the general hospital the next day. In October his complaint was acute diarrhea. He was moved to the general hospital October 21.* He was captured December 17, 1864 at Franklin, Tennessee, and imprisoned at Camp Douglas, Illinois. He died May 29, 1865 [10]*at Camp Chase, Ohio, and was buried in lot number 2007.* Also spelled **Speers, Spiers**

Speer, Sterling W., Private, 5'7, lived in Coosa County. He was captured July 4, 1864, at Chattahoochie, Georgia. He was imprisoned at Camp Douglas, Illinois, where he was paroled June 17, 1865.

Spivey, Aaron, Private, enlisted May 10, 1862, at Corinth, Mississippi. His home was in Coosa County.

Stearnes, M. R., Private, was paroled on May 31, 1865, at Talladega.

Stephens, J. W. H., Private, enlisted March 11, 1862, at Clopton, Alabama. Parole was granted April 1865 at Greensboro, North Carolina.

Stewart, Gideon T., Private, lived in Coosa County. He was hospitalized June 17, 1864, for 14 days in Macon, Georgia. [17]***G. D. Stewart*** *was listed on the regimental medical register June 2, 1864, with debilitas.* ***G. I. Stewart*** *was listed December 19, 1863, with acute diarrhea.* ***G. T. Stewart*** *was listed four times in 1864. On January 15, the diagnosis was morbi cutis and on March 10, acute rheumat. He was sent to the general hospital at Spring Hill March 11. On September 30, the diagnosis was acute diarrhea and on October 3, feb int quotid.*

COMPANY D

Stewart, James J., Private, enlisted September 6, 1863, Coosa County. He was 5'8, a farmer, and born 1845 in Tallapoosa County. [17]*He was listed on the regimental medical register March 7, 1864; diagnosis was catarrhus.* See Service Records for S. H. Clyett. Also spelled **Steward.**

Stewart, Nathaniel Wentley, enlisted September 17, 1861, age 26. While in Pensacola January 22, 1862, he was placed on sick furlough for 15 days and sent to Goodwater, Alabama. He was hospitalized in Mississippi during June 1862. He was captured at Nashville, Tennessee, December 15, 1864, and imprisoned at Camp Douglas, Illinois. [20]*He was born November 14, 1834, in Newton, Georgia. He was living in Coosa County in 1907.*

[17]**Stewart, Seaborn H.,** Lieutenant, enlisted as first sergeant September 17, 1861, at Montgomery. He was hospitalized in Mississippi during June 1862. He was appointed second lieutenant April 14, 1864. [17]*He was listed on the regimental medical register on April 27, 1864, diagnosis was feb int tert.* He was captured at Big Shanty, Georgia, June 15, 1864, and imprisoned at Johnson Island, Ohio, where he was paroled June 15, 1865. He was born in 1834, and his home was in Brickville, Alabama.

Stewart, Samuel S., Private, enlisted September 17, 1861, Montgomery, age 19. He was hospitalized in Mississippi during June 1862. [17]*He was listed on the regimental medical register on January 1, 1864, diagnosis was feb int tert. He was listed again in September, diagnosis ulcus.* He was captured December 15, 1864, Nashville, Tennessee, and imprisoned at Camp Douglas, Illinois. [30]*He was born and died in Goodwater, Coosa County. His father was Gideon T. Stewart.*

Stewart, William, Private, enlisted September 17, 1861, Montgomery, age 32. He was hospitalized in the general hospital in Mobile in the fall of 1862. He was granted a disability discharge November 5, 1862. He was born in Campbell County, Georgia.

Story, Newton A., Corporal, enlisted September 17, 1861, Montgomery, age 19. He died in the hospital in Mobile January 5, 1862. He was buried at Barrancas National Cemetery. Also spelled **Storey.**

[17]**Taylor, Evan,** Private, *was listed on the regimental medical register March 24, 1864, with acute dysentery.* He died in battle July 1, 1864, shot in the right temple. He was 18 1/2 years old and a farmer.

Taylor, George W., Private, enlisted November 6, 1861, Macon County. He was discharged December 1, 1862: provided a substitute. He was born in Coosa County in 1837.

Taylor, W. R. H., Private, was on the original muster roll for Company D September 17, 1861, age 20. He was discharged December 17, 1861.

Temple, B. Z., Private, 5'8, was paroled May 26, 1865 at Montgomery. [27]*He enlisted November 1863 at Montgomery. He was slighted wounded by a shell during the battle of Franklin, Tennessee, on November 30, 1864. He was captured that night while moving artillery. He was paroled May 24, 1865, at Montgomery. He was born in 1845 and died August 6, 1909. He is buried at the Confederate Memorial Park Cemetery, Mountain Creek, Alabama.*

Thaxton, D. S., was elected lieutenant September 17, 1861, and resigned December 23, 1861.

[17]**Thomas, C. G.,** *Private, was listed on the regimental medical register twice in December 1863: on the 3rd, diagnosis was feb int quotid and on the 14th, catarrhus. He was sick again January 4, 1864, with acute diarrhea. January 9, he was diagnosed as having a hernia. He was discharged January 14.*

Thompson, E. Z., Private, enlisted September 17, 1861, at Montgomery. He was 5'9, born 1846, and lived in Coosa County. [17]*He was listed on the regimental medical register four times in 1864. On January 26, the diagnosis was contusio, on February 7 and July 2, feb int tert, and on April 16, feb int quotid.* He was captured December 17, 1864, at Franklin, Tennessee, and was imprisoned at Camp Chase, Ohio.

Thompson, Cain Zebidee, Private, was captured December 17, 1864, at Franklin, Tennessee, and imprisoned at Camp Chase, Ohio. [20]*He was born January 17, 1844, Chambers County. Discharged June 6, 1865, he was living at Titus, Elmore County, Alabama, in 1907.*

Thornton, Horatio Marion, Private, enlisted September 17, 1861, at Montgomery, age 22. He was 5'8, and his home was Coosa County. He suffered wounds at the battle of Shiloh, Tennessee, in April 1862. [17]*He was listed on the regimental medical register three times in 1864. On June 21, the diagnosis was feb int quotid. On July 17, the diagnosis was acute dysentery, and he was moved to the general hospital the next day.* At the battle of Franklin, Tennessee, on November 30, he was slightly wounded in the left leg. He was captured December 17, 1864, at Franklin and imprisoned at Camp Chase, Ohio. Moved to Point Lookout during March 1865, he was paroled June 20, 1865. [20]*He was born March 7, 1838, at Meriweather, Georgia. He was living at Wetumpka in Elmore County in 1907.* [30]*He married Josephine Warrick and went by the name "Rash".*

Underwood, Joseph W., Private, [17]*was listed on the regimental medical register during September 1864, diagnosis was parotitis.* He was hospitalized at West Point, Mississippi, January 12, 1865. [30]*He was born in 1846 in Coosa County. He married Louisa J. Gilberte. He died in 1883 in Bossier Parish, Louisiana.*

Walker, S., Private, was hospitalized at Richmond, Virginia, May 28, 1864.

Walker, W. E., Private, enlisted March 17, 1862, at Greenville. He was paroled April 1865 at Greensboro, North Carolina.

Walker, W. W., Private, enlisted February 1, 1864, West Point.

Wall, James, Private, enlisted October 25, 1862, at Mobile. He was 5'10 and born in 1816 in Ireland.

Wall, John, Private, enlisted October 25, 1862, at Mobile.

Warick, Henry D., Private, enlisted September 17, 1861, at Montgomery, age 22. He died July 22, 1862, at Saltillo, Mississippi.

Warrick, James H., Private, enlisted September 7, 1861, and died in 1862 leaving father, Wiley Warrick.

Watford, B. C., Private, enlisted March 11, 1862, at Clopton.

Webb, Austin P., Private, [17]*was listed on the regimental medical register three times in 1864. On June 15, the diagnosis was debilitas, on August 13, acute diarrhea, and on September 4, nephretis. He was immediately moved to the general hospital.* His home was in Coosa County and was paroled May 20, 1865 in Talladega.

[17]***White, B. R.**, Private, was listed on the regimental medical register on January 1, 1864, diagnosis was catarrhus.*

White, Stephen, Private, died in 1864 leaving widow, Fanny White.

Whitehead, W. H., Private, enlisted March 11, 1862, at Clopton. He was granted a parole in April 1865 at Greensboro, North Carolina.

Wideman, A., Private, was discharged March 11, 1863.

Wiggins, C. C., Private, enlisted March 11, 1862, at Clopton,.

Wiggins, Joseph B., Private, [17]*was listed on the regimental medical register March 17, 1864, diagnosis was acute dysentery. He suffered a slight wound (right foot) August 14, 1864, during the siege of Atlanta, and was sent to the general hospital the next day.* He was paroled June 19, 1865, at Talladega.

Wilson, Benjamin E., Private, enlisted September 17, 1861, at Montgomery. [17]*He was listed on the regimental medical register with dysentery on August 13, 1864.*

Wilson, Henry, Private, enlisted December 6, 1861, at Montgomery. He was paroled April 1865 at Greensboro, North Carolina.

Wilson, Robert, Private, enlisted December 1, 1863, at Montgomery. He was paroled April 1865 at Greensboro, North Carolina.

Wright, J. D., Private, enlisted September 17, 1861, at Montgomery.

Yarborough, Thomas J., Private, [17]*was listed on the regimental medical register on July 6, 1864, diagnosis was feb int quotid, and was transferred to the general hospital the next day. He was sick again on July 19, diagnosis was feb remitt, and was transferred to the general* *hospital July 21.* He was captured December 15, 1864 in Nashville and was imprisoned at Camp Douglas, Illinois. He took the oath of allegiance and enlisted in the 6th US Volunteer Infantry April 1, 1865.

Yong, Aug, Private, lived in Randolph County. He was hospitalized at Macon, Georgia, May 21, 1864 for 2 days.

[17] *Young, Asa, Private, was listed on the regimental medical register on December 15, 1863, diagnosis was feb int tert. He reported sick January 5, January 27, February 9, and April 18, 1864, diagnosis was feb int quotid.* [20] *He was born October 10, 1834, at Liberty Hill, Troup County, Georgia. He enlisted January 6, 1863, at Mobile and was discharged February 4, 1864, at Macon. He was living at Joppa, Cullman County in 1907.*

Appendix VI. Company E

Alexander, W. A. J., Private, was at the surrender at Greensboro, North Carolina, April 26, 1865.
Ansbury, Frank, Private
Arnold, Thomas, Private, was declared missing after the battle of Shiloh, Tennessee, April 6, 1862.

[17]**Baas, B.,** Private, reported to the regimental medical unit December 31, 1863, diagnosis was feb int tert.
Bacon, John, Private, enlisted February 15, 1862, at Lacon, Alabama. [12]During the summer of 1862 he was listed as absent and sick. [1]He was born December 27, 1838, at Lawrenceville, Gwinett County, Georgia. He served until surrender in 1865 and was living in Weedowee, Randolph County, in 1907.
Bailey, Julian L., Private, enlisted September 20, 1862, at Camp Forney. [17]He reported to the regimental medical unit on December 25, 1863, diagnosis debilitas, and was placed on furlough on December 27 for 20 days. He reported again on March 27, 1864, with acute dysentery.
Bailey, Patrick G., Private, enlisted September 13, 1862, at Camp Forney or Roanoke. [17]He reported to the regimental medical unit January 12, 1864, diagnosis paronychia. He reported in May having sustained wounds, probably at the battle of Dalton, Georgia. His ring and middle fingers were amputated. [20]He was born January 22, 1838, Lawrenceville, Gwinett County, Georgia. In 1907 he was living in Randolph County.
Baker, W. H. H., Private, enlisted September 14, 1861, at Montgomery. A farmer he was 5'8 and born in 1843 Newton County, Georgia. He died in the hospital January 5, 1862, leaving father, Thomas Baker of Newton County.
Bales, Newton, Private, enlisted September 13, 1862, at Camp Forney. [17]He reported to the regimental medical unit five times in 1864. The first time was February 5, diagnosis contusio. In May, he sustained a severe wound to his finger. On June 29 the diagnosis was feb int quotid. On July 4 he sustained a slight head wound and was sent to the general hospital, when he was listed as 24 years old and a farmer. On August 30 the diagnosis was feb int quotid. He was paroled at Greensboro, North Carolina, May 1865. [20]He was born February 17, 1837 in Newman, Coweta County, Georgia. In 1907 he was living in Liberty in Blount County. Also spelled **Bayles.**
Barnes, Daniel S., Private, enlisted September 30, 1862, at Mobile. [26]He was born August 28, 1833. He died June 9, 1906, and is buried in an unmarked grave in Beulah Cemetery in Randolph County.

Barnett, Frances M., Private, enlisted January 27, 1862, at Greenville. [17]*He reported to the regimental medical unit February 23, 1864, diagnosis was feb int quotid.*

Barnett, R., Private

Barrett, Thomas V., Sergeant, September 14, 1861, at Montgomery. [18]*In September 1863 he was described as 32 years old, blue eyes, sandy hair, fair complexion, 6'1, a farmer, and a deserter.* He later rejoined his unit. [17]*He reported to the regimental medical unit on June 15, 1864 with acute diarrhea.*

Barton, Enoch, Private, was discharged December 16, 1861. [30]*He was born in 1818.* [33]*He died January 20, 1896. His wife, Martha C. Barton, applied for a pension.*

Barton, William F., Private, enlisted October 7, 1861, at Camp Davis.

Bedgood, Richmond, Private, enlisted January 27, 1862, at Greenville. He was 5'8 and born in 1811, Washington County, Georgia. [12]*During the summer of 1862 he was listed as absent and sick.* He was discharged November 25, 1862.

Bell, J. E., Private

Bellah, John W., Private, enlisted November 16, 1863, at Mobile. A mechanic, he was 5'7, born in 1821 in Morgan County, Georgia. [17]*On February 8, 1864, he reported to the regimental medical unit with neuralgia.*

Benefield, Caleb Cox, Private, enlisted September 30, 1862, at Mobile. [17]*He reported to the regimental medical unit twice with a diagnosis of feb int tert, on December 1, 1863, and March 19, 1864.* He was paroled at Greensboro, North Carolina, May 1865. [37]*He was born November 11, 1832, in Newton, Georgia. In 1921, he was living in Randolph County and stated that he was in the battles of Resaca, Atlanta, and Franklin. He also stated that he was captured in Nashville in December of 1864, but escaped.*

Benton, W. F., Private

Blair, John William, Corporal, enlisted September 14, 1861, at Montgomery. [12]*On the muster roll for July-August 1862, he was listed as absent on furlough July-August 1862.* [18]*In September 1863 he was described as 23 years old, gray eyes, light hair, fair complexion, 5'6, a mechanic, and a deserter.* [26]*He died December 1889 and was buried in an unmarked grave in Christian Church Cemetery in Randolph County.* [33]*His wife applied for a pension.* [30]*Blair was born December 19, 1839, Dekalb County, Georgia, to John C. And Margie Bird Blair. He was married to Sarah Ann Hairston His brother-in-law, Thomas Collier, was also in Company E. He died December 30, 1887.*

Bohannan, James, Private, enlisted September 13, 1862, at Camp Forney. [17]*He reported to the regimental medical unit on December 3, 1863,*

COMPANY E 259

diagnosis feb int quotid. He reported twice with a diagnosis of feb int tert, on January 14 and February 9, 1864. His diagnosis in May was a slight neck wound, probably occurred during the battle of Resaca, Georgia. On July 4 during the siege of Atlanta, he sustained a wound to the jaw caused by a minnie ball. He was listed as 22 years old. He was at the surrender at Greensboro, North Carolina, April 26, 1865.

Bohannan, Robert K., Private, enlisted September 13, 1862, at Camp Forney. [17] *He reported to the regimental medical unit on December 19, 1863, diagnosis feb int tert. He reported again September 23, 1864, with acute dysentery.* He was paroled June 1, 1865, at Talladega. Also listed as **R. B. Bohamon, R. R. Bohannan.**

Bohanan, W. R., Private, enlisted January 30, 1864. He was at the surrender April 26, 1865, at Greensboro, North Carolina.

Boyd, Elias M., Private, enlisted September 14, 1861, at Montgomery. He was hospitalized in Mississippi in June 1862. [12] *During the summer of 1862, he served on extra duty as a teamster. He was hospitalized at St. Mary's, LaGrange, Georgia, 4th Quarter 1863.* He required surgery in 1864 for the removal of a tumor. [26] *He was born July 12, 1829. He died June 15, 1904, and is buried in an unmarked grave in Paran Baptist Church Cemetery in Randolph County.*

Brantley, John H., Private, enlisted July 7, 1863, at Mobile. He was a farmer, 6'2, and born in 1828 in Dallas County.

Brazeal, Frances M., Private, enlisted May 14, 1862, Corinth, Mississippi. He was a farmer, 5'9, and born in 1841 in Campbell County, Georgia. [17] *He reported to the regimental medical unit on December 26, 1863, diagnosis was feb int tert, and on June 5, 1864, with acute diarrhea.*

Brazeal, James K. P., Private, enlisted at Montgomery September 14, 1861. [17] *He reported to the regimental medical unit June 28, 1864, with acute diarrhea.*

Brown, A. D., Private, enlisted May 10, 1863, at Mobile. A clerk, he was 5'11 and born in 1838 in Jackson, Michigan.

Bursen, David J., Private, was paroled May 15, 1865, at Talladega.

Bryon, Henry C., Private, [12] *He enlisted February 15, 1862, Leon, Butler/Crenshaw County.* He was discharged July 4, 1862.

Bush, W. M., Private

Butler, Augustus, Private, enlisted September 8, 1862, at Mobile.

Camp, Isaiah C., Private, enlisted September 14, 1861, at Montgomery. He was placed on sick furlough January 19, 1862, for 20 days and sent home to Randolph County. [18] *In September 1863 he was described as 24 years old, gray eyes, sandy hair, fair complexion, 5'8, a farmer, and a deserter.* At the end of the war, he was captured and released after taking the oath of allegiance. Also listed as **Isaac C. Camp.**

Caruthers, William W., Private, 5'11, was paroled May 24, 1865, at Greenville. [17]*He entered the regimental medical unit January 16, 1864, with rubeola. He reported again February 18, diagnosis feb int tert, and on March 17 with acute dysentery. On August 13 during the siege of Atlanta, his hand was severely wounded, and he was moved to a general hospital on the 15th.*

Cassels, G. H., Private, enlisted September 14, 1862, at Mobile. [17]*He entered the regimental medical unit on March 21, 1864, with rubeola and transferred to the general hospital in at Greenville the next day. He was listed as sick July 13, diagnosis debilitas. The next day he was granted a 30-day furlough.* He was paroled at Greensboro, North Carolina, May 18, 1865. Also spelled **Castles, Cassils.**

Cassels, Henry T., Private. [17]*reported to the regimental medical unit on March 6, 1864, diagnosis catarrhus. He was wounded (hip), July 28, 1864, at the battle of Ezra Church near Atlanta. He was transferred to the general hospital on August 15.* Also spelled **Castles, Cassils.**

Cassels, Mark, Private, enlisted November 25, 1863. He was born in 1821, Morgan County.

Cassettes, J. C., Private, died March 29, 1864, Spring Hill Hospital, at Mobile. [17]*He reported to the regimental medical unit twice in early 1864: January 14, diagnosis was feb int quotid, and February 23, feb int tert.* Also spelled **Cassels, Castles.**

Clark, William H., was appointed second lieutenant May 16, 1862.

Collier, Squire Thomas, Sergeant, enlisted September 14, 1861, at Montgomery. He was hospitalized in Mississippi in June 1862. [17]*He reported to the regimental medical unit with diagnosis feb int tert, five times, on December 19 and 20, 1863, on January 13, February 5, and April 7, 1864. He was moved to the general hospital on April 11. He was also sick February 21, diagnosis feb int quotid. On June 22 he reported to the regimental medical unit and was moved to a general hospital having sustained some type of wound.* [30]*He was born July 30, 1831, Moore County, North Carolina, to Thomas and Sarah Morris Collier. He was married to Nancy Blair. Her brother, John William Blair, was also in Company E. Collier died February 1905, and is buried in Funston Cemetery, Jones County, Texas.*

Combs, John J., Private, enlisted April 15, 1862, at Greenville. He died July 26, 1862 at the general hospital in Macon, Mississippi.

[17]***Conn, W. G.,*** *Private, reported to the regimental medical unit March 21, 1864, with acute dysentery. He was sick again April 2 with debilitas, and granted 30-day furlough the next day.*

Cooper, John G., Private, enlisted October 7, 1861, at Camp Davis. He was placed on sick furlough January 19, 1862, for 20 days and sent to Randolph County. He was hospitalized in Mississippi in June 1862.

[17]*He reported to the regimental medical unit on December 29, 1863, diagnosis was feb int tert. He was ill February 14, 1864, with neuralgia. He suffered some type of wound to his right foot August 7.* He was paroled at Greensboro, North Carolina, May 1865. Also listed as **J. L. Cooper.**

Copeland, Thomas J., Private, enlisted at Montgomery September 14, 1861. He was wounded at Shiloh, Tennessee, in April 1862 and placed on furlough June 1862. [5]*He was a standard bearer.* Also listed as **T. J. Coplan.**

Copeland, William C., Private, enlisted September 14, 1861, at Montgomery, and was discharged July 4, 1862: disability.

Crawford, Francis M., Private, enlisted January 27, 1862, at Greenville. He was assigned as Signal operator.

Cullins, G. W., Sergeant, [42]*died January 13, 1862.*

Cummings, William W., Private, died 1862, claim filed by widow, Sara Ann Cummings.

Cummings, James S., Private, died June 26, 1864, Macon, Georgia.

Dabney, G. A., Private, was placed on sick furlough January 10, 1862 for 20 days and sent to Randolph County. He died April 1862, at the battle of Shiloh, Tennessee.

Dabney, James L., Private, enlisted September 13, 1862, at Mobile. His home was in Roanoke, Randolph County. [17]*He reported to the regimental medical unit on August 7, 1864, diagnosis debilitas, and was transferred to the general hospital on August 13.* He died August 14, 1864, Texas Hospital, Opelika.

Dabney, John T., Private, enlisted August 28, 1862, at Iuka, Mississippi.

Daniel, Newton, Private, enlisted September 14, 1862, at Montgomery. [12]*He was granted a furlough for 15 days January 13, 1862, and sent to Troup County, Georgia.* [17]*He reported to the regimental medical unit twice in 1864. On March 19, the diagnosis was feb int quotid. On July 20 he was wounded at the battle of Peachtree Creek near Atlanta, and transferred to the general hospital the next day.* Also listed as **Newton Dane.**

Daniels, E. W., Private. Also listed as **Edward N. Daniel**

Daniels, George M., Private

Davis, David L., Private, enlisted September 14, 1862, at Montgomery. [12]*He was listed as sick and absent from duty during the summer of 1862.*

Davis, John H., Private, [17]*reported to the regimental medical unit in early May of 1864 with acute dysentery and then was listed as missing.* He was captured May 16, 1864, Resaca, Georgia. Transferred to Alton, Illinois, he was then sent to Camp Douglas, Illinois, where he died of smallpox November 19, 1864.

Dendy, William M., Private, enlisted March 10, 1863, at Greenville, and was paroled May 22, 1865, at Montgomery. Also listed as **H. M. Denby, William S. Dendy**

Dunn, John, Private, was captured May 16, 1864, Resaca, Georgia. He was transferred from Alton, Illinois, to Camp Douglas, Illinois, Illinois.

Earnest, John L., Private, enlisted February 14, 1862, at Greenville.

Earnest, Josiah, Private, [12]*He enlisted February 14, 1862, at Greenville.* He was discharged July 4, 1862.

Edwards, John W., Private, enlisted September 14, 1861, at Montgomery, and was born 1833, Troupe County, Georgia. See Service Records for David Blackman. [12]*He was listed as sick and absent from duty during the summer of 1862.*

Edwards, Samuel J., Private, enlisted September 22, 1861, Camp Davis. [42]*He was granted a 20 day furlough January 1, 1862, and sent to Randolph County.* He was hospitalized in Mississippi in June 1862. He was 6' and born in 1829, Butts County, Georgia.

Ellington, George W., Private, enlisted September 13, 1862, at Mobile. [17]*He reported to the regimental medical unit seven times in 1864. On January 6 and February 5, the diagnosis was feb int tert. On February 25 and June 23, the diagnosis was feb int quotid. On June 8 and in November, his complaint was acute diarrhea. On July 28, he sustained a leg wound at the battle of Ezra Church near Atlanta and was moved to a general hospital on July 31.* He was paroled at Greensboro, North Carolina, May 1865. [20]*He was born October 25, 1843, at Walton County, Georgia. In 1907 he was living at Gold Hill, Chambers County.* [24]*He died September 11, 1919, and is buried in Oak Bowers Cemetery in Lee County.*

Etheridge, Harrison P., Private, enlisted September 14, 1861, at Montgomery. He was hospitalized in Mississippi in June 1862.

[17]**Everdeen, J. W.**, *Private, reported to the regimental medical unit June 10, 1864, diagnosis feb int quotid, and was moved to a general hospital June 11. He is listed as killed on the field July 28, 1864, at the battle of Ezra Church near Atlanta.*

Faucett, Jesse, Private, enlisted September 13, 1862, [1]*Mobile. He was born January 11, 1844, Roanoke, Randolph County.* He was admitted to St. Mary's Hospital, West Point, Mississippi, January 10, 1865, after the Tennessee Campaign. [1]*He served until the surrender and was living in Roanoke in 1907.* [37]*In 1921, he was living in Roanoke. He stated that his place of birth was Covington, Newton County, Georgia, and that he fought at New Hope Church, Atlanta, Franklin, and Nashville.* [30]*His parents were Samuel and Harriett Anne Arnett Faucett, and his wife* was Ellen Manley. [26]*He died June 26, 1937, and was buried in Christiana Church Cemetery, Randolph County.*

Faust, Andrew J., Private, took the oath of allegiance at Nashville January 1865.

Fields, Green B., Private, enlisted January 27, 1862, at Greenville. He was granted a 20-day furlough June 11, 1862.

Field, P., Private, was hospitalized in Mississippi in June 1862.

Fincher, Alvey B., Private, enlisted September 14, 1861, at Montgomery.

Fincher, N. E., Private, enlisted March 13, 1863, and was paroled Greensboro, North Carolina, May 1865.

Fincher, Wiley Private, enlisted September 13, 1862, at Mobile, and died December 15, 1862, at Mobile.

Fincher, William A., Private, enlisted at Montgomery September 14, 1861. [17]*He reported to the regimental medical unit on December 26, 1863, diagnosis feb int tert. He reported to the medical unit three times in 1864, diagnosis feb int quotid: on February 14, on March 11, and on April 29. On March 14 he was transferred to the general hospital at Spring Hill in Mobile. In April he was listed as a Sergeant.* He was captured June 3, 1864, at Kennesaw Mountain, Georgia, and imprisoned at Camp Morton, Indiana, where he died January 22, 1865. The cause od death was inflammation of his lungs. [23]*He was buried at Greenlawn Cemetery, Indianapolis.*

Foster, James M., Private, enlisted September 30, 1862, at Mobile. [17]*He reported to the regimental medical unit with colica on February 23, 1864, and again on June 26, diagnosis feb int quotid. He suffered a head wound and was killed on the field August 15, 1864, during the battle of Atlanta.*

Fowler, O. D., Private

Ganutt, E. T., Private, enlisted May 9, 1864, at West Point. He was paroled at Greensboro, North Carolina, May 1, 1865.

[17]***Gauntt, D. F.,*** *Private, entered the regimental medical unit on November 20, 1864, and was moved to a general hospital on November 29. The diagnosis was parotitis.*

Gauntt, Elisha Luther, Private, enlisted at Montgomery September 14, 1861. He was placed on sick furlough January 1862 for 20 days and sent to Randolph County. He was discharged May 27, 1862: disability. He was listed as a sergeant in the master roster. [30]*His rank changed from private to sergeant to corporal. On August 1, 1863, he transferred to the Engineering Corps, also known as Company C, and Confederate Engineer Troops. He was wounded at the battle of Mobile, gunshot laterally through the hips. His unit surrendered at Citronelle Many 1865.* [30]*He applied for a pension.* [30]*He was born March 27, 1833,*

Lexington District, South Carolina. He married (1) Susan Burgess and (2) Sophia Meacham. He died February 17, 1905. He lived in Randolph County in the Rock Mills community. He was listed as 6'1, light complexion, blue eyes and light hair. Also spelled **Garnet.**

[1]***Garrnett, Elbert T.***, Private, was born April 24, 1845, near Bacon Level in Randolph County. He served until surrender and was living in Lineville in 1907. [37]In 1921, he was still living in Lineville and claimed his place of birth was Chambers County. He stated that he fought in battles from Dalton to Atlanta to Nashville and that he was wounded at New Hope Church in Georgia. May be **E. T. Ganutt** or **Elbert T. Garrnett.**

Green, B., Private, was hospitalized in Mississippi in June 1862.

Green, Tandy H., Corporal, enlisted September 14, 1862, at Montgomery. [12]He was listed as absent with leave on the muster roll for July-August 1862. [18]In September 1863 he was described as 28 years old, gray eyes, sandy hair, fair complexion, 6'1, a farmer, and a deserter. He later returned to his unit. [17]He reported to the regimental medical unit in May of 1864, suffering with acute dysentery, and was then listed as missing. He was captured May 14, 1864, at Resaca, Georgia. He was transferred from Resaca to Alton, Illinois; then from Alton to Camp Douglas, Illinois. In March 1865 he was transferred to Point Lookout for exchange. [20]He was born April 28, 1835, in DeKalb County, Georgia. In 1907 he was living in Cullman County.

[18]**Green, Thomas**, Private, was described in September 1863 as 48 years old, blue eyes, light hair, fair complexion, 5'9, a trader and a deserter.

Gunt, Thomas J., Private, [17]he reported to the regimental medical unit on December 18, 1863, diagnosis feb int quotid. He again reported to the hospital with acute diarrhea. He entered the hospital on April 5, 1864, diagnosis debilitas, and was moved to the general hospital (Ross Hospital in Mobile) on April 20. Also spelled **Gauntt.**

Guthry, G. S., Private, was discharged December 31, 1861.

Hames, Joshua, Private. [17]*J. Z. T. Hames* reported to the regimental medical unit on September 7, 1864, with acute diarrhea. Joshua was captured December 17, 1864, Nashville, and imprisoned at Camp Chase, Ohio. Also spelled **Haines.**

Harrell, Samuel H., Private, enlisted September 14, 1862, at Montgomery. [17]He reported to the regimental medical unit five times in 1864: first on January 14, diagnosis was feb int tert. Then June 23, the diagnosis was feb int quotid. On July 5, August 16, and November 11, he was suffering with acute diarrhea. He was paroled at Greensboro, North Carolina, in May 1865. [20]He was born December 15, 1831, in Tolbert county, Georgia, and was living in Roanoke, Alabama, in 1907.

COMPANY E 265

Harris, James Augustus, Private, enlisted January 29, 1862, at Greenville. He was 5'2, a farmer, and born in 1846 in Russell County. He was detailed as a signal operator. He was paroled at Greensboro, North Carolina, May 1865. [30]*He was born December 27, 1846, in Russell County. He moved to SanDiego in 1903 where he died April 27, 1928.*

Hathorn, Hugh, Private, enlisted September 14, 1861, at Montgomery. He was placed on sick furlough January 1, 1862, for 20 days and sent to Randolph County. He was discharged July 2, 1862, after hirig a substitute, Thomas Strickland.

Head, Richard, Private, enlisted September 14, 1861, at Montgomery. Wounded at Shiloh, Tennessee, April 6, 1862, he was hospitalized in Mississippi in June 1862. He was hospitalized again at Ross Hospital, Mobile September 2, 1863, diagnosis feb int tert. [17]*He reported to the regimental medical unit on December 21, 1863, diagnosis colica. He was sick again February 25, 1864, diagnosis feb remitt. He was diagnosed with acute dysentery on March 16 and June 15. He was hit by a shell on July 20, at the battle of Peachtree Creek near Atlanta. He suffered a severe wound to the left breast and was moved to a general hospital on July 21.* [1]*He was born February 17, 1839, in Atlanta. He lived in Rock Mills, Randolph County, in 1907.* [33]*He applied for a pension.* [26]*He died July 31, 1922, and is buried in an unmarked grave in Wehadbenn Primitive Baptist Cemetery in Randolph County.*

Head, Samuel J., Private, enlisted September 14, 1861, at Montgomery. On sick furlough December 20, 1861, for 20 days and sent to Randolph County. [17]*He reported to the regimental medical unit on February 19, 1864, diagnosis feb remitt.* He was captured September 21, 1864, at Atlanta and was imprisoned at Camp Douglas, Illinois. [30]*He survived the war.*

Heard, A. J., Private, enlisted July 6, 1863, at Mobile. He was a farmer, 5'9, and born in Heard County, Georgia. [17]***Thos. J. Heard** was listed on the records of the regimental medical unit on March 18, 1864, with acute diarrhea.*

Heath, Emmanuel, Private, died in 1862 at the Enterprise Hospital in Mississippi.

Hester, Jeremiah, Private, enlisted September 14, 1861, at Montgomery. [17]*He reported to the regimental medical unit on December 27, 1863, diagnosis feb int quotid. He was sent to the general hospital on July 6, 1864, diagnosis feb int tert.* [1]*He enlisted as 2nd Sergeant. Born October 10, 1836, in Wehaokee in Randolph County, he was living in Levelroad in 1907.* [26]*He died October 27, 1917, and is buried in an unmarked grave in Forrester Chapel Cemetery in Randolph County.*

Hester, J. H., Private, was hospitalized in Mississippi in June 1862. This could be either Jeremiah or John.

Hester, John, Sergeant, was granted a sick furlough January 1862 for 20 days and sent to Randolph County where he died sometime that year.

Hildebrand, Vanburen L., Private, enlisted January 8, 1862, at Camp Gladden, Florida. [17]*He reported to the regimental medical unit on December 1, 1863, diagnosis was feb int tert; on December 15, acute dysentery; and on March 8, feb int quotid. On August 4, 1864, during the siege of Atlanta, he sustained a severe wound to his right hand.* He was paroled at Greensboro, North Carolina, April 1865. [1]*He was born February 25, 1835, near Decatur, Dekalb County, Georgia. His parents were William and Sara Rapshear Hildebrand. He married Rena Ann Upchurch. He was living in Almond, Alabama, in 1907. He died ca 1892 and was buried at County Line Baptist Church, Mellow Valley, Alabama.* Also spelled **Heldebrand, Helterbran.**

Hill, J. J., Private, was wounded and placed on sick furlough June 1862.

Hodge, Bennett, Private, enlisted September 14, 1861, at Montgomery, and paroled at Greensboro, North Carolina, April 1865. [17]*He reported to the regimental medical unit on December 31, 1863, with an abscess. On June 4, 15, and 28, 1864, he reported to the medical unit with acute diarrhea. On July 28 at the battle of Ezra Church near Atlanta, he suffered a slight wound to his right arm, and was moved to the general hospital on July 31.*

Hodges, James M., Private, enlisted September 14, 1861, at Montgomery. He was granted a sick furlough January 30, 1862, for 20 days and sent to Randolph County. [5]*He was severely wounded at Shiloh, Tennessee, April 1862.* He was wounded in June 1862. [12]*He was listed as wounded and absent without leave during the summer of 1862.* He died December 3, 1863, in Randolph County

Hodges, John A., Private, enlisted September 13, 1862, at Mobile.

Hodges, William, Private, enlisted September 13, 1862, at Mobile. [17]*He reported to the regimental medical unit three times in 1864. On June 15, he was suffering from acute dysentery. On July 20 at the battle of Peachtree Creek near Atlanta, a minnie ball inflicted a slight wound to his right breast, and he was sent to the general hospital the next day. On August 13, the diagnosis was ferumculus.* [39]*He was wounded and captured at the battle of Franklin, Tennessee, November 30, 1864.* He was paroled at Greensboro, North Carolina, April 1865. [26]*He sustained wounds during the war and is buried in an unmarked grave in Concord Church Cemetery in Randolph County.* [33]*He applied for a pension (which indicates he died after 1896).*

[17]**Holder, A.,** Private, reported to the regimental medical unit July 13, 1864, diagnosis cholera mobus, and was moved to a general hospital.

[17]**Holder, I. J.**, *Private, reported to the regimental medical unit on July 28, 1864, having sustained a wound (left hip) at the battle of Ezra Church near Atlanta. He was moved to a general hospital on July 31.*

Holder, Jose Dempsey, Private, enlisted May 3, 1864, Roanoke, and was paroled at Greensboro, North Carolina, May 1865.

[17]**Holder, Jasper**, *Private, reported to the regimental medical unit on November 30, 1864, after suffering a severe wound to the left thigh at the battle of Franklin, Tennessee.*

Holder, John, Private, enlisted July 30, 1862. [17]*He was sent to the general hospital on February 11, 1864, diagnosis feb in tert. He reported to the regimental medical unit on June 15 with acute diarrhea.*

Holder, Joseph B., Private, [17] *reported to the regimental medical unit three times in 1864. On January 9, the diagnosis was feb int quotid, on February 1, feb int tert, and on June 15, feb int quotid.* He was captured December 17, 1864, Franklin, Tennessee where he had been wounded. Imprisoned at Camp Chase, Ohio, [10]*he died April 14, 1865 and was buried in lot number 1863 or 1843.*

Holder, Theophilas J., Private, enlisted September 14, 1861, at Montgomery. [18]*In September 1863 he was described as 19 years old, gray eyes, red hair, fair complexion, 6'1, a farmer, and a deserter.* He later returned to his unit. [17]*He was killed July 20, 1864, at the battle of Peach Tree Creek near Atlanta.*

[17]**Holdn, J. E.**, *Private, suffered a severe wound to his left thigh July 28, 1864, at the battle of Ezra Church near Atlanta. He was sent to the general hospital on July 31.*

Holland, Gilbert G., 2nd Lieutenant, was promoted to captain March 3, 1863, of the 9th Battalion.

Hollingsworth, Theopholas A., Private and musician, enlisted September 14, 1861, at Montgomery. He was wounded at Shiloh, Tennessee, April 1862 and hospitalized in Mississippi in June 1862. He received a disability discharge September 20, 1862, and was paroled at the end of war. [8]*His home was Pike County.*

Hood, Oscar A., Private, was granted a sick furlough in January 1862 for 20 days and sent to Randolph County. He died [42]at home January 18, 1862, leaving father, Stephen W. Hood.

Hornesby, James M., Private, enlisted at Montgomery. [42]*He was detailed to special duty, working on a brick oven, January 1862.* He was captured February 16, 1862, at Fort Donelson and imprisoned at Camp Douglas, Illinois. He was listed as missing after Shiloh, Tennessee, as he was captured April 8, 1862. He was again imprisoned at Camp Douglas, Illinois, and sent to Vicksburg for exchange in September 1862. [33]*He died December 3, 1862.* His widow applied for a pension.

Hornesby, Noah D., Private, enlisted September 14, 1861, at Montgomery. [12]*He was placed on detached duty as a nurse in the hospital during the summer of 1862.* He was employed as an assistant cook during April of 1863. [17]*He reported to the regimental medical unit on February 15, 1864, diagnosis feb int tert.* He was at Greensboro, North Carolina, May 1865. [1]*He was born November 19, 1832, at East Point in Fulton County, Georgia. He is listed as living in Roanoke, Alabama, in 1907.* [26]*He died May 21, 1921, and is buried in an unmarked grave in Friendship Cemetery in Randolph County.*

Huddleston, David Franklin, Private. See Company D.

Hudson, T. J., Private, enlisted November 17, 1861, at Mobile. [17]*He reported to the regimental medical unit on January 6, 1864, with acute diarrhea.* He was born in Henry County, Georgia. He was paroled at Greensboro, North Carolina, May 1865.

Hughley, John A., Private, enlisted February 10, 1862, at Greenville, and was discharged February 1863. He was born in 1827, Wilkes County, Georgia. Also spelled **Huguley**

Hunt, Gilbert, Private, enlisted September 14, 1861, at Montgomery, and was hospitalized in Mississippi during June 1862. [17]*He reported to the regimental medical unit twice with the diagnosis feb int tert, on December 30, 1863, and January 2, 1864. He was slightly wounded (hip) in May 1864, probably at the battle of Resaca, Georgia.*

Hutchins, James D., Private, enlisted September 14, 1861, at Montgomery. [17]*He reported to the regimental medical unit on January 15, 1864, diagnosis was feb int quotid.* He was captured December 15, 1864, at Nashville. He was then imprisoned at Camp Chase, Ohio, [10]*where he died February 4, 1865, and was buried in lot number 1041.* Also spelled **Hutchens**.

Hutchins, Henry H., Private, enlisted September 14, 1861, at Montgomery. Granted a sick furlough January 19, 1862 for 20 days, he was sent to Randolph County. He was wounded (shoulder) at Shiloh, Tennessee, April 1862. [17]*He reported to the regimental medical unit four times in 1864. On January 24, his complaint was acute diarrhea. On February 4, his diagnosis was feb int tert and he was moved to the general hospital at Spring Hill the next day. On June 6, his complaint was acute dysentery, and he was moved to the general hospital on June 9. On November 11, he had sustained an injury and was sent to a general hospital the next day.* He was hospitalized in Meridian, Mississippi, December 1864. Also spelled **Hutchinson**

[17]**John, Bradley P.**, Private, *reported to the regimental medical unit on December 1, 1863, diagnosis was feb int tert.*

Johnson, James, Private, was admitted to the Methodist Hospital in North Carolina in April 1865.
Johnson, Robert D., Private, enlisted September 14, 1861, at Montgomery. He was hospitalized in Mississippi during June 1862. [12]*He was listed on the muster roll for July-August 1862 as absent sick.* [6]*He died in 1862 in Okalona, Mississippi.* Also listed as **Johnston**
Johnston, J. H., Private, enlisted January 30, 1864, at Mobile. [17]*On June 8 and July 6, 1864, he reported to the regimental medical unit, diagnosis feb int tert, and was transferred to the general hospital immediately.* He was paroled at Greensboro, North Carolina, May 1865.
Jones, William A. A., musician, enlisted at Montgomery September 14, 1861.

Kinion, J. A., Private, enlisted March 12, 1862, at Greenville. He was paroled at Greensboro, North Carolina, May 1865.
Kinney, William, Private, was hospitalized in Mississippi June 1862.
Kinsey, Martin, Private, enlisted February 1, 1862, at Greenville.

Lee, S. M., Private, paroled May 20, 1865, at Talladega. [17]*He reported to the regimental medical unit three times in 1864. On June 5, his complaint was acute dysentery, and he was moved to the general hospital. On July 31, the complaint was feb int quotid, and on August 3, acute dysentery.*
Lee, William H., Private, [17]*reported to the regimental medical unit February 10, 1864, diagnosis was rubeola.*
Lew, Z. E., Private, was hospitalized in Mississippi during June 1862.

Major, L., Private, was hospitalized in Mississippi during June 1862.
Manley, Thomas A., Private, enlisted September 13, 1862, at Mobile. He was 5'6 and lived in Randolph County. [17]*He reported to the regimental medical unit on December 3, 1863, diagnosis was feb int quotid, on December 14, neuralgia, and on January 26, 1864, feb int tert. On March 17,* **Ad Manly** *entered the hospital with acute dysentery.* Manley was captured July 3, 1864, at Kennesaw Mountain, Georgia, and imprisoned at Camp Douglas, Illinois, where he took the oath of allegiance in March 1865.
Martin, Ransom V., Private, enlisted September 27, 1862, at Greenville. He was hospitalized in Mississippi in June 1862. [12]*He was listed on the muster roll for July-August 1862 as absent sick.* He transferred from Company E to K September 12, 1862.
Mathews, Simeon, Private, was hospitalized June 14, 1864, in Macon, Georgia. Granted a sick furlough, he was sent to Randolph County.

Mattox, B. P., Private, was granted sick furlough January 20, 1862, for 20 days and sent to Randolph County.

Mattox, J. C., Private, enlisted September 29, 1863, at Mobile. He was 5'9 and born at East Baton Rouge, Louisiana.

[18]**Maury, John**, Private, was described in September 1863 as 45 years old, black eyes, black hair, dark complexion, 5'7, a laborer, and a deserter.

May, Seth S., Private, enlisted January 27, 1862, at Greenville.

Mayfield, Battle W., Private, enlisted September 14, 1861, at Montgomery. He was 5'7 and was from West Point, Georgia. He was placed on sick furlough November 14, 1861, and sent to Randolph County. [17]*On June 29, he reported to the regimental medical unit with acute dysentery. On July 2, 1864, the diagnosis was feb int tert.* Captured July 3, 1864, at Kennesaw Mountain, Georgia, he was imprisoned at Camp Douglas, Illinois, where he was paroled May 17, 1865.

Mayo, Lovic W., Private, enlisted September 14, 1861, at Montgomery. [12]*He was listed on the muster roll for July-August 1862 as absent sick.*

McCall, J., Private, was listed under James B. of Company I

McDanel, K., Private, enlisted March 8, 1863, Roanoke. He was paroled at Greensboro, North Carolina, May 1865.

McDaniel, Bailey H., Private, enlisted September 13, 1862, at Mobile. [17]*He reported to the regimental medical unit on December 2, 1863, diagnosis feb int quotid. On December 30 he was granted a 20-day furlough. He reported again on February 12, 1864, diagnosis feb int tert, and on June 20, acute diarrhea.* He was paroled June 14, 1865, at Talladega. All Union records list him as **McDonald**.

McDaniel, Josiah, Private, enlisted September 13, 1862, at Mobile. [17]*He reported to the regimental medical unit on December 29, 1863, and February 19, 1864, diagnosis feb int quotid.* He was paroled at Greensboro, North Carolina, May 1865. Also spelled **McDanel, McDannell**

McDaniel, Samuel W., Private, enlisted September 13, 1862, at Mobile. [17]*He reported to the regimental medical unit on December 1 and 29, 1863, diagnosis was feb int quotid. He reported to the medical unit again on June 28, 1864, with acute diarrhea. He was admitted to the general hospital on July 3, diagnosis anasarca.* He was paroled at Greensboro, North Carolina, May 1865. Also spelled **McDanel**

McLeod, Angus M., Private, was born in 1829 in Butler County. He was discharged November 20, 1863: disability.

McWaters, Francis A., Private, enlisted October 1861, at Camp Davis. He was placed on sick furlough January 23, 1862, for 30 days and sent to Montgomery. He was detailed as a teamster. [17]*He entered the regimental medical unit twice in 1864. On January 6 the diagnosis was sub luxatio. On March 14, the diagnosis was feb int quotid.* [8]*His home was in Pike County.* He was paroled July 12, 1865, at Talladega. [20]*He* was born September 16, 1834, in Covington, Newton County, Georgia. In 1907 he was living in Tennille, Coffee County. Also listed as **J. A. McWaters, McWhorter.**

[17]***Mickle, Jerry**, Private, reported to the regimental medical unit three times in 1864. On January 9, the diagnosis was pleuritis, on January 17, neuralgia, and on February 19, feb int quotid. On July 28, he is listed as killed on field, at the battle of Ezra Church near Atlanta.*

Miller, Francis M., Private, [17]*reported to the regimental medical unit on February 8, 1864, diagnosis was hernia.* He was captured July 20, 1864, near Atlanta at the battle of Peachtree Creek. He was imprisoned at Camp Douglas, Illinois, where he was paroled June 13, 1865.

Miller, William Jackson, Private, enlisted September 14, 1861, at Montgomery and was from Randolph County. [17]*He reported to the regimental medical unit, diagnosis catarrhus, December 24, 1863, and February 4, 1864. He was ill January 23, 1864, diagnosis feb int quotid; March 16, acute dysentery; and November 12, feb int tert.* He was captured November 30, 1864, at Franklin, Tennessee, and imprisoned at Camp Douglas, Illinois, [1]*where he was paroled June 1865.* He was born March 8, 1841, at Locust Grove, Henry County, Georgia, and living in Warrior, Jefferson County, in 1907.

Milton, John F., Sergeant, enlisted September 14, 1861, at Montgomery. He was granted a 20-day sick furlough, January 13, 1862. He was hospitalized September 2-16, 1863. [17]*He reported to the regimental medical unit twice in 1864: May 28, the diagnosis was feb int tert and August 9, feb int quotid.* He was paroled May 1, 1865, Greensboro, North Carolina. Also spelled **Melton**

[17]***Minter, R. J.**, Private, reported to the regimental medical unit on January 26, 1864, with acute diarrhea. **R. F. Minter** reported to the regimental medical unit on July 3, diagnosis debilitas, and was moved to a general hospital the next day.*

Moon, J. G., Private, was placed on sick furlough January 1862 for 30 days, and sent to Randolph County. He died in 1862 leaving father, Rolly Moon.

Moon, Josiah F., Private, enlisted September 14, 1861, at Montgomery. Granted a sick furlough December 20, 1861 for 21 days, he was sent to Randolph County. He was hospitalized in Mississippi during June 1862. He died July 5, 1862, at the general hospital in Macon, Mississippi.

Moon, L. T., Private, died in the hospital January 15, 1862.

[42]**Moore, Josiah F.**, Private, enlisted September 14, 1861, at Montgomery.

Morris, Jefferrison, Private, was paroled June 20, 1865, at Talladega.

Motes, Bush W., Private, enlisted January 27, 1862, at Greenville. [12]*He was described as sick and absent from duty during the summer of 1862.*

Mulkey, R. S., Private, was discharged December 16, 1861.

[18]***Murry, Thomas***, *Private, was described in September 1863 as 47 years old, gray eyes, black hair, dark complexion, 5'9, a laborer, and a deserter.*

[17]***Neeley, John***, *Private, reported to the regimental medical unit on January 13, 1864, with acute diarrhea.*

Neely, William C., Private, enlisted November 16, 1863, at Mobile. He was 5'5 and born in 1845, Fayette County. He was hospitalized January 11, 1865, Meridian, Mississippi. [37]*He was born September 23, 1845, at Fairborn, Fayette County, Georgia. In 1921, he was living in Double Springs and stated that he had fought at Franklin, Nashville, Atlanta, Marietta, and Lovejoy.*

Newell, James C., Private, was hospitalized April 21, 1864, at Mobile Hospital. [17]*He reported to the regimental medical unit four times in 1864. On March 20, the diagnosis was feb int quotid, and on March 26, acute dysentery. On April 5, he was ill with chronic diarrhea and was moved to the general hospital on April 20. He reported to the medical unit again on November 8 with acute diarrhea.*

Newman, John M., Private, enlisted August 15, 1862, Tallapoosa. He died November 24, 1862, at Mobile Hospital #3.

Newman, Samuel, Private, enlisted September 14, 1861, at Montgomery. [17]*He reported to the regimental medical unit twice in 1864: February 11, the diagnosis was catarrhus, and September 6, acute diarrhea.*

[17]***Newman, Seaborn***, *Private, was slightly wounded in the left leg on November 30, 1864, during the battle at Franklin, Tennessee.*

Nichols, J., Private, was hospitalized January 29, 1865, Meridian, Mississippi.

Nixon, Shaw, Private, enlisted September 13, 1862, at Mobile, and deserted July 1, 1864. [17]*He reported to the regimental medical unit three times in 1864. On January 13, the diagnosis was feb int quotid. On January 27, the diagnosis was feb int tert. On November 3, the diagnosis was acute diarrhea.* Although his service record indicates that he deserted in July, he was back with his regiment in November.

Norred, Jasper, Private, enlisted September 13, 1862, at Mobile. He was paroled May 31, 1865, at Talladega. [18]*In September 1863 he was described as 24 years old, blue eyes, auburn hair, fair complexion, 5'10, a farmer, and a deserter.* Also spelled **Nurred**.

Norred, Lewis O., Private, enlisted September 13, 1862, at Mobile.

Osburn, John L., Private, enlisted September 14, 1861, at Montgomery. [12]*He was listed as sick and absent from duty June through December 1862.* Also listed as **J. F. Osborne** and **Orsburn**.

COMPANY E 273

Owen, Alphas D., Corporal, enlisted September 14, 1861, at Montgomery. [17]*On January 7, 1864, he reported to the regimental medical unit, diagnosis feb int tert. On February 15, 1864, he reported to the regimental medical unit, diagnosis sub luxatio, and transferred to the general hospital at Mobile on the 17th.* He was captured May 29, 1864, at Dallas, Georgia, imprisoned at Rock Island, Illinois, and released June 18, 1865. He was 6', born 1827, and lived at Cornhouse, Randolph County. Also listed as **Alfred B. Owen** and **Alfred D. Owen**

Owen, William F., Private, enlisted October 2, 1862, at Mobile. [17]*On February 22, 1864, he reported to the regimental medical unit, diagnosis feb int quotid. On July 20, 1864, he was reported killed at the battle of Peach Tree Creek near Atlanta.*

Pate, Robert S., Sergeant, enlisted September 20, 1861, at Camp Davis. He was discharged March 1, 1863, for promotion to second lieutenant. [17]*He reported to the regimental medical unit twice in 1864: on February 12, diagnosis was feb int quotid, and on July 29, acute diarrhea.* [1]*Born September 26, 1845, at Thomaston, Upson County, Georgia, he was living at Rock Mills, Randolph County in 1907. Conflicting information. Probably some pertains to R. S. Pate below.* [26]*He was born March 23, 1842, at Roanoke, Alabama. He died September 10, 1917, and was buried in an unmarked grave in Weedowee in Randolph County.*

Pate, R. S., 1st Lieutenant, enlisted September 14, 1861, at Montgomery, and was elected March 1862. He was granted furlough from Atlanta Hospital on September 28, 1864. When he was paroled at Greensboro, North Carolina, May 1, 1865, he was listed as a captain.

Pike, Thomas, Private, 5'10, was captured April 7, 1862, Pittsburg Landing, Tennessee. He was sent to Alton Prison in Illinois, then to St. Louis where he died August 13, 1862.

Pittman, J. M., Private, [17]*reported to the regimental medical unit three times in 1864. On January 15 and February 6, the diagnosis was feb int tert. He reported sick July 3, diagnosis anasarca, and was moved to the general hospital on July 4.* He died July 12, 1864, LaGrange, Georgia. [33]*His widow applied for a pension.*

Pool, Robert C., Private, 5'9, lived in Roanoke, Alabama. [17]*He reported to the regimental medical unit eight times in 1864. On January 14, the diagnosis was feb int tert. On February 3, he reported with rubeola and was moved to the general hospital at Spring Hill on the 5th. On February 24, the diagnosis was debilitas, as it was on March 9. He was again sent to the general hospital on Spring Hill on March 12. On April 17, the diagnosis was feb int tert. On June 3, the diagnosis was debilitas. On June 25, he reported with anasarca and sent to the general hospital the next day. On November 30 he suffered a severe* wound to his right leg at the battle of Franklin, Tennessee. He was captured December 17, 1864, Franklin, and as one of the wounded, was admitted to a hospital in Nashville. [9]*Surgery was performed on March 1, 1865, for a fracture of the middle right femur.* Imprisoned at Louisville, Kentucky, he was paroled June 1865.

Ray, William P., Private, enlisted September 14, 1861, at Montgomery. He suffered a severe wound to his hand at Shiloh, Tennessee, April 6, 1862. [6]*He died June 27, 1862, at Columbus, Mississippi, of typhoid fever.*

Reed, B. F., appointed Quartermaster January 7, 1862. He was elected first lieutenant on September 14, 1861, and captain by June 1862. [17]*He reported to the regimental medical unit on February 11, 1864, diagnosis debilitas. He was placed on furlough February 13 for 30 days.* Also spelled **Reid**.

Rhoades, William H., Private, was 5'6 and from Calhoun County. He was captured July 5, 1864, at Chattahoochie, Georgia, and imprisoned at Camp Douglas, Illinois, where he was paroled June 12, 1865. Also spelled **Rhoader, Rhodes**.

Robertson, Andrew Pickna, Private, enlisted September 14, 1861, at Montgomery. He was 5'6 and from Randolph County. Captured July 3, 1864, at Kennesaw Mountain, he was imprisoned at Camp Douglas, Illinois, where he was released June 16, 1865. [37]*He was born March 28, 1843, in Newborn, Georgia. His family moved to Alabama in 1847. He was living in Ashland in 1921.*

Robertson, Frank Copeland, Private, [30]*enlisted at Montgomery in 1861.* He was captured July 5, 1864, at Chattahoochie, Georgia, and imprisoned at Camp Douglas, Illinois. He applied for amnesty. He died February 3, 1865, of pneumonia and was buried in lot 658-2, Chicago City Cemetery. [30]*He was married to Martha Gant who applied for a pension April 14, 1892, and again June 16, 1898.* Also listed as **F. G. Roberts**

Robertson, George, Private, was granted a furlough extension in March 1863, at Mobile.

Robertson, James, Private, enlisted September 13, 1862, at Mobile.

Robertson, John D., Lieutenant, was promoted to first lieutenant July 27, 1862. He was severely wounded (knee) at the battle of Shiloh, April 1862. He resigned April 4, 1863.

Robinson, Joseph R., Private, enlisted August 20, 1863, at Mobile. He was 5'10 and born 1829, Putnam County, Georgia. He was hospitalized February 26, 1864, with measles. [17]*He reported to the regimental medical unit on April 25, 1864, diagnosis was feb int quotid. He reported again November 7, 1864, with acute diarrhea and was moved* to the general hospital on November 9. He was paroled at Greensboro, North Carolina. Also spelled **Robison**

[17]***Robison, F. C.***, Private, reported to the regimental medical unit three times with the diagnosis feb in tert; December 23, 1863, February 4, and April 12, 1864. *He reported twice in 1864: on January 15, diagnosis anasarca, and on June 20, diagnosis acute diarrhea. His widow applied for a pension.* Also listed as **S. F. C. Robison**

[17]***Robison, J. W.***, Private, reported to the regimental medical unit on September 7, 1864, diagnosis debilitas.

Ryan, H. C., Private

Samuel, N., Private, was hospitalized in June 1862.

Sanders, David, Private, [17]*reported to the regimental medical unit twice in June of 1864. On June 2 the diagnosis was catarrhus and diarrhea, and on June 20, diarrhea.* He was captured at Chattahoochie, Georgia, July 5, 1864,. He was imprisoned at Camp Douglas, Illinois, where he died September 28, 1864. He was buried at Chicago City Cemetery. Also spelled **Saunders**.

Sanders, James M., Private, enlisted October 7, 1861, at Camp Davis. He was placed on sick furlough January 19, 1862, for 20 days and sent to Randolph County. He was discharged on July 4, 1862: disability.

Sanit, George W., Private, was hospitalized at Ross Hospital in Mobile on September 2, 1863. [17]*He was killed on the field on July 28, 1864, at the battle of Ezra Church near Atlanta.*

Searcy, George W., Private, enlisted January 27, 1862, at Greenville.

Sheffield, E., Private, was paroled May 1865 in Montgomery.

Shellnut, Andrew J., Private, enlisted at Montgomery September 14, 1861. He was placed on sick furlough January 3, 1862, for 20 days and sent to Randolph County. [17]*He reported to the regimental medical unit December 19, 1863, diagnosis feb int tert. He reported sick six times in 1864 with various ailments. On January 19, the problem was rubeola. On January 21 and March 19, the complaint was acute dysentery. On June 4, the diagnosis was debilitas and on June 20, acute diarrhea.* He was severely wounded in the left hip on July 28, at the battle of Ezra Church near Atlanta. He was transferred to the general hospital on July 31. [24]*He was buried at the Stonewall Confederate Cemetery in Griffin, Georgia.* Also spelled **Shelnut, Shelmut**

Shellnut, James Thomas, Private, enlisted November 16, 1863, at Mobile. He was 5'4, a farmer, and born 1846 in Randolph County. [17]*On April 26, 1864, he reported to the regimental medical unit, diagnosis was catarrhus. In June he was sick twice with acute diarrhea, on the 4th and the 15th.* He was moved to the general hospital on June 16. **T. J. Shellnut** *reported to the regimental medical unit on February 3, 1864* *with rubeola. He was moved to the general hospital at Spring Hill in Mobile two days later.* [33]*He applied for a pension.* [37]*He was born June 11, 1845, in Randolph County. In 1921 he was living in Weedowee in Randolph County. He stated that he had been in battles at Franklin, Nashville, Marietta, and New Hope Church. He surrendered with General Joe Johnston in April 1865.* Also spelled **Shelnut**

Shelnut, William J., Private, enlisted September 13, 1862, at Mobile. [17]*He reported to the regimental medical unit three times, diagnosis feb in tert, December 28, 1863, January 30, and March 6, 1864. He also reported February 28, 1864, diagnosis feb int quotid.* He was captured May 28, 1864, at Dallas, Georgia, and imprisoned at Rock Island. Also spelled **Shelmet, Shemet, Shelmar, Shernet, Shelmutt, Shelnutt**

Sherren, J., Private, was paroled June 17, 1865 at Talladega.

Sherver, William, Private, was granted a furlough December 20, 1863, for 30 days to Randolph County. [17]*He reported to the regimental medical unit on June 25, 1864, diagnosis debilitas. He was sick October 6, 1864, with acute diarrhea, and was moved to the general hospital on October 15.* Also spelled **Shearer.**

Skinner, James M., Private, died from wound (stomach) received at Shiloh, Tennessee, April 6, 1862, leaving mother, E. M. Sisk.

Skipper, Hiram, Private enlisted September 14, 1861. He was appointed corporal July 15, 1862. [17]*He reported to the regimental medical unit twice in 1864, diagnosis feb int quotid, on February 28 and June 21. The last time he was immediately sent to the general hospital.* He was at the surrender at Greensboro, North Carolina, April 26, 1865.

Slaughter, John N. or W., Private, enlisted September 14, 1861, at Montgomery. [17]*He reported to the regimental medical unit on December 21, 1863, with acute dysentery. He reported sickl three times in 1864. On January 17, the diagnosis was feb int tert, and on July 29, feb int quotid. He reported the next day with acute dysentery.* He was captured December 15, 1864, at Nashville and imprisoned at Camp Douglas, Illinois.

Slaughter, Zachariah, Private, [17]*reported to the regimental medical unit with rubeola on March 10. He was moved to the general hospital at Spring Hill, in Mobile the next day.* He was hospitalized at LaGrange, Georgia, June 30, 1864.

[17]***Smith, R. E. P.**, Private, reported to the regimental medical unit on August 19, 1864, with acute dysentery.*

Smith, Charles A., Private, 5'3, enlisted January 28, 1862. He was paroled June 12, 1865, at Montgomery.

Smith, Josiah F., Private, enlisted October 12, 1862, at Mobile. [17]*He reported to the regimental medical unit several times in 1864. On January 2, January 6, and February 15, the diagnosis was feb int tert;*

and on June 15, feb int quotid. J. T. Smith reported to the medical unit after sustaining a severe shell wound to the left leg on July 20, at the battle of Peach Tree Creek near Atlanta. He was moved to the general hospital the next day. **J. F. Smith** died September 4, 1864.

Smith, Lewis B., Private, enlisted September 14, 1861, at Montgomery. He was 5'4, a farmer, and born 1841 in Fulton County, Georgia. [42]*He was granted a 20-day furlough January 13, 1862, and sent to Randolph County.* He was discharged October 20, 1862: disability. He was captured July 3, 1864, at Kennesaw Mountain, Georgia. He was imprisoned at Camp Douglas, Illinois, where he was paroled on March 14, 1865. He was hospitalized March 22, 1865, at Howard's Grove Hospital, Richmond, Virginia. From there he was granted a furlough for 30 days on March 28, 1865.

Smith, Milton, Private, enlisted September 13, 1862, at Mobile. [17]*He reported to the regimental medical unit three times in 1864. On June 4, his complaint was acute diarrhea. On June 15, the complaint was colica. On July 28, he reported to the hospital after a slight wound to his left hand, sustained at the battle of Ezra Church. He was moved to the general hospital on July 31.* He was hospitalized December 7, 1864, at Opelika.

[1]**Smith, Olin F.,** *Private, was born January 15, 1840, LaFayette, Chambers County. He was living in Roanoke, Alabama, in 1907.* [26]*He died September 22, 1920, and is buried in an unmarked grave in Paran Baptist Church Cemetery in Randolph County.*

Smith, Robert J., Private, enlisted March 8, 1862, at Leon, Butler/Crenshaw County. [12]*He was listed on the muster roll for July-August 1862 as absent sick.* [17]*He reported to the regimental medical unit December 20, 1863, diagnosis pneumonia.*

Spears, William C., Private, enlisted September 14, 1861, at Montgomery. He was wounded (leg) at Shiloh, Tennessee, where he was captured April 7, 1862. He was then imprisoned at Camp Chase, Ohio. He was transferred for exchange on August 25, 1862. He was again captured April 28, 1864, at Dallas, Georgia, and imprisoned at Rock Island, Illinois. Also listed as **William P.**

Spradling, Felix, Private, enlisted October 12, 1861, at Camp Davis. He was 5'4, a farmer, and born 1847 in Talladega. He received a gunshot wound to his lung at Shiloh, Tennessee, April 7, 1862, when he was captured. He was imprisoned at Camp Dennison where he died May 19, 1862. He was survived by Seaborn Spradling. [10]*He was buried in lot number 2145 with spelling of **Spaulding**.* [10]*Listed as first lieutenant.* Also spelled **Sprading, Spendling.**

Stays, J. E., Private, was paroled May 22, 1865, at Talladega.

Steel, Edgar, Private, enlisted July 4, 1863, at Mobile. He was 5'9, a merchant, and born 1827 at Columbia, New York.

Stell, R. S., Private, was captured at Nashville in December 1864. He died at Camp Douglas, Illinois, January 12, 1865, and was buried in lot number 480-2 Chicago City Cemetery.

Stephens, Thomas R., Private, enlisted November 16, 1863, at Mobile. [17]*He reported to the regimental medical unit twice in 1864 with rubeola, on January 17 and February 3. He was sent to the general hospital at Spring Hill in Mobile February 5.* He was captured May 27, 1864 in Dallas, Georgia, and imprisoned at Rock Island, Illinois, where he was paroled June 21, 1865. He was 5'5, a farmer, born 1846 in Georgia, and from Buchanon, Randolph County. Also spelled **Stevens.**

Stewart, Richard, Private, enlisted September 14, 1861, at Mobile, and was from Coosa County. He was captured December 15, 1864, at Nashville and imprisoned at Camp Douglas, Illinois.

Stitt, John T., Private, enlisted May 21, 1862, Monroe. [17]*He reported to the regimental medical unit twice in 1864. On January 28, the diagnosis was feb int quotid, and on March 22, feb int tert.* He was severely wounded at Dallas, Georgia, May 27, 1864, with fracture to right shoulder.

[17]***Stitt, C. G.,*** *Private, reported to the regimental medical unit three times in 1864, on January 25 and March 19, diagnosis feb int quotid, and on February 11, diagnosis feb int tert. On July 28, 1864, at the battle of Ezra Church near Atlanta, he was killed on the field. Also spelled **Still**.*

Stitt, Robert S., 1st Sergeant, enlisted September 14, 1861, at Montgomery. He was 5'9, and born in 1842 in Randolph County. He was elected second lieutenant in 1863. [17]*He reported to the regimental medical unit four times in 1864. On January 30 and February 12, the diagnosis was feb int tert and on February 29 and March 3, feb int quotid.* He was captured September 18, 1864, at Lovejoy, Georgia. He took the oath of allegiance during November 1864 promising to remain north of the Ohio River for the duration of the war. Also listed as **Sam Still**

Stitt, Thomas J., Private, enlisted September 14, 1861, at Montgomery. He was hospitalized in Jackson, Mississippi, March 20, 1862, for 10 days. His arm was severely wounded at Shiloh in April 1862. He was hospitalized at Mobile September 2, 1863 for 16 days. [17]*He reported to the regimental medical unit twice in 1864, diagnosis feb int quotid, on January 7 and August 3. He was slightly wounded (right thigh) on July 28, at the battle of Ezra Church. He was transferred to the general hospital three days later.* [26]*He was born February 9, 1844. He died September 23, 1896, and is buried in an unmarked grave in Beulah Cemetery in Randolph County.* Also listed as **T. J. Hill, Thomas J. Stith, Steth, Still.**

COMPANY E 279

Stone, Caleb, Private, enlisted September 30, 1862, at Mobile. [17]*He reported to the regimental medical unit with rubeola January 12, 1864. He reported to the hospital with rubeola February 3 and moved to the general hospital at Spring Hill at Mobile on February 5.* [30]*He was born in 1836 in South Carolina to Jeremiah and Sarah Johnson Stone. He died about 1904 in Carrolton, Georgia.*

Strickland, Thomas, Private, enlisted July 2, 1862, at Tupelo, Mississippi, as a substitute for Hugh Hathorn. [18]*He was described in September 1863 as 46 years old, blue eyes, dark hair, fair complexion, 6'2, a mechanic, and a deserter.*

Suggs, Elisha, Private, [17]*sustained a slight wound (thigh) in early May 1864, probably at the battle of Resaca, Georgia. He was severely wounded (left arm) by a shell on July 20, 1864, at the battle of Peach Tree Creek near Atlanta. He was transferred to the general hospital the next day.* He was captured April 23, 1865, at Talladega.

Swan, James Anderson, Private, enlisted September 13, 1862, at Mobile. [17]*He reported to the regimental medical unit four times in 1864, on January 20, diagnosis was feb int tert, on June 15 and November 15, feb int quotid, and finally on September 4, acute rheum. In the last case he was immediately moved to the general hospital.* [1]*He was born August 6, 1833 in Monroe County, Georgia.* He was paroled at Greensboro, North Carolina, May 1865 and was *living in Roanoke, Alabama, in 1907.* [33]*He applied for a pension.* [37]*He was born August 6, 1835, at Liberty Hill, Monroe County, Georgia. He was living in Roanoke in 1921. He state that he was in battles at Dalton, Resaca, Kennesaw Mountain, Atlanta and New Hope Church, and that he was honorably discharged in North Carolina.* Also spelled **Swann**.

Swan, S. L. G., Private, [37]*enlisted at Roanoke in 1864.* [17]*He reported to the regimental medical unit three times in 1864. On February 27, his illness was rubeola. He was immediately sent to the general hospital in at Mobile. On March 29, the diagnosis was feb int tert. On October 6, he complained of chronic diarrhea and was sent to the general hospital the next day.* He was hospitalized with rubeola February 27, 1864. He was paroled at Greensboro, North Carolina, May 1865. [37]*He was born November 31, 1845, at Dudleyville, Tallapoosa, County. In 1921 he stated that he was in battles at Resaca, Altoona, Missionary Ridge, wounded at Resaca, and discharged at end of war.* Also listed as **Saml. Swan**

Swan, Thomas H., Private, enlisted September 13, 1862, at Mobile. [17]*He reported to the general hospital twice, diagnosis feb int tert, on December 19, 1863, and on February 6, 1864. He was also ill January 9, 1864, diagnosis pleuritis, and in November his complaint was chronic diarrhea.*

Swann, Nathaniel G., Private, enlisted at Montgomery September 14, 1861. He was hospitalized in Mississippi in June 1862. He died [12]*at home in Randolph County June 27, 1862*, leaving widow or mother Sarah C. Swann.

Talley, John T., Private, enlisted September 14, 1861, at Montgomery. He was 6'2, born in 1841 and lived in Randolph County. [17]*He reported to the regimental medical unit twice with the same complaint, feb int quotid, December 20, 1863, and January 15, 1864. He reported to the hospital March 10, diagnosis feb remitt, and sent to general hospital at Spring Hill the next day. On April 28, the diagnosis was feb int tert. On July 28, at the battle of Ezra Church near Atlanta, he suffered a slight wound to his chin. He moved to the general hospital July 31. He was listed as a sergeant by January 15, 1864.* He was wounded at Franklin, Tennessee, November 30, 1864, and was captured December 17, 1864. He was then imprisoned at Camp Chase, Ohio, where he was paroled June 1865.

Talley, Thomas Didemus, Private, was captured May 27, 1864, at Dallas, Georgia, and imprisoned Rock Island, Illinois. After his release he was hospitalized March 23, 1865, at Richmond, Virginia, and furloughed March 24, 1865, for 30 days. [30]*He was born May 21, 1822, Morgan County, Georgia, son of Thomas and Susan Elizabeth Littleton Talley. He was a Baptist preacher before the war living in Randolph County. He married Martha Barnes. He moved to Texas after the war. He served a number of churches in that state until his death May 11, 1898, Hamilton, Texas.*

Taylor, Elijah N., Private, enlisted September 13, 1862, at Mobile, and was discharged December 17, 1862. [17]*He was listed as slightly wounded by a minnie ball to the right thigh, at the battle of Peach Tree Creek near Atlanta on July 20, 1864. He was transferred to the general hospital on the 21st.*

Taylor, Josiah M., Private, enlisted September 16, 1862. [18]*In September 1863 he was described as 32 years old, gray eyes, dark hair, fair complexion, 5'7, a farmer, and a deserter.* He later rejoined his unit. [17]*On December 3, 1863, he reported to the regimental medical unit, diagnosis anasarca. The next day, his complaint was acute dysentery. On December 23, his complaint was debilitas, and he was immediately moved to the general hospital. On February 3, he reported to the regimental medical unit with debilitas and moved to the hospital at Mobile on February 14. He reported to the hospital, diagnosis was phthisis pulmon, on both March 24 and April 3, 1864. He was discharged on April 1, 1864.*

Taylor, William, Private, enlisted January 27, 1862, at Greenville. He died September 27, 1862, at a Selma hospital.

Taylor, W. J., Private, enlisted March 13, 1863, at Mobile. [17]*He reported to the regimental medical unit on December 16, 1863, diagnosis feb int quotid. He reported to the hospital again on March 20, 1864, with acute diarrhea.* He was paroled at Greensboro, North Carolina, May 1865. [17]*W. H. Taylor reported to the medical unit December 28, 1863, diagnosis feb int tert. W. V. Taylor reported to the medical unit twice in 1864, diagnosis feb int tert, on January 3 and February 10. Wm. Taylor complained of acute dysentery on June 4, as did W. V. Taylor on July 2. Wm. Taylor complained on acute diarrhea on September 12.*

Teague, E. A., Private, [17]*reported to the regimental medical unit on June 1, 1864, diagnosis was debilitas. He received a slight wound to his left hand on July 28, 1864, at the battle of Ezra Church near Atlanta. He was moved to the general hospital on July 31.* He was granted a parole May 1865 at Talladega.

Tedder, William B., Private, [17] *reported to the regimental twice in 1864, diagnosis catarrhus, on March 20 and April 26.* He was captured July 5, 1864, at Marietta, Georgia, and imprisoned at Camp Douglas, Illinois. He was forwarded for exchange March 14, 1865.

[17]***Thomas, W. L.,*** *Private, reported to the regimental medical unit in early May 1864, in the vicinity of Resaca, Georgia, diagnosis was acute dysentery. He was then reported missing.*

[18]***Thomson, John,*** *Private, was described in September 1863 as 47 years old, blue eyes, dark hair, fair complexion, 6'2, a mechanic, and a deserter.*

[12]***Thorn, L. T.,*** *Private, died in the hospital January 15, 1862.*

Towles, O. D., Private, enlisted May 7, 1863, at Mobile. He was 5'11, a merchant, and born in 1835 in Chamber County.

Townsand, Harris, Private, enlisted September 14, 1861, at Mobile. He was captured April 7, 1862, at Shiloh, Tennessee, and imprisoned at Alton, Illinois. [17]*He reported to the regimental medical unit on January 14, 1864, diagnosis feb int quotid.* Also spelled **Townsend.**

Upchurch, Berry, Private, lived in Randolph County. [17]*On July 28, 1864, at the battle of Ezra Church, he was severely wounded in the right neck chest, and hip. He was transferred to the general hospital on July 31.* He was hospitalized August 2, 1864, at Macon, Georgia, with injury to wrist, shoulder, and back. He died August 9, 1864. [24]*He was buried at Rose Hill Cemetery, Grave 57, Macon, Georgia.* Also listed as **L. B.**

Upchurch, Harbord M., Private, enlisted at Montgomery September 14, 1861, from Randolph County. In June 1862 he was a wagon master. [17]*He reported to the regimental medical unit twice in 1864. On*

February 9, the diagnosis was feb int tert. On July 20, 1864, at the battle of Peach Tree Creek near Atlanta, he was hit in the left leg by a shell and slightly wounded. He was moved to the general hospital the next day. He was captured December 15, 1864, at Nashville, and imprisoned at Camp Douglas, Illinois, where he was paroled May 8, 1865. Also listed as **Harry Upchurch, Harvey Upchurch.**

Upchurch, J. W., Private, died at a hospital in Pensacola, Florida, January 16, 1862.

Upchurch, L., Private, enlisted November 13, 1863, at Mobile. He was 5'9, a farmer, and born 1845 in Henry County, Georgia.

Upchurch, Vinson P., Private, enlisted at Corinth, Mississippi, May 1862. He was hospitalized in Mississippi in June 1862. He was listed as absent sick on the muster rolls for July-August, September-October, and November-December, 1862. He died soon after. [25]*He was buried in Gainesville, Alabama.*

[17]**Vincent, Thomas**, *Private, reported to the regimental medical unit twice in 1864. On January 9, the diagnosis was feb int tert. On November 3, the complaint was acute diarrhea.* Also listed as **T. J. Vincent**

Vinson, J. C., Private, enlisted August 20, 1863, at Mobile. He was 5'8 and born 1844, Chambers County.

Vinson, Micager W., Private, enlisted at Montgomery September 14, 1862.

[17]**Vowell, Andrew**, *Private, reported to the regimental medical unit three times in 1864. In September, the diagnosis was constipatio. The next time was October 9 with some type of bruise or wound. He moved to the general hospital on October 15. He was severely wounded (right thigh) at the battle of Franklin, Tennessee, November 30. A. J. Vowill reported to the hospital with rubella on January 11, 1864.* Also listed as **A. M. Vowell**

Vowell, J. C., Private, enlisted October 8, 1863, at Mobile. [17]*He reported to the regimental medical unit January 10, 1864, diagnosis feb int quotid, and June 4, 1864, diagnosis was catarrhus.* He was hospitalized at Mobile October 26, 1864. He was paroled at Greensboro, North Carolina, May 1865. See Service Records for Henry Castles. Also spelled **Vowill.**

Waldon, W. W., Private, worked as nurse during January 1862. He was hospitalized in June 1862 and discharged July 24, 1862.

Watkins, James, Private, enlisted September 14, 1861, at Montgomery. He was on sick furlough January 5, 1862, for 20 days and sent to Coosa County. He was captured February 16, 1862, at Ft. Donelson. He was captured at Pittsburg Landing April 8, 1862, and imprisoned at Camp Douglas, Illinois. He was exchanged in September 1862. He received a disability discharge December 5, 1862. He was 5'8, a farmer, and born 1806 in Green County, Georgia.

Watson, F. M., Private, enlisted at Mobile, was 5'7, and born 1846 in Tallapoosa County.

Watson, Samuel H., Private, enlisted November 13, 1863, at Mobile. He was 5'8, a farmer, and born 1845 in Randolph County. [17]*He reported to the regimental medical unit on December 3, 1863, diagnosis catarrhus, and three times in 1864. On June 30 and July 1, his complaint was acute dysentery. On August 5, the diagnosis was feb int quotid.* He was paroled at Greensboro, North Carolina, May 1865. [37]*He was born November 2, 1845, Randolph County. In 1921 he was living in Heflin and stated he was in battles at Resaca, Altoona, Hopewell ant Franklin.*

[17]***Watts, Wm.***, *Private, reported to the regimental medical unit on November 3, 1864, diagnosis feb int quotid.*

Weathers, Benjamin Frank, 2nd Lieutenant, 6', enlisted September 1861, Randolph County. He was appointed second lieutenant September 14, 1861. He was promoted to first lieutenant January 10, 1862. He was temporarily appointed captain May 12, 1862, after the capture of Captain Wiley E. White, commanding officer of Company E. White was exchanged and returned to his company October 25, 1862, relieving Weathers of his position as captain. [17]*Weathers reported to the regimental medical unit three times in 1864, each time listed as a lieutenant. On March 3, the diagnosis was debilitas. On April 26, the diagnosis was acute dysentery, and he was moved to the general hospital the next day. On September 6, the diagnosis was feb int tert.* Lieutenant Weathers was captured November 30, 1864, at Franklin, Tennessee, and imprisoned at Rock Island, Illinois, where he was paroled June 17, 1865. [1]*He was born November 8, 1839, Fayetteville, Fayette County, Georgia,* [41]*to Isham Thomas and Sarah Thompson Weathers.* [1]*He was living in Roanoke, Alabama, in 1907 and* [37]*in 1921 when he stated that his family moved to Alabama in March of 1842.* [41]*He died March 18, 1832 and* [26]*is buried in an unmarked grave in Cedarwood Cemetery in Randolph County.*

Weathers, James A., Private, enlisted November 16, 1863, at Mobile. He was 6', a farmer, and born 1845 in Randolph County. [17]*He reported to the regimental medical unit on July 12, 1864, diagnosis feb remitt, and moved to the general hospital the next day.* He was paroled at Greensboro, North Carolina, May 1865. [1]*He was born November 8, 1845, Highshoals, Randolph County, and was living in Roanoke, Alabama, in 1907.* [37]*In 1921 he was living in Roanoke and stated that he had fought in battles at Resaca, New Hope Church, and Franklin. He was wounded twice...at Resaca and at New Hope Church.*

Weathers, Simeon, Private, enlisted September 30, 1862, at Mobile. [17]*On April 29, 1864, he was listed as a sergeant and reported to the regimental medical unit, diagnosis catarrhus. On June 13, he was listed as a corporal when he reported sick, diagnosis acute diarrhea.* He was hospitalized Columbus, Georgia, September 30-October 31, 1864. [20]*He was born March 3, 1842, at Roanoke in Randolph County. In 1907 he was living at Albertville, Marshall County.*

Weathers, Thomas, Private, enlisted September 14, 1861, at Montgomery. He was slightly wounded in thigh at Shiloh, Tennessee, April 1862 and in the hospital in June 1862. He was hospitalized with rheumatic fever in LaGrange, Georgia, August 1864. [17]*He reported to the regimental medical unit twice in 1863, diagnosis feb int quotid, on December 16, and 27. He reported to the medical unit six times in 1864: on February 28 and March 4, diagnosis feb int tert; on March 28 with acute dysentery; on June 15 with acute diarrhea; on July 2, diagnosis feb int quotid; and on November 11 with acute diarrhea.* He was paroled at Greensboro, North Carolina, May 1865. He was a private at Shiloh, Tennessee, a sergeant in 1864, and a first lieutenant when paroled in 1865. [1]*He was born February 3, 1844 at Hightower, Randolph County and living in Roanoke in 1907.* [26]*He died March 26, 1924, and is buried in an unmarked grave in Springfield Baptist Church Cemetery in Randolph County.* [37]*He was elected to first lieutenant in 1865 while in North Carolina. He was stationed at Danville River in North Carolina.*

[17]**Weavers, B. J.,** *1st Lieutenant, reported to the regimental medical unit on December 2, 1863, diagnosis was debilitas. He was transferred to the general hospital on December 8.*

Weaver, John T., Private, enlisted September 14, 1861, at Montgomery. He was granted a sick furlough January 15, 1862, for 20 days and sent to Randolph County. [12]*He was listed as sick and absent from duty during the summer of 1862.*

Weaver, R. H., Private, died January 15, 1862, in a Mobile hospital.

[10]**Whaley, Archibald,** *Private, died at Camp Chase, Ohio, on March 15, 1865, and was buried in lot number 1666.*

Wheeler, John, Private, enlisted September 14, 1861, at Montgomery. He was hospitalized in Mississippi in June 1862.

[17]**White, B. S.,** *Private, reported to the regimental medical unit on January 12, 1864 with neuralgia.*

White, David C., Private, enlisted November 16, 1863, at Mobile. He was 5'6, a farmer and born 1845 in Fulton County, Georgia. He was at Greensboro, North Carolina, May 1865. [26]*He was born November 19, 1841. He died January 20, 1929, and is buried in Green's Chapel in Randolph County.*

COMPANY E

White, Daniel C., Private, enlisted October 15, 1862. [17]*He reported to the regimental medical unit on July 24, 1864, having been severely wounded in his right arm and was* admitted to LaGrange hospital, July 25, 1864. [26]*He sustained wounds during the war and is buried in Cedarwood Cemetery in Randolph County.* [37]*He was born November 18, 1843, in Randolph County. In 1921 he was living in Weedowee and stated that he fought in battles at Dalton, Atlanta, and Jonesboro, Georgia, and at Danville, Virginia. He was captured at Atlanta and "quit the service" in April 1865 at Danville.*

White, Homer V., Private, enlisted September 22, 1861, at Camp Davis. He was placed on sick furlough January 12, 1862, for 8 days and sent to Randolph County. [17]*He reported to the regimental medical unit on December 26, 1863, diagnosis was subluxatis.*

White, Henry C., Private, enlisted September 14, 1861, at Montgomery. He was 5'10, a farmer, and born 1845, Randolph County. He died May 13, 1862, in Mississippi leaving father, William C. White.

[17]***White, Virgil S.**, Private, reported to the regimental medical unit twice in January 1864: on the 18th, diagnosis was constipacio and on the 31st, feb int tert.*

White, Wiley E., Captain, was elected September 14, 1861. He was granted 20 days leave December 17, 1861. After the battle of Shiloh, Tennessee, he was captured April 11, 1862, at Huntsville, Alabama. After imprisonment at Johnson Island, Ohio, he was sent to Vicksburg, Mississippi, on September 1, 1862 for exchange. He returned to his regiment October 25, 1862, and resumed his position as commanding officer of Company E. [17]*He reported to the regimental medical unit on March 16, 1864, diagnosis was feb remitt. On April 2, 1864, he reported, diagnosis feb in tert, and immediately transferred to the general hospital. On April 12 he was placed on furlough for 30 days.* He resigned October 25, 1864. He was born June 27, 1832, and died January 27, 1890.

Whorton, W. A., Private, died in 1863.

Wilkerson, Warren C., Private, enlisted March 1, 1862, at Greenville.

Williams, Basil B., Private, enlisted September 13, 1862, at Mobile. He was hospitalized in at Mobile September 2, 1863, for 7 days. [17]*He reported to the regimental medical unit three times in 1864. On February 10, the diagnosis was feb int tert. He was transferred to the general hospital on the 14th. On March 10, the diagnosis was feb int quotid and on March 11 debilitas. He was transferred to the general hospital at Spring Hill on March 12.* He was paroled at Greensboro, North Carolina, May 1865, and listed as 2nd Lieutenant when paroled. [10]*He was born December 9, 1839, at Forsyth County, Georgia.* Also spelled **Brazzell B., Bazzle Barney**

[17]**Williams, J. D.,** *Private, reported to the regimental medical unit on December 13, 1863, the diagnosis was odontalgia. He reported to the hospital three more times in early 1864. On January 4, the diagnosis was catarrhus and on January 7, rubeola. He was moved to the general hospital on January 15. On March 28, the diagnosis was feb int tert.*

Williams, Thomas Jefferson, Private, enlisted March 15, 1862, Roanoke. He was at Greensboro, North Carolina, May 1865. [10]*He was born May 11, 1833, at Montgomery. In 1907 he was living in Blount County.*

Willis, John, Private, died May 29, 1862 in at Mobile.

[18]**Winger, John,** *Private, was described in September 1863 as 46 years old, gray eyes, light hair, fair complexion, 5'7 a trader, and a deserter.*

Wood, David, Private, enlisted March 15, 1862, at Greenville. He was hospitalized in June 1862.

Young, Giles R., Private, enlisted September 14, 1861, at Montgomery. He was hospitalized in June 1862. [17]*On December 20, 1863, he reported to the regimental medical unit, diagnosis feb int tert. On January 14, the diagnosis was acute rheum, and on January 20, the diagnosis was orchitis.* Also spelled **Jiles.**

Young, Joel, Private, enlisted September 14, 1861, at Montgomery. [42]*He was on special detail as wagoner January 1862.* [5]*He was slightly wounded at Shiloh, Tennessee, in April 1862.* He was hospitalized in Mississippi in June 1862. [12]*He served on extra duty as a teamster during the summer of 1862.* He was placed on sick furlough from Dalton, Georgia, during the summer of 1864, with disease and sent to Buchanan, Randolph County for 30 days. [17]*He reported to the regimental medical unit three times in 1864. On February 28, the diagnosis was feb int tert. On April 26, the diagnosis was acute dysentery. On July 4 near Marietta, Georgia, he was severely wounded in the thigh. He was immediately sent to a general hospital where he died. He was listed as 23 years old and a farmer.*

Appendix VII. Company F

Able, J. A., Private, enlisted December 27, 1861, Jefferson County. He was hospitalized June 1862. Also listed as **J. H. Able.**

Adams, D., Private, Elba, was hospitalized January 1865 at Meridian, Mississippi. He was paroled at Greensboro, North Carolina, May 1865.

Addison, Abijah Minto, Sergeant, 5'7, enlisted at Montgomery September 17, 1861. [17]*He was wounded and reported to the regimental medical unit three times during the siege of Atlanta. On June 27, the diagnosis was vulnus cont; on July 4, shell fragment in left hip; and on July 20, at the battle of Peachtree Creek near Atlanta, a slight wound to his thigh.* Suffering from wounds, he was and admitted to a hospital in Meridian, Mississippi, March 1865. He was paroled at Montgomery June 19, 1865. [1]*He was born September 20, 1832, Lancaster County, South Carolina. He was living in Highland Home, Crenshaw County, in 1907 and* [37]*in 1921. At that time, he stated that he had fought at Shiloh, Farmington, Resaca, New Hope Church, Kennesaw Mountain and Peachtree Creek.*

[37]**Addison, Moses B.,** Private, enlisted March 4, 1864, at Greenville. [17]*He reported to the regimental medical unit twice in 1864, diagnosis was feb remitt: on March 11 and August 28. In March he was moved to the general hospital at Spring Hill at Mobile.* [1]*He was born March 4, 1846, in Lancaster County, South Carolina. Paroled at Greensboro, North Carolina, April 1865, he was living in Highland Home, Crenshaw County, in 1907 and* [37]*1921. In 1921, he stated that he fought at Atlanta.*

Albright, Charles, Private, enlisted September 17, 1861, at Mobile and was discharged December 6, 1861.

Alexander, Alexander, Private, enlisted October 24, 1862, at Camp Watts. He was granted a disability discharge at Mobile on November 16, 1862. He was born in 1826 in Germany and was a shoemaker.

Amason, C. O., Corporal, enlisted March 12, 1862, at Greenville. He was at the surrender at Greensboro, North Carolina, April 26, 1865.

Amason, W. F., Sergeant, enlisted March 12, 1862, at Greenville. He was at the surrender at Greensboro, North Carolina, April 26, 1865.

Anderson, Elijah, Private, died by April 1862, leaving father, Elijah. [17]*E. Anderson reported to the hospital on July 4, 1864, wounded in the left thigh. He was immediately sent to the general hospital at Atlanta. He was listed as 26 years old and in poor health.* **Elijah Anderson** was placed on sick leave January 12, 1865, for 15 days. Could this be the father and son listed here?

Anderson, J. H., Private, enlisted December 27, 1861, Jefferson County. He later transferred to Company C 58th Alabama.

Anderson, W., Private, died January 11, 1862, leaving father, Elijah Anderson. NOTE: Under **W. Sr.**, there is a **W. Anderson**, Co. F, missing at Battle of Shiloh and a **Williamson Anderson** whose death was reported April 11, 1862. Under **W. Anderson**, Co. F, there is **William Anderson** who died January 11, 1862; **Wm. Anderson Sr.**, Co. F, who died January 11, 1862; and **Williamson Anderson** with father Elijah. [10] *W. Anderson listed as died at Camp Douglas, Illinois, March 19, 1862.*

Anderson, W. D. S., Private, was discharged May 20, 1862.

Anderson, W. Sr., Private, enlisted September 17, 1861, and died April 11, 1862, at Shiloh, Tennessee.

[5]**Andrews, Wm.,** Private, was listed as missing after the battle of Shiloh, Tennessee, April 1862.

Armer, W. M., Private, enlisted March 13, 1862, at Greenville. He was paroled at Greensboro, North Carolina, at the end of the war.

Bailey, Wesley Fletcher, Corporal (5'8), enlisted September 17, 1861, Montgomery. [17]*He reported to the regimental medical unit December 16, 1863, with acute dysentery, and five times in 1864. On February 14, diagnosis was acute diarrhea; on April 4 and September 11, feb int tert. On June 23, he suffered with debilitas and on July 2, feb int quotid. Captured December 18, 1864, near Franklin, Tennessee, he was imprisoned and paroled at Camp Chase, Ohio.* [1]*He was born May 9, 1844, Alexandria, Louisiana. He was living in Mobile in 1907.*

Baker, J. H., Private, enlisted September 17, 1861, Montgomery and was discharged July 25, 1862.

Baker, James, Private, enlisted February 20, 1862, Montgomery. He was 5'8 and born 1816, Warren, Tennessee. [17]*Hit by a minnie ball, he was severely wounded in the breast on July 20, at the battle of Peachtree Creek near Atlanta. He was moved to the general hospital the next day.* A Confederate soldier named James Baker is buried in Greenwood Cemetery in Barnesville, Georgia.

Blair, G. M., Corporal, enlisted February 20, 1862, at Elba, Alabama. He was at the surrender at Greensboro, North Carolina, April 26, 1865.

Blaum, Stephen, Private, was discharged December 5, 1861.

Block, Abraham, Private, enlisted October 10, 1862. [17]*He reported to the regimental medical unit on January 12, 1864, diagnosis was paronychia. Captured December 17, 1864, at Franklin, he was imprisoned at Camp Chase, Ohio, where he was paroled March 29, 1865.*

Blount, C. W., Private, enlisted September 17, 1861, at Montgomery. He was 5"9 and his home was Rutherford County, Tennessee. [17]*He reported to the regimental medical unit three times with syphilis: on*

December 23, 1863, and on February 1 and September 4, 1864. In February he was moved to the general hospital at Spring Hill in Mobile. He was captured December 15, 1864, at Nashville and applied to take the oath of allegiance.

Blythe, M. M., Private, enlisted December 27, 1861, Jefferson County. He transferred to Company F, 58th Alabama. Also spelled **Blunt**.

Bobiford, J., Private.

Bock, F. R. W., Private, enlisted September 17, 1861, at Montgomery. He was 5'4, a clerk, and was born 1843 in Halsteia, Denmark. He was detailed in the hospital as a ward master during September 1862. [17]*He reported to the regimental medical unit on December 12, 1863, diagnosis was syphilis, and moved to the general hospital at Spring Hill in Mobile on December 19.* Also spelled **Boch**

Bofinger, George, Musician, enlisted November 19, 1862, at Mobile. Captured May 20, 1864, at Cassville, Georgia, he was imprisoned at Rockland, Illinois.

Bonham, James Thomas, Private, [17]*reported to the regimental medical unit on February 3, 1864, and moved to a hospital at Spring Hill on February 5. He reported to the hospital again on March 20 with debilitas and on April 18 with pneumonia. He reported to the hospital on January 4, diagnosis catarrhus.* He was captured December 16, 1864, Nashville and imprisoned at Camp Douglas, Illinois, where he died March 24, 1865. Cause of death was consumption. He is buried in lot number 998, Block 3, Chicago City Cemetery.

Boothe, W. D., Private, enlisted March 17, 1862, at Greenville. He was at the surrender at Greensboro, North Carolina, April 26, 1865.

Bowden, S. F., Sergeant, enlisted December 27, 1861, Jefferson County.

Boyd, J. M., Private, enlisted April 21, 1864, at Dalton, Georgia. He was at the surrender at Greensboro, North Carolina, April 26, 1865.

Boykin, D. S., Private, was discharged August 20, 1862: hired a substitute, Paul Callagy, to take his place.

Bradford, J. F., Private, was hospitalized at Macon, Georgia, where he was granted a furlough for 60 days, June 10, 1864, diagnosis was chronic diarrhea.

Brassill, George, Private, enlisted January 2, 1863, at Montgomery and died in a Mobile hospital July 13, 1863.

Bray, Henry B., Sergeant, 5'7, enlisted at Montgomery September 17, 1861. He was promoted from corporal to sergeant September 11, 1862. [17]*He suffered a slight wound to his side on July 20, 1864, at the battle of Peachtree Creek at Atlanta, and was sent to the general hospital on July 21.* He was at the surrender at Greensboro, North Carolina, April 26, 1865. He was paroled May 22, 1865, at Montgomery. [30]*He was born*

August 22, 1840, North Carolina. *After the war, he worked as a gas fitter in Montgomery. He died October 6, 1873.*

Broadway, Abner, Private, enlisted January 27, 1863, at Montgomery. *[17]He reported to the regimental medical unit twice with rubeola, on April 4 and June 25 in 1864. [1]He was born August 7, 1827, Montgomery. He was wounded at the battle of Chickamauga. He fought until the end of the war at Mobile. In 1907 he was living in Montgomery.* NOTE: He was probably in another unit for some part of the war, as the 17th Alabama did not fight at Chickamauga, nor was the 17th Alabama at Mobile at the end of the war. *[30]He was probably W. H. Broadway's uncle or brother.*

Broadway, J., Private, 5'6, paroled May 31, 1865, at Montgomery.

Broadway, Wade Hampton, Private, enlisted January 29, 1863, at Montgomery. *[17]He reported to the regimental medical unit on June 25, 1864, diagnosis feb int quotid. He was mortally wounded July 20, 1864, at the battle of Peachtree Creek.* He died August 4, 1864, Vining Station, Georgia, from a gunshot wound to his left lung. *[30]He was born 1829. He married Mary Frances Hicks.*

Brodnax, O. W., Private, was 5'9 and born in 1827 in Pike County, Florida. He was granted a disability discharge May 6, 1862.

[17]**Brown, N. F.,** Private, *reported to the regimental medical unit on February 15, 1864, diagnosis was feb int tert.*

[17]**Brown, O. F.,** Private, *reported to regimental medical unit on March 16, 1864, diagnosis rubeola, and was moved to the hospital in Greenville on March 18. He was also ill April 11, 1864, diagnosis catarrhus.* He was killed on July 20, 1864, at the battle of Peachtree Creek near Atlanta.

Brumley, Elias S., Private, enlisted December 27, 1861, Jefferson County. He transferred to 58th Alabama.

Bryant, William H., 2nd Lieutenant

Buckelew, Josephus, Private, enlisted January 1863. *[17]He reported to the regimental medical unit April 29, 1864, diagnosis was acute dysentery.* Also spelled **Buckalow.**

Buckley, D. J., Private, *[42]was detailed as a carpenter at O'Bannonville, January 1862.* He died April 6, 1862, Shiloh, Tennessee, from a wound to his breast.

Buckner, Leonard, Private, enlisted February 3, 1863, at Montgomery. His home was Coosa County. *[17]During September 1864 he reported to the regimental medical unit, diagnosis was haemorrhois.*

Bullard, Edward H., Private, enlisted March 7, 1863, at Mobile. *[1]He was born September 19, 1842, Henry County, Georgia. He was wounded on July 28, 1864, at the battle of Ezra Church in Georgia. He was discharged later in 1864.* At 6'1, he was paroled June 29, 1865, at Montgomery. *[1]In 1907 his residence was in Lapine, Crenshaw County.*

COMPANY F

[17]**Bullard, G. H.**, Private, reported to the regimental medical unit on April 25, 1864, diagnosis was catarrhus.

Bullard, Henry M., Private, enlisted May 25, 1863. He was 5'10 and a resident of Lowndes County. [17]He reported to the regimental medical unit four times in 1864. On February 21, the diagnosis was feb int quotid, on June 21, acute diarrhea, on June 26, acute dysentery, and on July 4, icterus. Captured December 18, 1864, at Franklin/Spring Hill, Tennessee, he was imprisoned at Camp Douglas, Illinois.

[17]**Burch, Josiah**, Private, reported to the regimental medical unit on March 17, 1864, diagnosis was rubeola. He was moved to the hospital in Greenville. He reported to the hospital again on April 6, 1864, diagnosis was debilitas. He was moved to a general hospital on April 22.

Burns, Edward, Musician. Also spelled **Brun.**

Burton, M. A., Private, enlisted February 28, 1862, at Pensacola, Florida. Captured February 16, 1862, at Fort Donelson, he was imprisoned at Camp Douglas, Illinois.

Butler, Thomas, Private, enlisted September 17, 1861. [42]He was granted a 20-day furlough January 9, 1862, and sent to Lowndes County.

Caffey, E. C., Corporal, enlisted March 12, 1862, Greenville. He was paroled at Greensboro, North Carolina, May 1865.

Caffey, W. V., Private, enlisted March 12, 1862, Greenville. He was paroled at Greensboro, North Carolina, May 1865.

Call, J. W., Sergeant, was paroled June 1, 1865.

Callagy, Paul, Private, enlisted August 20, 1862, at Mobile. He was a substitute for D. S. Boykin.

Campbell, William Bishop, Private, enlisted July 7, 1862, at Mobile. He was employed as a nurse. [17]He reported to the regimental medical unit on June 13, 1864, and was moved to the general hospital the next day. The diagnosis was org dis heart. He reported again to the hospital on July 31, 1864, diagnosis debilitas. [1]He was born January 1, 1836, Norfolk, Virginia. He was paroled at Macon, Georgia, and living in Mobile in 1907.

Carey, John, Private, [18]was described in September 1863 as 45 with blue eyes, black hair, fair complexion, 5'4, a laborer, and a deserter.

Carr, J., Private, enlisted January 1, 1863, Murphresboro, Tennessee.

Champion, Francis M., Private, was captured at Pittsburg Landing, Tennessee, April 1862. He died June 24, 1862, at a Union general hospital in Louisville, Kentucky. [30]He is buried in Cave Hill Cemetery in Louisville. His tombstone says he died April 28, 1862.

Champion, H. M., Private, enlisted September 17, 1861, at Montgomery. His placed on extra duty driving the regimental wagon. He was placed on medical furlough on January 17, 1862, for 20 days and sent to Pike County. He suffered a wound in his side at Shiloh, Tennessee, April 6, 1862. He was granted parole at Greensboro, North Carolina, May 1865.

Cheek, Randolph W., Private, [17]*suffering from rubeola, he reported to the regimental medical unit March 18, 1864, and moved to the hospital in Greenville March 21.* He was captured October 23, 1864, at Gaylesville, Alabama, and was imprisoned at Camp Douglas, Illinois. He died of pneumonia March 17, 1865, and was buried in lot 967 Block 3, Chicago City Cemetery. Also listed as **Cheap, Cheeks**.

Christy, James, Private, was 5'8, a mechanic, and born 1812 in Liverpool, England. He was granted a disability discharge on February 28, 1862.

Cluss, George, Private, enlisted June 21, 1863, at Mobile. He was born 1830 in France, a gardener, and 5'7. See Service Records for James Lake. [17]*He reported to the regimental medical unit on December 19, 1863, diagnosis was catarrhus.*

Coll, Hugh, Private, enlisted September 17, 1861, at Montgomery. He was paroled May 10, 1865, at Montgomery. He worked as a storekeeper. Also listed as **Call, Colb**

[17]**Collins, D.**, *Private, reported to the regimental medical unit on August 7, 1864, diagnosis was acute diarrhea.*

Collins, Jeremiah, Private, enlisted September 17, 1861, at Montgomery, his home. He was captured December 16, 1864, at Nashville, and imprisoned at Camp Douglas, Illinois. He was paroled May 1865 in Montgomery.

Conger, R. E., Private, enlisted August 17, 1862, Camp Watts. [17]*He reported to the regimental medical unit three times in 1864. On April 15, the diagnosis was anasarca, on July 30, acute diarrhea, and August 19, haemorrhois.* He was paroled at Greensboro, North Carolina, May 1865. Also spelled **Conyer**.

Connell, Dennis, Private, enlisted December 8, 1862. Mobile was his home. [17]*He reported to the regimental medical unit five times in 1864. On January 18, the diagnosis was ulcus; on February 29, odontalgia; on March 28, acute dysentery; on July 6, acute diarrhea; and on August 19, haemorrhois.*

Cook, O. H. P., Private, enlisted January 24, 1863, at Montgomery. [17]*He reported to the regimental medical unit three times in 1864. On February 19, the diagnosis was catarrhus, and on June 21, feb int quotid. On July 20, at the battle of Peachtree Creek, Georgia, he was hit in the neck by a minnie ball and was moved to the general hospital on July 21.* He was hospitalized at Macon, Georgia, on August 19, 1864, and at Meridian, Mississippi, January 2 and 3, 1865.

Cook, W. M., Private, enlisted 1862, at Greenville. He was paroled at Greensboro, North Carolina, May 1865.

Cordle, N. C., Private, enlisted December 27, 1861, Jefferson County. He was 5'11, born 1837 in Blount County, and died May 20, 1862. See personal papers for Hagood.

Cordle, W. C., Private, enlisted December 27, 1861, Jefferson County. He was 5'10, born in 1840 in Blount County, and died May 20, 1862. See personal papers for Hagood.

Courtney, B.F., Private, enlisted in 1862, at Greenville and paroled at Greensboro, North Carolina, May 1865.

Courtney, S. J., Private, enlisted March 12, 1862, at Greenville and paroled at Greensboro, North Carolina, May 1865.

Cowden, R. L., Private, enlisted December 27, 1861, Jefferson County. He was 6'2, born in 1828 in Jefferson County, and died in 1862. See Service Records for Hagood.

Cowden, W. D., Sergeant, enlisted December 27, 1861, Jefferson County. He transferred to Company C, 58th Alabama.

Cowley, John T., Private, enlisted 1861, at Montgomery (5'11). Captured April 7, 1862, at the battle of Shiloh, Tennessee, he was exchanged October 20, 1862, and discharged November 22, 1862. [17]*He reported to the regimental medical unit on January 5, 1864, diagnosis was sub luxatio. He reported again on June 15, 1864, diagnosis was varicocele.* Also listed **Cawley, Cowly.**

Craig, John N., Private, [42]*was a clerk at General Gladden Hospital while stationed at Pensacola.*

Croxton, Elijah Minter, Private, enlisted September 3, 1863, at Mobile. A farmer he was born in 1823 in Lowndes County. [17]*He reported to the regimental medical unit three times in 1864. On February 14, the diagnosis was acute diarrhea. On February 16, the diagnosis was feb int quotid. He was moved to a hospital in Mobile two days later. On June 18, the diagnosis was feb int quotid, and the next day, he was again moved to the general hospital. He was killed July 20, 1864, at the battle of Peachtree Creek, Georgia.*

Croxton, Robert A., Corporal, enlisted September 17, 1861, at Montgomery. [17]*He reported to the regimental medical unit December 20, 1863, diagnosis was feb int tert. As a sergeant, he reported to the hospital again July 31, 1864 and August 6, diagnosis acute diarrhea.* [2]*As a lieutenant, he died November 30, 1864, at the battle of Franklin, Tennessee. He was buried at McGavock Cemetery, Franklin, in section 69, lot #26, Alabama.*

Cumbie, J. T., Private, enlisted October 7, 1863, Chickamauga. He was paroled at Greensboro, North Carolina, May 1865.

Cumbie, W. A., 2nd Lieutenant, enlisted February 20, 1862, at Elba, Alabama. He was paroled at Greensboro, North Carolina, May 1865.

Cumbie, W. B., Private, enlisted March of 1862, Clopton, Alabama. He was paroled at Greensboro, North Carolina, May 1865.

[17]**Dailey, Wm.,** Corporal, reported to the regimental medical unit on April 1, 1864, diagnosis was feb int tert.

Dandy, W. W., Private, enlisted December 27, 1861, Jefferson County. [17]*He reported to the regimental medical unit twice in 1864. On January 17, the diagnosis was scorbutus, and on March 28, otorrhoea.* Also listed as **W. H., Wm. Dendy**

Davis, D. D., Private, enlisted September 17, 1862, at Montgomery. [17]*He reported to the regimental medical unit three times in 1864. On March 9, the diagnosis was gonorrhea; on June 3, acute dysentery; and on September 13, constipatio. In June he was moved to the general hospital.* Captured on December 15, 1864, Nashville, he was imprisoned at Camp Douglas, Illinois. His home was Honoraville.

Davis, R. L, Private, was captured at Island 10, Tennessee, April 8, 1862, and imprisoned at Camp Douglas, Illinois.

[17]**Deason, C.,** Private, suffered a back injury on July 20 at the battle of Peachtree Creek near Atlanta and was moved to the general hospital the next day.

Demony, A., Private, enlisted August 10, 1863, at Mobile, and was listed as sick in camp in August 1863.

Dempsey, Stephen, Private, was listed as missing after the battle of Shiloh, Tennessee, in April 1862.

[18]**Dennis, Ogburn,** Private, was listed in September 1863 as 35 with black hair and eyes, dark complexion, 5'5, a farmer, and a deserter.

Dickey, C. K., Private, enlisted March 12, 1862, at Greenville. He was paroled at Greensboro, North Carolina, May 1865.

[18]**Dickson, John,** Private, was listed in September 1863 as 47 with hazel eyes, dark hair, fair complexion, 5'10, a laborer, and a deserter.

Dinsey, Stephen, Private

Donnell, Cornelius O., Private, was granted a disability discharge on January 16, 1862.

Doyle, John, Private, [42]*He was placed on furlough for 15 days January 28, 1862, and sent to Montgomery.* He was wounded at Shiloh, Tennessee, in April 1862. [5]*He was reported captured.*

Dumas, Asa, Private, enlisted February 19, 1862, Greene County. He was 6 foot and lived at Stevenson. He was hospitalized June 1862. Captured May 13, 1864, near Dalton, Georgia, he was imprisoned at Camp Morton, Ohio. He was paroled May 20, 1865. He had transferred to Company F, 58th Alabama by the time he was captured.

COMPANY F

[17]**Duncan, G. W.**, *Private, reported to the regimental medical unit March 27, 1864, diagnosis feb int tert. He was sick June 17, 1864, diagnosis haematuria, and moved to the general hospital the next day.*

Edwards, John, Private, enlisted February 19, 1862, Greene County.

Evans, E. A., Private, enlisted September 17, 1861, at Montgomery. He was placed on sick furlough January 22, 1862, for 20 days and sent to Montgomery. [17]*He reported to the regimental medical unit on June 20, 1864, diagnosis was acute diarrhea.*

Fables, George, Private, 5'8, was born about 1846, at Montgomery. [17]*He reported to the regimental medical unit on January 8, 1864, diagnosis was catarrhus, and on April 28, acute diarrhea.* He lived in Montgomery and worked as a clerk. Captured December 16, 1864, Nashville, he was imprisoned at Camp Douglas, Illinois. Also listed as **Geo. P. Fabel, Geo. B. Faber, Geo. B. Falee.**

[17]**Fannin, J. H.**, *Private, reported to the regimental medical unit on March 16, 1864, diagnosis was rubeola. He was moved to the hospital in Greenville on the 18th. On April 24, 1864, he reported to the hospital again, diagnosis was pneumonia. He was sent to the general hospital three days later.* [24]*This may be I. Fanning buried in Linwood Community Cemetery in Columbus, Georgia.*

Farrell, Robert, Private.

Fields, Gabriel, Private, enlisted 1861, at Montgomery. He was granted a sick furlough January 2, 1862, for 20 days and sent to Montgomery. [17]*He reported to the regimental medical unit three times with diagnosis, feb int tert, December 26, 1863, January 14, 1864, and on June 4, 1864.*

Fitzallen, Nicholas, Private. See **N. Pizzala**

Forshee, Charles, Private, enlisted October 10, 1861, at Montgomery. He was 5'5, a farmer, and born in Upson County, Georgia. He was hospitalized during June 1862. [17]*He reported to the regimental medical unit on December 13, 1863, diagnosis pleuritis. He reported three times in 1864. On April 20, the diagnosis was feb int tert; on July 29, acute diarrhea; and on September 13, feb int quotid. On September 23, he was moved to the general hospital.* Captured December 15, 1864, Nashville, he was imprisoned at Camp Douglas, Illinois. Also spelled **Furshee, Forshea.**

Forshee, William, Private, enlisted October 10, 1861, at Montgomery. He was 5'8, a farmer, and born in Upson County, Georgia. He was granted a sick furlough during January 1862 for 20 days and sent to Montgomery County. [17]*He reported to the regimental medical unit on March 19, 1864, diagnosis was ischuria renalis. On April 27, 1864, the diagnosis was ulcus chronic, and he was moved to the general hospital* two days later. On June 13, 1864, he suffered a severe injury to his thigh. He was moved to the general hospital on June 14. He was paroled May 11, 1865. Also spelled **Forche, Forshe, Forhe, Forshea.**

Foshe, M. M., Private, was paroled in Montgomery, May 1865.

[17]**Gay, Stewart,** Private, is listed on the records of the regimental medical unit on June 1, 1864, with a severe wound to his thigh. He was moved to the general hospital the next day.

George, Emmett, Private, worked as clerk in January thru March of 1864. He was later promoted to captain.

Gleason, Cornelius, Private, enlisted September 17, 1862, at Montgomery.

Goodwin, Jordan D., Private, enlisted December 17, 1861, Jefferson County. He was hospitalized June 1862. He transferred to the 26th Alabama Company C.

Going, T., Private, was hospitalized and sent to Montgomery on an 18 day medical furlough November 12, 1861.

Goynes, H., Private, enlisted March 11, 1862, at Greenville. He was paroled at Greensboro, North Carolina, May 1865.

Goynes, J. T., Sergeant, enlisted March 13, 1862, at Greenville. He was paroled at Greensboro, North Carolina, May 1865.

Grayor, Henry T., Private, enlisted September 25, 1861, at Montgomery. [17]He reported to the regimental medical unit four times in 1864. On January 12, the diagnosis was feb int tert, on February 10, otorrhoea, on March 15, feb int quotid, and on April 9, feb int tert. He was hospitalized with wounds in Macon, Georgia, June 17, 1864. He was granted a furlough to Montgomery County, June 25. **H. T. Green,** Private, was hospitalized during June 1862. Hospitalized at Macon, a finger on his left hand was amputated June 24, 1864. He was granted sick furlough for 60 days and sent to Montgomery County. Also spelled **Graor, Greor, Greer**

Green, J., Private, enlisted at Greenville. He was paroled at Greensboro, North Carolina, May 1865.

Gregory, J. A., Private, enlisted during 1862, at Greenville. He was paroled at Greensboro, North Carolina, May 1865.

Griffin, Patrick, Private, enlisted April 1863. [17]He was severely injured in the face and neck, hit by a minnie ball on July 20 at the battle of Peachtree Creek, near Atlanta. He was sent to the general hospital on July 21.

Griffin, Waldo Y., Private, enlisted September 1, 1862, at Camp Watts. According to the muster roll for July-August 1863, he was in confinement at the Provost Marshall Guard House in Mobile.

Gullard, Martin, Private, enlisted August 27, 1863, at Mobile.

Hagood, J. H., Private, enlisted December 27, 1861, Jefferson County. He was hospitalized June 1862. He transferred to the 19th Alabama, Company K.

Hagood, J. M., Private, enlisted December 27, 1861, Jefferson County. He was absent with leave June 1862. He was granted a disability discharge December 30, 1862. He was for in Jefferson County in 1832.

Hagood, M. D., Private, enlisted December 27, 1861, Jefferson County. He was 5'11, a farmer, and born in 1838 St. Clair County. He died in 1862.

Hall, G. M., enlisted February 3, 1863. [30]*George Washington Hall was killed during the battle of Atlanta. His parents were Wilson West and Jane Bryant Hall. He was married to Mary Sumner. His brothers included Hardy and John Wilson Hall of Company F.*

Hall, Hardy R., Private, enlisted September 17, 1861, at Montgomery. [17]*He reported to the regimental medical unit four times in 1864. On January 10, the diagnosis was acute bronchitis and March 15, feb int quotid. On July 20, he was shot through the middle finger of his left hand at the battle of Peachtree Creek, Georgia. The finger was later amputated. On November 20 diagnosis was nephritis, and he moved to the general hospital on November 29.* [30]*His parents were Wilson West and Jane Bryant Hall. He was married to Sarah Hall. His brothers included George Washington and John Wilson Hall of Company F.*

Hall, J. A., Private, enlisted September 24, 1862, at Montgomery. According to the September-October 1863 muster roll, Hall was sick in the hospital and under arrest.

Hall, John Wilson, Private, enlisted January 27, 1863. [17]*He was listed on the regimental medical unit records in May 1864 as missing and as having acute dysentery.* He was captured June 24, 1864, Calhoun, Georgia, and imprisoned at Alton, Illinois. He was a member of the Crenshaw County Confederate Veterans' Association in 1890. [30]*His parents were Wilson West and Jane Bryant Hall. He was married to Elizabeth Jones. His brothers included George Washington and Hardy R. Hall of Company F.*

Halprin, Thomas, 2nd Lieutenant, was furloughed after being wounded September 29, 1864. [17]*He suffered a severe injury to his right thigh on July 28, 1864, at the battle of Ezra Church near Atlanta. He was moved to the general hospital on July 31.* As listed in the Macon Daily Telegraph, he died August 21, 1864, and is buried in the old City Cemetery. Also listed as **Halpin, Halfrin.**

Halso, J. A., Private, [10]*was born June 23, 1823, in Dumplin County, North Carolina. He was living in Butler County in 1907.*

Halso, John William, Private, enlisted 1862, at Mobile. [17]*He reported to the regimental medical unit on June 15, 1864, diagnosis was acute dysentery, and on September 21, icterus, when he was sent to the* *general hospital.* He was paroled at Greensboro, North Carolina, May 1865. [28]*He attended the Confederate Veterans Reunion in Greenville August 21, 1897. He was listed in Company C.* [7]*He registered as a veteran in Butler County July 4, 1906.* [30]*He was born June 23, 1823 and died October 24, 1918, at Pigeon Creek in Butler County.*

Halso, Stephen, Private, enlisted October 3, 1862, Camp Watts, and discharged March 26, 1862. He reenlisted in Company F October 3, 1862. [17]*He reported to the regimental medical unit on July 6, 1864, diagnosis feb int quotid. He suffered severe injuries in his shoulders on July 20 at the battle of Peachtree Creek, Georgia. According to the hospital records, he was left on the field.*

Harrison, Martin, Private, enlisted September 17, 1861, at Montgomery. He was detailed as waggoner to the Chief Quarter Master during June 1862. [17]*He reported to the regimental medical unit December 2, 1863, diagnosis was pneumonia, and December 18, diagnosis was chronic rheum and chronic diarrhea. He was granted a disability discharge December 21.*

Hartley, Joseph F., Private, was hospitalized June 1862.

Hickman, H. W., Private.

[17]***Hickman, J. M.,*** *Private, reported to the regimental medical unit on September 16, 1864, diagnosis was feb remitt. He was moved to the general hospital the next day.*

Hicks, A. J., Private, enlisted December 13, 1861, at Greenville. He was paroled at Greensboro, North Carolina, April 1865.

Hogan, M., Private, was paroled in 1865 at Selma.

Holland, Davis, Private, enlisted April 3, 1863, at Mobile, and was hospitalized March 1-August 31, 1864, at Greenville. Captured December 15, 1864, Nashville, he was imprisoned at Camp Chase, Ohio. He died of pneumonia January 29, 1865, and was buried in lot 614 block 2 Chicago City Cemetery.

Howell, W. T., Private, enlisted March 17, 1862, at Greenville. He was paroled at Greensboro, North Carolina, April 1865.

Huffman, A. J., Private, enlisted August 2, 1862, at Montgomery. He was paroled at Greensboro, North Carolina, April 1865.

Huffman, B. H., Sergeant, enlisted March 12, 1862, at Greenville. He was paroled at Greensboro, North Carolina, April 1865.

Imms, H., Private, wounded, was granted a sick furlough from a hospital in Meridian, Mississippi, January 12, 1865.

James, William R., Private, enlisted November 4, 1863, at Montgomery. He was hospitalized in Montgomery during November 1864.

COMPANY F

Johnson, T. J., Private, enlisted December 27, 1861, Jefferson County. Also spelled **Johnston.**

Johnston, Charles, Private, enlisted 1863, at Mobile. He was 5'8, a clerk, and born in 1840 in Baton Rouge, Louisiana.

Johnston, Windon T., Private, enlisted June 12, 1864, at Mobile. [17]*He reported to the regimental medical unit four times in 1864. On March 21, the diagnosis was acute diarrhea, and on April 5, catarrhus. On April 20, the diagnosis was pleuritis. He was sent to the general hospital two days later. In October, the diagnosis was debilitas, and he was moved to the general hospital on October 31st.*

Jolly, J. H., Private, enlisted March 17, 1864, at Elba. He was paroled at Greensboro, North Carolina, April 1865.

Jones, H., Private, died at Camp Douglas, Illinois, [10]*May 3, 1862.*

Jones, James Newton, Private, enlisted at Montgomery November 27, 1861. [1]*He was born December 6, 1844, Strata, Montgomery County. He was captured at Resaca, Georgia, during May 1864. He was exchanged March 1865. In 1907 his residence was Montgomery.* [17]*The regimental medical unit records indicate that he was suffering with acute dysentery in May of 1864, and he was listed as missing.* [37]*In 1921 he stated that he was born in Lowndes County. He was at the battle of Shiloh and the bombardment of Pensacola. He was captured near Cassville, Georgia and sent to Buck Island, Ohio. He was exchanged from the hospital and sent to Richmond in early 1865. He was sent home in March.*

Jones, Jasper W., Private, enlisted January 27, 1862, at Montgomery. He was born in 1845 in Lowndes County. [17]*He reported to the regimental medical unit March 7, 1864, diagnosis was abscessus and April 8, 1864, vulnus contusum.* Captured on May 20, 1864, at Cassville, Georgia, he was imprisoned at Rock Island, Illinois. Suffering from battle wounds, he was granted a sick furlough from a hospital in Meridian, Mississippi, on March 18, 1865.

[1]***Jones, John William,*** Private, enlisted April 1862, at Montgomery. [17]*The regimental medical unit records indicate that he suffered a severe injury to his right arm on July 20, at the battle of Peachtree Creek near Atlanta. He was moved to the general hospital on July 31 where his arm was amputated.* [1]*He was paroled in Montgomery during May 1865. In 1907 he was living in Montgomery.* [37]*He was born near Sillero, Montgomery County, June 7, 1834. In 1921, he wrote that he fought at Cassville, and from Resaca to Atlanta. He also wrote that he lost his right arm at Peachtree Creek July 20, 1864.*

Jones, Owen, Corporal, enlisted September 25, 1861, at Montgomery. He was granted a sick furlough January 7, 1862, for 20 days and sent to Lowndes County. He was wounded in the thigh at Shiloh, Tennessee,

April 1862. [17]*The regimental medical unit records indicate that he suffered a severe injury to his right wrist on July 28, 1864, probably at the battle of Ezra Church in Georgia. He was moved to the general hospital on July 31. Wounded during the Tennessee campaign December 1864, he was hospitalized in Meridian, Mississippi, January 1865. He was granted a sick furlough March 17, 1865.*

Jones, William, Private, was imprisoned at Camp Douglas, Illinois, [10]*where he died May 3, 1862.*

[17]***Jones, William,*** *Private, reported to the regimental medical unit on December 1, 1863, diagnosis was debilitas. He was granted a furlough on December 4. He reported to the hospital January 10 and July 3, 1864, diagnosis was phlegmon.*

Jones, William K., Private, was wounded (thigh, severely) and missing after the battle of Shiloh, Tennessee, April 1862. He died at Camp Douglas, Illinois, leaving father, Joshua Jones. Seems to be two **William K. Jones.** Second one was moved to the hospital in Macon, Georgia, on May 22, 1864. His foot had been amputated. He was granted a furlough on May 23, for 60 days. [17]*W. K. Jones reported to the regimental medical unit on April 11, 1864, diagnosis feb int tert. The regimental records indicate that in May 1864, he suffered a slight wound to this foot, probably at the battle of Resaca. The above furlough was probably granted to recuperate from the wound.*

Jones, W. S, Corporal, suffering from wounds, was admitted to the hospital at Meridian, Mississippi, March 24, 1865.

[17]***Jones, W. T.,*** *Private, reported to the regimental medical unit on March 20, 1864, diagnosis feb int quotid.*

[20]***Jusilce, John Hartwell****, enlisted in 1861, and later transferred to Company G, 2nd Georgia. He was captured at Egypt, Mississippi. Born July 24, 1838, in Newton County, Georgia, he was living in Elmore County in 1907.*

Karr, John N., Private, enlisted August 28, 1862, at Mobile. He was 6'1 and born in 1830 in Montgomery.

Keith, Daniel, Private, enlisted September 8, 1862, Camp Watts. [17]*He reported to the regimental medical unit on June 22, 1864, diagnosis was haemorrhois. He was moved to the general hospital the same day.*

Kelly, Edward, Private, enlisted September 17, 1862, at Montgomery.

Kerr, Newton J., Private, died January 26, 1862, at Mobile.

Kettner, G., Private, enlisted March 15, 1862, at Greenville. He was paroled at Greensboro, North Carolina, April 1865.

Kilgore, James M., Private, was discharged December 5, 1861.

Krimmel, G, Private, enlisted April 20, 1863, at Mobile. He was 6' a shoemaker, and born in 1817, Virtenburg.

Larkins, J. S., Private, enlisted November 1862, at Greenville. He was paroled at Greensboro, North Carolina, April 1865.

Layton, Joseph, Private, enlisted June 21, 1863, at Mobile. He was 5'5, a laborer, and born in 1818 in Maine. Personal papers for Krimmell. [17]*He was wounded (abdomen) July 2, 1864. He was sent to the general hospital the next day.* **Jas. Leighton,** Private, reported to the regimental medical unit on February 4, 1864, diagnosis sub luxatis. Also spelled **Laton, Leighton.**

Ledbetter, J. D., Private, was captured December 28, 1864, at Egypt Station, Mississippi. He was imprisoned at Alton Prison in Illinois, and sent to Camp Lookout for exchange during February 1865. He died March 18, 1865, at a Richmond Hospital. Also spelled **Leadbetter.**

Lee, James L., Private, enlisted 1863, at Montgomery. [17]*He reported to the regimental medical unit twice in 1864. On February 19, the diagnosis was catarrhus, and on October 9, icterus. He was moved to the general hospital October 18.* Captured December 15, 1864, at Nashville, he was imprisoned at Camp Douglas, Illinois.

Lee, Wayne E., 2nd Lieutenant, was hospitalized during June 1862.

Lewis, J. E., Private, enlisted August 1, 1862, at Camp Watts. Also listed as **J. A.** [17]*Jas. Lewis reported to the regimental medical unit on February 2, 1864, diagnosis was ulcus. J. E. Lewis reported to the regimental medical unit on February 23, 1864, chronic ulcus. J. A. Lewis reported to the hospital twice in 1864 with a diagnosis of ulcus and chronic ulcus, on March 6 and April 15. He was moved to the general hospital on April 18. J. H. Lewis reported to the hospital on July 6, 1864, with chronic ulcus. He was moved to the general hospital on July 9. J. A. Lewis is listed on the regimental medical unit records as severely injured in the right ankle on July 28, 1864, wounded at the battle of Ezra Church near Atlanta. He was sent to the general hospital July 31.* [20]*James A. Lewis, was born November 5, 1842, in Barbour County. He enlisted August 1862. He was discharged July 28, 1864, near Atlanta - loss of leg. He was living in Enterprise, Coffee County, in 1907.* [27]*James Allen Lewis, born November 5, 1842, in Barbour County. He enlisted August 1, 1862, at Camp Watts. He served extra duty as a driver for an artillery battery, July - August 1863. He married Laura A. Hubbard, October 3, 1884. He died November 11, 1912, and was buried at the Confederate Soldiers Home of Alabama Cemetery Row 2, lot 16B1.*

Lloyd, C. C., Captain, resigned January 7, 1862.

Love, S. A., Private, enlisted December 27, 1861, Jefferson County. He was hospitalized in Mississippi during June 1862.

Love, Thomas, Musician, enlisted July 21, 1863, at Mobile. He was born in 1840 at Mussoja, Alabama.

Lovett, Joseph, Private, enlisted September 17, 1861, at Montgomery. Granted sick furlough January 11, 1862, for 20 days, he was sent to Butler County. Also spelled **Lovits, Lovet.** [17]*He reported to the regimental medical unit twice with a diagnosis of feb int tert: on December 17, 1863, and June 22, 1864. He reported to the hospital three times in July of 1864. On July 1, the diagnosis was acute diarrhea, and on July 14, colica. On July 20, he was severely wounded in the hand, at the battle of Peachtree Creek, near Atlanta. He was moved to the general hospital on July 21. **Jas. Lovett** reported to the hospital twice in 1864 with the diagnosis feb int tert: on February 15 and June 25. This may have been Joseph.*

Lovett, Pierce, Private, enlisted March 7, 1863, at Mobile. Captured July 4, 1864, at Chattahoochie, Georgia, he was imprisoned at Camp Douglas, Illinois, [1]where he died December 10, 1864. Also spelled **Lorreth, Lorett, Lovitt.**

Lowrie, W. W., Private, was captured April 26, 1865, at Greenville. [17]*Wiley Lowry reported to the regimental medical unit with gonorrhea three times in 1864: On February 15, February 17, and March 4.*

Lowry, L., Private, enlisted December 27, 1861, Jefferson County.

MacRae, Joseph, Private, died January 25, 1862, leaving father, John, of Lowndes County.

Maher, Patrick, Private, 5'8, lived in Wellsborough, New York. [17]*He reported to the regimental medical unit March 30, 1864, diagnosis was acute dysentery.* Captured July 4, 1864 near Chattahoochie, Georgia, he was imprisoned at Camp Douglas, Illinois, where he was paroled May 15, 1865. Also spelled **Mahon, Magher.**

Manning, Thomas, Private, was working as brick layer during January 1862.

Marlow, Daniel, Private, enlisted September 24, 1862, at Montgomery. He was hospitalized during June 1862. [17]*He reported to the regimental medical unit twice in 1864. On March 19, the diagnosis was feb int tert, and on April 20, feb int quotid. The hospital records indicate that he was killed on the field on July 28, 1864, at the battle of Ezra Church, near Atlanta.* Also spelled **Marler, Mailar, Marlar.**

Martin, Henry, Private, was captured April 6, 1862, Shiloh, Tennessee. He was imprisoned at Camp Dennison, Ohio, where he died May 17, 1862, of a gunshot wound, buried in lot 1. [10]*It is also recorded that he died at Camp Chase, Ohio, May 17, 1862. He was buried in lot number 2143.* Also spelled **Henry Mastin.**

[17]Martin, J. M., *Private, reported to the regimental medical unit February 24, 1864, diagnosis was acute rheum.*

Martin, William J., Private, enlisted August 14, 1862, at Camp Watts. [17]*He reported to the regimental medical unit four times in 1864. On April 27, the diagnosis was chronic rheumatism, on august 9, acute diarrhea, on September 6, acute rheumatism, and on November 3, acute rheum.* Captured December 15, 1864, at Nashville, he was imprisoned at Camp Chase, Ohio. Also listed as **W. J., J. W. Martin.**

Mastin, Peter B. Jr., 1st Lieutenant, was hospitalized during June 1862. [30]*He resigned when the regiment moved to Mobile.* July 18, 1863, his father submitted a request that Peter Mastin Jr. be appointed colonel and given command of a regiment. See letter in compiled service records for Peter Mastin Jr.

Matthews, Albert Timothy, Sergeant, enlisted September 17, 1861, at Montgomery, and was discharged July 5, 1862. [20]*He was born September 16, 1834, in Covington, Newton County, Georgia. He was living in Coffee County in 1907.*

McCampbell, J., 2nd Lieutenant, enlisted January 1, 1863, Murphreesboro, Tennessee. He was paroled at Greensboro, North Carolina April 1865.

McCann, G. W., Private, enlisted November 6, 1861, at Montgomery. He was a telegraph operator at Pensacola, Florida, in January 1862 and in Artesia, Mississippi, in June 1862.

McCarthy, Charles, Private, enlisted June 1863, at Mobile. A tailor, he was born in 1834, Ireland. He was discharged August 17, 1863.

McCarver, George W., Private, enlisted December 27, 1861, at Greenville. He was hospitalized during June 1862. He transferred to Company B 58th Alabama.

McClentick, Robert, Private, enlisted December 8, 1862, at Mobile.

McCormack, Ben, Private, enlisted June 18, 1863, at Mobile. He was 6'2 and born in 1827 in Pinkno, Alabama. [17]*He reported to the regimental medical unit on November 3 1864, diagnosis was acute diarrhea. He was moved to the general hospital November 14.* Also listed as **D. B. McCormick.**

McCrae, Joseph, Private, died in the hospital January 25, 1862.

McCreight, J. O., Private, enlisted August 5, 1862, Camp Watts. He was hospitalized in the summer of 1863. [17]*He reported to the regimental medical unit on June 21, 1864, diagnosis acute diarrhea.* He was paroled at Talladega, May 23, 1865.

McCreight, Robert A., Private, enlisted August 20, 1862, at Camp Watts. He was 5'6 and lived in Tallapoosa. [17]*He reported to the regimental medical unit on June 16, 1864, diagnosis debilitas. The next day he was sent to the general hospital. He was severely injured in the arm on July 20, 1864, probably at the battle of Peachtree Creek, Georgia. He was* *sent to the general hospital the next day.* Captured December 16, 1864, at Nashville, he was imprisoned at Camp Douglas, Illinois. Also listed as **R. R.** and **McCrite.**

McCreight, W. Y., Private, enlisted June 15, 1862, at Camp Watts. [17]*He reported to the regimental medical unit on December 23, 1863, diagnosis catarrhus. He reported to the hospital several times in 1864. On January 7, the diagnosis was acute rheum, and on April 26, neuralgia. On July 8, he was immediately sent to the general hospital, diagnosis chronic diarrhea. On August 30, the diagnosis was acute diarrhea, and in September, acute dysentery.* He was paroled May 22, 1865, Talladega. Also spelled **McCright.**

McGentry, James, Private, enlisted August 1, 1862, at Camp Watts. Suffering from wounds, he was admitted April 1, 1865, to Yandell Hospital, Meridian, Mississippi. He surrendered, as part of a detached detail, at Citronelle, Alabama. He was paroled at Gainesville, Alabama, May 1865.

McGlennon, P. M. C., Private, enlisted December 8, 1862, at Mobile.

[17]**McGinty, Jas.,** *Private, reported to the regimental medical unit June 24, 1864, diagnosis was feb int quotid, and July 2, 1864, debilitas. He was moved to the general hospital the next day.* Also *spelled* **Magintey.**

[17]**McGintey, Thomas,** *Private, reported to the regimental medical unit on February 3, 1864, diagnosis was ulcus. He was moved to the general hospital at Spring Hill in Mobile two days later.*

McHugh, John, Private, enlisted September 17, 1861, at Montgomery. Also spelled **McCugh.**

McKay, T. J., Private, enlisted February 1, 1863, at Montgomery. [17]*He reported to the regimental medical unit on July 28, 1864, after sustaining a slight wound to his right shoulder at the battle of Ezra Church near Atlanta. He was sent to the general hospital on July 31st. He was severely injured in the left knee on November 30, 1864, at the battle of Franklin, Tennessee.* He was captured December 18, 1864, at Franklin, and was moved to a Nashville hospital. He died February 27, 1865, and was buried in lot number 12283, Nashville City Cemetery. His widow was Sarah A. McKay. Also listed as **Thomas J. McKel, McKey, Mackey.**

McLellan, Charles W., Junior Master Sergeant, enlisted October 13, 1861, at Mobile. He transferred to the 17th from the 21st Alabama. He was paroled April 20, 1865, Greensboro, North Carolina.

McMann, William, Private, enlisted December 21, 1862, at Mobile.

McMillin, Charles B., Private, enlisted at Montgomery September 17, 1861. [17]*He reported to the regimental medical unit on January 20, 1864, diagnosis was phlegmon, and on February 1, furumculus. He was* killed July 20, 1864, at the battle of Peachtree Creek near Atlanta. Also spelled **McMillan, McMillen.**

McMillan, James G., Private, died in the hospital January 2, 1862.

[18]**McName, William,** Private, was listed in September 1863 as 46, black eyes, black hair, fair complexion, 5'9, a bricklayer, and a deserter.

Measles, J. A., Private, enlisted March 12, 1862, at Greenville.

Mickler, W. C., Private, enlisted February 20, 1862, at Elba, Alabama. He was hospitalized January 15, 1865, at Meridian, Mississippi, with a wound. He was paroled at Greensboro, North Carolina, April 1865. Also listed as **C. W. Michell.**

Miller, Edward C., Private, enlisted September 17, 1861. He was 5'10 and born in 1839 in Montgomery, father James. He was placed on sick furlough on January 9, 1862, for 20 days. He died January 12, 1862. Miller's service record includes a furlough permit and a letter to his father from Colonel J. W. Watts.

Milner, W. J., Major, was paroled at Greensboro, North Carolina, April 20, 1865.

Mings, James W., Private, enlisted September 30, 1861, at Montgomery. He suffered a slight head wound at Shiloh, Tennessee, in April 1862. [17]*He reported to the regimental medical unit three times in 1864. On March 19, the diagnosis was morbi cutis, on June 18, feb int tert, and on June 27, anemia.* He was severely wounded (left side) July 28, at the battle of Ezra Church. He was moved to the general hospital on July 31. He was killed September 18, 1864, at Forsyth, Georgia and [34]*is buried in Forsyth Cemetery, Confederate section, Forsyth, Georgia.*

Monfee, Francis, Private, enlisted September 17, 1861, at Montgomery. He was an orderly to Lieutenant Colonel Ryan. [17]*He reported to the regimental medical unit twice in 1864; on March 28, diagnosis was gonorrhea, and on April 2, syphilis prim.* Captured July 4, 1864, Chattahoochie, Georgia, he was imprisoned at Camp Douglas, Illinois, where he died of smallpox, December 11, 1864. Also spelled **Montue, Morfee.**

Monk, R. S., Private, enlisted September 15, 1862, at Camp Watts. [17]*He reported to the regimental medical unit on January 4, 1864, diagnosis was abscessus. He reported to the regimental medical unit on August 9, 1864, diagnosis was acute dysentery.* Also listed as **R. F., R. T. Monk.**

[17]**Montgomery, John,** *was wounded twice in 1864. On July 28 at the battle of Ezra Church, he was slightly wounded in the left knee. He was sent to the general hospital on July 31. He was severely wounded in the left hand on November 30 at the battle of Franklin, Tennessee.* Note: this may be John Montgomery listed in Company A.

[18]**Moody, A. C.,** *Private, was listed in September 1863 as 36, dark eyes, brown hair, fair complexion, 6'4, a blacksmith, and a deserter.*

[18]**Moody, W.**, Private, was listed in September 1863 as 20, gray eyes, dark hair, fair complexion, 5'8, a farmer, and a deserter.

Moore, W. H., Sergeant, enlisted September 17, 1861, at Montgomery. [17]He was wounded twice in 1864. In May, probably at the battle of Resaca, Georgia, he was severely injured in his hand. On November 30 at the battle of Franklin, Tennessee, he was slightly wounded in the neck. He was paroled May 1, 1865, Greensboro, North Carolina. He was promoted to first lieutenant. Also listed as **W. T.**

[17]**Morris, W. F.**, Private, reported to the regimental medical unit on June 13, diagnosis was acute diarrhea. He was moved to the general hospital on June 14. Note: This may be William Morris listed in Company B.

Moseley, William, Private, sustained a wound through his lung. Captured at Shiloh, Tennessee, he was imprisoned at Camp Dennison, Ohio, where he died April 27, 1862.

Moseley, William H., Private, sustained a stomach wound at Shiloh, Tennessee, April 1862, and was reported missing.

Mothershead, W. Y., Private, enlisted February 21, 1863, at Montgomery. He died September 2, 1864, at the hospital in Macon, Georgia.

[1]**Mothershed, David B.**, Private, was born September 14, 1832, Pike County. He was granted a disability discharge in October 1862. He was living in Petry, Crenshaw County, in 1907. [17]He suffered a severe wound to his leg on July 20, at the battle of Peachtree Creek, near Atlanta. He was moved to the general hospital on July 21.

Murphy, Samuel P., Private, was 6', a farmer, and born in 1842, Chambers County. [17]He reported to the regimental medical unit three times in 1864. On February 1, the diagnosis was odontalgia. On March 11, his illness was rubeola. The next day he was sent to the hospital at Spring Hill, Alabama. On April 1, the diagnosis was debilitas. The next day he was granted a 20 day furlough. Service Records for Samuel Pettis.

Mustin, William, Private, enlisted February 4, 1863, at Montgomery. [17]He is listed on the regimental medical unit records five times in 1864. On March 9, the diagnosis was feb int quotid and on April 9, feb int tert. On June 3, the diagnosis was acute dysentery, and he was sent to the general hospital the next day. He suffered a slight wound to his left calf on July 4. The wound was dressed on the field. He was then sent to the general hospital. He was listed as a farmer and 38 years old. On November 5, the diagnosis was acute rheum. He was sent to the general hospital on November 16. He was paroled at Greensboro, North Carolina, April 1865. **Also spelled Muston.**

Naftel, Albert S., Private, was discharged April 22, 1863.

COMPANY F

Nordhausen, Adolph, Corporal, enlisted October 5, 1861, at Montgomery. [17]*He reported to the regimental medical unit January 7, 1864, diagnosis ulcus, and February 2, 1864, diagnosis chronic ulcus.* He was hospitalized February 14, 1864, at Mobile and then sent to Greenville. He was hospitalized August 15, 1864, at Macon, Georgia. Captured December 18, 1864, at Franklin, Tennessee, he was imprisoned at Camp Douglas, Illinois. He took oath of allegiance, March 29, 1865.

Norman, W. R., Private, enlisted May 30, 1864, at Montgomery. He was paroled at Greensboro, North Carolina, April 1865.

O'Brien, Andrew, Captain, was elected September 17, 1861. He was granted 10 days leave, June 26, 1862. [17]*He reported to the regimental medical unit on January 4, 1864, diagnosis contusio. He suffered a severe wound to his left foot and his right ankle on July 28, 1864.* He was placed on sick furlough July 29, 1864, after being wounded near Lovejoy Station, Georgia.

O'Brian, R., Private, [17]*reported to the regimental medical unit June 11, 1864, diagnosis scorbutis. He suffered a severe flesh wound (left hip) August 11, 1864. He was moved to the general hospital the next day.*

O'Brian, Thomas S., Sergeant, enlisted at Tupelo, Mississippi, June 22, 1862. He was 5'10, born 1840, and was from Charleston, South Carolina. He was appointed second lieutenant June 26, 1862. [17]*He reported to the regimental medical unit twice in January 1864, on the 12th the diagnosis was feb int tert, and on the 30th feb int quotid.* Captured July 20, 1864, at the battle of Peachtree Creek near Atlanta, he was imprisoned at Johnson Island and paroled June 15, 1865, Sanduskey, Ohio. Note: OWR. Vol. 38-3, pg. 942: listed as Asst. Inspector General. Also listed as **F. S. O'Brien.**

O'Connor, E., Private, suffered a severe neck wound at Shiloh, Tennessee, April 1862. He was listed as missing.

Odom, L. S., Private, enlisted September 21, 1861, at Montgomery. He was 5'6 and detailed as a nurse on muster roll for January-February 1862. He was listed as missing at Tupelo during the summer of 1862. [17]*He reported to the regimental medical unit December1 and 21, 1863, diagnosis pneumonia.* He was paroled at the end of the war. Also spelled **Odam**

Ogburne, Dennis, Private, enlisted October 7, 1862, Chattanooga.

O'Hara, Patrick, Private, was 5'5 and born in 1829, Galway County, Ireland. [17]*He reported to the regimental medical unit on June 13, 1864, diagnosis acute diarrhea. He was sent to the general hospital the next day.* Captured December 17, 1864, at Franklin, Tennessee, he was imprisoned at Camp Douglas, Illinois. Also spelled **O'Hare.**

Ollman, Lewis, Private, enlisted December 18, 1862, at Mobile. [18]*In 1863 he was listed as 45, hazel eyes, black hair, dark complexion, 5'9, a carpenter, and a deserter.*

[17]**Owen, Hill,** *Private, reported to the regimental medical unit February 11, 1864, diagnosis was paronychia.* This may be **Thomas H. Owen.**

Owen, James Madison, Private, enlisted at Montgomery September 17, 1861. [17]*He reported to the regimental medical unit June 8, 1864, diagnosis acute dysentery. He moved to the general hospital the next day.* Captured December 15, 1864, Nashville, he was imprisoned at Camp Douglas, Illinois. He mustered into 5th US Volunteer Infantry. [1]*He was born July 5, 1843, at Sandy Ridge, Lowndes County. In 1907 he was living in Montgomery.*

Owen, Thomas F., Private, enlisted September 14, 1863, at Mobile. He was 5'11, a farmer, and born in 1845 in Montgomery County. [17]*He reported to the regimental medical unit on February 27, 1864, diagnosis paronychia. He reported again on April 1, diagnosis debilitas, and was granted a 20 day furlough. On July 13, the diagnosis was phlegmon. He was slighted wounded in the right arm on July 20, at the battle of Peachtree Creek near Atlanta. He was moved to the general hospital the next day.* He was paroled May 20, 1865. Is this **T. F.** or **T. H Owen**?

Parham, H. T., Private, was placed on sick furlough January 17, 1862, for 20 days and sent to Montgomery. He died in 1862 leaving widow Elizabeth Parham.

Pebworth, T. J., Private, was discharged December 17, 1861.

Pettus, Samuel, Private, enlisted November 1, 1863, at Mobile. [17]*He reported to the regimental medical unit December 8, 1863, diagnosis feb int quotid. He reported to the hospital four times in 1864. On March 21, the diagnosis was febris remitt. He was sent to the general hospital at Greenville on March 23. On June 20, the diagnosis was feb remitt. He was sent to the general hospital the same day. On June 22, his complaint was feb int tert. On September 25, the diagnosis was pneumonia. He was moved to the general hospital the next day.* He was at the surrender at Greensboro, North Carolina, April 26, 1865. [37]*He was born October 12, 1846, in Montgomery. In 1921 he was living in Hope Hull and stated that he fought at Resaca, New Hope Church, Kennesaw Mountain, Peachtree Creek and Atlanta.*

Pizzala, Nicholas, Private, [42]*enlisted January 29, 1862, Camp Gladden, Florida.* He was captured February 16, 1862, at Fort Donelson. Captured Pittsburg Landing, Tennessee April 7, 1862, he was listed at Camp Douglas, Illinois August 15, 1862. Member of Lewis Guards. He was sent to Vicksburg for exchange July 6, 1862. He took oath of allegiance on September 1862, signed Niccola Pizzala. Also listed as **Nicholas Fitzallen, N. Pittzeller(Co. A), N. Pizzeler, Nichoas Pitzeller, N. Pizallo, Nicholas Pozzola.** Note: This is more than one individual here.

Pomels, H, Private, enlisted February 28, 1863, at Mobile.

[17]***Radford, George T.****, Private, reported to the regimental medical unit twice with a diagnosis of feb int tert, December 17, 1863, and October 9, 1864. On October 15, he moved to the general hospital. He reported to the hospital January 11, 1864, diagnosis catarrhus. Also spelled* ***Rodford.***

Rany, B., Private, was admitted to Way Hospital, Meridian, Mississippi, after the retreat from Nashville. Wounded, he was placed on furlough January 13, 1865.

Reese, W. N., Private, enlisted December 27, 1861, Jefferson County. He was discharged July 5, 1862. He transferred to the 58th Alabama.

Reese, J. P., Private, enlisted December 27, 1861, Jefferson County. He was 5'11, a farmer, and born in 1840 in Blount County. He died during 1862, leaving father, Jesse. Also spelled **Reice.**

Richberg, R. E., Private.

Rivers, Frank, Private, enlisted September 24, 1862, at Montgomery. He was listed as deserter September 29, 1862, Mobile.

Robertson, A. F. E., elected 1st Lieutenant September 17, 1861. Captured at Shiloh, Tennessee, he died of wounds on April 24, 1862. [10]***Archis Robinson****, 1st Lieutenant, died April 29, 1862, at Camp Chase, Ohio.*

[18]***Robertson, John****, Private, was listed in September 1863 as 45, blue eyes, dark hair, fair complexion, 5'9, a laborer, and a deserter.*

Robertson, Edward, Private, enlisted July 7, 1863, at Mobile.

Rooney, Bernard, Private, enlisted May 20, 1863, Meridian, Mississippi. He was born in 1815 in Ireland, a gardener, and 5'7. [17]*He reported to the regimental medical unit twice in December 5, 1863. On the 15th, the diagnosis was nephritis, and on the 28th, ebrietas. He also reported to the hospital four times in 1864. January 1, the diagnosis was lumbago, January 2, 1864, lumbago, March 10, feb int quotid, and June 2, contusio.* After the retreat from Nashville, he was hospitalized January 13, 1865, at Meridian, Mississippi. He was paroled May 10, 1865, Meridian. See Service Records for Krimmell. Also spelled **Rhoney, Roaney, Rany, Roney, Rony.**

Roper, V. B., Private, enlisted December 27, 1861, Jefferson County. He transferred to the 58th Alabama Company C.

Royal, Hardy A., Private, enlisted July 23, 1863, at Mobile. A farmer he was born in 1845 in Lowndes County where he lived. [17]*He reported to the regimental medical unit on June 29, 1864, diagnosis feb int tert. He* reported sick July 8, diagnosis feb int quotid. He was moved to the general hospital the same day. Captured December 15, 1864 in Nashville, he was imprisoned at Camp Douglas, Illinois. [1]Born July 22, 1845, Lowndes County, he was paroled at Camp Douglas, Illinois, May 1865. His home was in Lapine, Crenshaw County, in 1907. [15]He is buried at Rocky Mount Cemetery in Crenshaw County. [37]In 1921 he was living in Lapine and stated that he fought at New Hope Church, Peachtree Creek and Franklin.

Rushton, Basil Manly, Private, was discharged March 9, 1863. He died February 23, 1864 in a Montgomery hospital. [30]He was born 1827, Edgefield County, South Carolina, to Moses and Sarah Posey Rushton. His wife was Sarah Elizabeth Urquhart.

Rushton, James H., Sergeant, was at the surrender at Greensboro, North Carolina, April 1865. [30]He was in 1840 to Moses and Sarah Posey Rushton. He died March 10, 1884.

Rushton, William H. P., Private, enlisted January 27, 1863, at Montgomery. [17]He reported to the regimental medical unit on December 23, 1863, diagnosis odontalgia. He reported to the hospital again on April 23, 1864, with pneumonia. He was moved to the general hospital two days later. Captured December 21, 1864 at Columbia, Tennessee, he was imprisoned at Camp Chase, Ohio, [10]where he died February 3, 1865 and is buried in lot number 1026. [30]He was born in 1835, Georgia, to Moses and Sarah Posey Rushton.

Russell, T. J., Private, enlisted March 12, 1862, at Greenville,

Sawyers, C. D., Private, enlisted March 13, 1862, at Greenville.

Scaife, Joel, Private, died February 17, 1864, of congestive chill. [17]The regimental medical unit records indicate that he was sick January 25, 1864, diagnosis ulcus. He was sick again February 9, diagnosis feb remitt, and was moved to the general hospital at Mobile February 14. **Joel Seefee**, a Confederate soldier, was buried at Magnolia Cemetery in Mobile, row 11, grave 32.

Scarborough, Hardy, Private, enlisted February 25, 1863, at Mobile. [18]In September 1863 he was listed as 33, black eyes, black hair, fair complexion, 5'6, a farmer, and a deserter.

Scogin, E. B., Corporal, enlisted March 13, 1862, at Greenville. He was paroled at Greensboro, North Carolina, April 1865.

Scott, James W., Private, was discharged December 5, 1861.

Sharp, Archie, F., Private, was hospitalized May 1864 at St. Mary's Hospital in LaGrange, Georgia. [17]He reported to the regimental medical unit on June 21, 1864, diagnosis feb int quotid, and on August 16, diagnosis acute diarrhea. He was paroled May 20, 1865 in Montgomery.

[17]**Sharpe, F. H.**, Private, reported to the regimental medical unit twice in 1864. March 29, the diagnosis was scabies and September 11, acute dysentery.

Sharp, James M., Sergeant, enlisted September 17, 1861, at Montgomery. During July/August 1863, he was placed in charge of drivers for the battery. [17]He reported to the regimental medical unit on February 25, 1864, diagnosis feb int tert. He was paroled May 1865 in Montgomery.

Sharp, John O., Private, enlisted September 17, 1861, at Montgomery. He was assigned extra duty as driver for a battery. [17]He reported to the regimental medical unit on December 21, 1863, diagnosis feb int tert. He reported to the regimental medical unit five times in 1864. January 9, diagnosis was acute diarrhea, and he was moved to the general hospital on January 20. March 14, the diagnosis was furunculous, March 19, syph consec, August 11, neuralgia, and August 16, a wound to the left foot. The wound was received during the siege of Atlanta. He was a member of the Crenshaw County Confederate Veterans' Association in 1890.

Sharp, Moses, [17]reported to the regimental medical unit on February 10, 1864, with meningitis. Two days later he was moved to the hospital at Spring Hill in Mobile. He died February 14, 1864, inflammation of brain.

[17]**Sharpe, T. B.**, Private, reported to the regimental medical unit April 2, 1864, diagnosis scabies. He was sent to the general hospital April 18.

Shaver, Jacob, Private, enlisted July 5, 1862, at Mobile. He was 5'6, born in 1841 in Germany, a printer from Montgomery. [17]He reported to the regimental medical unit three times in 1864. January 9, the diagnosis was feb int quotid, March 24, acute dysentery, and June 6, acute diarrhea. He was sent to the general hospital June 9. He was severely wounded in the left cheek July 2, 1864. The ball was extracted at the brigade hospital, and he was then sent on to Atlanta. At that time he was listed as a farmer and 27 years old. Captured December 15, 1864 in Nashville, he was imprisoned at Camp Douglas, Illinois where he applied for the oath of allegiance January 1865.

Shaver, W. H., Private, 5'6, was from Montgomery County. On July 14, 1864, at Dalton, Georgia, he applied for medical furlough for 7 weeks to Olustee, Pike County.

Shea, John, Private, enlisted October 25, 1862, at Mobile. He was 5'7, a laborer, and born in 1817 in Kerry County, Ireland. [17]He died from a head wound May 1864, probably at the battle of Resaca, Georgia.

[18]**Shelby, Hugh**, Private, was listed in September 1863 as 45, blue eyes, gray hair, fair complexion, 5'8, a tailor, and a deserter from the Confederate Army.

Shell, Thomas Jepthia, Private, [20]*enlisted February 1862 in Montgomery.* [10]*He was born March 25, 1830, near Madison in Morgan County.* [17]*He reported to the regimental medical unit March 11, 1864, diagnosis was anasarca.* He was paroled May 20, 1865, Montgomery. [20]*He was living in Iverness, Bullock County in 1907.*

Sheets, Lewis T., Private, enlisted December 27, 1861, Jefferson County. He was 5'11, a farmer, and born in 1839 in Jefferson County. He died July 1, 1862, [6]*in Okolona, Mississippi,* leaving wife Malisa.

Shields, Hugh, Private, enlisted December 25, 1862, Obanonville.

Shoemaker, W. H., Private, enlisted September 17, 1861, at Montgomery. He was placed on sick furlough January 1862 for 20 days and was sent to Morgan County. He was discharged July 5, 1862.

Shunackel, William, Musician, enlisted September 17, 1861. [17]***William Shoenacker**, musician, was wounded and reported to the regimental medical unit on July 28, 1864, after the battle at Ezra Church.* Also listed as **Shonocker.**

Sill, John, Private, was captured December 15, 1864, at Nashville. He was imprisoned at Camp Chase, Ohio, where he was paroled May 1865. He was 5'6 and lived in Mobile.

Skipper, Morgan, Private, was hospitalized June 6, 1864 with gunshot wound to his hand ([17]*severe injury to his thumb and finger*). He was furloughed to Montgomery on June 10, 1864. His service records are almost unreadable.

Skipper, William, Private, enlisted at Montgomery. He was promoted to second lieutenant on September 16, 1861.

Smith, A. J., Private, enlisted February 20, 1862, at Elba, Alabama. He was paroled at Greensboro, North Carolina, April 1865.

Smith, John, Private, enlisted October 27, 1862, at Camp Watts. [18]*In 1863 he was described as 46 years old, gray eyes, gray hair, fair complexion, 5'7, a steamboat hand, and a deserter.*

Smyly, Robert Edwin Paul, was appointed master sergeant May 1862. He transferred to Company H, 17th Alabama November 26, 1861. He applied for lieutenancy in the artillery. He was given a letter of recommendation by Colonel Watts.

Sperry, John T., Private, enlisted December 18, 1862, at Mobile. He was arrested as deserter January 1863.

Stacy, Henry, Private, enlisted July 1, 1863, at Mobile. He was 5'4, a clerk, and born in 1845 in Montgomery County. [17]*W. H. Stacy reported to the regimental medical unit on March 16, 1864, diagnosis syph prim. He was immediately moved to the general hospital at Montgomery. He reported again to the hospital on July 4, 1864, diagnosis acute diarrhea.* He was hospitalized at Howard's Grove, Richmond, Virginia, March 12, 1865, and furloughed for 30 days March 18, 1865.

COMPANY F

[17]**Stigol, John,** Private, reported to the regimental medical unit twice during January 1864. On the 8th, the diagnosis was feb int quotid, and on the 22nd, paronychia.

Steigell, Reuben, Private, [17]reported to the regimental medical unit three times in the summer of 1864. On June 23, the diagnosis was pneumonia, on June 26, acute dysentery, and on July 1, feb int quotid. He was captured July 3, 1864, near Marietta, Georgia. He was imprisoned at Camp Douglas, Illinois. [10]He died January 12, 1865, and was listed in Company A. Also listed as **Steegel, Stegall, Stigol.**

Stewart, J. W., Private, died January 3, 1862.

Stoudenmeir, D., Private, enlisted March 8, 1861, at Elba, Alabama. He was paroled at Greensboro, North Carolina, April 1865.

Strickland, Andrew Benjamin, Private, [20]enlisted September 1862 in Mobile. [17]He reported to the regimental medical unit on February 25, 1864, diagnosis was feb int tert, and on March 26, 1864, feb int quotid. He was wounded July 28, 1864, at the battle of Ezra Church near Atlanta. The injury was a severe wound to his left arm and amputation above the wrist was required. [10]He was sent home September 7, 1864. He was paroled May 20, 1865, at Montgomery. [1]He was born near Milledgeville, Georgia, on October 10, 1826, and living in Bullock County in 1907. Note: He was also listed as a member of Company I.

Suggs, G. W., Private, enlisted October 19, 1861. He was a carpenter, 5'11, and born in 1837 in Raleigh, North Carolina.

Tankersley, J. R., Private, enlisted February 13, 1863, at Montgomery. He was paroled at Greensboro, North Carolina, April 1865.

Tarver, Hamilton, Private, was hospitalized in June 1862

Taylor, A. B., Private, enlisted December 27, 1861, Jefferson County. He was hospitalized in June 1862. He transferred to Company C 58th Alabama and was promoted to sergeant.

Taylor, J. A. J., Private, enlisted December 27, 1861, Jefferson County.

Taylor, Jesse H., Private, enlisted December 27, 1861, Jefferson County. He was 5'10, a farmer and born in 1841 in Jefferson County. He died in 1862 leaving widow Malinda Taylor. See Service Records for M. D. Hagood.

Taylor, T. B., Private, enlisted December 27, 1861, Jefferson County. He was born in 1841 in Jefferson County. He was hospitalized June 1862. He was granted a disability discharge January 1, 1863.

Taylor, W. M., Private, enlisted December 27, 1861, Jefferson County. He was hospitalized June 1862. He transferred to the 58th Alabama, Company C, and was promoted to sergeant.

Taylor, W. B., Private, enlisted September 17, 1861, at Montgomery. He was placed on sick furlough on December 20, 1861, for 20 days and sent to Montgomery County. [17]*He reported to the regimental medical unit on April 13, 1864, diagnosis feb int quotid.* He was paroled June 12, 1865, in Montgomery.

Terry, Thomas, Private, enlisted September 17, 1861, at Montgomery. [17]*He reported to the regimental medical unit on July 7, 1864, diagnosis phlegmon.* Captured December 18, 1864 at Spring Hill, Tennessee, he was imprisoned at Camp Chase, Ohio, [10]*He died at Camp Chase March 21, 1865, and is buried in lot 1729.*

Thomas, W. O., Private, [42]*died January 23, 1862, in the hospital while stationed at Pensacola.*

Thompson, George P., Private, enlisted March 28, 1862, Corinth. He was 5'9, a farmer, and born in 1841 in Autauga County. [17]*He reported to the regimental medical unit on February 7, 1864, diagnosis was scabies, and was sent to a hospital in Mobile on the 14th.* He was hospitalized at Montgomery on August 12, 1864. [17]*He also reported to the regimental medical unit on November 2, 1864, diagnosis was acute diarrhea.* He was paroled June 5, 1865.

Thompson, John E., Private, enlisted March 28, 1862, Corinth. He was 6'1, a farmer, and born in 1844 in Lowndes County.

Thorn, Edward, Private, enlisted September 17, 1862, at Montgomery.

Tichenor, J. T., was appointed Chaplain October 2, 1861. He served heroically at the battle of Shiloh, April 7 and 8, 1862. He resigned May 24, 1862. See letter of resignation in his service record. Later became president of Auburn University.

Torpey, John, Drummer, enlisted December 8, 1862, at Mobile. [18]*In September 1863 he was described as 19 years old, gray eyes, dark hair, fair complexion, 5 foot, a trader, and a deserter.* Captured July 4, 1864 near Kennesaw Mountain, Georgia, he was imprisoned at Camp Douglas, Illinois. He was transferred to New Orleans for exchange on May 4, 1865. Also spelled **Tobery, Tobey.**

Truss, C. C., Private, enlisted December 27, 1861, Jefferson County. In June 1862 he was occupied repairing muskets at Iuka. He transferred to the 58th Alabama, Company C.

Tucker, J. M., Private, was granted a medical furlough for 20 days and sent to Montgomery on January 13, 1862. He died of a stomach wound received at Shiloh, Tennessee on April 6, 1862.

Vann, E. T., Private, enlisted May 28, 1862, at Corinth. He was 6 foot, a farmer, and born in 1825 in Jefferson County. He was hospitalized June 1862. He was granted a disability discharge December 31, 1862.

Vann, S. T., Private, enlisted December 27, 1861, Jefferson County. He was hospitalized June 1862.

Waldo, Charles M., Private, enlisted February 28, 1862, at Pensacola, Florida. He was 5'6, a tailor, and born in 1828 in New York, New York. [17]*He reported to the regimental medical unit December 17, 1863, diagnosis ebrietas, and June 20, 1864, diagnosis acute diarrhea.* Captured July 1, 1864, Marietta, Georgia, he was imprisoned at Camp Morton, Indiana, where he was paroled May 23, 1865.

Walker, Daniel W., Private, was captured December 15, 1864 in Nashville. He was imprisoned at Camp Douglas, Illinois, where he was paroled May 1865.

[17]***Walker, William,*** *Private, reported to the regimental medical unit December 11, 1863, diagnosis was acute rheumatism. He reported three times in 1864. On January 20, diagnosis was vulnus inscism. On July 28, he suffered a slight wound in his right side at the battle of Ezra Church near Atlanta. He was sent to the general hospital on July31. He also reported to the hospital on November 5, diagnosis acute dysentery.*

Ward, A. B., Private, was hospitalized June 1862.

[17]***Ward, James,*** *Private, reported to the regimental medical unit on December 2, 1863, diagnosis was catarrhus. He was moved to the general hospital December 4.*

Ward, Tarleton, Private, [17]*reported to the regimental medical unit on February 7, 1864, diagnosis was ambustio.* He surrendered at Meridian, Mississippi, and was paroled May 1865 at Mobile.

Ward, W. T., Private, was hospitalized June 1862.

Ware, A. B., Private, enlisted December 27, 1861, Jefferson County. He transferred to the 58th Alabama, Company C, where he was promoted to corporal.

Ware, W. T., Private, enlisted December 27, 1861, Jefferson County. He was 5'9, a farmer, and born in 1836 in Jefferson County. He was discharged December 31, 1862.

Watson, A. F., was appointed surgeon May 6, 1862, and division surgeon July 22, 1864 at Atlanta. He was furloughed from the hospital July 22, 1864. Also listed as **S. A. Watson**

Way, David, Private, was hospitalized during the Atlanta campaign July 24, 1864, with wound to his left lung.

Webb, C. C., Private, enlisted September 17, 1861, at Montgomery. [17]*He reported to the regimental medical unit on April 29, 1864, diagnosis acute dysentery. He suffered a severe wound (right thigh) August 11 during the battle of Atlanta and was sent to the general hospital the next day.* He was paroled at Greensboro, North Carolina, April 1865.

Webb, W. H., Private, enlisted September 17, 1861, at Montgomery. He was placed on sick furlough January 4, 1862, for 20 days and sent to Pike County. [17]*He reported to the regimental medical unit December*

11, 1863, diagnosis was morbi cutis, and on April 16, 1864, diagnosis catarrhus.

Welsh, James, Private, enlisted March 20, 1863, at Mobile. [17]He was severely wounded on both sides July 20. The regimental medical unit records indicate that he was left on the field at the battle of Peachtree Creek near Atlanta.

[17]**Whisker, D. W.,** Private, reported to the regimental medical unit on March 19, 1864, diagnosis was feb in tert.

[17]**White, G. D.,** Private, reported to the regimental medical unit on December 2, 1863, diagnosis catarrhus.

White, J. C., Private, enlisted August 15, 1862, at Camp Watts. [17]He reported to the regimental medical unit March 25, 1864, diagnosis acute dysentery.

Williams, A., Private, enlisted February 20, 1862, at Elba, Alabama.

Williams, C. W., Private, was furloughed for 15 days March 6 in either 1863 or 1864.

Williams, Henry C., Private, enlisted September 17, 1862, at Montgomery. [17]He reported to the regimental medical unit four times in 1864. On February 28 and March 3, the diagnosis was scabies. On July 7, the diagnosis was feb remitt and on August 13, feb int quotid. Captured December 15, 1864, in Nashville, he was imprisoned at Camp Douglas, Illinois where he was paroled June 1865. He lived in Montgomery County.

Williams, Isaiah, Corporal, was discharged December 17, 1861.

Wilson, M. W., Corporal, enlisted September 17, 1861, at Montgomery. He was 5'9, a carpenter, and born in 1833 in Truro, Nova Scotia. He received a disability discharge June 12, 1862.

Wooten, J. T., Captain, enlisted February 20, 1862, at Elba, Alabama.

[10]**Worley, W. H.,** Private, died April, 27, 1862 while imprisoned at Camp Chase, Ohio, and was buried in lot number 2129.

Yarbrough, Henry Pleasant, Private, enlisted September 6, 1863, at Mobile. He was 5'8, a farmer, and born in 1845 in Autauga County. [17]He reported to the regimental medical unit three times in 1864. March 22, diagnosis was rubeola, April 28 and June 18, acute diarrhea. March 23, he was moved to the general hospital at Greenville. [30]After the battle of Franklin, he remained in Franklin with the burial detail. When he arrived in Tupelo after the retreat from Tennessee, he was furloughed home to Montgomery where he remained for a long convalescing period. He was paroled June 7, 1865 in Montgomery. [1]He was born June 4, 1845, in Autaugaville. He was detailed as a sharpshooter. In 1907 his residence was in Montgomery. [15]He was buried at Rocky Mount Cemetery in Crenshaw County, 1845 - 1934. He was a member of the Crenshaw County Confederate Veterans' Association in 1890.

Appendix VIII. Company G

Anderson, G. W., Private, enlisted June 17, 1863, Calhoun County. [17]*He reported to the regimental medical unit on July 7, 1864, diagnosis was acute dysentery, and on August 18 and September 6, 1864, acute diarrhea.* He was at the surrender at Greensboro, North Carolina, April 26, 1865.

Anderson, J. P., Private, enlisted December 27, 1861, Jefferson County. He was 5'6 and born in 1845 in Jefferson County. [12]*He was hospitalized during the summer of 1862.* He died July 5, 1864, at Penn Hospital, Georgia.

Austin, D. W., Private, enlisted February 28, 1862, at O'Bannonville, Florida. He was hospitalized during the summer of 1862.

Barker, Jesse M., Private, enlisted September 10, 1861, at Montgomery. [42]*He was on special duty as a wagoner January 1862.* His home was in Barbour County. [12]*The muster roll for July-August 1862 listed Barker as on detached service.* [17]*He reported to the regimental medical unit on July 16, 1864, diagnosis feb int quotid.* He was at the surrender at Greensboro, North Carolina, April 26, 1865.

Baton, J. C., Private, enlisted September 7, 1862, Coffee County. [17]*He reported to the regimental medical unit December 19, 1863, diagnosis was pneumonia, and June 13, 1864, acute diarrhea.* He died July 7, 1864, at the hospital in Macon, Georgia.

Benton, G. B., Private.

[18]**Boon, Jere**, *Private, was described in September 1863 as 32 years old, gray eyes, light hair, fair complexion, 5'2, a painter, and a deserter from the Confederate Army.*

Broadwaters, Thomas J., Private, enlisted at Montgomery September 10, 1861. [17]*He reported to the regimental medical unit June 10, 1864, with acute dysentery and was sent to the general hospital the next day. On July 28, 1864, he suffered a slight wound (left thigh) at the battle of Ezra Church near Atlanta. He was sent to the general hospital on the 31st.* He was at the surrender at Greensboro, North Carolina, April 26, 1865.

[17]**Brown, Jackson**, *Private, reported to the regimental medical unit three times in 1864: on June 20, diagnosis was debilitas, on June 21, feb int quotid, and in September, debilitas.*

Brown, Thomas, Private, 5'5, enlisted October 20, 1862, at Mobile. [17]*He reported to the regimental medical unit July 6, 1864, diagnosis was feb int tert. He was transferred to the general hospital the next day.* After leaving the Confederate Army, he took the oath of allegiance to the Union October 25, 1864. [1]*His home was in Mountain Creek, Alabama.*

Bryant, W. S., Private, enlisted August 10, 1862, Russell County. [17]*He reported to the regimental medical unit on September 13, 1864, diagnosis was feb int tert.* He was at the surrender at Greensboro, North Carolina, April 26, 1865. Also spelled **Briant**.

Bullington, James O., Private, [17] *reported to the regimental medical unit on February 2, 1864 with rubeola. He was sent to the general hospital at Spring Hill near Mobile three days later. He returned to the regimental medical unit June 16, 1864,* after he was wounded (left hand) during the fighting at Kennesaw Mountain. The next day he moved to Ocmulgee Hospital, Macon, Georgia.

Burton, G. D, Musician, enlisted October 1, 1861, at Montgomery.

Burton, R. J., Private, [17]*reported to the regimental medical unit June 25, 1864, diagnosis was feb int quotid, and was sent to the general hospital the next day.*

Bussey, James C., Corporal, enlisted September 10, 1861, at Montgomery. He was 5'9 and born in 1825 in South Carolina. [12]*He was hospitalized during the summer of 1862.* [30]*He died in 1903 and was buried in the Texas State Cemetery, Austin, Texas.*

Bussey, J. M., Private, [12]*enlisted September 10, 1861.* [42]*He was granted a 15-day furlough January 1, 1862, and a 20-day furlough January 14, 1862, and sent to Uchee, Russell County.* He was 5'8, born in 1841 in South Carolina, and died April 1862 at Shiloh, Tennessee.

Calle, Cornelius, Private, enlisted October 2, 1862, at Mobile. He was hired by R. W. Johnson as a substitute. [17]*He reported to the regimental medical unit November 9, 1864, diagnosis pneumonia.* Also spelled **Call**.

Carbo, W. M., Private.

Carden, William Tarentine, Private, enlisted at Montgomery September 10, 1861. *He was wounded at Shiloh, Tennessee, in April 1862.* He was hospitalized during June 1862. [12]*He was listed as sick in the hospital on the muster roll for July-August 1862.* [26]*He was discharged at Corinth, Mississippi, June 1863.* Note: he was probably discharged in June 1862. He was paroled in Columbus, Mississippi, May 25, 1865. [26]*He was born January 29, 1840, in Russell County. He was living in Silligent, Lamar County in 1907.* [30]*His parents were Randolph and Elizabeth Thompson Cardin. His wife was Sarah Sandlin. He died December 17, 1919.* [30]*He applied for a pension in 1893 when he stated that he was wounded in the head, hip and side. His wife applied for a pension in 1920. She stated that William T. was visiting in Oklahoma when he died.*

Carley, J., Private, died July 5, 1862, Camp Douglas, Illinois. Note: He was probably captured at Shiloh, Tennessee, in April 1862.

COMPANY G

Carlisle, M. J., Private, a farmer, was born in 1833 in Talbot County, Georgia. He was granted a disability discharge October 25, 1862.

Cassidy, J. L., Private, was 5'8 and born 1829 in South Carolina. He was employed as a clerk by Major General Maury. He was paroled at Greensboro, North Carolina, May 1865. See service record for David Blackman of 54th Ala.

Chadwick, Ambrose H., Private, enlisted at Montgomery September 10, 1861. His home was in Russell County. [17]*He reported to the regimental medical unit twice in 1864. On January 31, the diagnosis was catarrhus, and on June 3, acute dysentery. He moved to the general hospital on June 4th.* Captured December 15, 1864, Nashville, he was imprisoned at Camp Douglas, Illinois.

Chadwick, Augustus H., Private, [12]*enlisted September 10, 1861, Montgomery.* He was hospitalized during June 1862. He died June 1, 1862, in a hospital at Okolona, Mississippi.

Chadwick, John L., Private, enlisted September 10, 1861, at Montgomery. [17]*J. H. Chadwick reported to the regimental medical unit on July 18, 1864, diagnosis acute diarrhea.* He was paroled at Greensboro, North Carolina, May 1865.

[17]***Chadwick, R.**, Private, reported to the general hospital on August 10, 1864, with acute dysentery.* Note: This is probably either **Rufus or Rickerson**.

[17]***Chadwick, R. K.**, Private, reported to the regimental medical unit with acute diarrhea on December 21, 1863, and August 26 and September 4, 1864.* This could be **Rufus Chadwick**.

Chadwick, Rickerson, Private, enlisted at Montgomery September 10, 1861. He was 5'8, a farmer, and born in 1834 in South Carolina. He was hospitalized during August 1862. He was granted a disability discharge the same month. He died August 24, 1864, at a hospital in Lauderdale Springs, Mississippi.

Chadwick, Rufus N., Private, 5'8, enlisted November 10, 1862, Russell County where he was born in 1834. He was paroled at Greensboro, North Carolina, May 1865.

Chappell, Abram, Private, enlisted September 10, 1861, at Montgomery. He was hospitalized during June 1862. Captured December 15, 1864, Nashville, he was imprisoned at Camp Douglas, Illinois. [30]*In April 1865 he signed the Oath of Allegiance and enlisted in the 5th US Regiment. He was sent to garrison forts on the Plains. He returned to Alabama and owned land there by 1870.* He was born ca 1824 in Tennessee. He was living in Russell County, Alabama at the beginning of the war. His wife was Elizabeth Candler. Two of his sons, William and John Henry Chappell were also in the 17th. He died in 1903.

Chappell, John Henry, Private, was from Russell County. He was hospitalized for one week in Macon, Georgia, summer of 1864. [17]*He reported to the regimental medical unit four times in 1864. On June 6 and in September, the diagnosis was feb int tert. On July 1, the diagnosis was acute dysentery, and he was sent to the general hospital on July 7. On November 3, the diagnosis was acute diarrhea.* [37]*He was born May 24, 1848, near Opelika, Lee County. In 1921 he was living in Phoenix City, Alabama, and stated that he fought at Dalton, Marietta, Atlanta, and Franklin.* [30]*He was the son of Abram and Elizabeth Chappell.*

Chappell, William Jackson, Private, enlisted March 1, 1864. [1]*He lived in Avondale.* [30]*He was the son of Abram and Elizabeth Chappell. He was in 1844 in Russell County.*

Childers, E. A., Private, enlisted September 1862. He was hospitalized in Mobile during November 1862.

Clark, J. P., Sergeant, enlisted March 5, 1862, at Pensacola. A merchant, he was born in 1820 in Hartford, Connecticut. [17]*He reported to the regimental medical unit on August 6, 1864, with acute diarrhea.* He was granted a parole June 7, 1865, at Montgomery.

Clark, Richard, Private, [17]*reported to the regimental medical unit three times in the spring of 1864. On March 7, the diagnosis was rheumat chronic, on March 21, acute dysentery, on April 2; rheumat chronic, when he was sent to Demopolis to recuperates.*

Covington, W. T., Private, was discharged April 20, 1863.

Crenshaw, James E., Private, enlisted at Montgomery September 10, 1861. He was born 1838 in Henry County, Georgia. He was discharged December 1861: disability.

Cummings, Samuel James, Lieutenant, enlisted October 25, 1861. He was placed on sick leave for 10 days January 29, 1862. He was granted a disability discharge May 12, 1862. He resigned August 13, 1862, in anticipation of his appointment as adjutant on September 1, 1862. On the July and August muster roll for the 17th Alabama, he is listed as absent, attending the session of legislature. He was furloughed from the hospital (in the Atlanta area) June 1864 after being wounded. He was listed as absent due to illness August 27, 1864. From Burnt Corn in Monroe County on January 1, 1865, he submitted his resignation "on account of ill health and having been elected to the legislature."

Davis, James D., Private, enlisted September 14, 1861, at Montgomery. He was placed on medical furlough January 15, 1862, for 15 days and sent home to Uchee, Russell County, Alabama. He was discharged July 4, 1862.

Davison, John, Private, died 1863 leaving widow, Martha Davison.

Dean, C. B., Private, enlisted December 27, 1861, Jefferson County. [12]*He was hospitalized during the summer of 1862.*

Dees, John L., Private, lived in Neshoba County, Mississippi. [17]*He reported to the regimental medical unit five times in 1864. On March 31 and April 1, the diagnosis was debilitas, and he was sent to the general hospital on April 9. On June 4, the diagnosis was acute diarrhea, June 21, acute dysentery, and June 27, acute diarrhea. He was sent to the general hospital June 28. Also spelled* **Deas**

Dewett, J. R., Private, enlisted September 3, 1862, at Choctaw. [17]*He reported to the regimental medical unit three times in 1864. On January 30, the diagnosis was feb int tert. On February 2, the diagnosis was rubeola, and he was sent to the hospital at Spring Hill in Mobile on February 5. On July 4, the diagnosis was feb int quotid. Also spelled* **Dewitt.**

Dewett, William, Private, [17]*reported to the regimental medical unit three times in 1864. On January 7, the diagnosis was feb int tert, on June 23, feb int quotid, and on August 28, acute diarrhea.*

[17]**Donnigan, G. T.,** *Private, reported to the regimental medical unit on December 22, 1863, diagnosis acute diarrhea.*

Dowd, Samuel, Private, enlisted October 4, 1861, at Montgomery. He was hospitalized during June. [12]*The muster roll for July-August 1862 lists dowd as sick in the hospital.*

Dudley, J., Private, died during the war.

[17]**Dunagin, G. S.,** *Private, reported to the regimental medical unit twice in 1864. January 28, the diagnosis was opthalmia, and March 30, acute dysentery. Also spelled* **Dunnegan.**

[17]**Dunnegan, T. A.,** *Private, reported to the regimental medical unit April 28, 1864, diagnosis feb int quotid.*

Edward, E. H., Private, enlisted December 27, 1861, Jefferson County. He was hospitalized during June 1862. He transferred to the 58th Alabama, Company C.

Edwards, Ransom W., Private, enlisted December 27, 1861, Jefferson County. He was hospitalized during June 1862.

Elbern, Joseph W., Corporal, enlisted at Montgomery September 10, 1861. He was granted a medical furlough January 6, 1862, and sent home to Uchee, Russell County, Alabama, for 20 days. [17]*He was severely wounded in the right leg July 28, 1864, at the battle of Ezra Church near Atlanta. After reporting to the regimental medical unit, he was transferred to the general hospital on July 31. Also spelled* **Elbon, Elborne.**

Elder, James, enlisted September 10, 1861, Montgomery, and was from Russell County. He worked as a teamster during the spring of 1863. He was a deserter from the Confederate Army and took the oath of allegiance to the Union on September 9, 1864.

[17]**Elder, Thomas**, Private, reported to the regimental medical unit December 12, 1863, diagnosis debilitas. He was granted a 20 day furlough December 17. He returned to the regimental medical unit twice in August 1864. On the 7th, the diagnosis was acute diarrhea and the 18th, acute rheum.

Elliot, John, Private, enlisted December 27, 1861, Jefferson County. He was born 1841 in Jefferson County.

Elliot, M. L., Private, enlisted December 27, 1861, Jefferson County.

[17]***Ellis, G. W.**,* Private, reported to the regimental medical unit on January 6, 1864, diagnosis was feb int tert.

Evans, William, Private, enlisted October 6, 1863, at Mobile. [17]*He reported to the regimental twice in 1864. In September, the diagnosis was constipation, and on November 3, feb int tert.*

Ferrill, J. W. O., Private.

Finley, William G., Private, enlisted December 27, 1861, Jefferson County. He was discharged by December 1862: overage. He was 6', a carpenter, and born in South Carolina [30]*February 7, 1814. His parents were Emanuel and Rebecca Whitmire Finley. He married (1) Elizabeth Cox and (2) Margaret Dean. He was living in Pinson, Jefferson County, in 1880. He died October 20, 1889.*

Franklin, Wiley, Private, enlisted February 15, 1862, at Greenville. He was detailed to the regimental hospital June 1862.

Geeslin, Benjamin F., Private, enlisted September 1861 at Montgomery. He was absent with leave October 1, 1861 to June 1862. [42]*The January returns for the 17th Alabama indicate that Geeslin had been granted a furlough October 1, 1861, and sent to Society Hill, Macon County. By January he had not returned and was listed as a deserter.* He was discharged July 4, 1862. Also spelled **Gesslin.**

Gilchrist, William, Private. See William Kilcrease

Gill, N. M., Private, enlisted December 27, 1861, Jefferson County.

Gillespie, J. M., Private, enlisted December 27, 1861, Jefferson County. He transferred to the 58th Alabama.

Glover, W. F., Private, was a Signal Operator.

Glover, J., Private

Goff, Matthew, Private, enlisted September 12, 1861, at Montgomery. He was born 1834. He was wounded July 28, 1864, at the battle of Ezra Church near Atlanta. [9]*He suffered a fracture of the head and anatomical neck of left humerous. Surgery was performed on the head and neck through straight incision posteriorly. Surgeon was S. V. D.*

COMPANY G

Hill, CSA. *Goff died September 14, 1864.* He was buried at Stonewall Cemetery, Griffin, Georgia.
Going, John C., Private, enlisted December 27, 1861. He was hospitalized June 1862, and was discharged July 4, 1862. Also listed as **J. C. Goines.**
Goodwin, J. D., Private, enlisted December 27, 1861, Jefferson County. [11]*He died June 2, 1862,* [25]*at Gainesville.* [12]*The muster roll for July-August 1862 states that he died in Greenville.*
[17]**Grace, J. S.,** Private, reported to the regimental medical unit on August 10, 1864, diagnosis was acute diarrhea.
Graham, J. S., Private.
Gray, J. J., Private, enlisted December 27, 1861, Jefferson County. He was hospitalized during June 1862.
Gray, Riley, Private, was wounded in leg and hip at Shiloh, Tennessee, in April of 1862.
Gray, T. J., Private, enlisted September 10, 1861, at Montgomery. He was hospitalized during June 1862.
[5]**Gray, W. R.,** *was listed as severely wounded at Shiloh, Tennessee, in April of 1862.* Note: this may be Riley Gray listed above.
[12]**Grimes, J. C.,** Private, enlisted December 27, 1861, Jefferson County. He was discharged July 2, 1862,
Guin, William Preston, Private, was granted a parole at Selma at end of war. [17]*He reported to the regimental medical unit three times in 1864. March 28, the diagnosis was chronic hepatitis, and he was sent to the general hospital in Greenville. August 10, the diagnosis was debilitas, and on August 19, diagnosis constipatio.* [30]*His brother-in-law, Sellars, was in the same company.* Also spelled **Gwin, Guinn, Guynn.**
Gunn, J. T., Private, a farmer, was born in Muscogee County, Georgia. He died June 23, 1863, leaving mother, Lauren Gunn, and widow, G. T. Gunn. See papers in his service file.
Gunter, E. A., Private.

Haggins, H. C., 1st lieutenant, enlisted October 17, 1861, Marengo County. He was paroled at Greensboro, North Carolina, April 1865.
Hall, G. S., Private, was granted a parole at Talladega, May 1865.
Hamner, E. C., Private, [17]*reported to the regimental medical unit on April 25, 1864, diagnosis acute dysentery.* He died June 1864 in an Atlanta hospital.
Hancock, H. J., Private, enlisted [12]*December 27, 1861,* Jefferson County. He was hospitalized during June 1862.
Harris, Elijah, Private, was hospitalized at Mobile February 17, 1864. While he was hospitalized at St. Mary's Hospital, LaGrange, Georgia, he was granted a furlough to Wildewood, Alabama, June 15, 1864. [17]*He*

reported to the regimental medical unit on January 14, 1864, diagnosis was debilitas, and on February 1, 1864, diagnosis dyspepsia. He was granted a parole at Talladega June 1865.

Harris, J. A., Private, was a Signal Operator. [17]*He reported to the regimental medical unit on September 11, 1864, diagnosis was abscessus.*

Harris, William J., Private, [17]*reported to the regimental medical unit February 5, 1864, diagnosis febris remitt, and was transferred to the general hospital in Greenville February 8.* He was paroled at Greensboro, North Carolina, May 1865.

Hartness, Robert E. H., Private.

[42]***Haskins, David R.***, *Private, was granted a 20-day furlough January 6, 1862, and sent to Uchee, Russell County.*

Hatley, F. M., Private, enlisted at Macon County. He was hospitalized during June 1862.

Hayes, W. F., Private, was hospitalized during June 1862.

Hearn, Warren F., Private, [17]*reported to the regimental medical unit on April 26, 1864, diagnosis feb int quotid.* He was captured December 15, 1864, at Nashville and was imprisoned at Camp Douglas, Illinois. He died January 8, 1865, of pneumonia, and was buried in lot number 417 Block 3 Chicago City Cemetery. Also spelled **Herron**.

Heath, Benjamin W., Private, was a hospital nurse.

Henry, Hiram, Private, enlisted August 10, 1863, Randolph County. [17]*He reported to the on December 7, 1863, diagnosis dyspepsia, and was transferred to the general hospital on December 10. He returned to the medical unit on February 8, 1864, diagnosis rubeola, and was transferred to the general hospital at Greenville the same day. He returned on September 21, and moved to the general hospital on September 23.*

[17]**Horn, G. L.**, *Private, reported to the regimental medical unit on August 8, 1864, diagnosis herpes circinatus.*

Hoskins, David R., Musician, was granted a medical furlough on January 1862 for 20 days and sent to home to Uchee, Russell County. He was discharged June 1862.

Howard, William L., drummer, was discharged April 3, 1863.

Huddleson, J. S., Private, enlisted December 27, 1861, Jefferson County. [12]*On the muster roll for July-August 1862, he was listed as sick in the regimental hospital. It also stated that the previous muster roll had erroneously listed him as a deserter.*

Hudson, R., Private, enlisted October 1863, Monroe County. [18]***Reuben Hudson*** *was described in 1863 as 33 years old, blue eyes, light hair, fair complexion, 5'10, a farmer, and a deserter from the Confederate Army.*

COMPANY G 327

Huggins, W. P., Private, enlisted October 17, 1862, Marengo County. [17]*He reported to the regimental medical unit four times in 1864. On June 3 and August 19, diagnosis was acute diarrhea, on September 11, ulcus, and on November 3, debilitas. In November, he was transferred to the general hospital. After July he was listed as a sergeant.*

Hughes, W. F., Private, enlisted December 27, 1861, Jefferson County.

Hunt, J. D., Private, was born 1845, Russell County. [17]*He reported to the regimental medical unit on December 4, 1863, diagnosis feb int quotid. He returned on June 17, 1864, with acute diarrhea and transferred to the general hospital the next day. He returned on July 2, diagnosis debilitas, and was transferred to the general hospital on the 6th. Captured December 28, 1864, at Egypt Station, he was imprisoned at Alton, Illinois, and released May 1865.* See Service Records for David Blackman, Private, Co. F, 54th Alabama.

Hunt, W. R., Private, enlisted May 12, 1862, Russell County. [12]*He was listed as absent without leave on the July-August muster roll.* He was born 1840 in Gwinett County, Georgia, and died October 2, 1863 [6]*at Mobile.*

Huton, James, Private, lived in Clarke County. He was hospitalized May 22, 1864, Macon, Georgia.

[17]***Hutto, James,** Private, reported to the regimental medical unit three times in 1864. On February 2, the diagnosis was rubeola, and he moved to the general hospital at Spring Hill near Mobile. On April 14, the diagnosis was feb int quotid, and in September, acute diarrhea.* Probably James Huton and Hutto are the same.

[17]***Jackson, Stephen,** Private, reported to the regimental medical unit on January 23, 1864, with rubeola, and on April 12, diagnosis feb int quotid. He was severely wounded in the face and groin on August 27, 1864, during the Battle of Atlanta, and died August 28.*

Jackson, William, Private, was 5'9, born in 1811, and died in December 1861.

James, J. J., Private, enlisted December 27, 1861, Jefferson County. He was reported as sick in the hospital during June 1862 and reported dead in December 1862.

Johnson, Henry Mathews C., Private, enlisted September 10, 1861. He was born 1837 and died January 5, 1862. Large file

Johnson, L. S., Master Sergeant, enlisted April 7, 1861, at Montgomery. He was a doctor and born 1842 in Putnam County, Georgia. Captured February 15, 1862, at Fort Donelson, he was imprisoned at Camp Douglas, Illinois. [17]*He was severely wounded (thigh) July 20, 1864, at the battle of Peachtree Creek near Atlanta, where he was captured.*

Johnson, Robert Walker, Sergeant, enlisted May 12, 1862. He was born 1840 in Russell County and was a substitute for Cornelius Calle. [20]*He was born January 25, 1840, in Meriweather, Georgia. He was living in Russell County in 1907.*

Johnson, Walter O., Private, enlisted October 10, 1861, at Montgomery. He was 5'7, a farmer, and born in 1844 in Russell County. He was hospitalized during June 1862. [12]*He was erroneously listed as a deserter on the May-June 1862 muster roll.* [17]*He reported to the regimental medical unit April 16, 1864, diagnosis was acute dysentery. He was wounded in the left leg and right arm on July 1, 1864. He was sent to the general hospital in Atlanta where his arm was amputated. He died July 30, 1864, Forsythe County, Georgia, and was buried in Forsythe Confederate Cemetery, Georgia.* See Service Records for Wm. Kilcrease

[17]**Johnson, Wm.**, Private, reported to the regimental medical unit four times in 1864. On March 5, the diagnosis was feb int quotid; June 5, acute dysentery; July 7, acute diarrhea; and November 11, pneumonia.

Jones, T. P., Private, enlisted December 27, 1861, Jefferson County. He transferred to the 58th Alabama.

Justice, A. T., Private, enlisted October 10, 1862, Dale County.

Justice, John, Private, was granted a medical furlough January 25, 1862 for 15 days and sent home to Himes, Russell, County. [1]*Lived in Tallahassee.* [12]*He transferred to Captain Warner's Sharpshooters July 2, 1862.* Also spelled **Justass, Justiss.**

[17]**Kaunne, Jno.**, Private, reported to the regimental medical unit on April 1, 1864, diagnosis debilitas. On April 19 he was granted a furlough for 15 days.

[17]**Kelly, James Polk**, Private, [20]*enlisted February 15, 1863, at Mobile.* [17]*He was wounded in the left knee during the fighting at Kennesaw Mountain. He was admitted to the general hospital in Atlanta on July 2, 1864, where his leg was amputated. He was paroled at Columbus, Georgia, during 1865.* [20]*A farmer, he was born January 15, 1845, in Macon County. In 1907 he was living at Society Hill in Macon County.* [37]*In 1921 he was living at Auburn and stated that he fought at Resaca and Kennesaw Mountain where he was wounded on July 2 and lost his leg.*

Kilgrease, William, Private, enlisted September 1862, at Montgomery. [17]*He reported to the regimental medical unit on March 10, 1864, diagnosis feb int tert, and on April 10, 1864, acute diarrhea.* He was 5'9 and born 1827 in Jones County, Georgia. He was granted a parole at May 1865. Also spelled **Killcrese, Gilchrist, Kilcrease, Killcrease.**

[1]**Kinyon, Austin Burress**, was born July 16, 1845, in Dallas County. He was wounded at Atlanta during the summer of 1864. He was sent to the

hospital in Eufaula until the end of the war. He was living in Mobile in 1907. [17]He reported to the regimental medical unit four times in 1864. On March 21, the diagnosis was chronic ulcus; on June 5, acute dysenteria; on June 25, debilitas; and on July 19, ulcus. Also spelled **Kenyon.**

Kirbo, M, Private, enlisted April 5, 1862, Russell County. [12]*He was hospitalized during the summer of 1862.* He was 6', a farmer, and born 1839 in Hancock County, Georgia. See Service Records for Kilcrease.

[17]***Laney, M. M.**, Private, reported to the regimental medical unit on July 1, 1864, diagnosis was acute dysenteria. On November 9, he was listed as a sergeant when he reported to the hospital with constipatio.*

Leonard, B. F., 1st Lieutenant, appointed July 25, 1861.

Leonard, G. F., 2nd Lieutenant, appointed July 25, 1861.

[17]***Leonard, Martin**, Musician, reported to the regimental medical unit on March 26, 1864, diagnosis was morbi cutis.*

Lollis, James, Private, was placed on medical furlough on January 27, 1862, for 15 days and sent to Crawford, Alabama.

Lollis, John, Private, enlisted September 10, 1861. He was granted a medical furlough on January 1, 1862, for 15 days and sent to Crawford, Alabama. He was discharged July 4, 1862.

Lollis, W. A., Private, enlisted October 1, 1861, at Montgomery. He was granted a medical furlough on January 12, 1862, for 15 days and sent to Crawford, Alabama. [25]*He died August 1, 1862, at Gainesville.* He is listed as **Wm. A. Sollers, A. Sollers, Lallas.**

[42]***Long, L. M.**, Sergeant, was granted a 20 day furlough December 27, 1861.*

Lowrie, Henry G., Private, [17]*reported to the regimental medical unit three times in 1864. On June 23, the diagnosis was feb int quotid; on August 6, acute diarrhea; and in September, constipatio.* He was captured at Greenville in April 1865.

Lowry, Bruce, Private, died November 18, 1863.

[18]***Lucery, James**, Private, was described in 1863 as 46 years old, blue eyes, dark hair, fair complexion, 5'10, a laborer, and a deserter from the Confederate Army.*

Lunsford, Blanton S., Private, a teamster, enlisted September 10, 1861, at Montgomery. He was placed on medical furlough January 21, 1862, for 20 days and sent to Himes, Russell County. [17]*On December 24, 1863, he reported to the regimental medical unit, diagnosis gonorrhea, on October 9,1864, debilitas, and on November 7, 1864, a hernia.*

Madison, J. S., Private, enlisted October 1862, Marengo County.

[17]**Mapp, J. B.**, Private, reported to the regimental medical unit four times in 1864. On March 9, the diagnosis was catarrhus; on August 4, feb int quotid; on September 6, acute diarrhea, and on November 5, acute diarrhea. Also spelled **Napp.**

[17]**Martin, A. P.**, Captain, died on the field on July 28, 1864, at the battle of Ezra Church near Atlanta.

Martin, Alfred P., Private, enlisted September 24, 1863, at Mobile. He was 6'1, a farmer, and born 1826 in Choctaw County. He was wounded and captured July 28, 1864, at Ezra Church near Atlanta. [9]*His left leg was amputated July 28, 1864.* He hospitalized in a Union hospital until December 28, 1864, when he was transferred to the Provost Marshall. He was imprisoned at Camp Douglas, Illinois, where he died January 27, 1865. He was buried in lot number 17, Range 2, Cave Hill Cemetery, Louisville, Ky.

Martin, Isaac, Private, enlisted September 12, 1862, Choctaw County.

Martin, John, Private, enlisted October 12, 1862, Choctaw County. He was granted a parole at Greensboro, North Carolina, May 20, 1865. [17]*He reported to the regimental medical unit on June 3 and 13, 1864, diagnosis was acute diarrhea.*

Mayer, Lewis, Musician, November 6, 1861, at Montgomery. He was 5'8 and born 1824 in Denmark. Captured February 16, 1862, Ft. Donelson, he was imprisoned Camp Douglas, Illinois. Returned to duty April 26, 1862.

McCary, J. A., Private

McDowell, Robert, Private, was discharged December 5, 1861.

McIntyre, J. L., Captain, enlisted June 24, 1862, Tupelo, Mississippi. [17]*As a lieutenant he reported to the regimental medical unit on July 1, 1864, diagnosis was chronic rheum.* He was at the surrender at Greensboro, North Carolina, April 26, 1865. Also spelled **McIntire.**

McTyire, W. C., 2nd Lieutenant, April 14, 1862, at Greenville. He was granted a parole at Greensboro, North Carolina, April 1865.

McVay, George, Private, enlisted November 1, 1861, at Montgomery. He was 5'3, a farmer, and was born in 1837 in Upson or Muscogee County, Georgia. He was granted a disability discharge July 2, 1862.

Meek, D. M., Private, was wounded in leg at Shiloh, Tennessee, April 1862.

Montague, Henry, Private, was a Courier. [30]*He transferred to the 17th Alabama Infantry October 22, 1862.*

[17]**Moore, James**, Private, reported to the regimental medical unit on March 24, 1864, with acute diarrhea.

Morgan, Frank M., Private, enlisted September 1, 1863, Mobile. He was 5'10 and born in 1821 in Greene County, Mississippi. [17]***Frank Morgan** reported to the regimental medical unit April 20, 1864, with acute dysentery. F. M. contracted pneumonia in December 1863 and sent to*

the general hospital. He reported to the hospital again January 28, 1864, diagnosis was nephritis, and November 13, 1864, catarrhus.
Frank M. died May 24, 1864, in Atlanta. F. M. was detailed as a carpenter in Mobile earning $3 per day. He was admitted to St. Mary's Hospital, West Point, Mississippi, January 1865.
Mortard, C. Private, was hospitalized with wounds January 25, 1865, Meridian, Mississippi.
Mote, James, Private, enlisted September 10, 1861, at Montgomery. He died in 1862. [12]*On the muster roll for July-August 1862, it was stated that he had erroneously been listed as a deserter on the previous muster roll.*
Myrick, John, Private, enlisted December 27, 1861, Jefferson County. He was hospitalized during June 1862.

Nail, R. H., Private, enlisted December 27, 1861, Jefferson County. He transferred to the 58th Alabama.
Nelson, W., Private, was hospitalized August 28, 1864, Richmond.
Nixon, E. P., Private, was granted a disability discharge January 20, 1862.

O'Ferrel, J. W., Private, enlisted October 1, 1861, at Montgomery. He was 5'7 and born in 1830, Barbour County. He was granted a furlough on June 20, 1862, for 21 days. On October 20, 1862, he was granted a discharge. Also spelled **O'Farrell**
Otts, John, Private, enlisted September 15, 1862, at Mobile. [17]*He reported to the regimental medical unit on March 10, 1864, diagnosis haemorrhois, and on March 11, acute dysentery. He was transferred to the general hospital at Spring Hill at Mobile on March 12. He reported to the hospital again on July 14, diagnosis ascites.*

Pace, G. W., Private, was granted a disability discharge January 15, 1862.
Pace, Joseph W., Private, enlisted September 4, 1862, Choctaw County. He was hospitalized February 14, 1864, Mobile, diagnosis was an ulcer. [17]*He reported to the regimental medical unit on February 5,1864, diagnosis febris remitt, and was transferred to the general hospital in Greenville on February 14.*
[18]**Painter, Robert,** *Private, was described in 1863 as 29 years old, blue eyes, dark hair, fair complexion, 5'6, a farmer, and a deserter from the Confederate Army.*
[17]**Parker, Jesse,** *Private, reported to the regimental medical unit on June 1, 1864, diagnosis feb remitt, and sent to the general hospital the next day.*
Partin, J. R., Private, was hospitalized with wounds, January 20, 1865, Meridian, Mississippi.

Paul, William, Private, enlisted July 24, 1864, Green County. [17]*He reported to the regimental medical unit on November 3, 1864, diagnosis catarrhus.* He was paroled May 1865 at Greensboro, North Carolina.

Phillips, John J., Private, was 5'8, a gardener, and born in 1824 in London, England. [17]*He reported to the regimental medical unit six times in 1864. On March 7, diagnosis was feb int quotid. He reported twice with acute rheum, on March 20 and April 7. He suffered with acute dysentery in June and was transferred to the general hospital on the 9th. On July 20, at the battle of Peachtree Creek during the Atlanta campaign, he was hit by a minnie ball to the right shoulder. After reporting to the regimental medical unit, he was transferred to the general hospital. He had a case of acute diarrhea and reported to the regimental medical unit on November 8 and transferred to the general hospital on the 28th.* Captured December 22, 1864, at Columbia, Tennessee, he was imprisoned at Camp Chase, Ohio. He took the oath of allegiance to the Union on January 13, 1865. He was from Mobile County.

Plunkett, J. C., Private, enlisted December 27, 1861, Jefferson County.

Pointer, Robert, Private, enlisted August 17, 1862, Marengo County.

Polk, James K., Private, 5'5, [17]*reported to the regimental medical unit twice in 1864 with acute diarrhea: on June 2 and August 19.* He was on a roll of deserters from the Confederate Army who took oath of allegiance to the Union and promised to stay north of the Ohio River. Home was Paulding County, Georgia.

Porter, Joe Day, Private, enlisted September 10, 1861, at Montgomery. He was granted a parole at May 1, 1865, Greensboro, North Carolina. [10]*He was born September 10, 1844, in Wilkerson County, Georgia He was living in Barbour County in 1907.* [37]*In 1921 he was living in Eufaula when he stated he had been slightly wounded at Shiloh and fought at Atlanta, Franklin and Nashville.*

Porter, John T., Private, enlisted September 10, 1861, at Montgomery. [42]*He was granted a furlough for 20 days October 1, 1862, and sent to San Fort.* [17]*He reported to the regimental medical unit on February 27, 1864, diagnosis acute diarrhea.* He was at the surrender at Greensboro, North Carolina, April 26, 1865. He was 5'7, a farmer, and born in 1842 in Wilkerson County, Georgia.

Porter, J. R., Private, enlisted September 10, 1862, Butler County. [17]*He reported to the regimental medical unit on December 2, 1863, diagnosis syph seco. He reported to the hospital on February 15, 1864, diagnosis was vulnus cont, and on April 28, scorbutus. On June 22, 1864, he returned to the hospital, diagnosis feb cont, and was transferred to the general hospital the same day.* He was placed on medical furlough January 21, 1865, for 60 days and sent to Georgiana, Alabama. He was granted a parole June 1, 1865.

COMPANY G

[17]**Porter, Ross**, Private, reported to the regimental medical unit on March 11, 1864, diagnosis catarrhus. This may be **J. R. Porter**.

Porter, W. M., Private, enlisted February 11, 1863, Russell County. [20]He was born in 1833 in Wilkerson County, Georgia. He was paroled in Greensboro, North Carolina, May 1865. He was living at Headland, Henry County, in 1907

Preddy, T. W., Private, [42]was granted a 20-day furlough to Society Hill, Macon County, January 1, 1862.

Preston, W. H., Private, was granted a parole at May 24, 1865, Talladega.

Pruitt, C.C., Private, enlisted in Marengo County. [17]He reported to the regimental medical unit on December 2, 1853, diagnosis feb remitt. He was granted a parole June 20, 1865, at Demopolis.

Pruitt, Francis M., Private, [17]reported to the regimental medical unit in September of 1864, diagnosis feb int tert. He was captured December 15, 1864, Nashville. He was imprisoned at Camp Douglas, Illinois, where he died of frost bite February 5, 1865. He was buried in lot number 694-2 at Chicago City Cemetery. Also spelled **Prewitt**

Pruitt, Miles S., Private, enlisted October 17, 1862, Choctaw County. [17]He reported to the regimental medical unit in early May 1864 when severely wounded in his hand. He was paroled May 1, 1865, Greensboro, North Carolina. [20]He was born November 19, 1839, Lauderdale, Mississippi. In 1907 he was living at St. Stephens, Washington County, Alabama. Also listed as **M. L. Pruitt**.

[17]**Pursewell, W. S.**, Private, was wounded in the mouth and jaw on July 28, 1864, during the battle of Ezra Church near Atlanta. He was sent to the general hospital on July 31.

Ragland, Thomas, Captain, was elected September 25, 1861. His records indicate that he was paid $130 per month through 1862 and 1863. Various acquisition records and receipts exist until his death in Georgia. [17]He was killed on the field of battle on July 28, 1864, at the battle of Ezra Church near Atlanta.

Reid, J. P., Private, enlisted December 27, 1861, Jefferson County. [25]He is buried in Magnolia Cemetery in Mobile.

[17]**Richardson, G. A.**, Private, was diagnosed with rubeola on February 4, 1864, and moved to the general hospital at Spring Hill near Mobile the next day.

[17]**Richardson, Geo. J.**, Private, was severely wounded in his left side on July 24, 1864, and sent to the general hospital the next day.

Ridgell, W., Private, enlisted October 20, 1862, Dale County. He died May 27, 1863, at Mobile leaving widow Susan. Also spelled **Rigel**.

Roberts, Robert, Private, [17]reported to the regimental medical unit on July 20, 1864, with a slight wound to his hip, at the battle of Peachtree Creek *near Atlanta.* He was transferred to a general hospital at Macon, Georgia, *the next day.*

Roberts, William, Private, was hospitalized August 29, 1864, at Mobile. The lower third of his right arm had been amputated, and he was placed on medical furlough for 60 days.

Rodgers, Moses, Private, enlisted December 27, 1861, Jefferson County. He was hospitalized February 25, 1864; diagnosis was rubeola.

[18]*Rodgers, Edward, Private, was described in 1863 as 46 years old, dark eyes, dark hair, dark complexion, 5'6, a laborer, and a deserter from the Confederate Army.*

Rodgers, M. P., Private, enlisted December 27, 1861, Jefferson County

Roland, J. S., Private, enlisted May 12, 1862, Russell County. He was 5'8 and born in 1834 in Montgomery County. Also spelled **Rolan**

Roquemore, J. M., Sergeant, was 5'5 and born in 1828 in Georgia. [42]*He was granted a 15 day furlough, January 4, 1862, and sent to Russell County.* He was captured at Shiloh, Tennessee, in April 1862. He suffered a gunshot wound to hip. He was imprisoned at Camp Dennison, Ohio, where he died May 16, 1862, leaving widow, Mary.

Rumbley, H. M., Private, transferred to Company G from Company H as first sergeant July 10, 1862. See Company H for more information.

Sassa, J., died March 29, 1862, Camp Douglas, Illinois.

Sasser, John W., Private, enlisted September 10, 1861, at Montgomery. He was granted a medical furlough January 20, 1862, for 21 days and sent to Russell County. [17]*He reported to the regimental medical unit on December 3, 1863, diagnosis gonorrhea.* He was granted a parole at Greensboro, North Carolina.

Sasser, Joseph J., Private, enlisted September 10, 1861, at Montgomery. He was born in 1833 in Stewart County, Georgia, 6', and a farmer. Missing at Shiloh, Tennessee, April 1862, he was imprisoned Camp Douglas, Illinois. He was granted a parole May 1865, at Greensboro, North Carolina. See Service Records for Wm. Kilcrease. [17]*Jo. Sasser reported to the regimental medical unit on December 30, 1863, diagnosis was herpes circ, and on January 1, 1864, morbi cutis.*

Sasser, W. P., Private, enlisted February 3, 1863, Russell County. He was granted a parole at Greensboro, North Carolina.

[18]*Savage, James, Private, was described in 1863 as 46 years old, blue eyes, dark hair, dark complexion, 5'8, a laborer, and a deserter from the Confederate Army.*

Saxon, John, Private, was discharged October 12, 1863.

[17]*Screws, Wm., Private, reported to the regimental medical unit on December 9, 1864, diagnosis phlegmon.*

Sellars, Hardy, Private, enlisted in 1862, Clark County.

Sellers, Andrew, Private, died February 26, 1864, leaving widow, Josephine J. He was buried in Magnolia Cemetery, row 11, grave 36.

Shaffer, Anthony, Private, was hospitalized February 17, 1864, in Mobile for 30 days. He was captured May 22, 1864, at Cartersville, Georgia, and imprisoned at Rock Island, Illinois. Also spelled **Schoffer, Schover**

Sharpton, Alexander, Private, enlisted at Montgomery, September 10, 1861. He was granted a medical furlough January 16, 1862 for 20 days and sent to Langford. [17]*He reported to the regimental medical unit three times in 1864. On January 16, the diagnosis was feb int tert. On June 23, his complaint was acute diarrhea. On August 15, he was admitted with a chest wound received at the siege of Atlanta.*

Sharpton, William E., Private, enlisted at Montgomery, September 10, 1861. He was 6' and from Wayne County, Tennessee. He was a nurse at the hospital during January 1862. [17]*On December 20, 1863, he reported to the regimental medical unit, diagnosis feb int quotid, and transferred to the general hospital two days later. On July 28, 1864, he sustained a severe wound to the face, at the battle of Ezra Church in the Atlanta area. After reporting to the regimental medical unit, he was moved to the general hospital on July 31.* He surrendered May 15, 1865, at Pulaski, Tennessee, and took the oath of allegiance to the Union May 20, 1865.

[17]**Shaver, S.**, *Private, reported to the regimental medical unit on February 3, 1864, diagnosis feb int tert.*

[17]**Shaw, John**, *Private, reported to the regimental medical unit on July 28, 1864. He had been wounded (right thigh and left arm) at the battle of Ezra Church in the Atlanta area. He was transferred to the general hospital on July 31.*

Shepperd, James B., Private

Simmons, A. D., Private, enlisted September 10, 1861, at Montgomery. His residence was Russell County. Captured December 15, 1864, Nashville, he was imprisoned at Camp Douglas, Illinois.

Smith, Burwell J., Corporal, was discharged December 28, 1861. [37]*He was born February 28, 1838, in Hancock, Georgia. His family moved to Alabama in 1839 or 1840. In 1921 he stated that he was at the bombardment of Pensacola and fought at Resaca, Kennesaw Mountain and Atlanta. He hired a substitute after his first enlistment and returned home in 1862. He later volunteered in the artillery. Family and property matters allowed him to be discharged a second time. He rejoined the artillery after the battle of Chickamauga. He escaped imprisonment at the end of the war at Columbus, Georgia, and was later paroled. A personal letter is attached to the 1921 Confederate Soldiers Census record.*

Smith, Charles J., Sergeant, enlisted September 10, 1861, at Montgomery. He was 5'6 and born in 1839. He was captured December 15, 1864, Nashville. He was imprisoned at Johnson Island, Ohio, where he was granted a parole in June 14, 1865.

Smith, W., Private, was captured at Fort Donelson, February 6, 1862. He was imprisoned Camp Douglas, Illinois, where he died March 29, 1862.

Sollies, W. A., Private See Lollies

Spears, G. W., Private, enlisted February 21, 1862, at Greenville. [12]*He was listed as hospitalized on the July-August 1862 muster roll.* He was dropped from the rolls November 1862. Left widow Caroline B. Also spelled **Speer**.

Spinks, William, Private, enlisted in 1861, at Montgomery. [12]*He was listed as absent on furlough on the muster roll for July-August 1862.* [17]*He was killed during the battle for Kennesaw Mountain on June 23, 1864, by a minnie ball to the head.* He was survived by his widow, Susan Ann Spinks.

Stegall, Peter, Private, enlisted February 21, 1862, at Montgomery. [12]*He was discharged July 2, 1862.* [6]*He died of typhoid fever July 22, 1862.* Also spelled **Steagall, Steayall**

Stokes, Thomas, Private, was hospitalized at Jackson, Mississippi, March 20, 1862, for 10 days.

Sullivan, P. G., Private, enlisted December 27, 1861, Jefferson County.

Tate, John F., Lieutenant, was appointed second lieutenant, October 25, 1861. He was promoted to first lieutenant May 17, 1862. He was appointed captain July 28, 1864, after the death of his commanding officer, Captain Thomas Ragland. He was appointed lieutenant colonel April 20, 1865. He was paroled at May 1865, Greensboro, North Carolina.

Taylor, John, Private, was hospitalized February 22, 1864, in Mobile with gun shot wound. He was granted a medical furlough March 22, 1864, for 60 days.

Teat, J. H., Private, enlisted September 10, 1861, at Montgomery. He was hospitalized during June 1862.

[17]**Templeton, J. F.**, *Private, reported to the regimental medical unit on June 25, 1864, diagnosis feb int quotid. He was sent to the general hospital the next day. Could possibly be* **S. F. Templeton**.

[17]**Templeton, S. F.**, *Private, reported to the regimental medical unit on June 6, 1864, diagnosis acute diarrhea. Could possibly be* **J. F. Templeton**.

[17]**Tetre, J. H.**, *Private, reported to the regimental medical unit on June 8, 1864, diagnosis acute dysentery. He was transferred to the general hospital the next day. Could this be* **J. H. Teat**?

Thead, Columbus A., Private, enlisted 1862. [17]*He reported to the regimental medical unit on December 1, 1863, diagnosis catarrhus. He reported to the hospital twice with acute diarrhea, on June 15 and November 3, 1864. In June he was moved to the general hospital the next day.* Captured December 15, 1864, in Nashville, he was imprisoned Camp Douglas, Illinois. His home was in Choctaw.

Thomas, Moses, Private, enlisted December 27, 1861, Jefferson County.

[17]***Thomas, T. C.,*** *Private, reported to the regimental medical unit on July 4, 1864, diagnosis fracture. He was sent to the general hospital the next day. On August 13, 1864, he returned to the hospital with some type of wound.*

Thompson, James, Private, was granted a medical furlough January 15, 1862, for 15 days and sent home to Sandfort, Russell County, Alabama. He was wounded at Shiloh, Tennessee, April 8, 1862, where he was captured. He died April 18, 1862, on his way to St. Louis for imprisonment.

[17]***Thompson, W.,*** *Private. Wm. Thompson reported to the regimental medical unit on June 3, 1864, with acute dysentery. Wm. P. Thompson reported to the regimental medical unit on June 13, 1864, with acute diarrhea. W. Thompson reported to the regimental medical unit on June 25, 1864, diagnosis was feb int quotid, and on July 13, debilitas. W. W. Thompson reported to the regimental medical unit on August 7, 1864, diagnosis feb int quotid. W. D. Thompson reported to the regimental medical unit on September 4, 1864, diagnosis acute rheum, and was transferred to the general hospital the next day.* Note: These entries may possibly include more than one individual.

[22]***Threadgill, J.,*** *died at Augusta, Georgia, and is buried in the Confederate Cemetery in Marietta, Georgia.*

Treadway, Henry C., Private, enlisted January 30, 1865. He was granted a parole at May 1865 at Greensboro. Also spelled **Treadman.**

Treadway, George W., Private, was captured December 15, 1864, in Nashville and imprisoned at Camp Douglas, Illinois.

Treadway, James M., Private, enlisted at Montgomery, September 10, 1861. He served as a nurse. [17]*He reported to the regimental medical unit on December 4, 1863, diagnosis was gonorrhea, and on April 12, 1864, feb int quotid.* [26]*He was born September 1818 and died September 27, 1898. Burial was at Antioch Cemetery in Randolph County.* Also spelled **Tradaway.**

Tulville, George W., Private, was captured December 15, 1864, Nashville. He was imprisoned at Camp Douglas, Illinois, where he was paroled June 1865. His home was in Russell County.

Tutt, William D., Lieutenant, was appointed second lieutenant May 20, 1862, and appointed first lieutenant July 17, 1862. [17]*He reported to the* regimental medical unit on December 1, 1863, diagnosis was rheumat chronic. He was granted a 20 day furlough on December 14. He reported to the hospital again on July 1, 1864, diagnosis was feb int quotid. He was transferred to the general hospital on July 3. He was slightly wounded (left shoulder) at the battle of Franklin, Tennessee.

Walker, James P., Sergeant, was discharged January 19, 1862: disability.
Walton, L. M., Sergeant, was placed on medical furlough in January of 1862 for 20 days.
Warren, David G., Private, enlisted December 27, 1861, Jefferson County.
White, J. F., Private, enlisted September 10, 1861, at Montgomery.
Wilkerson, Freeman W., Private, enlisted December 29, 1862, Columbus, Georgia. [17]*He reported to the regimental medical unit four times in 1864. On February 3, the diagnosis was rubeola, and he was transferred to the hospital at Spring Hill in Mobile on February 5. On June 15, the diagnosis was acute diarrhea. He was transferred to the general hospital in Macon, Georgia, the next day. On November 3, the diagnosis was feb int quotid, and on November 8, feb int tert.* He was granted a parole May 1865 in Greensboro, North Carolina. His home was in Russell County.
Williams, D. M., Private, enlisted September 10, 1861, at Montgomery. He was a musician in the band. He was hospitalized during June 1862. Also listed as **D. H., D. W.**
Williams, J. C., Private, enlisted December 27, 1861, Jefferson County. He was hospitalized during June 1862. He transferred to the 58th Alabama.
Williamson, A. W., Private, enlisted December 27, 1861, Jefferson County. He died at Okolona, Mississippi, June 8, 1862.
[17]**Wilson, J. A.**, *Private, reported to the regimental medical unit twice in 1864. On June 4, the diagnosis was acute dysentery. On July 1, he was severely wounded in the right hip and transferred to the general hospital in Atlanta. He was a farmer and born in 1846.* **James Wilson** *reported to the hospital on February 2, 1864, with rubeola. He was transferred to the general hospital in Spring Hill at Mobile on the 5th.*
Wilson, W. C., Private, enlisted September 10, 1861, at Montgomery. He was placed on medical furlough January 28, 1862, for 20 days and sent to Himes in Russell County. [17]*He reported to the regimental medical unit on September 11, 1864, diagnosis acute diarrhea.* **W. W. Wilson** *reported to the hospital on July 9 with acute dysentery.*
Wimberley, L. W., Private, enlisted September 23, 1863, at Mobile. He was 5'9, a farmer, and born in 1825 in Wayne County, Mississippi. He was granted a disability discharge October 25, 1863.
Wimberley, J. L., Private, enlisted September 1, 1862, at Choctaw.

Winn, W., Private, was hospitalized during June 1862. [12]*He died July 1, 1862, in the hospital in Columbus, Mississippi.*

Woodard, W. J., Private, enlisted July 5, 1863, Russell County. [17]*He reported to the regimental medical unit five times in 1864. On January 13, the diagnosis was catarrhus, and on the 23rd, feb int tert. On February 3, the diagnosis was rubeola, and he was transferred to the general hospital in Spring Hill near Mobile on the 5th. On March 29, the diagnosis was acute dysentery, and on August 4, acute diarrhea.* He was paroled at Greensboro, North Carolina, April 1865. Also spelled **Woodward.**

[17]**Wynn, H. T.,** *Private, reported to the regimental medical unit on February 20, 1864, diagnosis feb int quotid.*

Wynn, Lycurgus, Private, lived in Chambers County. Captured December 15, 1864 in Nashville, he was imprisoned Camp Douglas, Illinois where he was paroled June 1865.

Wynn, R. A., Sergeant, enlisted September 1, 1861, at Montgomery. [17]*On November 9, 1864, he reported to the regimental medical unit, diagnosis acute diarrhea. On April 5,* **Richard Wynn** *reported to the regimental medical unit, diagnosis herpes cire*

Wynne, Clem, Private, enlisted February 3, 1863, Russell County. [17]*He reported to the regimental medical unit three times in 1864. On April 2, the diagnosis was gonorrhea, and on August 28, feb remitt. On September 4, the diagnosis was acute diarrhea, and he was transferred to the general hospital on the 18th.* He was granted a parole at Greensboro, North Carolina, April 1865.

Wynne, John T., Corporal, enlisted September 10, 1861, at Montgomery. [17]*On December 5, 1863, he reported to the regimental medical unit, diagnosis feb int tert, listed as sergeant. On December 20, the diagnosis was feb int quotid, listed as private. On January 29, 1864, the diagnosis was feb int tert, listed as 5th sergeant. On March 4, the complaint was debilitas, listed as corporal. On March 19, the complaint was debilitas, listed as a private. On June 15, the diagnosis was acute diarrhea, listed as a private. On July 24, he was severely wounded in the right thigh, listed as sergeant.*

Wynne, Lemuel, Private, September 10, 1861, at Montgomery. He was hospitalized in Greenville February 29, 1864. He was hospitalized in Macon, Georgia, on July 22, 1864, and transferred to a hospital in Russell County. [17]*He reported to the regimental medical unit seven times in 1864. He reported with gonorrhea on January 6 and March 27. His complaint was fever twice, January 27, feb int tert, and June 30, feb remitt.* He was wounded twice: on July 20, at the battle of Peachtree Creek, slight wound to side; and on August 10 at the siege of Atlanta, slight flesh wound to left arm. He returned to the hospital with *acute diarrhea on August 23.* [37]*He was born February 13, 1842, Monroe County, Georgia. In 1921 he was living in Girad, Alabama. He stated he fought at the battle of Shiloh and in skirmishes at Dalton, Atlanta, and at Peachtree Creek where he was wounded. He was in North Carolina at the end of the war and was told to get home "by the best way we could."*

Wynne, William H., Private, enlisted September 10, 1861, at Montgomery. [12]***Wm. Wynne** died July 1, 1862, Columbus, Mississippi.* [17]***W. H. Wynn** reported to the regimental medical unit on July 24, 1864, diagnosis debilitas.*

York, G. W., Private, died May 27, 1864 in an Atlanta Hospital. [17]*He reported to the regimental medical unit on February 15, 1864, diagnosis was feb int quotid.*

Appendix IX. Company H

Albea, S. P., Private, enlisted February 28, 1862, at Dallas County. [32]*He transferred to another unit.*

Andress, George D., Private, enlisted November 25, 1861, at Camp Davis. He was hospitalized during June 1862 and died August 25, 1862. Elizabeth Andress filed for death benefits in 1862. [40]*He was born in 1836 at Ridge Road in Monroe County, son of William Francis and Elizabeth Davison Andress. His brother, Hugh, was also a member of Company H.*

Andress, Hugh Mercer, Private, enlisted September 16, 1862, at Mobile. He was mortally wounded in the groin and pelvis at Shiloh, Tennessee, April 1862. Elizabeth Andress, mother, filed for death benefits. His brother, George, was also a member of Company H.

Andress, James, Private, enlisted October 25, 1861, at Camp Davis. He suffered a severe head wound at Shiloh, Tennessee, in April 1862 and died on July 18. [40]*He was born in 1823, son of Isaac and Polly Nettles Andress. He was married to Amelia East.*

Andress, Redden McCoy, Lieutenant, enlisted October 25, 1861, at Camp Davis. He was slightly wounded at Shiloh, Tennessee, April 1862. He was hospitalized during June 1862. [17]*He reported to the regimental medical unit February 9, 1864, diagnosis was contusio, and March 10, vulnus contusio. He was granted a furlough March 19 for 15 days. On July 20, 1864, at the battle of Peach Tree Creek, he was hit by a minnie in the left arm. He died the next day in the brigade hospital,* leaving widow P. E. Andress who filed for his pay. [30]*Family tradition states that his slave buried Andress in a lady's rose garden in Atlanta. However, the site was never found. He was born December 25, 1834, Pineville, Monroe County, son of Stephen Singleton and Susan McCoy Andress. He was married to Elizabeth Parthenia Riley. His brother, Stephen, also served in Company H.*

Andress, Stephen Decatur, Private, enlisted August 25, 1863, at Mobile. [17]*He reported to the regimental medical unit December 21, 1863, diagnosis catarrhus. He was sick again February 7, 1864, diagnosis otorrhoea, and March 2, with tonsillitis.* [40]*He was born August 12, 1827, in Pineville, Monroe County, son of Stephen Singleton and Susan McCoy Andress. He died December 25, 1896, and was buried at Andress Cemetery in Pineville. His brother, Redden, also served in Company H.*

Andress, William R., Corporal, enlisted October 25, 1861, at Mobile. He was 5'11 and born 1835 in Monroe County. [30]*He was son of Isaac and Polly Nettles Andress, and brother of James.* [4]*He died in Meridian, Mississippi, at the Confederate Hospital on April 25, 1862.* [32]*He was listed as a 4th corporal.*

Anthony, J. C., Private, enlisted March 29, 1862, Burnt Corn, Monroe County. He was at the surrender at Greensboro, North Carolina, April 26, 1865.

Ballard, John, Private, enlisted May 10, 1862, Corinth, Mississippi. [17]*He reported to the regimental medical unit April 15, 1864, diagnosis rubeola. He was sent to the general hospital April 18.* He was seriously wounded in the lungs and back during May 1864, at the battle of New Hope church in Georgia. He died July 5, 1864.

Barnes, A. J., Private, enlisted February 28, 1862, at Dallas County. [32]*He transferred to another unit.*

Barnes, Jasper N., Private, enlisted February 28, 1862, at Dallas County. In 1863 he worked as a carpenter and as mechanic receiving extra pay. [20]*He was born April 26, 1835, at Montevallo, Shelby County. He enlisted after the battle at Shiloh, Tennessee. Captured at Resaca, Georgia, May 5, 1864, he was imprisoned at Indianapolis until May 1864. In 1907 he was living at Plantersville, Shelby County.* [32]*He transferred to another regiment.*

Barnes, Robert J., Private, [17]*reported to the regimental medical unit on January 16, 1864, diagnosis feb int tert.* He died February 5, 1864, at Mobile. He was buried in the Magnolia Cemetery, Mobile, row 12, grave 37.

Barnes, Thomas J., Private, [36]*enlisted December 21, 1863 at Mobile* and was from Monroe County. [17]*He reported to the regimental medical unit on February 5, 1864, diagnosis was feb int quotid, on April 18, 1864, parotitis, and during September, oedema.* Captured December 15, 1864, at Nashville, he was imprisoned at Camp Douglas, Illinois. [32]*He transferred to another unit.*

Baseley, Anderson, Private, was discharged December 5, 1861.

Baxley, Jesse, Private, [36]*enlisted February 16, 1864, at Mobile.* [17]*He reported to the regimental medical unit three times in 1864. March 10, the diagnosis was rubeola, April 10, parotitis, and July 3, debilitas.*

Bayles, Wash J., Private, enlisted October 12, 1862, Monroe County. [17]*He reported to the regimental medical unit December 4, 1863, diagnosis feb int quotid. He reported to the regimental medical unit five times in 1864. February 10, diagnosis was debilitas. He moved to the general hospital on the 14th. March 19, diagnosis was acute diarrhea, and March 30, feb int quotid. April 16, his diagnosis was chronic diarrhea, and he moved to the general hospital on the 20th. August 11, he suffered a severe injury to his right knee, and he was transferred to the general hospital the next day.* [41]*He died September 22, 1864, and is buried at Macon, Georgia, Rose Hill Cemetery, grave 423.*

Beadlescomb, W., Private, enlisted February 28, 1862, at Dallas County. He was discharged July 29, 1862. Also spelled **Bradlescomb**

[36]**Belcher, E. M.**, Private, enlisted September 14, 1863, Butler County. [17]*He reported to the regimental medical unit three times in 1864. January 16, the diagnosis was chronic rheum, June 25, feb remitteus, and June 28, feb int quotid. He was transferred to the general hospital June 28.* Also spelled **Belsher**.

Biggs, Tulley J., Private, enlisted October 15, 1862, Monroe County. [17]*He reported to the regimental medical unit seven times in 1864. For four times the diagnosis was feb int tert: February 21, March 21, April 27, and in September. January 25, the diagnosis was icterus, and August 16, acute dysentery. November 30, at the battle of Franklin, Tennessee, he suffered a slight injury to his left knee.* [32]*At some point he was promoted to first corporal.* Captured December 17, 1864, Franklin, Tennessee, he was imprisoned at Camp Chase, Ohio. Also spelled **Briggs**.

Biggs, William J., Corporal, enlisted October 25, 1861, at Shorter. He was hospitalized during June 1862. He was granted a furlough, August 29, 1862. [17]*He reported to the regimental medical unit on January 16, 1864, diagnosis feb int tert.* He was paroled at Greensboro, North Carolina, April 1865. [37]*He was born January 30, 1844. In 1921, he stated he was in battles at Shiloh, Atlanta, Franklin and Nashville.* [40]*He died November 27, 1921, and is buried in Rumbley Cemetery at Peterman, Alabama.*

Billings, Jethro W., Private, enlisted March 1863, at Mobile. [17]*He reported to the regimental medical unit four times in 1864. On January 8, diagnosis was acute rheum. On January 27 and March 18, the diagnosis was feb int quotid. In May he was slightly injured (hip),* [32]*at the battle of New Hope Church in Georgia.* He was hospitalized during November 1864 in Montgomery. Also spelled **Billiness**.

Black, James, Private, enlisted October 25, 1861, Macon. He suffered a slight wound to his foot at Shiloh, Tennessee in April 1862. He was hospitalized during June 1862. His mother was Mary Black.

Black, John W., Corporal, enlisted October 25, 1861, at Shorters. He was born in 1816 in North Carolina, 6 feet tall and a farmer. He was placed on sick furlough January 20, 1862, for 20 days. He was discharged on May 26, 1862, disability. He re-enlisted on October 25, 1862, at Camp Davis. [17]*He reported to the regimental medical unit twice with diagnosis feb int quotid: on December 13, 1863, and January 30, 1864. He reported to the medical unit four times with diagnosis feb int tert: December 28, 1863, and January 2, March 7, and November 13, 1864. He was wounded twice in 1864. On July 2, he was slightly wounded (right shoulder). He was sent to the general hospital July 31.* [32]*In July,* he was wounded at Poor House in Atlanta. At some point he was promoted to 4th sergeant. He was injured in the left foot and right thigh at the battle of Franklin, Tennessee, November 30, 1864, and captured December 17. He was moved from a Louisville prison to Camp Chase, Ohio, March 10, 1865, where [10]*he died March 20, buried in lot 1721.*

Bloxam, H. C., Corporal, enlisted October 25, 1862, at Camp Davis.

Bodiford, Israel, Private, was hospitalized with bronchitis February 3, 1864, at Ross Hospital, Mobile. He was sent to the general hospital in Montgomery February 17.

Boland, J., Private, was hospitalized during June of 1862.

[36]***Boon, John,*** Private, enlisted December 31, 1863, at Mobile. [17]*He was injured (back and right side) July 28 and was sent to the general hospital July 31.* [32]*The injury occurred at the battle of Poor House in Atlanta.*

Booth, W. K., Private, enlisted February 28, 1862, Dallas County. [12]*On the muster roll for July-August 1862, he was listed on detached service in Montgomery.* He was 6'1 and born in 1837.

Bradbury, J. W., Private, enlisted October 25, 1861, at Shorter. He was hospitalized during the month of June 1862. [17]*He reported to the regimental medical unit June 5, 1864, diagnosis acute dysenteria, and September 13, 1864, diagnosis was feb int quotid. He was suffered an injury to the middle finger of his left hand on August 10, 1864. The finger was later amputated.* [32]*The injury occurred at Kennesaw Mountain.* He was 6'1 and was paroled June 6, 1865, at Montgomery. Also spelled **Bradberry.**

Bradly, John, Private, [36]*enlisted November 1863 at Camden, Wilcox County.* [17]*He reported to the regimental medical unit four times in 1864. January 5, the diagnosis was feb int tert; January 16, feb int quotid; February 9, vulnus cont; and April 25, feb int quotid.*

Brady, William R., Private, was captured May 15, 1864, at Sugar Valley, Georgia, near Resaca. He was imprisoned at Alton, Illinois. He was discharged June 10, 1864, at Alton and enlisted in U.S. Navy.

Brent, W. T., Private, enlisted October 25, 1861, at Shorter. He was 5'6, born in 1840, and lived in Monroe County. He was granted a medical furlough January 6, 1862 and sent to Claiborne for 25 days. He was hospitalized during June 1862 while in Mississippi. [17]*He reported to the regimental medical unit four times with the diagnosis of feb int quotid: December 14, 1863, January 10, and 17, and July 31, 1864. He also reported to the hospital twice with feb int tert: June 2 and September 30, 1864. October 9 of the same year, he was back in the hospital with acute diarrhea. He was sent to the general hospital on October 15. He was wounded in the left leg at the battle of Franklin, Tennessee, on*

COMPANY H 345

November 30, 1864. He surrendered at Citronella, Mobile County May 14, 1865.

Britleing. A, Private, enlisted August 2, 1863, at Mobile. He was 5'5, a farmer, and born in 1845 in Lauderdale, Mississippi. See personal papers for M.S. Holcombe. Also spelled **Brighting**.

Brown, J. N., Private, enlisted October 10, 1862, Monroe County. [32]*He was discharged.*

[18]**Brown, John**, *Private, was listed in 1863 as 45 years old with blue eyes, dark hair, dark complexion, 5'11, a laborer, and a deserter.*

Brown, N. R., Private, enlisted October 25, 1861, at Shorter. He was hospitalized during June 1862. Captured December 15, 1864, Nashville, he was imprisoned at Camp Douglas, Illinois. He died March 22, 1865, of pleurisy and is buried in lot number 995, Block 3, Chicago City Cemetery.

Brown, William J., Private, was discharged November 22, 1862.

Brudberry, M., Corporal.

Buck, J. W., Private, enlisted February 28, 1862, at Dallas County. He transferred to another regiment.

Burnett, Oliver Simpson, Private, enlisted November 16, 1861, at Montgomery and was from Lafayette. Captured December 25, 1864, Pulaski, Tennessee, he was imprisoned at Camp Chase, Ohio. [30]*He was born September 24, 1837.* [32]*He transferred to the regimental band.*

Burney, W. T., Private, enlisted September 9, 1861, at Memphis. [12]*He transferred to the Virginia Corps.* He was 5'6 and born 1845 in Jasper County, Georgia.

Campbell, A., Private, enlisted February 28, 1862, at Dallas County. He was discharged April 25, 1862.

Campbell, A. B., Private. [32]*He transferred to another unit.*

Campbell, A. S., Private, enlisted February 28, 1862, at Dallas County. He was hospitalized during June 1862. [32]*He transferred to another unit.*

Campbell, Charles, Private, enlisted February 28, 1862, at Dallas County. He was hospitalized during June 1862. [32]*He transferred to another unit.*
Note: Charles Campbell is also listed as a member of the 58th Alabama.

Campbell, J. K., Private, enlisted February 28, 1862, at Dallas County. He was hospitalized during June 1862. [32]*He transferred to another unit.*
Note: J. K. Campbell is also listed as a member of the 58th Alabama.

Campbell, W. J., Private, enlisted February 28, 1862, at Dallas County. He was hospitalized during June 1862. [32]*He transferred to another unit.*
Note: W. J. Campbell is also listed as a member of the 58th Alabama.

Carr, Patrick, Private, enlisted October 25, 1861, at Camp Davis. His home was in Monroe County. He was hospitalized at Macon, Georgia, July 8, 1864. [17]*He reported to the regimental medical unit three times* with the diagnosis feb int quotid: December 2, 1863, March 28 and April 10, 1864. He reported sick twice with feb int tert: December 28, 1863, and January 1, 1864. He reported sick twice with diagnosis feb remitt: January 16, and February 6, 1864.

Carter, Charles Newton, Private, enlisted October 25, 1861, at Camp Davis. He was discharged July 5, 1862. [20]*He re-enlisted in the 54th Alabama. He was born December 12, 1838, at Mt. Willing in Lowndes County. He was living in Mexia, Monroe County, in 1907.*

Carter, James W., Private, enlisted October 25, 1861, at Camp Davis. His home was Monroe County. He was hospitalized during June 1862. [17]*He reported to the regimental medical unit six times in 1864. January 5, the diagnosis was tonsilitis; February 25, lumbago; March 5, lumbago; April 28, catarrhus; June 15, acute diarrhea; and July 29, debilitas.* He was paroled at Greensboro, North Carolina, May 1865.

Chisholm, Neal K., Private, enlisted May 10, 1862, at Corinth, Mississippi. [36]*On the Muster Roll for his company for the period of December 1863 through February 1864, he was listed as absent since the last muster roll.* [17]*He reported to the regimental medical unit on December 13, 1863, diagnosis feb int tert. He reported sick three times with diagnosis feb int quotid, January 27, February 14, and March 28, 1864..* [9]*He was wounded July 20, 1864, at Atlanta* (Peachtree Creek), *diagnosis fracture of the frontal.* Note: Chisholm was captured at Peachtree Creek and was immediately sent to a Union hospital in Nashville. *On September 5, bone fragments were removed. On October 6, diagnosis was pyaemia. He died on November 12, 1864,* in a Nashville Union hospital of a scalp wound. He was buried in the Nashville City Cemetery, and later moved to Mt. Olivet Cemetery. He was born in 1829 and his mother's name was Margaret.

Coleman, Joseph, Private, enlisted November 23, 1862, at Mobile. [17]*He reported to the regimental medical unit December 1, 1863, diagnosis was catarrhus, January 9, 1864, morbi cutis, and again April 6, parotitis. November 7, the diagnosis was catarrhus, and he was transferred to the general hospital November 26.* Also listed as **J. A., J. H. Coleman.**

[18]**Conner, John,** Private, *was described in 1863 as 46 years old with blue eyes, light hair, fair complexion, 5'8, a painter, and a deserter.*

Connolly, John, Private, was listed as a deserter. [18]***John Connell,*** *Private, was described in 1863 as 46 years old with gray eyes, auburn hair, fair complexion, 5'7, and a laborer.*

Craig, J. M., Private, enlisted February 28, 1862, Dallas County. [32]*He transferred to another unit.* Note: May be James M. Craig in Company H 58th Alabama.

Craker, Calvin W., Private, [17]*reported to the regimental medical unit on June 10, 1864, diagnosis acute dysenteria. He was transferred to the general hospital the next day. Also spelled **Kraker**.*

Cummings, Samuel McL., drummer, enlisted September 25, 1861. He was born February 1848. On April 15, 1862, his mother, Susan Cummings, requested that her son be discharged for several reasons. She cited his age, her need for him to help her run the farm, and because of the impact of the battle of Shiloh. She wrote a letter to her son's commanding officer and another to President Jeff Davis.

Daggett, George A., Private, enlisted October 25, 1861, Macon County. He was born in 1833. He was granted a medical furlough January 8, 1862, for 20 days and sent to Burnt Corn, Monroe County. He was hospitalized during June 1862 in Mississippi. He died July 10, 1862, at Meridian, Mississippi, leaving widow Martha L. Also spelled **Doggette**.

Dailey, Jacob, Private, enlisted October 10, 1862, Monroe County. He was hospitalized during June 1862 in Mississippi. [32]*He was discharged.*

Dailey, James T., Private, enlisted October 10, 1862, Monroe County. He was 5'11 and born in Monroe County. [17]*He reported to the regimental medical unit December 6, 1863, diagnosis was dyspepsia, and November 6, 1864, diagnosis pneumonia.*

Daily, Fielding Straughn, Private, enlisted January 10, 1864, at Mobile. [17]*He reported to the regimental medical unit October 9, 1864, diagnosis acute diarrhea. He was moved to the general hospital on the 15th. He suffered a slight head wound November 30, 1864, at the battle of Franklin, Tennessee.* [40]*He was born January 1, 1846, son of John Hill and Margaret Straughn Daily. He married Georgia English. He died October 29, 1934, and was buried at Philadelphia Baptist Church, Tunnel Springs in Monroe County.*

Daily, S. F., Private, was a resident of Monroe County and was paroled at Greensboro, North Carolina, May 1865. Note: Is this **F. S. Daily**?

Danas, J. W., Private

Daniel, John M., Private, [36]*enlisted February 11, 1864, at Pollard, Alabama.* [17]*He reported to the regimental medical unit April 12, 1864, diagnosis was acute dysenteria.*

Daniel, N., Private, enlisted February 28, 1862, Dallas County. Note: May have transferred to Company H 58th Alabama.

Daniel, R., Private, enlisted February 28, 1862, Dallas County. Note: May have transferred to Company H 58th Alabama.

[17]***Davis, James***, *Private, reported to the regimental medical unit on December 23, 1863, diagnosis feb int quotid.*

[17]**Davis, Jno. T.**, *Private, was severely wounded in the left thigh on August 15, 1864. He was moved to the general hospital the same day.*

[36]**Davis, John. R.**, *Private, enlisted November 4, 1863, Camden, Wilcox County.* [17]*He reported to the regimental medical unit June 23, 1864, the diagnosis was vul cont vel lac.* [32]*He was killed during the siege of Atlanta August 1864.*

Davison, J. N., Corporal, enlisted October 25, 1862, at Camp Davis. He was hospitalized during June 1862 in Mississippi. [17]*He reported to the regimental medical unit December 12, diagnosis was catarrhus, and December 23, 1863, feb int quotid. He reported sick four times in 1864. January 11, diagnosis was feb int tert, and February 1, debilitas. He was placed on furlough February 3. March 11, diagnosis was feb int tert. He was moved to the general hospital at Spring Hill in Mobile the next day. June 21, the diagnosis was v. inscisum. He was moved to the general hospital the same day. July 28, 1864, he was listed as killed on field, at the battle of Poor House in Atlanta.*

Davison, James Miller, Sergeant, enlisted October 24, 1862, at Camp Davis. [17]*He reported to the regimental medical unit January 10, 1864, diagnosis catarrhus. He reported again March 22 and April 16, 1864, diagnosis feb int tert. On August 6, diagnosis was v. cont., right thigh (wounded by a shell fragment). He was wounded in the thigh November 30, 1864, at the battle of Franklin, Tennessee* (within a few feet of the famous gin house). Captured December 17, 1864, at Franklin, Tennessee, he was imprisoned at Camp Chase, Ohio. [1]*He was sent to Point Lookout, Maryland, March 1, 1865, and exchanged April 6, 1865. He was paroled April 6, 1865. He was born December 14, 1844, Scotland, Monroe County. He was living in Brewton, Alabama, in 1907.* [37]*In 1921 he stated he was in battles at Shiloh, Resaca, New Hope church, Poor House, Peachtree Creek and Franklin, and that he was wounded at Franklin and Kennesaw Mountain.* According to *Memorial Record of Alabama*, James Davison was the son of William and Mary J. McMillan Davison. After the war, he studied to be a lawyer and later entered politics.

Davison, W. M., Private, was discharged December 5, 1861.

[17]**Dean, James**, *Private, reported to the regimental medical unit June 23, 1864, diagnosis was feb int quotid.*

Dean, Jeremiah J., Private, [17]*reported to the regimental medical unit, diagnosis constipatio. He was slightly wounded in the left hip July 28, 1864, possibly at the battle of Ezra church near Atlanta. He was transferred to the general hospital July 31.* Also spelled **Deen**.

Deason, W. M., Private, [42]*was granted a 15-day furlough January 15, 1862, to Stockton, Alabama.* [25]*He died January 27, 1862, and is buried in Magnolia Cemetery in Mobile.*

Dees, Abner, Private, ³⁶*enlisted January 30, 1864, at Camden, Wilcox County.* He was 5'2, born 1818, and lived in Monroe County. He was admitted to Ross Hospital, Mobile, diagnosis was asthma, April 14, 1864, and released May 9, 1864. ¹⁷*He reported to the regimental medical unit June 19, 1864, diagnosis asthma.* He was moved to the general hospital the next day. He was paroled June 16, 1865, at Mobile. Also spelled **Dease, Deen, Deseree, Deese.**

Dees, Joel, Private, ³⁶*enlisted January 30, 1864, at Camden, Wilcox County.* ¹⁷*He reported to the regimental medical unit three times in 1864. March 22, diagnosis was catarrhus, and March 26, asthma.* He was transferred to the general hospital at Greenville the next day. November 3, the diagnosis was feb int tert. He was captured December 15, 1864, at Nashville and imprisoned at Camp Douglas, Illinois, where he was paroled June 6, 1865. He was from Neshoba, Mississippi. Also listed as **Jewell Dees, Joseph Dees.**

Deese, C. T., Private, enlisted May 10, 1862, at Corinth, Mississippi. ¹⁷*He reported to the regimental medical unit three times in 1864. January 2, the diagnosis was feb int quotid, June 6, acute dysenteria, and April 15, asthma.* He was transferred to the general hospital April 18. The regimental medical unit lists him as having been killed July 20, possibly at the battle of Peach Tree Creek, near Atlanta. Also spelled **Deas, Dease, Dees**

Dennis, J. U., Private, enlisted February 28, 1862, Dallas County. ¹²*J. N. Dennis died June 13, 1861.*

Densler, W. H., Private, was discharged April 25, 1862.

Duncan, J. F., Private, was hospitalized in Richmond in 1863.

Dunn, Anthony Wayne, Private, enlisted September 8, 1863, at Mobile. He was 6'2 and born 1819 in Washington County. ¹⁷*He reported to the regimental medical unit four times in 1864. February 19, diagnosis was acute diarrhea, April 23, feb int quotid, and June 13, acute dysenteria.* He was moved to the general hospital the next day. He was slightly wounded in his right arm and wrist July 28, and was moved to the general hospital on the 31st. He was paroled at Greensboro, North Carolina, May 1865.

Dyke, Lewis H., Private, ³⁶*enlisted September 9, 1863, Shelby County.* He was listed as sick in quarters on the muster roll for December 1863 through February 1864. ¹⁷*He reported to the regimental medical unit on December 5, 1863, diagnosis ascites, and was immediately sent to the general hospital. He reported to the hospital again February 23, 1864, diagnosis oedema, and March 3, anasarca.* He was transferred to the general hospital March 12. He was paroled May 15, 1864, at Louisville, Kentucky. His home was in Shelby County. Also listed as **S. H. Dycke.**

Eddins, Francis Marion, Private, enlisted October 25, 1861, at Camp Davis and was from Wilcox County. He was hospitalized August 15, 1864, Macon, Georgia. [17]*He reported to the regimental medical unit three times in 1864. June 5, diagnosis was acute dysenteria, July 7, chronic diarrhea, and November 3, acute diarrhea.* [2]*He is buried at McGavock Cemetery, Franklin, Tennessee, section 69, lot number 28. Note: He died at battle of Franklin, Tennessee, on November 30, 1864.* [30]*He was born ca 1841, Wilcox County, son of William Riley and Nancy King Eddins.*

[17]**Eddins, J. M.,** *Private, reported to the regimental medical unit on June 18, 1864, diagnosis chronic diarrhea.*

Eddins, John Rufus, Private, enlisted October 25, 1861, Camp Shorter. [17]*He reported to the regimental medical unit three times with diagnosis feb int quotid: on December 2, and December 26, 1863, and on March 31, 1864.* He was listed as a corporal on the hospital records. Captured July 20, 1864, at the battle of Peachtree Creek near Atlanta, he was imprisoned at Camp Douglas, Illinois. He was received at a hospital in Richmond, Virginia, February 9, 1865. [30]*He was November 15, 1837, at Pineapple, Wilcox County, son of William Riley and Nancy Manning Eddins. He married Emiline L. Beard. He died December 21, 1921, and was buried in Stranger Cemetery, Falls County, Texas.*

Eddins, Riley Harrison, Private, enlisted October 25, 1861, at Camp Davis. He was granted a medical furlough January 28, 1862, for 20 days and sent to Pineapple. [17]*He reported to the regimental medical unit on June 4, 1864, diagnosis acute diarrhea, and on July 21, 1864, diagnosis V inscisum.* He was paroled at Greensboro, North Carolina, May 1865. [30]*He was born ca 1845, Wilcox County, son of William Riley and Nancy King Eddins. He married A. A. Williams.*

Elrod, L. D., Private, was hospitalized September 7, 1864, Macon, Georgia.

Elton, Henry, Private, was captured December 15, 1864, Nashville, and imprisoned at Camp Douglas, Illinois.

[30]**Emmett, John,** *Private, in September 1863 was described as 45 years old, hazel eyes, dark hair, fair complexion, 5'8, a mason, and a deserter.*

Emmett, W. H., Private, enlisted October 13, 1862, Monroe County. [17]*He reported to the regimental medical unit three times in 1864. On February 6, the diagnosis was feb int tert, on June 21, acute diarrhea, and on November 13, feb int tert.* He was paroled June 19, 1865, at Mobile.

Erwin, J.C., Private, enlisted February 28, 1862, Dallas County. He was hospitalized during June 1862 in Mississippi. Note: May have transferred to Company H 58th Alabama. Also spelled **Ervin**

COMPANY H 351

Falkenberry, Dearon, Private, was 5'8, a farmer, and born 1822 in Monroe County. [17]*He reported to the regimental medical unit six times in 1864. January 1, diagnosis was debilitas, and he was granted a 15 day furlough. February 6, March 9, and June 27, the diagnosis was acute diarrhea, and April 16, constipatio. July 28 at Ezra Church near Atlanta, he suffered a severe injury to his right knee and was moved to the general hospital July 31.* He died August 1864, Macon, Georgia. According to the *Macon Daily Telegraph,* June 26, 1866, Falkenberry was buried in the Old Cemetery in Macon. Probably Deason or David. [30]*He was the son of Israel and Tabitha Williams Falkenberry, and spouse of Eliza Ann Nettles.* Also spelled **Falkingbury, Faulkenberry.**

Farnell, Robert F., Private, [36] *enlisted January 1863 in Mobile,* his home. [17]*Regimental medical unit records indicate that he reported to the hospital four times in 1864. January 4, diagnosis was feb int tert, January 23, catarrhus, June 5, acute diarrhea, and June 15, acute dysenteria. He was moved to the general hospital June 16.* He was admitted to the hospital in Macon, Georgia, July 29, 1864 and placed on medical furlough August 17, 1864, for 20 days. He was placed in a hospital in Meridian, Mississippi, December 20, 1864.

Foster, John S., Private, [17]*reported to the regimental medical unit on February 21, 1864, diagnosis was rubeola, and was moved to the general hospital in Mobile immediately. He reported sick August 26, 1864, diagnosis was icterus. Jno. H. Foster reported sick August 6, 1864, diagnosis acute diarrhea. Jno. J. Foster reported sick April 13, diagnosis feb int quotid.* He was hospitalized June 6, 1864, Macon, Georgia. His home was Mobile.

Foster, W.H., Private, enlisted February 28, 1862 Dallas County. He was hospitalized during June 1862 in Mississippi. [32]*He transferred to another unit.* Note: May have transferred to Company H, 58th Alabama.

Fountain, Henry P., Private, enlisted October 25, 1861, at Camp Davis. He was hospitalized during June 1862 in Mississippi. [17]*He reported to the regimental medical unit on December 18, 1863, diagnosis was feb int tert. On March 18, 1864, the diagnosis was acute dysenteria. He was listed as a sergeant on the regimental medical unit records.* Captured December 15, 1864, Nashville, he was imprisoned at Camp Douglas, Illinois. Also listed as **H. S. Foster**

Fountain, W. H., Private, enlisted September 10, 1862, at Mobile. [17]*He reported to the regimental medical unit December 6, 1863, diagnosis was debilitas. He reported three times in 1864. January 21, diagnosis was feb int quotid, February 10, dysenteria, and March 19, feb int tert.* He was hospitalized at Meridian, Mississippi, January 12, 1865, after the retreat from Nashville. He was suffering from wounds and was granted a furlough. Also spelled **Fontaine.**

Gammon, E. W., Private, [36]*enlisted August 18, 1863, Talladega.* [17]*He reported to the regimental medical unit March 30, 1864, diagnosis was feb int quotid.* He died [10]*April 9, 1864,* [6] *in Greenville,* his home. Also listed as **E. H. Gammon.**

Gayle, R. D., Private, enlisted September 1, 1863, at Mobile. His home was in Cahaba. [36]*On the muster roll for December 1863 through February 1864 he listed on detached duty – ordnance.* He was detailed from the company October 13, 1863, considered unfit for field service. [17]*He reported to the regimental medical unit on September 23, 1864. The diagnosis was strictula urethra, and he was immediately sent to the general hospital.* Also spelled **Gagle, Yugle.** See Service Records for F. W. Seddons.

[1]***Giddeus, Pickney,*** *Private, was born October 20, 1836, in Conecuh County. He transferred to 2nd Regt. Confederate Engineers, August 5, 1863. His home was in Pineapple, Wilcox County, in 1907.*

Goldman, L., Private, enlisted February 28, 1862, Dallas County. On the muster roll for September-October 1862, He was listed as sick in quarters.

Goodwin, M., Private, enlisted February 28, 1862, Dallas County. He was discharged August 1862 - furnished J. T. Harbrooke as substitute. He was paroled at Selma May 1865.

Goodwin, W. P., Private.

Goodwin, W. R., Private.

Gordon, J. J., Private, enlisted October 25, 1861, at Camp Davis. He was detailed as a nurse in the hospital June 1862. [12]*He died August 1, 1862.* He was born in 1861, Dallas County.

Gowing, T., Private, was granted a sick furlough November 12, 1862, for 18 days and sent to Montgomery.

Grace, J. A., Private, enlisted April 1864, at Rome, Georgia and was from Monroe County. [17]*He reported to the regimental medical unit on June 15, 1864, diagnosis feb int tert, and transferred to the general hospital the next day.* He was paroled at Greensboro, North Carolina, May 1865.

Graves, J. H., Private, enlisted February 28, 1862, Dallas County. [32]*He transferred to another unit.* Note: May have transferred to Company H, 58th Alabama.

Graves, J. T., Private, enlisted February 28, 1862, Dallas County. [32]*He transferred to another unit.* Note: May have transferred to Company H, 58th Alabama.

Green, A. P., Private, enlisted February 28, 1862, Dallas County. On the muster roll for September-October 1862, he was listed as sick in quarters. [32]*He transferred to another unit.* Note: May have transferred to Company H, 58th Alabama.

Haines, Nathaniel, Private, died August 28, 1864.
Hall, George T., Private, [17]*was wounded July 4, 1864, during the Atlanta campaign.* He was moved to the general hospital the next day where they amputated his left thumb and forefinger. [32]*His wound was received at Vinings Stations, Georgia.* He was captured December 15, 1864, Nashville, and imprisoned at Camp Douglas, Illinois. He was paroled in Montgomery in May 1865. He was 5'7 and from Monroe County. [37]*He was born July 8, 1849, Camden, Wilcox County.* In 1921 he stated that he was at the battle of Resaca, wounded at Peachtree Creek, and captured at Nashville when he was imprisoned for five months.
Hall, R. C., Private, enlisted February 28, 1862, Dallas County. He was granted a disability discharge May 18, 1862. He was born 1839 in Dallas County.
Hanella, F., Private, was hospitalized during June 1862 in Mississippi.
Harbrock, John T., Private, transferred from Company D as a substitute for M. Goodwin. [36]*He enlisted November 25, 1862, in Mobile where he lived.* He was hospitalized on October 1863. [36]*He was hospitalized on the muster roll for December 1863 through February 1864.* He was granted a 60 day furlough from Lauderdale, Mississippi, January 31, 1865. Note: This was probably to allow him to recuperate after the retreat from Nashville. Also listed as **A. T. Harbrock**
Harrell, C. L., 2nd Lieutenant, enlisted February 28, 1862, Dallas County. He enrolled conscripts in Huntsville during November and December 1862. [32]*He was promoted to captain of company H, 58th Alabama.* Also spelled **C. S. Harroll**
Harrell, E. F., Private, enlisted February 28, 1862, Dallas County. On the muster roll for November-December 1862, he was listed as sick in quarters. [32]*He transferred to another unit.* Note: May have transferred to Company H, 58th Alabama.
Harrell, F. E., Private, enlisted February 28, 1862, Dallas County. [32]*He transferred to another unit.*
Harrell, S. J., Private, enlisted February 28, 1862, Dallas County, and reenlisted September 17, 1862.
[36]**Harris, James,** Private, enlisted February 15, 1864, at Camden, Wilcox County. He was listed as hospitalized on the muster roll for December 1863 through February 1864. [17]*He reported to the regimental medical unit March 11, 1864, diagnosis was feb int quotid. He was moved to the general hospital at Spring Hill in Mobile the next day.*
Harris, Nathaniel, Private, [36]*enlisted February 15, 1864, at Camden, Wilcox County.* He was hospitalized on the muster roll for December 1863 through February 1864. [17]*He reported to the regimental medical unit on March 11, 1864, diagnosis was feb int quotid. He moved to the*

general hospital at Spring Hill in Mobile the next day. He was admitted to Ross Hospital August 17, 1864, diagnosis chronic diarrhea. He died August 28, 1864, and was buried in Magnolia Cemetery in Mobile, row 16, grave 8.

[17]**Harvel, U. H.**, *Private, reported to the regimental medical unit February 21, 1864, diagnosis was rubeola. He was moved to the general hospital at Mobile the same day. He reported sick again April; diagnosis was acute diarrhea.*

Harvel, W. D., Private, enlisted December 7, 1863, at Mobile. [36]*He was listed as hospitalized on the muster roll for December 1863 through February 1864.* [17]*He suffered a slight wound to his left forefinger July 28, 1864. He was moved to the general hospital on the 31st. He reported to the regimental medical unit November 12, 1864, diagnosis acute diarrhea.* He was paroled at Greensboro, North Carolina, May 1865. Also spelled **Harville.**

Hauser, J. H., Private, enlisted February 28, 1862, at Dallas County.

Hilton, Henry, Private, [36]*enlisted November 23, 1863, Mobile. He was hospitalized on the muster roll for December 1863 through February 1864.* [17]*He reported to the regimental medical unit December 7, 1863, diagnosis feb int quotid. He reported to the regimental medical unit four times in 1864. The diagnosis was acute dysenteria January 10, and September 30. February 21, diagnosis was rubeola, and he was moved to the general hospital in Mobile the same day. He suffered a slight wound to his left breast July 2, at the battle of Ezra Church near Atlanta. He was moved to the general hospital July 31.* He was captured December 16, 1864, at Nashville and imprisoned at Camp Douglas, Illinois. Also spelled **Helton.**

Hinson, J. M., Private, enlisted November 22, 1861, Camp Gladden. Also spelled **Henson.**

Hinson, John W., Ordnance Sergeant, enlisted November 15, 1861, Pensacola. He was wounded at Shiloh, Tennessee, April 6, 1862. He was hospitalized during June 1862 in Mississippi. He was admitted to Ross Hospital in Mobile September 27, 1863, diagnosis feb int tert, and released October 2, 1863. [36]*On the muster roll for December 1863 through February 1864, he was listed on detached duty – ordnance on city redoubt.* [17]*He reported to the regimental medical unit in September of 1864 and November 3, 1864, diagnosis was feb int tert. He was sent to the general hospital on November 26.* [32]*He died at Mount Pleasant, Tennessee, November 1864.*

Hixon, Samuel, Private, enlisted August 28, 1863, at Mobile. He was 5'8, born in 1821, and was a resident of Monroe County. [17]*He reported to the regimental medical unit January 10, 1864, diagnosis pneumonia.*

He was moved to the general hospital January 14, where he died January 16, 1864.

[18]**Hohan, John,** Private, was listed in 1863 as 45 years old, with gray eyes, black hair, dark complexion, 5'8, and a laborer. [32]*He deserted.*

Holiday, J. W., Private, was granted a medical furlough from a hospital in Meridian, Mississippi, January 13, 1865.

Hornback, William F., Private, enlisted October 12, 1862, at Mobile. [36]*On the muster roll for December 1863 through February 1864, he was listed as absent without leave.* [17]*He reported to the regimental medical unit March 21, 1864, diagnosis catarrhus. He suffered a severe wound to his arm May 1864,* [32]*at the battle of Resaca, Georgia.* He was hospitalized November 9, 1864, at Mobile.

Houser, Frank. H., Private, enlisted March 1, 1862, Selma, ward master. He was hospitalized during June 1862 in Mississippi.

Howard, G. T., Private, enlisted February 28, 1862, at Dallas County. Note: May have transferred to Company H, 58th Alabama.

Hughes, James, Drummer, was captured at Kennesaw Mountain, Georgia, July 3, 1864, and imprisoned at Camp Douglas, Illinois. Also listed as **Joseph Hughes**

Hughey, J. S., Private, enlisted February 28, 1862, Dallas County. Note: May have transferred to Company H, 58th Alabama.

Jenkins, A. E., Private, enlisted February 1864, Monroe County. He was paroled at Greensboro, North Carolina, April 1865. [17]*Suffering with acute diarrhea, he reported to the regimental medical unit April 15 and July 9, 1864.*

Jenkins, James S., Private, was born 1819, Colleton District, South Carolina. He was granted a disability discharge on March 22, 1862. He served as acting assistant surgeon during the month of January 1862.

Jenkins, W., Private, suffering from wounds, was admitted to Way Hospital, Meridian, Mississippi, January 11, 1865, after the retreat to Mississippi.

[18]**Johnson, Joseph,** Private, was listed in 1863 as 48 years old with gray eyes, dark hair, dark complexion, 5'8, and a laborer. [32]*He deserted.*

Johnson, L., Private, enlisted September 17, 1862, at Mobile. He was hospitalized during June 1862 in Mississippi. [32]*He transferred to another unit.*

Johnson, Lydall, Musician, was discharged on December 27, 1861.

[18]**Jones, John,** Private, was listed in 1863 as 47 years old with gray eyes, light hair, fair complexion, 5'6 and a carpenter. [32]*He deserted.*

[36]**Jones, Wiley W.,** Private, enlisted November 3, 1863, at Camden, Wilcox County. [17]*He reported to the regimental medical unit three times in 1864. On March 19, the diagnosis was acute diarrhea, on April 16,*

dyspepsia, and on July 9, debilitas. ³⁰He enlisted November 12, 1862, at Mobile. He was discharged May 1865. He was born November 12, 1823, Brooklyn, Conecuh County, to Elbert and Elizabeth Bensley Jones. His twin brother, William Henry, was in Company B. He married (1) Mary, (2) Leah Louiza Collins. He died June 3, 1904, and was buried in Covington County.

Kearley, A., Private, ³⁶enlisted February 11, 1864, Camden, Wilcox County. ¹⁷He reported to the regimental medical unit March 22, 1864, diagnosis was rubeola. He was sent to the general hospital the same day. He reported sick April 24, 1864, diagnosis was debilitas. He died May 23, 1864, at Greensboro, Georgia.

Kearley, T. J., Private, enlisted March 29, 1862, Burnt Corn. ¹⁷He reported to the regimental medical unit December 15, 1863, diagnosis feb int quotid. He reported sick with feb int tert January 25, February 17, and June 20, 1864. On June 21, diagnosis was acute diarrhea.

Keenum, George W., Private, ³⁶enlisted August 11, 1863. ¹⁷He reported to the regimental medical unit three times in 1864. January 18, diagnosis was ebrietas, February 14, acute diarrhea, and April 21, catarrhus. He was captured December 16, 1864, at Nashville and imprisoned at Camp Douglas, Illinois. Also spelled **Kennen, Keenam, Keenham, Kenan.**

¹⁸**Kelly, John**, Private, was listed in 1863 as 46 years old with blue eyes, brown hair, fair complexion, 5'7, and a molder. He deserted.

Kelly, Thomas, Private, was 5'11, and lived Dalton County. He was hospitalized at West Point, Mississippi, January 10, 1865.

Kelly, W. W., Private, enlisted February 28, 1862, at Dallas County. He was hospitalized during June 1862 in Mississippi. He died ¹⁷July 10, 1862, leaving mother, Catherine Jewell Kelly.

Kendrick, S., Private, enlisted October 23, 1862, Conecuh. A farmer, he was 5'10 and born in 1836, Butler County. He was granted a disability discharge November 18, 1862.

Kidd, James, Private, enlisted August 18, 1862, at Mobile. ³²He transferred to another unit.

Killcrease, J. S., Private, ³⁶enlisted August 20, 1862, at Mobile. On the muster roll for December 1863 through February 1864, he was listed as absent. He was 5'10, born 1822 in Baldwin County, and a millwright. ¹⁷**J. L. Kilcrease** reported to the regimental medical unit April 14, 1864, the diagnosis was dysuria.

Killough, R. L., Private, enlisted February 28, 1862, at Dallas County. He was hospitalized during June 1862 in Mississippi. ¹²On the muster roll for July-August 1862, he was listed as absent sick. He was discharged October 19, 1862. Also spelled **Kelo**

COMPANY H

Kirby, T. N., Private, wounded, was admitted to Way Hospital at Meridian, Mississippi, January 18, 1865, after the retreat from Nashville.

Kirkham, William L., Private, [36]*enlisted July 29, 1863, at Linden. He was hospitalized at June 23, 1864, in Macon, Georgia. His home was Murray County.* [17]*He reported to the regimental medical unit December 8, 1863, diagnosis was catarrhus. He reported sick three times in 1864. January 6, diagnosis was acute dysenteria, June 22, anasarca, and September 21, acute Rheum. He was moved to a general hospital June 22 and September 27.*

Kirkland, N. M., Private

Knight, Thomas, Private, [36]*enlisted February 16, 1864, at Mobile.* [17]*He reported to the regimental medical unit March 20, diagnosis was sub luxatio. He reported sick again August 26, diagnosis feb int tert. He was suffering with acute diarrhea during September.* He was wounded at Franklin, Tennessee (November 30, 1864), in the right arm and leg. He was captured December 17, 1864, at Franklin and imprisoned at Camp Chase, Ohio. [20]***Thomas Wilborn Knight** enlisted December 1861, at Mobile. He was born November 23, 1830, near Stone Mountain, Campbell County, Georgia. Discharged in May 1865, Meridian, Mississippi, he was living in Winston County in 1907.*

Ladd, W. J., Private, enlisted August 25, 1863, at Mobile. He was 5'9 and born 1823 in Anson County, North Carolina. [13]*He was wounded at New Hope Church in Georgia in 1864.* [17]*He reported to the regimental medical unit seven times in 1864. January 20 and March 30, diagnosis was catarrhus. February 8, diagnosis was feb int quotid, and April 20, feb int tert. August 30 and again in September, the diagnosis was acute diarrhea. Chronic diarrhea on October resulted in his being moved to the general hospital on the 7th.* Also listed as **W. L., Wm. Ladd**

Lassiter, W. D., Private, enlisted February 28, 1862, at Dallas County. [12]*He was listed as absent without leave during the summer of 1862.*

Lewis, Thomas F., Private, enlisted October 25, 1861, at Shorters. Captured April 7, 1862, at Shiloh, Tennessee, where he was wounded severely in the thigh, he was sent to the prison at Camp Chase, Ohio. He rejoined his unit on September 16, 1862. Also spelled **Louis.** He was discharged March 8, 1863.

[18]***Lonally, James,** Private, was listed in September 1863 as 45 years old, blue eyes, black hair, fair complexion, 6'1, a laborer, a deserter.*

Manahan, Patrick, Private, was paroled May 1865 at Montgomery. [17]*He reported to the regimental medical unit December 30, 1863, diagnosis was pneumonia, and April 19, 1864, diagnosis acute dysenteria. He* suffered a slight wound to his shoulder in May 1864, possibly at the battle of Resaca, Georgia. Also spelled **Monahan**.

[18]**Manger, Jerry**, was listed in September 1863 as 46 years old with gray eyes, brown hair, fair complexion, 5'7, a laborer, and a deserter.

Marshall, W. H., Private, enlisted August 25, 1863, at Mobile. He was 6'1 and born 1825 in Mecklenburg, Virginia. He was granted a medical furlough from LaGrange hospital for 30 days, typhoid pneumonia. [17]*He reported to the regimental medical unit March 30, 1864, diagnosis was acute diarrhea, and April 14, 1864, catarrhus.* Also listed as **W. L. Marshall**.

Massey, J. M., Private, enlisted August 23, 1863, at Mobile. He was 5'8 and born 1825 in Monroe County. [17]*He reported to the regimental medical unit twice in 1864. On March 16, the diagnosis was rubeola. He was sent to the general hospital at Greenville on the 18th. In October, the diagnosis was debilitas. He was moved to the general hospital October 21.* Captured November 30, 1864, Franklin, Tennessee, he was imprisoned at Camp Douglas, Illinois. He died March 6, 1865, and was buried in lot number 895-3 Chicago City Cemetery.

Mathews, John, Private, was paroled at May 30, 1865. [17]*He reported to the regimental medical unit July 14, 1864, diagnosis acute diarrhea.*

Maynard, J., Private, enlisted February 28, 1862, at Dallas County. He was granted a disability discharge July 4, 1862. Also spelled **Mayner**.

McCorveys, A. B., 2nd Lieutenant, was wounded at Shiloh, Tennessee, in April 1862, slight head wound. He resigned June 16, 1862.

McCorvey, Neil, Private, was wounded at Shiloh, Tennessee, April 1862. [17]*He reported to the regimental medical unit July 2, 1864, diagnosis acute dysenteria.* He was admitted to the general hospital at Macon, Georgia, July 8, 1864, and placed on furlough July 17. Also spelled **McCorvy**

McDaniel, John, Private, enlisted October 3, 1863, Greenville. A farmer, he was 5'6 and born 1818 in Washington County, Georgia. He was granted a disability discharge November 20, 1863. He was admitted to the Mobile Hospital April 21, 1864, and returned to duty May 4.

McMahan, James, Private, was born 1809. [36]*On the muster roll for December 1863 through February 1864 he was listed on detached duty – carpenter for the city ordnance.* He was placed on medical furlough, May 28, 1864, for 60 days, acute rheumatism.

McMillan, Benjamin Franklin, Sergeant, enlisted October 25, 1862, at Camp Davis. [36]*On the muster roll for December 1863 through February 1864, he was listed on extra duty – clerk in the adjutant's office.* [17]*He reported to the regimental medical unit December 2, 1863, diagnosis catarrhus. He reported sick January 14, 1864, diagnosis sub luxatio.*

He was killed at Franklin, Tennessee, November 30, 1864, and [39]buried at McGavock Cemetery, section 68, lot 2.

McMillan, Malcolm, Private, enlisted October 25, 1861, at Camp Davis. He was hospitalized during June 1862 in Mississippi. He was placed on medical furlough January 13, 1865.

McMillan, Murdock, Private, enlisted September 16, 1862, at Mobile. He was discharged November 1, 1862, - provided Celest Oliver as his substitute.

McMillan, R. N., Private, [36]*enlisted March 17, 1862. On the muster roll for December 1863 through February 1864 he was listed on extra duty – clerk to the regimental surgeon.* [17]*He reported to the regimental medical unit on December 23, 1863, diagnosis sub luxatio.* He was hospitalized with wounds at Meridian, Mississippi, after the retreat from Nashville. He was granted a medical furlough January 13, 1865.

McMillan, W. H., Sergeant, enlisted October 25, 1861, at Camp Davis. He was hospitalized during June 1862 in Mississippi. He was promoted to 5th Sergeant July 24, 1862. He was elected 2nd Lieutenant March 17, 1863. [17]*He reported to the regimental medical unit December 23, 1863, diagnosis debilitas, rank first lieutenant. He was granted a 15 day furlough December 25. He reported again on January 20, 1864, rank second lieutenant and on February 14, rank third lieutenant. Diagnosis last two times was feb int tert. On July 28, 1864, he was wounded in the left shoulder and chest. He died in the brigade hospital on the 31st.* [32]*He suffered the fatal wounds at Poor House in Atlanta.*

McMillan, William W., Captain, enlisted October 25, 1861, at Camp Davis. His home was in Scotland, Monroe County, where he was born in 1834. He was appointed captain October 25, 1861. He was granted a furlough June 23, 1862, for 10 days. [17]*He reported to the regimental medical unit December 17, 1863, diagnosis feb int tert. He reported sick again February 9, 1864, diagnosis icterus. He was granted a furlough for 20 days on the 15th. On July 2, the diagnosis was acute dysenteria; which resulted in his being transferred to the general hospital on the 4th. He suffered a slight wound to his left hand July 28, at the battle of Ezra Church near Atlanta. He was sent to the general hospital on the 31st. He was severely wounded in the left thigh and hand November 30, 1864, at the battle of Franklin, Tennessee.* Captured December 17, 1864, Franklin, Tennessee, he was imprisoned at Camp Chase, Ohio. Once released he returned to Scotland, a 30 day trip by wagon, train, and on foot. He died March 1895 and was buried in Old Scotland Cemetery, Monroe County.

McNeil, James N., Private, enlisted August 25, 1863, at Mobile. He was 5'8, born 1819 in Clarke County, and a farmer. [17]*He reported to the regimental medical unit June 15, 1864, diagnosis acute diarrhea. He* suffered a severe flesh wound (left thigh) July 28, 1864, at the battle of Ezra Church near Atlanta. He transferred to the general hospital on the 31st. He was hospitalized at March 28, 1865, Meridian, Mississippi. He transferred April 9, 1865, to Macon, Georgia, diagnosis was impetigo. He was captured during April 1865.

[18]**McQuirk, Thomas**, was described in September 1863 as 46 years old, hazel eyes, brown hair, fair complexion, 5'7, a blacksmith, and a deserter.

Monk, James A., Private, was discharged December 5, 1861. [32]*He transferred to another unit*

Morris, Jesse, Private, enlisted August 31, 1863, at Mobile. He was 5'10 and born 1823 in Monroe County. Captured at Chattahoochie, Georgia, July 4, 1864, he was imprisoned at Camp Douglas, Illinois. He died of pneumonia January 28, 1865, and was buried in lot number 593-2 Chicago City Cemetery.

Morris, Preston A., Private, was captured July 3, 1864, Marietta, Georgia. He was imprisoned at Camp Douglas, Illinois, where he was paroled May 16, 1865.

Morris, W. D., Private, enlisted October 10, 1862, Monroe County. [18]*He was listed in September 1863 as 24 years old with gray eyes, light hair, fair complexion, 5'8, a farmer, and a deserter.*

[1]**Mothershed, David B.**, enlisted September 1862 at Montgomery. He was discharged October 1862. He was born February 21, 1843, Lowndes County. He was living in Brantley in 1907.

[17]**Murphy, J. J.**, Private, reported to the regimental medical unit December 14 and 17, 1863, diagnosis was colica. He reported sick February 28,1864, diagnosis was rubeola, and March 2, diagnosis was pneumonia. He was moved to a Mobile general hospital March 2 where he died March 10, 1864. He was buried at Magnolia Cemetery in Mobile, row 12, grave 49.

Murphy, N. A., Private, enlisted September 16, 1862, at Mobile. He was discharged October 12, 1862 - furnished W. F. Hornback as substitute.

Murray, James Henry, Private, enlisted November 25, 1861, Camden, Wilcox County. He was hospitalized February 25, 1864, at Mobile. He was granted a furlough March 22, 1864, for 60 days. [17]*He reported to the regimental medical unit five times in 1864. February 8, the diagnosis was contusio, February 18, acute dysenteria, June 4, acute diarrhea, June 16, feb remitt, and June 18, feb int quotid.* [20]*He was paroled at Greensboro, North Carolina, April 1865. He was living in Escumbia in 1907.* [37]*He was born November 24, 1845, in Buena Vista, Monroe County. In 1921 he was living in Flomaton. He stated that he was at Bentonville, North Carolina.* Also spelled **Murry**.

Nettles, William T., Private, enlisted August 25, 1863, at Mobile. [17]*He reported to the regimental medical unit three with diagnosis of feb int tert, December 16, 1863, February 14 and April 20, 1864. He reported sick June 19, diagnosis was debilitas, and was moved to the general hospital the next day.* He was discharged at Montgomery at the end of the war. [30]*Nettles was born February 3, 1823, near Claiborne, Monroe County, to Joseph and Elsie Nichols Nettles. He married Mary Margaret Dubose. After the was Nettles was a farmer, active in politics and a civil engineer for the county. He died December 28, 1909, and was buried in the Philadelphia Baptist Cemetery, Tunnel Springs, Monroe County.*

Newberry, W. T., Private, enlisted October 25, 1861, at Camp Davis. He was appointed corporal December 1, 1862. He was placed on sick furlough January 6, 1862, for 20 days and sent to Monroeville. [17]*He reported to the regimental medical unit December 10 and December 27, 1863, diagnosis feb int quotid. He reported sick eight times in 1864. January 11 and February 9, diagnosis was feb int quotid. January 27, March 20, and April 24, diagnosis was feb int tert. February 28 and March 7, diagnosis was debilitas. In May 1864, he suffered a severe injury to his side,* [32]*possibly during the battle of Resaca, Georgia.*

O'Brien, M., Private, enlisted September 4, 1862, at Mobile. He was due pay from February 28, 1862, as substitute for R. S. Sharp. He was detailed for special order #17 September 1863 and returned to command October 1863. He was hospitalized May 19, 1864 and deserted May 25, 1864.

[17]**Odione, George,** Private, *reported to the regimental medical unit August 13, 1864, diagnosis was acute diarrhea, and September 21, 1864, feb int tert. He was transferred to the general hospital September 23.* Also spelled **Odiorne.**

[36]**Odione, W. W.,** Private, enlisted January 31, 1863, Mobile. On the muster rolls for December 1863 through February 1864, he was listed on detached duty – sharp shooter. [17]*He reported to the regimental medical unit December 10, 1863, complaint catarrhus. He reported sick again June 21, 1864, complaint acute diarrhea. He was wounded (right foot) during the battle of Peachtree Creek near Atlanta July 20, 1864. He was sent to the general hospital the next day.* **William W. Ordianne,** 5'6, was paroled May 17, 1865. **William W. Ordime** was 5'11, a mechanic, and born 1839 in Coosa County. He was granted a disability discharge December 31, 1861.

Oliver, Celest, Private, enlisted December 1, 1862, Mobile. [17]*He reported to the regimental medical unit July 3, complaint was hemeralopia, July 31, haemorrhois, and August 20, 1864, hemoralphia.* [32]*He was* wounded at New Hope Church in Georgia. He died October 14, 1864. He was a substitute for M. M. McMillan.

Perry, Reuben, Corporal, enlisted October 25, 1862, at Camp Davis. [17]*He reported to the regimental medical unit December 11, 1863, complaint was acute dysentery. He reported sick seven times in 1864. January 20, diagnosis was feb int quotid. February 7 and 27, and March 28, diagnosis was feb int tert. In September his complaint was acute dysentery. Finally November 20, his complaint was acute diarrhea. He was moved to the general hospital on the 29th.*

Phillips, W., Private, enlisted September 20, 1862, Butler County. He was 5'2, born 1828 in Harris County, Georgia, and a farmer. He was granted a disability discharge November 18, 1862.

Pickens, W. A., Private, enlisted February 28, 1862, Dallas County. Note: May have transferred to Company H, 58th Alabama.

Pitts, Harry W., Private, was hospitalized at West Point, Mississippi, January 13, 1865 after the retreat from Nashville.

Preston, J. E., Private, enlisted October 25, 1861, at Shorter. He had pay due as a sergeant from January 16, 1862. He applied for promotion to lieutenant January 17, 1862. [32]*He transferred to another unit.*

Raiford, L. H., Private, enlisted February 28, 1862, Dallas County. He was paroled May 1865 at Greensboro, North Carolina. He was born about 1844 in Alabama. [32]*He transferred to another unit.* Also spelled **Radford.**

[36]**Rains, James,** Private, enlisted December 31, 1863, Mobile. [17]*He reported to the regimental medical unit January 12, 1864, diagnosis was vulnus contusio.* [37]*He was born March 16, 1846, in Monroe County. He stated in 1921 that he had been in battles at New Hope Church, Peachtree Creek and Atlanta. He stated he was on furlough during January 1865. He could not get back to his regiment because it was in North Carolina. "I and 14 other soldiers including W. J. Robison, the 1st lieutenant of my company. They asked Montgomery if they could send a train to get us and they told him they couldn't. So he told us that we would hafta go back home."*

Raines, Thomas H., Private, enlisted October 25, 1861, at Camp Davis. He suffered a breast wound at Shiloh, Tennessee in April 1862. [12]*He was listed as sick and absent from duty during the summer of 1862.* [17]*He reported to the regimental medical unit three times in 1864. March 29, diagnosis was odontalgia. In May, possibly at the battle of Resaca, Georgia, he suffered a severe wound to his arm. September 30, diagnosis was debilitas.* He was declared unfit for field service and assigned as teamster November 19, 1864. He was paroled May 15,

1865, at Montgomery. [37]*He was born in 1844. In 1921 he stated that he was wounded at Shiloh and was in battles at Resaca and Nashville.*

Rasco, R. C. W., Private, enlisted February 28, 1862, Dallas County. [32]*He transferred to another unit.* Note: May have transferred to Company H, 58th Alabama.

Reagan, Robert, Private, enlisted October 9, 1862, Monroe County. [13]*Deserted.* [18]*In 1863 he was listed as 24 years old with gray eyes, light hair, fair complexion, 5'8, and an overseer.*

Reynoldson, John G., Private, was in the hospital at Macon, Georgia, during June 1864.

Reynoldson, John T., Private.

Richardson, J. W., Private, enlisted March 29, 1862, Burnt Corn, Monroe County, Alabama. [36]*On the muster rolls for December 1863 through February 1864 he was listed on detached duty – sharp shooter.* [17]*He reported to the regimental medical unit four times in 1864. January 6, diagnosis was feb int tert, July 8, feb int quotid, and August 8 and 28, diagnosis was acute diarrhea.* He was captured September 1, 1864, Jonesboro, Georgia. [32]*J. W. Richardson Jr. was discharged. J. W. Richardson Sr. was promoted to 4th corporal August 1864.*

Riley, Jeremiah, Private, [36]*enlisted February 18, 1863. He was listed as sick in quarters the same month.* He was a resident of Conecuh County. Captured December 15, 1864, at Nashville, he was imprisoned at Camp Douglas, Illinois, where he was paroled June 1865. [17]*Jere Riley reported to the regimental medical unit January 18, 1864, diagnosis was feb int tert. February 28, J. R. Riley reported sick. March 3, J. H. Riley reported sick, diagnosis parotitis.*

Riley, Lafayette R., Private, enlisted November 25, 1862, at Mobile. [17]*He reported to the regimental medical unit December 19, 1863, diagnosis was feb int tert, and December 21, abscessus.* [37]*He was born October 28, 1844, in Monroe County and was living in Monroe County in 1921. At that time, he stated he was in battles at Pensacola, Spring Hill, Franklin and Nashville. In the fall of 1863, he transferred to Company G in the 4th Alabama Cavalry.*

[17]***Riser, P.,*** Private, reported to the regimental medical unit October 9, 1864, diagnosis was debilitas. He moved to the general hospital on the 15th.

Rives, B. S., Private, enlisted October 25, 1861. He was 6' and born 1817 at Bodford, Virginia. He was granted a disability discharge December 31, 1861.

Rives, John H, Private, enlisted October 25, 1861, at Camp Davis. He was granted a medical furlough February 4, 1862, for 20 days and sent to Pineapple. His arm was slightly wounded at Shiloh, Tennessee in April 1862. Because he was wounded in the left thigh and permanently disabled, he was granted a furlough January 21, 1865, for 60 days and sent to Allentown, Wilcox County. Also spelled **Reives**.

Roark, R. H., Private, enlisted February 28, 1862, Dallas County. He was promoted to third sergeant February 28, 1862. [32]He transferred to another unit.

Roberts, E. M., Private, was killed at Shiloh, Tennessee, April 6, 1862.

[36]**Roberts, G. W.**, Private, enlisted November 5, 1863, in Mobile. [17]He reported to the regimental medical unit January 3, 1864, diagnosis vulnus contusum.

[17]**Roberts, Y. W.**, Private, reported to the regimental medical unit June 9, 1864, diagnosis was epilepsia.

Robinson, N. J., Private, enlisted February 28, 1862, Dallas County. [12]He was listed as sick and absent from duty during the summer of 1862. [17]He reported to the regimental medical unit December 1, 1863, diagnosis was catarrhus. He reported again January 17,1864, diagnosis was dyspepsia, and March 21 with chronic diarrhea. He reported to the hospital three times with hepatitis, March 29, June 1 and July 7. He was wounded (intestines) July 20 and died in the brigade hospital the next day. [32]This occurred at the battle at Poor House in Atlanta. Also spelled **Roberson, Robison**.

Robison, William Jesse, 1st Lieutenant, enlisted March 25, 1862, at Fort Pillow. He was 5'10 and born 1835. He was appointed first lieutenant on June 11, 1862. He was granted a medical furlough August 13, 1864, and sent to Monroe County. He was captured May 4, 1865, at Citronella, Mobile County, and paroled June 16, 1865, at Mobile. [17]He reported to the regimental medical unit four times in 1864. In May, he received a slight wound to the neck, possibly at the battle of Resaca, Georgia. July 2, diagnosis was feb int quotid. August 15, he was suffering with chronic diarrhea and was immediately sent to the general hospital. November 30, he received a severe wound to his right hand at the battle of Franklin, Tennessee. His forefinger was amputated. [30]He was born April 22, 1835. His father was Jesse Robison. He married Elizabeth Jane Marshall. He died September 27, 1894, and was buried at McConnico Cemetery. When he died he was tax collector of Monroe County.

Rodgers, Charles, Private, [36]enlisted December 7, 1863, in Mobile. On the muster rolls for December 1863 through February 1864, he was listed as sick in quarters. [17]He reported to the regimental medical unit December 10, 1863, diagnosis was debilitas, and January 10, 1864, otalgia. May be the **Charles Rogers** buried in Confederate Cemetery in Newnan, Coweta County, Georgia, on May 24, 1864.

Rodgers, William, Private, enlisted August 25, 1863, at Mobile. A farmer he was 6'1 and born in 1819 in Monroe County. He was hospitalized

February 22 to March 13, 1864, in Mobile with measles. He was reported unfit for field duty May 30, 1864. He was hospitalized June 14, 1864, Macon, Georgia, with bronchitis. He was granted a furlough July 2, 1864, for 30 days sent to Wilcox County. He was paroled at Selma. [17]*He reported to the regimental medical unit three times in 1864. January 27 and June 13, diagnosis was catarrhus. June 14, he was moved to the general hospital. March 26, diagnosis was pneumonia. He was sent to the general hospital the next day.* Also spelled **Willis Rogers**

Rogers, H. C., Private, enlisted February 28, 1862, Dallas County.

Rogers, J. H., Private, was hospitalized January 13, 1865, Meridian, Mississippi, after the retreat from Nashville.

Rolen, J. W., Private, enlisted October 14, 1862, Pike County. He died sometime in 1862, leaving widow M. A. Also spelled **Rolling.**

Roller, A. J., Private, enlisted February 28, 1862, Dallas County. He was 5'6 and born 1833 in Dallas County.

[18]***Ross, John**, Private, was listed in September 1863 as 46, blue eyes, light hair, fair complexion, 6'1, bricklayer, and a deserter.*

Rothacker, Jacob, Private, enlisted May 7, 1863, at Mobile. He was 5'5, a baker, and born 1845 in Prussia. [32]*He transferred to another unit.*

[20]***Rowlen, James Vincent**, Private, was born December 15, 1846 in Cotton Valley, Macon County. He enlisted just before the battle of Shiloh, Tennessee. He reenlisted April 7, 1863, in Company D, 7th Cavalry. He was captured and paroled in Line Creek Swamp in May 1865.* [30]*He has three markers on his grave. From foot to head of grave, the unit on marker is "Co. H, 17 Regt. Ala. Inf". Standing at head of grave, the marker reads "Co. D, 7 Ala Cav." Laying down at head of grave, the unit marker is "PVT. Co. H 1 Ala Inf."*

Rumbley, Hector McMillan, Private, enlisted October 25, 1861, Camp Davis. He was 5'8 and a clerk. He transferred to Company G from Company H as first sergeant July 10, 1862. He suffered a leg wound at Shiloh, Tennessee, April 1862. [30]*He was wounded at Atlanta.* He also served in the 58th Alabama, Company C. He was paroled May 20, 1865, at Columbus, Georgia. He was born September 27, 1828, son of Richard Henry and Mary McMillan Rumbley. He married Emma S. Sowell. He died December 21, 1893, and is buried in Old Evergreen Cemetery, Evergreen, Alabama. His brothers, Richard Henry and Thomas Anson Rumbley, were also in Company H.

Rumbley, Richard Henry, Private, [36]*enlisted February 6, 1863, Monroe County. On the muster rolls for December 1863 through February 1864, he listed on extra duty – sharp shooter.* [17]*He reported to the regimental medical unit four times in 1864. July 5, the diagnosis was feb int quotid, August 7, feb int quotid, September 7 and November 3,* the diagnosis was debilitas. He was moved to the general hospital on November 4. He was paroled at Montgomery May 27, 1865. His service record is listed under R. H. Bumbley. [30]*He was the son of Richard Henry and Mary McMillan Rumbley. His brothers, Hector McMillan and Thomas Anson Rumbley, were also in Company H. After the war, he worked as a farmer and merchant. His death occurred June 18, 1897, killed in a robbery attempt at his store. The assailant was later captured and hanged.*

Rumbley, Thomas Anson, Private, enlisted September 6, 1861, at Old Scotland. [36]*On the muster rolls for December 1863 through February 1864, he listed on extra duty – sharp shooter.* [17]*He reported to the regimental medical unit December 7, diagnosis was feb int quotid, and December 24th, 1863, catarrhus. He reported sick with tonsillitis January 5, 1864.* He was paroled May 1865, Greensboro, North Carolina. [30]*Family tradition states that he walked all the way home from North Carolina.* [37]*In 1921 he stated he was a first lieutenant, and he was in battles at Shiloh, Iuka, Corinth, Resaca to Atlanta, Franklin, and Nashville.* [30]*He was born August 3, 1838, Monroe County, son of Richard Henry and Mary McMillan Rumbley. He died July 9, 1928, and was buried at Puryearville Cemetery, Burnt Corn, Monroe County. He married Alabama Crook. He was at the surrender at Greensboro, North Carolina, April 26, 1865. Rumbley walked home from North Carolina to Alabama. He was a farmer and highly respected surveyor of Monroe County for many years. His brothers, Richard Henry and Hector McMillan Rumbley, were also in Company H.*

Russell, Charles H., Private

Russell, H. C., Private, was in a Mobile hospital with chronic rheumatism. [17]*He was reported to the regimental medical unit December 17, 1863, with acute rheumatism, and February 14, 1864, with debilitas.*

Rutherford, J. J., Private, enlisted September 11, 1863, at Mobile. A farmer, he was 6'2 and born 1824 in Anderson County, South Carolina. [17]*He reported to the regimental medical unit March 17, 1864, diagnosis rubeola, and was transferred to the general hospital in Greenville. He reported sick April 21, diagnosis morbi cutis.*

Salter, George W., Private, was detailed as cook at a hospital in Mobile during January 1862.

Salter, Simon, Private, was discharged December 16, 1861.

Sharp, R. S., Private, enlisted February 28, 1862, Dallas County. He was discharged September 4, 1862 - provided M. O'Brien as his substitute.

Sims, W. M., Private, enlisted November 16, 1861, Camp Gladden. [32]*He transferred to another unit.*

Sinquefield, James, Private, enlisted October 25, 1861, at Camp Davis, a resident of Monroe County. He was hospitalized June 1, 1864, Macon, Georgia. [36]*During December 1863 through February 1864, he was hospitalized in Mobile.* [17]*He is listed on the regimental medical unit records three times in 1864. January 8 and February 5, diagnosis was feb int tert. August 26, diagnosis was constipatio.*

Slaughter, Samuel H., Private, enlisted May 27, 1863, at Mobile. [36]*On the muster rolls for December 1863 through February 1864, he was listed as sick in his quarters in Mobile.* [17]*He reported to the regimental medical unit three times with diagnosis of feb int quotid: December 15, 1863, January 20, 1864, and February 28. He was placed on sick furlough January 24 for 15 days. He was moved to the general hospital February 29. Diagnosis was debilitas March 5, April 4, and July 4, 1864. April 16, he was granted a medical furlough for 30 days and on July 14 for another 30 days. June 21, the diagnosis was acute diarrhea, and in October, pneumonia.* A farmer, he was born 1845 in Monroe County. He was paroled at Greensboro, North Carolina, April 1865.

Small, E., Private, enlisted February 28, 1862, Dallas County. [32]*He transferred to another unit.* Note: May have transferred to Company H, 58th Alabama.

Smith, Hiram W, Sergeant, [36]*enlisted February 7, 1863, in Monroe County.* [17]*He reported to the regimental medical unit twice in 1864. January 15, the diagnosis was abscessus and February 7, feb int tert.* He was wounded at Franklin, Tennessee, November 30, 1864. He was captured December 16, 1864, at Nashville. He died January 30, 1865, at the Nashville Hospital, gangrene from stump of left leg. He was born in 1844 and was from Grove Hill, Clarke County.

Smith, J. M., Private, enlisted May 10, 1862, Corinth, Mississippi. [12]*He was listed as sick and absent from duty during the summer of 1862.* [10]*He died September 13, 1862.*

Smith, John, Private, enlisted May 10, 1862, Corinth, Mississippi. He was hospitalized February 20, 1864, for 4 days.

[17]***Smith, John Davison,*** *Sergeant, reported to the regimental medical unit five times in 1864. February 15, diagnosis was abscessus, February 26, tonsilitis, and March 28, debilitas. March 2, diagnosis was feb int tert, and he was sent to the general hospital at Mobile on March 7. In May 1864, possibly during the battle of Resaca, Georgia, he received a severe injury to his arm. It was eventually amputated.* [30]*He was born in 1831. He enlisted August 1861 at Claiborne, Monroe County. He was wounded in the arm when he tried to pull a wounded comrade out of the line of fire.* He was born November 24, 1832, son of John W. and Mary (Polly) Davison Smith. He married Rebecca Ann Capell. He died April

12, 1900 and is buried at Old Scott Presbyterian Church Cemetery, Monroe County.

Smith, Joseph, Private, was discharged July 5, 1862.

[18]**Smith, Peter,** Private, was described in September 1863 as 46, hazel eyes, light complexion, dark hair, 5'9, a laborer, and a deserter.

[17]**Smith, S.**, Private, reported to the regimental medical unit June 18, 1864, diagnosis was feb int quotid. He moved to the general hospital June 19.

Smith, William H., Private, enlisted August 25, 1863, at Mobile. He was 5'8, a farmer, and born in 1845, Monroe County. He was hospitalized nine days in Macon, Georgia, January 1864. [17]He reported to the regimental medical unit December 8, 1863, diagnosis was acute dysentery. He reported sick four times in 1864. February 18, diagnosis was feb int quotid, March 22 and 25, catarrhus and in October, hydrocele. He moved to the general hospital October 21.

[17]**Smith, William,** Private, reported to the regimental medical unit April 26, 1864, diagnosis was parotitis. **W. L. Smith** reported to the regimental medical unit three times in 1864. January 13, diagnosis was feb int tert, April 18, morbi cutis, and June 15, feb int quotid. **W. W. Smith** reported to the regimental medical unit July 6, 1864, diagnosis was acute diarrhea, and moved to the general hospital July 13.

Smith, William L., Corporal, lived in Monroe County. He was captured December 15, 1864, at Nashville, and imprisoned at Camp Douglas, Illinois, where he was paroled June 20, 1865.

Smyly, C. F., Private, enlisted February 28, 1862, Dallas County. He was hospitalized during June 1862 in Mississippi. [32]He transferred to another unit.

Snead, A., Private, enlisted February 28, 1862, Dallas County. [17]He is listed as sick and absent from duty during the summer of 1862. [32]He transferred to another unit. Also spelled **Sneed.**

[36]**Speed, James F.**, Private, enlisted September 18, 1863, Sumter County. [17]He reported to the regimental medical unit five times in 1864. January 4, diagnosis was catarrhus, March 16, rubeola, June 15, acute diarrhea and in August and September, acute dysentery.

Stacy, E. M., Private, enlisted October 13, 1862, Monroe County. He was 6' and lived in Monroe County. Captured Citronelle, Mobile County, May 4, 1865, he was paroled July 6, 1865, at Mobile. Also listed as **M. and Manning Stacy.**

Stallworth, N. C., Private, enlisted October 10, 1862, Monroe County. [32]He was discharged.

Stevens, W., Private, died January 18, 1862, [32]at Pensacola.

Stewart, G. W., Private, enlisted February 28, 1862, Dallas County. He was discharged July 2, 1862. His mother was Martha A. Stewart.

COMPANY H

[18]**Swany, P.**, Private, was described in September 1863 as 47, blue eyes, light hair, fair skin, 5'9, a laborer, and a deserter.

Talbert, George W., Private, enlisted October 25, 1861, at Camp Davis. He was 5'10, a farmer, and born 1833 in Monroe County. He was hospitalized during June 1862 in Mississippi. He died [12]*July 12, 1862,* leaving father, Rawlings Talbert. [25]*He is buried at Gainesville.*

Talbert, James, Private, enlisted May 10, 1862, Corinth. He died July 26, 1862, leaving father, Rawlings Talbert. [25]*He is buried at Gainesville.*

Tanns, W., Private, was hospitalized at Meridian, Mississippi, January 27, 1865, after the retreat from Nashville.

[20]**Tatum, Richard T.**, was born January 11, 1847, at Midway, Monroe County. He enlisted April 7, 1864, at Pollard. He was living in Monroe County in 1907. [17]*He reported to the regimental medical unit July 1, 1864, the diagnosis was rubeola, and September 30, 1864, furunculous.*

Templin, Abraham, Private, enlisted March 25, 1862, at Mobile. He was 6', a farmer, and born in 1841 in Monroe County. [13]*He died during the war.*

Templin, Charles, Corporal, enlisted March 15, 1862, Bethel, Tennessee. He was 5'10, a farmer, born in 1844 in Coosa County. He was a resident of Monroe County. He was listed as fourth corporal on the muster roll for September/October 1862 and demoted to private on the muster roll for November/December 1862. He worked as a teamster while in the Confederate Army. [17]*He reported to the regimental medical unit March 21, April 11, and July 29, 1864, the diagnosis was syphilis. He also reported sick July 13, complaint anemia.* He was paroled at Greensboro, North Carolina, April 1865. Also listed as **C. Templer.**

Templin, Henry, Private, enlisted October 25, 1861, at Camp Davis. He was hospitalized during June 1862 in Mississippi. [17]*He reported to the regimental medical unit December 14, 1863, diagnosis feb int quotid.* [13]*He was killed at Peachtree Creek, Georgia, July 20, 1864.*

Thames, John, Private, enlisted October 4, 1862, Monroe County. Diagnosed as having opthalmia, he was considered unfit for field service. [36]*He was listed as a nurse on the muster rolls for December 1863 through February 1864.* He served as ward master in Mobile in April 1864. [17]*The regimental medical unit records list two entries for Thames in 1864. On February 1, the diagnosis was debilitas and he was furloughed on the 4th for 20 days. On March 22, the diagnosis was strumus opthalmia and he was moved to the general hospital in Mobile two days later.* He was listed as a prisoner of war in Meridian, Mississippi, in May 1865.

Thames, Newby C., Private, enlisted October 25, 1861, at Camp Davis. He was hospitalized June 1862 in Mississippi. [36]*He was hospitalized in Mobile on the muster rolls for December 1863 through February 1864.* [13]*He was wounded at the battle of Poor House in Atlanta.* [17]*He reported to the regimental medical unit twice in January 1864. On the 4th, diagnosis was feb int tert and on the 9th, abscessus. February 10 and April 25, 1864, his complaint was dysentery. In February he was transferred to the general hospital.* He was paroled at Greensboro, North Carolina, April 1865.

Thomas, N. C. or Newby C., Private, records are under N. C. Thames. Impossible to know which name is correct.

Turberville, J., Private, enlisted August 31, 1863, at Mobile. He was 6', a farmer, and born 1840 in Milledgeville, Georgia. [32]*He transferred to another unit.*

Vickery, J. J., Private, 5'10, enlisted January 11, 1862, Camp Gladden. He was hospitalized during June 1862 in Mississippi. [17]*He reported to the regimental medical unit four times in 1864. January 14, diagnosis was morbi cutis, February 29, feb int tert, April 3 and August 5, feb int quotid.* He was captured September 14, 1864, near Jonesboro, Georgia. He was granted parole June 19, 1865, in Montgomery. Also spelled **Vickry, Vickney.**

Waters, C. H., Private, was discharged December 10, 1861.

Weisinger, E., Private, enlisted February 28, 1862, Dallas County. [12]*On the muster roll for July-August 1862, he was listed as absent sick.*

Weisinger, James K., Private, enlisted February 28, 1862, Dallas County. He was 5'6, a student, and born 1844 in Dallas County. He was granted a disability discharge October 27, 1862.

West, W. P., Private, was 5'11, a teacher, and born 1839 in Autauga County. He sustained an injury to his spine, probably at Shiloh, Tennessee. He was discharged May 18, 1862.

Westbrook, A. G., Private, enlisted February 28, at Dallas County. He was discharged July 5, 1862.

Whatley, Edward W., Private, enlisted September 25, 1862, Monroe County. He was 5'8 and lived in Monroe County. [18]*In September 1863, he was described as 27, dark eyes, dark complexion, black hair, 5'7, a farmer, and a deserter.* Captured December 15, 1864, at Nashville, he was imprisoned at Camp Douglas, Illinois, where he was paroled May 1865. Also spelled **Wadley.**

Whatley, W. H., Private, was paroled May 25, 1865, at Talladega.

White, Thomas, Private, enlisted November 22, 1862, as a substitute for W. D. Lassiter. [32]*He transferred to another unit.*

Wicks, Charles, Private, enlisted June 1, 1863, at Mobile, and served as nurse. Captured May 20, 1864, at Hightower, Georgia, he was imprisoned at Rock Island. He died December 12, 1864, and is buried in lot number 1665. Also spelled **Wickes**

Wiggins, Jno. T., Private, enlisted October 25, 1861, at Camp Davis. He was 5'3, a farmer, and born 1843 in Monroe County. [12]*On the muster roll for July-August 1862, he was listed as absent sick.* He was hospitalized during June 1862 in Mississippi. He died on the Mobile and Ohio Railroad September 30, 1862, leaving father, Robert O. Wiggins.

Wiggins, M. Lafayette, Private, enlisted May 11, 1862, Corinth. [17]*He reported to the regimental medical unit on December 19, 1863, January 31 and February 15, 1864, diagnosis feb int quotid. He also reported sick January 5, diagnosis feb int tert.* He was killed during the battle of Peachtree Creek on July 20, 1864.

Wiggins, N. J., Private, enlisted October 25, 1861, at Camp Davis and was discharged July 25, 1862.

Wiggins, T. S., 2nd Lieutenant, elected September 25, 1861, and resigned June 18, 1862. Obviously he rejoined his unit as [17]*he reported to the regimental medical unit in Georgia June 13, 1864, diagnosis debilitas. He was sent to the general hospital the next day.* A letter is on file at the Alabama Archives that Wiggins' lawyer wrote to Thomas M. Owens October 28, 1905. The letter claims that Wiggins rejoined the 17th Alabama at Resaca. From there he fought at New Hope, Kennesaw Mountain, Atlanta, Franklin, and Nashville. At Nashville, he lost his diary with dates, movements, names, etc. It was in his saddlebags that were carried to the rear when "we were surrounded and captured." From his letter it can be determined that he was in the cavalry from 1862 to 1864, and he fought in middle Tennessee during that time.

Wirtingel, E. B., Private, was paroled June 1865 at Selma.

Wright, William H., Private, enlisted May 25, 1863, at Mobile. He was 5'11, a farmer, and born 1827 in Lincoln, Georgia.

Wynager, E., Private, was hospitalized during June 1862 in Mississippi.

Appendix X. Company I

Adams, Abner, Private, was hospitalized in Jackson, Mississippi, from October 25, 1864 to December 1, 1864, diagnosis was chronic diarrhea. [17]He reported to the regimental medical unit five times in 1864. January 28, February 13, and March 18, diagnosis was feb int tert; on February 23, feb int quotid; and April 23, catarrhus.

[8]**Adams, Bunk**, Private, was from Pike County.

[8]**Adams, Early**, Private, was from Pike County. [17]December 16, 1863,and January 22, 1864, while in Mobile; he reported to the regimental medical unit, diagnosis was feb int tert. He reported sick while in Georgia April 29, diagnosis was abscessus and July 9, acute diarrhea. He was killed July 20, 1864, at the battle of Peach Tree Creek near Atlanta.

Adams, John W., Private, enlisted September 16, 1861, Montgomery. He was hospitalized in Mississippi during June 1862.

Adams, Robert B., Private, enlisted September 16, 1861, at Montgomery. He was 5'10 and born 1835, Montgomery County. He received a disability discharge December 31, 1861, after suffering from a gunshot wound to his right hand at Pensacola. [8]He was from Pike County.

Adison, M., enlisted March 7, 1864, at Greenville. He was at the surrender at Greensboro, North Carolina, April 26, 1865.

Alford, Hillard Judge, Private, enlisted August 22, 1862, at Camp Watts. [8]He was from Pike County. [17]He reported to the regimental medical unit in Mobile February 13, 1864, diagnosis was fibris remittens. On April 27, 1864, he reported sick again, diagnosis abscessus. He was paroled at Greensboro, North Carolina, May 1865. [1]He was born December 30, 1837, in Montgomery County. He was living in Bullock County, Alabama, in 1907. Also listed as **Alfred.**

[10]**Allen, J.**, Private, died a prisoner at Camp Douglas, Illinois, March 11, 1862.

Allen, James, Private, was 6', a farrier, and born 1816 in Putnam, Georgia. He was discharged April 1862 after being wounded at the battle of Shiloh, Tennessee.

[8]**Allen, Jessie**, Private, was from Pike County. He died at Pensacola in 1861, probably from disease.

[17]**Ansley, B. F.**, Private, reported to the regimental medical unit March 19, 1864, diagnosis was feb int quotid, and June 4, acute diarrhea.

[20]**Banks, Abner**, Private, enlisted January 1862 at Camp Cantey. He was born in Edgefield County, South Carolina, October 20, 1833. [17]He reported to the regimental medical unit in Mobile March 22, 1864, diagnosis catarrhus. [20]Paroled May 1865 at Petersburg, South Carolina, he was living in Enterprise in 1907.

[17]**Barley, J. T.**, *Private, reported to the regimental medical unit in September 1864 with acute diarrhea.*
Barnett, Joseph F., Sergeant, enlisted at Montgomery September 16, 1862. [8]*He died in service in Mobile in 1862.* His father was James S. Barnett.
Baskin, John C., Private, enlisted December 16, 1861, at Montgomery. [8]*He resigned at Pensacola, Florida, probably in early 1862.*
Bicker, R. A., Private.
Bickerson, R., Private.
Bickerstaff, R. J., Private, died January 11, 1864, [6]*at Mobile.*
Bickerstall, R. A., Private, enlisted January 20, 1863. [17]*He reported to the regimental medical unit September 5, 1864, diagnosis was acute diarrhea.* He was at the surrender at Greensboro, North Carolina, April 26, 1865.
Bolin, John A., Private, enlisted March 23, 1862, at Corinth, Mississippi. He was hospitalized during June 1862 in Mississippi. He was buried in the Stonewall Jackson Cemetery in LaGrange, Georgia. Note: He probably died in 1864 when his regiment was in Georgia.
Bone, John, Private, died of typhoid and pneumonia June 22, 1864, St. Mary's Hospital, LaGrange, Georgia. [17]*He reported to the regimental medical unit March 7, 1864, diagnosis acute dysenteria; and March 15, rubeola. He was transferred to the general hospital March 30.* He was buried at the Confederate Cemetery, LaGrange, Georgia.
Bones, John Samuel, Captain, enlisted May 11, 1861. He was promoted to captain when Captain A. M. Collins resigned May 1862. [17]*He reported to the regimental medical unit April 15, 1864, diagnosis was feb int quotid. July 13, diagnosis was acute diarrhea. July 20, he was severely wounded in the left thigh at the battle of Peach Tree Creek near Atlanta. He was moved to the general hospital the next day.* Suffering from wounds, he was granted a discharge during the spring of 1865, and listed as a "Retired Invalid Officer."
Boyle, Jackson, Private, enlisted August 23, 1862, Mobile. On the muster roll for September-October 1862, he was listed as absent without leave since August 28, 1862.
Brady, J. A., Private, 5'3, was paroled May 22, 1865, at Montgomery.
Brady, James A., Private, enlisted September 23, 1863, Autauga County. He was 5'11, a mechanic, and born 1822 in Jefferson, Georgia.
Brady, William R., Private, enlisted September 23, 1863, Autauga County. He was 5'8, a farmer, and born 1843 in Coosa County. [17]*He reported to the regimental medical unit in May 1864 with acute diarrhea and then was listed as missing.* He was captured at Resaca, Georgia, May 15, 1864, and imprisoned at Alton, Illinois, where he enlisted in the Union Navy.

COMPANY I

[17]**Bristoe, J. H.**, Private, reported to the regimental medical unit June 21, 1864, with acute diarrhea.

Bristow, J. N., Private. See Service Records for David Blackman, Company F, 54th Alabama.

Bristow, James W., Private, enlisted February 4, 1863. He was 6 foot tall, a carpenter, and born 1827 in Talliaferro, Georgia. [17]*He reported to the regimental medical unit December 14, 1863, with acute diarrhea. He returned to the medical unit four times in 1864. March 15, 1864, diagnosis was acute dysenteria, April 16, feb int quotid, and August 4, parotitis. In September, diagnosis was feb int quotid, and he was immediately moved to the general hospital.* He was at the surrender at Greensboro, North Carolina, April 26, 1865.

Brooks, Samuel W., Private, enlisted December 27, 1861, at Greenville. [12]*He was placed on detached duty by General Forney.*

Brown, Enoch F., Private, enlisted September 19, 1863, Georgiana. He was 5'9, a farmer, and born 1845 in Sumter County, Georgia. [17]*He reported to the regimental medical unit February 22, 1864, diagnosis was rubeola. He moved to the general hospital the next day.* He was paroled at Greensboro, North Carolina, May 1865.

Brown, John W., Private, enlisted December 27, 1861, at Greenville and was discharged July 5, 1862.

Browning, William, Private, was discharged December 16, 1861.

Brumby, T. P. G., enlisted and was appointed first lieutenant September 1, 1861. He was discharged May 14, 1862.

[20]**Carlisle, Robert K.**, Private, enlisted October 1862 in Eufaula. He was born in Jaspar, Georgia, May 20, 1832, and living in Newton, Dale County, in 1907. [17]*He reported to his regimental medical unit December 13, 1863, in Mobile and July 3, 1864, in Georgia, diagnosis was neuralgia.*

Carlisle, Thomas J., Private, was captured on April 7, 1862, at Pittsburg Landing, Tennessee, after being wounded in the hip. Imprisoned at Camp Chase, Ohio, he was exchanged August 25, 1862. [17]*While in Mobile he reported to the regimental medical unit December 10, 1863, diagnosis feb int quotid, and January 30, 1864, feb int tert.* He was killed by a musket ball May 1864 in Georgia, possibly at the battle of Resaca.

Carlisle, William I., Corporal, was 5'8 and born 1829 in Marlborough District, South Carolina. He was granted a disability discharge in 1862. [8]*He was from Pike County.*

Cheatham, James, Private, enlisted September 16, 1861, at Montgomery. He was hospitalized June 1862. [17]*He reported to the regimental medical unit on three occasions in 1864. June 2, diagnosis was acute* diarrhea. *July 28, he received a wound in the back, at the battle of Ezra Church near Atlanta. August 9, diagnosis was feb int tert.* He was listed as second sergeant when paroled at Greensboro, North Carolina, May 1865. [8]*He was from Pike County.* [20]*In 1907 he was living in Pickens County.* Also spelled **Chatham**.

Christian, William T., Private, [5]*was listed as missing after the battle of Shiloh, Tennessee, on April 6, and* died on April 17, 1862, at a Union hospital in St. Louis, Missouri.

Cogburn, Jesse M., Private, enlisted September 16, 1861, at Montgomery. He was hospitalized during June 1862 and died July 28, 1862, at a hospital in Columbus, Mississippi. Also spelled **Cockburn**.

Coleman, Francis M., Private, enlisted March 14, 1862, at Corinth, Mississippi. He was 6', born 1834, and a carpenter. He was granted parole May 18, 1865, at Montgomery.

Collins, A. Marion, Captain, resigned May 16, 1862, after leading his company at the battle of Shiloh. [8]*He was from Pike County.*

Combey, Anderson D., Private, enlisted December 15, 1863, at Montgomery. A farmer, he was 5'10 and born in 1845 in Randolph County. His home was Randolph County. [17]*He reported to the regimental medical unit five times in 1864. March 4, diagnosis was rubeola, and he was moved to the general hospital the next day. April 19, diagnosis was constipatio, June 21, phlegmon, and July 19, feb int quotid. July 28, he was slighted wounded in his left fore finger, at the battle of Ezra Church near Atlanta. He was moved to the general hospital July 31.* Captured on December 15, 1864, at Nashville, he was imprisoned at Camp Douglas, Illinois. Also listed as **Comdey, Andrew Combey, Anderson Cumbey, Cumby,**

Combie, Charles, Private, enlisted January 1, 1863, Roanoke, Randolph County. [17]*He reported to the regimental medical unit June 13, 1864, diagnosis was debilitas.*

Copeland, Joseph A., Private, enlisted October 16, 1861, at Montgomery. He was hospitalized in Mississippi during June 1862. [17]*While in Mobile, he reported to the regimental medical unit twice in 1864. On January 24, diagnosis was acute bronchitis, and March 20, acute dysenteria.*

[17]***Curry, W. H. H.***, *Private, reported to the regimental medical unit June 6, 1864, diagnosis was feb int tert.*

Davis, Anson L., Private, was captured December 15, 1864, at Nashville.

Davis R. L., Private, enlisted September 1, 1862, Mobile, and was from Lowndes County. [17]*He reported to the regimental medical unit November 8, 1864, diagnosis was acute diarrhea.* He was captured December 5, 1864, at Nashville and imprisoned at Camp Douglas,

Illinois, [1]*where he was paroled June 20, 1865. He was living in Honoraville, Crenshaw County, in 1907.* [30]*He was born January 10, 1831, Fairfield County, South Carolina.* [15]*He died January 9, 1931, and is buried at Salem Church of Christ in Crenshaw County. Early in the war he had been in Company A.*

[17]**Davis, R. M.**, Private, reported to the regimental medical unit during September 1864, diagnosis was acute diarrhea.

Dorman, John A., Private, enlisted September 16, 1861, at Montgomery. He was listed as missing after the battle at Shiloh, Tennessee, April 7, 1862. [12]*He was discharged August 22, 1862.*

Doster, J. N., Private, was discharged on December 16, 1861.

[17]**Doswell, Isaac M.**, Private, reported to the regimental medical unit four times in 1864. On April 1, diagnosis was feb int tert. On July 31, August 7, and September 4, diagnosis was acute diarrhea.

[17]**Doswell, William**, Private, reported to the regimental medical unit December 11, 1863, diagnosis was debilitas.

Downing, Joseph T., Private, enlisted September 14, 1861, at Montgomery. He was 5'10 and born 1843. He died May 9, 1862, at Corinth, Mississippi, leaving father, James B. Downing. [8]*He was from Pike County.*

Dozewell, Thomas P., Private, [17]*reported to the regimental medical unit April 5, 1864, diagnosis catarrhus. He reported sick June 18, 1864, diagnosis chronic diarrhea. He was moved to the general hospital the next day. He was captured December 15, 1864, at Nashville and imprisoned at Camp Douglas, Illinois.* Also spelled **Doswell**

[37]**Draughon, Joel**, Private, enlisted January 1863 at Newton, Dale County. He was born February 6, 1846, in Newton. [17]*He reported to the regimental medical unit July 8, 1864, rubeola, and was immediately moved to the general hospital.* [37]*In 1921 he was living in Newton, Alabama, and stated that he fought at Franklin and Nashville.*

[1]**Driver, Allen J.**, Private, was born March 19, 1836, at LaFayette, Chambers County. He served until the surrender and was living in Roanoke, Alabama, in 1907.

[17]**Eddins, C. S.**, Private, reported to the regimental medical unit September 1864 with acute dysentery.

Edwards, W. J., Private, enlisted May 19, 1862, at Montgomery. He was paroled at Greensboro, North Carolina, in the spring of 1865.

Falk, James, Private, was hospitalized at the prison hospital Camp Dennison, Ohio.

Falk, W. R., Private, was exchanged at Vicksburg in 1862 after the battle of Shiloh, Tennessee. He was at Camp Dennison, Ohio, in October 1862.

He was paroled May 1865 at Montgomery. [17]*Robert Faulk reported to the regimental medical unit in early October 1864 with acute diarrhea.*

Faulkner, William J., Private, enlisted September 14, 1861, at Montgomery. He was placed on duty as a carpenter. He was granted a medical furlough January 5, 1862 for 20 days and sent home to Pike County. Also spelled **Falconer.**

Furshee, Charles, Private. May be **Charles Forshee** of Company F.

Garlington, T. C., Private, was captured at Raleigh, North Carolina, April 1865.

Gibson, D. M., Private, enlisted February 1862 at Greenville. [17]*He reported to the regimental medical unit three times in 1864. June 23, diagnosis was feb int tert; July 3, acute diarrhea; and on September 11, acute dysentery. In September he was moved to the general hospital.* He was hospitalized February 2, 1865, at Way Hospital, Meridian, Mississippi, with wounds.

Gillmore, Joseph L., Sergeant, suffered a head wound and died at Shiloh, Tennessee, April 6, 1862. [8]*He was from Pike County.* Also spelled **Gilmne.**

Gilmore, Albert M., Private, enlisted December 27, 1861, at Greenville.

Gilmore, James J., Private, enlisted December 27, 1861, Greenville. He was hospitalized in Mississippi during June 1862. [12]*He was discharged August 19, 1862.* Also listed as **J. G. Gilmore**

Gilmore, James W., Private, died in 1862.

Gleason, E., Private, is listed on the muster roll for July-August 1862 as sick in the hospital in Macon, Mississippi. He was listed on the muster roll for September-October 1862 as a deserter. He was transferred from the 5th Alabama April 22, 1862, but never reported to the 17th Alabama.

[17]**Goodwin, H. C.**, *Private, reported to the regimental medical unit, diagnosis was chronic diarrhea, and transferred to the general hospital June 20, 1864.*

Goodwin, W. C., Private.

Grant, H. H., Private.

Gray, Daniel J., Private, enlisted September 14, 1861, at Montgomery. [17]*He reported to the regimental medical unit three times in 1864. February 26 and March 4, diagnosis was constipatio. During October he was sick with pneumonia. He was transferred to the general hospital on October 21.* He was paroled at Greensboro, North Carolina, May 1865. Documentation in his service record states that the 5th Alabama claimed that he was a deserter. Gray claimed that he was a member of the 17th Alabama.

Gray, John C., Private, enlisted September 24, 1862, Mobile. He was hospitalized in Greenville, February 29, 1864. [17]*He reported to the* regimental medical unit eight times in 1864. January 27, diagnosis was bronchitis, and on February 14, indigestio. March 28 and April 1, diagnosis was ascites. June 6, diagnosis was acute diarrhea, July 12, acute dysentery, and August 6, feb int quotid. November 20, diagnosis was chronic rheum, and he was moved to the general hospital November 29, 1864. He took the oath of allegiance March 1865.

Green, B. R., Private, [17]reported to the regimental medical unit April 26,1864, diagnosis was feb int quotid. In May, possibly at the battle of Resaca, Georgia, he suffered a wound to his back. He died in September 1864. Also listed as *P. R. Green*

[17]**Green, D. I.**, Private, reported to the regimental medical unit April 3, diagnosis was oedema, and again August 10, 1864,when diagnosis was anasarca.

Green, William S., Private, enlisted November 14, 1861, at Montgomery. He was hospitalized in Mississippi during June 1862. [17]*W. S. Greer suffered a severe head wound in May of 1864, possibly at Resaca, Georgia.* [8]*Green lost an eye in battle.* He was granted a parole at Greensboro, North Carolina, May 1865.

Grimsley, John P., Private, was ordnance sergeant at Battery Huger off Mobile. [17]*He reported to the regimental medical unit three times in December of 1863. On the 11th, diagnosis was colica, the 18th odontalgia, and the 20th, anthrax. In 1864, he reported to the hospital with acute diarrhea, August 19 and September 21.*

Guthrie, Andrew C., Sergeant, enlisted at Montgomery September 16, 1861. He was ordnance sergeant at Battery Huger off Mobile. Captured December 15, 1864, at Nashville, he was imprisoned at Camp Douglas, Illinois. He died January 27, 1865, and was buried in lot 616-2 Chicago City Cemetery. [8]*He was from Pike County.*

Guthrie, Asbury, Private, died May 11, 1862, at Guntown, Mississippi. [8]*A. J. Guthrie held the rank of 5th sergeant and was from Pike County.* Also spelled **Ashbury Guthrie**.

Haiden, A., Private, was granted a furlough for one month from Mississippi June 1862.

Hale, George W., Corporal, enlisted September 5, 1861, at Montgomery. He worked as a teamster. He was captured February 16, 1862, at Fort Donelson, Tennessee, and again April 8, 1862, at Pittsburg Landing, Tennessee. He was imprisoned at Camp Douglas, Illinois. [17]*He reported to the regimental medical unit January 21, 1864, diagnosis mobi cutis, and February 7, 1864, acute rheum. He suffered a severe injury to his ankle in May 1864 in Georgia, possibly during the battle of Resaca.* [17]*He reported to the regimental medical unit in September 1864, diagnosis was acute diarrhea. He reported again to the hospital*

November 6 and was sent to the general hospital, diagnosis was acute bronchitis. Also spelled **Hail, Hale, Hayle.**

Hale, John, Private, [8]*was from Pike County.* [5]*He was listed as missing after the battle of Shiloh, Tennessee, April 1862.* [30]*He was born ca 1839 in Alabama, son of Richard F. and Mary Hale.* Also spelled **Hayle, Hail.**

Hall, James C., Private, enlisted September 17, 1861, at Montgomery. [17]*He reported to the regimental medical unit February 14, 1864, diagnosis was debilitas.* He was captured May 30, 1864, Dallas, Georgia.

Hall, R, Private, [17]*reported to the regimental medical unit four times in 1864. March 10, diagnosis was debilitas; April 5, phlegmon; September 18, feb int tert; and September 30, acute diarrhea.* September 18, he was sent to the general hospital.

Hamilton, James A., Private, enlisted at Montgomery. He was hospitalized in Mississippi during June 1862 and [12]*died at home in Pike County, July 11, 1862.*

Hammonds, Wylie H., Private, enlisted September 29, 1861, at Montgomery. He suffered wounds at Shiloh, Tennessee, in April 1862. He was listed as a deserter June 28, 1862. Captured at July 20, 1864, at Peachtree Creek near Atlanta, he was imprisoned at Camp Douglas, Illinois.

[17]**Hardee, William F.,** *Private, reported to the regimental medical unit December 1, 1863. Diagnosis was sudites, and he was discharged December 11.*

Harden, Allen, Private, enlisted September 14, 1861, Montgomery. He was placed on furlough June 1862. On the muster roll for September-October 1862, he was listed as sick in the hospital in Mobile. [8]*He was from Pike County.* Also spelled **Hardin.**

Harden, Elijah, Private, enlisted May 1, 1862, Corinth, Mississippi. He died September 26, 1863 at a Mobile hospital, valvula disease. He was buried at Magnolia Cemetery, Mobile, row 14, grave 50.

Harden, Henry, Private, was born 1846 in Macon County, was 5'5, and a farmer. He was granted a disability discharge December 31, 1861.

Harden, Jacob, Private, enlisted May 1862, Corinth, Mississippi. He died [12]*in the hospital July 11, 1862,* leaving E. Hardin, widow.

Harris, J. P., Private, [1]*enlisted March 1864 at Montgomery.* [8]*He was known as Press and was from Pike County.* [17]*He reported to the regimental medical unit twice in 1864. April 20, diagnosis was pneumonia; he was sent to the general hospital the next day. September 23, diagnosis was catarrhus, and he was sent to the general hospital the same day.* He was admitted to St. Mary's Hospital, West Point, Mississippi, January 18, 1865, after the retreat from Nashville. He was granted parole at Greensboro, North Carolina, May 1865. [1]*He was born*

July 15, 1846, in Sumter County, Georgia. He was living in Bullock County in 1907.

Harris, John T., Private, enlisted September 16, 1861, at Montgomery. He was hospitalized in Mississippi during June 1862. [17]*He reported to the regimental medical unit three times in December 1863. On the 12th, diagnosis was feb int tert; on the 18th, icterus; and on the 24th, debilitas. He was placed on sick furlough on the 27th for 25 days. He reported sick three times in 1864. February 14, diagnosis was acute diarrhea; April 1, feb int tert; and April 4, feb remittus.* He did not survive the war.

Harris, Samuel H., was appointed captain June 1862. See so. #42-1, 62-2 at Alabama Archives. He transferred to the 1st Alabama on August 10, 1862. Also listed as **Samuel L.**

Harris, William T., Private, was granted a medical furlough January 5, 1862, for 20 days and sent home to Pike County. He was wounded in the neck at the battle of Shiloh, Tennessee, April 6, 1862. [17]*He was wounded twice July 1864. On the 20th at Peachtree Creek near Atlanta, he suffered a slight wound to his hip and was sent to the general hospital the same day. On the 28th at Ezra Church near Atlanta, he was severely wounded in the right leg and was sent to the general hospital on the 31st.* [8]*He was killed at the battle of Franklin, Tennessee, November 30, 1864.*

[17]**Hays, George**, Sergeant, *reported to the regimental medical unit August 10, 1864, diagnosis was acute diarrhea.*

Head, A. F. I., Corporal, enlisted March 29, 1862, at Camp Watts. He was born 1827 in LaFayette County, Georgia. He was granted a disability discharge May 1862.

Head, Adolphus M., Private, enlisted September 16, 1861, at Montgomery. He was hospitalized in Mississippi during June 1862. [8]*He was called Dolf and was from Pike County.* [17]*He suffered a wound to his arm July 20, 1864, at the battle of Peach Tree Creek near Atlanta. He was sent to the general hospital on the next day.*

Head, Oliver J., enlisted November 11, 1863, Mobile. He was a farmer and born 1819 in Jasper County, Georgia. [17]*He reported to the regimental medical unit three times in 1864. June 3, diagnosis was acute dysenteria; in September, feb int tert; and November 3, acute diarrhea. He was moved to the general hospital November 4.* He was admitted to Way Hospital, Meridian, Mississippi, March 25, 1865, diagnosis debilitas.

[9]**Head, W. S.**, *Private, was born in 1837. He was shot in the left shoulder September 8, 1863. The head of the humerous with fragments of bone were removed. On January 1, 1864, the doctor reported that he was nearly well and promised to have full recovery.*

Head, William J., Private, enlisted at Corinth, Mississippi, March 24, 1862. He was on furlough June and July 1862 and died in the hospital July 11, 1862.

Head, William L., Private, enlisted September 16, 1861, at Montgomery. He was born in 1828 and was a farmer. He was hospitalized during June 1862. He was wounded August 1863. He was admitted to Way Hospital, Meridian, Mississippi, with wounds and chronic diarrhea. He was discharged March 25, 1865.

Hewry, J., Private, was hospitalized in Mississippi during June 1862.

Hickman, J. M., Private, enlisted at Greenville. He was granted parole at Greensboro, North Carolina, May 1865.

Hill, Charles, Private, died in the hospital January 5, 1862. [8]*He was from Pike County.*

Hogan, George W., Private, enlisted September 16, 1861, at Montgomery. He was listed as a cook in January 1862 and as a nurse in June 1862. [17]*He reported to the regimental medical unit April 14, 1864, diagnosis was catarrhus.* He was captured May 30, 1864, at Dallas, Georgia, and imprisoned at Rock Island, Illinois, [10]*At Rock Island he died of pneumonia August 8, 1864, and is buried in lot number 1407.*

Hogan, William, Private, enlisted September 16, 1861, at Montgomery. [17]*He reported to the regimental medical unit on December 10, 1863, diagnosis was catarrhus. He returned to the medical unit twice in 1864. May 1, diagnosis was acute dysenteria, and November 10, acute diarrhea.* Captured at December 17, 1864, Franklin, Tennessee, he was imprisoned at Camp Chase, Ohio.

Hogan, Wyatt, Private, was discharged October 16, 1861.

Huey, Joseph D., Private.

Hunt, John D., Private, was born 1845 in Georgia and was 5'8. Captured at May 30, 1864, Dallas, Georgia, he was imprisoned at Rock Island, Illinois, [10]*where he died August 11, 1864.* [17]*J. B. Hunt reported to the regimental medical unit April 23, 1864, diagnosis was acute dysenteria. Jno. Hunt reported to the medical unit January 1, 1864, diagnosis was feb int tert.* Also listed as **John B. Hunt, John W. Hunt**

Jackson, Joseph B., Private, enlisted September 16, 1861, at Montgomery. He was promoted to corporal. [17]*He reported to the regimental medical unit December 28 and 29, 1863, diagnosis sub luxatio. He suffered an injury to his left hip on July 28, 1864, at the battle of Ezra Church near Atlanta. He was sent to the general hospital on the 31st. He reported to the medical unit in October and was sent to the general hospital on the 31st.* He was paroled at Greensboro, North Carolina, in April 1865. [8]*He was from Pike County.* [1]*He was born February 22, 1847, in Bullock County where he was living in 1907.*

Jenkins, James E., Private, enlisted April 10, 1862, at Pollard, Alabama. [17]*He reported to the regimental medical unit August 11, 1864, diagnosis acute diarrhea.* He was granted parole in May 1865 at Greensboro, North Carolina. [20]*Born in Bullock County near Inverness February 22, 1847, he was living in Bullock County in 1907.*

Johnson, Alfred, Private, was a teamster from Dale County. He was born in 1844 at Decatur, Georgia, and was 5'9. [17]*He was severely wounded in the left shoulder July 20, 1864, at the battle of Peach Tree Creek near Atlanta.* He was sent to the general hospital the next day.

Johnson, William, Private.

Joiner, Thomas B., Private, enlisted September 16, 1861, at Montgomery. He was hospitalized in Mississippi during June 1862. He was hospitalized September 2, 1863, for twelve days. [17]*He reported to the regimental medical unit on December 9, 1863, diagnosis feb int quotid. He reported to the unit three times with diagnosis feb int tert: January 5, January 19, and April 2, 1864. He also reported to the medical unit three times with gonorrhea: January 22, February 21, and March 21, 1864. Most entries in the regimental register listed him as a corporal.*

Jones, Seborn, Private, enlisted September 8, 1863, Henry County. A farmer, he was born in 1820 in Henry County. Captured May 30, 1864, at Dallas, Georgia, he was imprisoned at Rock Island, Illinois. He died August 11, 1864, [10]*and was buried in lot number 1405 at Rock Island.*

King, John, Private, enlisted March 13, 1863, Mobile. He was paroled at Greensboro, North Carolina, in April 1865.

Lancaster, John Austin, Second Lieutenant, [17]*reported to the regimental medical unit January 31, March 29, and July 5, 1864, with the same diagnosis, feb int tert.* He was badly wounded at Franklin, Tennessee, November 30, 1864. He was paroled in May 1865. [30]*He was born December 1839, Troup County, Georgia, and died March 6, 1904, Elmore County, Alabama.*

Laney, Fielder, Private, enlisted March 24, 1862, at Corinth, Mississippi. He died July 4, 1862, at Macon, Mississippi.

[17]**Laney, S. F.**, *Private, reported to the regimental medical unit on April 6, 1864, diagnosis feb int tert.*

Laney, S. Thomas, Private, enlisted November 14, 1861, Montgomery. He was granted a medical furlough January 13, 1862, for 20 days and sent home to Pike County. He was hospitalized in Mississippi during June 1862. He was wounded (gunshot through his left hand) [17]*in May 1864, possibly at the battle of Resaca, Georgia.*

Leathers, James M., Private, was captured at December 15, 1864, Nashville, and imprisoned at Camp Douglas, Illinois.

Love, George T., Private, was killed at Shiloh, Tennessee, April 7, 1862. [8]*He was from Pike County.*

[12]***May. George W.***, *Private, enlisted December 27, 1861, Greenville.*

McCarver, George W., Private, enlisted December 27, 1861, Mobile. He was hospitalized the summer of 1862. He was 5'9 and born in 1829 in East Baton Rouge, Louisiana. [20]*Captured November 1864, he was imprisoned at Johnson Island, Ohio. He volunteered for the Union Army and went to the frontier to fight the Indians. He was living in Fayette County in 1907.*

McCall, James B., Private, enlisted December 27, 1861, at Greenville. He worked as a carpenter. He helped build the hospital in Mobile and repaired wagons. [17]*He reported to the regimental medical unit twice in 1864. June 6, diagnosis was debilitas, and he was immediately sent to the general hospital. June 19, diagnosis was acute bronchitis, and he was sent to the general hospital the next day.*

McCrary, William H., Private, [27]*enlisted September 14, 1862, at Montgomery. He was born in 1847.* [17]*While in Georgia, he reported to the regimental medical unit June 23 1864, diagnosis was acute dysentery; and July 5, debilitas. July 28,1864, he suffered a severe wound to his face, at the battle of Ezra Church near Atlanta. He was moved to the general hospital at Macon, Georgia, on July 31, where he* [8]*lost an eye. He was granted a furlough for 30 days.* [27]*He was paroled after the surrender on June 8, 1865. He was 5'6, brown hair, gray eyes, and dark complexion. He died January 14, 1910, and was buried at Confederate Memorial Park Cemetery, Alabama.* Also spelled **McCreary.**

McDaniel, B. O., Private, was discharged December 16, 1861.

McGowin, James, Private, [17]*reported to the regimental medical unit on December 10, 1863, diagnosis was abscessus. He reported five times in 1864. January 19, February 14, and June 18, diagnosis was feb int tert. February 17, diagnosis was gonorrhea, and July 17, feb int quotid.* He was captured at December 15, 1864, Nashville, and was imprisoned at Camp Douglas, Illinois.

McGowin, Peter, Private, died December 20, 1863, Spring Hill in Mobile. [30]*He was born October 30, 1833, son of Samuel and Martha (Patsy) Mason McGowin. His wife was Nancy Floyd He died of typhoid fever and is buried in the Foshee Cemetery in Grab Mill, Alabama.* Note: Grab Mill is not listed on current maps. However, there is a Grab Mill Creek in Conecuh County.

McKilln, F. G, Private, was hospitalized January 12, 1865, at Meridian, Mississippi, and then transferred to Marion, Alabama.

McLane, Henry A., Private, enlisted September 16, 1861, at Montgomery. He was 5'8, a farmer, and born in 1840 at Tallapoosa, Alabama. [8]*He was from Pike County.* [17]*He reported to the regimental medical unit July 16, 1864, diagnosis was feb int quotid.* [30]*McLane was born May 23, 1830. He married (1) Mary Elizabeth Beverly and (2) Mrs. W. R. Copeland. He died February 19, 1911, and is buried in Brundidge, Alabama. He probably is brother of Samuel McLane of Company I.*

McLane, Sam A., Private, was hospitalized September 2, 1863, Mobile. He was placed on medical furlough September 18, 1863. He was hospitalized again on January 18, 1865, Mobile. He was placed on medical furlough February 6, 1865, after the retreat from Nashville. [30]*He was born ca 1834 and probably was the brother of Henry A. McLane of Company I.*

McLaurine, Christopher, Sergeant, enlisted September 16, 1861, at Montgomery. He was appointed second lieutenant May 14, 1862. He was elected first lieutenant August 29, 1862, and assigned September 5, 1862. February 5, 1862, while in Pensacola, he was granted a medical furlough for 20 days and sent home to Pike County. [17]*He reported to the regimental medical unit four times in 1864. January 31, diagnosis was feb int tert. In early May, he received a slight wound to his leg while fighting in Georgia, possibly at the battle of Resaca. July 2, diagnosis was feb int quotid. In September it was colica.* [8]*He was killed at the battle of Franklin, Tennessee, November 30, 1864.* According to a brother who wrote in <u>Confederate Veteran</u>, McLaurine *"was slightly wounded at Shiloh, Tennessee, and was mortally wounded while leading his company in a charge at Franklin, Tenn. His cap, pierced by a bullet, was found after the charge, and that is the only thing we heard of him after this battle."*

[17]**McLaurin, J. M.**, Lieutenant, reported to the regimental medical unit March 17, 1864, diagnosis was feb int tert.

McLear, G. R., Private, was hospitalized June 6-June 10, 1864, Macon, Georgia. His home was Pike County. **McLeod** sustained a gunshot wound to his left knee on July 4, 1864. He was placed on medical furlough September 1, 1864, from Augusta, Georgia, and sent to Pike County. **McLear** was 5'8 and was granted parole in May 1865 at Montgomery. Also listed as **G.R. McLeod, G. R. McCloud.**

[17]**McLeod, G. R.**, Private, reported to the regimental medical unit July 4, 1864, diagnosis was feb remit, and immediately was sent to the general hospital.

[17]**McLeod, J. R.**, Private, reported to the regimental medical unit June 20, 1864, diagnosis was acute diarrhea.

McQuester, E. A., Private, was placed on medical furlough January 5, 1862, and June 20, 1862, for 20 days and sent home to Tallapoosa.

McVay, Morgan, Private, [37]*enlisted in February of 1862 in Mobile. He was hospitalized with rubeola, February 18, 1864, Mobile. He was placed on medical furlough March 15, 1864 for 60 days.* [17]*December 1, 1863, and January 4 and 18, and February 13, 1864, he reported to the regimental medical unit, diagnosis was catarrhus. February 13, he was moved to the general hospital in Greenville. February 17, he returned to the medical unit with rubeola and was transferred to the general hospital in Mobile. He suffered a slight wound to his arm July 20, 1864, at the battle of Peach Tree Creek near Atlanta. He reported to the medical unit with acute diarrhea November 3.* Captured December 15, 1864, at Nashville, he was imprisoned at Camp Douglas, Illinois. He was hospitalized February 28, 1865, Richmond and placed on medical furlough March 6, 1865, for 30 days. [8]*He was from Pike County.* [37]*He was born January 24, 1843, in Crawford, Georgia. In 1921 he was living in Troy and stated that he had fought at Peachtree Creek in Georgia and at Nashville.* Also spelled **McVey, McVeigh, McVery.**

McWhorter, Ezekiel A., Private, enlisted September 16, 1861, at Montgomery. He was hospitalized September 9, 1863, Mobile. He retired September 26, 1863. He rejoined his unit later as [17]*he is listed in the regimental medical unit register seven times after December 1, 1863. He reported sick December 17, 1863, and April 11, and June 5, 1864, diagnosis feb int quotid. He also reported sick February 14 and March 7, 1864, diagnosis feb int tert. January 19, diagnosis was splinitis. He died on the field July 28, 1864, at the battle of Ezra Church near Atlanta.*

[8]**McWhorter, William,** *was killed at the battle of Atlanta during the summer of 1864.*

Meadows, H., Private, was hospitalized in June 1862.

[17]**Miller, Henry**, *Private, reported to the regimental medical unit in Mobile December 25, 1863, diagnosis acute dysenteria and February 23, 1864, syphilis primary. He was wounded in the left leg and ankle August 3 during the Atlanta campaign. He transferred to the general hospital on August 8, 1864.*

[8]**Moon, John T.**, *died at Pensacola, Florida, during 1861.*

Moore, Daniel, Private, enlisted at Bruceville, Macon County, on February 3, 1863. He was born in Edgefield County, South Carolina, in 1824. He had dark hair and dark eyes. (Document in Alabama Archives submitted by Mrs. Mary Moore McKee.) [17]*He reported to the regimental medical unit three times in 1864. On March 17, diagnosis was feb int tert, on April 5, acute diarrhea, and on April 18, acute dysenteria.*

Moore, John, Corporal, was 6'3 and born in 1828 in Munroe County, Georgia. He died January 2, 1862, at Pensacola, leaving widow Aley or Elcey I. Moore of Pike County.
Munchus, James W., Private, enlisted December 27, 1861, at Greenville. He was 5'8 and born, in Russell County. He was discharged December 31, 1862, reason: under age.
Murphy, B. F., Private, enlisted February 9, 1863, at Greenville and was paroled May 1865 at Greensboro, North Carolina.

[17]***Norsworthy, Lafayette L.***, Private, reported to the regimental medical unit three times in 1864. March 18, diagnosis was feb int tert; and April 27, acute diarrhea. In May, he suffered a wound to his thumb, possibly at the battle of Resaca, Georgia. Also spelled **Northsworthy**.

Ozier, James Uriah, Private, enlisted September 16, 1861, at Montgomery. He was placed on medical furlough January 5, 1862, for 20 days and sent home to Montgomery County. He was hospitalized June 1862. [12]*On the muster roll for July-August 1862, he was listed as sick in the hospital.* He worked as a ward master in the hospital October 3, 1862. He worked as a nurse during November and December of 1862 and March and April of 1863. He was a ward master from May to October of 1863. [17]*He reported to the regimental medical unit June 15, 1864, diagnosis was acute diarrhea.* **James E. Ozier** *reported to the hospital March 21, diagnosis acute dysenteria.* **J. W. Ozier** *suffered a slight head wound May 1864, possibly at the battle of Resaca, Georgia.* Captured December 15, 1864, Nashville, he was imprisoned at Camp Douglas, Illinois, where he was released on June 20, 1865. [8]*He was from Pike County.* [30]*He was born December 1835, Montgomery County, son of Perry and Clarissa Jones Ozier. He married Susannah Adams. He died January 2, 1902, and was buried at Salem Cemetery, Pike County.* Also listed as **John Ozier**.
Ozier, J. N., Private, enlisted November 11, 1864, at Montgomery. [17]*He reported to the regimental medical unit December 3, 1864, diagnosis was ulcus.* He was paroled in May 1865 at Greensboro, North Carolina.

Pace, D. C. M., Private, was discharged December 16, 1861.
Padgett, John, Private, enlisted September 16, 1861, at Montgomery. He was hospitalized five days September 8, 1863, at Mobile with fever. [17]*He reported to the regimental medical unit twice with catarrhus December 1 and 26, 1863. He also reported sick, diagnosis feb int quotid, January 2 and June 18, 1864. He was moved to the general hospital June 19.* [8]*He was from Pike County.* Also spelled **Pagett, Paggett**

Parish, Tyra, Private, enlisted March 24, 1862, Corinth, Mississippi. He was 6', and born in 1838 in Pike County. [5]*He was wounded at Shiloh, Tennessee, April 7, 1862.* He was hospitalized in Mississippi during June 1862. He died August 27, 1862, in a Mobile hospital leaving father, William M. Also listed as **F. Parish**, and as **Lyre Parish, Tira Parish**.

Parish, William J., Private, enlisted February 20, 1862, Newbern.

[12]***Parker, William***, *Private, enlisted December 27, 1861, Newbern.*

Pearson, Philip, Private, enlisted December 26, 1861, Newbern. He was discharged July 4, 1862.

[17]***Pierce, Geo.***, *Private, reported to the regimental medical unit March 16, 1864, diagnosis chronic rheum.*

Pierce, John, Private, was captured at July 4, 1864, Marietta, Georgia. He was imprisoned at Camp Chase, Ohio. He died November 11, 1864, [10]*and is buried in lot number 446.*

Pitts, Adoniram J., Private, enlisted November 10, 1861. He sustained a leg wound at Shiloh, Tennessee, April 7, 1862. He was appointed fourth corporal on October 20, 1862. He was hospitalized July 9, 1864, Macon, Georgia. [17]*He reported to the regimental medical unit December 30, 1863, diagnosis feb int quotid, and June 18, 1864, feb int tert. He suffered a wound to his little finger, right hand, July 20, 1864, at the battle of Peach Tree Creek near Atlanta.* The wound required amputation. Captured at December 19, 1864, Columbia, Tennessee, after the battle at Nashville, he was imprisoned at Camp Chase, Ohio. He was from Union Springs, Bullock County.

Poodin, K. C., Private.

Porter, J., Private.

Potter, J. R., Private.

Prater, William F., Private, enlisted December 20, 1861, at Newbern.

Price, James, Private, enlisted December 20, 1861, at Newbern.

Rainer, Joel H., Private, enlisted September 16, 1861, at Montgomery. He was elected second lieutenant July 25, 1862. [5]*He was wounded at Shiloh, Tennessee, April 6, 1862.* [17]*He reported to the regimental medical unit June 16, 1864, diagnosis chronic hepatitis.* [20]*He was detailed to General George D. Johnson's staff at Montgomery in October 1864.* He was hospitalized at Meridian, Mississippi, January 14, 1865, after the retreat from Nashville. He was listed as captain when granted parole May 1865, Greensboro, North Carolina. [1]*He was born January 17, 1829 in Sampson County, North Carolina.* [20]*He was living in Union Springs, Bullock County, in 1907.*

Rawls, Oliver Lieke, Private, enlisted at Montgomery, September 16, 1861. [17]*He reported to the regimental medical unit in Mobile December 20,*

1863, diagnosis abscessus. He was slightly wounded in the right thigh July 28, 1864, at the battle of Ezra Church near Atlanta. He was granted parole in May 1865 at Greensboro, North Carolina. [8]*He was from Pike County.* [1]*He was born August 24, 1828, in Wilcox County. He was living in Montgomery in 1907.* Also spelled **Rauls, Ralls**

Rawls, C. L., Private, was hospitalized at LaGrange, Georgia, and returned to duty June 14, 1864.

Ready, S. W., Private, enlisted September 26, 1863, at Mobile. He was 5'5 and born in 1845 in Pike County. [17]*He reported to the regimental medical unit five times in 1864. February 10 and April 1, diagnosis was rubeola. June 21 and August 6, diagnosis was feb int quotid. He was moved to the general hospital June 21. June 15, his complaint was acute dysenteria.* He was granted parole in May 1865 at Greensboro, North Carolina.

Roberds, William R., Private, enlisted September 16, 1861, at Montgomery. He was born in 1845 in Coosa County, a farmer, and 5'10. He was hospitalized in Mississippi during June 1862. He was hospitalized February 14-February 22, 1864, in Mobile. [17]*He reported to the regimental medical unit November 15, 1864, diagnosis feb int tert.* He was granted parole May 1865 at Greensboro, North Carolina. Also spelled **Robarts, Robberds, Robbins, Roberts, Robins**.

[17]**Roberts, W. B.**, Private, *reported to the regimental medical unit in September 1864, diagnosis hepatitis.* Note: This is probably William R. Roberds above.

Robertson, John S., Private, enlisted December 20, 1861, Newbern. He was 5'6 and born in 1846 in Scotland. He was discharged December 20, 1862, reason: under 18. Also spelled **Roberson**.

Rotten, William O., Private, was discharged December 16, 1861.

Rowell, R. N., Corporal, was discharged December 16, 1861.

Russell, C. F., Private, enlisted December 20, 1861, Newbern. He was 6', born in 1842, Fayette County. He died May 15, 1862, in the hospital at Okolona, Mississippi.

Russell, J. J., Private, enlisted December 20, 1861, Newbern. He was admitted to the hospital March 2, 1862. He was hospitalized June 1862. He had not returned to his company by the September/October 1862 muster roll.

Russell, Reuben, Private, enlisted December 20, 1861, Newbern. He was sent to the Interior Hospital in July 1862. He appeared in Fayette County, Alabama, August 13, 1862, as a witness. Still not on the muster roll for September-October 1862.

Saunders, John Henry, Private, enlisted September 16, 1861, at Montgomery. A farmer, he was 5'7, born [1]*September 9, 1837,*

Edgefield County, South Carolina. While in Pensacola, he was granted a medical furlough December 10, 1861 for 20 days and sent home to Pike County. He was wounded slightly at Shiloh, Tennessee, April 7, 1862. He was dropped from the rolls as deserter. Obviously he rejoined his company as [17]*he is listed on the regimental medical records in 1864. March 15, diagnosis was debilitas; April 2, feb int tert; and November 16, feb int quotid.* [1]*Service ended when he was given a furlough in December 1864. Was living in Trussville, Jefferson County, in 1907.*

Saunders, Jno., Private, was hospitalized February 4, 1865, at Meridian. [8]*He was from Pike County.* May be John Henry above.

Scarborough, John T., Musician, died May 9, 1862, at a hospital in Corinth, Mississippi, leaving father, Thomas B. Scarborough, of Pike County. [30]*He was born ca 1842 in Alabama.*

Schofield, John James, Private, enlisted September 6, 1863, Mobile. [17]*He reported to the regimental medical unit February 18, 1864, with rubeola and was moved to the general hospital in Mobile February 20. He returned to the medical unit July 24, diagnosis acute diarrhea.* [1]*He was paroled at Greensboro, North Carolina, April 1865. He was born October 22, 1844, in Pickens County. He was living in Lapine, Crenshaw County, in 1907* [37]*and in 1921. In 1921 he stated that he had fought at New Hope Church, Jonesboro where he was wounded, Peachtree Creek, and Atlanta.*

[17]**Sewell, John**, Private, *reported to the regimental medical unit on February 13, 1864, diagnosis feb int tert.*

Shaw, Thomas, Private, enlisted December 20, 1861, Newbern. He was discharged July 23, 1862.

[20]**Shell, Thomas Jepthia**, Private, *enlisted February 1862 in Montgomery. Born March 25, 1830, near Madison in Morgan County, he was living in Inverness, Bullock County.* [17]*He reported to the regimental medical unit on March 11, 1864, diagnosis anasarca.* [1]*He served until the end of the war and was paroled at Montgomery.*

Slaughter, H. T., Lieutenant, was granted a leave of absence for 15 days in January 1862. He resigned May 14, 1862.

Slaughter, W. R., Sergeant, lived Union Springs, Bullock County. He was discharged January 24, 1862.

Smart, Martin, Private, was 5'10 and born in 1843 in North Carolina. He died of pneumonia December 31, 1861, leaving father, W. W. Smart.

Smith, Elijah A., Private, enlisted December 20, 1861, Newbern.

Smith, Elijah M., Private, enlisted December 20, 1861, Newbern. He was 5'10 and born in 1821, Pendleton District, South Carolina. He was discharged October 31, 1862, reason: over 40 years old.

COMPANY I

Smith, James D., Private, enlisted December 20, 1861, Newbern. At 5'6 he was discharged December 20, 1862, reason: under 18. He died in 1863 at Lauderdale Springs, Mississippi. Also listed as **T. D. Smith**.

Smith, John O., Private, was 5'11, a farmer and was born in 1832 in Montgomery County. He was discharged November 19, 1862, reason: provided a substitute.

Smith, John H., Private, enlisted March 24, 1862, Corinth, Mississippi. A farmer he was 5'11 and born 1838 in Pike County. He died in Okolona, Mississippi, July 4, 1862, leaving widow, Mary Ann Smith.

[17]*Smith, Rich*, Private, reported to the regimental medical unit April 9, 1864, diagnosis was feb int quotid.

Smith, Saul, Private, enlisted September 16, 1861, at Montgomery. He transferred to the Sharpshooters July 1, 1862. Captured July 3, 1864, at Marietta, Georgia, he was imprisoned at Camp Douglas, Illinois. He enlisted in 5th US Volunteers April 14, 1865, and deserted the Union Army on April 30, 1866.

Smith, Thomas N., Private, enlisted December 20, 1861.

Smith, W., Private.

Smith, William W., Private, enlisted November 26, 1863. He was a farmer, born 1845 in Montgomery, and from Union Springs, Bullock County. [17]*He reported to the regimental medical unit December 12, 1863, diagnosis acute diarrhea. He reported sick again February 13 and June 9, 1864. Diagnosis was feb int tert. He was moved to the general hospital June 11. In September he reported sick with acute diarrhea.* Captured December 17, 1864, at Franklin, he was hospitalized in a Union hospital at Nashville with frost bite on the right foot January 20, 1865. [9]*He had the first four toes of his right foot and the first three toes of his left foot removed February 11, 1865. March 9, 1865, his right leg was amputated. June 16, 1865, he died of exhaustion,* leaving father, Nathaniel Smith. He was buried in lot number 13936 at the Nashville City Cemetery. Later his remains were moved to Mt. Olivet Cemetery in Nashville.

Spoon, James H., Private, enlisted May 14, 1862, at Montgomery. A merchant he was 5'10 and born in 1842 in Muscogee County, Georgia. He died in Pensacola, Florida, January 16, 1862, leaving widow, Mary C. Spoon.

Spoon, John E., Private, enlisted at Montgomery. [5]*He was wounded at Shiloh, Tennessee, April 7, 1862.* He was discharged July 4, 1862. [8]*He was from Pike County.*

Stanford, W., Private

Starr, John, Private, enlisted September 11, 1862, Mobile.

Stewart, Reuben A. J., Private, enlisted December 20, 1861, Newbern. He was 5'8 and born in 1845, Fayette County. He was discharged December 20, 1862, reason: under 18. Also listed as **R. Y. Stewart Street, A. J.**, Private.

Strom, H. S., Private, was born in Pike County. He died August 4, 1862, a head wound received at battle of Shiloh, Tennessee, April 6, 1862 leaving mother, Lucy Strom.

Stuart, William R., Private, [17]*reported to the regimental medical unit three times in 1864. February 25, diagnosis was catarrhus; June 6, acute diarrhea; and June 13, feb int tert. He was sent to the general hospital June 14.* Also spelled **Stewart**.

Thigpen, Daniel M., enlisted January 31, 1863. He was admitted to Ross Hospital in Mobile October 5, 1863, diagnosis was debility, and November 4, 1863, chronic diarrhea. He was placed on sick furlough December 1863, for 30 days. He returned to the hospital February 14, 1864, diagnosis ulcer.

Thomas, G. W., Private, enlisted June 4, 1861, at Montgomery, from Shelby County. He was hospitalized June 23, 1864, and deserted July 19, 1864. [17]*The regimental medical records state that he reported to the regimental medical unit June 22, 1864, diagnosis hernia, was moved to the general hospital the same day.* He was granted parole May 26, 1865 at Talladega.

Thomas, Ira, Private, enlisted September 16, 1861, at Montgomery. He was appointed third sergeant August 17, 1862. He was Ordnance Sergeant at Battery Huger in Mobile. [17]*He reported to the regimental medical unit December 18, 1863, diagnosis feb int quotid.*

Thomas, W. T., Private, enlisted April 10, 1864, at Montgomery. [17]*He reported to the regimental medical unit August 7, 1864, diagnosis acute diarrhea.* He was paroled at Greensboro, North Carolina, April 1865. He died May 19, 1930, at the Beauvoir Confederate Soldiers Home.

Thompson, Augustus L., Private, enlisted September 16, 1861, at Montgomery. He was 5'10, a farmer, and born in 1843 in Baldwin County, Georgia. He received a disability discharge in 1862. He was known as Gus.

[17]***Thurman, W. D.**, Private, reported to the regimental medical unit December 15, 1863, diagnosis was pleuritis. He reported twice in 1864, diagnosis feb int tert: February 28 and March 11.*

Townsand, Jefferson C., Private, enlisted September 14, 1861, at Montgomery. He was discharged July 4, 1862. [8]*He was from Pike County.*

Turner, Benjamin Howard, Sergeant, enlisted September 16, 1862, Montgomery. [8]*He was from Pike County.* [17]*He reported to the* regimental medical unit three times in 1864. February 4 and 11, diagnosis was feb int tert, and July 11, phlegmon. ²He was killed at the battle of Franklin, Tennessee, November 30, 1864, and buried in McGavock Cemetery, section 69, number 25.

Turner, John H., Private, enlisted April 21, 1862, Pike County. He was 5'9, born 1840, Pike County, and a farmer. He was granted a medical furlough August 11 to October 11,1862. [17]*He reported to the regimental medical unit January 1, 1864, diagnosis debilitas, and January 22, 1864, diagnosis feb int tert. He was severely wounded, left thigh, July 28, at the battle of Ezra Church near Atlanta. He was transferred to the general hospital July 31.*

[17]**Turner, Thomas**, Private, reported to the regimental medical unit December 30, 1863, diagnosis feb int quotid.

Ward, John W., Private, enlisted September 16, 1861, at Montgomery. He was hospitalized at Mobile September 4, 1863, for 1 month.

Ward, Sampson M., Private, enlisted September 16, 1861, at Montgomery, 5'9. [17]*He reported to the regimental medical unit, diagnosis feb int tert, December 13, 1863, and January 18 and 30, March 1, April 18, and June 23, 1864. He also reported to the hospital February 26, diagnosis feb int quotid. He suffered a slight wound, right thumb, July 20, 1864, at the battle of Peach Tree Creek near Atlanta.* He was granted parole June 8, 1865 at Montgomery.

Ware, Thomas, Private, was hospitalized in Mobile September 9, 1863, for two months. He was granted parole May 18, 1865. [17]*He reported to the regimental medical unit twice in 1864. February 23, diagnosis debilitas, he was sent to the general hospital at Mobile the next day. April 16, diagnosis was oedema.*

[17]**Watson, Thomas**, Private, reported to the regimental medical unit on December 26, 1863, diagnosis catarrhus. He reported to the hospital again on February 21, 1864, diagnosis feb int tert.

[17]**Weaver, James R.**, Private, was killed on July 20, 1864, at the battle of Peach Tree Creek near Atlanta. *J. R. Weaver reported to the regimental medical unit June 4, 1864, diagnosis acute diarrhea. This could be either James R. or John R. Weaver.*

Weaver, John R., Private, 5'10, captured at July 20, 1864, Atlanta. He was imprisoned at Camp Douglas, Illinois, where he was granted parole June 17, 1865.

[8]**Weaver, William**, Private, was killed at the battle of Shiloh, Tennessee, April 7, 1862.

Whaley, Archibald, Private, enlisted August 17, 1863, Coosa County. He was 6'1, a farmer, and born 1819 in Jaspar County, Georgia. [17]*He reported to the regimental medical unit three times when diagnosis was* *catarrhus, December 29, 1863, and on January 22 and March 22, 1864. He also reported June 2, 1864, with acute dysenteria.* He was sent to the general hospital the next day. He was hospitalized in Jackson, Mississippi, for 2 weeks August 20, 1864. Captured at December 19, 1864 at Columbia, Tennessee, he was imprisoned at Camp Chase, Ohio, where he died of rheumatism March 5, 1865. He is buried in lot 1666.

Whittles, James M., Private, lived in Lowndes County. [17]*He reported to the regimental medical unit on March 25, 1864, diagnosis rubeola, and was transferred to the general hospital in Greenville on March 31. He was wounded in May 1864, possibly at the battle of Resaca, Georgia.* Also spelled **Whiddle.**

White, John L., musician, enlisted September 9, 1861, Montgomery, age 19. He was detailed as a musician in the regimental band July 6, 1862. He was captured at Nashville December 16, 1864, and imprisoned at Camp Chase, Ohio.

White, William, Private, was discharged December 16, 1861.

Wilkes, Johnsy, Private

Williams, Malachi C., Private, enlisted August 9, 1862, at Montgomery. He was hospitalized in Mobile in March and April of 1863. He was placed on medical furlough from Mobile October 16, 1863 for 30 days. [17]*He reported to the regimental medical unit December 5, 1863, diagnosis was feb int quotid, and July 1, 1864, feb remit.* Captured December 15, 1864, Nashville, he was imprisoned at Camp Douglas, Illinois, where he applied for oath of allegiance. He was hospitalized March 22, 1865 at Howard's Grove in Richmond, Virginia. He was transferred to Camp Lee March 25, 1865. [8]*He was from Pike County.*

Williams, Stanford J., Private, enlisted September 16, 1861, at Montgomery, from Cherokee County. [17]*He reported to the regimental medical unit six times during 1864. February 29, march 1, and July 5, diagnosis was feb int tert, April 14, paronychia, and June 6 and June 15, acute diarrhea.* Captured December 15, 1864, at Nashville, he was imprisoned at Camp Douglas, Illinois, where he was paroled June 6, 1865. [8]*He died in 1908.*

Williford, John T., Private, enlisted September 16, 1861, at Montgomery. He was 5'11 and lived in Pike County. [17]*He reported to the regimental medical unit December 12 and 19, 1863, diagnosis feb int tert. He also reported sick in 1864. January 21, diagnosis was catarrhus. March 28, and June 23, diagnosis was feb int quotid.* He was granted a medical furlough August 2, 1864, from Dalton, Georgia, (typhoid pneumonia) for 60 days and sent home to Hilliard, Pike County. [17]*He was severely wounded November 30, 1864, at the battle of Franklin, Tennessee. An injury to his left thigh required an immediate amputation.* Captured December 17, 1864 at Columbia, Tennessee, he was imprisoned at

COMPANY I 395

Camp Chase, Ohio. From there he transferred to Point Lookout for exchange. He was paroled from Point Lookout June 22, 1865. He was listed corporal in 1864.

[17]**Wooten, Thomas E.**, *Private, reported to the regimental medical unit on December 27, 1863, diagnosis was pleuritis. He is also listed on the regimental medical register six times in 1864. January 25, diagnosis was feb int tert; February 22, feb int quotid; February 5 and April 22, catarrhus; July 9, acute diarrhea; and September 4, a hernia.*

[17]**Wright, J. P.**, *Sergeant, reported to the regimental medical unit April 13, 1864, diagnosis was feb int quotid.* [8]*Sergeant **Jep Wright** was from Pike County.*

Wright, Thomas, Private, enlisted September 16, 1861, at Montgomery. He was sent to the hospital May 27, 1862. He was hospitalized in Mississippi during June 1862. By October 1862 he had not been heard from.

Wright, William J., Sergeant, enlisted September 16, 1861, at Montgomery. He was paroled in May 1865 at Montgomery. [17]*He reported to the regimental medical unit December 8, 1863, diagnosis feb int quotid, and November 8, 1864, acute diarrhea. He suffered at head wound May 1864, possibly at the battle of Resaca, Georgia.*

Young, G. G., Private, enlisted November 11, 1863, Montgomery. He was paroled May 26, 1865 at Montgomery. He was a farmer and born in 1818 in Putnam County, Georgia.

[17]**Young, G. H.**, *Private, reported to the regimental medical unit February 11, 1864, diagnosis was acute dysenteria.*

[17]**Young, M. L.**, *Private, reported to the regimental medical unit June 1, 1864, diagnosis acute dysenteria. He was sent to the general hospital the same day.*

Appendix XI. Company K

Albritton, John E., Private, enlisted September 9, 1861, at Montgomery. He was born in 1840 and died before April 21, 1862.

Albritton, Pleasant L., Private, enlisted September 9, 1861, at Montgomery. He died in 1862 at a hospital in Lauderdale Springs, Mississippi.

Allen, J., Private, was captured at Shiloh, Tennessee, April 1862. He was imprisoned at Camp Douglas, Illinois, where he died.

Allen, Noah, Private, enlisted January 27, 1862, at Greenville.

Allen, Washington, Private, enlisted January 27, 1862, at Greenville.

Ballard, John A., Private, enlisted September 9, 1861, at Montgomery. [5]*He was severely wounded at Shiloh, Tennessee, and was admitted to a Union hospital April 6, 1862. His arm was amputated at the shoulder the next day. He recovered and was sent to a Union prison April 27. He died June 28, 1862, of smallpox, in prison at St. Louis, Missouri.* [9]*He was born in 1837*

Barganier, William J., Private, [17] *reported to the regimental medical unit eight times in 1864. February 18, diagnosis was pleuritis. March 9 and 29, and April 23, diagnosis was feb int quotid. June 18 and July 4, diagnosis was acute diarrhea, August 13, acute dysenteria, and in September, icterus.* He was captured December 15, 1864, Nashville and was imprisoned at Camp Douglas, Illinois. He died February 21, 1865, and was buried in lot number 843, Chicago City Cemetery. [20]*He was born September 12, 1825,* [30]*son of Jesse and Nancy Slater Barganier.*

[20]**Barnes, Michael H.**, enlisted October 1862 at Selma. He was placed on detail to make whiskey for the duration of the war. His home was Plantersville, Chilton County, in 1907. He was born February 2, 1842, Shelby County.

Barrett, Andrew J., Private, enlisted March 3, 1863, at Mobile. His home was Butler County. [17]*He reported to the regimental medical unit December 18, 1863, diagnosis was debilitas, and was granted a medical furlough December 21 for 20 days. He reported to the regimental medical unit six times in 1864. March 22 and April 28, diagnosis was feb int tert, and June 11, acute diarrhea. June 21, diagnosis was feb int quotid, and he moved to the general hospital the same day. August 18, he reported sick again, diagnosis debilitas, and October 3, acute diarrhea.* He was captured December 15, 1864, at Nashville and imprisoned at Camp Douglas, Illinois. Also listed as **A. J. Barnett.**

Barrington, William W., Private, enlisted October 1, 1862, at Mobile. [17]*He reported to the regimental medical unit July 14, 1864, diagnosis was colica.* He was paroled at Montgomery on June 19, 1865. [30]*He was born January 5, 1829, in Henry County, Georgia, to Willis and Cebelle*

Mathews Barrington. He married Rhoda Weaver. [1]At 6'2, he was living in Rutledge, Crenshaw County, in 1907. [30]He died April 26, 1909, and was buried in Black Rock Cemetery.

Bedgood, John, Private, enlisted February 26, 1862, at Mobile. [17]He reported to the regimental medical unit November 6, 1864, diagnosis was feb int quotid. He was captured April 25, 1865, at Greenville and paroled May 6, 1865.

Bedgood, Samuel, Private, enlisted February 24, 1863, at Greenville. [17]He reported to the regimental medical unit three times in December 1863. On the 8th, diagnosis was feb int quotid, on the 16th, icterus, and on the 23rd, debilitas. The next day he was granted a medical furlough for 15 days. He reported sick again June 18, diagnosis acute dysenteria. He suffered a severe wound to the right forehead July 28, 1864, at the battle of Ezra Church during the Atlanta campaign. He was moved to the general hospital July 31.

Bennett, Jeremiah, Private, enlisted September 7, 1861, at Montgomery. He died January 5, 1862, while serving in Pensacola, leaving father Elijah Bennett.

Benson, William C., Private, enlisted September 7, 1862, at Mobile and was 5'10. He suffered a gunshot wound to his right foot, [17]July 24, 1864, and was sent to the general hospital July 31 during the Atlanta campaign. He was admitted to Way Hospital, Meridian, Mississippi, February 4, 1865, after the retreat from Nashville. He was transferred to Lauderdale Hospital where he was placed on medical furlough for 60 days on February 28, 1865, and sent to Greenville. Parole was granted at Montgomery, June 8, 1865.

Black, Ezekiel, Corporal, enlisted September 7, 1862, at Mobile and was from Butler County. [17]He reported to the regimental medical unit three times in 1864. In May he suffered a severe wound to his finger, possibly during the battle of Resaca. He reported sick July 2, diagnosis acute dysenteria, and moved to the general hospital the next day. August 19, diagnosis was acute diarrhea. He was captured December 15, 1864, at Nashville and imprisoned at Camp Douglas, Illinois.

Black, F. M., was discharged March 19, 1863.

Black, John C., Private, enlisted February 26, 1863, at Mobile. He was born in 1845 in Butler County and was 5'11. He was granted a disability discharge on May 23, 1863. [28]He attended a Confederate Veterans Reunion in Greenville, August 21, 1897, [7]and registered as a veteran in Butler County July 4, 1906.

Black, Joseph S., Private, enlisted February 26, 1863, at Mobile. [17]He reported to the regimental medical unit six times in 1864. On January 28 and March 19, diagnosis was feb int tert. On February 20 and August 2, diagnosis was feb int quotid. On July 29, diagnosis was acute diarrhea and on July 30, debilitas. He was captured December 16, 1864, Nashville, and imprisoned at Camp Douglas, Illinois.

Black, Robert W., Private, enlisted October 17, 1863, at Greenville. He was 5'11, a farmer, and born in 1822, Butler County.

Blackman, George W., Private, enlisted September 9, 1861, at Montgomery. [17]*He reported to the regimental medical unit January 18, 1864, diagnosis was abscessus.* He was five foot tall and was granted a parole June 1, 1865, at Montgomery. Also spelled *Blackmon.*

Blackman, Hardy J., Private, enlisted September 9, 1861, at Montgomery and died in the hospital January 1, 1862.

Boan, Frederick S., Sergeant, enlisted September 9, 1861, at Montgomery. He was granted a medical furlough January 5, 1862, and sent to Butler County for 20 days. He was 5'8, born in 1834 Butler County, and a school teacher.

Boan, Samuel S., Private, enlisted September 7, 1862, at Mobile. He was 5'8 and born in 1844 Butler County. He had light complexion, black eyes and red hair. He was discharged May 27, 1862, and again on May 15, 1863, reason given: chronic hepatitis and general debility.

[17]***Boatright, Pat***, *Private, reported to the regimental medical unit on December 12, 1863, diagnosis was acute dysentery. He reported sick twice in September; diagnosis was feb int tert and feb int quotid.*

Bonnett, Andrew J., Private, enlisted September 9, 1861, at Montgomery. He was hospitalized June 22, 1864, at Macon, Georgia. His home was in Butler County.

[7]***Briggs, L. E.***, *registered as a veteran in Butler County on July 4, 1906.*

[17]***Brinkley, John***, *Private, was severely injured in his left hand July 28, 1864, at the battle of Ezra Church during the Atlanta campaign.*

Brooks, William R., Private, enlisted January 20, 1863, Mobile. He was assigned as a signal and telegraph operator.

Buckman, George, Private.

Buffington, James R., Private, enlisted October 12, 1862, Clark County. [18]*In September 1863, his name was on a list of deserters. He was described as 21 years old, gray eyes, dark hair, fair complexion, 5'8, and a farmer.* He was wounded June 25, 1864, at Kennesaw Mountain. He was admitted to Ocmulgee Hospital in Macon, Georgia, where he was placed on furlough and sent home to Clarke County. Wounded, he was admitted to the First Mississippi Hospital in Jackson, Mississippi, November 8, 1864.

Bullard, John A., Private, was reported missing after the battle at Shiloh, Tennessee, April 1862.

Bunkley, Burrell J., Corporal, enlisted August 27, 1862, at Montgomery. [17]*He reported to the regimental medical unit January 23, 1863, diagnosis debilitas. He was placed on sick furlough for 15 days*

January 24. He reported sick February 29, March 3, and July 5, diagnosis feb int quotid. He was slightly wounded on his left leg November 30, 1864, at the battle of Franklin, Tennessee. He was at the surrender at Greensboro, North Carolina, April 26, 1865.

Bunkley, J. R., Private, [12]enlisted September 9, 1861. He was from Pike County. [17]He reported to the regimental medical unit December 9, 1864, diagnosis was feb int quotid.

Burke, J., Private, was discharged December 5, 1861.

Burke, John, Private, enlisted April 2, 1863, at Mobile. [18]In September 1863, his name was on a list of deserters. He was described as 47 years old, blue eyes, gray hair, fair complexion, 5'8, and a laborer.

Burke, P. J., Private, enlisted September 9, 1861, at Montgomery.

Burnett, Thomas J., Captain, enlisted September 9, 1861, at Montgomery. He was promoted to major May 1, 1862. [17]He was severely wounded (his chest and left arm) July 28, 1864, at the battle of Ezra Church in Georgia. He was moved to the general hospital July 31. [35]He never fully recovered from his wounds. He was born in Greenville, August 30, 1826. He died October 8, 1887, and was buried in Old Cemetery in Greenville. He was paroled May 17, 1865, at Montgomery.

Cates, Needham, Private, was 6 feet tall and granted a parole June 7, 1865, at Montgomery. [30]He was born in 1818 in Edgefield District, South Carolina. His family moved to Alabama after 1820. He was married to Lucinda Manning. He served about two years and was discharged November 21, 1863, chronic liver disease. He died in 1884, Lowndes County and is buried in an unmarked grave in Daniel Cemetery, Butler County. The cemetery is located off state road 185 between Greenville and Fort Deposit. His brother, Josiah, was in Company C of the 17th Alabama.

Cavine, George B., Private, enlisted September 9, 1862, at Mobile. He was a laborer, 5'6, and born in 1845, Levy, Florida. [17]He reported to the regimental medical unit four times in 1864. June 3 and August 23, diagnosis was acute diarrhea. In September, diagnosis was feb int quotid and November 13, catarrhus. He was captured December 17, 1864, at Franklin, Tennessee, and imprisoned at Camp Douglas, Illinois. See Papers for George Philyaw. Also spelled **Cavane, Cavone, Cavene, Cavens**

Cheatham, John H., Private, enlisted September 9, 1861, at Montgomery. He was sick at home during August 1862. He served as a teamster and ambulance driver. He died December 11, 1863, General Hospital, Miller Spring, Mobile. He was born in 1820.

Cheatham, William F., Private, enlisted September 7, 1862, at Mobile. [17]He reported to the regimental medical unit three times in 1864 with

COMPANY K 401

acute diarrhea, August 13, September 21, and November 15. He was discharged from the hospital in Augusta, Georgia, April 17, 1865. [37]He was born August 30, 1844, Fort Deposit, Lowndes County. In 1921 he was living in Greenville and stated that he fought at Resaca, Peachtree Creek, New Hope Church, Franklin, and Nashville.

Clark, James T., Private, enlisted September 1, 1861, at Montgomery. He was placed on sick furlough January 14, 1862, for 20 days and sent to Butler County. His name was on a list of sick in the hospital June 1862 and discharged July 27, 1862.

Cleghorn, Henry S., Private, enlisted September 9, 1861, at Montgomery.

Cleghorn, Jno. P., Private, was discharged April 20, 1863

Cleghorn, Samuel O., Private, enlisted September 1, 1862, at Greenville. A farmer, he was 5'8 and born in 1832 in Montgomery County.

Clements, W. H., Private, enlisted September 1, 1861, at Montgomery. He died January 5, 1862 in a hospital.

Clorr, John, Sergeant, enlisted October 1, 1861, in Macon County. He suffered a wound to his knee at Shiloh, Tennessee, April 6, 1862. He was discharged March 2, 1863.

Coatney, William R., Private, enlisted September 9, 1861, at Montgomery. He was working as a cook in a hospital in northeast Mississippi during June 1862. He was transferred to the 1st Battalion Alabama Artillery by order of general headquarters, Spring 1863. Also listed as **William J. Coatney**

Cody, Columbus Jefferson, 2nd Lieutenant, enlisted September 9, 1861, at Montgomery. He was born in 1838. His home was Millville, Alabama. [17]He reported to the regimental medical unit twice in 1864 while in Georgia. On June 25 diagnosis was debilitas, and he was sent to the general hospital the same day. He was hospitalized July 28 with a slight wound to the back received at the battle of Ezra Church during the Atlanta Campaign. He was sent to the general hospital to recuperate July 31. Captured December 15, 1864, at Nashville, he was imprisoned at Sandusky, Ohio. Parole was granted June 16, 1865, at Johnson's Island, Ohio.

Cody, Jackson V. B., Private, enlisted September 9, 1861, at Montgomery. He was hospitalized in Mississippi June 1862. He was acting ordinance sergeant July 1, 1863 to October 31, 1863. [17]He reported to the regimental medical unit March 11 and March 19, 1864, diagnosis feb int tert. He later transferred to the Confederate Navy.

[17]**Codey, W. V.,** Private, reported to the regimental medical unit February 22, 1864, diagnosis was acute dysenteria.

Coker, William P., Private, enlisted March 5, 1862, at Mobile. [17]He reported to the regimental medical unit December 25, 1863, diagnosis was feb int tert. He reported sick four times in 1864. January 8, diagnosis was catarrhus, February 3, feb int tert, March 28, acute dysenteria, and April 5, chronic diarrhea. April 19, he was sent to the general hospital. He was paroled at Greensboro, North Carolina, May 1865.

Coleman, Benjamin A., Private, [17]*reported to the regimental medical unit July 5, 1864, diagnosis catarrhus, and August 7, diagnosis acute diarrhea.* He was granted a parole at Montgomery May 1865. Also spelled **Colman.**

Coleman, Walter, Sergeant, enlisted September 9, 1861, at Montgomery. He was granted a sick furlough January 5, 1862, while at Pensacola, and sent to Butler County for 20 days. [12]*He was listed as sick in an unknown hospital on the muster roll for July-August 1862.* Captured July 28, 1864, during the battle of Ezra Church in Atlanta, he was imprisoned at Camp Chase, Ohio. [43]*He was born December 15, 1840, son of Walter Leak and Caroline Bibb Coleman. He died October 2, 1881.*

Cook, W. F., Corporal, enlisted October 10, 1862, at Talladega. [33]*He died July 1884. His wife applied for a pension.*

Crawford, Robert L., Private.

Crenshaw, Edward, 2nd Lieutenant, enlisted at Montgomery, September 9, 1861. He transferred from Company C, 26th Alabama, to Company K, 17th Alabama in early 1862. [5]*On May 15, 1862, ill with typhoid fever, he was taken home to recover. He returned to his regiment June 28.* He then transferred from Company K to Company C, 17th Alabama. *In March 1863, he joined the newly reorganized 9th Alabama Battalion where he was elected captain of Company B.* [30]*He was born 1842, Butler County, Alabama, son of Walter Henry and Sarah Anderson Crenshaw. He died in 1911.*

Cubsted, Azberry, Private, enlisted September 1, 1861, at Montgomery and was discharged December 5, 1861.

Cubsted, John, Private, enlisted September 1, 1861, at Montgomery and was discharged December 5, 1861.

Cunningham, Hillery H., Private, was a resident of Greenville. [17]*After being wounded (arm) July 20 at the battle of Peach Tree Creek during the Atlanta campaign, he was hospitalized July 22, 1864, at Macon, Georgia. He was again wounded (back) November 30 at the battle of Franklin, Tennessee.*

Daniel, Frederick F., Private, enlisted September 9, 1861, at Montgomery. [17]*He reported to the regimental medical unit December 12, 1863, diagnosis was feb int quotid; and June 14,1864, diagnosis was acute diarrhea. He was sent to the general hospital June 15.* Captured November 30, 1864, at Franklin, Tennessee, he was imprisoned at Camp Douglas, Illinois.

Davis, Francis, Private, enlisted 1863, at Mobile and was from Honoraville. [17]*He reported to the regimental medical unit January 8, 1864, diagnosis pneumonia, and November 11, 1864, diagnosis acute diarrhea.* Captured December 15, 1864, at Nashville, he was imprisoned at Camp Douglas, Illinois.

Defee, William T., Private, enlisted September 9, 1861, at Greenville. He was 5'11 and born in 1828, Twiggs County, Georgia. Also spelled **Dufie.**

Deloney, William C., Private, enlisted May 18, 1863, at Mobile. [17]*He reported to the regimental medical unit twice in December 1863. On the 5th diagnosis was feb int tert, and on the 22nd feb congestive. He was sent to the general hospital on the 22nd.* [20]*He was born May 1, 1845, in Georgia. He was discharged in 1864; diagnosis was brain fever. In 1907 he was living in Castleberry, Conecuh County.*

Dewberry, William, Private, enlisted September 9, 1861, at Montgomery. He was born 1839. He was placed on sick furlough for 20 days and sent to Butler County in 1862. . [5]*He was severely wounded* and declared missing after the battle at Shiloh, Tennessee, April 6, 1862.

[17]**Donaldson, A. W.,** Private, reported to the regimental medical unit June 14, 1864, diagnosis was feb int tert. He was sent to the general hospital the next day.

Donaldson, John W., Private, enlisted September 9, 1861, at Montgomery. [17]*He reported to the regimental medical unit December 3, 1863, January 2, and August 3, 1864, diagnosis was feb int quotid. He also reported sick January 29, 1864, diagnosis feb int tert, and April 4, diagnosis acute diarrhea.* Captured December 16, 1864, at Nashville, he was imprisoned at Camp Douglas, Illinois. Also spelled **Donalson, Donelson, Donnelson**

Donalson, William H., Private, enlisted at Montgomery, September 9, 1861. He was born in 1824.

Dunigan, J. T., Private, was granted a furlough January 1865 from a hospital in Meridian, Mississippi, after the retreat from Nashville.

Dunklin, William Turner, enlisted September 9, 1861, at Montgomery as 4th sergeant. He was appointed 2nd lieutenant. The muster roll for September-October 1862 indicates that he transferred Company B. He was captured December 15, 1864, at Nashville and imprisoned at Johnson Island, Ohio, where he was paroled June 16, 1865. [10]*He was born June 1, 1843, at Greenville. He was living in Butler County in 1907* [37]*and in 1921. He stated that he fought at Shiloh, New Hope Church, Franklin, and Nashville.* Note: See Company B for more information.

Durden, W. W., Sergeant, enlisted September 19, 1861, at Montgomery. He was wounded during the Atlanta campaign and hospitalized August

17, 1864, at Macon, Georgia. He was granted parole in Greensboro, North Carolina, May 1865.

Ellington, Joseph Malachi, Private, enlisted September 16, 1862. [17]*He reported to the regimental medical unit twice in 1864. On March 30, diagnosis was debilitas, and on April 7, feb int tert. He was paroled May 30, 1865 at Montgomery.* [1]*He resided in Luverne in 1907. He was born March 31, 1838, Butler County.* [30]*He was born in 1838 in Butler County, the son of Joseph and Emily Patterson Ellington. He married Emalina Knight. After the war, he was a prominent farmer in Crenshaw County, living close to his birthplace.*

Ellis, Radford, Private, enlisted, at Mobile. [17]*He reported to the regimental medical unit twice in 1864. March 26, diagnosis was feb int tert and April 21, feb int quotid. In May 1864, he was killed by a minnie ball to the heart, probably at the the battle of Resaca, Georgia.*

Farrow, Samuel, Private, enlisted January 27, 1862, at Greenville.

Farrow, W. G., Corporal, enlisted September 1861 at Montgomery. He was born about 1837 and died before June 1862.

[17]**Ficklin, A. B.,** Private, reported to the regimental medical unit January 20, 1864, diagnosis was feb int tert. Note: Could be **E. B. Ficklin,** below.

[17]**Ficklin, E. B.,** Private, reported to the regimental medical unit December 18, 1863, and February 20, 1864, diagnosis was feb int quotid. He reported sick December 27, 1863, and April 29, 1864, diagnosis feb int tert. He also reported sick June 24, 1864, diagnosis anasarca. He was sent to the general hospital the same day.

Ficklin, Christopher, Private, enlisted March 1863, at Mobile.

Ficklin, Joseph R., Private, enlisted September 16, 1862, at Montgomery. [17]*He reported to the regimental medical unit December 13, 1863, diagnosis feb int tert. He reported sick January 31, March 10, and October 3, 1864, diagnosis feb int quotid. He was moved to the general hospital October 7. He also reported sick March 29, 1864, with rubeola and was sent to the general hospital in Greenville.*

Ficklin, Smylie, Private, enlisted October 1, 1861, Macon County. He was hospitalized in Mississippi June 1862.

Fife, John Henry, Private, enlisted October 17, 1863, at Greenville. A farmer, he was 5'11 and born in 1845, in Butler County. [17]*He suffered a slight ankle wound July 20, 1864, at the battle of Peach Tree Creek during the Atlanta campaign. He was sent to the general hospital the next day.* [28]*He attended the Confederate Veterans Reunion in Greenville August 21, 1897.* [37]*He was born October 20, 1845, in Butler County. In 1921 he was living in Chapman and stated that he fought at*

Resaca, New Hope Church, and Peachtree Creek. He also stated that he was home with wounds when the war ended. See Service Records for Robert Black.

Floyd, Robert A., Private, enlisted September 9, 1861, at Montgomery.

Fort, George W., Private, enlisted September 9, 1861, at Montgomery. He was hospitalized in Mississippi June 1862. [17]*He reported to the regimental medical unit January 9, 1864, diagnosis was acute diarrhea.* He was captured September 1864 at Jonesboro, Georgia, and imprisoned at Camp Douglas, Illinois. He enlisted in 5th US Volunteers April 1865.

Fronabager, John P., Private, enlisted September 1861, at Montgomery. [5]*He was severely wounded at Shiloh, Tennessee, April 1862.* He was discharged on June 22, 1862. Could be **Fronzberger.**

Gafford, James Milton, Private, enlisted September 9, 1861, at Montgomery. He was placed on sick furlough January 5, 1862 for 20 days and sent to Butler County. He was transferred to the 1st Confederate Regiment November 1862.

Gafford, Richard H., Private, enlisted January 27, 1862, at Greenville. He was 5'10 and lived in Butler County. During June 1862, he was hospitalized in Mississippi. He was imprisoned in Louisville, Kentucky. He took the oath of allegiance in September 1864 and joined the US Volunteers.

Gafford, G. M., Private, was granted a furlough June 1862.

Galloway, Nathan, Private, [17]*reported to the regimental medical unit on April 6, 1864, diagnosis catarrhus.* He was captured May 30, 1864, at Dallas, Georgia, and was imprisoned at Rock Island, Illinois, [27]*June 7, 1864. He was transferred for exchange February 25, 1865. He was admitted to Jackson Hospital in Richmond, Virginia, March 6, 1865, diagnosis debilitas.* He died October 25, 1914, at age 73. [7]*He registered as a veteran in Butler County July 4, 1906.*

Golden, Emanuel, Private, enlisted October 25, 1862, Pike County. He was born in 1831, Warren County, Georgia. He was discharged May 13, 1863, general debility and dyspepsia. He died in Texas about 1915.

Golson, George F., Private, enlisted September 9, 1861.

Golson, James Augustus, Private, enlisted April 25, 1864. [17]*He reported to the regimental medical unit in September 1864, diagnosis icterus, and October 9, 1864, diagnosis acute diarrhea. He was sent to the general hospital October 15.* He was paroled at Greensboro, North Carolina May 1865. [7]*He registered as a veteran in Butler County July 4, 1906.* [20]*He was living in Conecuh County in 1907. He was born April 4, 1847, Orangeburg, South Carolina.* [37]*His family moved to Alabama in 1854. In 1921 he was living at Fort Deposit and stated that he fought at Rome,*

*Atlanta, and Peachtree, Georgia, and Franklin and Nashville, Tennessee. Also spelled **Gohlson***

Golson, John C., Private, enlisted September 9, 1861, at Montgomery. He was listed on sick furlough on the muster roll for May-June 1863. [17]*He reported to the regimental medical unit August 13, 1864, and November 5, 1864, diagnosis acute diarrhea.* Also spelled **Gohlson, Golsen.**

Gore, Samuel J., Private, enlisted September 9, 1861, at Montgomery. [17]*He reported to the regimental medical unit several times in 1864. January 5, diagnosis was acute dysenteria; January 29, feb int tert; March 22, feb int quotid; and June 6, acute diarrhea. He was severely wounded in the left thigh July 24, 1864, during the Atlanta campaign.* He died August 14, 1864. See Manuscript #1911.

Haigler, James, Private, enlisted September 22, 1862. He was a farmer, born in Butler County. He was granted a disability discharge December 31, 1862. He was buried in Melton Cemetery, Winn Parish Louisiana.

Hammonds, Wylie H., Private, enlisted September 29, 1861, at Montgomery. [5]*He was severely wounded at Shiloh, Tennessee, April 1862.* [17]*He reported to the regimental medical unit March 19, diagnosis was acute diarrhea, and April 7, feb int tert.* He was captured July 20, 1864, at the battle of Peach Tree Creek in Atlanta and imprisoned at Camp Douglas, Illinois. Also listed as **Henry W. Hammonds, Hewitt Hammonds, Jerry W. Hammonds, H. W. Hammonds,** and **Hammons.**

Harrison, Daniel, Private, enlisted September 9, 1862, at Montgomery. He was promoted to Corporal May 1863. [17]*He reported to the regimental medical unit December 4, 1863, and January 4, 1864, diagnosis was feb int tert. He reported sick again February 4, 1864, diagnosis was feb int quotid, and March 26 with acute dysentery. June 3 and November 6, 1864, diagnosis was hydrocele. He was transferred to the general hospital June 6 and November 16.* He was admitted to Petgrew Hospital, Raleigh, North Carolina, April 10, 1865. He was granted a parole at Greensboro, North Carolina. [7]*He registered as a veteran in Butler County July 4, 1906.* [43]*He was born April 3, 1842, son of Jonathan and Barbara Harrison. He died April 23, 1909.*

Harrison, George W., Private, enlisted October 10, 1862, at Mobile. [17]*He reported to the regimental medical unit March 12, 1864, diagnosis debilitas, and was transferred to the general hospital at Spring Hill, Mobile. He reported sick again July 1, 1864, diagnosis anasarca.*

Harrison, James W., Private, enlisted September 9, 1861, Montgomery. He was captured at Pittsburg Landing, Tennessee, April 1862. He was imprisoned at Camp Douglas, Illinois, where he died May 17, 1862.

Harrison, J. J. N., Private, enlisted September 9, 1861, at Montgomery and died during 1862. [5]*He was listed as missing at Shiloh, Tennessee, in April 1862.*

Harrison, King S., Private, enlisted September 16, 1862, at Mobile. [17]*He reported to the regimental medical unit December 5, 1863, and March 11, 1864, diagnosis anasarca. He reported sick four more times in 1864. January 20, diagnosis was feb int tert. February 2, diagnosis was debilitas, and he was moved to the general hospital at Spring Hill on February 7. He reported again March 22, diagnosis acute diarrhea. He was wounded in May, at the battle of Resaca, Georgia.* He was captured May 30, 1864, at Dallas, Georgia, and imprisoned at Rock Island, Illinois.

Harrison, Levi, Private, enlisted September 9, 1861, at Montgomery and was from Butler County. He was granted a sick furlough November 14, 1861 for 60 days and sent to Butler County. He was hospitalized in Mississippi June 1862. [17]*He reported to the regimental medical unit December 13, 1863, March 30, and April 3, 1864, diagnosis feb int tert. He suffered a severe injury to his groin July 28, 1864, at the battle of Ezra Church during the Atlanta campaign. He was sent to the general hospital July 31* and admitted to another hospital August 24, 1864. He was hospitalized again January 30, 1865, at Meridian, Mississippi, after the retreat from Nashville. Also spelled **Hanson.**

Harrison, Thomas E., Private, enlisted January 27, 1862, at Greenville.

Harrison, William, Private, enlisted March 3, 1863, Mobile. [17]*W. Harrison reported to the regimental medical unit April 13, 1864, acute diarrhea. W. H. Harrison reported sick June 13, 1864, diagnosis acute dysenteria. W. M. Harrison reported sick August 16, 1864, diagnosis acute diarrhea. Wm. Harrison suffered a slight wound to his left hand July 28, 1864, at the battle of Ezra Church during the Atlanta campaign. He was sent to the general hospital on July 31.*

Harston, Thomas M., Private.

Hartley, Anderson C., Private, enlisted September 10, 1862, Butler County. He was assigned as a signal operator. [28]*He attended a Confederate Veterans Reunion at Greenville August 21, 1897.* [7]*He registered as a veteran in Butler County July 4, 1906.*

Harvill, William, Private, enlisted September 4, 1861, at Montgomery. He was listed as sick in the hospital on the muster roll for July-August and September-October 1862. Also spelled **Harvell.**

Harvill, Samuel T., Private, enlisted September 4, 1861, at Montgomery.

Hastings, Charles M., Private, enlisted January 27, 1862, at Greenville.

Hastings, Jeremiah W., Private, enlisted January 27, 1862, at Greenville.

Hasting, John B., Private, enlisted September 7, 1862, at Mobile. [17]*He reported to the regimental medical unit June 4, 1864, diagnosis chronic* ulcus and was sent to the general hospital the next day. He was hospitalized August 20, 1864, at Shelby Springs, Alabama.

Hastings, B. W., Private, was discharged September 27, 1863.

Haystring, John B., Private, enlisted September 2, 1862, Mobile. He was discharged in 1863.

Heaton, Frank M., Private, enlisted September 1861, at Montgomery and was discharged December 5, 1861.

Highpins, William, Private.

Hinson, William C., Private, enlisted September 9, 1861, at Montgomery. [12]*He was discharged July 6, 1862.*

Hodge, Thomas P., Private, enlisted September 7, 1862, at Mobile and was from Butler County. [17]*He reported to the regimental medical unit four times in 1864. On January 23, diagnosis was catarrhus; February 21, feb int quotid; April 11, feb remitt; June 14, acute dysenteria. He was transferred to the general hospital April 13 and June 15.* He was captured July 20, 1864, at Peachtree Creek in Atlanta. He was hospitalized July 28, 1864, at Chattanooga, Tennessee, [9]*where his leg was amputated July 29. He was released to a Union prison, November 30, 1864,* at Camp Douglas, Illinois. He was released and admitted to a Richmond Hospital, March 22, 1865. He was captured at Richmond April 3. On May 9 he was put aboard the Steamer Mary Powell headed for Point Lookout, Maryland. At Point Lookout he was transferred to a hospital May 12. He was paroled June 26 at Point Lookout..

Holland, Davis Furman, Private, [30]*enlisted April 3, 1863, Mobile.* [17]*He reported to the regimental medical unit December 18, 1863, January 21 and March 21, 1864, diagnosis feb int quotid. He also reported to the regimental medical unit March 31, 1864, diagnosis was rubeola. He was transferred to the general hospital in Greenville the same day.* He was captured at Nashville on December 15, 1864, and sent to Camp Douglas, Illinois. He died of pneumonia while in prison January 24, 1865. He was buried in block 2, grave #D14Chicago City Cemetery. [30]*He was born in 1827 in North Carolina. He married Rosanna Rebecca Ellington.* Also listed as **David Holland, David Davis.**

Holman, Caspers W., Private, [17]*reported to the regimental medical unit in September 1864, diagnosis abscessus.* He was captured December 15, 1864, at Nashville and imprisoned at Camp Douglas, Illinois. He died there January 26, 1865 and is buried in lot number 570 Block 2, Chicago City Cemetery. Also spelled **Capers, Hollmon.**

Huggins, James L., Private, enlisted September 9, 1861, at Montgomery, age 22. He died in 1862 leaving widow, Diana P. Huggins.

Huggins, R. Bennett, Private, enlisted January 27, 1862, at Greenville. He was hospitalized in Mississippi June 1862.

Huggins, William N., Private, enlisted January 27, 1861, Warrington, Florida. He was hospitalized in Mississippi June 1862 and was granted a disability discharge in fall of 1862. He was 6'4 and born in 1830 in Butler County. He was paroled June 1865 at Montgomery.

Hughes, Singleton D., Private, enlisted September 9, 1861, at Montgomery, age 24. He was hospitalized in Mississippi June 1862. He died of disease July 1862 leaving his father, Wilson Hughes.

Hughes, William W., Private, enlisted September 9, 1861, at Montgomery, age 22. [17]*He reported to the regimental medical unit December 7, 1863, diagnosis feb int quotid. He reported sick again February 1 and April 13, 1864, diagnosis feb int tert.* He was killed in May 1864, injured in back and lungs, possibly at the battle of Resaca, Georgia.

Hurston, Thomas M., Private, enlisted September 9, 1862, at Mobile and resided in Butler County. [17]*He reported to the regimental medical unit December 7, 1864, diagnosis was feb int quotid.* He was captured December 15, 1864, at Nashville and imprisoned at Camp Douglas, Illinois. He died [10]*March 14, 1865,* and is buried in lot number 540, Block 3, Chicago City Cemetery. Also listed as **Thomas Haston**

Huse, D., Private, enlisted May 12, 1862, at Mobile. He was granted a parole at Greensboro, North Carolina, April 1865. (Note: This is probably **D. Hughes**)

Hussey, John, Private, enlisted August 25, 1862, at Mobile. [18]*In September 1863 he was described as 23 years old with gray eyes, dark hair, fair complexion, 6'1, a farmer, and a deserter.* [17]*He reported to the regimental medical unit July 10, 1864, diagnosis was acute diarrhea.* He was granted a parole May 11, 1865, at Montgomery.

Jefcoat, Daniel C., Private, enlisted April 21, 1863, at Mobile. He died August 30, 1863, at Spring Hill, Mobile. He was buried at Magnolia Cemetery in Mobile, row 14, grave 42, listed as D. G. **Jeffoard.**

Joiner, Linsay, Private, enlisted March 3, 1863, at Mobile.

Jones, Charles C., Private, enlisted September 14, 1861, at Montgomery. He was hospitalized in Mississippi June 1862.

Jones, Joseph S., Private, enlisted September 9, 1861, at South Butler. He was granted a sick furlough January 5, 1862, for 20 days and sent to Butler County. [12]*He was discharged July 5, 1862.*

Jordan, George W., Private, enlisted September 9, 1861, at Montgomery, age 18. [5]*He was severely wounded at Shiloh, Tennessee, April 1862.* [17]*He reported to the regimental medical unit January 21, 1864, diagnosis parotitis.* He was captured April 6, 1865, at Greenville.

Kanne, John, Private, enlisted December 12, 1862, at Mobile. He was captured May 20, 1864, at Cassville, Georgia, and imprisoned at Rock Island, Illinois. Also spelled **Kanna, Kanner, Knonor, Konor.**

Kelly, J. H., Private.

Kerbee, James D., Private, enlisted September 4, 1861, at Montgomery, age 32. He was hospitalized in Mississippi June 1862. [12]*He was discharged August 18, 1862.* Also spelled **Kirbee.**

Kern, Simon Moses, Private, enlisted August 1863, at Greenville. He was 5'2, a farmer and born in 1821 in Germany. [17]*He suffered a slight head wound in May 1864 at the battle of Resaca, Georgia.* He was granted a parole May 30, 1865, at Montgomery. [28]*He attended the Confederate Veterans Reunion in Greenville August 21, 1897.* [30]*He was born April 10, 1820 in the Bavarian town of Bochingen-Pfalz to Ludwig and Rosina Lehman Kern. He married Rachel Elizabeth Bates and settled in Butler County. He died of pneumonia November 23, 1904, and is buried at Greenville's Magnolia Cemetery.*

King, Thomas C., 1st Sergeant, enlisted at Montgomery, September 9, 1861, age 28. He was 5'9 and born in 1832 in Luverne. He was granted a disability discharge November 21, 1862.

Kipper, A. S., Private, was hospitalized in Mississippi June 1862.

Kirpatrick, William M., Private, enlisted September 1861, at Montgomery and was discharged December 5, 1861.

Knight, Lawrence Sanson, Private, enlisted September 9, 1861, at Montgomery. He was granted a medical furlough January 5, 1862, for 20 days and sent to Butler County. He was hospitalized in Mississippi June 1862. He was detailed to the army floating battery during May and June 1863. [17]*He reported to the regimental medical unit December 5, 1863, diagnosis catarrhus, and March 14, 1864, diagnosis feb int quotid. He reported to the regimental medical unit June 21 after being* [1]*wounded at Kennesaw Mountain. He lost his left arm at the shoulder.* He retired January 20, 1865, and [1]*was paroled April 20, 1865. He was living in Luverne, Crenshaw County, in 1907* [37]*and in 1921. He stated that he fought at Pittsburg Landing and Resaca and took part in the retreat to Atlanta.* [1]*He was born January 15, 1846, in Pike County, son of William and Mary Sansom Knight.*

Lauderdale, J., Private, enlisted March 1, 1863, at Mobile. He was paroled at Greensboro, North Carolina, May 1865.

Lee, Zachariah, Private, enlisted January 27, 1862, at Greenville.

Lepper, Joseph, Private. See **Seppes**

Lester, Eli, Private, enlisted at Mobile April 26, 1863. [17]*He reported to the regimental medical unit March 22, 1864, diagnosis was debilitas.* [7]*He* registered as a veteran July 4, 1907, [20] and was living in Butler County. He was born September 15, 1843, Marbary, South Carolina.

Leysath, Erskine J., Private, enlisted September 9, 1861, at Montgomery, age 18. He was hospitalized in Mississippi June 1862 and was granted a disability discharge July 27, 1862.

Logan, Stewart H., Private, enlisted August 24, 1862, at Coosa County. [17] He reported to the regimental medical unit January 10, 1864, diagnosis was acute diarrhea.

Long, Henry J., Private, enlisted September 9, 1861, at Montgomery, age 24. He was granted a sick furlough January 5, 1862 for 20 days and sent to Butler County. [17] He reported to the regimental medical unit December 11, 1863, diagnosis feb int tert. He reported again to the hospital June 1 and July 7, 1864, diagnosis phlegmon. Hospital records list him as killed on the field July 28, 1864, at the battle of Ezra Church during the Atlanta campaign. Also listed as **H. S. Long.**

Majors, Henry, Private, enlisted September 1, 1861, at Montgomery. He was born in Lowndes County, father Lemuel D. Majors. He was wounded at Shiloh, Tennessee, April 1862 and died June 3, 1862.

[5] **Majors, J. D.**, Private, was wounded at Shiloh, Tennessee in April 1862.

Majors, Samuel D., Private, enlisted September 9, 1861, at Montgomery. He was 5'10 and born June 15,1818, Twiggs County, Georgia. He was granted a disability discharge June 8, 1863. [7] He was living in Butler County in 1907.

[7] **Majors, S. J.**, Private, registered as a veteran in Butler County July 4, 1906.

Mall, J. J., Private, possibly J. J. Nall of 37th regiment.

Martin, James A., Private, enlisted September 23, 1862, at Mobile. [17] He reported to the regimental medical unit February 29 and March 5, 1864, diagnosis was feb int quotid. He was moved to the general hospital at Spring Hill in Mobile March 14. He was captured July 4, 1864, near Chattahoochie, Georgia, and imprisoned at Johnson Island, Ohio. He was transferred for exchange on May 4, 1865. [20] He was born December 4, 1838, Butler County where he was living in 1907

Martin, James L., Lieutenant, enlisted December 4, 1861, at Warrington. [17] He reported to the regimental medical unit January 19, 1864, diagnosis feb int tert; February 13, 1864, feb int tert; and August 19, 1864, acute diarrhea. He was slightly wounded on his right hand November 30, 1864, at the battle of Franklin, Tennessee. He was listed as a sergeant on the regimental medical unit records. He was paroled at Greensboro, North Carolina.

Martin, John M., Private, enlisted September 9, 1861, at Montgomery. He was hospitalized in Mississippi June 1862. [17] He reported to the regimental medical unit June 15, 1864, diagnosis was acute diarrhea. Captured December 15, 1864, at Nashville, he was imprisoned at Camp Douglas, Illinois. [30]*He was born June 30, 1842. He died February 2. 1912, and buried at Thorp Spring Cemetery in Texas.* Also listed as **J. W. Martin.**

Matthews, William J., Private, enlisted February 23, 1862, Abbeville. He was captured May 30, 1864, at Dallas, Georgia, and imprisoned Rock Island, Illinois.

McCane, Thomas A., Lieutenant, enlisted September 9, 1861, at Montgomery. He was wounded at Shiloh, Tennessee, April 1862. He was promoted to captain July 26, 1862. [17]*He reported to the regimental medical unit August 18 and September 4, 1864, diagnosis was acute diarrhea.* Captured November 30, 1864, at Franklin, Tennessee, he was imprisoned at Johnson Island, Ohio. He was released from Johnson Island May 29, 1865.

McCory, James R., Private, enlisted September 9, 1861, at Montgomery, age 20.

McCoy, Wm. J. R. W., Private, enlisted September 9, 1861, at Montgomery, age 31. [17]*He reported to the regimental medical unit seven times in 1864. February 14 diagnosis was acute dysenteria. February 25 and March 7, diagnosis was abscessus. June 18, diagnosis was acute diarrhea. July 2, July 31, and August 10, diagnosis was anasarca. He was sent to the general hospital August 22.* He was captured April 27, 1865, at Greenville. *Also listed as* **W. J. R., W. J. R. W, W. R., W. V., W. V. R., and Wm.**

McCoy, William H., Private, was on furlough June 1862 and died within the year.

McKellar, Felix G., Private, enlisted September 9, 1861, at Montgomery, age 18. He was served as the regiment postmaster. [17]*He reported to the regimental medical unit eight times in 1864. January 6 and February 3, diagnosis was feb int tert. January 18, March 8, and August 4, diagnosis was feb int quotid. June 8 and July 2, diagnosis was anemia. August 17, diagnosis was acute diarrhea.*

McKellar, James W., Private, [12]*enlisted September 9, 1861.* He reenlisted May 6, 1863, at Mobile. He died September 17, 1863, in Mobile survived by his father, Alexander McKellar.

McKinney, E. H., Private, enlisted September 5, 1862. [17]*He reported to the regimental medical unit August 26, 1864, diagnosis was acute diarrhea.* He was granted a parole at Greensboro, North Carolina, May 1865.

Mercer, Alexander, Private, enlisted September 7, 1862, at Mobile and was from Butler County. [17]*He reported to the regimental medical unit August 26, 1864, diagnosis was acute diarrhea.* Captured December 15, 1864, at Nashville, he was imprisoned Camp Douglas, Illinois. [30]*He* *served as witness for J. C. Boggus of Company C July 9, 1909.* [43]*He was bprn July 31. 1836, and died October 12, 1918. He was buried in Mercer Cemetery five miles northwest of Luling, Texas.*

Meredith, E. W., Private, enlisted September 9, 1861, at Montgomery, age 19. He was wounded in the spine at Shiloh, Tennessee, April 1862.

Moore, William J., Private, enlisted February 26, 1863, at Mobile.[17]*He reported to the regimental medical unit December18, 1863, diagnosis feb int quotid. He reported to the regimental medical unit ten times in 1864. January 15 and March 11, diagnosis was rubeola. He was transferred to the general hospital in Greenville on March 19. March 28 and April 1, diagnosis was debilitas. He was granted a 15 day sick furlough April 15. June 23, diagnosis was acute diarrhea. July 20, he was wounded, minnie ball to neck, at the battle of Peachtree Creek in Atlanta and sent to the general hospital the next day. He reported sick again August 17, diagnosis acute dysenteria; September 4, acute diarrhea; and November 5, acute dysenteria. He was suffered a severe wound to the right hand at the battle of Franklin, Tennessee November30.* He was 5'6 and granted parole June 17, 1865, at Montgomery.

Morgan, Benjamin F., Private, enlisted February 23, 1863, at Mobile, occupation carpenter.

Morse, W. J., Private, was paroled June 19, 1865, at Montgomery.

Moseley, Robert, Private, enlisted September 9, 1861, at Montgomery, age 29. He suffered a severe wound to his thigh (probably during the battle of Shiloh, Tennessee). He was listed as missing after Shiloh in April 1862.

Mosely, John L., Private, enlisted September 9, 1861, at Montgomery, age 22. He was killed April 7, 1862, at Shiloh, Tennessee, head wound.

Mosley, Ransom, Private, enlisted February 26, 1863, at Mobile. [17]*He reported to the regimental medical unit December 19, 1863, and on June 15 and August 5, 1864, diagnosis feb int quotid. He reported sick December 26, 1863, diagnosis meningitis. He also reported sick July 1, 1864, diagnosis feb int tert.* He was captured April 26, 1865, at Greenville. Also spelled **Masley.**

Mosely, Thomas J., Private, enlisted August 30, 1862, Chambers County. He died September 25, 1863, at Spring Hill Hospital in Mobile. He was buried at Magnolia Cemetery, row 5, grave 42.

Mullala, J., Private, enlisted March 23, 1862, at Talladega. He was paroled May 1865 at Greensboro, North Carolina.

[1]**Mulkey, Seaborn R.**, *Private, was born in 1821 in Henry County, Georgia. He was living in Roanoke, Randolph County, in 1907.*

Murphy, A. D., Private, enlisted March 12, 1862, at Mobile. He was 6'2, farmer, and born in 1838 at Montgomery County. He died July 2, 1862, Lauderdale County, Mississippi, leaving widow, Sarah Murphy.

Newton, Amos, Private, was born about 1846. [17]*He reported to the regimental medical unit March 21, 1864, diagnosis was acute diarrhea.* He died June 6, 1864, Georgia.

Newton, Benjamin Jaspar, Private, enlisted at Montgomery, September 9, 1861. He was on sick furlough during May and June 1863. [17]*He reported to the regimental medical unit December 12, 1863, diagnosis acute diarrhea. He reported to the regimental medical unit five times in 1864. January 30, diagnosis was catarrhus; February 11, neuralgia; and March 29, acute dysenteria. April 1, diagnosis was debilitas. April 13, he was placed on sick furlough for 30 days. June 20, diagnosis was chronic diarrhea and he was sent to the general hospital.* He served on provost duty at Camp Wright, Macon, Georgia, during November and December 1864. He was paroled June 1865 at Montgomery. [28]*He attended the Confederate Veterans Reunion in Greenville August 21, 1897.* [29]*He died January 18, 1899.* [30]*He was buried at Ebenezer Cemetery, Butler County. He was born August 1, 1834, Robeson County, North Carolina.*

Newton, Thomas Edmund, Private, enlisted at Montgomery, September 9, 1861. He was mustered in as a 2nd Corporal. He was promoted from 2nd Corporal to 1st Corporal July 27, 1862. He was granted sick furlough January 14, 1862, for 15 days and sent to Butler County. [17]*He was slighted wounded in the left knee July 28, 1864, at the battle of Ezra Church in the Atlanta campaign. He was sent to the general hospital July 31.* He was captured April 26, 1865, at Greenville. [28]*He attended the Confederate Veterans Reunion in Greenville August 21, 1897.* [30]*He was born November 2, 1839 in Butler County. He died January 12, 1905 and was buried in Damascus Cemetery in Butler County.*

[17]**Newton, W. A.,** Private, *reported to the regimental medical unit March 18, diagnosis was acute dysenteria.* (Note: this may be **Amos Newton** above or this may be Walter Amos Newton.)

Norris, John A., Private, enlisted September 9, 1861, at Montgomery and discharged December 5, 1861.

Norsworthy, William J., Private, was discharged April 16, 1863. [41]*He was born November 18, 1828, and died March 6, 1907. He was buried at Fort Dale Cemetery, Greenville, Alabama.*

Odam, A., Private, was hospitalized July 20, 1864, at Macon, Georgia. He transferred to a hospital in Butler County, September 22, 1864. He was captured at Greenville April 26, 1865. Also listed as **Alatha L. Odom.**

COMPANY K 415

Odam, John, Private, enlisted February 27, 1863, at Mobile. [17]*He reported to the regimental medical unit December 17, 1863, and January 13, 1864, diagnosis was catarrhus. He reported sick five more times in 1864. February 12, diagnosis was feb int quotid; March 10, acute diarrhea; March 11, rubeola; July 31, acute colitis; and August 3, acute diarrhea. He was sent to the general hospital at Spring Hill, Mobile, March 12.* He was captured December 15, 1864, at Nashville and imprisoned at Camp Douglas, Illinois, [10]*where he died January 21, 1865.* **Also spelled Odom, Odum.**

Olden, James, Private, was captured December 15, 1864, at Nashville and imprisoned Camp Douglas, Illinois. He died of pneumonia, January 21, 1865, and was buried in lot number 547-2, Chicago City Cemetery.

Odom, L. S., Private, enlisted September 17, 1861, at Montgomery. He was 5'6 and detailed as a nurse in 1862 and listed as missing at Tupelo, Mississippi. He was paroled June 2, 1865, at Montgomery.

Pardue, G. H., Private, was wounded and hospitalized April 4, 1865, at Meridian, Mississippi.

Parmer, J. W., Private, [17]*reported to the regimental medical unit December 18, 1863, diagnosis sub luxitia. He reported sick four times in 1864. April 25, diagnosis was feb int quotid; July 7, lumbago; October 9, debilitas; and November 5, feb int tert. He was moved to the general hospital October 15.* He was 5'10 and was paroled June 6, 1865, at Montgomery. [28]*He attended the Confederate Veterans Reunion in Greenville August 21, 1897.* Also listed as **J. M., Jno., J. N. Parmer, and Palmer**

Pate, Samuel, Private, enlisted January 27, 1862, at Greenville.

Payne, John S., Sergeant, enlisted September 9, 1861, at Montgomery, age 20. He was granted a furlough in June 1862 for 20 days.

Payne, William J., Private, enlisted September 9, 1861, at Montgomery, age 20. He was detailed as a nurse January 1862. He was promoted to 5th Sergeant May 1, 1863. [17]*He reported to the regimental medical unit February 13, 1864, diagnosis indigestis, and April 11, diagnosis feb int quotid.* He was discharged from LaGrange Hospital, Georgia, June 23, 1864. He was captured December 17, 1864, Franklin, Tennessee, and was imprisoned at Camp Douglas, Illinois. He died February 6, 1865, (diagnosis rheumatism) and was buried in lot number 717-3, Chicago City Cemetery.

Peach, William F., Private, enlisted August 22, 1862, Pike County. [17]*He reported sick December 1, 1863, diagnosis feb int tert, and December 23, 1863, diagnosis debilitas. He reported sick January 9, 11864, diagnosis debilitas. He reported sick again March 27 and April 1,*

1864, diagnosis phthisis pulmon. He was discharged from the army April 9, 1864.

Peagler, George W., Private, enlisted September 9, 1861, at Montgomery, age 17. He was 5'7 and born in 1844, Butler County. He was promoted to 2nd corporal June 23, 1862. He was granted a sick furlough August 20, 1862 for 30 days. He was promoted to 5th sergeant November 25, 1862. A discharge was granted December 1, 1862 - provided a substitute.

Peagler, Martin G., Private, enlisted September 9, 1861, at Montgomery, age 19.

Pentecost, Leonidas, 2nd Lieutenant, enlisted September 9, 1861, at Montgomery, age 35. He was born 1829. He was elected 2nd lieutenant September 9, 1861, promoted to 1st lieutenant July 30, 1862. [17]*He was wounded in May 1864, at the battle of Resaca.* He was listed as captain when paroled at Greensboro, North Carolina, May 1, 1865.

Perdue, Alex, Private, was captured at Nashville December 15, 1864, and sent to Camp Douglas, Illinois. He was paroled June 1, 1865.

Perdue, Foster, Private, [17]*reported to the regimental medical unit June 6, 1864, diagnosis debilitas. On June 9 he entered* St. Mary's Hospital in LaGrange, Georgia, where he died June 21, 1864.

Perdue, James A., Private, enlisted July 30, 1863, at Greenville. He was 5'9, a farmer, and born in 1845 in Butler County.

Perdue, James E. W., Private, enlisted February 23, 1863, at Mobile. He was 5'11, born in 1823 in Butler County. He was granted a disability discharge (asthma and general debilty) May 23, 1863. He was hospitalized December 20, 1863, Miller Hospital at Spring Hill.

Perdue, Lorenzo B., Private, enlisted September 9, 1861, at Montgomery, age 18. [17]*He reported to the regimental medical unit February 12 and March 20, 1864, diagnosis feb int quotid. He reported sick August 16, diagnosis acute diarrhea.* He was 5'6 and was paroled May 30, 1865, at Montgomery. Also listed as **L.P. Perdue**.

Perdue, Payton, Private, enlisted May 5, 1862, at Lowndes County. He transferred to Richmond, October 27, 1862. [17]*He reported to the regimental medical unit December 1, 1863, diagnosis feb int tert. He reported to the regimental medical unit four times in 1864. April 19, diagnosis was feb int tert; July 5, debilitas; and June 14, acute dysenteria. He was moved to the general hospital the next day. He suffered a severe wound to his left hand July 28, 1864, at the battle of Ezra Church near Atlanta. He was sent to the general hospital July 31.* He was captured April 27, 1865, at Greenville. [28]*He attended the Confederate Veterans Reunion in Greenville August 21, 1897.*

[17]**Perdue, Tully**, Private, reported to the regimental medical unit June 4, 1864, and was sent to the general hospital June 9.

Perdue, W. E., Private, [17]*He reported to the regimental medical unit seven times in 1864. January 9, diagnosis was haemorrhois; February 22, acute dysenteria; June 3 and 11, acute diarrhea; August 19, debilitas; and in September, lumbago.* He was hospitalized with chronic diarrhea November 10, 1864, at Jackson, Mississippi, and transferred December 21, 1864. He was captured April 26, 1865, at Greenville.

Perry, John T., Private, enlisted September 9, 1861, at Montgomery. He was placed on sick furlough January 14, 1862 for 20 days and sent to Butler County. He was discharged March 1, 1863.

Perry, M. F., Private, was paroled May 24, 1865, at Talladega.

Philyaw, George W., Private, enlisted January 23, 1862, at Warrington, Florida. He was a substitute for T. F. Pottey. He was appointed musician September 13, 1862. Captured September 5, 1864, at Jonesboro, Georgia, he was imprisoned at Camp Douglas, Illinois, where he was paroled June 2, 1865. Also spelled **Philjaw.**

Pickens, W. A., Private, enlisted February 3, 1863, at Greenville. He was discharged October 12, 1863.

Pitts, John, Private, enlisted September 9, 1861, at Montgomery. He was discharged July 5, 1862.

Pollard, Nathaniel, Private, enlisted May 5, 1863, Mobile.

[17]***Pollard, Daniel**, Private, reported to the regimental medical unit March 20, diagnosis feb int tert. (Note: This may be **William D. Pollard**.)*

Pollard, William Daniel, Private, enlisted July 13, 1863, at Greenville. He was 5'10, a farmer, and born in 1845 in Butler County. [17]*He reported to the regimental medical unit March 27, 1864, diagnosis was rubeola. He was sent to the general hospital in Greenville the same day.* He was captured December 15, 1864, at Nashville, and imprisoned at Camp Douglas, Illinois. His home was in Butler County. [28]*He attended a Confederate Veterans Reunion in Greenville August 21, 1897.* [1]*He was born March 16, 1845. He was living in Honoraville, Pike County, in 1907.* [37]*In 1921 he was living in Luverne and stated that he fought at Franklin and Nashville.*

Potter, Thomas F., Private, enlisted September 9, 1861, at Montgomery. He was discharged January 27, 1862 - provided a substitute.

Potter, William, enlisted September 7, 1861, at Montgomery. He was detailed as a musician.

Prewitt, H. H., Private, was paroled at Greensboro, North Carolina, May 1865.

Prewitt, J. W, Private, was paroled at Greensboro, North Carolina, May 1865.

Ray, Andrew J., Private, lived in Talladega County. He was hospitalized August 3, 1864, at Macon, Georgia. He was paroled at Greensboro, North Carolina, May 1865.

Ray, John, Private, was 5'9. He was captured June 18, 1864, at Marietta, Georgia, and hospitalized in a Union hospital in Nashville until October 16, 1864. Later imprisoned at Camp Chase, Ohio, he died [10]*on June 19, 1865, and is buried in lot number 2048.*

Redfield, Syd, died June 4, 1862.

Reeves, C. W., Private, died while in the Confederate Army.

Reeves, Jesse W., Private, enlisted November 14, 1862, at Mobile. He died September 11, 1863, in Miller Spring Hospital at Mobile.

Register, Stephen W., Private, enlisted October 9, 1862, in Pike County. [18]*In September 1863 he was described as 23 years old, gray eyes, dark hair, dark complexion, 5'9, a farmer, and a deserter.* Also spelled **Regooter.**

Reid, Hillory, Private, enlisted September 9, 1861, at Montgomery. He was detailed as a hospital steward. [17]*He reported to the regimental medical unit December 14, 1863, diagnosis debilitas, and granted a 15 day furlough December 17.* He was paroled at Greensboro, North Carolina, May 1865. [1]*He was born April 28, 1840, in Butler County. In 1907 he was living in Evergreen, Conecuh County.*

Rhodes, John, Private, enlisted November 26, 1861, at Warrington, Florida. [12]*He was listed on the muster roll for July-August 1862 as absent sick in an interior hospital.*

Riley, George W., Corporal, was 5'11, born in 1833, Orangeburg District, South Carolina. He was promoted to 5th sergeant June 23, 1862, and to 2nd lieutenant March 6, 1863. [17]*He reported to the regimental medical unit June 15, 1864, diagnosis acute diarrhea, and was sent to the general hospital the same day. He was slightly wounded in the face July 28, 1864, at the battle of Ezra Church near Atlanta. He was severely wounded (right arm) November 30, 1864, at the battle of Franklin, Tennessee.*

Roach, D. C., Private, was discharged April 3, 1863. [17]*He reported to the regimental medical unit July 1, 1864, diagnosis catarrhus, and November 3, 1864, diagnosis acute colitis. He was sent to the general hospital the next day.* He took the oath of allegiance April 22, 1865.

Robbins, Stephen, Private, enlisted January 27, 1862, at Greenville. [20]*He was born February 14, 1845, Covington County. He was paroled May 20, 1865, at Chinagrove, North Carolina. He was living in Covington County in 1907.* **Also spelled Robins.**

Rogers, William James, Private, enlisted September 9, 1861, at Montgomery. He was 5'9 and born *in* 1833, in Duplin County, North Carolina. He was granted a disability discharge June 19, 1863. [1]*He was* born April 18, 1833, and was living in Pigeon Creek, Crenshaw County, in 1907. [37] His place of birth was Duplin, North Carolina. He lived in Texas from 1875 to 1890. He stated that he fought at Shiloh and transferred to Company B, 59th Alabama Regiment in 1863.

Roundtree, Adam Wainwright, Private, enlisted August 23, 1862, Pike County. [1] He first entered service February 1862 in Company K, 1st Alabama. He was later discharged and enlisted in the 17th Alabama. He was born November 2, 1843, in Talbot County, Georgia. Paroled at Hamburg, South Carolina, he was living in Banks, Pike County, in 1907.

[17] **Roundtree, Atwright W.,** Private, reported to the regimental medical unit January 31 and February 25, 1864, diagnosis feb int tert. [1] He was born in 1834. He was paroled at the end of the war and was living in Banks, Pike County, in 1907.

Rozier, John Lee Brown, Private, enlisted September 9, 1861, at Montgomery. [17] He reported to the regimental medical unit five times in 1864. On January 2, diagnosis was catarrhus; January 30, constipacio; on February 5, feb int quotid; and August 28, debilitas. He was slighted wounded (chin) July 28, at the battle of Ezra Church near Atlanta. He was granted a furlough at Meridian, Mississippi, February 6, 1865, for 60 days and sent to Millville. [30] He was born in 1828, Georgia. He married Rebecca Berry and died in 1869 in Pensacola, Florida. Also listed as **D. B., J. L. B., J. L. B. Z., Rosier, Rasier, John Lamb Brown Rozier.**

Sanders, W. J., Private, enlisted September 9, 1861, at Montgomery, 29.

Scott, James M., Private, enlisted January 27, 1862, at Montgomery.

Scott, William, Private, enlisted September 9, 1861, at Montgomery, age 21. He was granted a furlough in June until July 1862. He was sick in the hospital from July to December 1862. [17] He reported to the regimental medical unit December 16, 1863, diagnosis catarrhus. He reported sick again January 17, 1864, diagnosis diptheria. He was sent to the general hospital January 20. He died at Miller Hospital in Spring Hill, Alabama, January 21, 1864. He was buried in Magnolia Cemetery, row 12, grave 12.

Seale, James K., Private, enlisted September 9, 1861, at Montgomery. He was detailed as a musician in the regimental band July 6, 1862. [28] He attended the Confederate Veterans Reunion in Greenville August 21, 1897.

Seawright, George A., Private, enlisted September 9, 1861, at Montgomery, age 22. He was promoted to 2nd Ssrgeant in March 1863. [17] He reported to the regimental medical unit March 13 and April 6, 1864, diagnosis feb int quotid. He was slightly wounded on his right side *July 28, 1864, at the battle of Ezra Church in the Atlanta campaign. He was sent to the general hospital July 31.* Captured December 15, 1864, in Nashville, he was imprisoned at Camp Douglas, Illinois. His home was Butler County. [28]*He attended the Confederate Veterans Reunion in Greenville August 21, 1897.* [7]*He registered as a veteran in Butler County July 4, 1906.* [24]*He was born September 1, 1843. He died December 14, 1915, and was buried in Magnolia Cemetery in Greenville.* Also spelled **Searight.**

Seawright, John R., Private, enlisted September 9, 1861, at Montgomery. [17]*He reported to the regimental medical unit January 11, 1864, diagnosis was feb int tert. He reported again February 11, 1864, diagnosis feb int quotid, and was sent to the general hospital February 21. He was wounded slightly on the left hip July 28, 1864, at the battle of Ezra Church during the Atlanta campaign. He was sent to the general hospital the next day.* He was granted a parole at Greensboro, North Carolina, May 1865. [11]*He was born September 1, 1843, at Fall Branch, Orangeburg District, South Carolina. He was captured at the battle of Nashville and paroled at the end of the war.*

Seppes, Joseph, Private, was 6'2. Also listed as **Lepper.**

[17]*Sevannet, A., Private, reported to the regimental medical unit November 3, 1864, diagnosis was debilitas.*

Shealey, Wilson E., Private, enlisted February 26, 1863, at Mobile. He was six feet tall, a farmer, and born in 1835 in Chambers County. He was granted a discharge February 28, 1863 - provided a substitute.

Shell, George Daniel, Private, applied for sick furlough July 14, 1864. [28]*He attended the Confederate Veterans Reunion held in Greenville August 21, 1897.* [30]*He was born January 1846 and died March 19, 1909 in Pigeon Creek in Butler County. His father was Thomas Barnes Shell, listed below.* [41]*He married Elizabeth Riles.*

Shell, Thomas Barnes, Private, enlisted October 24, 1863, at Greenville. [17]*He reported to the regimental medical unit January 5 and April 23, 1864, diagnosis was chronic rheum. Each time he was sent to the general hospital the next day. He also reported sick March 20, 1864, diagnosis chronic diarrhea.* He was 5'7, a farmer, and born 1818 in Laurens District, South Carolina. [30]*His son was George D. Shell, see above. He died February 11, 1865, at Pigeon Creek in Butler County* [15]*and is buried at Mt. Zion Cemetery, Crenshaw County.* [41]*He married Martha Adaline Parker. He survived the battles of Franklin and Nashville. He was sent home ill arriving February 10, 1865, and died the next day.*

Shepherd, W. C., Private, [17]*reported to the regimental medical unit four times in 1864. On January 8, February 29 and March 5, diagnosis was*

COMPANY K

rheumatism, and April 20, acute dysenteria. He was paroled May 30, 1865 at Montgomery. Also spelled **Sheppard**.

Sheppard, J. M., Private, enlisted September 9, 1861, at Montgomery and died in 1862.

Sheppard, Thomas H., Private, enlisted September 9, 1861, at Montgomery, age 20. He was promoted to 4th corporal July 27, 1862, and to 3rd corporal November 1862. [17]*He reported to the regimental medical unit four times in 1864. January 17, diagnosis was feb int tert, and February 5, feb int quotid.* He was slightly wounded in the heel in May, at the battle of Resaca. August 14 while in Atlanta, he suffered a slight wound to his right arm. Hospital records listed him as a corporal in May and August. He was a 1st sergeant by the surrender at Greensboro, North Carolina, April 1865, when he was granted a parole. Also spelled **Shephard**.

Sheppard, William F., Private, enlisted September 9, 1861, at Montgomery, age 20. He died of disease July 7, 1862 in the general hospital in Okolona, Mississippi.

Simms, William A., Private, enlisted February 2, 1863, at Greenville. [17]*He reported to the regimental medical unit three times in 1864. January 8 diagnosis was debilitas; March 10, acute dysenteria; April 25, catarrhus.* He was captured at Macon, Georgia, April 1865. Also listed as **Sumers**.

Sims, W. H. S., Private, enlisted September 9, 1861, at Montgomery, age 23. [17]*He reported to the regimental medical unit March 31, 1864, diagnosis was feb int tert.*

Skipper, Alexander, Private, enlisted September 9, 1861, at Montgomery, age 18. He died November 21, 1863, at the general hospital, Miller Spring Hill, in Mobile.

Skipper, Joseph, Private, enlisted September 9, 1861, at Montgomery, age 21. [17]*He reported to the regimental medical unit April 19, 1864, diagnosis was feb int quotid, and June 6, 1864, acute diarrhea.* Also spelled **Scipper**.

Sloane, J. B., Private, enlisted September 9, 1861, at Montgomery, 35. [17]*He reported to the regimental medical unit December 11, 1863, diagnosis was feb int quotid. He also reported sick four times in 1864. On January 1, diagnosis was acute dysenteria; February 14, feb int quotid; April 15, feb int tert; and July 4, acute diarrhea.* Captured December 15, 1864, at Nashville he was imprisoned at Camp Douglas, Illinois, where he died of smallpox February 11, 1865.

Smith, George W., Private, enlisted March 13, 1863, at Mobile. [17]*He reported to the regimental medical unit five times in 1864. April 9 diagnosis was feb int quotid; April 10, scorbutis; June 23, acute diarrhea; August 6, neuraglia; and September 10, constipatio.*

Captured December 15, 1864, at Nashville, he was imprisoned at Camp Douglas, Illinois, where he was paroled at the end of the war. His home was Butler County.

Smith, John B., Private, enlisted November 11, 1863, at Greenville. [17]*He suffered a slight wound to his hand May 1864, at the battle of Resaca, Georgia. He reported to the regimental medical unit in October 1864. On the 6th, diagnosis was debilitas. He was sent to the general hospital on the 15th. Later in the month diagnosis was acute diarrhea. He was again sent to the general hospital on the 31st.* He was 6'1 and born in 1846 in Decatur County, Georgia. He was paroled at Greensboro, North Carolina, May 1865.

Smith, J. W., Private, enlisted October 17, 1863, at Montgomery. At the end of the war he was paroled at Greensboro, North Carolina.

Smith, William J., Private, enlisted September 9, 1861, at Montgomery, age 20. He was discharged December 5, 1861.

Solomon, Francis M., Private, enlisted September 9, 1861, at Montgomery, age 20 and died of disease June 22, 1862.

Staggers, John N., Private, enlisted September 9, 1861, at Montgomery. He was 5'6, a farmer, and born in 1846, Butler County. He was captured February 16, 1862 at Fort Donelson and imprisoned at Camp Douglas, Illinois. He was captured again December 17, 1864, at Franklin, Tennessee, and sent to prison at Camp Chase, Ohio where he was paroled June 12, 1865. **J. W. Staggers** was missing after the battle of Shiloh, Tennessee. [17]*J. Staggers was wounded in June 1864 during the Atlanta campaign. J. W. Staggers received a slight wound to his left fore finger on July 28, 1864, at the battle of Ezra Church during the Atlanta campaign. He was sent to the general hospital on July 31. Jno. M. Staggers received a flesh wound to the right thigh on November 30, 1864, at the battle of Franklin, Tennessee.* Note: this may be two people.

Staggers, R. M., Private, was captured April 8, 1862, at Pittsburg Landing, Tennessee, and sent to prison at Camp Douglas, Illinois.

Steward, J. J., Private, enlisted September 1863, at Mobile. He was granted a parole at Greensboro, North Carolina, May 1865. Note: May be **James J. Steward** of Co. D

Strickland, Samuel B., Private, enlisted September 7, 1862, at Mobile. He was 5'10, a farmer, and born in 1827 in Johnson County, North Carolina, He was granted a disability discharge December 13, 1862. [17]*He reported to the regimental medical unit five times in 1864. On February 11, diagnosis was feb int tert; February 28 and March 6, catarrhuApril 25, parotitis; and on June 18, feb int quotid.* Also spelled **Stricklin**

COMPANY K 423

Stubbs, Alexander G., Private, enlisted September 6, 1862, Butler County. He was an ordinance sergeant at the city redoubts at Mobile. [17]*He reported to the regimental medical unit September 21, 1864, diagnosis feb int quotid.* He reported sick again in October of 1864, diagnosis acute diarrhea. He was sent to the general hospital October 21. He was hospitalized at Jackson, Mississippi, November 8, 1864, and placed on medical furlough December 24, 1864. At the end of the war he was granted a parole at Greensboro, North Carolina.

Swaner, Amariah, Private, enlisted June 5, 1864, at Greenville (5'11). He was discharged June 3, 1863 - provided a substitute.

[17]***Swanner, H.**, Private, was wounded in June 1864 at Kennesaw Mountain.*

Taylor, John H., Corporal, enlisted September 9, 1861, at Montgomery. He was promoted from 4th corporal to 3rd corporal July 27, 1862. Promoted from 2nd corporal to 4th sergeant March 16, 1862. [17]*He reported to the regimental medical unit on April 27, 1864, diagnosis acute dysenteria.* He was captured by May 19, 1865, at Grenada, Mississippi.

Thigpen, George W., Private, enlisted September 9, 1861, at Montgomery. He was 5'10 and born in 1841 in Butler County. He was granted a medical furlough January 1, 1862, for 15 days and sent to Butler County. He was granted a disability discharge [12]*July 27, 1862.*

Thornton, Willis D., Private, enlisted April 9, 1863, at Mobile. [17]*He reported to the regimental medical unit on March 20, 1864, diagnosis was feb int tert.* Captured at Egypt Station, Mississippi, December 28, 1864, he was imprisoned at Alton, Illinois. He was transferred for exchange to Point Lookout, Maryland, February 21, 1865, and was captured April 3, 1865, at Richmond.

[17]***Thorrington, W. D.**, Private, reported to the regimental medical unit on April 11, 1864, diagnosis was feb int quotid.*

Tierney, Frank, Private, enlisted September 9, 1861, at Montgomery. He was detailed as an ordinance sergeant while stationed at Mobile. He was granted a parole at Greensboro, North Carolina.

Tippett, J. M., Private, enlisted September 9, 1861, at Montgomery. He was captured at Shiloh, Tennessee, April 6, 1864, after being severely wounded in leg. He was imprisoned Camp Douglas, Illinois, where he died as result of his wound on May 5, 1862.

Van, James W., Private, [17]*He reported to the regimental medical unit on March 18, 1864, diagnosis rubeola, and was sent to the general hospital the next day.* Captured December 15, 1864, at Nashville, he was imprisoned at Camp Douglas, Illinois.

Vaughn, James, Private, was captured July 3, 1864, at Kennesaw Mountain, Georgia. He was imprisoned Camp Douglas, Illinois, where he died of pneumonia January 20, 1865. He was buried in lot number 513-2, Chicago City Cemetery.

Vernon, Obadiah C., Private, enlisted September 9, 1861, at Montgomery. [17]*He reported to the regimental medical unit twice in 1864. January 14, diagnosis was feb int tert and March 21, feb int quotid.* He was captured December 15, 1864, at Nashville. He was imprisoned at Camp Douglas, Illinois, where he died of pneumonia March 18, 1865. He was buried in lot number 976-3, Chicago City Cemetery.

Vernon, J. C., Private, was captured December 15, 1864, at Nashville and was imprisoned Camp Douglas, Illinois.

Wallace, George, Private, enlisted September 9, 1861, at Montgomery. He was hospitalized in Mississippi June 1862. He was captured July 20, 1864, Atlanta at the battle of Peach Tree Creek. He was then sent to prison at Camp Douglas, Illinois.

Watson, William J., Private, enlisted September 9, 1861, at Montgomery.

Watson, William V. R., Private, enlisted October 1, 1861, Macon County. He was absent from the regiment during the period April 13, 1862 to October 23, 1862 due to wounds in stomach and foot received at Shiloh, Tennessee. He is listed as a sergeant in 1862. He applied for promotion to lieutenant in 1863. He was born in New Jersey and was a salesman in New York in 1861. He was highly recommended by his superiors. There are very interesting letters in his file. Documents list his promotion to a lieutenant by July 12, 1864.

Weaver, Isaac, Private, enlisted October 8, 1862, at Mobile. He was a farmer, 6 feet tall, and born in 1835 in Montgomery County.

Whidden, Elias, Private, enlisted September 7, 1862, at Mobile. [17]*He was mortally wounded in the left hip July 28, 1864, at the battle of Ezra Church near Atlanta. He died at the brigade hospital the next day.*

Whidden, Noah W., Private, enlisted June 25, 1863, at Mobile. He was 5'8, a farmer, and born 1817 in Darlington District, South Carolina. [17]*He reported to the regimental medical unit March 29, 1864, diagnosis rubeola. He was immediately moved to the general hospital at Greenville.* He was paroled June 19, 1865. Spelled and signed on parole papers as **Whiddon.**

Whisker, Daniel W., Private, enlisted September 9, 1861, at Montgomery. [17]*He reported to the regimental medical unit five times in 1864. February 29 and March 7, diagnosis was anthrax; March 19, feb int tert; and April 26, feb int quotid. He reported to the regimental medical unit June 14, diagnosis feb int tert, and sent to the general hospital the next day.* His home was Monroe County. He was captured December

15, 1864 in Nashville and imprisoned at Camp Douglas, Illinois, where he was paroled June 1865.

Wight, J. M., Private, enlisted September 9, 1861, at Montgomery. This may be **J. M. Wright** buried at Barrancas National Cemetery.

Wilburn, James, Private, enlisted September 9, 1861, at Montgomery. He was born in 1836. He was killed at Shiloh, Tennessee (wound to abdomen) in April 1862.

Wilber, J., Private, died June 16, 1862 in Macon, Mississippi.

Wilkes, J., Private, died in Macon, Mississippi. [6]*He died June 16, 1862.*

Wilkinson, Benjamin F., Private, enlisted September 7, 1862, at Mobile. [17]*He reported to the regimental medical unit three times in 1864. March 11, diagnosis was acute dysenteria; June 18, acute diarrhea; and June 27, feb int quotid. He was moved to the general hospital June 28.* He was 5'11and paroled June 17, 1865, in Montgomery. Also spelled **Wilkson, Wilkerson.**

Wilkinson, Joshua, Private, enlisted September 7, 1862, at Mobile. [17]*He reported to the regimental medical unit January 18, 1864, diagnosis was catarrhus.* His home was in Butler County. He was captured December 15, 1864, in Nashville and imprisoned Camp Douglas, Illinois. Also spelled **Wilkerson.**

Williams, Daniel, Private, enlisted September 9, 1861, at Montgomery. He was listed as missing after the battle of Shiloh, Tennessee, April 1862. He was captured and sent to City General Hospital in St. Louis, Missouri, where he died of a gunshot wound April 29, 1862. [10]*He was buried in lot number 10121 in St. Louis.* [30]*He was born November 14, 1838, son of Henry Goodman and Permelia Lee Cross Williams. In the 1860 Census, he was listed as a teacher.*

Williams, Reason, Private, enlisted September 9, 1861, at Montgomery.

Wilson, Allen, Private, enlisted February 9, 1863, at Mobile. [17]*He reported to the regimental medical unit December 1, 1863, diagnosis meningitis, and was moved to the general hospital December 3.* He died December 10, 1863 at Miller Spring Hill Hospital in Mobile.

Wynsdick, T. R., Private, enlisted September 9, 1861, at Montgomery.

Yarborough, James D., Private, enlisted August 26, 1862, at Montgomery. [17]*He reported to the regimental medical unit three times in 1864. March 21, diagnosis was rubeola, and he was sent to the general hospital in Greenville the next day. April 12, diagnosis was debilitas. He was granted a furlough April 18 for 30 days. August 7, diagnosis was feb int tert.*

Appendix XII. Medical Glossary

The following is a list of illnesses recorded in the medical journal, *The Register of the Sick and Wounded of the 17th Alabama Volunteers,* for the period December 1, 1863 to November 30, 1864.

Abscessus	A swollen, inflamed, infected area of the body where pus collects
Acute	An illness of sudden or recent onset or one that has reached a crisis
Ambustio	Latin for a burn or scald
Anasarca	Generalized swelling, large amounts of fluid in the intercellular parts of the body
Anemia	Below normal red blood cell count
Anthrax	Infectious bacterial disease usually contracted from infected animals or animal products
Ascites	Accumulation of thin, watery fluid in the abdominal cavity. Often due to liver disease or heart or kidney failure.
Asthma	Respiratory disease
Bronchitis	Inflammation of one of more bronchi
Catarrhus	Inflammation of mucous membrane, most commonly in the nose and throat, sometimes accompanied by fever. The majority of cases of catarrhus occurred during the months of December 1863 through May 1864 at the rate of an average of 28 per month.
Cephalalgia	Pain in the head, headache
Cholera	Acute infection of the small intestine. Spread by infected water or food. Often fatal.
Chronic	Persisting over a long period
Colica	Colic, pertaining to the colon, severe abdominal pain
Colitis	Inflammation of the colon
Congestion of brain	Abnormal accumulation of blood in the brain.
Constipatio	Infrequent or difficult evacuation of feces
Contusio	Bruise or injury without a break in skin
Cutis	Skin
Debilitas	A condition of the body in which there is a weakening of the vital signs
Diarrhea	Abnormal frequency or liquidity of fecal discharge. Over three/fifths of the cases of diarrhea were reported during the months of May, June and August 1864

Diphtheria	An acute infectious disease of the upper respiratory tract. Possibly fatal.
Dysentery	Any of various disorders marked by inflammation of the intestines. More than half the cases were reported during the months of May and June 1864.
Dyspepsia	Impairment of digestive functions, usually pain following meals.
Dysuria	Painful or difficult urination
Ebriata	Drunkenness
Epilepsia	A disease of the nervous system
Erysipelas	Acute contagious skin infection caused by streptococci, characterized by inflammation of the skin and accompanied by a fever.
Feb	Febris, the Latin word for fever
Feb Congestiv	Congestive fever, probably malaria.
Feb Int	Intermittent fever, an attack of malaria or other fever characterized by intervals of elevated temperature separated by intervals of normal temperature.
Feb Int Quotid	An intermittent fever, as described above, that occurs daily
Feb Int Tert	An intermittent fever, as described above, that occurs every three days, probably malaria.
Feb Remitt	Remittent fever, in which the diurnal variation is 2 degrees, but never falls to normal, could be malaria
Febris Typhoides	Typhoid fever
Fistula	Disease of the digestive system
Fractura	Breaking of a bone
Furunculous	A painful inflamed nodule formed in the skin called a boil.
Gonorrhea	Sexually transmitted infection
Haematuria	Blood in the urine
Hemeralopia	Day Blindness
Hemorrhois	A varicose dilatation of a vein, heavy bleeding
Hepatitis	Inflammation of the liver
Hernia	Protrusion of a loop of an organ thru an abnormal opening
Herpes	Inflammatory skin disease characterized by the formation of clusters of small vesicles
Hydrocele	Disease of the urinary tract
Icterus	Jaundice
Indigestis	Indigestion
Irritatios Spinalis	Irritation of the spine

MEDICAL GLOSSARY

Ischuria	Suppression or retention of urine
Lithitis	Formation of abnormal concretions within the body, calcification
Lumbago	Pain in the lumbar region (lower back)
Meningitis	Viral infection causing inflammation of the meringues, the three membranes that envelope the brain and spinal cord
Morbi cutis	A skin disease
Nephretis	Inflammation of the kidneys
Neuralgia	Pain, which extends along the course of one or more nerves
Odontalgia	Toothache
Oedema	Edema, massive generalized swelling, large amounts of fluid in the intercellular tissue spaces of the body. Probably due to kidney or heart failure
Opthalmia	Severe inflammation of the eye
Orchitis	Inflammation of a testis. May be associated with other diseases such as mumps or tuberculosus.
Org Dis of the Heart	Organic disease of the heart
Otalgia	Earache
Otitis	Inflammation of the ear
Otorrhoea	Disease of the ear
Parotitis	An inflammation of the parotid gland that is near the ear. A common cause is mumps.
Paronychia	A painful pus-producing nflammation involving folds of tissue surrounding the nails of toes or fingers
Parrychia	Toxic nodular goiter
Pertussis	An acute, highly contagious infection of the respiratory tract. Also known as whooping cough.
Phlegmon	An inflammatory swelling such as a boil or abscess which could lead to gangrene.
Phthisis Pulom	Wasting away of the body, especially lungs, tuberculosis. Any debilitating lung or throat infection, severe cough, or asthma.
Pleuritis	Pleurisy, inflammation of the membrane of the lungs
Pneumonia	Inflammation of the lungs
Psoriosis	A common chronic skin disease
Pulmonary	Pertaining to the artery conveying blood from lungs to the heart
Quotid	Daily
Remitt	Remittent, having periods of abatement

Renalis	Pertaining to the kidneys
Rheum/Rheumat	Any watery or catarrhal discharge
Roseola	Rose colored rash as may be seen in diseases such as measles.
Rubeola	An acute, usually an infectious, disease, ither measles or German measles
Scabies	Contagious dermatitis of humans caused by the itch mite
Scorbutis	Scurvy caused by lack of vitamin C. Symptons: weakness, spongy gums and hemorrhages under the skin.
Splinitis	May be splenitis, an inflammation of the spleen
Strictula Urethra	Decrease in canal carrying urine from bladder
Sub Luxatio	Luxatio, dislocation of some part of the body
Surdites	Deafness
Syphilis	Chronic infectious sexual disease
Tert	Tertian, every other day or intermittent
Tonsillitis	Inflammation of the tonsils
Ulcus	Ulcer
Vulnus	A wound
Vulnus Sclopet	A wound caused by a gunshot
Vulnus Contusium	A wound caused by a blow

Appendix XIII. Battle Casualties

A. Introduction

The casualty lists clearly depict the reality of the war. This section lists the known (777) casualties in the battles involving the 17th Alabama Infantry. The list includes wounded, captured, missing, and killed. It is important to remember that these are the only names found on record. There may be many other names on records not yet uncovered. There are also many unknown soldiers who died on the battlefield, men who fell unnoticed by fellow soldiers, men lost forever to their families.

The list is organized into the four major campaigns involving the 17th Alabama: Shiloh, Atlanta, Franklin and Nashville. Within each campaign, the list is organized by company to present an overview of the impact suffered by a given company in each campaign.

B. Shiloh

The battle of Shiloh, Tennessee, took place on April 6 and 7, 1862. The total casualties listed below are 143 men: Company A – 14, Company B – 13, Company C – 8, Company D – 10, Company E – 19, Company F – 19, Company G – 9, Company H – 12, Company I – 19, and Company K – 20.

Anderson, W.	Pvt	A	Shiloh	Captured
Brown, John R.	Pvt	A	Shiloh	Captured
Davis, Ransom	Pvt	A	Shiloh	Captured, exchanged
Ferris, James M.	Sgt	A	Shiloh	Wounded
Hutson, Daniel	Pvt	A	Shiloh	Wounded, captured, d. 4/16/62 at Paducah, KY
Moon, David N.	Pvt	A	Shiloh	Captured. D. 5/1/62 at Louisville, KY
Moore, Daniel	Pvt	A	Shiloh	Wounded, missing
Sadler, C. E.	Cpt	A	Shiloh	Wounded
Shanks, A. M.	Pvt	A	Shiloh	Wounded
Shields, Milton	Pvt	A	Shiloh	Wounded
Smith, W. B.	Pvt	A	Shiloh	Captured, d. 6/10/62, Camp Douglas, IL
Taylor, Samuel B.	Sgt	A	Shiloh	Wounded
Weatherford, Stephen	Pvt	A	Shiloh	Wounded
Wetherford, James	Pvt	A	Shiloh	Wounded, captured, d. 4/18/62 on Steamer Imperial
Cararthan, Joseph	Pvt	B	Shiloh	Wounded
Deal, William J.	Pvt	B	Shiloh	Wounded, d. 4/17/62
Galloway, Eli	Pvt	B	Shiloh	Wounded
Garrett, Henry C.	Pvt	B	Shiloh	Wounded, exchanged 11/30/62
Johns, John B.	Pvt	B	Shiloh	Wounded
Kirvin, John F.	Pvt	B	Shiloh	Missing
Lee, John D.	Pvt	B	Shiloh	Wounded, captured, exchanged
Owens, Robert Philip	Pvt	B	Shiloh	Wounded

Pearson, James H.	Pvt	B	Shiloh	Killed
Porter, Thomas M. J.	Lt	B	Shiloh	Wounded
Sheppard, James	Pvt	B	Shiloh	Wounded
Vardell, Milton G.	Sgt	B	Shiloh	Wounded
Warren, George W.	Pvt	B	Shiloh	Wounded, captured, exchanged
Connor, William H.	Pvt	C	Shiloh	Wounded
Frost, James	Pvt	C	Shiloh	Wounded
Hernden, William	Pvt	C	Shiloh	Wounded, d.
Holland, J. H.	Pvt	C	Shiloh	Killed
Mapes, John W.	Pvt	C	Shiloh	Wounded
Milton, Jacob C.	Pvt	C	Shiloh	Wounded, captured, exchanged
Shirlock, J. T.	Pvt	C	Shiloh	Wounded
Sims, Robert M.	Pvt	C	Shiloh	Wounded
Bryant, William	Pvt	D	Shiloh	Wounded
Causey, G. B.	Pvt	D	Shiloh	Captured, d. 10/10/62, Camp Douglas, IL
Connor, David	Pvt	D	Shiloh	Captured
Crew, William C.	Pvt	D	Shiloh	Killed
Lauderdale, John F.	Sgt	D	Shiloh	Wounded
Lewis, William Pinckney	Pvt	D	Shiloh	Killed
McNair, Daniel	Pvt	D	Shiloh	Wounded, captured, d. 4/23/62, Camp Dennison, OH
Oliver, H. M.	Pvt	D	Shiloh	Missing
Rush, Warren	Lt	D	Shiloh	Wounded
Thornton, Horatio	Pvt	D	Shiloh	Wounded
Arnold, Thomas	Pvt	E	Shiloh	Missing
Copeland, Thomas J.	Pvt	E	Shiloh	Wounded
Dabney, G. A.	Pvt	E	Shiloh	Killed
Head, Richard	Pvt	E	Shiloh	Wounded
Hodges, James M.	Pvt	E	Shiloh	Wounded
Hollingsworth, Theopholas A.	Pvt	E	Shiloh	Wounded
Hornesby, James M.	Pvt	E	Shiloh	Captured, exchanged
Hutchins, Henry H.	Pvt	E	Shiloh	Wounded
Pike, Thomas	Pvt	E	Shiloh	Captured, d. 8/13/62, St. Louis, MO
Ray, William	Pvt	E	Shiloh	Wounded
Skinner, James M.	Pvt	E	Shiloh	Killed
Spears, William C.	Pvt	E	Shiloh	Wounded, captured, exchanged
Spradling, Felix	Pvt	E	Shiloh	Wounded, captured, d. 5/19/62, Camp Douglas, IL
Stitt, Thomas	Pvt	E	Shiloh	Wounded
Townsend, Harris	Pvt	E	Shiloh	Captured
Watkins, James	Pvt	E	Shiloh	Captured, exchanged
Weathers, Thomas	Pvt	E	Shiloh	Wounded
White, Wiley E.	Cpt	E	Shiloh	Captured, exchanged
Young, Joel	Pvt	E	Shiloh	Wounded
Anderson, William	Pvt	F	Shiloh	Missing

BATTLE CASUALTIES 433

Name	Rank	Co.	Battle	Notes
Anderson, William Sr.	Pvt	F	Shiloh	Wounded, d. 4/11/62
Buckley, D. J.	Pvt	F	Shiloh	Killed
Champion, F. M.	Pvt	F	Shiloh	Captured, d. 6/24/62 Louisville, KY
Cowley, John T.	Pvt	F	Shiloh	Captured, exchanged
Dempsey, S.	Pvt	F	Shiloh	Missing
Doyle, John	Pvt	F	Shiloh	Wounded
Hayle, George W.	Cpl	F	Shiloh	Captured
Jones, Owen	Cpl	F	Shiloh	Wounded
Jones, William K.	Pvt	F	Shiloh	Wounded, captured, d.
Martin, Henry	Pvt	F	Shiloh	Wounded, captured, d. 5/13/62, Camp Dennison, OH
Mings, James W.	Pvt	F	Shiloh	Wounded
Moseley, William	Pvt	F	Shiloh	Wounded, captured, d. 4/27/62, Camp Dennison, OH
Moseley, William H.	Pvt	F	Shiloh	Wounded, missing
O'Connor, E.	Pvt	F	Shiloh	Missing
Pizzala, Nicholas	Pvt	F	Shiloh	Captured, exchanged
Robertson, A. F. E.	Lt	F	Shiloh	Wounded, captured, d. 4/24/62, Camp Chase, OH
Tucker, J.	Pvt	F	Shiloh	Killed
Bussey, J. M.	Pvt	G	Shiloh	Killed
Carden, William T.	Pvt	G	Shiloh	Wounded
Gray, Riley	Pvt	G	Shiloh	Wounded
Gray, W. R.	Pvt	G	Shiloh	Wounded
Meek, D. M.	Pvt	G	Shiloh	Wounded
Roquemore, J. M.	Pvt	G	Shiloh	Wounded, captured, d. 5/16/62, Camp Chase, OH
Rumbley, H. M.	Pvt	G	Shiloh	Wounded
Sasser, Joseph J.	Pvt	G	Shiloh	Captured
Thompson, James	Pvt	G	Shiloh	Wounded, captured, d. 4/18/62, on his way to St. Louis
Andress, Hugh	Pvt	H	Shiloh	Killed
Andress, James	Pvt	H	Shiloh	Wounded, d. 7/18/62
Andress, R. M.	Lt	H	Shiloh	Wounded
Black, James	Pvt	H	Shiloh	Wounded
Hinson, John W.	Sgt	H	Shiloh	Wounded
Lewis, Thomas F.	Pvt	H	Shiloh	Wounded, captured
McCorvey, A. B.	Lt	H	Shiloh	Wounded, resigned 6/16/62
McCorvey, Neil	Pvt	H	Shiloh	Wounded
Raines, Thomas H.	Pvt	H	Shiloh	Wounded
Rives, John H.	Pvt	H	Shiloh	Wounded
Roberts, E. M.	Pvt	H	Shiloh	Killed
West, W. P.	Pvt	H	Shiloh	Wounded, discharged 5/18/62
Allen, James	Pvt	I	Shiloh	Wounded, discharged
Carlisle, Thomas J. J.	Pvt	I	Shiloh	Captured, exchanged
Champion, H. M.	Pvt	I	Shiloh	Wounded
Christian, Wm. T.	Pvt	I	Shiloh	Listed as missing. Was captured, d. 4/17/62 in St. Louis

Name	Rank	Co.	Battle	Notes
Dorman, John A.	Pvt	I	Shiloh	Missing
Falk, W. R.	Pvt	I	Shiloh	Captured, exchanged
Gillmore, Joseph L.	Sgt	I	Shiloh	Killed
Hale, John	Pvt	I	Shiloh	Missing
Hammonds, Wylie	Pvt	I	Shiloh	Wounded
Harris, William T.	Pvt	I	Shiloh	Wounded
Love, George	Pvt	I	Shiloh	Killed
McLaurine, Christopher	Pvt	I	Shiloh	Wounded
Parish, Tyra	Pvt	I	Shiloh	Wounded, d. 8/27/62 at Mobile
Pitts, Adoniram	Pvt	I	Shiloh	Wounded
Rainier, Joel H.	Pvt	I	Shiloh	Wounded
Saunders, John Henry	Pvt	I	Shiloh	Wounded
Spoon, John E.	Pvt	I	Shiloh	Wounded, discharged 7/4/62
Strom, H. S.	Pvt	I	Shiloh	Wounded, d. 8/4/62
Weaver, William	Pvt	I	Shiloh	Killed
Allen, J.	Pvt	K	Shiloh	Captured, d. at Camp Douglas, IL
Ballard, John A.	Pvt	K	Shiloh	Wounded, captured, d. 6/28/62
Clorr, John	Sgt	K	Shiloh	Wounded, missing
Dewberry, William	Pvt	K	Shiloh	Wounded
Fronabager, John P.	Pvt	K	Shiloh	Wounded, discharged 6/22/62
Hammonds, Wylie	Pvt	K	Shiloh	Wounded
Harrison, J. J. N.	Pvt	K	Shiloh	Missing
Harrison, James W.	Pvt	K	Shiloh	Captured, d. 5/17/62 Camp Douglas
Jordan, George W.	Pvt	K	Shiloh	Wounded
Majors, Henry	Pvt	K	Shiloh	Wounded, d. 6/3/62
Majors, J. D.	Pvt	K	Shiloh	Wounded
McCane, Thomas A.	Lt	K	Shiloh	Wounded
Meredith, E. W.	Pvt	K	Shiloh	Wounded
Moseley, Robert	Pvt	K	Shiloh	Wounded, missing
Moseley, John	Pvt	K	Shiloh	Killed
Staggers, R. M.	Pvt	K	Shiloh	Captured
Tippett, J. M.	Pvt	K	Shiloh	Wounded, captured, d. 5/5/62
Watson, William	Pvt	K	Shiloh	Wounded
Wilburn, James	Pvt	K	Shiloh	Killed
Williams, Daniel	Pvt	K	Shiloh	Wounded, captured, d. 4/29/62, St. Louis, MO

C. Atlanta Campaign

For the 17th Alabama and Cantey's brigade the Atlanta campaign began in May 1864 at Resaca and continued until the capture of Atlanta by General Sherman in early September. Total casualties listed below are 384 men: Company A – 27, Company B – 39, Company C – 38, Company D – 31, Company E – 55, Company F – 51, Company G – 23, Company H – 40, Company I – 39, and Company K – 41.

Name	Rank	Co.	Battle	Notes
Banks, James	Pvt	A	Resaca	Wounded

BATTLE CASUALTIES

Name	Rank	Co.	Battle	Status
Blankenship, Eli	Pvt	A	Ezra Church	Wounded
Bodiford, Alex	Pvt	A	Atlanta	Wounded
Brown, John	Pvt	A	Cassville	Captured, sent to Rock Island, IL
Brown, Joseph	Pvt	A	Cassville	Captured, sent to Rock island, IL
Buck, James	Pvt	A	Resaca	Wounded
Davis, Joseph	Pvt	A	Chattahoochie	Captured
Fonville, James B.	Pvt	A	Chattahoochie	Captured, sent to Camp Morton
Gingles, Harry S.	Pvt	A	Ezra Church	Wounded
Harris, George	Pvt	A	Marietta	Captured, sent to Camp Douglas, IL
Hartley, Hiram G.	Sgt	A	Ezra Church	Wounded
Holcombe, Milton S.	Pvt	A	Ezra Church	Wounded
Hudson, Joseph	Pvt	A	Kennesaw Mtn.	Wounded
King, James S.	Pvt	A	Ezra Church	Wounded
Leach, Richard	Pvt	A	Peachtree Creek	Killed
Lee, Ollin Talbot B.	Pvt	A	Marietta	Captured, sent to Camp Douglas, IL
McShores, William	Pvt	A	Peachtree Creek	Wounded
Roberson, Alfred B.	Sgt	A	Ezra Church	Wounded
Shanks, J. J.	Pvt	A	Resaca	Wounded
Shanks, James Jordan	Pvt	A	Resaca	Wounded
Shanks, John W.	Pvt	A	Ezra Church	Wounded
Shields, Milton J.	Pvt	A	Ezra Church	Wounded
Taylor, Dixon L.	Pvt	A	Ezra Church	Wounded
Taylor, John	Pvt	A	Peachtree Creek	Wounded
Taylor, Samuel B.	Cpl	A	Peachtree Creek	Wounded, captured, d. 10/20/64
Taylor, William A. B.	Pvt	A	Ezra Church	Wounded
Thornton, John E.	Pvt	A	Ezra Church	Wounded
Beesley, Abraham	Pvt	B	Resaca	Wounded
Black, William H.	Pvt	B	Atlanta	Wounded
Blackman, Chapman	Pvt	B	Ezra Church	Wounded and died
Braswell, William	Pvt	B	Kennesaw Mtn.	Wounded
Braswell, William	Pvt	B	Resaca	Wounded
Clark, James R.	Pvt	B	Resaca	Wounded
Coleman, Jesse	Pvt	B	Resaca	Wounded
Deans, John J.	Pvt	B	Ezra Church	Wounded
Doswell, W. J.	Pvt	B	Resaca	Wounded
Griffin, John B.	Pvt	B	Ezra Church	Wounded
Jackson, George L.	Pvt	B	Ezra Church	Captured, sent to Camp Douglas, IL
Johns, John B.	1 Lt	B	Atlanta	Wounded
Jordan, Nathan	Pvt	B	Resaca	Wounded, d. 7/19/64
Kirksy, Willis D.	Pvt	B	Peachtree Creek	Wounded, d. 8/5/64
Majors, Daniel M.	Pvt	B	Atlanta	Wounded
Majors, James	Pvt	B	Ezra Church	Killed
Majors, Joseph	Pvt	B	Atlanta	Killed
Manley, Charles J.	Pvt	B	Atlanta	Wounded
Maxey, William	Pvt	B	Resaca	Wounded
McClure, George H.	Pvt	B	Peachtree Creek	Killed

McIntire, J. C.	Pvt	B	Atlanta	Wounded	
McPherson, J. W.	Pvt	B	Peachtree Creek	Killed	
Moreland, James S.	Pvt	B	Resaca	Captured, sent to Johnson Island, IL	
Owens, Robert E.	Pvt	B	Ezra Church	Wounded	
Parker, Benjamin	Pvt	B	Resaca	Killed	
Parker, William	Pvt	B	Atlanta	Wounded	
Phillips, John W.	Pvt	B	Dallas	Captured, sent to Rock Island, IL	
Rambo, John R.	Pvt	B	Resaca	Killed	
Rhodes, James W.	Pvt	B	Resaca	Wounded	
Rigsby, Benjamin	Pvt	B	Ezra Church	Wounded	
Rigsby, Phil D.	Pvt	B	Atlanta	Wounded	
Robbins, Solomon E.	Pvt	B	Ezra Church	Wounded	
Stallings, Henry C.	Pvt	B	Ezra Church	Wounded	
Stanley, W. H.	Pvt	B	Ezra Church	Killed	
Stanley, William H.	Pvt	B	Chattahoochie	Wounded	
Tyner, Josiah	Pvt	B	Ezra Church	Wounded	
Tyner, Josiah	Pvt	B	Resaca	Wounded	
Walker, Felix G.	Pvt	B	Peachtree Creek	Captured, sent to Camp Douglas, IL	
Williamson, S. J.	Pvt	B	Ezra Church	Wounded	
Armstrong, Max	Pvt	C	Ezra Church	Killed	
Bell, Jere	Pvt	C	Ezra Church	Wounded	
Cornathan, George	Pvt	C	Peachtree Creek	Wounded	
Davis, Isaiah	Pvt	C	Kennesaw Mtn.	Wounded	
Dendy, Buford	1 Lt	C	Peachtree Creek	Wounded	
Frost, W. H.	Pvt	C	Resaca	Wounded, d. in 6/64	
Goodson, Peter	Pvt	C	Atlanta	Killed	
Grayden, William A.	Pvt	C	Peachtree Creek	Wounded	
Harrison, John A.	Pvt	C	Ezra Church	Killed	
Harrison, Moses J.	Pvt	C	Resaca	Wounded	
Hester, L. A.	Pvt	C	Resaca	Killed	
Johnson, J. E.	Pvt	C	Peachtree Creek	Killed	
Long, Henry J.	Pvt	C	Ezra Church	Killed	
Lowery, George W.	Pvt	C	Stone Mtn.	Captured, sent to Camp Chase, OH	
Miller, Isaiah G.	Pvt	C	New Hope	Captured	
Milton, William	Pvt	C	Resaca	Wounded	
Morgan, James W.	Pvt	C	Resaca	Wounded	
Nichols, Christopher	Pvt	C	Atlanta	Wounded	
Parker, Gardner G.	Pvt	C	Ezra Church	Wounded	
Perdue, J. H.	Pvt	C	Resaca	Wounded	
Peterson, Thomas A.	Pvt	C	Ezra Church	Wounded	
Pollard, Everett	Pvt	C	Atlanta	Wounded	
Powell, John L.	Pvt	C	Peachtree Creek	Wounded	
Russell, Samuel Tines	Pvt	C	Resaca	Wounded	
Seale, Cornelius H.	Pvt	C	Resaca	Wounded	
Seale, Henry O.	Pvt	C	Peachtree Creek	Captured, sent to Camp Douglas, IL	
Singleton, John W.	Pvt	C	Kennesaw Mtn.	Wounded	

BATTLE CASUALTIES 437

Name	Rank	Co.	Battle	Status
Skipper, George	Pvt	C	Atlanta	Wounded
Smith, William R.	Pvt	C	Ezra Church	Wounded
Spradley, James E.	Pvt	C	Atlanta	Wounded
Spradley, Manning C.	Pvt	C	Peachtree Creek	Wounded
Stanley, C. D.	Pvt	C	Ezra Church	Wounded
Stewart, Hillery	Pvt	C	Kennesaw Mtn.	Captured, sent to Camp Douglas, IL
Tally, Josiah	Pvt	C	Ezra Church	Wounded
Thornton, H.	Pvt	C	Peachtree Creek	Wounded
Trainum, James F.	Pvt	C	New Hope	Captured, sent to Camp Douglas, IL, d. 1/3/65
Turner, Joseph	Pvt	C	New Hope	Captured
Williamson, S. J.	Pvt	C	Ezra Church	Wounded
Adkins, John F.	Sgt	D	Ezra Church	Wounded
Adkins, Rufus G.	Pvt	D	Peachtree Creek	Wounded
Banister, David	Pvt	D	Kennesaw Mtn.	ccmo
Banister, William M.	Pvt	D	Ezra Church	Wounded, d. 8/4/64
Bryant, Z. T.	Pvt	D	Peachtree Creek	Wounded
Clisby, Samuel H.	Pvt	D	Peachtree Creek	Killed
Conner, William J.	Pvt	D	Jonesboro	Captured, sent to Camp Douglas, IL
Cook, Wiley H.	Pvt	D	Ezra Church	Wounded
Darden, William W.	Cpl	D	Ezra Church	Wounded
Easterling, E.	Pvt	D	Ezra Church	Wounded
Edwards, T.	Pvt	D	Resaca	Wounded
Gillilond, William	Pvt	D	Atlanta	
Graham, Thomas M.	Pvt	D	Kennesaw Mtn.	Wounded
Hester, Alfred L.	Pvt	D	Ezra Church	Wounded
Hester, John A.	2 Lt	D	Dallas	Captured, sent to Johnson Island, OH
Huddleston, T. M.	Pvt	D	Resaca	Wounded
Ingram, Samuel J.	Pvt	D	Ezra Church	Wounded, Captured, sent to Camp Douglas, IL
Johnson, J. L.	Pvt	D	Resaca	Killed
Kinkade, William B.	Pvt	D	Ezra Church	Wounded
Konkle, John	Pvt	D	Resaca	Wounded
Lake, James M.	Pvt	D	Ezra Church	Wounded
Lindsay, Noah J.	Pvt	D	Jonesboro	Captured, sent to Camp Douglas, IL
Macon, William H.	Pvt	D	Peachtree Creek	Wounded
Mullaney, William J.	Pvt	D	Atlanta	Wounded
Peoples, J. A.	Pvt	D	Ezra Church	Killed
Prickett, James W.	Pvt	D	Peachtree Creek	Wounded
Rawls, William B.	Pvt	D	New Hope	Captured, sent to Rock Island, IL
Richardson, W. C.	Pvt	D	Peachtree Creek	Killed
Smallwood, James A. I.	Pvt	D	Peachtree Creek	Killed
Speer, Sterling W.	Pvt	D	Chattahoochie	Captured, sent to Camp Douglas, IL
Stewart, Seaborn H.	Lt	D	Big Shanty	Captured, sent to Johnson Island, OH
Bailey, Patrick G.	Pvt	E	Resaca	Wounded
Bohannan, James	Pvt	E	Atlanta	Wounded

Name	Rank	Co.	Battle	Status
Bohannan, James	Pvt	E	Resaca	Wounded
Cassels, Henry T.	Pvt	E	Ezra Church	Wounded
Cooper, John G.	Pvt	E	Atlanta	Wounded
Daniel, Newton	Pvt	E	Peachtree Creek	Wounded
Davis, John H.	Pvt	E	Resaca	Captured, sent to Camp Douglas, IL
Dunn, John	Pvt	E	Resaca	Captured, sent to Camp Douglas, IL
Everdeen, J. W.	Pvt	E	Ezra Church	Killed
Fincher, William A.	Pvt	E	Kennesaw Mtn.	Captured, sent to Camp Morton, IN, d. 1/22/65
Foster, James M.	Pvt	E	Atlanta	Killed
Green, Tandy H.	Pvt	E	Resaca	Captured, sent to Camp Douglas, IL
Head, Richard	Pvt	E	Peachtree Creek	Wounded
Head, Samuel J.	Pvt	E	Atlanta	Captured, sent to Camp Douglas, IL
Heldebrand, Vanburen	Pvt	E	Atlanta	Wounded
Hodge, Bennett	Pvt	E	Ezra Church	Wounded
Hodges, William	Pvt	E	Peachtree Creek	Wounded
Holder, I. J.	Pvt	E	Ezra Church	Wounded
Holder, Theophilas	Pvt	E	Peachtree Creek	Killed
Holdn, J. E.	Pvt	E	Ezra Church	Wounded
Hunt, Gilbert	Pvt	E	Resaca	Wounded
Manley, Thomas A.	Pvt	E	Kennesaw Mtn.	Captured, sent to Camp Douglas, IL
Mayfield, Battle W.	Pvt	E	Kennesaw Mtn.	Captured, sent to Camp Douglas, IL
Mickle, Jerry	Pvt	E	Ezra Church	Killed
Miller, Francis M.	Pvt	E	Peachtree Creek	Captured, sent to Camp Douglas, IL
Owen, Alphas D.	Pvt	E	Dallas	Captured, sent to Rock Island, IN
Owen, William F.	Pvt	E	Peachtree Creek	Killed
Rhoades, William H.	Pvt	E	Chattahoochie	Captured, sent to Camp Douglas, II.
Robertson, Andrew P	Pvt	E	Kennesaw Mtn.	Captured, sent to Camp Douglas, IL
Robertson, Frank	Pvt	E	Chattahoochie	Captured, sent to Camp Douglas, IL, d. 2/3/65
Sanders, David	Pvt	E	Chattahoochie	Captured, sent to Camp Douglas, IL
Sanit, George W.	Pvt	E	Ezra Church	Killed
Shellnut, Andrew J.	Pvt	E	Ezra Church	Wounded
Shelnut, William J.	Pvt	E	Dallas	Captured, sent to Rock Island, IN
Smith Lewis B.	Pvt	E	Kennesaw Mtn.	Captured, sent to Camp Douglas, IL
Smith, J. T.	Pvt	E	Peachtree Creek	Wounded
Smith, Milton	Pvt	E	Ezra Church	Wounded
Spears, William C.	Pvt	E	Dallas	Captured, sent to Rock Island, IN
Stephens, Thomas R.	Pvt	E	Dallas	Captured, sent to Rock Island, IN
Stitt, John T.	Pvt	E	Dallas	Wounded
Stitt, C. G	Pvt	E	Ezra Church	Killed
Stitt, Robert S.	Pvt	E	Lovejoy	Captured
Stitt, Thomas J.	Pvt	E	Ezra Church	Wounded
Suggs, Elisha	Pvt	E	Peachtree Creek	Wounded
Talley, John T.	Pvt	E	Ezra Church	Wounded
Talley, Thomas D.	Pvt	E	Dallas	Captured, sent to Rock Island, IN

BATTLE CASUALTIES

Taylor, Elijah N.	Pvt	E	Peachtree Creek	Wounded
Teague, E. A.	Pvt	E	Ezra Church	Wounded
Tedder, William B.	Pvt	E	Marietta	Captured, sent to Camp Douglas, IL
Upchurch, Berry	Pvt	E	Ezra Church	Captured, sent to Camp Douglas, IL, d. 8/9/64
Upchurch, Harbord M.	Pvt	E	Ezra Church	Wounded
Weathers, James A.	Pvt	E	New Hope	Wounded
Weathers, James A.	Pvt	E	Resaca	Wounded
White, Daniel C.	Pvt	E	Atlanta	Wounded
Young, Joel	Pvt	E	Marietta	Wounded
Addison, Abijah Minto	Pvt	F	Kennesaw Mtn.	Wounded
Addison, Abijah Minto	Pvt	F	Peachtree Creek	Wounded
Anderson, Elijah	Pvt	F	Kennesaw Mtn.	Wounded
Baker, James	Pvt	F	Peachtree Creek	Wounded
Bofinger, George	Pvt	F	Cassville	Captured, sent to Rock, Island, IL
Bray, Henry B.	Sgt	F	Peachtree Creek	Wounded
Broadway, W. H.	Pvt	F	Peachtree Creek	Killed
Brown, O. F.	Pvt	F	Peachtree Creek	Killed
Bullard, Edward H.	Pvt	F	Ezra Church	Wounded, discharged
Cook, O. H. P.	Pvt	F	Peachtree Creek	Wounded
Dumas, Asa	Pvt	F	Dalton	Captured, sent to Camp Morton, OH
Forshee, William	Pvt	F	Kennesaw Mtn.	Wounded
Gay, Stewart	Pvt	F	Lost Mountain	Wounded
Griffin, Patrick	Pvt	F	Peachtree Creek	Wounded
Halfrin, Thomas	2 Lt	F	Ezra Church	Wounded
Hall, H. P.	Pvt	F	Peachtree Creek	Wounded
Halso, Stephen	Pvt	F	Peachtree Creek	Wounded
Johns, John B.	Lt	F	Ezra Church	Wounded
Jones, James Newton	Pvt	F	Cassville	Captured, sent to Buck Island, OH
Jones, Jasper W.	Pvt	F	Cassville	Captured, sent to Rock Island, IL
Jones, John William	Pvt	F	Ezra Church	Wounded
Jones, Owen	Pvt	F	Ezra Church	Wounded
Jones, W. K.	Pvt	F	Resaca	Wounded
Layton, Joseph	Pvt	F	Marietta	Wounded
Lewis, A.	Pvt	F	Ezra Church	Wounded
Lovett, Joseph	Pvt	F	Peachtree Creek	Wounded
Marlow, Daniel	Pvt	F	Ezra Church	Killed
McKay, T. J.	Pvt	F	Ezra Church	Wounded
McMillin, Charles B.	Pvt	F	Peachtree Creek	Killed
Mings, James W.	Pvt	F	Forsyth	Killed
Monfee, Francis	Pvt	F	Chattahoochie	Captured, sent to Camp Douglas, IL
Montgomery, John	Pvt	F	Ezra Church	Wounded
Moore, W. H.	Pvt	F	Resaca	Wounded
Mothershead, David B.	Pvt	F	Peachtree Creek	Wounded
Mustin, William	Cpt	F	Chattahoochie	Wounded
O'Brian, R.	Pvt	F	Atlanta	Wounded

O'Brian, Thomas S.	Sgt	F	Peachtree Creek	Captured, sent to Johnson Island, OH
O'Brien, Andrew	Pvt	F	Ezra Church	Wounded
Owen, Thomas F.	Pvt	F	Peachtree Creek	Wounded
Sharp, John O.	Pvt	F	Atlanta	Wounded
Shaver, Jacob	Pvt	F	Chattahoochie	Wounded
Shea, John	Pvt	F	Resaca	Wounded
Shunackel, William	Mus	F	Ezra Church	Wounded
Skipper Morgan	Pvt	F	Marietta	Wounded
Strickland, Andrew B.	Pvt	F	Ezra Church	Wounded
Torpey, John	Pvt	F	Kennesaw Mtn.	Captured, sent to Camp Douglas, IL
Waldo, Charles M.	Pvt	F	Marietta	Captured, sent to Camp Morton, Ind.
Walker, William	Pvt	F	Ezra Church	Wounded
Way, David	Pvt	F	Atlanta	Wounded
Webb, C. C.	Pvt	F	Atlanta	Wounded
Welch, James	Pvt	F	Peachtree Creek	Wounded
Broadwaters, Thomas	Pvt	G	Ezra Church	Wounded
Bullington, James O.	Pvt	G	Kennesaw Mtn.	Wounded
Elbern, Joseph W.	Cpl	G	Ezra Church	Wounded
Goff, Matthew	Pvt	G	Ezra Church	Wounded, d. 9/14/64
Holcombe, Edward P.	Col	G	Resaca	Wounded
Jackson, Stephen	Pvt	G	Atlanta	Killed
Johnson, L. S.	Sgt	G	Peachtree Creek	Wounded, captured
Johnson, Walter	Pvt	G	Kennesaw Mtn.	Wounded
Kelly, James Polk	Pvt	G	Kennesaw Mtn.	Wounded
Martin, A. P.	Cpt	G	Ezra Church	Killed
Martin, Alfred P.	Pvt	G	Ezra Church	Wounded, captured, sent to Camp Douglas, IL, d. 1/27/65
Phillips, John J.	Pvt	G	Peachtree Creek	Wounded
Pruitt, Miles S.	Pvt	G	Resaca	Wounded
Pursewell, W. S.	Pvt	G	Ezra Church	Wounded
Ragland, Thomas	Cpt	G	Ezra Church	Killed
Roberts, Robert	Pvt	G	Peachtree Creek	Wounded
Shaffer, Antony	Pvt	G	Cartersville	Captured, sent to Rock Island, IL
Sharpton, William E.	Pvt	G	Atlanta	Wounded
Shaw, John	Pvt	G	Ezra Church	Wounded
Spinks, William	Pvt	G	Kennesaw Mtn.	Killed
Thomas, T. C.	Pvt	G	Atlanta	Wounded
Wynne, John T.	Sgt	G	Atlanta	Wounded
Wynne, Lemuel	Pvt	G	Peachtree Creek	Wounded
Andress, R. M.	Lt	H	Peachtree Creek	Killed
Ballard, John	Pvt	H	New Hope	Wounded, d. 7/5/64
Barnes, J. N.	Pvt	H	Resaca	Captured, sent to Indianapolis
Bayles, W. J.	Pvt	H	Atlanta	Killed
Billings, Jethro	Pvt	H	New Hope	Wounded
Black, John W.	Pvt	H	Ezra Church	Wounded
Boon, John	Pvt	H	Ezra Church	Wounded

BATTLE CASUALTIES

Name	Rank	Co.	Battle	Status
Bradbury, J. W.	Pvt	H	Atlanta	Wounded
Brady, William R.	Pvt	H	Resaca	Captured, sent to Alton, IL
Chisholm, Neal H.	Pvt	H	Peachtree Creek	Killed
Davis, Jno. T.	Pvt	H	Atlanta	Wounded
Davis, John R.	Pvt	H	Atlanta	Wounded
Davison, J. N.	Cpl	H	Ezra Church	Killed
Davison, James Miller	Sgt	H	Kennesaw Mtn.	Wounded
Dean, Jeremiah J.	Pvt	H	Ezra Church	Wounded
Dees, C. T.	Pvt	H	Peachtree Creek	Killed
Dunn, Anthony Wayne	Pvt	H	Ezra Church	Wounded
Eddins, John R.	Pvt	H	Atlanta	Captured, sent to Camp Douglas, IL
Falkenberry, Dearon	Pvt	H	Ezra Church	Killed
Hall, George T.	Pvt	H	Chattahoochie	Wounded
Hilton, Henry	Pvt	H	Ezra Church	Wounded
Hornback, William F.	Pvt	H	Resaca	Wounded
Ladd, W. J.	Pvt	H	New Hope	Wounded
Manahan, Patrick	Pvt	H	Resaca	Wounded
McMillan, W. H.	Sgt	H	Ezra Church	Killed
McMillan. William W.	Cpt	H	Ezra Church	Wounded
McNeil, James N.	Pvt	H	Ezra Church	Wounded
Morris, Jesse	Pvt	H	Chattahoochie	Captured, sent to Camp Douglas, IL, d. 1/28/65
Newberry, W. T.	Pvt	H	Resaca	Wounded
Odione, W. W.	Pvt	H	Peachtree Creek	Wounded
Raines, Thomas H.	Pvt	H	Resaca	Wounded
Richardson, J. W.	Pvt	H	Jonesboro	Captured
Robinson, N. J.	Pvt	H	Peachtree Creek	Wounded
Robison, William Jesse	1 Lt	H	Resaca	Wounded
Smith, John Davison	Sgt	H	Resaca	Wounded
Templin, Henry	Pvt	H	Peachtree Creek	Killed
Thames, Newby C.	Pvt	H	Ezra Church	Wounded
Vickery, J. J.	Pvt	H	Jonesboro	Captured
Wicks, Charles	Pvt	H	Hightower	Captured, sent to Rock Island
Wiggins, M. Lafayette	Pvt	H	Peachtree Creek	Killed
Adams, Early	Pvt	I	Ezra Church	Killed
Adams, Early	Pvt	I	Peachtree Creek	Wounded
Bones, John Samuel	Cpt	I	Peachtree Creek	Wounded
Brady, William R.	Pvt	I	Resaca	Captured, sent to Alton, IL
Carlisle, Thomas J.	Pvt	I	Resaca	Killed
Cheatham, James	Pvt	I	Ezra Church	Wounded
Combey, Anderson D.	Pvt	I	Ezra Church	Wounded
Green, B. R.	Pvt	I	Resaca	Wounded
Green, William S.	Pvt	I	Resaca	Wounded
Hall, James C.	Pvt	I	Dallas	Captured
Hammonds, Wylie H.	Pvt	I	Peachtree Creek	Captured, sent to Camp Douglas, IL
Harris, William T.	Sgt	I	Ezra Church	Wounded

Harris, William T.	Sgt	I	Peachtree Creek	Wounded
Head, Aldolphus M.	Pvt	I	Peachtree Creek	Wounded
Hogan, George W.	Pvt	I	Dallas	Captured, sent to Rock Island
Jackson, Joseph B.	Pvt	I	Ezra Church	Wounded
Johnson, Alfred	Pvt	I	Peachtree Creek	Wounded
Jones, Seborn	Pvt	I	Dallas	Captured, sent to Rock Island
Laney, S. Thomas	Pvt	I	Resaca	Wounded
McCrary, William H.	Pvt	I	Ezra Church	Wounded
McLaurine, Christopher	Sgt	I	Resaca	Wounded
McLeod, G. R.	Pvt	I	Marietta	Wounded
McVay, Morgan	Pvt	I	Peachtree Creek	Wounded
McWhorter, Ezekiel A.	Pvt	I	Ezra Church	Killed
McWhorter, William	Pvt	I	Atlanta	Killed
Miller, Henry	Pvt	I	Atlanta	Wounded
Norsworthy, L. L.	Pvt	I	Resaca	Wounded
Ozier, James Uriah	Pvt	I	Resaca	Wounded
Pierce, John	Pvt	I	Marietta	Captured, sent to Camp Chase, OH
Pitts, Adoniram J.	Pvt	I	Peachtree Creek	Wounded
Rawls, Oliver Lieke	Pvt	I	Ezra Church	Wounded
Schofield, John James	Pvt	I	Jonesboro	Wounded
Smith, Saul	Pvt	I	Marietta	Captured, sent to Camp Douglas, IL
Turner, John H.	Pvt	I	Ezra Church	Wounded
Ward, Sampson M.	Pvt	I	Peachtree Creek	Wounded
Weaver, James R.	Pvt	I	Peachtree Creek	Killed
Weaver, John R.	Pvt	I	Peachtree Creek	Captured, sent to Camp Douglas, IL
Whittles, James M.	Pvt	I	Resaca	Wounded
Wright, William J.	Sgt	I	Resaca	Wounded
Begood, Samuel	Pvt	K	Ezra Church	Wounded
Benson, William C.	Pvt	K	Atlanta	Wounded
Brinkley, John	Pvt	K	Ezra Church	Wounded
Buffington, James R.	Pvt	K	Kennesaw Mtn.	Wounded
Burnett, Thomas J.	Cpt	K	Peachtree Creek	Wounded
Cody, Columbus J.	2 Lt	K	Ezra Church	Wounded
Coleman, Walter	Sgt	K	Ezra Church	Captured, sent to Camp Chase, OH
Cunningham, Hillery	Pvt	K	Peachtree Creek	Wounded
Durden, W. W.	Sgt	K	Atlanta	Wounded
Ellis, Radford	Pvt	K	Resaca	Wounded
Fife, John Henry	Pvt	K	Peachtree Creek	Wounded
Fort, George W.	Pvt	K	Jonesboro	Captured, sent to Camp Douglas, IL
Galloway, Nathan	Pvt	K	Dallas	Captured, sent to Rock Island, IL
Gore, Samuel J.	Pvt	K	Atlanta	Wounded
Hammonds, Wylie H.	Pvt	K	Peachtree Creek	Captured, sent to Camp Douglas, IL
Harrison, King S.	Pvt	K	Dallas	Captured, sent to Rock Island, IL
Harrison, King S.	Pvt	K	Resaca	Wounded
Harrison, Levi	Pvt	K	Ezra Church	Wounded
Harrison, William	Pvt	K	Ezra Church	Wounded

Name	Rank	Co.	Battle	Status
Hodge, Thomas P.	Pvt	K	Peachtree Creek	Captured, sent to Camp Douglas, IL
Hughes, William W.	Pvt	K	Resaca	Killed
Kanne, John	Pvt	K	Cassville	Captured, sent to Rock Island, IL
Kern, Simon Moses,	Pvt	K	Resaca	Wounded
Knight, Lawrence S.	Pvt	K	Kennesaw Mtn.	Wounded
Long, Henry J.	Pvt	K	Ezra Church	Killed
Martin, James A.	Pvt	K	Chattahoochie	Captured, sent to Johnson Island, OH
Moore, William J.	Pvt	K	Peachtree Creek	Wounded
Pentecost, Leonidas	1 Lt	K	Resaca	Wounded
Perdue, Payton	Pvt	K	Ezra Church	Wounded
Philyaw, George W.	Pvt	K	Jonesboro	Captured, sent to Camp Douglas, IL
Ray, John	Pvt	K	Marietta	Wounded, captured, sent to Camp Chase, IL, d. 6/19/65
Riley, George W.	Cpl	K	Ezra Church	Wounded
Rozier, John L. B.	Pvt	K	Ezra Church	Wounded
Seawright, George A.	Pvt	K	Ezra Church	Wounded
Seawright, John R.	Pvt	K	Ezra Church	Wounded
Sheppard, Thomas H.	Pvt	K	Atlanta	Wounded
Sheppard, Thomas H.	Pvt	K	Resaca	Wounded
Staggers, John W.	Pvt	K	Ezra Church	Wounded
Vaughn, James	Pvt	K	Kennesaw Mtn.	Captured, sent to Camp Douglas, IL, d. 1/20/65
Wallace, George	Pvt	K	Peachtree Creek	Captured, sent to Camp Douglas, IL
Whidden, Noah W.	Pvt	K	Ezra Church	Killed

D. Franklin

The battle of Franklin, Tennessee, took place one late afternoon on November 30, 1864. Total casualties listed below are 76 men: Company A – 10, Company B – 8, Company C – 7, Company D – 11, Company E – 9, Company F – 4, Company G – 2, Company H – 11, Company I – 6, and Company K – 8.

Name	Rank	Co.	Battle	Status
Adams, Vincent	Pvt	A	Franklin	Wounded
Bozeman, Walter	Pvt	A	Franklin	Wounded
Davis, James T.	Pvt	A	Franklin	Wounded
Davis, Robert F.	Pvt	A	Franklin	Wounded
Hartly, Green B.	Lt	A	Franklin	Wounded
Hartley, Hiram G.	Lt	A	Franklin	Killed
Hawkins, Robert F.	Pvt	A	Franklin	Wounded
Shanks, James Jordan	Pvt	A	Franklin	Family tradition states he was killed
Verdery, Samuel A.	Lt	A	Franklin	Wounded
Wright, Jas. M.	Pvt	A	Franklin	Wounded
Biggs, Tulley	Pvt	B	Franklin	Wounded
Davis, Sam	Pvt	B	Franklin	Killed
Ewing, Samuel	Pvt	B	Franklin	Wounded
Hamric, John F. M.	Pvt	B	Franklin	Captured November 30, 1864

Holliman, James H.	Pvt	B	Franklin	Captured November 30, 1864
Owens, Robert Philip	Pvt	B	Franklin	Died after battle, buried at Rosehill Cemetery, Columbia
Porter, Thomas M. J.	2 Lt	B	Franklin	Captured November 30, 1864
Williamson, John	Pvt	B	Franklin	Wounded
Brooks, L. M.	Pvt.	C	Franklin	Wounded
Dugan, James F.	Pvt	C	Franklin	Wounded
Harrison, Moses J.	Pvt	C	Franklin	Killed
Posey, George H.	Pvt	C	Franklin	Killed, buried at McGavock Cemetery
Stanley, James B.	Pvt	C	Franklin	Wounded
Stewart, D. M.	Pvt	C	Franklin	Killed
Wyche, George D.	Pvt	C	Franklin	Wounded 11/30 and captured 12/17-18 at Franklin
Groce, Joshua J.	Chp	D	Franklin	Wounded 11/30 and captured 12/17-18 at Franklin, died
Graham, Thomas M.	Pvt	D	Franklin	Wounded and captured
Jones, William R.	Pvt	D	Franklin	Killed
Lauderdale, J. S.	Pvt	D	Franklin	Killed, buried at McGavock Cemetery
Mitchell, Thomas H.	Pvt	D	Franklin	Captured November 30, 1864
Monk, John Samuel	Pvt	D	Franklin	Killed, buried at McGavock Cemetery
Mullaney, William J.	Pvt	D	Franklin	Wounded
Patterson. E.	Pvt	D	Franklin	Wounded and captured
Prickett, William W. F.	Pvt	D	Franklin	Wounded. May have been Puckett
Temple, B. Z.	Pvt	D	Franklin	Wounded, captured November 30, 1864
Thornton, H.	Pvt	D	Franklin	Wounded, captured, sent to Camp Morton
Hodges, William	Pvt	E	Franklin	Wounded and captured
Holder, Jasper	Pvt	E	Franklin	Wounded and captured
Holder, Joseph B.	Pvt	E	Franklin	Wounded 11/30 and captured 12/17-18 at Franklin
Miller, William Jackson	Pvt	E	Franklin	Captured November 30, 1864
Newman, Seaborn	Pvt	E	Franklin	Wounded
Pool, Robert C.	Pvt	E	Franklin	Wounded 11/30 and captured 12/17-18 at Franklin
Talley, John T.	Pvt	E	Franklin	Wounded and captured
Vowell, Andrew	Pvt	E	Franklin	Wounded
Weathers, Benjamin	1 Lt	E	Franklin	Captured November 30, 1864
Croxton, R. A.	Pvt	F	Franklin	Killed, buried at McGavock Cemetery
McKey, T. J.	Pvt	F	Franklin	Wounded 11/30 and captured 12/17-18 at Franklin
Montgomery, John	Pvt	F	Franklin	Wounded
Moore, W. H.	Sgt	F	Franklin	Wounded
Lynn, L. W.	Pvt	G	Franklin	Captured
Tutt, William D.	Pvt	G	Franklin	Wounded
Black, J. W.	Pvt	H	Franklin	Wounded 11/30 and captured 12/17-18 at Franklin
Brent, W. T.	Pvt	H	Franklin	Wounded
Daily, Fielding	Pvt	H	Franklin	Wounded

BATTLE CASUALTIES

Davison, James Miller	Sgt	H	Franklin	Wounded 11/30 and captured 12/17-18 at Franklin
Eddins, Francis M.	Pvt	H	Franklin	Killed, buried at McGavock Cemetery
Knight, Thomas	Pvt	H	Franklin	Wounded 11/30 and captured 12/17-18 at Franklin
Massey, J. M.	Pvt	H	Franklin	Captured November 30, 1864
McMillan, Benjamin	Lt	H	Franklin	Killed
McMillan, William W.	Cpt	H	Franklin	Wounded 11/30 and captured 12/17-18 at Franklin
Robison, William Jesse	Lt	H	Franklin	Wounded
Smith, Hiram	Sgt	H	Franklin	Wounded 11/30 and captured 12/17-18 at Franklin
Harris, William T.	Pvt	I	Franklin	Killed
Lancaster, John Austin	Pvt	I	Franklin	Wounded
Martin, James L.	Sgt	I	Franklin	Wounded
McLaurine, Christopher	Pvt	I	Franklin	Killed
Turner, Benjamin H.	Pvt	I	Franklin	Killed, buried at McGavock Cemetery
Williford, John T.	Cpl	I	Franklin	Wounded
Bunkley, Burrell J.	Pvt	K	Franklin	Wounded
Cunningham, Hillary	Pvt	K	Franklin	Wounded
Daniel, Frederick F.	Pvt	K	Franklin	Captured November 30, 1864
McCane, Thomas A.	Pvt	K	Franklin	Captured November 30, 1864
Moore, William J.	Pvt	K	Franklin	Wounded
Riley, George W.	Lt	K	Franklin	Wounded
Staggers, Jno. M	Pvt	K	Franklin	Wounded
Staggers, John N.	Pvt	K	Franklin	Captured 12/17-18 at Franklin

E. Nashville

The battle of Nashville, Tennessee, took place on December 15 and 16, 1864. Total casualties listed below are 171 men: Company A – 7, Company B – 21, Company C – 29, Company D – 26, Company E – 7, Company F – 20, Company G – 8, Company H – 12, Company I – 16, and Company K – 25.

Blankenship, Eli	Pvt	A	Nashville	Captured, sent to Camp Douglas, IL
Davis, Ransom	Pvt	A	Nashville	Captured
Dean, Sumter	Pvt	A	Nashville	Captured, sent to Camp Douglas, IL
Edwards, Lyman D.	Cpl	A	Nashville	Captured, sent to Camp Douglas, IL
Hatcher, William J.	Pvt	A	Nashville	Wounded
Taylor, John	Pvt	A	Nashville	Captured, sent to Camp Douglas, IL
Tomlinson, William B.	Pvt	A	Franklin	Captured at Franklin after Nashville
Autrey, Benjamin F	Pvt	B	Nashville	Captured, sent to Camp Douglas, IL, d. 2/1/65
Carathan, Joseph	Pvt	B	Nashville	Captured, sent to Camp Douglas, IL
Coleman, George	Pvt	B	Nashville	Captured, sent to Camp Douglas, IL, d. 3/26/65
Coleman, Jesse	Pvt	B	Nashville	Captured, sent to Camp Douglas, IL
Decken, William	Pvt	B	Nashville	Captured, sent to Camp Douglas, IL

Name	Rank	Co.	Location	Notes
Deens, William H.	Pvt	B	Nashville	Captured, sent to Camp Douglas, IL, d. 3/16/65
Fowler, William A. O.	Pvt	B	Nashville	Captured, sent to Camp Douglas, IL
Garrett, James B.	Pvt	B	Nashville	Captured, sent to Camp Douglas, IL
Garrett, N. G.	Pvt	B	Nashville	Captured
Griffin, Samuel L.	Pvt	B	Nashville	Captured, sent to Camp Douglas, IL, d. 2/5/65
Leslie, Charles W.	Pvt	B	Nashville	Captured, sent to Camp Douglas, IL
Majors, Benjamin	Pvt	B	Nashville	Captured, sent to Camp Douglas, IL
Mims, Basil M.	Pvt	B	Nashville	Captured, sent to Camp Douglas, IL
Norris, Alexander	Pvt	B	Nashville	Captured, sent to Camp Douglas, IL
Norris, William A.	Pvt	B	Nashville	Captured, sent to Camp Douglas, IL
Parker, John T.	Cpl	B	Nashville	Captured, sent to Camp Douglas, IL
Shea, Patrick	Pvt	B	Nashville	Captured, sent to Camp Douglas, IL
Thomas, Daniel	Pvt	B	Nashville	Captured, sent to Camp Douglas, IL, d. 1/11/65
Walston, Andrew J.	Pvt	B	Nashville	Captured, sent to Camp Chase, OH
Williams, Benjamin	Pvt	B	Nashville	Captured, sent to Camp Douglas, IL, d. 2/15/65
Williams, William	Pvt	B	Nashville	Captured, sent to Camp Douglas, IL
Alford, J. R.	Pvt	C	Nashville	Captured, sent to Camp Chase, OH
Bailey, J. T.	Pvt	C	Nashville	Captured, sent to Camp Douglas, IL
Bolling, John Jr.	Cpt	C	Nashville	Captured, sent to Johnson Island, OH
Braydon, William E.	Pvt	C	Nashville	Captured, sent to Camp Douglas, IL
Brooks, Leonard M.	Pvt	C	Nashville	Captured, sent to Camp Douglas, IL
Chambers, John E.	Pvt	C	Nashville	Captured, sent to Camp Douglas, IL
Chambers, William F.	Pvt	C	Nashville	Wounded captured, sent to Camp Douglas, IL, d. 2/3/65
Cheatham, W. A.	Pvt	C	Nashville	Captured, sent to Camp Douglas, IL, d. 4/22/65
Creach, Sidney S.	Pvt	C	Nashville	Captured, sent to Camp Douglas, IL, d. 2/1/65
Creech, Francis L.	Pvt	C	Nashville	Captured, sent to Camp Douglas, IL
Dendy, Buford W.	2 Lt	C	Nashville	Captured, sent to Johnson Island, OH
Driver, James M.	Sgt	C	Nashville	Captured, sent to Camp Douglas, IL
Flowers, J. D.	Pvt	C	Nashville	Captured, sent to Camp Douglas, IL
Frost, James	Pvt	C	Nashville	Captured, sent to Camp Douglas, IL, 4/8/65
Henderson, Isaiah P.	Pvt	C	Nashville	Captured, sent to Camp Chase, OH
Lowery, J. H.	Pvt	C	Nashville	Captured
Milton, William	Pvt	C	Franklin	Captured at Franklin after Nashville
Owens, Miami J.	Pvt	C	Nashville	Captured, sent to Camp Douglas, IL
Pace, William B.	Pvt	C	Nashville	Captured, sent to Johnson Island, OH
Parker, Gardner G.	Pvt	C	Nashville	Captured, sent to Camp Douglas, IL, d. 5/5/65
Perry, Benjamin	Pvt	C	Nashville	Captured, sent to Camp Douglas, IL, d. 2/2/65
Peterson, Thomas	Pvt	C	Nashville	Captured, sent to Camp Douglas, IL
Peterson, William R.	Pvt	C	Nashville	Captured, sent to Camp Chase, OH
Rhodes, George W.	Pvt	C	Nashville	Captured, sent to Camp Chase, OH, d.

BATTLE CASUALTIES 447

				2/2/65
Rhodes, George W.	Pvt	C	Franklin	Captured at Franklin after Nashville
Seale, Cornelius H.	Pvt	C	Nashville	Captured, sent to Camp Douglas, IL
Stringer, Anderson T.	Pvt	C	Nashville	Captured, sent to Camp Douglas, IL
Troutman, Newton C.	Pvt	C	Nashville	Captured, sent to Camp Chase, OH
Willis, James Thomas	Pvt	C	Nashville	Captured, sent to Camp Douglas, IL
Adkins, Rufus G.	Pvt	D	Nashville	Captured, sent to Camp Douglas, IL
Buckelew, James	Pvt	D	Nashville	Captured, sent to Camp Douglas, IL
Burnett, J. R.	Pvt	D	Nashville	Captured
Cook, Wiley H.	Pvt	D	Nashville	Captured, sent to Camp Douglas, IL
Downs, Shelley	Pvt	D	Nashville	Captured, sent to Camp Douglas, IL
Durden, Anderson J.	Pvt	D	Nashville	Captured, sent to Camp Douglas, IL, d. 1/20/65
Fleming, William J.	Cpl	D	Nashville	Captured, sent to Camp Douglas, IL
Harmon, James B.	Pvt	D	Nashville	Captured, sent to Camp Douglas, IL
Hollingshead, Moses	Pvt	D	Nashville	Captured, sent to Camp Douglas, IL
Hull, William D.	1 Lt	D	Nashville	Captured, sent to Johnson Island, OH
Jackson, James T.	Pvt	D	Nashville	Captured, sent to Camp Douglas, IL
Lane, Henry S.	Pvt	D	Nashville	Captured
Lane, John H.	Pvt	D	Nashville	Captured
Letlow, Bulger	Pvt	D	Nashville	Captured, sent to Camp Chase, OH
Letlow, Thomas B.	Pvt	D	Nashville	Captured, sent to Camp Douglas, IL
Mills, Charles	Pvt	D	Nashville	Captured, sent to Camp Douglas, IL
Pate, Thomas M.	Pvt	D	Nashville	Captured, sent to Camp Douglas, IL
Pruett, George J.	Pvt	D	Nashville	Captured, sent to Louisville
Smith, William H. W.	Pvt	D	Nashville	Captured, sent to Camp Douglas, IL
Spear, James A.	Pvt	D	Franklin	Captured at Franklin after Nashville
Stewart, Nathaniel W.	Pvt	D	Nashville	Captured, sent to Camp Douglas, IL
Stewart, Samuel S.	Pvt	D	Nashville	Captured, sent to Camp Douglas, IL
Thomas, D.	Pvt	D	Nashville	Captured
Thompson, Cain Zebidee	Pvt	D	Franklin	Captured at Franklin after Nashville
Thompson, E. Z.	Pvt	D	Franklin	Captured at Franklin after Nashville
Yarborough, Thomas J.	Pvt	D	Nashville	Captured, sent to Camp Douglas, IL
Benefield, Caleb Cox	Pvt	E	Nashville	Captured
Faust, Andrew J.	Pvt	E	Nashville	Captured
Hames, Joshua	Pvt	E	Nashville	Captured, sent to Camp Chase, OH
Hutchins, James D.	Pvt	E	Nashville	Captured, sent to Camp Chase, OH, d. 2/4/65
Stell, R. S.	Pvt	E	Nashville	Captured, sent to Camp Douglas, IL, d. 1/12/65
Stewart, Richard	Pvt	E	Nashville	Captured, sent to Camp Douglas, IL
Upchurch, Harbord M.	Pvt	E	Nashville	Captured, sent to Camp Douglas, IL
Bailey, Wesley F	Pvt	F	Franklin	Captured at Franklin after Nashville
Block, Abraham	Pvt	F	Franklin	Captured at Franklin after Nashville
Blount, C. W.	Pvt	F	Nashville	Captured
Bonham, James T.	Pvt	F	Nashville	Captured, sent to Camp Douglas, IL, d. 3/24/65

Name	Rank	Co.	Place	Notes
Bullard, Henry M.	Pvt	F	Franklin	Captured at Franklin after Nashville
Davis, D. D.	Pvt	F	Nashville	Captured, sent to Camp Douglas, IL
Fables, George	Pvt	F	Nashville	Captured, sent to Camp Douglas, IL
Forshee, Charles	Pvt	F	Nashville	Captured, sent to Camp Douglas, IL
Holland, Davis	Pvt	F	Nashville	Captured, sent to Camp Douglas, IL, d. 1/29/64
Martin, William J.	Pvt	F	Nashville	Captured, sent to Camp Chase, OH
McCreight, Robert A.	Pvt	F	Nashville	Captured, sent to Camp Douglas, IL
Nordhausen, Adolph	Pvt	F	Franklin	Captured at Franklin after Nashville
O'Hara, Patrick	Pvt	F	Franklin	Captured at Franklin after Nashville
Owen, James Madison	Pvt	F	Nashville	Captured, sent to Camp Douglas, IL
Perdue, Alex	Pvt	F	Nashville	Captured, sent to Camp Douglas, IL
Royal, Hardy A.	Pvt	F	Nashville	Captured, sent to Camp Douglas, IL
Rushton, William H. P.	Pvt	F	Columbia	Captured, sent to Camp Chase, OH
Sill, John	Pvt	F	Nashville	Captured, sent to Camp Chase, OH
Terry, Thomas	Pvt	F	Spring Hill	Captured, sent to Camp Chase, OH
Walker, Daniel W.	Pvt	F	Nashville	Captured, sent to Camp Douglas, IL
Chadwick, Ambrose	Pvt	G	Nashville	Captured, sent to Camp Douglas, IL
Phillips, John J.	Pvt	G	Columbia	Captured, sent to Camp Chase, OH
Pruitt, C. C.	Pvt	G	Nashville	Captured, sent to Camp Douglas, IL
Smith, Charles J.	Sgt	G	Nashville	Captured, sent to Johnson Island
Thead, Columbus A.	Pvt	G	Nashville	Captured, sent to Camp Douglas, IL
Treadway, George W.	Pvt	G	Nashville	Captured, sent to Camp Douglas, IL
Tulville, George W.	Pvt	G	Nashville	Captured, sent to Camp Douglas, IL
Wynn, Lycurgus	Pvt	G	Nashville	Captured, sent to Camp Douglas, IL
Barnes, Thomas J.	Pvt	H	Nashville	Captured, sent to Camp Douglas, IL
Brown, N. R.	Pvt	H	Nashville	Captured, sent to Camp Douglas, IL
Burnett, Oliver S.	Pvt	H	Pulaski	Captured, sent to Camp Chase, OH
Dees, Joel	Pvt	H	Nashville	Captured, sent to Camp Douglas, IL
Elton, Henry	Pvt	H	Nashville	Captured, sent to Camp Douglas, IL
Fountain, Henry P.	Pvt	H	Nashville	Captured, sent to Camp Douglas, IL
Hall, George T.	Pvt	H	Nashville	Captured, sent to Camp Douglas, IL
Hilton, Henry	Pvt	H	Nashville'	Captured, sent to Camp Douglas, IL
Keenum, George W.	Pvt	H	Nashville	Captured, sent to Camp Douglas, IL
Riley, Jeremiah	Pvt	H	Nashville	Captured, sent to Camp Douglas, IL
Smith, William	Cpl	H	Nashville	Captured, sent to Camp Douglas, IL
Whatley, Edward W.	Pvt	H	Nashville	Captured, sent to Camp Douglas, IL
Combey, Anderson D.	Pvt	I	Nashville	Captured, sent to Camp Douglas, IL
Davis, R. L.	Pvt	I	Nashville	Captured, sent to Camp Douglas, IL
Dozewell, Thomas P.	Pvt	I	Nashville	Captured, sent to Camp Douglas, IL
Guthrie, Andrew C.	Sgt	I	Nashville	Captured, sent to Camp Douglas, IL
Hogan, William	Pvt	I	Franklin	Captured at Franklin after Nashville
Leathers, James M.	Pvt	I	Nashville	Captured, sent to Camp Douglas, IL
McVay, Morgan	Pvt	I	Nashville	Captured, sent to Camp Douglas, IL
Olden, James	Pvt	I	Nashville	Captured, sent to Camp Douglas, IL
Ozier, James Uriah	Pvt	I	Nashville	Captured, sent to Camp Douglas, IL

Name	Rank	Co	Place	Notes
Pitts, Adoniram J.	Pvt	I	Nashville	Captured, sent to Camp Chase, OH
Smith, William W.	Pvt	I	Franklin	Captured at Franklin after Nashville, buried at Mt. Olivet in Nashville
Whaley, Archibald	Pvt	I	Columbia	Captured, sent to Camp Chase, OH, d. 3/5/65
White, John L.	Pvt	I	Nashville	Captured, sent to Camp Chase, OH
Williams, Malachi C.	Pvt	I	Nashville	Captured, sent to Camp Douglas, IL
Williams, Stanford J.	Pvt	I	Nashville	Captured, sent to Camp Douglas, IL
Williford, John T.	Pvt	I	Columbia	Captured, sent to Camp Chase, OH
Barganier, William J.	Pvt	K	Nashville	Captured, sent to Camp Douglas, IL
Barrett, Andrew J.	Pvt	K	Nashville	Captured, sent to Camp Douglas, IL
Black, Ezekiel	Cpl	K	Nashville	Captured, sent to Camp Douglas, IL
Black, Joseph S.	Pvt	K	Nashville	Captured, sent to Camp Douglas, IL
Cavine, George B.	Pvt	K	Franklin	Captured at Franklin after Nashville
Cody, Columbus	2 Lt	K	Nashville	Captured, sent to Sanduskey, OH
Davis, Francis	Pvt	K	Nashville	Captured, sent to Camp Douglas, IL
Donaldson, John W.	Pvt	K	Nashville	Captured, sent to Camp Douglas, IL
Dunklin, William T.	2 Lt	K	Nashville	Captured, sent to Johnson Island, OH
Holland, D. Furman	Pvt	K	Nashville	Captured
Holman, Caspers W.	Pvt	K	Nashville	Captured, sent to Camp Douglas, IL
Hurston, Thomas M.	Pvt	K	Nashville	Captured, sent to Camp Douglas, IL
McKay, T. J.	Pvt	K	Nashville	Captured, buried at Mt. Olivet, Nashville
Martin, John M.	Pvt	K	Nashville	Captured, sent to Camp Douglas, IL
Mercer, Alexander	Pvt	K	Nashville	Captured, sent to Camp Douglas, IL
Odam, John	Pvt	K	Nashville	Captured, sent to Camp Douglas, IL
Payne, William J.	Pvt	K	Franklin	Captured at Franklin after Nashville
Pollard, William Daniel	Pvt	K	Nashville	Captured, sent to Camp Douglas, IL
Seawright, George A.	Pvt	K	Nashville	Captured, sent to Camp Douglas, IL
Seawright, John R.	Pvt	K	Nashville	Captured
Sloane, J. B.	Pvt	K	Nashville	Captured, sent to Camp Douglas, IL
Van, James W.	Pvt	K	Nashville	Captured, sent to Camp Douglas, IL
Vernon, J. C.	Pvt	K	Nashville	Captured, sent to Camp Douglas, IL
Vernon, Obadiah C.	Pvt	K	Nashville	Captured, sent to Camp Douglas, IL, d. 3/18/65
Whisker, Daniel W.	Pvt	K	Nashville	Captured, sent to Camp Douglas, IL

Bibliography

Books

1907 Alabama Confederate Soldier Census. Cullman, AL: Gregath Publishing Co.

Bergeron, Arthur W. Jr. *Confederate Mobile.* Oxford, Ms: University Press of Mississippi, 1991.

Brewer, Willis. *Brief Historical Sketches of Military Organizations of Alabama.* University, AL: Alabama Civil War Commission, 1862.

Bridges, Robert S., Editor. *Confederate Military History.* Wilmington, NC: Broadfoot Publishing Co., 1987:Volumes VIII and IX.

Chisolm, J. Julian, M. D. *A Manual of Military Surgery, for the use of Surgeons in the Confederate States Army.* Columbia, SC: Evans and Cogswell, 1864.

Connelly, Thomas L. *Autumn of Glory, The Army of Tennessee.* Baton Rouge, LA: Louisiana State University Press, 1971.

Connelly, Thomas L. & James Lee McDonough. *Five Tragic Hours, The Battle of Franklin, Tennessee.* Knoxville, TN: University of Tennessee Press, 1983.

Cox, Jacob D. *The March to the Sea, Franklin and Nashville.* Wilmington, NC: Broadfoot Publishing Company, 1989.

Cunningham, H. H. *Doctors in Gray, The Confederate Medical Service.* Baton Rouge, LA: Louisiana State University Press, 1993.

Crute, Joseph H. Jr. *Units of the Confederate States Army.* Midlothian, VA: Derwent Books, 1987.

Daniel, Larry J. *The Battle of Shiloh.* The National Park Series

DuBose, Joel E. *Notable Men of Alabama.* Reprint of 1904 edition, ed. 1976.

Farmer, Margaret P. *Record of Confederate Soldiers, 1861-1865, Pike County, Alabama.* Pike County Civil War Centennial Commission, 1962.

Hahn, Marilyn Davis. *Butler County in the Nineteenth Century.* Birmingham, AL: privately printed, 1978.

Hague, Parthenia Antoinette. *A Blockaded Family.* Lincoln, NB: University of Nebraska Press, 1991.

The Heritage of Butler County, Alabama. Clanton, AL: Heritage Publishing Consultants, 2001.

Herren, Dianne S. *Randolph County, Alabama, and the Confederacy.* Woodland, AL: Southern Roots, 1992

Hewett. Janet B., Editor. *The Roster of Confederate Soldiers, 1861-1865.* Wilmington, NC: Broadfoot Publishing Co., 1995.

Hood, John Bell. *Advance and Retreat: Personal Experiences in the United States and Confederate States Armies.* Bloomington, IN: 1959, Reprint of 1880 edition
Horn, Stanley F. *The Army of Tennessee.* New York, NY: The Bobbs-Merrill Company, 1941.
Ingmire, Frances & Carolyn Ericson. *Confederate POWs Buried in Northern Cemeteries.* Nacogdoches, TX: privately published, 1984.
Ingmire, Frances. *Confederate POWs: Soldiers and Sailors who died in Federal Prisons and Military Hospitals in the North.* Nacogdoches, TX: privately published, 1984.
Johnston, Joseph E. *Narrative of Military Operations.* New York, NY: D. Appleton and Company, 1874
Laney, Mildred Smith. *Confederate Veterans, Buried in Clay, Cleburne, and Randolph Counties.* Anniston, AL: privately published 1987.
Lipscomb, W. L. *A History of Columbus, Mississippi, During the 19th Century.* Birmingham, AL: Press of Dispatch Printing, 1909.
Lonn, Ella. *Desertion during the Civil War.* New York: The Century Co. 1928.
Martin, Bessie. *Desertion of Alabama Troops from the Confederate Army.* New York, NY: AMS Press, 1966.
Massey, Mary Elizabeth. *Ersatz in the Confederacy.* Columbia, SC: University of South Carolina Press, 1952.
McMillan, Malcolm C. *Alabama Confederate Reader.* University, AL: University of Alabama Press, 1863.
McMurry, Richard M. *John Bell Hood and the War for Southern Independence.* Lincoln, NB: University of Nebraska Press, 1992.
Medical and Surgical History of the Civil War. Wilmington, NC: Broadfoot Publishing Co., 1999.
Memorial Record of Alabama. Madison, WS: Brant and Fuller, 1893.
The Monroe Journal Centennial Edition, 1866-1966. Monroe County, AL: privately published, 1966.
Owen, Thomas A. *History of Alabama and Dictionary of Alabama Biography.* Spartanburg, SC: The Reprint Co., Publishers, 1978.
Pearce, George F. *Pensacola During the Civil War.* Gainesville, FL: University Press of Florida, 2000.
Rambo, William. *Service records of Veterans Buried at the Confederate Soldiers Home of Alabama.* Privately printed, 1992.
Thompson, Illene & Wilbur. *Journey to Egypt Station.* Privately printed, 1997.
Sifakis, Stewart. *Who Was Who in the Confederacy.* New York, NY: Facts on File, 1988.
Sword, Wiley. *Embrace an Angry Wind.* New York, NY: Harper Collins, 1991.

UDC, Georgia Division. *Confederate Graves Roster.* Privately printed, 1999.
War of the Rebellion: A Compilation of the Official Records of the Union and Confederate Armies. Washington, DC: 1880-1902.
Watkins, Raymond W. *Deaths of Confederate Soldiers in Confederate Hospitals.* Meridian, MS: Lauderdale County Department of Archives and History, 1989.
Watkins, Raymond W. *Confederate Burials,* Volume II. Meridian, MS: Lauderdale County Department of Archives and History, 1992.
Weitz, Mark. *A Higher Duty.* Lincoln, NB: University of Nebraska Press, 2000.
Woodhead, Henry. *Echoes of Glory, Civil War Battle Atlas.* Alexandria, VA: Time-Life Books, 1996.
Woodsworth, Steven. *Jefferson Davis and His Generals.* Laurence, NE: University of Nebraska Press, 1990.
Zorn, William A. *Hold at All Hazards, The Story of the 29th Alabama Infantry Regiment.* Greenville, SC: A Press, 1987.

Articles
Brewer, Rev. George E. "Thomas Coke Bragg" *The Alabama Historical Quarterly,* Spring and Summer 1942.
"A Captured Letter." *Southern Bivouac* June 1886: 67.
"Col. H. P. Yarborough." *Montgomery Advertiser,* 1931.
"Confederate Soldiers Buried in the Old Cemetery." *Butler County Historical and Genealogical Society Quarterly,* March 1989:3.
"Confederate Veterans Reunion." *The Greenville Advocate,* Greenville, Alabama, March 10, 1897.
Crenshaw, Edward. "The Diary of Edward Crenshaw." *The Alabama Historical Quarterly,* Fall 1930:261.
"The Heirs of Anderson Seale." *Butler County Historical and Genealogical Society Quarterly,* April 1997: 27.
"The Independent American." *Pike County Civil War News,* Troy, Alabama, November 18, 1864.
Jones, Joseph. "Roster of Medical Officers of the Army of Tennessee." *Southern Historical Papers,* Book 22 (1894): 165.
"Letter written by Major Thomas Burnett." *Marietta, Georgia, Journal,* November 13, 1924.
"List of Deserters." *The Independent,* Gainesville, Alabama, September 5, 1863.
Pickett, Laura Kate. "Thomas Watts." *Confederate Veteran* XXXVII, 1929: 210-211.
"Registered Soldiers (Confederate Veterans)." *The Greenville Advocate,* Greenville, Alabama, July 11, 1906.

"Roster of Confederate Veterans Reunion at Greenville, Alabama, August 21, 1897." *The Living Truth*, Greenville, Alabama, August 21, 1897.
Seckler, Anne. "The Battle of Franklin." Publication unknown, November 1864.
Ward, Lewis Y. "From Montgomery to Durham Station: A Short History of the 17th Alabama Infantry Confederate States of America." *Montgomery Genealogical Society*, Spring 2000: 2.
Weathers, B. F. "War History of General Weathers." *Roanoke Leader*, Roanoke, Alabama, 1931.

Manuscripts

17th Alabama Infantry, Company H Muster Roll, December 1, 1863 – February 29, 1864. 17th Alabama Regiment, Box 9x, Alabama Archives, Montgomery, AL.
17th Alabama Muster Rolls. SG024896, Folder 21, Alabama Archives, Montgomery, AL.
17th Alabama Regiment Folder. Butler County Historical Society Research Room, Butler County Library, Greenville, AL
17th Alabama Regiment Muster Roll, June 30, 1862 – August 31, 1862. Shiloh National Park, Shiloh, TN
1907 Confederate Veterans. Survivors' Questionnaire. Alabama Archives, Montgomery, AL.
The Alabama 17th, Isaac Taylor Tichenor and a Sabbath Event. SG024895, Folder 11, Alabama Archives, Montgomery, AL.
Alabama Confederate Soldiers and Sailors Who Died as POWs. SG11134, SG11135, Alabama Archives, Montgomery, AL.
Bolling, John. Letters written to his wife from Tupelo, Mississippi, June 9 and 13, 1862. Duke University, Rare book, Manuscript and Special Collection, Durham, NC.
Bray, Henry. Letters, written to his mother from Florida, January 29 and February 19, 1862. Transcribed and edited by W. Mark Anderson. Folder 7N Box 26, Alabama Archives, Montgomery, AL.
Bray, Henry. Letter, written to his brother from Corinth, Mississippi, May 17, 1862. Transcribed and edited by W. Mark Anderson. Folder 7N Box 26, Alabama Archives, Montgomery, AL.
Bray, Henry. Letters, written to his mother from Tupelo, Mississippi, June 13 and 23 and July 3, 1862. Transcribed and edited by W. Mark Anderson. Folder 7N Box 26, Alabama Archives, Montgomery, AL.
Bray, Henry. Letter, written to his mother from Mobile, November 4, 1862. Transcribed and edited by W. Mark Anderson. Folder 7N Box 26, Alabama Archives, Montgomery, AL.

BIBLIOGRAPHY

Burnett, Thomas Jefferson. Letters, written to his wife from Corinth, Mississippi, March 23 and May 20, 1862. Pearce Civil War Collection, Navarro College, Corsicana, TX.

Burnett, Thomas Jefferson. Letters, written to his wife from Mobile, Alabama, October 4, 1862. Pearce Civil War Collection, Navarro College, Corsicana, TX.

Burnett, Thomas Jefferson. Letters, written to his wife from Georgia, April 30, May 9, May 21, June 15, and June 18, 1864. Pearce Civil War Collection, Navarro College, Corsicana, TX.

Civil War and Reconstruction Casualties. SG11134 – SG11137, Alabama Archives, Montgomery, AL.

Civil War Folder. Butler County Historical Society Research Room, Butler County Library, Greenville, AL

Crenshaw, Edward. *The Battle of Shiloh,* "Report of Killed and Wounded, and Missing in the 17th Alabama Regiment commanded by Colonel R. C. Fariss in the Engagement of the 6th and 7th of April." SG024896, Folder 1, Alabama Archives, Montgomery, AL.

Croxton, Robert. Letter written to his brother July 31, 1864 from the Atlanta area. SG024896, Folder 1, Alabama Archives, Montgomery, AL.

Davison, James M. Letter written to Thomas M. Owen, November 4, 1905. SG024896, Alabama Archives, Montgomery, AL.

Dubose, John W. (1930). *History of Seventeenth Alabama Infantry.* SG024896, Folder 4, Alabama Archives, Montgomery, AL.

Family Folders. Butler County Historical Society Research Room, Butler County Library, Greenville, AL

Hospitals, Augusta, Georgia. SG11143, Folder 13, Alabama Archives, Montgomery, AL.

Hospitals, Columbus, Mississippi: Alabama Deaths. SG024896, Folder 8, Alabama Archives, Montgomery, AL.

"Letter from Jessie McQuigg to his sister, Sallie McQuigg." Tutwiler Collection, Birmingham Public Library, Birmingham, AL

List of Officers and Men of Company H, 17th Alabama. SG024896, Folder 3, Alabama Archives, Montgomery, AL.

Listing of Confederate Soldiers' (McGavock) Cemetery, Franklin, Tennessee. SG11134, SG11135, Alabama Archives, Montgomery, AL.

McGowin, Peter. Letters written to his wife from Mobile, June 14, and September 16, 1863. Source unknown.

McGowin, Peter. Letter written to his brothers from Mobile, December 10, 1863. Source unknown.

McMillan, Capt. W. W., Personal sketch. *Reminiscences of the War of 1861.* SG024896, Folder 5, Alabama Archives, Montgomery, AL.

Motherhead, F. I. Letter written to his cousin from City Hall Hospital, Macon, Georgia, July 23, 1864. SG024896, Folder 1, Alabama Archives, Montgomery, AL.

Murphy, Virgil S. *Diary, November 30 1864 – February 17, 1865.* University of North Carolina. Wilson Library, Chapel Hill, NC

Murphy, Virgil S. Letter written to his cousin from Rome, Georgia, April 27, 1864. Kennesaw Mountain National Park, Kennesaw Mountain, GA.

Murphy, Virgil S. Letter written to his cousin from Kennesaw Mountain, Georgia, June 21, 1864. Kennesaw Mountain National Park, Kennesaw Mountain, GA.

Murphy, Virgil S. Letter written to his cousin from Montgomery, Alabama, November 29, 1865. Kennesaw Mountain National Park, Kennesaw Mountain, GA.

Register of Sick and Wounded of the 17th Alabama Volunteers, handwritten. National Archives, Washington, D. C., 1907, filed as Chapter VIII, Vol. 5.

Robertson, Frank. Letters written to his wife from Mobile, Alabama, during 1863, and from Pascagoula, Mississippi and from Georgia in 1864. Private Collection.

Sanders, J. B. Papers. Mississippi State Archives, Jackson, MS.

Thompson, James Alford. Letters written to F. W. Crenshaw from Saltillo, Mississippi, July 20, 1862, and from Mobile, March 15 and May 26, 1863. Originals in possession of Crenshaw Family, Greenville, AL

Thompson, James Alford. Letters written to his wife, Mary, from Mobile December 6, 1862, and from Atlanta, August 24, 1864. Originals in possession of Thompson Family, Greenville, AL

Tichenor, Rev. J. T. Letter written to Thomas Watts from Camp Watts near Corinth, Mississippi, April 18, 1862. SG024896, Folder 1, Alabama Archives, Montgomery, AL.

Watts, Thomas. "January 1862 Return, 17th Alabama." Shiloh National Park, Shiloh, TN, Unpublished.

Watts, Governor Thomas. Letters from Watts. SG24872, Reels 20-22, Alabama Archives, Montgomery, AL.

Wiggins, Thomas. Letter written to Thomas M. Owen, October 28, 1905. SG024896, Unnumbered folder, Director's Office: Correspondence, Alabama Archives, Montgomery, AL.

Microfilm

1921 Alabama Confederate Soldiers Census.

Compiled Service Records of Confederate Soldiers Who Served in Organizations in Alabama.

INDEX

1

16th Alabama, 120
18th Alabama, 43
19th Alabama, 44
1st Alabama, 62, 120
1st Louisiana Regulars, 44

2

21st Alabama, 62, 65
26th Alabama, 62, 86, 88
27th Alabama, 120
29th Alabama, 62, 65, 70, 82, 88
2nd Texas, 44

3

33rd Alabama, 120
35th Alabama, 120
37th Mississippi, 65, 88, 89

4

45th Alabama, 120
49th Alabama, 120

5

55th Alabama, 120
57th Alabama, 120
5th Georgia, 38

9

9th Alabama, 44

A

Aaron: William, 13, 143
Able: J., 287
Aceman: J. M., 143
Ackerman, 143
Acree: Joseph S., 13
Acreman: G. M., 143

Adams: Abner, 373; Bunk, 373; D., 123, 287; Early, 373, 441; John, 143, 229; John B., 28; John W., 373; John Z., 143; Martin, 13; Robert B., 28, 373; Solomon, 13, 143; Stephen, 13, 143; Vincent, 143, 443
Addison: Abijah, 24; Abijah Minto, 287, 439; Moses B., 123, 287
Adison: M., 124, 373
Adkins: John F., 229, 437; John T., 19, 229; Rufus G., 229, 437, 447
Alabama and Florida RR, 61
Albea, 235; S. P., 341
Albright: Charles, 24, 287
Albritton: John, 29; John E., 397; P. L., 29; Pleasant L., 397
Alexander: Alexander, 287; Permelia, 230; W. A., 143; W. A. J., 123, 257; W. H., 229; William E., 143
Alford: H. J., 124; Hillard Judge, 373; J. R., 199, 446
Alfred. See Alford
Allen: J., 373, 397, 434; James, 373, 433; Jessie, 373; Noah, 397; Washington, 397
Altoona, 80, 95
Altoona Mountain, 80
Amason: C. O., 123, 287; W. F., 123, 287
Anderson: Brig. Gen. Patton, 44; Elijah, 287, 439; F. F., 123, 229; G. W., 124, 319; H., 199; J. H., 287; J. P., 319; Sarah, 402; W., 24, 144, 288, 431; W. D. S., 288; W. Sr., 288; William, 432, 433
Andress: Elizabeth, 341; G. D., 26; George D., 341; H. M., 51; Hugh, 433; Hugh M., 26; Hugh Mercer, 341; Isaac, 341; James, 51, 341, 433; Lt., 80; R. M., 26, 51, 58, 433, 440; Redden McCoy, 341; Stephen Decatur, 341; Stephen

Singleton, 341; W. R., 26; William Francis, 341; William R., 341
Andrews: Daniel W., 144; Marion J., 17; Wm., 288
Andsly: Benjamin T., 144
Ansbury: Frank, 257
Ansley: B. F., 373; J. C., 122, 169; J. H., 169; John A., 15; John S., 122, 169; Josiah, 169
Ansly, 144
Anthony: J. C., 124, 342
Arant: Calvin L., 122, 169; Elvin P., 15, 169; Frances, 189
Armer: W. M., 123, 288
Armstrong: Henry, 199; Max, 199, 436
Army of Pensacola, 38
Army of Tennessee, 66, 74, 75, 76, 86, 94, 99, 100, 101, 102, 103, 105, 113, 114, 115, 116, 117, 118, 119, 120, 121, 125
Army of the Cumberland, 75, 76, 82, 88, 100, 113
Army of the Ohio, 76, 102, 103, 105, 113
Arnett: Harriet Anne, 262
Arnold: M., 199; Thomas, 257, 432; Thos., 21
Ashworth: William M., 229
Atchinson: Theophilus, 17
Atkinson: Theophilus, 199
Austin: D. W., 319
Autrey: Arias, 144; Benjamin F., 169, 445; Elmo, 13
Avant: Wm., 144

B

Baas: B., 257
Bacon: John, 257
Bailey: Geo. W., 17; George M., 199; J. T., 199, 446; Julian L., 257; Patrick G., 257, 437; Wesley F., 24, 288, 447
Baird: Isaac R., 170
Baker: J. H., 24; J. N., 288; James, 288, 439; W. H., 21; W. H. H., 257
Baldwin: Jesse, 170

Balentine: Isaac, 19; Isack, 229
Bales: Newton, 123, 257
Ballard: John, 342, 440; John A., 29, 397, 434
Balt: Erasmus, 13
Baltzer: Daniel, 13
Banister: David, 229, 437; John J., 230; William M., 230, 437
Banks: Abner, 373; James, 434; James P., 144
Bannister: D. M., 230; J. J., 230
Barganier: Jesse, 397; Slater, 397; William J., 397, 449
Barker: Jesse, 124; Jesse M., 25, 319
Barley: J. T., 374
Barnes: A. J., 342; Daniel S., 257; J. N., 440; Jasper N., 342; Jethrow, 200; Julius, 170; Michael H., 397; Robert J., 342; Thomas J., 342, 448
Barnett: Frances M., 258; James S., 374; Joe, 55; John B., 19, 230; Joseph F., 374; R., 258
Barrett: Andrew J., 397, 449; J. R., 170; Melvin T., 15, 170; Ruffin, 170; T. J., 16, 18, 170; T. M., 170; Thomas V., 258; Thos. D., 20; William R., 170
Barrington: William W., 397; Willis, 398
Barton: Enoch, 21, 258; M. C., 170
Baseley: Anderson, 342
Baskin: John, 374
Baswell: James, 171
Bates: Rachel Elizabeth, 410
Baton: J. C., 319
Battle: E. C., 144
Baxley: Jesse, 342
Bay Shore Battery, 63
Bayles: W. J., 440; Wash J., 342
Beadlescomb: W., 343
Beasley: Sophronia, 183
Beauregard, 49, 50, 53, 59, 99, 114, 115, 118, 119; P. G. T., 42; Pierre G., 95
Bedgood: John, 398; Richmond, 258; Samuel, 398
Beesley: Abraham, 435; Abram, 170

INDEX 459

Begood: Samuel, 442
Belcher, 83, 243; E. M., 343
Bell: J. E., 258; Jere, 200, 436
Bellah: JOhn, 258
Belton: Sol. D., 200
Benefield: Caleb Cox, 123, 258, 447
Bennett: G. H., 123; G. M., 230; Jeremiah, 29, 398
Bensley: Elizabeth, 181, 356
Benson: J. R., 4; James R., 9; William C., 398, 442
Benton: G. B., 319; W. F., 258
Berry: F. M., 200; William, 200
Bethel Station, TN, 39, 43
Beverly: Mary Elizabeth, 385
Bibb: Caroline, 402
Bicker: R. A., 374
Bickerson: R., 374
Bickerstaff: R. J., 374
Bickerstall: R. A., 124, 374
Big Shanty, 95
Biggs: Tulley, 443; Tulley J., 343; W. J., 26, 124; William J., 343
Billings: Jethro, 440; Jethro W., 343
Bishop: Columbus F., 15; Columbus T., 171
Black: Ezekiel, 398, 449; F. M., 398; J., 200; J. W., 444; James, 26, 343, 433; James A., 171; James H., 15; Jas., 51; Jno. M., 26; John, 26; John C., 398; John W., 343, 440; Joseph, 449; joseph S., 398; Robert W., 399; William H., 171, 435; Wm. H., 15
Blackman: Chapman, 15, 171, 435; George W., 29, 399; Hardy, 29; Hardy J., 399
Blair: Frank P., 97; G. M., 123, 288; J. W., 21; Jasper, 122, 171; John W., 258; Nancy, 260
Blankenship: Abner J., 19, 230; Eli, 144, 435, 445
Blaum: Stephen, 288
Block: Abraham, 288, 447
Blount: B. F., 3, 9; C. W., 24, 288, 447
Bloxam: H. C., 26, 344
Blunt, 289

Blythe: M. M., 289
Boan: Frederick, 29; Frederick S., 399; Samuel S., 399
Boatwright: pat, 399
Bobiford: J., 289
Bobo: F., 200
Bock: F. R., 24; F. R. W., 289
Bodeford: Stephen, 13
Bodiford: Alex, 435; Alexander, 144; Aley, 144; Isham, 144; Israel, 344; John Jasper, 145; William Preston, 145
Bodright: P., 200
Bofinger: George, 289, 439
Boggs: Isah, 200
Boggus: Henry J., 17, 200; James Carter, 200
Bohamon: R. B., 259
Bohanan: James, 123; W. R., 123, 259
Bohannan: James, 258, 437, 438; R. R., 259; Robert K., 259
Bolan: Michael J., 9
Boland: J., 344
Bolin: John A., 374
Bolling: Jno., 58; John, 7, 12, 17, 18, 446; John A., 54, 55; John Jr., 201
Bone: John, 374
Bones: Jno. S., 58; John Samuel, 28, 374, 441
Bonham: James T., 447; James Thomas, 289
Bonnell: Andrew J., 29
Bonnett: Andrew J., 399
Boon: Jere, 319; John, 344, 440
Boonsville, Mississippi, 6, 54, 58
Booth: W. K., 344
Boothe: W. D., 123, 289
Boswell: T. J., 123, 230
Boutwell: William Arnold, 145; William. Arnold, 13
Bowden: J. S., 122, 171; S. F., 289
Boyd: Elias, 21; Elias M., 259; J. M., 123, 289
Boykin: D. S., 289, 291
Boyle: Jackson, 374
Boyles: W. J., 26
Bozeman: Walter, 122, 145, 443

Bradbury: J. W., 26, 344, 441
Bradford: J. F., 289; T. H., 201
Bradlescomb, 343
Bradley: William E., 201
Bradly: John, 344
Brady: J. A., 374; James A., 374;
  William, 344; William R., 374,
  441
Bragg, 18; Braxton, 5, 11, 14, 16, 33,
  34, 38, 75; Capt., 4; General, 52,
  58; T. C., 20, 230; Thomas C., 19
Branch: Noah, 146
Brantley: John H., 259
Brassill: George, 289
Braswell: William, 435; Wm., 15
Braswill: William, 171
Bray: Henry, 24, 38, 52, 56, 67, 68,
  123, 289, 439; Private, 63
Braydon: William E., 201, 446
Brazeal: Frances M., 259; James K.
  P., 259
Braziel: James P., 21
Brent: Joseph, 15, 171; W. T., 26,
  344, 444
Brewer: Judson, 171
Briant: C. G., 230; Cyrus E., 97; J.
  G., 230
Briggs: L. E., 399; Tulley, 343
Bright: J. C., 13, 146; J. L., 58
Brinkley: John, 399, 442
Bristoe: J. H., 375
Bristow: J. N., 375; James W., 124,
  375
Britleing: A., 345
Broadnax: O. W., 290
Broadwater: T. J., 124
Broadwaters, 440; Thomas, 440;
  Thomas J., 25, 319
Broadway: Abner, 290; J., 290; W.
  H., 290, 439
Brooks: John T., 146; L. M., 444;
  Leonard M., 201, 446; Samuel E.,
  172; Samuel W., 375; Thomas J.,
  146; W. F., 172; William R., 399;
  Wm. F., 15
Brown: A., 123, 231; A. D., 259;
  Colonel, 34, 35, 36; Enoch F., 124,
  375; H. G., 201; J. A., 201; J. N.,

345; Jackson, 319; John, 146, 345,
  431, 435; John R., 13, 146; John
  W., 375; Joseph, 146, 435; N. B.,
  26; N. F., 290; N. R., 345, 448; O.
  F., 290, 439; Thomas, 319;
  William J., 345
Browning: William, 375
Broxton: George W., 146
Brudberry: M., 345
Brumby: T. P. G., 28, 375
Brumley: Elias S., 290
Bruner: Anne, 157; J. D., 123; J. W.,
  231; Margaret E., 162; Suvilla,
  157
Bryant: Jane, 297; John D., 231; John
  L., 231; Lt., 57; W. S., 124, 320;
  William, 19, 231, 432; William H.,
  290; Zac, 231, 437
Bryon: W. M., 259
Buck: George W., 146; J. K., 146; J.
  W., 345; James, 146, 435; T. W.,
  146
Buckelew: James, 231, 447;
  Josephus, 290
Buckley: D. J., 290, 433
Buckman: george, 399
Buckner, 62; Leonard, 290; S. B., 64
Buell: Don Carlos, 42
Buffington: A. E., 122; Alfred E.,
  146; George J., 172; James R.,
  399, 442; S. E., 146; T. P., 122;
  Thomas P., 147
Buist: James, 201
Bullard: Edward H., 290, 439; G. H.,
  291; Henry M., 291, 448; John A.,
  399
Bullington: James O., 320, 440
Bunkley: B. J., 124; Burrell J,, 399;
  Burrell J., 445; J. R., 400
Burch: Josiah, 291
Burgess: Susan, 264
Burk: James S., 231; William L., 231
Burke: J., 400; James D., 231; John,
  400; P. J., 29, 400
Burks: Columbus A., 201
Burnett, 58; Capt., 38, 91; Captain,
  53; J. R., 447; Major, 6, 77, 79, 84,
  91, 95; O. S., 26; Oliver S., 345,

INDEX

448; T. J., 4, 31; Thomas J., 6, 12, 17, 29, 30, 44, 72, 88, 400, 442
Burney: W. T., 345
Burns: Edward, 291
Bursen: David J., 259
Burson: David J., 21
Burton: Benjamin F., 17; G. D., 320; M. A., 291; R. J., 320
Bush: John B., 231; W. M., 259
Bussey: J. C., 25; J. M., 320, 433; James, 25; James C., 320
Butler: Augustus, 259; Thomas, 24, 291

C

Caffey: Alberto H., 231; E. C., 123, 291; W. V., 123, 291
Caigle: N. H., 232
Call: Hugh, 292; J. W., 291; Sergeant, 57
Callagy: Paul, 291
Callaway: Henry H., 147; J. W., 232; Joseph W., 19
Calle: Cornelius, 320, 328
Calvin: D. K., 147; DeVan, 147
Calvin Kraker, 347
Camp: Isaiah C., 259; Izah C., 21
Camp Cantey, 69
Camp Forney, 63, 67
Camp Gladden, 38
Campbell: A., 345; A. B., 345; A. S., 345; Charles, 345; J. K., 345; W. J., 345; William Bishop, 291
Canady: William, 13
Candler: Elizabeth, 321
Cannon: Abraham, 172; W. S., 147
Cansey, 232
Cantey: General, 65, 77; James, 6, 11, 62, 99
Cantey's Brigade, 62, 65, 74, 77, 78, 79, 82, 84, 86, 87, 88, 90, 99, 103
Cany: John O., 147
Capell: Rebecca Ann, 367
Caple: William L., 202
Cararthan: Joseph, 431
Carathan: George B., 172; Joseph, 172, 445

Carbo: W. M., 320
Carden: William T., 320, 433; William. T., 25
Carey: John, 291
Carley: J., 320
Carlisle: J. B., 232; M. J., 321; Robert, 232; Robert k., 375; Thomas, 433; Thomas J., 441; Thomas J. J., 375; William I., 375
Carman: D. A., 232
Carnes: J. F., 147
Carnethan: Joseph, 15
Carony: Green B., 19
Carr: J., 291; Patrick, 345
Carter: A. W., 202; C. M., 26; Charles Newton, 346; J., 26; James, 346; James W., 124
Caruthers: William W., 260
Cassells: G. H., 123
Cassels: G. H., 260; Henry T., 260, 438; Mark, 260
Cassettes: J. C., 260
Cassidy: J. L., 124, 321
Cassils, 260
Cassville, 78, 80
Castlebury: J. W. P., 172
Castles, 260
Cater: Josiah, 17, 202
Cates: Lucinda, 239; N., 400
Caton: Alfred D., 15, 172
Causey: G. B., 232, 432; J. W., 147, 232
Cavine: George B., 400, 449
Cawthron: G. W., 147
Cedartown, 95
Chadwick: Ambrose, 448; Ambrose H., 321; Augustus, 25, 321; John L., 25, 124, 321; R., 321; R. K., 321; Rickerson, 25, 321; Rufus N,, 124; Rufus N., 321
Chambers: John E., 202, 446; William F., 202, 446
Champion: F. M., 291, 433; H. M., 24, 123, 291, 433
Chancellor: Mary Anne, 225
Channel: G. W., 232
Chappell: Abram, 25, 321; John H., 322; W. J., 322

Cheap: Randolph, 292
Cheatham: D. H., 122, 202; James, 28, 124, 375, 441; John, 29; John H., 400; W. A., 446; William Alexander, 202; William F., 400
Cheek: Randolph, 292
Childers: E. A., 322
Chisholm: Margaret, 346; Neal H., 346, 441
Christian: William H., 232; William T., 376
Christy: James, 292
Clark: J. P., 322; James R., 172, 435; James T., 29, 401; Richard, 322; William H., 260
Clarke: John, 147
Cleeman: William, 13
Cleghorn: Henry S., 29, 401; Jno., 401; Samuel O., 401
Clements: W. H., 29, 401
Clesby: S., 232
Clisby: Saml H., 232; Samuel, 437; Stephen, 232
Clorr: John, 401, 434
Clow: John, 31
Cluman: William, 147
Cluss: George, 292
Clyatt: Thomas H., 232
Clyett: S. H., 232
Coatney: William, 401; William R., 29
Cobstead: Azberry, 402
Cocheran: F. G., 147
Cocherel: J. W., 147
Cochran: George Washington, 147
Codey: W. V., 401
Cody: C. J., 58; Columbus, 29, 449; Columbus J., 442; Columbus Jefferson, 401; Jackson V. B., 401; Jackson V. P., 29
Cogburn: Jesse M., 28; Jesse T., 376
Coker: William P., 124, 401
Colb: Hugh, 292
Coleman: Benjamin A., 402; Charles, 15, 172; Francis M., 376; Geo. T., 15; George, 445; George T., 173; J., 346; J. R., 173; James, 202; Jesse, 15, 173, 435, 445; Jospeh,
346; Walter, 29, 402, 442; Walter Leak, 402
Coley: J., 147
Coll: Hugh, 24, 292
Collier: C., 19; Jugertha E., 232; Squire T., 20, 260; Thomas, 260
Collins: A. M., 4, 27; A. Marion, 28, 376; Jeremiah, 24, 292; Leah, 356
Coltin: Whitman, 13
Columbus, MS, 54, 59
Colvin: D. K., 147
Combey: Anderson D., 376, 441, 448; Andrew, 376
Combie: Charles, 376
Combs: John J., 260
Company A, 13, 14, 62, 71, 122
Company B, 15, 62, 72, 122
Company C, 17, 54, 67, 111, 122
Company D, 18, 123
Company E, 36, 71, 123
Company F, 38, 67, 68, 89, 102, 123
Company G, 24, 71, 124
Company H, 35, 63, 65, 71, 80, 99, 104, 124, 125
Company I, 37, 68, 124
Company K, 37, 62, 71, 124
Cone: F. S., 31
Conger: R. F., 123, 292
Conn: W. G., 260
Connell: Dennis, 292; John, 346
Connelly: John, 202
Conner: David A., 233; James, 233; John, 346; William H., 17, 202; William J., 437; William S., 233
Connolly: John, 346
Connor: David, 432; George, 173; William H., 432
Conway: John, 173
Cook: J. D., 173; James Russell, 173; O. H., 439; O. H. P., 292; Serena, 183; W. F., 233, 402; W. M., 123, 292; Wiley, 233; Wiley H., 437, 447
Cooley: Jno. S., 233
Cooper: John G., 123, 260, 438
Copeland: Joseph A., 376; Mrs. W. R., 385; Thomas, 432; Thomas J.,

INDEX 463

21, 261; William C., 261; Wm. C., 21
Cordle: N. C., 293; W. C., 293
Corinth, 39, 41, 42, 43, 44, 45, 47, 50, 51, 52, 53, 54, 55, 56, 59
Corley: Andrew B., 202; Benjamin, 233
Cornathan: George, 122, 203, 436
Corprell: Charles, 234
Cotrell: Y. J., 148; Young A., 13
Cottingham: Alex H., 148; James W., 148
Cotton: Eldred M., 148; Whitman, 148
Courtney: B. F., 123, 293; S. J., 123, 293
Covington: W. T., 322
Cowden: R. L., 293; W. D., 293
Cowles: A. D., 148; F. A., 148; Thomas, 13
Cowley: John T., 293, 433
Cox: Elizabeth, 324; James A., 123, 234; Odom, 203
Craig: J. M., 346; John N., 293
Craker: Calvin, 347
Crawford: Francis M., 261; Robert L., 402
Creach: Sidney, 203; Sidney S., 17, 446
Creech: Francis L., 446; Francis Lafayette, 203
Crenshaw, 44, 48, 51, 57; Edward, 29, 31, 44, 58, 63, 66, 402; F. W., 57, 67; Howell, 173; James, 25; James E., 322; Lt., 37, 47, 50, 57; Walter Henry, 402
Cretrett: J. C., 148
Crew: William C., 19, 234, 432
Crook: Alabama, 366
Cross: Permelia Lee, 425
Croxton: Elijah Minter, 293; R. A., 444; Robert, 92; Robert A., 24, 293
Crumpter: Paschal A., 19, 234
Cubstead: Azbury, 29; John, 29, 402; John W., 173
Cullens: George W., 20
Cullins: G. W., 261

Cumbey: Anderson, 376
Cumbie: J. T., 123, 293; W. A., 123, 293; W. B., 123, 294
Cummings: G., 64; James S., 261; S. J., 4, 26; Samuel, 26, 52; Samuel J., 8; Samuel James, 322; Samuel McL., 347; Susan, 347; William W., 261
Cummins: J. L., 234
Cunningham: Hillary, 445; Hillery, 442; Hillery H., 402; W. R., 203
Curry: W. H. H., 376

D

Dabney: G. A., 261, 432; Garlin, 21; James L., 261; John T., 261
Daggett: George A., 347
Dailey: Jacob, 347; James T., 347; Wm., 294
Daily: Fielding, 444; Fielding Straughn, 347; John Hill, 347; S. F., 124, 347
Dalton, GA, 76, 79, 80, 95, 96
Damper: Elija, 203
Danagan: James, 234
Danas: J. W., 347
Dandy: W., 294
Daniel: Edward N., 261; Elizabeth, 184; Frederick, 29; Frederick F., 402, 445; John M., 347; N., 347; Newton, 21, 261, 438; R., 347
Daniels: E. W., 261; George M., 261
Darden, 235; William W., 123, 437
Davidson: J. S., 122, 204; T. F., 13, 148
Davis: Alfred, 17; Anson L., 376; Bradley D., 173; D. D., 294, 448; David, 408; David L., 21, 261; Francis, 403, 449; Harriet Allis, 216; Isaiah, 204, 436; James, 347; James D., 25, 322; James M., 13; James Madison, 148; James T., 148, 443; Jasper Horrie, 174; Jno. T., 348, 441; John H., 261, 438; John R., 348, 441; John W., 15; Joseph, 149, 435; Joseph G., 122; Joseph Greene, 13; Joseph I., 149;

Joseph L., 149; Joseph T., 13;
Lewis, 174; R. C., 149; R. G., 204;
R. J., 204; R. L., 294, 376, 448; R.
M., 377; Ransom, 431, 445;
Ransom L., 149; Robert F., 149,
443; Sam, 174, 443
Davison, 107; Elizabeth, 341; J. N.,
26, 348, 441; James M., 26, 106,
131, 137; James Miller, 348, 441,
445; John, 322; Martha, 322;
Mary, 367; W. M., 26, 348;
William, 348
Day: B. F., 149; James A. W., 149;
James F., 149; William B., 149
Deal: J. F., 174; James, 15; William,
431; William J., 174
Dean: C. B., 323; J. M., 13; James,
348; James R., 149; Jeremiah, 441;
Jeremiah J., 348; Margaret, 324;
R., 13; Sumter, 149, 445
Deane, John J., 174
Deans: J. J., 234; Jeptha J., 174; John
J., 174, 435; John Jefferson, 234
Deason: C., 294; W. M., 26, 348
Decken: William, 174, 445
Deen: Capt., 4; Jeptha, 15, 16; Wm.
K., 15
Deens: J. J., 234; John J., 174;
William H., 174, 446
Dees: Abner, 349; C. T., 441; J. H.,
122, 175; Jewell, 349; Joel, 349,
448; John L., 323; Joseph, 349; W.
R., 175
Deese: C. H., 26; C. T., 349
Defee: William C., 403; William T.,
29
Defraites: John, 149
Deloney: William, 403
Demony: A., 294
Dempsey: S., 433; Stephen, 294
Dendy: Buford, 436; Buford W., 17,
204, 446; Lawson, 122, 204; W.,
294; William M., 262; William S.,
262
Denis: J. J., 175
Dennis: J. N., 349; J. U., 349;
Ogburn, 294
Denniston: John, 150

Densler: W. H., 349
Derden: Andrew, 235
desertion, 73, 88, 90, 134
DeSoto, MS, 65
Dewberry: Thomas, 175; William,
29, 403, 434
Dewett: J. R., 323; William, 323
Dickens: Jas., 175; W. J., 175; Wm.,
175
Dickey: C. K., 123, 294
Dickson: John, 294
Dinsey: Stephen, 294
Dixon: J. R., 234
Dodge: Grenville M., 97
Dodson: George W., 204; James E.,
234; N. J., 204
Donaldson: A. W., 403; John W., 29,
403, 449; William H., 29
Donalson: E. R., 150; William H.,
403
Donnell: Cornelius, 294
Donnigan: G. T., 323
Dorman: Ephraim, 150; John A., 28,
377, 434
Dorson: George W., 204
Doster: J. N., 377
Doswell: Isaac, 377; W. J., 175, 435;
William, 377
Doughty: Sarah Permelia, 224
Dovroon: J. N., 91
Dowd: Samuel, 323
Dowdy: B. W., 58
Downing: James B., 377; Joseph T.,
28, 377
Downs: Joshua, 19, 234; Shelley, 19,
447; Shelley E., 234
Doyle: John, 294, 433
Dozewell: Thomas P., 377, 448
Draughon: Joel, 377
Driver: Allen J., 377; James M., 204,
446; John, 204; John W., 17
DuBose: John Witherspoon, 43, 44,
62
Dudley: J., 323
Duffie: W. G., 123, 234
Dugan: James, 17; James F., 205,
444

Duke: George H., 234; George W., 19
Dukes: James F., 17, 205
Dumas: Asa, 294, 439
Dunagin: G. S., 323
Duncan: G. W., 295; J. F., 349
Dunigan: J. T., 403
Dunklin: Turner, 31; W. T., 58, 175; William T., 29, 449; William Turner, 81, 403; Wm., 31
Dunn: Anthony W., 124; Anthony Wayne, 349, 441; John, 262, 438
Dunnegan: T. A., 323
Durden: Anderson, 234; Anderson J., 447; W. W., 29, 124, 403, 442; William W., 19; William Watson, 235
Dycke: S. H., 349
Dyer: J. B., 13, 150
Dyke: Lewis H., 349

E

Earnest: James, 17; James J., 205; John L., 262; Josiah, 262
Eason: John Clark, 235
East: Amelia, 341
Easterling: Celia Ann, 213; E., 235, 437; William B,, 122; William B., 175
Eddings: C. F., 150
Eddins: C. S., 377; F. M., 26; Francis, 350; Francis M., 445; J. B., 26; J. M., 350; John R., 350, 441; R. H., 26, 124, 350
Edgar: A., 175; Adams H., 15
Edings: C. T., 13
Edward: C. L., 123, 235; E. H., 323
Edwards: F. M., 150; John, 295; John W., 21, 262; Lyman C., 150, 445; Ransom W., 323; Samuel J., 262; T., 235, 437; W. J., 124, 377; William, 13, 122, 150
Elbern: Joseph, 440; Joseph W., 25, 323
Elder: James, 25, 323; Thomas, 324

Ellington: George W., 123, 262; Joseph, 404; Joseph M., 404; Rosanna Rebecca, 408
Elliot: A. M., 205; John, 324; M. L., 324
Ellis, 81; G. W., 324; Radford, 404, 442
Elrod: L. D., 350
Elton: Henry, 350, 448
Emmett: W. H., 350
English: Georgia, 347
Erving. See Ewing
Erwin: J. C., 350
Esom: James Marion, 235
Etheridge: Harrison, 21; Harrison P., 262
Eubanks: Jesse H., 15
Evans: Andrewson, 57; E. A., 24, 295; Lemuel, 150; T. J., 150; William, 324
Everdeen: J. W., 262, 438
Everton: Margaret, 238
Ewing: Jonathan, 175; Nancy Turner, 175; Samuel, 443; Samuel T., 175
Ezra Church, 24, 25, 77, 78, 90, 92, 97

F

Fabel: George P., 295
Faber: George B., 295
Fables: George, 295, 448
Fagan: Nicholas, 176
Fail: Boling, 176; H. W., 176
Fails: Irene, 212
Falee: Geo. B., 295
Fales: L., 205
Falk: James, 377; W. R., 377, 434
Falkenberry: David, 351; Dearon, 351, 441; Israel, 351
Falkner: Nancy, 178
Fannin: J. H., 295
Fariss: R. C., 4, 5; Robert C., 11
Farmington, 51
Farnell: Robert F., 351
Farrell: Robert, 295
Farris: Colonel, 52; Lieut. Col., 44; R. C., 3; Robert C., 43

Farrow: Maj., 44; Samuel, 404; W. G., 404
Faucett: Jesse, 262; Samuel, 262
Faulk: Robert, 378
Faulkenberry: D., 91
Faulkner: William J., 28, 378
Faust: Andrew J., 263, 447
Ferrill: J. W., 324
Ferris: James M., 150, 431
Ficklin: A. B., 404; Christopher, 404; E. B., 404; Joseph R., 404; Smylie, 404
Field: P., 263
Fields: Gabriel, 24, 295; Green B., 263; M. J., 150
Fife: John Henry, 404, 442
Fincher: Alex B., 21; Alvey B., 263; N. E., 123; Wiley, 263; Wiley E., 263; William, 21; William A., 263, 438
Finley: Emanuel, 324; G. W., 324
Finnell: Jesse M., 150
Fleming: John, 235; William J., 235, 447; Wm. J., 19
Flowers: Henry, 176; J. D., 205, 446
Floyd: E. H., 150; Robert A., 405
Fonville: James B., 150, 435
Foreville: J. B., 151
Forney: J. H., 64, John H., 11, 62
Forrest, 114, 116; Nathan Bedford, 50, 100
Forshee: Charles, 295, 378, 448; William, 295, 439
Fort: George W., 29, 405, 442
Fort Apalachee, 62
Fort Barrancas, 33, 34, 36, 39
Fort Gindrat, 68
Fort McRee, 33, 34, 35, 39
Fort Pickens, 33, 34, 35, 36
Fortner: Nancy, 178
Foshe: M. M., 296
Foster: H. S., 351; Hosey W., 15; J. M., 235; James M., 263, 438; Joel E., 235; John, 351; W. H., 351
Fountain: H. S., 26; Henry P., 351, 448; P. C., 26; W. H., 351
Fowler: O. D., 263; William A., 176, 446; Wm. A., 15

Franklin, 99, 102, 103, 104, 105, 107, 108, 110, 111, 112, 113, 114, 117, 118; B. J., 176; Wiley, 324
Free: William B., 176
Fronabager: John P., 405, 434
Frost: Henry, 17, 205; James, 205, 432, 446; Joseph, 206; Josiah, 17, 206; W. H., 206, 436
Fulton: Ann Elizabeth, 196
Furshee: Charles, 378

G

Gafford: Frances, 215; G. M., 405; James Milton, 405; Milton, 29; Richard H., 405; Thomas G., 17
Galaway: H. J., 123, 236
Gallaway: Walter C., 176
Galloway: C., 176; Eli, 15, 176, 431; Nathan, 405, 442
Gammon: E., 352
Gandy: G. L., 151; William, 176
Gant: G. T., 151; Martha, 274
Gantham: Jno., 176
Ganus: Thomas J., 206
Ganutt: E. T., 263
Gardner: John, 15, 176
Garlington: T. C., 378
Garnet, 264
Garrett: Henry, 16, 431; Henry C., 177; J. D., 177; James B., 177, 446; N. G., 446; N. J, 177; Nathan G., 16; Nathaniel G., 177; Thomas J., 122, 177; W. G., 177; William G., 177
Garrnett: Elbert T., 264
Gary, 236; Augustus S., 19
Gauntt: A. T., 151; D. F., 263; E. T., 123; Elisha L., 20; Elisha Luther, 263
Gay: Augustus S., 236; Stewart, 296, 439
Gayle: R. D., 352
Geeslin: Benjamin, 25; Benjamin F., 324
George: Emmett, 296
Gibson: D. M., 378; M. B., 151
Giddeus: Pickney, 352

Gill: J., 151; John, 14; Marion, 14; N. M., 324
Gillaland, 236
Gillelund: Wm., 19
Gillespie: J. M., 324
Gilliland, 236
Gillilond: William, 123, 236, 437
Gillmore: Albert M., 378; Joseph L., 378, 434
Gilmore: J. G., 378; James J., 378; James W., 378
Gingles: Harry S., 151, 435
Gladden: Adley Hogan, 35; Camp, 137; General, 44, 137
Gladden's Battery, 62
Gladden's Battery, 47
Gladden's Brigade, 38
Gleason: Cornelius, 296; E., 378
Glenn: John, 19
Glover: Alfred L., 236; J., 324; W. F., 324
Goff: Matthew, 25, 324, 440
Goines: J. C., 325
Going: John C., 325; T., 296
Golden: Emanuel, 405
Goldman: L., 352
Goldsmith: J. C., 122, 177
Golson: george, 405; George F., 29; James A., 124; James Augustus, 405; John C., 29, 406
Goodman: W. R., 151
Goodson: C., 206; Peter, 17, 206, 436
Goodwin: H. C., 378; Henry C., 151; J. D., 325; Jordan D., 296; M., 352; M. W., 14; W. C., 378; W. P., 352; W. R., 151, 352; Wiley, 151; William, 151
Gordon: J. J., 26, 352
Gore: Samuel, 29; Samuel J., 406, 442
Gowing: T., 352
Goynes: H., 123, 296; J. T., 123, 296
Grace: J. A., 124, 352; J. S., 325
Grachak: R. I., 151
Graham: J. S., 325; Thomas M., 236, 437, 444
Graibeck: Ripley J., 206

Grant: H. H., 378
Grantham: George, 177; John, 177; Thomas J., 177; Thos. J., 16; Wm., 16
Graves: J. H., 352; J. T., 352
Gray: Daniel, 28; Daniel J., 124, 378; J. J., 325; John C., 378; Riley, 325, 433; T. J., 25, 325; W. R., 325, 433
Grayden: Henry Sterling, 206; William A., 207, 436
Grayor: H. T., 24; Henry T., 296
Green: A. P., 352; B. R., 379, 441; D. I., 379; Doctor J., 151; Edward, 207; H. T., 296; J., 123, 296; James, 16, 178; Tandy H., 21, 264, 438; Thomas, 264; William S., 124, 379, 441
Greensboro, 119, 120, 121, 122, 124
Greer: W. S., 379
Gregg: James M., 151
Gregory: J. A., 123, 296
Gresham: Whitten R., 19, 236
Griffin: John B., 435; John H., 16, 178; Patrick, 296, 439; Samuel L., 178, 446; Waldo Y., 296
Grimmer: E. M., 123, 236
Grimsley: John P., 379
Griswold: Clemmons R., 16, 178; Frances, 189; Oba, 16; Obediah, 178
Grizzle: Frances, 189
Groce: Joshua J., 9, 236, 444
Guin: H. M., 236; William P., 325
Gullard: Martin, 296
Gulledge: A. J., 237; J. A., 237; W. A. J., 237
Gunn: J. T., 325
Gunt: Thomas J., 264
Gunter: E. A., 325
Guthrie: A. J., 379; Albert M., 28; Andrew C., 379, 448; Asbury, 379
Guthry: G. S., 264

H

Hadmond: James, 19
Haggins: H. C., 124, 325

Hagins: Benjamin, 178
Hagood: J. H., 297; J. M., 297; M.
  D., 297
Haiden: A., 379
Haigler: James, 406
Haines: Nathaniel, 353
Hairston: Sarah Ann, 258
Hale: George, 28; George W., 379;
  John, 380, 434
Halfrin: Thomas, 439
Hall: Benton, 207; G. M., 297; G. S.,
  325; George T., 353, 441, 448;
  George Washington, 297; H. P.,
  24, 439; Hardy R., 297; J. A., 297;
  J. M., 297; James, 28; James C.,
  380, 441; John A., 178; John
  Wilson, 297; M. H., 152; Marshall,
  14; R., 380; R. C., 353; Sarah,
  297; Wilson West, 297
Hallford: Julius, 178
Halprin: Thomas, 297
Halso: J. A., 297; John William, 123,
  297; Stephen, 16, 298, 439
Hambrick: F. A., 13, 14, 58, 152;
  John F. N., 16
Hamer: D. P., 237
Hames: J. Z. T., 264; Joshua, 264,
  447
Hamilton: James A., 380
Hammock: T. J., 237; W. T., 237
Hammond: James B., 237
Hammonds: Henry W., 406; Hewitt,
  406; Jerry W., 406; Wylie, 28,
  434, 441; Wylie H., 29, 380, 406,
  442
Hamner: E. C., 325
Hamric: John F. M., 178, 443
Hamrick: George H., 178; J. M. F.,
  178
Hamson: S. C., 152
Hancock: H. J., 325
Hanella: F., 353
Hanny: D. J., 237
Harbrock: A. T., 353; John T., 353
Hardee: William F., 380
Harden: Allen, 28, 380; Elijah, 380;
  Henry, 380; Jacob, 380
Hardy: W. R., 178

Harmon: James B., 237, 447
Harper: Henry S., 17
Harrell: C. L., 58, 353; E. F., 353; F.
  E., 353; S. J., 353; Sam, 21;
  Samuel H., 123, 264
Harrington: H. M., 237
Harris: Elijah, 325; George, 152,
  435; J. A., 326; J. P., 124, 380;
  James, 353; James A., 123, 265;
  James F., 237; James M., 237;
  James Peter, 380; John F., 237;
  John T., 28, 381; Joseph A., 152;
  Nathaniel, 353; S. S., 57; Samuel,
  381; William J., 124; William T.,
  381, 434, 441, 445; William. J.,
  326
Harrison: Benjamin, 97; Daniel, 29,
  124, 406; George M., 406; J., 152,
  207; J. J. N., 29, 407, 434; James,
  29; James W., 406, 434; Jno., 58;
  John A., 17, 207, 436; John R.,
  207; Jonathan, 406; King S., 407,
  442; Levi, 29, 407, 442; Lt., 91;
  Martin, 24, 298; Moses, 17; Moses
  J., 208, 436, 444; Thomas E., 407;
  W., 407; William, 407, 442;
  Williamson, 208
Harroll: C. S., 353
Harston: Thomas M., 407
Hartley: Anderson C., 407; H. G., 13;
  Hiram G., 152, 435, 443; Joseph
  F., 298
Hartly: Green B., 152, 443
Hartnell: William, 178
Hartness: Robert E. H., 326
Harvel: U. N., 354; W. D., 124, 354
Harvill: Samuel, 29; Samuel T., 407;
  William, 29, 407
Hasting: John B., 407
Hastings: B. W., 408; Charles M.,
  407; Jeremiah, 407
Haston: Thomas, 409
Hatcher: W. J., 14; William J., 152,
  445
Hathorn: Hugh, 265
Hatley: F. M., 326
Hauser: J. H., 354

Hawkins: H. S., 14; Hanel S., 152; J. S., 153; James, 14; James A., 153; Joseph, 153; R. F., 14; Robert F., 153, 443; S. M., 153; Vansant, 153; Vincent Thomas, 153
Hawthorn: Hugh, 21; John R., 16
Hawthorne: John R., 178
Hayes: W. F., 326
Hayle: George W., 24, 433
Haynes: Henry C., 237
Hays: Geo., 179; George, 381; Mary, 225
Haystring: John B., 408
Head: A. F. I., 381; Adolphus M., 28, 381, 442; Oliver J., 208, 381; Richard, 21, 265, 432, 438; Samuel, 21; Samuel J., 265, 438; W. S., 381; William, 382; William L., 28
Heard: A. J., 265; J. W., 122, 179
Hearn: W. A., 122; Warren F., 326
Heath: Benjamin W., 326; Emmanuel, 265; George, 153
Heaton: Frank M., 29, 408
Hefcoat: Daniel C., 409
Heinbaak: W. T., 153
Heldebrand: Vanburen, 123, 438
Heller: M., 237
Henderson: Isaiah H., 208; Isaiah P., 446; James A., 237; John H., 208; Josiah H., 17; W. E., 179, 238
Hendrick: Elijah W., 153; J. M., 179
Hendricks: Tapley, 208; Yapley, 17
Hendrix: James, 19; Jones, 238; William, 179
Henry: Hiram, 326
Herbert: R. L., 208
Hernden: William, 18, 208, 432
Hester: Abram, 238; Alfred L., 19, 437; Alfred Lafayette, 238; D., 208; Daniel E., 18; George F., 238; J. H., 265; Jeremiah, 21, 265; Jno. A., 58; John, 20, 266; John A., 19, 20, 238, 437; L. A., 436; Louis, 208; Louis A., 18
Hewry: J., 382
Hickman: H. W., 298; J. M., 124, 298, 382

Hicks: A. J., 123, 298
Highpins: William, 408
Hildebrand: Vanburen L., 266; William, 266
Hill: Charles, 382; J. J., 266
Hilton: Henry, 354, 441, 448
Hines: Thomas, 238; Thomas G., 19
Hinson: J. M., 354; John W., 354, 433; William C., 29, 408; Wm. C., 31
Hinton: T. A., 238
Hixon: Samuel, 354
Hochmeister: Fritz, 238
Hodge: Bennett, 123, 266, 438; David L., 179; Thomas P., 408, 443
Hodges: Bennett, 21; David L., 16; G. M., 179; James M., 21, 179, 266, 432; John A., 266; William, 123, 266, 438; William., 444
Hogan: George W., 28, 382, 442; M., 298; William, 28, 382, 448; Wyatt, 28, 382
Hohan: John, 355
Holcomb, 81; Milton, 154
Holcombe, 6, 58, 435; Capt., 49; E. P., 4, 13, 44; Edward P., 5, 14, 120, 122, 440; Lt. Col., 77, 80
Holder: A., 266; I. J., 267, 438; Jasper, 267, 444; John, 267; Jose D., 123; Jose Dempsey, 267; Joseph B., 267, 444; Theophilas, 438; Theophilas J., 267; Theophilus, 21
Holdn: J. E., 267, 438
Holfain: Thos., 58
Holiday: J. W., 355; Newtin, 14
Holiman: James W., 238
Holladay: W. J., 154
Holland: D. Furman, 449; David, 408; David J., 208; Davis, 298, 448; Davis Furman, 408; Gilbert G., 267; H., 209; J. H., 209, 432; Robert M., 19, 238
Holliday: A. F., 154; George W., 154; Nathan F., 154; Newton J., 154
Holliman: James H., 179, 444

Hollimond: James F., 239
Hollingshead: Eleanor, 144; J., 238; Moses, 239, 447
Hollingsworth: T., 21; Theopholas A., 267, 432
Holloday: H. F., 154
Holman: Caspers W., 408, 449
Homes: W. T., 239
Hood, 90, 93, 94, 95, 96, 99, 100, 101, 102, 103, 104, 105, 111, 112, 113, 114, 115, 116, 118, 119, 121; General, 93; John Bell, 12, 79, 87, 88, 89, 99; Onan A., 21; Oscar A., 267; Stephen W., 267
Horis: J. M., 239
Horn: Bright, 239; D. W. B., 239; G. L., 326
Hornback: W. F., 360; William F., 355, 441
Hornbeck: Pvt., 80
Hornesby: J. M., 21; James M., 267, 432; Noah D., 123, 268
Hornsby: Noah, 21
Hoskins: David R., 326
Houser: Frank H., 355
Hover: Henry J., 179
Howard: G. T., 355; Henry Malone, 154; John D., 18, 209; Mary Jane, 239; William L, 326
Howell: W. T., 123, 298
Hubbard: Laura, 301
Huddleson: J. S., 326
Huddleston: David F., 239, 268; T. M., 239, 437; Thomas, 134; William Berry, 239
Hudmon: James Neal, 239
Hudson: C. H., 179; F. C., 179; Francis M., 179; James, 155; Joseph, 155, 435; Pvt., 80; R., 326; T. J., 123, 268; William W., 179; Wm. W., 16
Huey: Joseph, 382
Huffman: A. J., 123, 298; B. H., 298
Huggins: James L., 29, 408; R. Bennett, 408; W. P., 327; William N., 409
Hughes: B., 240; D., 409; James, 355; Joseph, 355; N., 122, 179;
Singleton, 29; Singleton D., 409; W. F., 327; William, 155; William W., 29, 409, 443; Wilson, 409
Hughey: J. S., 355
Hughley: John A., 268
Hull: Joseph B., 19, 240; M. G., 240; Nathaniel, 19; Nathaniel G., 240; Thad, 240; W. D., 58; William D., 19, 240, 447
Hungerpillar: Rosana, 193
Hunt: Gilbert, 21, 268, 438; J. D., 327; John, 382; W. R., 327
Hurd: T. J., 155
Hurley: Michael, 155
Hurston: Thomas M., 409, 449
Huse: D., 124, 409
Hussey: John, 409
Hutchens: Henry, 21; J. D., 21
Hutchins: Henry H., 268, 432; James D., 268, 447
Hutchinson: Henry H., 268
Huton: James, 327
Hutson: Daniel, 155, 431
Hutto: James, 327

I

Imms: H., 298
Impressment, 5, 6, 73, 134
Ingram: Samuel, 240, 437; Samuel A., 19

J

Jackson: A. J., 155; B. F., 240; Brig. Gen., 47, 51; Geo. L., 15; George L., 180, 435; Hilrey, 240; J. S., 240; James T., 240, 447; Jno. K., 38, 43; John K., 11, 14; Joseph, 28; Joseph B., 124, 382, 442; M. S., 155; Stephen, 327, 440; W. L., 155; William, 327; William B. Jr., 209; William M., 240; William S., 155; Wm. M., 19
James: J. J., 327; William H., 180; William R., 298
Jay: James W., 18, 122, 209
Jenkins: A. E., 124, 355; D. S., 241; J. S., 9, 26; James S., 355; Jenkins

E., 124, 383; Ralph, 26; S. C., 35;
Samuel W., 241; W., 355;
William, 21
Jernigan: D. P., 180; J. P., 122;
William, 122, 180
John: Bradley P., 268
Porter, 332
Johns: John B., 180, 431, 435, 439
Johnson: Alfred, 383, 442; Daniel R.,
180; Geo. S., 16; George, 180;
Henry M., 25; Henry Mathews C.,
327; J., 209; J. A., 241; J. B., 58; J.
E., 436; J. F., 241; J. L., 241, 437;
James, 269; James H., 16, 18, 180;
Joseph, 355; Joseph S., 241; Julius
F., 18; L., 26, 355; L. S., 25, 327,
440; Lydall, 355; R. W., 25;
Robert, 21; Robert D., 269; Robert
Walker, 328; S. A., 26; Samuel A.,
19, 241; T. J., 299; Thomas, 241;
Walter, 440; Walter O., 328; Wm.,
241, 328, 383
Johnsten: Joseph, 241
Johnston, 49, 101, 241; A. S., 46;
Albert S., 41; Charles, 299; Enoch
G., 155; General, 78; J H.., 123; J.
H., 269; James D., 156; Joseph,
13; Joseph E., 76, 80, 82, 83, 86,
87, 88, 95, 119, 120, 121; Windon
T., 299
Joiner: Linsay, 409; Thomas B., 28,
383
Jolley: Henry M., 16
Jolly: Hardy, 180; J. C., 123, 241; J.
H., 123, 299
Jones: Charles C., 409; D. P., 156;
David P., 14; Elbert, 181, 356;
Elizabeth, 297; Char, 30; H., 299;
Isham, 180; J. B., 122, 209; J. P.,
52, 57; James Newton, 299, 439;
Jasper W., 299, 439; John, 355;
John E., 180; John William, 299,
439; Joseph S., 30, 409; Julius, 19,
241; Owen, 24, 299, 433, 439;
Seborn, 383, 442; Sol, 13; T. P.,
328; Theodore, 98; Thomas B., 16;
W., 156, 300; W. H., 180; W. K.,
300, 439; W. R., 3, 10; W. T., 300;
Wiley W., 355; William, 181, 300;
William A. A., 269; William K.,
300, 433; William R., 241, 444
Jonesboro, 78, 93
Jonyes: J. S., 241
Jordan: George W., 30, 409, 434;
Nathan, 181, 435; Thomas, 181
Jordon: J. M., 181; John F., 181
Jourdan: James M., 181
Judge: Thomas J., 22
Justice: A. T., 328; John, 328; John
Hartwell, 300

K

Kanne: John, 410, 443
Kaough: James, 156
Karr: John N., 300
Kaunne: Jno., 328
Kearley: A., 124, 356; T. J., 356
Keenum: George W., 356, 448
Keith: Daniel, 300
Kelley: Franklin, 156
Kelly: Andrew J., 18, 209; Edward,
300; J. H., 410; J. M., 122, 181;
James Polk, 328, 440; John, 356;
John H., 18; Thomas, 356; W. W.,
356
Kelsoe: Daniel, 181
Kendrick: J. H., 209; R., 122, 209;
S., 356
Kennedy: Benjamin F., 156; William
L., 156
Kennesaw Mountain, 14, 77, 78, 82,
84, 85, 86, 95
Kent: T. A., 209; T. J., 210
Kerbee: James D., 30, 410
Kern: Ludwig, 410; Simon Moses,
410, 443
Kerr: Newton J., 300
Kershratter: James, 241
Kettner: G., 123, 300
Keyes: John W., 10
Kidd: James, 356
Kilcrease: J. L., 356
Kilgore: James M., 300
Kilgrease: William, 328
Killcrease: J. S., 356

Killough: R. L., 356
Kimbro: J. B., 181; J. P., 181
Kimbrough: T. H., 241; Thomas. M., 19; William D., 181
Kincade: Wm. B., 19
King: Ellis, 156; James S., 156, 435; Jas. L., 14; John, 124, 383; Nancy, 350; Thomas, 31; Thomas C., 29, 410; William E., 156
Kinion: J. A., 123, 269
Kinkade: William B., 241, 437
Kinney: William, 269
Kinsey: Martin, 269
Kinyon: Austin Buress, 328
Kipper: A. S., 410
Kirbee, 410
Kirbo: M., 329
Kirby: T. N., 357
Kirkham: William L., 357
Kirkland: Calvin, 242; J., 242; N. M., 357
Kirksey: Isaac M., 182; William D., 16
Kirksy: Willis D., 181, 435
Kirpatrick: William M., 30, 410
Kirven: John F., 16
Kirvin: John F., 182, 431
Kitchens: John, 21
Kite: Bankston, 210
Knight: Emalina, 404; Lawrence S., 443; Lawrence Samson, 410; Samson L., 30; Thomas, 357, 445; Thomas Wilborn, 357; William, 410
Konkle: John, 242, 437
Krimmel: G., 300
Kuykendall: J. H., 122, 182; William D., 242

L

Lacoste: L., 242
Ladd: W. J., 357, 441
Lake: James M., 242, 437
Lancaster: John Austin, 383, 445; Lt., 58
Lane: Henry S., 242, 447; James M., 242; John H., 242, 447; Nancy, 191
Laney: Fielder, 383; George, 210; M. M., 329; S. F., 383; S. Thomas, 383, 442
Largo: Lafayette, 210
Larkins: J. S., 123, 301
Lary: LaFayette, 18, 210
Lassiter: W. D., 357
Lauderdale: J., 124, 410; J. S., 243, 444; John F., 242, 432; John T., 19
Lauderdale, MS, 59
Lawrence: D. S., 156; David S., 14; James M., 156; Jasper, 14, 156; Joseph, 157
Layton: Joseph, 301, 439
Leach: Richard, 14, 435; Richard F., 157
Leathers: James M., 383, 448
Lecroy: William D., 123, 243
Ledbetter: J. D., 301; James M., 19, 243
Lee: Geo. W., 15; George, 16; George W., 182; James L., 301; John D., 16, 182, 431; John H., 122, 123, 182, 243; Oliver, 14; Ollin Talbot B., 157, 435; S. M., 269, W. H., 14; W. H. C., 157; Wayne E., 301; William H., 269; William W., 19; Wm., 16; Zachariah, 410
Leflore: J. W., 182
Lehman: Rosina, 410
Leighton: Jas., 301
Leonard: B. F., 25, 329; G. F., 25, 329; Martin, 329
Leslie: Charles W., 182, 446
Lester: Eli, 410
Letlow: Andrew J., 243; Bulger, 19, 447; Bulger F., 243; Thomas B., 243, 447; Thos. B., 19
Lew: Z. E., 269
Lewis: A., 439; B. G., 123, 243; D. C., 243; D. J., 157; G. F., 243; H. H., 244; J., 301; James A., 157; James Allen, 301; James H., 244; Jas H., 19; John H., 16; M. P., 244;

Richard, 244; T. F., 26, 51; Thomas F., 357, 433; William Pinckney, 244, 432; Wm. P., 19
Leysath: Erskine, 30; Erskine J., 411
Lim: J. B., 182
Lindsay: Noah J., 244, 437
Lindsey: William M., 244
Linsey: William, 19
Lintern: H., 210
Littlejohn: W. B., 244
Living: W. J., 210
Livingston: Abraham Richard, 244; Richard, 244
Lloyd: C. C., 4, 8, 301; Cary C., 17
Loftin: J. W., 182
Logan: John A., 97; Major General, 97; Stewart H., 411
Lollis: James, 329; John, 25, 329; W. A., 25, 329
Lonally: James, 231, 234, 241, 245, 247, 251, 357
Lone Mountain, 83
Long: Henry J., 30, 411, 436, 443
Lord: Lewis M., 18
Lorroon: G., 244
Lost Mountain, 84, 95
Love: George, 434; George T., 384; S. A., 301; Thomas, 302
Lovett: Jas., 302; Joseph, 24, 302, 439; Pierce, 302
Lowery: George W., 210, 436; H. B., 210; J. H., 211, 446; James, 210; Mary, 218; R. B., 211; Thomas H., 211; Wiley, 211
Lowrie: Henry G., 329; W. W., 302
Lowry: Bruce, 329; L., 302; Wiley, 302
Lucas: Lorenzo, 244; William M., 245
Lucery: James, 329
Ludlow, 243
Lunsford: Blanton, 25; Blanton S., 329
Lynn: L. B., 183; L. D., 183; L. W., 444; N. B., 182, 245

M

Macon: William H., 245, 437; Wm. H., 19
MacRae: Patrick, 302
Madison: J. S., 329
Maher: Patrick, 302
Major: Daniel, 16; Jonathan, 183; L., 269
Majors: Benjamin, 183, 446; Daniel M., 183, 435; Henry, 30, 411, 434; J. D., 411, 434; James, 183, 435; James Cornelius, 183; John, 183; Jonathan, 184; Joseph, 184; Joseph, 435; S. J., 411; Samuel D., 30, 411; Susan, 183
Mall: J. J., 411
Manahan: Patrick, 357, 441
Maney: William, 122, 211
Manger: Jerry, 358
Manley: Ad, 269; Charles, 184; Charles J., 16, 435; Ellen, 263; Joseph, 184; Thomas A., 269, 438
Manning: Lucille, 400; Nancy, 350; Thomas, 302
Maoro: R. P., 245
Mapes: John W., 211, 432; William James, 211
Mapp: J. B., 330
Marlow: Daniel, 302, 439
Marshall: Elizabeth Jane, 364; W., 358
Martin: A. P., 330, 440; Alfred P., 330, 440; Henry, 302, 433; Isaac, 330; J. M., 303; James A., 411, 443; James L., 29, 124, 411, 445; John, 124, 330; John M., 30, 411, 449; Ransom V., 269; William J., 303, 448
Mash: David J., 211
Mason: Henry P., 245; James B., 245; L. B., 245
Massey: J. M., 358, 445
Mastin: Gas T., 157; Henry, 302; Peter B. Jr., 303; Z. T., 157
Mathew: John L., 16

Mathews: Cebelle, 398; John, 358; John L., 184; Mary M., 183; Simeon, 269
Matthews: Albert T., 24; Albert Timothy, 303; William J., 412
Mattox: B. P., 270; Benj., 21; J. C., 270
Maury: Dabney, 62; Dabney H., 11; General, 64, 65, 74; John, 270
Maxey: William, 122, 184, 435; Wm., 16
May: Seth S., 270
Mayer: Lewis, 330
Mayfield: B. W., 21; Battle W., 270, 438
Maynard: J., 358
Mayner, 358
Mayo: Elisha M., 19, 245; Louie, 21; Lovic W., 270
McCall: C. O., 245; J., 270; James B., 384
McCampbell: J., 123, 303
McCane: T. A., 31, 58; Thomas, 10, 30; Thomas A., 12, 29, 412, 434, 445
McCann: G. W., 303
McCarthy: Charles, 303
McCarver: George, 303; George W., 384
McCary: J. A., 330
McCaskell: F. R., 122, 184
McClentick: Robert, 303
McClure: George H., 184, 435
McCook: D. A., 123, 245
McCord: George, 157
McCormack: Ben, 303; John D., 18, 211
McCormick: D. B., 303
McCorvey: A. B., 26, 433; Neil, 51, 358, 433
McCorveys: A. B., 51, 358
McCorvy, 358
McCory: James R., 30, 412
McCoy: Susan, 341; William H., 412; William J. R., 30; Wm. J. R. W., 412
McCrae: Joseph, 303; W. W. L., 157

McCrary: John A., 18, 212; William H., 384, 442
McCree: W. W., 157
McCreight: J. O., 303; Robert A., 303, 448; W. Y., 304
McCullough: George, 245
McDanel: K., 123, 270
McDaniel: B. O., 384; Bailey H., 270; John, 358; Josiah, 123; Samuel, 123, 270
McDonald: Bailey H., 270; Josiah, 270
McDowell: Robert, 330
McElrath: James, 246
McEntyre: J. L., 157
McFerrin: James, 157; Martha, 162
McGentry: James, 304
McGintey: Thomas, 304
McGinty: Jas., 304
McGlennon: P. M. C., 304
McGowan: James, 384; Peter, 384
McGowin: Peter, 68, 69
McHugh: John, 24, 304
McIlrath, 246
McIntire: J. C., 185, 436; J. L., 58; J. M., 184; John N., 122, 184
McIntyre: J. L., 8, 25, 124, 330; J. N., 212
McKay: T. J., 304, 439, 449
McKelay: S. M., 246
McKellar: Felix G., 30, 412; James W., 412
McKey: T. J., 92, 444
McKilln: F. G., 384
McKinney: E. H., 124, 412
McKinsey: J. T., 122, 185; William, 122, 185
McLane: Henry A., 28, 385; James, 242; Sam A., 385
McLaurin: C., 58; J. M., 385
McLaurine: Christopher, 28, 385, 434, 442, 445
McLear: G. R., 385
McLellan: Charles W., 123, 304; George F., 212
McLeod: Angus M., 270; G. R., 385, 442; J. R., 385
McMahan: James, 358

INDEX

McMann: William, 304
McMillan, 26, 54, 63, 77, 79, 80, 83, 84, 91, 95, 96, 107; B. F., 26, 83; Benjamin, 445; Benjamin Franklin, 358; Captain, 10, 35, 37, 42, 45, 46, 47, 50, 51, 63, 65, 79, 90, 99, 104, 105, 107, 113, 117, 118; James G., 305; M. M., 362; Malcolm, 359; Mary, 365, 366; Mary J., 348; Murdock, 359; R. N.., 359; W. H., 91; W. H., 8, 26, 359, 441; W. W., 3, 7, 12, 25, 27, 58, 77, 126; William W., 359, 441, 445
McMillin: Charles B., 304, 439
McMillon: Charles, 24
McNair: A. H., 246; Daniel, 246, 432; John B., 19, 123, 246
McName: William, 305
McNeil: James N., 359, 441
McPhearson: J. W., 185
McPherin: Jas., 14
McPherson: Arnold, 185; J. W., 436
McQueen: George W., 157; Norman, 19; Norman L., 246
McQuester: E. A., 385
McQuirk: Thomas, 360
McShoe: William, 14
McShores: William, 158, 435
McTyire: W. C., 330
McTyre: W. C., 124
McVay: George, 330; Morgan, 386, 442, 448
McWaters: Francis A., 270; J. A., 271
McWhorter: Ezekiel A., 28, 386, 442; William, 386, 442
Meacham: Sophia, 264
Meadows: H., 386
Measles: J. A., 305
Meek: D. M., 433
Melton: J. P., 212
Memphis and Charleston Railroad, 100
Mercer: Alexander, 412, 449; Noah, 212; Seth, 212
Meredith: E. W., 30, 413, 434
Messenger: Sarah Odella, 230

Michell: C. W., 305
Mickle: Jerry, 271, 438
Mickler: W. C., 123, 305
Miller: Edward, 24; Edward C., 137, 305; Francis M., 271, 438; Henry, 386, 442; Isaiah G., 18, 212, 436; J. T., 212; T. J., 212; William Jackson, 271, 444; Wm. J., 21
Mills: Charles, 246, 447; R. B., 185
Milner: A. J., 8; W. J., 123, 305
Milton: Berryman, 212; Jacob C., 18, 212, 432; John F., 21, 123, 271; R. B., 213; William, 436, 446; William L., 213
Mims: Basil M., 185, 446
Mings: James W., 24, 305, 433, 439
Miniard: John, 16
Minoyard: John, 185
Minter: R. F., 271; R. J., 271
Mitchell: Luther C., 246; P. H., 246; Thomas H., 246, 444
Mizzels: Joseph, 246
Mobile, 39, 60, 61, 62, 63, 64, 66, 68, 69
Mobile and Ohio Railroad, 42, 43, 54, 57, 61, 63, 64, 65, 68, 100
Monahan, 358; Pvt., 80
Monfee: Francis, 24, 305, 439
Monk: James, 360; John Samuel, 247, 444; Joseph, 247; R., 305
Monroe: Benjamin P., 19
Montague: Henry, 330
Monterey, 45, 51
Montgomery: John, 305, 439, 444; John A., 122, 158
Moody: A. C., 305; W., 306
Moon: David N., 158, 431; J. G., 271; J. J. C., 213; John G., 21; John T., 386; Josiah, 271; Josiah F., 21; L. T., 271; Levi T., 21; Rolly, 271; W. L., 13; W. M., 3; William L., 8, 158
Moore: Allen, 185; Augustus W., 16, 185; Col. J. C., 44; Daniel, 158, 386, 431; J. G., 122, 185; James, 330; John, 387; W., 306; W. H., 24, 123, 439, 444; William J., 413, 443, 445

Moorer: Mancil R. P., 158; Mansin, 14
Moreland: Capt, 81; James, 8; James L., 58; James S., 17, 185, 436
Moreno: S. A., 57
Morfee: Monfee, 305
Morgan: Benjamin F., 413; F. M., 330; Frank M., 330; J. E., 213; J. W., 213; James W., 213, 436; John A., 213; Thomas, 213
Morison: S., 16
Morris: Jefferrison, 271; Jesse, 360, 441; John M., 16, 185; Lt. Colonel, 83; Preston A., 360; Sarah, 260; W. D., 360; W. F., 306; William L., 122, 185; Wm. J., 16
Morrison: John A., 158
Morrow: Abram S., 186
Morse: W. J., 413
Mortard: C., 331
Moseley: John, 434; John L., 30; Robert, 30, 413, 434; Sgt. Bob, 47; William, 122, 186, 306, 433; William H., 306, 433
Mosely: C. L., 186; John L., 413; Thomas J., 413
Mosley: Chapman L., 16; Ransom, 413
Mote: James, 25, 331
Motes: Bush W., 271
Mothershead: David B., 439; W. I., 89; W. Y., 306
Mothershed: David B., 306, 360
Mulkey: R. S., 272; Seaborn R., 413
Mullala: J., 124, 413
Mullaly, 247
Mullaney: William J., 247, 437, 444
Munchus: James W., 387
Munroe: Benjamin P., 247
Murphey: S. G., 158; V. S., 11, 12
Murphy: A. D., 414; B. F., 124, 387; Col., 78; Colonel, 58, 74, 77, 85, 86, 99; J. J., 360; James G., 14, 122, 158; Major, 44, 45; N. A., 360; Samuel P., 306; Sarah, 414; V. S., 3, 5, 52, 54, 66, 77, 83, 108; Virgil S., 77

Murray: James H., 124; James Henry, 360
Murry: Thomas, 272
Musgrove: John W. Jr., 247; John W. Sr., 247
Musslewhite: J. E., 123, 248
Mustin: William, 123, 306, 439
Myrick: John, 331

N

Naftel: Albert S., 306
Nail: R. H., 331
Napier: Luisiana, 245
Narton: William F., 258
Nashville, 99, 100, 101, 102, 103, 105, 107, 111, 112, 113, 114, 116, 117, 118
Navy Yard, 33, 35, 37, 39, 43
Nealy: Benja. C., 14
Neeley: John, 272
Neely: William C., 272
Nelson: W., 331
Nettles: Eliza Ann, 351; Polly, 341; W. T., 361
New Hope, 78, 80, 85, 95
Newberry: W. T., 26, 361, 441
Newell: James C., 272
Newman, 21; C. B., 158; John M., 272; Joseph C., 158; S. M., 159; S. N., 159; Samuel, 272; Seaborn, 272, 444; William, 159
Newton: Amos, 414; Benjamin Jaspar, 30, 414; T. E., 31; Thomas, 30; Thomas Edmund, 414; W. A., 414
Nicholas: Jasper P., 16; Shadrack, 18
Nichols: Christopher, 214, 436; J., 272; James, 186; Jasper N., 186; S., 214
Nixon: E. P., 331; Shaw, 272
Nordhausen: Adolph, 307, 448
Norman: W. R., 123, 307
Norred: Jasper, 272; Joshua, 21; Lewis O., 272; Rebecca, 143
Norris: A. F., 248; Alex F., 16; Alexander, 186, 446; B. L., 248; Esum, 15; John A., 30, 414; John

F., 15, 186; W. H., 186; William
A., 16, 186, 446
Norsworthy: L. L., 442; Lafayette L.,
387; William J., 414
Northcut: H. L., 214
Norwood: James M., 248; Jas. M., 19
Numan: William, 14

O

O'Bannonville, 38
O'Brian: R., 307, 439; Thomas S.,
307, 440
O'Brien: A. L., 4, 58; Andrew, 24,
49, 307, 440; Andrew L., 23;
Capt., 57, 91, 92; F. S., 307; M.,
361, 366; T. S., 58
O'Brien's Company, 63
O'Connor: E., 307, 433
O'Ferrel: J. W., 331
O'Ferrell: J.W., 25
O'Hara: Patrick, 307, 448
O'Neal: Edward, 7. ; Edward A., 12,
86, 88, 89, 91, 96
Odam: A., 414; John, 415, 449
Odiomi, 248
Odione: George, 361; W. W., 361,
441
Odioran: William W., 248
Odom: Alatha L., 414; L. S., 24, 30,
307, 415; William, 214
Ogburn: W. H., 248
Ogburne: Dennis, 307
Olden: James, 415, 448
Oliver: Celest, 359, 361; H. M., 248,
432
Ollman: Lewis, 308
Ordianne: G. H., 159
Osburn: John L., 21, 272
Otts: John, 331
Overton: H. G., 159
Owen, 24; Alfred, 273; Alphas D.,
273, 438; Alphus, 21; Hill, 308;
James, 24; James Madison, 308,
448; L. C., 159; Thomas, 24, 308;
Thomas F., 440; W. F., 248;
Wade, 14; William F., 273, 438

Owens: Henry, 159; Hugh, 159;
Miami J., 214, 446; Robert E.,
187, 436; Robert G., 16; Robert
Philip, 431, 444; Robert Phillip,
187; Wade, 159
Ozier: J. N., 124, 387; J. W., 387;
James E., 387; James N., 28;
James Uriah, 387, 442, 448; John,
387

P

Pace: D. C. M., 387; G. W., 214,
331; Joseph W., 214, 331; Russell
F., 122, 214; Thomas E., 18, 214;
William B., 18, 214, 446
Packer: Robert F., 159
Padgett: John, 28, 387
Painter: Robert, 331
Palland: T. B., 215
Palmer: A. L., 122, 187; H. G., 187;
H. J., 187; J., 415; John, 159; M.
B., 160; M. R., 160; R,, 187
Palmetto, 94, 95
Palmore: Jno., 160; John, 159; M. R.,
160
Pardue: G. H., 415
Parham: H. T., 308
Parish: Lyre, 388; Tyra, 388, 434;
William J., 388
Parker: Benjamin, 15, 17, 187, 436;
Gardner G., 18, 215, 436, 446;
Jesse, 331; John T., 15, 187, 446;
Lieut, 81; Lt., 80; Margaret, 190;
Martha Adaline, 420; W. W., 122,
215; Wm., 188, 436
Parmer, 187; J., 415; Mary Jane, 239;
R., 215; R. F., 122, 187; Senie
Vergilin, 239
Partin: J. R., 331
Pate: R. S., 21, 123, 273; Robert S.,
273; Samuel, 415; Thomas M.,
248, 447; Thos. M., 19; William
A., 19, 248
Patterson: E., 444; Emily, 404
Paul: William, 124, 332
Paylant: Andrew H., 19

Payne: Ira E., 18; Ira Ellis, 215; J. E.,
215; John, 31, 215; John K., 17;
John S., 188, 415; William J., 30,
415, 449
Peach: William F., 415
Peachtree Creek, 28, 78, 86, 88, 89
Peacock: J. A., 160; Jno. J., 14; John
A., 160; M., 160; Simon, 123, 248
Peagler: George W., 30, 416; Martin,
30; Martin G., 416
Pearson: D., 160; David, 160; James
H., 16, 188, 432; Philip, 388
Pebworth: T. J., 308
Peek: Benjamin F., 19
Pelew: J. R., 123, 248
Pennington: L., 248
Pensacola, 41, 42, 43, 44, 52, 59, 63,
64
Pentecost: L. M., 31, 58; Leonidas,
10, 29, 31, 124, 416, 443
Peoples: Benjamin, 248; J. A., 249,
437; John, 19, 249
Perdue: Alex, 416, 448; Foster, 416;
J. H., 215, 436; James, 416;
Lorenzo, 30, 416; Morris W., 160;
Payton, 416, 443; Tully, 416; W.
E., 417; Whitman, 14
Perkins: Martha, 181
Perry: Benjamin, 215, 446; James,
18, 216; John, 216; John T., 30,
417; M. F., 417; R., 26; Reuben,
362; Robert, 216; Robt., 17;
William, 216
Perryman: W. D., 4; Walter D., 17,
18, 54, 216
Peterson: Thomas, 446; Thomas A.,
216, 436; William R., 216, 446;
William T., 17
Pettis: Samuel, 123, 308
Pettry: D., 160
Petty: J. A. H., 216; James A. M., 18,
216
Phillips: John J., 332, 440, 448; John
W., 188, 436; W., 362
Philpot: S. W., 14
Philyaw: George W., 417, 443;
Thomas J., 18, 216
Pickenpack: E. J., 160

Pickens: W. A., 362, 417
Pickett: Jas. W., 19
Pierce: Frank M., 18, 217; Geo., 388;
John, 388, 442; R. W., 217; W. R.,
217
Pike: Thomas, 21, 273, 432
Pimell: C. C., 160
Pine Mountain, 84
Pinkett: J. W., 249
Pinto Island Battery, 62, 63
Pitman: Absolum, 217
Pittman: J. M., 273; J. W., 160;
Robert C., 16, 188; William, 188
Pitts: Adoniram, 388, 434, 442, 449;
David, 188; Davis W., 188; H. W.,
160; Harry, 362; Harvey E., 160;
Henry W., 14; John, 30, 417
Pittsburg Landing, 41, 42, 45, 46, 49,
50
Pizzala: Nicholas, 308, 433
Plunkett: J. C., 332
Pointer: Robert, 332
Polk: James K., 332; Leonidas, 11,
84
Pollard, 61, 63, 65, 66, 73, 77;
Daniel, 417; Everett, 217, 436;
Nathaniel, 417; T. B., 217;
William Daniel, 417, 449
Pomels: H., 309
Poodin: K. C., 388
Pool: A., 249; Fannie, 22; Robert C.,
273, 444
Poor: Newton M., 249
Poor-House, 90, 91
Porter: J., 388; J. R., 332; Joe Day,
25, 124, 332; John T., 25, 124;
Ross, 333; Tho. M. J., 16; Thomas
M. J., 188, 432, 444; W. M., 124,
333
Posey: George H., 217, 444
Potter: J. R., 388; Thomas F., 30,
417; William, 30, 417
Powell: Andrew, 249; D. M., 217;
Edmond J., 19; Edmund, 249;
Henry, 26; J., 249; J. W., 122, 189;
James F., 217; Jno. L., 58; John L.,
18, 122, 217, 436; William F.,
160; William H., 18, 218

Prater: William F., 388
Preddy: T. W., 333
Preston: J. E., 26, 362; W. H., 333
Prewitt: H. H., 124; H.. H., 417; J. W., 124, 417
Price: Frederick, 249; George J., 249; James, 388
Prickett: James W., 249, 437; W. F., 249, 444
Pridgeon: S. J., 160
Proctor: Nancy, 195
Pruett: George J., 250, 447; H. H., 250
Pruitt: C. C., 333, 448; Francis M., 333; Miles S., 124, 333, 440; Willaim T., 160
Puckett, 249
Purdey: J. H., 250
Pursewell: W. S., 333, 440
Pylant: A. H., 250

R

Radford, 362; George T., 309
Ragland: Capt., 91; Thomas, 4, 6, 23, 25, 333, 440; Thos., 4, 58
Raiford: L. H., 124, 362
Rainer: Joel, 28; Joel H., 388
Raines: J. H., 58; James, 125; Pvt., 80; T. H., 26; Thomas H., 362, 433, 441
Rainier: Joel H., 124, 434; John H., 29
Rains: James, 362; Thomas, 51
Rambo: John R., 16, 189, 436
Ramsay: James M., 189; Neal O., 18
Ramsey: James M., 16
Randbar: J. L., 161
Rany: B., 309
Rapshear: Sara, 266
Rasco: R. C. W., 363
Rawles: J. C., 250; J. P., 250
Rawls: C. L., 389; Oliver L., 28, 124; Oliver Lieke, 388, 442; William B., 250, 437; Wm. B., 19
Ray: Andrew, 124; Andrew J., 418; John, 418, 443; William, 432; William P., 274

Rayburn: Richard, 18
Ready: S. W., 124, 389
Reagan: Robert, 363
Redd: Joshua, 16, 189
Redfield: Syd, 418
Reed: B. F., 8, 20, 22, 274
Reese: Elizabeth Jane, 224; J. P., 309; W. N., 309
Reeves: C. W., 418; Jesse W., 418; William, 250
Register: Stephen W., 418
Reid: hillory, 418; Hillory, 30, 124; J. P., 333
Resaca, 14, 17, 78, 79, 80, 82, 95, 96
Reves, Wm., 19
Reynolds: McCode, 161
Reynoldson: John G., 363; John T., 363
Rhoades: William H., 274, 438
Rhodes: George w., 218; George W., 218, 446; J. A., 219; James W., 189, 436; John, 418; John D., 218; Newton N., 189
Rice: M., 58; M. J., 10; Wm. P., 21
Richardson: G. A., 333; Geo. J., 333; J. W., 363, 441; W. C., 250, 437; W. H., 26
Richberg: R. E., 309
Ridgell: W., 333
Riese, 251; Henry, 250
Rigsby: Benjamin, 189, 436; Noah, 189; Phil D., 189, 436; Philo D., 122
Riley: Elizabeth Parthenia, 341; George W., 418, 443, 445; Jeremiah, 363, 448; Lafayette R., 363; William, 123, 250
Riser: P., 363
Rison: F. A., 161
Rivers: Frank, 309
Rives: B. S., 26, 51, 363; J. H., 26, 51; John H., 363, 433; Pvt., 80
Roach: D. C., 418
Roark: R. H., 364
Robbins: Howell R., 250; Solomon E., 190, 436; Stephen, 418
Roberds: William R., 28, 124, 389

Roberson: Alfred B., 161, 435;
  Frank, 161; J. L., 122, 190; N. F.,
  122, 190
Roberts: A. F. E., 23; E. M., 26, 51,
  364, 433; F. G., 274; G. W., 364;
  J. D., 22; Robert, 333, 440; W. B.,
  389; William, 334; William P.,
  251; Y. W., 364
Roberts, William, 19
Robertson: A. F. E., 309, 433; Alfred
  B., 161; Andrew, 21; Andrew P.,
  438; Andrew Pickna, 274; Edward,
  309; Frank, 64, 69, 86, 274, 438;
  George, 274; J. D., 20; J. M., 23;
  James, 274; John, 309; John D.,
  274; John S., 389; Josiah, 19;
  William M., 251
Robinson: Alford, 13; Alfred B., 161;
  Archis, 309; F. C., 275; Frank,
  161; Joseph, 123; Joseph R., 274;
  Josiah, 251; N. J., 364, 441
Robison: Alfred B., 161; J. W., 275;
  Jesse, 364; Lt., 80, 83; N. J., 91; S.
  F. C., 275; W. J., 58, 125; William
  Jesse, 83, 364, 441, 445
Rodgers: Charles, 364; Edward, 334;
  H., 218; M. P., 334; Moses, 334;
  W., 218; William, 364
Rogers: Charles, 364; H. C., 365; J.
  H., 365; W., 218; William James,
  30, 418; Willis, 365
Roland: J. S., 334
Rolen: J. W., 365
Roller: A. J., 365
Rolling, 365
Rooney: Bernard, 309
Roper: V. B., 309
Roquemore: J. M., 334, 433
Rose: J. A., 219
Rothacker: Jacob, 365
Rotten: William O., 389
Roundtree: Adam Wainwright, 419;
  Atwright, 419
Rowell: R. N., 389
Rowlen: James Vincent, 365
Royal: Hardy A., 309, 448
Rozier: John L. B., 30, 419, 443

Rumbley: A., 108; H. M., 51, 334,
  365, 433; R. H., 365; Richard
  Henry, 365, 366; Thomas A., 83,
  124; Thomas Anson, 366
Rumbly, 26
Ruse: Henry, 251
Rush, 58; George W., 251; John B.,
  19; Warren R., 19, 251, 432
Rushton: B. M., 310; J. H., 123, 310;
  William H. P., 310, 448
Russell: C. F., 389; Charles H., 366;
  H. C., 366; Henry, 219; J. J., 389;
  Mose R., 251; Reuben, 389;
  Samuel Tines, 219, 436; T. J., 310
Rutherford: J. J., 366; Samuel, 123,
  251
Ryan: H. C., 275; John, 57

S

Sadler, 15; C. E., 13, 14, 58, 161,
  431; Lt., 47
Sadler's Company, 63
Salter: G. W., 26; George W., 366; J.
  C., 26; Simon, 26, 366
Saltillo, MS, 41, 57, 63
Samuel: N., 275
Sanders: David, 275, 438; J. B., 87,
  92, 94; James M., 275; Thomas J.,
  18; W. J., 30, 419
Sanit: George W., 275, 438
Sansom: Mary, 410
Sapp: Allen H., 219; John A., 219
Sassa: J., 334
Sasser: John W., 25, 124, 334;
  Joseph J., 25, 124, 334, 433; W.
  P., 124, 334
Saunders: Jno., 390; John Henry, 28,
  389, 434
Savage: James, 334
Sawyers: C. D., 310
Saxon: John, 334
Scaife: Joel, 310
Scallion: Augustus, 14
Scallions: A. D., 161
Scarborough: Hardy, 310; John T.,
  390; Thomas B., 390
Schley: Jacob, 162

INDEX

Schofield: John J., 124; John James, 390, 442; John M., 76, 102, 103, 105, 107, 113
Scipper: Samuel, 219
Scogin: E. B., 123, 310
Scott: James M., 419; James W., 310; S. H., 190; William, 30, 419
Screws: Benjamin, 13; Wm., 334
Scruggs: E. F., 190; J. W. F., 190
Seale: Cornelius H., 219, 436, 447; Elias, 219; Henry O., 219, 436; Henry R., 17; James K., 30, 419; Martha, 203; O. E., 220
Searcy: George W., 275
Seawright: George A., 30, 419, 443, 449; John, 30; John R., 124, 420, 443, 449
Seefee: Joel, 310
Sellars: Hardy, 334
Sellers: Andrew, 335; Daniel B., 190; Hewitt M., 162; Hugh M., 162; William J., 162
Selman: Thomas B., 162; Thomas D., 162
Seppes: Joseph, 420
Sevannet: A., 420
Sewell: John, 390
Sexton: A. C., 162; A. E., 162
Shackleford: Louisa M., 167
Shaffer: Anthony, 335, 440
Shank: Sargt, 81
Shanks: A. M., 122, 162, 431; G. P., 162; G. W., 163; J. J., 435; James Jordan, 162, 435, 443; John, 122, 162; John W., 163, 435; John Wesley, 163; Jordan, 13; Marshall Henry, 163; Mary Catherine, 143; Robert M., 162
Sharp: Archie F., 310; James, 24, 92; James E., 251; James M., 311; Jas. G., 19; John O., 24, 311, 440; Moses, 311; R. S., 366
Sharpe: F. H., 311; T. B., 311
Sharpton: Alexander, 25, 335; J. G., 251; William E., 25, 335, 440
Shaver: Jacob, 311, 440; S., 335; W. H., 311

Shaw: John, 335, 440; Joseph P., 251; Thomas, 390; William, 19; William J., 251
Shea: John, 311, 440; Patrick, 190, 446
Shealey: Wilson E., 420
Shearer, 276
Sheets: Lewis T., 312
Sheffield: E., 275
Shelby: Hugh, 311
Shell: G. E., 190; George D., 420; Thomas Barnes, 420; Thomas Jepthia, 312, 390
Shelley: Charles M., 12, 13, 96, 99, 103, 104
Shelley's Brigade, 99, 113, 116, 119, 120
Shellnut: Andrew J., 275, 438; James Thomas, 275; T. J., 275
Shelmet: Andrew, 21
Shelnut: William J., 276, 438
Shepherd: J. T., 220; Thomas, 31; W. C., 420
Sheppard: J. M., 30, 421; James, 190, 432; Thomas, 30; Thomas H., 124, 421, 443; William F., 30, 421
Shepperd: James B., 335
Sherl, 190
Sherman, 76, 99; William T., 65, 83, 84, 85, 87, 90, 92, 93, 94, 95, 96, 99, 120
Sherren: J., 276
Sherver: William, 276
Shields: Hugh, 312; Milton, 435; Milton J., 163
Shiloh, 9, 15, 39, 41, 43, 45, 46, 48, 49, 50, 51, 52, 53, 54, 57, 59
Shine: Wm. P., 190
Shirlock: J. T., 220, 222, 432
Shoemaker: W., 24; W. H., 312
Shoenacker: William, 312
Shores: W. M., 163; William H., 163
Shorter: Col. Eli. S., 43
Shreves: J. S., 191
Shunackel: William, 24, 312, 440
Sill: John, 312, 448
Sills: John H., 122, 163
Simmons: A. D., 25, 335

Simms: William A., 421
Simpson: A. J., 20, 123, 251
Sims: Julius F., 220; Robert, 432; Robert M., 18, 220; W. H. S., 30, 421; W. M., 366
Sinclair: Daniel, 251
Singer: John, 191
Singleton: John W., 18, 220, 436
Sinquefield: James, 26, 367
Sisk: E. M., 276; J. N., 191
Skinner: James, 21; James M., 276, 432
Skipper: Alexander, 30, 421; George, 220, 437; Hiram, 21, 123, 276; J. W., 220; James H., 252; John W., 17; Joseph, 30, 421; Morgan, 312, 440; William, 23, 24, 312
Slater: Nancy, 397
Slaughter: H. T., 390; J. E., 63; James E., 11; John, 21, 276; L. E., 64; Samuel, 367; Samuel H., 124; W. R., 390; Zachariah, 276
Sloan: D. B., 164; Hugh, 164
Sloane: J. B., 30, 421, 449
Small: E., 367
Smallwood: James A., 437; James A. I., 252
Smalwood: W. F., 122, 191
Smart: Martin, 390
Smith: A. J., 123, 312; Amanda Elizabeth, 208; Burwell J., 335; C. A., 252; Charles A., 276; Charles J., 25, 336, 448; Elijah, 390; Elizabeth, 224; F. C., 191; George W., 421; Henry, 14; Hiram, 367, 445; J. H., 122, 191; J. M., 367; J. T., 277, 438; J. W., 124, 252, 422; James, 391; Jas., 191; Jeff, 220; John, 312, 367, 391; John A., 221; John B., 124, 422; John Davison, 367; John Davison., 441; John W., 367; Joseph, 368; Josiah F., 276; Lewis, 21; Lewis B., 277, 438; Milton, 277, 438; Moses, 14; Nathaniel, 391; Olin F., 277; R. E. P., 276; Rich, 391; Robert J., 277; S., 368; Saul, 28, 391, 442; Thomas, 391; Thomas J., 18; W., 252, 336, 391; W. B., 164, 431; W. P., 14; William, 18, 368, 422, 448; William H., 19; William H. W., 252, 447; William J., 30; William N., 221; William R., 122, 221, 437; William W., 391, 449
Smyly: C. F., 368; Robert Edwin Paul, 312
Smyth: A. C., 221; Andrew C., 18; Edna Permelia, 216; Robert J. Sr., 221
Snead: A., 368
Solomon: Francis M., 30, 422
Sowell: Emma S., 365; Robert L., 221
Spanish River Battery, 63
Spanks: Geo. P., 14; John, 14; Monne, 14
Spear: James A., 252, 447
Spears: G. W., 336; William, 277; William C., 432, 438; Wm. C., 21
Speed: James F., 368
Speer: Sterling W., 252, 437
Speers, 252
Sperry: John T., 312
Spiers, 252
Spinks: William, 25, 336, 440
Spivey: Aaron, 252; J. J., 164; Joshua, 14
Spoon: James H., 28, 391; John E., 391, 434
Spradley: G. H., 221; James E., 122, 437; James Erwin, 221; Manning C., 222, 437; Samuel, 222
Spradling: Felix, 277, 432; Seaborn, 277
Spradly: Thomas Harrison, 222
Spurlock: John T., 18; Thomas, 122; Thomas J., 220, 222
Stacy: E. M., 368; Henry, 312; Manning, 368; W. H., 312
Staggers: J. W., 422; Jno. M, 422; Jno. M., 445; John N., 30, 422, 445; John W., 443; R. M., 422, 434
Stallings: Archa M., 122, 191; Archie M., 16; Daniel, 191; Henry Chambers, 191, 436; J. L., 122,

INDEX 483

191; J. T., 122, 191, 222; Jas., 191;
  Jo, 191; R. R., 222
Stallworth: N. C., 368
Standaland: Lawson, 222
Stanfords: W., 391
Stanley: C. D., 223, 437; Henry, 192;
  James B., 111, 112, 223, 444;
  James Henry, 223; Jno. T., 192;
  W. H., 192, 436; William H., 192,
  436; Wm. Henry, 16
Stanly: J. T., 122, 223
Starr: John, 391
Stays: J. E., 277
Stearnes: M. R., 252
Steel: Edgar, 278
Stegall: Peter, 336
Steigell: Reuben, 313
Stell: R. S., 278, 447
Stephens: J. W. H., 123, 252; James,
  192; Roswell, 192; S. W., 122,
  192; Thomas R., 278, 438
Stevens: Edward, 17, 223; W., 368;
  W. C., 26
Steward, 253; J. J., 124, 422
Stewart: B. F., 164; Benja. F., 14;
  Charles, 192; D. M., 223, 444; E.
  M., 223; G. D., 252; G. I., 252; G.
  W., 368; Geo. W., 19; Gideon T.,
  252; Hillery, 223, 437; J. W., 313;
  James J., 253; John M., 164; Lewis
  C., 16, 192; Nathaniel W., 19, 253,
  447; R. Y., 392; Reuben A. J.,
  392; Richard, 278, 447; S. C., 192;
  Samuel D., 20; Samuel S., 253,
  447; Sanders S., 20; Seaborn H.,
  253, 437; Seaborn M., 19;
  William, 253; William D., 16, 192;
  William M., 164; Wm., 20
Stigol: John, 313
Still: Sam, 278
Stith: Thomas J., 278
Stitt: C. G., 278, 438; John T., 278,
  438; Robert S., 20, 278, 438;
  Thomas, 21, 432, 438; Thomas J.,
  278
Stokes: Thomas, 336
Stone: Caleb, 279
Storey: Newton A., 19

Story: Newton A., 253
Stoudenmeir: D., 123, 313
Straughn: Margaret, 347
Street: A. J., 392
Strickland: Andrew Benjamin, 313;
  Samuel B., 422; Thomas, 279;
  THomas, 265
Stringer: Anderson T., 223, 447;
  Robert J. A., 224; Robt. J. K., 18
Stringfellow: George, 164; Thomas
  W., 164
Strom: H. S., 392, 434; Lucy, 392
Stuart, 192; Anne, 235; William R.,
  392
Stubbs: Alexander G., 124, 423
Stuckey: John Q., 224
Suggs: Elisha, 279, 438; G. W., 313
Sullivan: E., 164; Elbert, 14; J. W.,
  164; James M., 164; P. G., 336
Swan: James A., 123; James
  Anderson, 279; S. L. G., 123, 279;
  Saml, 279; Thomas H., 279
Swaner: Amariah, 423; F. M., 193
Swann: Nathaniel, 21, 280
Swanner: H., 423

T

Talbert: G. W., 26; George W., 369;
  James, 369; Rawlings, 369
Tales: L., 224
Taliaferro: Edward T., 122; Edward
  Taylor, 164
Talley: John, 21; John T., 280, 438,
  444; Littleton, 18; Thomas D.,
  280, 438
Tally: Josiah, 224, 437
Tankersley: J. R., 123, 313
Tanns: W., 369
Tarver: Hamilton, 313
Tate: Capt., 91; Jno. F., 58; John F.,
  8, 25, 124, 336; W. D., 58
Tatum: Richard, 369
Taylor: A. B., 313; Charles P., 164;
  D. B., 14; Dixon L., 165, 435;
  Elijah N., 280, 439; Evan, 253;
  Evens, 20; George, 21; George T.,
  165; George W., 253; I. H., 31; J.

A. J., 313; J. M., 14; James P.,
165; Jesse H., 313; John, 14, 165,
336, 435; John H., 30, 423; John
P., 165; Joseph M., 165; Josiah M.,
280; Samuel B., 165, 431, 435; T.
B., 313; W., 281; W. B., 24, 313;
W. Henderson, 122, 193; W. J.,
123; W. M., 313; W. R. H., 253;
William, 16, 193, 281; William
Alexander, 166, 435; William H.,
122; William Hillary, 193; Wm. R.
H., 20
Teague: E. A., 281, 439
Teat: J. H., 25, 336
Tedder: William B., 281, 439
Temple: B. Z., 254, 444
Templer: C., 369
Templeton: J. F., 336; S. F., 336
Templin: Abraham, 369; Charles,
124, 369; Henry, 369, 441
Terraptin: Henry, 26
Terry: Thomas, 24, 314, 448
Tetre: J. H., 336
Thagard: Andrew J., 122, 224;
Frances, 227; Mary Jane, 219; W.
R., 224
Thames: John, 369; N. C., 26;
Newby C., 124, 370, 441
Thaxton: D. S., 254; Dixon S., 19, 20
Thead: Columbus A., 337, 448
Thigpen: Daniel M., 392; David M.,
166; George, 30; George W., 423
Thomas: C. G., 254; D., 447; Daniel,
193, 446; E. D., 180; G. W., 28,
392; George, 75, 76, 88, 100, 102,
103, 108, 113, 114, 115; Ira, 28,
392; James M., 16, 193; Moses,
337; Newby C., 370; Sarah Jane,
200; T. C., 337, 440; W. L., 281;
W. O., 314; W. T., 124, 392; Wm.
H., 20
Thompson: Augustus L., 28, 392;
Cain Zebidee, 254, 447; Calvin C.,
122; Calvin Clay, 224; E. Z., 254,
447; George P., 314; Harriet, 150;
James, 337, 433; James A., xiii;
James Alford, 57, 67, 68, 92, 225;
James S., 166; John E., 314; John

J., 18; John Jefferson, 225; W.,
337; Warren, 225; Zebeder, 20
Thomson: John, 281
Thorenton: Horatio, 20
Thorn: Edward, 314
Thornton: H., 225, 437, 444; Horatio,
432; Horatio Marion, 254; John,
193; John E., 166, 435; K. H., 225;
R. N., 226; Willis D., 423
Thorrington: W. D., 423
Threadgill: J., 337
Thurman: W. D., 392
Tichenor: Chaplain, 48; I. T., 3, 48;
Isaac T., 9; J. T., 314
Tierney: Frank, 30, 124, 423
Till: D. G., 193; Daniel, 193; G. D.,
193; William, 14; William T., 166
Tippett: J. M., 30, 423, 434
Tisdale: Marshal S., 16; Marshall,
193; Samuel, 193
Tobery, 314
Tobey, 314
Tobias: Mary, 195
Tomlinson: J. C., 166; J. S., 166;
William B., 167, 445
Torpey: John, 314, 440
Towles: O. D., 281
Townsand: Harris, 281, 432;
Jefferson, 28; Jefferson C., 392;
Samuel W., 193
Townsend: Harris, 21; Samuel, 16
Tradaway, 337
Trainem: Joseph, 226
Trainman, 226
Trainum: James F., 226, 437
Trainwin, 226
Traweek: Ripley J., 226
Trawick: L. W., 226; LaFayette, 17
Treadman, 337
Treadway: George W., 337, 448;
Henry C., 124, 337; James M., 25,
337
Troutman: Newton, 18; Newton C.,
226, 447; Sol. H., 226; Soloman
H., 18
Truss: C. C., 314
Tucker: J., 433; J. M., 314; W. H.,
226

INDEX

Tulville: George W., 337, 448
Tupelo, 117, 118, 119, 124
Tupelo, MS, 54, 56, 57, 58, 61
Turberville: J., 370
Turner: Benjamin H., 445; Benjamin Howard, 392; John H., 393, 442; Joseph, 226, 437; Mary Elizabeth, 201; Thomas, 393; William, 167
Tutt: William D., 337, 444
Tyner: Elijah, 16; Elijah S., 193; John A., 16; Joseph, 194; Josiah, 122, 194, 436; T. C., 122, 227; Wiley H., 194

U

Underwood: Joseph W., 254
Upchurch: Berry, 281, 439; Harbord M., 281, 439, 447; Harry, 282; Harvey, 282; Hobson, 21; J. W., 282; John, 21; L., 282; Rena Ann, 266; Vinson, 282

V

Van: James W., 423, 449
Van Echlin: Charles M., 31
Vann: E. T., 314; S. T., 314
Vardell: Milton G., 16, 122, 194, 432
Vardelle: R. J., 194
Varnell, 167
Vaughan: Samuel, 21
Vaughn: James, 424, 443
Verdell, 194
Verdery: S. A., 58; Samuel A., 167, 443
Vernell: Calvin, 14; Calvin C., 167
Vernelle, 167
Vernon: J. C., 424, 449; Obadiah, 30, 424
Vice: John R., 227
Vickery: J. J., 370, 441
Vincent: T. J., 282; Thomas, 282
Vines: William, 227
Vinson: J. C., 282; Micager W., 282; Micajah, 21
Vowell: Andrew, 282, 444; J. C., 123, 282

W

Wadkins: James, 21
Walden: W. W., 21
Waldo: Charles M., 315, 440
Waldon: W. W., 282
Walker: Daniel, 448; Daniel W., 315; Felix G., 16, 194, 436; Frank L., 14; Franklin L., 167; James P., 338; Napolean B., 122, 167; S., 255; W. E., 123, 255; W. W., 255; William, 315, 440
Wall: Andrew J., 194; Elizabeth, 183; James, 255; John, 255
Wallace: A. G., 227; Abram, 122; Abram F., 18, 227; George, 30, 424, 443; H. F., 227; John, 17; Samuel G., 18, 227; Samuel H., 194
Waller: W. S., 195
Walling: H. C., 195
Walston: Andrew J., 446
Walthall, 99, 102, 103, 113, 115, 116, 117; Edward C., 12, 79, 99
Walthall's Division, 78, 90, 99, 102, 104, 119
Walton: L. M., 338; W. A., 227; William A., 10, 122
Ward: A. B., 315; J. M., 228; James, 315; James N., 227; John W., 28, 195, 393; Sampson M., 28, 393, 442; Soloman A., 195; Tarleton, 315; W. T., 315
Ware: A. B., 315; David, 16, 195; Thomas, 393; W. T., 315
Warick: Henry D., 255
Warren: David G., 338; George W., 16, 195, 432
Warrick: Henry J., 20; James H., 255; Josphine, 254; Wiley, 255
Warrington, 36, 37
Washburn: Alice, 238
Waters: C. H., 370
Watford: B. C., 255
Watkins: James, 282, 432
Watson: A. F., 10, 315; A. M., 195; Anderson J., 16; Andrew J., 195; Christina, 144; F. M., 167, 283;

Gilbert, 195; H. F., 58; J., 122, 195; J. A., 228; J. G., 195; J. M., 167; J. R., 195; J. S., 195; Jas. S., 195; Jesse M., 16, 195; John A., 167; Samuel H., 123, 283; Sergeant, 49; Thomas, 393; William, 196, 434; William J., 30, 424; William V. R., 30, 424; Wm. V. R., 31
Watts: Attorney General Thomas, 48; Col., 27, 31; Colonel, 34, 35, 37, 38, 43, 44, 45, 52; Governor, 65, 73, 74, 82, 96, 101, 134; T. H., 3; Thomas, 6, 11, 23; Thomas H., 4; Tom, 48; Wm., 283
Way: David, 315, 440
Weatherford: Stephen, 14, 167, 431
Weathers: B. F., 20, 58; Benjamin, 102, 125, 444; Benjamin F., 22, 283; James A., 123, 283, 439; Lieutenant, 36; Simeon, 284; Thomas, 21, 123, 284, 432
Weaver: D. F., 167; Isaac, 424; J. M., 228; James, 21; James R., 393, 442; John, 21; John R., 393, 442; John T., 284; R. H., 284; Rhoda, 398; Richard, 21; William, 393, 434
Weavers: B. J., 284
Webb: Austin P., 255; C. C., 24, 123, 315, 440; W. H., 24, 315
Weeks: C. M., 228; W. A., 196
Weisinger: E., 370; James, 370
Welch: James, 440; Theresa, 218
Welsh: James, 316
West: W. P., 370, 433
Westbrook: A. G., 370
Westley: Rogers, 228
Wetherford: James, 168, 431
Whaley: Archibald, 284, 393, 449
Whatley: Edward W., 370, 448; W. H., 370
Wheeler: Col. Joseph, 44; John, 21, 284
Whetsone: Joseph, 20
Whidden: Elias, 424; Noah W., 424, 443

Whisker: D. W., 316; Daniel W., 30, 424
White: B. R., 228, 255; B. S., 284; Daniel C., 285, 439; David C., 123, 284; Fannie, 22; G. D., 316; Henry C., 21, 285; Homer V., 285; J. C., 316; J. F., 25, 338; James, 14, 168; John L., 28, 394, 449; Stephen, 255; Thomas, 370; Virgil S., 285; W. E., 4, 95; Wiley, 432; Wiley E., 7, 20, 22, 285; William, 394; William C., 285
Whitehead: W. H., 123, 255
Whitmire: Rebecca, 324
Whittles: James M., 394, 442
Whorton: W. A., 285
Wicks: Charles, 371, 441
Wideman: A., 255
Wigg: W. K., 196
Wiggins: C. C., 255; J. E., 196; J. T., 26; James C., 122, 196; Jno. T., 371; Joseph B., 255; M. Lafayette, 371, 441; N. J., 26, 371; T. S., 26, 371; W. D., 168; William K., 196; Wm. H., 16
Wight: J. M., 30, 425
Wilber: J., 425
Wilbur: James, 30
Wilburn: James, 425, 434
Wilkerson: Freeman W., 124, 338; Warren C., 285
Wilkes: J., 425; Johnsy, 394
Wilkinson: Benjamin F., 425; Joshua, 425
Williams: A., 316; A. A., 350; A. M., 122, 168; B., 58; B. B., 285; Basil B., 123; Benjamin, 196, 446; C. W., 316; D., 338; D. M., 25; Daniel, 30, 425, 434; G. W., 168; Geo. W., 14; Henry C., 316; Henry G., 425; Isaiah, 316; J. C., 338; J. D., 286; John, 168; M. W., 196; Malachi C., 394, 449; Reason, 30, 425; Stanford, 449; Stanford J., 28, 394; Tabitha, 351; Thomas, 15, 196; Thomas Jefferson, 286; William, 196, 446

INDEX

Williamson, 123; A. W., 338; J. W., 122, 228; James B., 196; John, 16, 196, 444; John W., 197; Madison, 16; R. M., 13, 168; S. E., 16; S. J., 197, 436, 437; Stephen James, 197; T. J., 197; Thomas, 122, 123, 197; William, 18
Williford: John T., 28, 394, 445, 449
Willioughby: William, 197
Willis: James S., 18; James Thomas, 228, 447; John, 286
Willoughby: William, 122
Wilson: Allen, 425; Benjamin E., 255; David R., 168; Elias, 20; Henry, 123, 255; J. A., 338; M. W., 24, 316; Robert, 123, 255; W., 338; W. C., 25
Wimberley: J. L., 338; L. W., 338
Wingate: W. A., 168
Winger: John, 286
Winn: W., 339
Wirtingel: E. B., 371
Withers: J. M., 11, 57
Withers Division, 43, 57
Wood: David, 286; J., 197; Samuel McN, 197
Woodard: W. J., 339
Woodward: W. J., 124
Wooten: J. T., 316; Thomas E., 395

Worley: W. H., 316
Worthington: Alex, 16; William A., 197; Wm. A., 16
Wright: J. D., 255; J. M., 425; J. P., 395; James N., 168; Jas. M., 168, 443; Jep, 395; Joseph T., 168; Stephen M., 122, 228; Thomas, 28, 395; William H., 371; William J., 28, 395, 442
Wyche: George D., 228, 444; J. D., 228
Wynager: E., 371
Wynn: H. T., 339; Lycurgus, 339, 448; R., 339; R. A., 25
Wynne: Clem, 124, 339; John T., 25, 339, 440; Lemuel, 25, 339, 440; William H., 25, 340
Wynsdick: T. R., 30, 425

Y

Yarborough: Henry P., 125; James D., 425; Thomas J., 255, 447
Yarbrough: Henry Pleasant, 316
Yong: Aug, 256
York: G. W., 340
Young: Asa, 256; G., 395; Giles R., 286; J. Berry, 197; Jiles, 21; Joel, 21, 286, 432, 439; M. L., 395

www.ingramcontent.com/pod-product-compliance
Lightning Source LLC
Chambersburg PA
CBHW051334230426
43668CB00010B/1254